# Handbook For Teaching Introductory Psychology

edited by

**Ludy T. Benjamin, Jr.**
*Texas A & M University*

**Robert S. Daniel**
*University of Missouri-Columbia*

**Charles L. Brewer**
*Furman University*

**LEA** LAWRENCE ERLBAUM ASSOCIATES, PUBLISHERS
1985   Hillsdale, New Jersey                    London

Lawrence Erlbaum Associates, Inc., Publishers
365 Broadway
Hillsdale, New Jersey 07642

ISBN 0-89859-561-4
LC Card Number 85-6758

Printed in the United States of America
10  9  8  7  6  5  4  3  2  1

# Table of Contents

# Preface

Introductory psychology continues to be one of the most popular courses on college campuses today, enrolling an estimated 1.5 million students annually. It is possibly the most popular elective course among college students and, some sources say, among high school students as well. It is impossible to say just how many people teach the introductory psychology course. One indicator is that publishers of introductory texts send to college instructors approximately 8,000 complimentary texts and to high school teachers 2,000 books geared to those students. It is clear that a great many people are involved with introductory psychology, either as instructor or student.

For the student, sources are plentiful with more than 100 introductory psychology texts in the current market. Most have a study guide for the student, some have a learning objectives program, and some offer students a collection of readings to supplement the coverage in the text. However, for the instructor, the situation is not nearly as bountiful. Publishers provide test-item files, now available on floppy disks, which contain an abundance of multiple-choice questions, some of which are well written, but many of which are unusable because of their ambiguity or the fact that they deal with the most trivial details. Publishers also make available booklets called instructor's manuals, which usually contain a list of films, suggested readings, sample lecture outlines, and a few classroom demonstrations to accompany the various chapters in the textbook.

Considering the number of graduate students and new instructors who are involved in teaching the introductory psychology course, it is surprising that better teaching aids are not available. Few books on the teaching of psychology have ever existed, and several from the 1960s and 1970s are now out of print.

In recent years, the American Psychological Association has taken a more active role in this kind of publishing, producing two important books, *Psychology Teacher's Resource Book* and *Activities Handbook for the Teaching of Psychology.* In 1980, the APA also initiated the G. Stanley Hall Lecture Series, a program of annual lectures specifically designed to provide content updates for teachers of introductory psychology and covering the topics typically included in a survey course in general psychology. Those lectures are published annually in book form by the APA. The Educational Affairs Office of APA also publishes two newsletters: *High School Psychology Teacher* (formerly *Periodically*), which, although intended primarily for high school teachers, is useful for instructors at any level; and *Network,* which is for instructors at two-year colleges.

Yet the most important happening for teachers of psychology occurred earlier, in 1974, when APA's Division Two, on the Teaching of Psychology, initiated publication of its journal, *Teaching of Psychology.* It has provided a means by which teachers can share their philosophies and their techniques with their colleagues in academia. The journal, by providing a publication outlet, has stimulated a great deal of research on teaching that otherwise might not have been done. Further, it has given greater visibility to the teaching profession and conveyed the importance of the teaching enterprise in psychology. That it is a respected publication is evidenced by its ranking 30th of 99 psychology journals in a recent survey, published in the *American Psychologist,* that rank ordered the journals based on the frequency of citation.

In 1985, *Teaching of Psychology* (*ToP*) begins its twelfth year of publication. Robert Daniel, of the University of Missouri, was the founding editor and has guided the journal through its first eleven years. With his retirement, the journal passes to a new editor, Charles Brewer, and to a new publisher, Lawrence Erlbaum Associates. This transition phase was partly a stimulus for this book. We recognized that over the years, *ToP* has included a number of articles on the subject of teaching the introductory course. These articles have dealt with the questions that commonly face teachers of this course, questions about course formats, goals, evaluation procedures, class size, team teaching, use of student assistants, textbook selection, and so forth. It seemed unlikely that many people would have all volumes of *ToP* and so might not have access to these articles.

With the advice of the Executive Committee of Division Two, it was decided to publish this handbook to provide a readily accessible collection of articles on teaching introductory psychology. Articles were selected for inclusion because of their value to teachers of the introductory course, but much of the information is relevant for teachers of other courses as well. The book will be most useful for those teaching at the college level, but high school teachers also will find much of value in these pages. Our aim was to include articles that will help assiduous teachers to become better informed, more effective, and more efficient in their challenging but joyous work. Even regular readers of *ToP* will find this collection helpful, because it brings together in a single volume a plethora of material.

We have selected a total of 89 articles, and divided them into two sections. The first section, "Issues and Approaches," contains 43 articles covering a wide range of topics. Some relate to the purpose and nature of the introductory course; others concern specific approaches to teaching that course. Several articles deal with beginning students' conceptions and misconceptions of psychology; others explore ways to increase students' motivation. One group of articles is devoted to different approaches for individualizing instruction; others cover the use of student teaching assistants and testing.

Section II, "Demonstrations and Activities," is a collection of 46 articles that describe specific activities, demonstrations, class projects, and experiments that are appropriate for the course in introductory psychology. These activities may be useful in other courses as well. In fact, a number of them were planned originally for use in more advanced courses. The activities in this section are grouped into such topical areas as physiological psychology, perception and sensory processes, social psychology, personality, and so forth. Almost all of these demonstrations and activities can be conducted in the classroom or laboratory with minimal or no equipment.

This book contains the work of many dedicated teachers. We are grateful to all of them for putting their ideas in print and for their permission to reprint their work in this volume. We also wish to thank those individuals who served as reviewers for the journal and thus have played a part in producing this book. All royalties from the sale of this book will be paid directly to the treasury of Division Two of the APA and will be used to promote its many important activities. We would like to acknowledge the substantial help of Jack Burton, of Lawrence Erlbaum Associates, in making this resource a reality.

Like many of our colleagues, we share an excitement in teaching the introductory course in psychology. There is a satisfaction experienced in that course that seems unique. We hope that all who use this book will, like the Clerk of Oxford in Chaucer's *Canterbury Tales*, "gladly learn and gladly teach."

Ludy T. Benjamin, Jr.
Robert S. Daniel
Charles L. Brewer

# Section I
# Issues and Approaches in Teaching
# Introductory Psychology

# 1. COURSE ORGANIZATION

## Introductory Psychology: Should it be Taught As a General Survey Course?

David J. Senn
*Clemson University*

"Psychology: Hot course on Campus" (Newsweek, 1973); "Will Success Spoil Psychology?" (Chronicle of Higher Education, 1974)—these headlines, and others, verify what psychology instructors have been experiencing over the past several years. Psychology is one of the hottest subject areas on campus. Cates (1973) reported that bachelor's degrees in psychology are expected to rise to 79,000 per year by the end of the 1970's, representing a growth of 114% during this decade. Moreover, three-fourths of all course enrollments are students not majoring in psychology. Clearly, interest in psychology is growing dramatically among all undergraduate students.

This phenomenal growth forces us to take a look at undergraduate curricula and the objectives they are trying to meet. We might logically start with the first course in the program—the introductory psychology course. A recent national study sponsored by the APA (Kulik, 1973) concluded that this course is an almost universal offering at colleges and universities throughout the country; 99% of all universities, 98% of liberal arts colleges, 100% of state colleges, and 98% of two-year colleges offer it. Obviously, the notion of an introductory survey is firmly entrenched in the undergraduate curriculum.

The majority of published articles dealing with the teaching of introductory psychology are concerned with various instructional methods as seen in the bibliographies of Johnson and Daniel (1974) and Jones, Saff and Daniel (1974). Few articles question whether introductory psychology should be taught, or, if taught, whether it should be taught as a general survey course. Based on his national questionnaire survey of the early 1970's, Kulik (1973) reported that "only one department chairman reported that his department had abandoned the introductory course. Instituted in its place were three lower-division courses in specific areas of psychology which did not count toward the major. By 1970, a few other distinguished schools had abandoned the broad introductory survey in favor of lower-level content courses" (p. 23). Although there is considerable diversity in the content areas emphasized and in the organizational format of most introductory courses, these differences are seldom communicated to other professionals in the field.

The purpose of this paper is threefold. First, a brief review of some of the major objectives of the introductory psychology course is given. Second, the assumption that introductory psychology should be taught as a general survey course is questioned, and a possible alternative to that style of

A rating study from two institutions indicates that students assess the survey course less favorably than they do the alternative proposed.

teaching is suggested. Finally, a summary of a follow-up evaluation after four years in this proposed alternative is reviewed and contrasted with the results from a similar evaluation of another institution's traditional general psychology course.

### Goals and Objectives for Introductory Psychology

In his 1964 Presidential Address to Division 2, MacLeod (1965) suggested four criteria by which each course in the psychology curriculum should be evaluated: (1) it should transmit to the new generation some of the significant components of our culture, (2) it should present the world in which we live as a challenge to thought and action, (3) it should contribute to the growth of the individual as a person, and (4) it should help to prepare the individual for a career in the broadest sense of the term "career." Applying MacLeod's general criteria to the introductory psychology course, what outcomes would be expected by most instructors?

McKeachie (McInish & Coffman, 1970) has identified three broad goals for students in introductory psychology courses: improved attitudes and skills, greater knowledge, and better personal adjustment. With regard to the first goal, students are expected to gain an appreciation and understanding of scientific methods and be able to apply these methods to problems of human behavior. The student should also be able to formulate testable hypotheses about behavior and be critical of assumptions involved in generalizations about behavior. In keeping with the second goal, a student should not only know something of the content of psychology, but he should also be able to apply these concepts in new situations. Finally, according to McKeachie, psychology has some knowledge which can contribute to the productivity, happiness, and social effectiveness of the average person. With particular reference to the introductory psychology course, these three goal areas can be stated more specifically as ten course objectives (Walker & McKeachie, 1967): (1) communicate elementary concepts, (2) communicate facts in support of the concepts, (3) introduce the student to the full range of subject matter, (4) integrate course material, (5) communicate basic attitudes of the discipline, (6) communicate the intrinsic interest of the subject matter, (7) present the newest developments of the field, (8) provide individual guidance and monitoring, (9) develop selected intellectual skills, and (10) provide a suitable identification model for the student.

## Should Introductory Psychology be Taught as a Survey Course?

When any curricular component is accepted by 98% to 100% of the colleges and universities in this country, changes and alternatives to the curriculum must be offered with a great deal of caution. Nevertheless, it is recommended that the traditional survey be replaced in many schools by lower-level content courses offered in specific areas. One possible set of such courses would be as follows:

**Psychobiology and Conditioning.** A study of the principles of classical and instrumental conditioning and the physiological bases of sensation, motivation, and instinctive behavior.

**Human Intelligence, Thought and Memory.** The study of human behavior emphasizing information processing. The principles of human learning, perception, and memory and their relation to intelligence, problem solving, concept formation, attention, and thinking.

**Life-Span Growth and Development.** An examination of development from conception through aging and death. An analysis of pertinent theories and research related to changes in physical growth and to the development of language, intellectual, social and moral behavior.

**Personality and Social Behavior.** Consideration of the basic similarities and differences among persons in their reactions to the physical and social environment. The influence of others upon one's behavior as a participant in social groups.

Other viable combinations of content courses are also possible. The set of courses outlined above is modeled after the Monmouth College (Illinois) introductory curriculum. Other schools have also adopted similar combinations of introductory courses. For example, Knox College (Illinois), in its set of four lower-level content courses, places a heavier emphasis on the experimental analysis of behavior. At the University of California at San Diego (Kulik, 1973), human information processing, developmental psychology, and social psychology are the introductory-level offerings. All three courses have a strong laboratory emphasis. Undoubtedly, there are other institutions that have also implemented similar content courses in lieu of the traditional introductory survey.

Arguments in support of such an introductory curriculum are many. First, most course objectives for introductory psychology can be met as well as, and usually better, by this format than by the conventional course. This observation is true of at least nine of the ten objectives specified by Walker and McKeachie (1967). The one exception is objective three—introduce the student to the full range of subject matter. In reality, this objective is rarely met in the conventional course. Frequently, the introductory survey represents a systematic point of view, e.g., humanistic emphasis, experimental analysis of behavior orientation, a natural science or social science focus, fundamental laboratory or experimental techniques. Within the same departmental program these various orientations often co-exist. The curriculum recommended here recognizes these existing differences and gives students (and faculty) a choice among them.

The general survey course is criticized frequently by students because it is said to lack coherence. A bewildering array of topics is presented in succession with little or no integration. Although the recommended curriculum will not necessarily eliminate this problem, it has the potential of greatly reducing it, thereby improving the experience of most students. Even though 75% of students in a typical introductory course take at least one more course in psychology (Walker & McKeachie, 1967), only a few will become majors. Therefore, the first course must be a coherent experience in itself. It would appear that the lower-level topical courses would provide this kind of meaningful experience most successfully.

Another point in support of the recommended curriculum is that a large number of college students have taken an introductory psychology course in high school. Many of these students were assigned a conventional survey text in that course. In the recent evaluation of introductory psychology by Clemson University students (reported below), 45% of the 220 respondents indicated that they had taken an introductory psychology course in high school. This rapid rise in pre-college instruction together with the popularization of psychology in the media is producing an increasingly sophisticated group of students in the first course.[1] It is suggested that the specific, content-oriented courses proposed in this paper will fulfill the needs of beginning students better than the traditional survey introduction to the field.

If the recommended restructuring takes place, faculty instructors will probably experience less frustration in reaching their course objectives. Most instructors are torn between the opposing forces of breadth and depth. To balance these forces in a rapidly growing field becomes a more formidable challenge each year (Kulik, 1973). Faculty who have taught in the proposed format attest to the fact that these frustrations can be reduced noticeably and that students can be "turned on" by the new introductory curriculum. Without question, the lower-level topical courses appear to stimulate the appetite of students for more advanced courses in the field.

It should also be noted that resource materials are becoming increasingly available for introductory courses of this nature. Numerous "packages" have been modularized so that instructors may select the components they feel are most appropriate. In addition, topical paperbacks and reprint series have become abundant in almost all areas. As more alternatives to organizing the first course become known, there will undoubtedly be a corresponding increase in the availability of appropriate resource material.

Finally, if some "common core" instruction is desired among courses in the introductory curriculum, this objective can be met easily. For example, if it is felt that each course should contain the basic principles of learning or the fundamental elements of experimental design, these "core" areas can be taught in each introductory course as they apply to that area. Not only has such an arrangement been found to be effective, but instructors also agree that these core areas are taught more effectively in the new topical courses than in the previous survey format. If a uniform orientation for each student is desired, common reading material can be assigned by all introductory instructors.

Two major criticisms against the recommended curriculum deal with the comprehensiveness of the students' introduction to the field and the more complex scheduling problems created by having multiple introductory courses. Both are valid criticisms. But it is highly questionable whether students in the traditional course really receive a comprehensive view of the field. Generally, some areas of psychology are emphasized to the exclusion of others. A more fundamental question is whether a comprehensive overview is really all that important. With regard to the second criticism, it is readily acknowledged that scheduling problems become more apparent with the introduction of new courses. However, the problems created by the new format are minimal unless very few course sections are available at one time. And, as with upper division offerings, academic advisers need to be prepared to discuss the alternative courses with the student so that the latter can make an informed choice among them.

In summary, the arguments in support of an introductory topical curriculum seem to outweigh those arguments against such a curriculum. Those who have taught students in both formats report that the new curriculum is an excellent way in which to initiate students into psychology.

### Evaluation of the Introductory Psychology Experience by Undergraduates at Two Institutions

**Characteristics of Respondents.** Ratings of a general survey course were made by 220 Clemson University undergraduates. Similar ratings of three topical introductory courses were performed by 100 students at Monmouth College (Illinois). In addition to rating their respective introductory courses, respondents from both schools stated their preference for a general survey or a topical format and all completed a scale measuring their attitudes toward psychology. At both institutions, questionnaires were completed anonymously by students during regularly scheduled class sessions and were administered by their course instructors.

Respondents in the two samples were similar in the proportion of males and females. In addition, 25% of each sample were psychology majors. But they differed in two respects. The Clemson sample was more heavily populated with juniors and seniors, whereas the Monmouth students were more evenly distributed across all four classes. The average number of courses taken in psychology was also somewhat greater at Clemson ($M = 4.0$) than Monmouth ($M = 3.0$). These two sets of differences are, of course, interrelated.

**Evaluation Questionnaire.** The questionnaires completed by students at both schools were composed of three parts. Part I was a rating of the introductory course(s) they had taken. Fourteen semantic differential scales with seven-points each were included in the course rating. Scales included such adjectives or phrases as excellent, interesting, meaningful, increased interest in psychology, difficulty of content, would recommend to other students, and continue in psychology curriculum. Eleven scales with clear positive and negative weightings were used to derive an overall rating for the course. The possible range of scores was 11-77 with a score of 44 representing a neutral rating.

Part II of the questionnaire requested a preferential rating on nine, seven-point scales between a single "general" course and one or two "specific" courses. Students were instructed to indicate which type of course structure they would have preferred as an introductory psychology student. The nine items rated included the following concepts (in sentence form): interest, usefulness, performance, learning the most, application of psychological principles, most stimulating (for majors and non-majors), and preferred format. The possible range of scores was 9-63 with a score of 36 indicating an equal preference for the two types of introductory formats.

Part III was an "Attitude Toward Psychology" scale devised by McKeachie and his colleagues (McInish & Coffman, 1970, pp. 131-133). The scale, constructed specifically for use in the introductory course, was composed of twenty Likert-type items. Each item was rated on a 5-choice, agree-disagree continuum. Therefore, the possible range of scores on this scale was 20-100.

**Results and Discussion.** The three major parts of the evaluation questionnaire were analyzed according to six characteristics of the respondents: sex, cumulative grade point average, academic class level, college major, number of psychology courses taken, and presence or absence of a high school psychology course. Evaluative ratings across these respondent variables were remarkably similar within each respective institution. That is, students within each school made highly homogeneous ratings regardless of the characteristic listed above. One internal difference of interest is that at Monmouth College male respondents evaluated the topical Psychobiology and Conditioning course more highly than did females but the opposite was true for the Human Intelligence, Thought and Memory course. The Personality and Social Behavior course was rated about equally by the two sexes.

The major differences among respondents were obtained in the introductory course(s) ratings *between* the two institutions. Table 1 summarizes some of these differences.

### Table 1
### Summary of Average Evaluative Ratings of General Survey and Topical Introductory Psychology Courses

| Introductory Courses | Sample Size | Overall Course Rating[a] | Preference: Survey vs. Topical[b] | Attitude Toward Psychology[c] |
|---|---|---|---|---|
| Survey Course (Clemson): General Psychology | 220 | 56.23 | 37.15 | 72.91 |
| Topical Courses (Monmouth): All Topical Courses Combined | 100 | 61.80 | 42.16 | 75.27 |
| Psychobiology and Conditioning | 40 | 61.48 | 43.58 | 75.08 |
| Human Intelligence, Thought & Memory | 66 | 60.48 | 41.21 | 74.45 |
| Personality & Social Behavior | 20 | 66.80 | 48.30 | 81.10 |

[a]A neutral course rating = 44.00; high scores reflect favorable course rating.
[b]Equal preference = 36.00; high scores indicate preference for topical courses.
[c]Neutral attitude toward psychology = 60.00; high scores reflect favorable attitude.

In regard to the evaluative ratings of the courses themselves, the first psychology course was rated favorably by students at both schools. Moreover, the students at Monmouth rated their three topical introductory courses more highly than students at Clemson rated their general survey course. When the mean rating of the general survey course (56.23) was tested against the combined rating of the three topical courses (61.80), the latter was found to be significantly higher than the former, $t(318) = 4.37, p < .01$. It should be noted that the size of introductory course sections at the two institutions was comparable. The statistically significant difference was obtained in spite of the fact that students at Clemson had received higher course grades in their survey course than students at Monmouth had received in their topical courses. In addition, the content of all three topical courses was rated as more difficult than that of the survey course. Thus, in terms of the courses themselves, these data offer substantial student support and credibility to the recommendation that courses be taught in a topical format.

Part II of the questionnaire asked respondents to state their preferences on each of nine items for one or the other of the course formats. Clemson students made these ratings *without* knowing what the more "specific" courses might be. That is, they were given no illustrative course titles or descriptions. Yet, they rated the two formats almost equally ($M = 37.15$, where no preference = 36.00), but with a slight tendency to prefer the topical course format. Monmouth students, who were very familiar with the topical emphasis, rated this format significantly more favorable ($M = 42.16$) than did the Clemson students, $t(318) = 3.18, p < .01$. Thus, regardless of the type of introductory course taken, all students were receptive to and indicated a preference for the topical introductory format. An interesting consistency between both student samples was also noted. Respondents from both institutions indicated that the topical courses were more preferred for those who planned to major in psychology than for those who did not plan to do so.

The last part of the questionnaire attempted to assess students' attitudes toward psychology in general. Students at both schools expressed moderately favorable attitudes in this regard. As can be seen in Table 1, Monmouth students had more favorable attitudes ($M = 75.27$) than did Clemson students ($M = 72.91$) where a mean of 60.00 represents a neutral attitude. This difference was statistically significant, $t(318) = 2.23, p < .05$.

One can only conjecture from the present data how much influence the first college psychology course had on these students' attitudes. A plausible hypothesis would state that such a relationship exists and that the positive influence would be greater in a content-centered introductory course than in a general survey course. Data from the present study give some support to this hypothesis. It should also be remembered that students at Monmouth, on the average, had taken fewer psychology courses. If their exposure had been comparable to that of Clemson students, their attitudes toward psychology might have been even more favorable. This notion appears reasonable since the greater the number of courses taken at either institution, the more positive was the attitude expressed toward psychology in general. For categories "less than 3", "4-6," and "greater than 7" courses, respectively, the attitudinal means for Clemson students were 71.17, 75.59, 75.81, and for Monmouth students 74.26, 77.67, and 78.67.

In conclusion, both types of introductory courses discussed in this paper are probably doing a good job of familiarizing students with the field of psychology. Both types obtain good student evaluations and help produce favorable attitudes toward the discipline. Students in both curricula want the courses continued. On a 7-point scale, the general survey course was rated 5.60 in terms of its retention in the curriculum, whereas the three topical introductory courses were rated 6.53, 6.09, and 6.05. Although both introductory formats were evaluated favorably, the new topically oriented introductory courses received the superior rating on *all* evaluative criteria in this study. Surely we must give serious consideration to this alternative structure for teaching introductory psychology. As far as the educational consumer is concerned, the topical introductory course cannot be ignored.

## References

Cates, J. Baccalaureates in psychology: 1969 and 1970. *American Psychologist,* 1973, *28,* 262-264.

Federici, L., & Schuerger, J. High school psychology students versus non-high school psychology students in a college introductory class. *Teaching of Psychology,* 1976, *3,* 172-174.

Johnson, M., & Daniel, R. S. (Eds.). Comprehensive annotated bibliography on the teaching of psychology at the undergraduate level through 1972. JSAS *Catalog of Selected Documents in Psychology,* 1974, *4,* 108. (Ms. No. 735).

Jones, C. S., Saff, J. L., & Daniel, R. S. Annotated bibliography on the teaching of psychology 1973. *Teaching of Psychology,* 1974, *1,* 75-79.

Kulik, J. A. *Undergraduate eduction in psychology.* Washington, DC: American Psychological Association, 1973.

McInish, J. R., & Coffman, B. *Evaluating the introductory psychology course.* Reading, MA: Addison-Wesley, 1970.

MacLeod, R. B. The teaching of psychology and the psychology we teach. *American Psychologist,* 1965, *20,* 344-352.

Psychology: Hot course on campus. *Newsweek,* May 21, 1973, pp. 105-107.

Walker, E. L., & McKeachie, W. J. *Some thoughts about teaching the beginning course in psychology.* Belmont, CA: Brooks/Cole, 1967.

Will success spoil psychology? *The Chronicle of Higher Education,* September 30, 1974, p. 3.

## Notes

1. This assertion may be qualified by future research on pre-college instruction. For example, Federici and Schuerger (1976) recently reported that 35 students who had taken high school psychology did not enter the college level introductory course knowing any more about the field than 79 students without such a background.

2. This article is based on a paper presented as part of a symposium entitled "The General Psychology Course: To Be or Not To Be," at the annual meeting of the Southeastern Psychological Association, Atlanta, March 1975.

3. The author would like to thank Charles J. Meliska, A. Dean Wright, and William M. Hastings of Monmouth College (Illinois) for their assistance in collecting data for this study. Their helpful comments on an earlier version of this paper are acknowledged as are those of David J. Marx of Clemson University.

# Psychological Seduction: Effective Organization of the Introductory Course

Gerard Lenthall
and David Andrews
*Keene State College*

Have you given any thought to reorganizing your syllabus? Consider these suggestions that are based on established principles.

Consider what we do when confronted with a novel and complex stimulus (roughly equivalent to the introductory psychology course for the average student). We seek out the familiar forms—a face here, a tree there; we identify the boundaries, progressively exploring less familiar sections and integrating what we find with those pieces already familiar in a process akin to Piaget's equilibration—assimilation and accomodation.

When an artist or performer creates an engaging work, he concocts a potion of the familiar and unfamiliar, the common and the foreign. The audience is repeatedly drawn ever deeper into unknown territory and then repeatedly returned toward the more familiar. Ideally, on completion of the work, the audience exits with an integrated sense of the whole, one which extends beyond itself, changing and influencing their lives. So too must the introductory psychology course build on the known, repeatedly drawing the student from familiar to unfamiliar and from concrete to abstract, until at the end there exists an integrated whole that also extends beyond itself.

Obviously many factors contribute to the success of an introductory psychology course. This paper will look at the order of presentation of topics as an important and generally ignored variable. As teachers and clinician (G.L.), we are aware of the need to accept people where they are (entry level behavior) and, starting from there, to work toward our goals (exit behavior). Change agents generally do best if they begin by accomodating their approach to the client's current level and concerns (Watzlawick, 1974). To tap client motivation a change agent's proposals either have to "make sense" to the client, i.e. meet her or his felt needs, or else they have to draw on credit and trust that the change agent has accumulated from prior successes.

In the teaching of psychology nowhere are these dicta ignored more than in the introductory survey course, where teachers consistently inflict upon students courses designed on the Procrustean principle of what *a priori* seems logical. Typically, the introductory course begins with a brief general introduction into the history of modern psychology, along with some discussion of research and the scientific method. It then systematically proceeds up the hierarchy of living systems, building from the smaller biological units on up to larger social units. Having gotten underway with a physiological orientation (brain & behavior and then sensation & perception), generally such courses go on to learning and later to emotion and motivation. Finally, more than halfway through the semester, there appear those topics that initially seem to "make sense" to the average beginning student— namely human development, personality and abnormal behavior, and assessment and intervention. Last of all and often rushed through at the end of a busy semester comes social psychology, a student favorite.

In designing a one semester introductory psychology survey course, we confront two contradictory alternatives. One of these is to follow the conventional building blocks sequence outlined above, which appears as option A in the list below.

Option A.
    Psychology as a science.
    Biological and perceptual processes.
    Learning and information processing.
    Developmental processes.
    Emotion, motivation and consciousness.
    Personality and abnormal behavior.
    Social Psychology.

Option B.
    Social psychology.
    Personality and abnormal behavior.
    Emotion, motivation and consciousness.
    Developmental processes.
    Learning and information processing.
    Biological and perceptual processes.
    Psychology as a science.

Option C.
    Personality and abnormal.
    Learning and information processing.
    Psychology as a science.
    Developmental processes.
    Biological processes.
    Emotion and motivation.
    Consciousness.
    Perceptual processes.
    Social psychology.

Option D.
    Psychology as a science.
    Personality and selected intervention (anticipates learning).
    Learning and information processing and language.
    Abnormal behavior (applies learning; anticipates biological).
    Biological processes.
    Emotion and motivation (applies biological; anticipates social).

Consciousness (applies biological; anticipates perceptual).
Perceptual processes.
Social psychology (application of perceptual).
Developmental processes (integrative section; draws on all of above).
Psychology as a science (integrative reprise).

The other alternative is to reverse the conventional order by beginning with social psychology, followed by the individual, and eventually ending with the biological underpinnings to behavior. This reverse sequence appears as option B in the list above. In rejecting the latter approach, Hilgard, Atkinson, and Atkinson (1979) say that to begin with "soft" areas and then end up with "hard" ones initially promotes a false expectation of what psychology is all about and thus results in student disillusionment. Although they therefore recommend the conventional strategy, I suspect that their students' entry level cognitive skills and general background of knowledge (if not motivation) enable them to master a course sequence that our students, for the most part, find extremely difficult. Below we suggest a third sequence of topics that we have found engages the average student while still maintaining quality. This new sequence appears as option C.

At the first class meeting, having begun by asking, "What is psychology?," we follow up by asking "What are the causes of human behavior?" The ensuing discussion makes for a natural transition into personality theory and then, if one chooses, into abnormal behavior. (Here we may also include some discussion of personality assessment and of the intervention approaches of theorists who view behavior primarily as being dispositional.) Not only are personality and psychopathology highly interesting to most beginning students, but also these subjects involve examining how individuals learn behavior patterns and how behavior is changed, thus preparing students for learning more about learning. When next we present learning as an area basic to an understanding of modern psychology, students, having already been exposed to the influence of learning upon individual behavior, are motivated to master this material. At this time we may also refer to behaviorally-oriented intervention methods as exemplifying the concrete application of unlearning existing behaviors and/or learning of new behavior patterns. The related areas of memory and concept formation and problem-solving follow. We next consider how psychologists approach problems in their own work. (If one chooses to introduce simple statistical concepts, then it's probably best to wait until the students have had several success experiences, and until one has earned the credibility to lead them past the paralysis of their all too prevalent math anxiety.)

Next we explore issues of learning versus biological development (heredity vs environment) in a developmental psychology context that makes intuitive sense to most students. These include IQ assessment, life-span human development, and language. These issues can serve as a lead-in to exploring the biological foundations of behavior, a topic that can be anticipated in discussion of the role of neurotransmitters in the abnormal psychology section of the course. The introduction to physiological psychology provides necessary background for understanding emotion, motivation, and consciousness. On the one hand, students generally have a lot to say about what makes them feel happy or what motivates them to do such things as go to college,

and they certainly have a lot to say about such topics as dreaming, drugs, and hypnosis. On the other hand, they can now approach these topics in a more sophisticated manner. In the final section of the course, discussion of perceptual processes precedes social psychology, a sequence that has historical justification. The semester closes with a topic that students find themselves applying to their daily lives.

In this new option C both the beginning and the ending topics of the semester are of prime interest to students. Nowhere is there a critical mass of the abstract or the counterintuitive that dries up student interest. In following such a format, we have found that students remain interested, work hard, seem to understand more, and do at least as well as with the conventional format of option A. Moreover, we find ourselves needing to spend less time doing remedial work with students.

Since psychology is *not* linear, one might begin the course at a number of places. Regardless of which sequence one chooses, what is important is the principle of beginning with students where they are in terms of entry level knowledge and interest. Where students' cognitive functioning is such that they need concrete examples plus help in integrating diverse material, the idea of juxtaposing areas of application with learning, physiological, and perceptual processes is a sound one.

One modification of the sequence proposed above might be to begin in the conventional manner with discussion of psychology as a science and then move on to a unit involving personality, learning, and selected intervention processes, followed by abnormal psychology, biological processes, and thereafter paralleling option C, except that the course ends with study of developmental processes as an integrative section, something that is usually lacking. Such a sequence appears as option D in the list.

One needs criteria by which to judge the efficacy of a given course sequence. Keeping in mind the principle that the sequencing of the course material should be designed to fit the student, we have selected the following criteria to guide us:

1. Students' entry level interests, skills, and knowledge should be used as a foundation for building comprehension and motivation.
2. One section of the course should flow readily into the next and should be perceived as doing so. The resulting coherence should contribute to greater understanding of any given topic and its relationship to the whole.
3. Students should feel some need to learn "hard" material prior to being exposed to it. Then, having become familiar with it, they should have some opportunity to apply it. There is much more overlap among the "tough" and "tender" areas than is usually clear to the introductory student. Such an integrated presentation manifests this overlap while sustaining student interest. Within these constraints there should be some effort to avoid clustering of "hard" and "soft" areas of psychology.

How do the four sequences presented above compare in terms of these proposed criteria? First, in terms of considering students' entry level behavior, including interests, option A scores lowest, but the other three options score well. Second, in terms of flow of topics and student perception of natural progression, options A and B rate as poor, and options C and D score well. Third, in terms of anticipating "hard" areas and then applying them immediately afterwards, only options C and D score well. Finally, since many students find integration of diverse material difficult—and the nature of traditional introductory psychology courses only adds to this difficulty—it should be noted that option D has the added merit of ending the semester with an integrative section.

Although the criteria presented above are hardly an exhaustive list, we submit that we need to be explicit about our criteria for selecting among various topic sequences for the introductory course. It is surprising that practitioners in a field which concerns itself with human motivation and learning have chosen to rely on only one set sequence for presenting their discipline.

In conclusion, we hope that this paper will generate discussion on how to improve a course that frequently resembles a quick European tour ("Paris on Monday, Rome on Tuesday, London on Wednesday") at a time integration in the field of psychology is increasing.

### References

Hilgard, E. R., Atkinson, R. L., & Atkinson, R. C. *Introduction to psychology* (7th Ed.). New York: Harcourt, Brace, and Jovanovich, 1979.

Watzlawick, P., Weakland, J., & Fisch, R. *Change: Principles of problem formation and problem resolution.* New York: Norton, 1974.

# Conceptual Interrelationships Based on Learning in Introductory Psychology

Robert F. Stanners
and Larry T. Brown
*Oklahoma State University*

Multidimensional scaling analysis of students' organization of concepts yields insights for restructuring the course.

The major purpose of the present experiment was to investigate the conceptual memory structure resulting from learning in a fairly typical introductory psychology course. A central assumption of the study was that the memory representation of conceptual units from learning material acquires an increasingly complex network of interrelationships as learning progresses. A second assumption was that individuals have conscious access to information about interrelationships among the concepts and can make judgments about them in an accurate and consistent way. Although the basic idea of an interrelated knowledge structure goes back a considerable period of time (Bartlett, 1932; Bruner, 1966; Gagné, 1965), quantitative attempts to depict the nature of conceptual interrelationships are comparatively recent. A two-fold problem is involved in efforts to depict conceptual structure: (a) the assessment of the strength of the interrelationships between concepts and (b) a method of evaluating the strength values to provide useful information about conceptual structure.

An early approach to the first aspect of the problem was that of Johnson (1964, 1965) who used the degree of overlap in free associations to physics concepts as a way of assessing the strength of the relationships among the concepts in the subjects' memories. Concepts with many associations in common (e.g., velocity and speed) were taken to be closely related. Since then studies with an educational orientation have used similarity judgments among concepts (Johnson, 1967, 1969; Stasz, Shavelson, Cox & Moore, 1976), graph construction methods (Shavelson, 1974, 1975), and card sorting (Shavelson, 1975). Some of the procedures for evaluating measurements of the interrelationships among

the concepts have been simple comparisons of averaged free association overlap indexes (Johnson, 1964), or similarity judgments (Johnson, 1967, 1969; Shavelson, 1972), as well as more elaborate procedures such as multidimensional scaling (Shavelson, 1972) and hierarchical clustering (Shavelson, 1974, 1975).

Fenker (1975) attempted to depict the memory representation of conceptual interrelationships among a group of experimental design concepts and also a group of measurement concepts. The subjects were taken from an undergraduate course in experimental design and measurement. Similarity judgments were made on pairs of concept labels, and the judgments were subjected to multidimensional scaling. An interesting innovation used by Fenker was a reference concept map which was produced by scaling the judgments of a group of faculty and graduate students in the measurement area. A comparison of the reference concept structure with that of the undergraduates after the relevant material had been covered in class showed little correspondence. In a second experiment in which students were given specific instructions to pay attention to the relevant concepts and their interrelationships, the correspondence between the reference concept structure and the one for the undergraduates improved.

In the present study, we attempted to determine whether a meaningful and consistent representation could be produced for a set of highly abstract and rather loosely defined concepts taken from personality theory. If a useful representation could be produced for this set of concepts, it would seem to be a positive indicator that most psychological concepts encountered in the introductory course could be handled by a concept-comparison approach. A reference structure was produced from concept judgments made by graduate students to facilitate the identification of specific areas of misunderstanding among introductory psychology students. Some specific attention was given to the issue of consistency of judgment. Any approach to representing knowledge as a system of interrelationships makes an important but heretofore untested assumption that there is some (greater than chance) degree of consistency among subjects in their individual patterns of concept relationships. If subjects were highly idiosyncratic in the way in which they assessed interrelationships among concepts, then a group depiction of the concept structure could be highly misleading. The group depiction would not represent any common scheme within the group, but, in the absence of any test, such an interpretation would very likely be placed on it. The method used in the present study for testing the consistency assumption could also be put to another useful purpose, namely, a statistical rather than simply a descriptive comparison of the concept structures produced by different groups of subjects.

**Method.** Eleven "concepts" from the area of personality theory were selected for study. Each was presented in the form of a statement or conceptual label:

A. Each individual is unique.
B. Behavior is unconsciously motivated.
C. The trait approach to the study of personality.
D. The humanistic approach to the study of personality.
E. Early developmental experiences are important to personality.
F. The individual's personality is highly structured.
G. Personality is a product of learning.
H. Inborn (i.e., genetic) factors play a major role in personality
I. The self-concept is important to personality.
J. The social learning approach to the study of personality.
K. Freud's approach to the study of personality.

Each statement was paired with every other, yielding 55 pairs. The pairs were arranged in four orders and typed in booklets (labeled Forms A, B, C, and D) with one member of each pair directly above the other. To the left of each pair was a blank for the student's rating. The ordering of the pairs in each form was random with the restriction that no statement appear in more than two consecutive pairings. Each statement appeared in the upper and lower positions of a pairing an equal number of items—for example, "Each individual is unique" appeared first when paired with five of the statements and second when paired with the other five statements. The upper and lower positions were assigned separately for each of the four forms.[1]

The booklets were completed by 23 undergraduate students enrolled in introductory psychology and 20 psychology graduate students. Each undergraduate had taken a quiz on the unit of the course concerned with personality theory 4 to 11 days prior to participating in the task and had received a grade of "C" or better. The reading assignment for the unit material included the chapter on personality theory and assessment (Chapter 12 in *Introduction to Psychology* by Brown & Weiner, 1979). Further, the students had received two or three lectures on personality theory. Each of the 11 concepts was discussed in the text and/or in lecture.

The undergraduate students were volunteers who were promised extra credit toward their course grade for participating in the task. Each of the 20 graduate students, also volunteers, had had at least one graduate course in personality theory.

Each booklet was presented with a cover sheet containing detailed instructions for performing the ratings. Briefly, the instructions requested that the student judge the members of each pair of statements for the "closeness" of their connection by assigning the numbers 1 through 7. A "1" was to be used if "the two aspects of personality theory you are judging are very closely connected" and a "7" if "the two aspects of personality theory you are judging are quite unconnected." It was stressed that, although the two members of a pair might not have been "treated in your textbook or in your lecture material as relating to the same approach to the study of personality," this didn't necessarily mean that they were not rather closely connected. The instructions were reiterated in shortened form on the rating booklet.

Each of the four forms was distributed with approximately equal frequency. Although the graduate students performed the task on their own, and hence we don't know how much time they spent on it, the undergraduates required between 10 and 25 minutes.

**Results.** The sets of paired-statement comparisons were the input to the multidimensional scaling procedure. The present study used the COSPA computer program (Schönemann, James, & Carter, 1979) which is based on Horan's (1969) model. This algorithm allows the testing of two assumptions which are very important in interpreting scaling results. The first of these is the common space (consistency) assumption. For each subject a statistic is calculated with which a goodness-of-fit test can be performed on how well the data of the subject fit the coordinate system derived from the complete group of subjects. The test is based on the rejection of the hypothesis that there is a random relationship between the subject's coordinates and the group coordinate space. The test for the complete group is a binomial test which is applied to the number of individual subject tests for which the random hypothesis can be rejected. From the perspective of psychological applications, the test of the common space assumption allows the investigator to ascertain whether the subjects are capable of making the two-way judgments in a somewhat common fashion. The second assumption is referred to as the diagonality assumption. The concern here is whether the dimensions derived from the scaling can be interpreted as independent. The testing is done by a two-stage procedure very similar to that used for the common space assumption.

The assumptions of Horan's model were satisfied for both sets of data. In the case of the undergraduates there were 13 subjects out of a total of 23 whose common space statistics met or exceeded the .10 level. Using the binomial test the probability of getting 13 or more out of 23 events significant at or beyond the .10 level is less than .001. For the test of the diagonality assumption in the undergraduate group the proportion was 6/23, $p < .05$ by the binomial test. The test of the common space assumption for the graduate students produced a proportion of 20/20, $p < .001$, and the diagonality test produced 8/20, $p < .001$.

Kruskal and Wish (1978, p. 9) have noted that "When multidimensional scaling does yield useful insights, these often result from examining the configuration." Accordingly, we held the dimensionality of the scaling to a level (three dimensions) which allowed fairly easy graphical depiction but which, according to our inspection, also allowed the important relationships in the data to be shown. The Schönemann et al. (1979) algorithm operates in such a way that a higher dimensional solution does not change the dimensions which are extracted from a lower dimensional solution. Therefore, rescaling the present data with four or more dimensions could not invalidate but only (possibly) supplement the present results. The results of the scaling in graphical form are presented in Figures 1 and 2. It should be noted that the vertical dimension is indicated by the length of the line from the point to the X, Z plane and not by the relative heights of points.

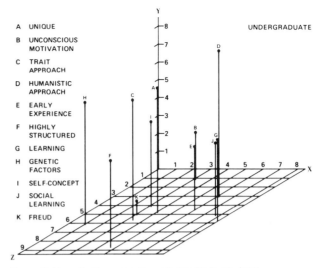

Figure 2. Coordinate space for undergraduate students

comparing the groups on the proportions of subjects who have common space statistics which meet or exceed the criterion value. In the undergraduate group this proportion is 7/23 and in the graduate student group, 20/20, $t(41) = 7.09$, $p < .001$. By this comparison, the groups are somewhat different.

Another possibly useful question is whether the fit of the individual undergraduates to their own coordinate system is any different from the fit of the individual graduate students to their group coordinates. For the undergraduates the appropriate proportion is 13/20 and for the graduate student, 20/20; $t(41) = 4.11$, $p < .001$. There is, therefore, a difference in fit in favor of the graduate students.

**Discussion.** The tests of the common space assumption in the present experiment provide some encouragement for the use of multidimensional scaling of similarity judgments as a way of depicting the memory representation of interrelationships among highly abstract concepts. Common space was present in both groups, although, as might be expected, the degree of consistency was higher for the group which had the greater amount of exposure to the material. Insofar as applications to educational situations are concerned, the present test of common space appears to be a fairly strong one in that the course format was quite typical of a large variety of undergraduate courses, and the concepts were highly complex. Since the map for each group was clearly not an amalgam of idiosyncratic individual results but reflected some common knowledge, the next question to ask is, are the maps interpretable with respect to the subject matter. In many respects the maps appear to be quite plausible depictions of the interrelationships among the concepts, and the similarities and differences between them seem to be at least somewhat interpretable.

Inspection of the graduate map (Figure 1) shows that many of the concepts form clusters corresponding to the basic approaches to the study of personality (given above). Thus, "unique" and "self concept" are located in the area of "humanistic approach," "unconscious motivation" is not far from "Freud," and "learning" and "social learning" are nearly coincident. The "trait approach" forms a separate "cluster" of

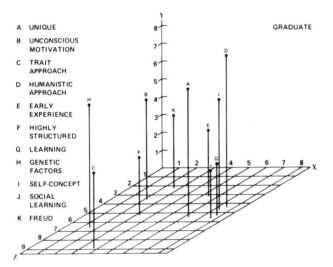

Figure 1. Coordinate space for graduate students

In comparing the maps for the undergraduates and graduate students there appears to be some similarity but also some differences. The statistical approach to the question of differences between the groups was implemented by a feature of the Schönemann et al. (1979) program which allows an external coordinate system to be substituted for the one derived from the data. The coordinate system based on the graduate students seemed to be the more plausible choice to use as a reference system because of their greater amount of education and presumably higher level of knowledge. When the coordinates of the graduate students were used with the undergraduate data, the test for the common space assumption produced a proportion of 7/23, $p < .01$; the relationship between the graduate student coordinate system and the undergraduate data is clearly not a random one. The test for the diagonality assumption produced 5/23, $p < .07$.

Although there is some similarity (a nonrandom degree) between the graduate student group coordinate system and the individual undergraduate systems, it may be asked whether this degree of similarity is as high as the degree of similarity between the group coordinate system for the graduate students (the reference system) and the individual graduate students. This difference can be assessed by its own. With exceptions to be noted, a similar patterning holds for the undergraduates (Figure 2). It is also true that "genetic factors" and "early experience" occupy roughly comparable positions in the two maps.

When compared with the concepts in the graduate map, those in the undergraduate map appear diffusely distributed, i.e., there is less tendency for grouping to occur. The greater formal training of the graduate students has apparently (and predictably) resulted in a tighter conceptual clustering of related concepts and a clearer distinction among unrelated concepts. Of special diagnostic importance (see below), the undergraduates showed little linkage between Freud's approach to personality and the notion of unconscious motivation. Indeed, the undergraduates didn't interpret Freud as showing a very close relationship to any of the other personality concepts. The same is true of the humanistic approach which, in contrast to the graduate student map, was conceived as only distantly related to the self-concept and the notion of individual uniqueness. A third concept which bore little relation to other concepts for the undergraduates was that pertaining to the role of genetic factors in personality. Even the graduate students tended to place this concept in relative isolation from other concepts. Neither group of students conceptualized genetic factors as bearing much relationship to early developmental experiences.

The present method for depicting memory representation provides a fairly clear, comprehensive view of how students interrelate groups of concepts gleaned from their reading and other course work. When compared with the instructor's own conceptualization of the topic, and/or with data from a criterion group (in the present study, psychology graduate students), such a mapping could provide information valuable in the selection and presentation of course materials. In the present instance, it appears that the introductory course could have done more to relate both Freud and the humanistic approach to other aspects of personality theory. It is as though both Freud and the humanistic approach were assigned slots largely unconnected with anything else in the field of personality. It is probable this could be prevented in the future by spending more time relating, as opposed to simply describing, the various approaches to the study of personality.

There were inadequacies, too, in the conceptualization of the role of genetic factors in personality; the textual and lecture materials apparently failed to stress sufficiently the presumed "instinctive" nature of unconscious impulses. Of perhaps even broader importance, neither the course work of the undergraduates nor that of the graduate students appear to have given emphasis to the importance of genetic factors in the programming of early developmental experiences, and learning in general (e.g., Alcock, 1975, chap. 9).

We chose a cluster type of approach to the interpretation of the results rather than an approach which placed emphasis on the labeling of the dimensions, because labeling appeared overly speculative at this stage of the research. Perhaps, as more data of the same general type are collected, labeling of the dimensions will become a useful interpretive maneuver.

The overall results of the present experiment indicate that people can make consistent and meaningful comparisons of pairs of abstract and complex concepts. Multidimensional scaling then allows one to generate the full set of relationships from the pair-judgments. Some potential extensions of this approach to other educational topics would be the comparison of different instructional formats (Would different formats yield different maps?), retention of concepts (Would conceptual maps change over a retention interval?), and the comparison of student ability levels.

## References

Alcock, J.  *Animal behavior: An evolutionary approach.* Sunderland, MA: Sinauer Associates, 1975.

Bartlett, F. C.  *Remembering: A study in experimental and social psychology.* New York: Macmillan, 1932.

Brown, L. T., & Weiner, E. A.  *Introduction to psychology.* Cambridge, MA: Winthrop, 1979.

Bruner, J. S.  *Toward a theory of instruction.* Cambridge, MA: Harvard University Press, 1966.

Fenker, R. M.  The organization of conceptual materials: A methodology for measuring ideal and actual cognitive structures. *Instructional Science* 1975, *4*, 33-57.

Gagné, R. M.  *The conditions of learning.* New York: Holt, Rinehart, and Winston, 1965.

Horan, C. B.  Multidimensional scaling: Combining observations when individuals have different perceptual structures. *Psychometrika*, 1969, *34*, 139-165.

Johnson, P. E.  Associative meaning of concepts in physics. *Journal of Educational Psychology*, 1964, *55*, 84-88.

Johnson, P. E.  Word relatedness and problem solving in high-school physics. *Journal of Educational Psychology*, 1965, *56*, 217-224.

Johnson, P. E.  Some psychological aspects of subject-matter structure. *Journal of Educational Psychology*, 1967, *58*, 75-83.

Johnson, P. E.  On the communication of concepts in science. *Journal of Educational Psychology*, 1969, *60*, 32-40.

Kruskal, J. B., & Wish, M.  Multidimensional scaling. Sage university paper on quantitative applications in the social sciences, 07-011, 1978. Beverly Hills, CA: Sage Publications.

Schönemann, P. H., James, W. L., & Carter, F. S.  Statistical inference in multidimensional scaling: A method for fitting and testing Horan's model. In J. C. Lingoes, E. E. Roskam & I. Borg (Eds.), *Geometric representation of relational data.* Ann Arbor, MI: Mathesis Press, 1979.

Shavelson, R. J.  Some aspects of the correspondence between content structure and cognitive structure in physics instruction. *Journal of Educational Psychology*, 1972, *63*.

Shavelson, R. J.  Methods for examining representations of a subject-matter structure in a student's memory. *Journal of Research in Science Teaching*, 1974, *11*, 231-249.

Shavelson, R. J.  Construct validation: Methodology and application to three measures of cognitive structure. *Journal of Educational Measurement*, 1975, *12*, 67-85.

Stasz, C., Shavelson, R. J., Cox, D. L., & Moore, C. A.  Field independence and the structuring of knowledge in a social studies minicourse. *Journal of Educational Psychology*, 1976, *68*, 550-558.

## Notes

1. Copies of the paired statements may be obtained by writing the first author.
2. Our sincere appreciation is due Dr. James M. Price for invaluable assistance on the quantitative portions of the present study.

# The Introductory Psychology Course in the Eighties

John K. Bare
*Carleton College*

Introductory courses and texts need
to be more effectively oriented toward
cognitive goals and liberal education.

Many are convinced that psychology has extraordinary promise and an eager audience. In 1969, Miller said, "In my opinion, scientific psychology is potentially one of the most revolutionary intellectual enterprises ever conceived by man" (p. 1063). "In the years ahead, we must not only extend and deepen our understanding of mental and behavioral phenomena, but we must somehow incorporate our hard-won knowledge more effectively in the vast social changes that we all know are coming" (p. 1063). "The heart of the psychological revolution will be a new and scientifically based conception of man as an individual and as a social creature" (p. 1067).

In 1972, Anastasi said, "psychologists. . .can contribute to the effective solution of human problems. . .by the planned and active dissemination of psychological knowledge throughout society" (p. 1095).

In 1978, Haber and Runyon said, "we consider psychology and the allied sciences of behavior disciplines of surpassing importance. We believe that they hold the key to the survival of the species" (pp. 225-226).

In 1980, Hilgard and Atkinson, writing about the 7th edition of the introductory text of which they were two of the authors, said, "primarily students want to know what is relevant to their lives, their futures, and the problems confronting society" (p. 119).

Has any of our potential in this direction been realized? In 1974 Lazarus said, "Many professors of psychology have been saying that the traditional design of introductory psychology is no longer appropriate for the typical present-day student, and I am sure they are right. The course used to be filled mainly by psychology majors expecting to go on to graduate study. Now most college students want some exposure to psychology, not primarily for career purposes, but for intellectual and personal development, and because they sense that psychology has something important to say about their lives. Yet academic psychology seems reluctant to reflect this change in values in the textbooks it uses. With rare exceptions, writers of new textbooks seem determined to follow the traditional pattern of including a smattering of everything. New texts proliferate, but most follow the time-honored formula, sometimes jazzed up a bit or written in a livelier style, but otherwise with little basic change over previous winners in the textbook sweepstakes. Some. . . cheat the student out of an opportunity to discover psychology as it is, a broad, divergent, turbulent, yet serious scientific discipline that is capable of contributing much about human problems and is not merely common sense or a bunch of cliches" (pp. 41-42).

In 1979 Wrightsman and Sigelman said, "In writing the fifth edition of 'Psychology: A Scientific Study of Human Behavior', we set for ourselves the challenge of how best to "give psychology away" in George Miller's terms, without throwing it away. Those familiar with previous editions will readily see that this is a new book. We felt that many introductory texts (including previous editions of our own), although solid, failed somehow to engage students and bring home the immense value of psychology as a route to understanding themselves, other people, and the human condition" (p. 247).

**Audience Characteristics.** Can we describe any of the characteristics of the audience? Hobbs (1962) in his memorable article entitled "Sources of Gain in Psychotherapy" said, "Man constantly engages in building and repairing and extending and modifying cognitive structures that help him make personal sense of the world. The individual has got to have a cognitive house to live in to protect himself from the incomprehensibilities of existence as well as to provide some architecture for daily experiencing. He has to build defenses against the absurd in the human condition and at the same time find a scheme that will make possible reasonably accurate predictions of his own behavior and of the behavior of his wife, his boss, his professor, his physician, his neighbor, and of the policeman on the corner. He must adopt or invent a personal cosmology" (p. 46).

Our cognitive houses will continue to be built, repaired, extended, and modified whether or not a course in psychology is part of our experience. Social changes will occur under a wide variety of conditions no matter what may be taught in psychology courses. The human species will survive without the help of psychology. But will psychology make its contributions in these areas? For some, this is one of the most important issues in the eighties.

We must be clear about the problem. It is not a matter of "simplistic popularizations" versus a "scientific discipline" (Lazarus, 1974); the serious teacher finds too many misconceptions in their students to compound their problems of instruction by echoing simplistic views. It is not "scientific discipline" versus "personal development" (Kasschau & Wertheimer, 1974); the discipline has something to say, derived from its principles, about the personal development of each of us. It is not "knowledge of self" versus "knowledge of others" or "principles" versus "applications" (Bare, 1971); principles of behavior are true for all of us if at all, and it is their extension to personal applications that we seek. The question is rather whether, in our instruction, a systematic effort will be made to specify for our students the consequences of well-founded psychological principles for their cognitive houses, their conceptions of man, and our social problems.

**Psychology as an Intimate Discipline.** Is there something unique to psychology and its students that gives the discipline its special mission while simultaneously making the accomplishment of that mission very difficult? I believe there is. First, psychology talks about us in an intimate way as no other discipline does. Biology talks about genes, but it is never my genes the way that my cognitions are my cognitions. Socio-economic classes are abstract even though I am part of one. Second, none of us has ever met a person who didn't believe in something. The beliefs provide the myths that we mix with facts to build that cognitive house. Psychology must make its contribution acknowledging the inevitability of belief. Third, humans treasure their uniqueness. As Bronowski puts it, "I wants to be a self, and you want to be another; we want our selves to be distinguishable; neither of us wants to be a duplicate copy of the other" (1965, p. 10). And it may be, as Bronowski warns, a person. . . "does not merely want to be unique, a different self from you and me; he wants to be a riddle that no one else can read" (p. 13). Psychology will have to find a way to help unique selves enter the world of other selves. Finally, we recognize that all beginning students are already psychologists in the sense of having been observers of their own behavior and that of others all of their lives. When the discipline confirms their observations they may respond that they knew *that* all the time, and when it countermands their misconceptions, they are remarkably resistant to being convinced otherwise (Vaughan, 1977; Gutman, 1979).

What generalizations, developed out of our systematic study of the human creature, might be included? There are many, from Miller's (1969) conceptions of man to bystander intervention and the laws that seem to govern it (Latane, 1981).

At one level, we might paraphrase Kluckhohn and Murray (1961): "I am like all others, like some others, and like no other." We might even add that we are like all others in that we all demonstrate processes and principles of behavior and share a common physiology; we are like some others in the experiences we have shared and in the outcomes of those experiences; and, we are like no other in the unique combination, sequencing, and timing of the experiences we have had.

We might follow the suggestion of Anastasi (1972) who would have us identify and disseminate *"orienting concepts,* ideas that are widely shared, well established, and thoroughly corroborated within both basic research and technology" (p. 1096). She suggests six such concepts and implicitly asks us to identify more: the fact that situations typically involve a multiplicity of variables, including those not immediately obvious like the Hawthorne effect, social expectancy, and the self-fulfilling prophecy; the concept of *interaction,* in the sense that the effect of any single variable may vary as a function of a second; the *overlapping* of distributions, in the sense that whenever whatever groups are compared on whatever variable, there are overlapping ranges of scores; the *multidimensionality* of individual and group differences and the need for assessments in terms of trait patterns; the surprising amount of *modifiability of behavior* and the breadth of the limits set by heredity; and concepts of *decision theory* to provide "basic training in decision making" (p. 1097).

Neisser (1975) would suggest: that the information from the surrounding world is patterned and redundant and we compare the types of information we receive; that there is wide latitude in choosing which aspects of the information will be picked up, which we accomplish both by orienting our receptors and the process of attention; that cognitive struc-

tures are developed by "the repeated application of particular cognitive strategies" that lead "to the formation of permanent systems for handling, relating, and retrieving information" (p. 161); and that "much of our cognitive activity consists of the manipulation and reorganization of representations" of the entities of the world, and "the most important of these are our representations of ourselves and other people, operating within a larger encompassing cognitive structure of social relations" (p. 161).

We might narrow our focus and demonstrate to our students that our perceptions are not often veridical and are heavily influenced by our cognitions and emotions; that we attribute the behavior of others to enduring personality characteristics and attribute our own to the situation and its vagaries (and whether intended or not, such a process helps us at least save face); that if we saw the behavior of others primarily as a consequence of environmental variables of which we are a part and not as a consequence of their inadequacies we would provide them with a greater sense of dignity; that emotional components of attitudes can be conditioned so easily that such attitudes are virtually accidental; that we frequently demand of children intellectual tasks for which their development has not yet prepared them; that there *are* ways of improving our efficiency at learning and remembering; and that we cannot opt out of being responsible in part for the behavior of others, for we have helped to create that behavior.

**The Introductory Course.** If we are to undertake the effort described here, the most important place for it to be made is in the introductory course, commonly taken by a large majority of *all* students enrolled in post-secondary education. The central instructional feature of most introductory courses is the text, and to accomplish the goals we seek, the material that can make its contribution to our lives must appear there. Now, by and large, it does not. Instead, reviewers (Lefton, 1974; Cafferty, 1975), and authors (Hilgard & Atkinson, 1980; Thompson, 1978; Baron & Byrne, 1977) expect the text to be comprehensive and up-to-date, reflecting the discipline as it is today. The result is that introductory texts differ little from one another; after an introductory chapter they range from genes to gurus, the all-or-none law to archetypes, and imprinting to intra-psychic change. (All terms were taken from the same introductory text index.) Indeed, after a survey, Irion concluded, "the picture emerges of an introductory course of fairly standard content that is usually taught in conventional ways" (1976, p. 7). Either the explosion of knowledge must bring this trend to a halt or the text must become longer and more and more fractionated. The student will learn less and less about more and more—this while Brown and Herrnstein caution us, "It may not be possible to be encyclopedic and also thought-provoking, interesting, and honest (1975, p. 139). In the present texts, even the order of the topics is insensitive to making the material speak to the human condition. A colleague has demonstrated this fact very convincingly. He organizes his course by following the chapters of the text from last to first, and much prefers it this way.

How might the course and the text be structured? There is no need to desert an empirical, data-based approach, but the coverage of the topics could readily be germane to the student's cognitive house. The chapter on perception might include a discussion of those modifiable by experience and those that are not, thus beginning to fill out the ways in which we are alike and those in which we are different. The study of the nervous system might emphasize not only its fixed capabilities and functions but its plasticity, thereby demonstrating that experience can alter structure and function. The learning chapter could display not only the ways in which both classical and operant conditioning have produced some of our behavior by the same principles that operate in animals, but the ways in which our cognitions can modify the learning outcomes, thus confirming a role for ideas and values in behavior. The chapter on heredity could convince the students that "either-or" is never a fruitful way to think about problems because interaction between heredity and environment is always present. In short, it is not the factual content of the texts that is most troublesome, it is the focus of the material that they present.

We must not be naive about what would be required to produce the changes we envision. There is considerable evidence (Lux & Daniel, 1978) to suggest that the core curriculum in psychology in four-year institutions is very much like that at the universities. Introductory texts are likely to be written by university scholars. It follows that it is the faculties of the universities who must be convinced that psychology has something of significance to say to the introductory student.

A second difficulty lies in the economics of the introductory text. In 1977 it was estimated that a well-illustrated text would cost up to a quarter of a million dollars to produce (Fischer & Lazerson, 1977). Publishers follow a "win-stay-lose-shift" strategy under these conditions, and once a winner is found, changes are slow in coming. To help solve this problem, we who adopt the texts must make the publishers responsive to the changes that must occur if psychology is to make a contribution to mankind in the eighties.

## References

Anastasi, A. The cultivation of diversity. *American Psychologist*, 1972, *27*, 1091-1099.

Bare, J. K. *Psychology: Where to begin.* Washington, DC: American Psychological Association, 1971.

Baron, R. A., & Byrne, D. Understanding understanding. The authors speak. *Teaching of Psychology*, 1977, *4*, 209.

Bronowski, J. *The identity of man.* Garden City, NY: The Natural History Press, 1965.

Brown, R., & Herrnstein, R. J. Teacher's pet. The authors speak. *Teaching of Psychology*, 1975, *2*, 139-140.

Cafferty, T. P. General psychology seasoned with schwitzgebel. A reviewer speaks. *Teaching of Psychology*, 1975, *2*, 91-92.

Fischer, K. W., & Lazerson, A. Managing a textbook versus plagiarizing it. *Teaching of Psychology*, 1977, *4*, 198-199.

Gutman, A. Misconceptions of psychology and performance in the introductory course. *Teaching of Psychology*, 1979, *6*, 159-161.

Haber, A., & Runyon, R. P. Behavior bazaar. The authors speak. *Teaching of Psychology*, 1978, *5*, 225-226.

Hilgard, E. R., & Atkinson, R. L. Life begins at 27. . . The authors speak. *Teaching of Psychology*, 1980, *7*, 119-120.

Hobbs, N. Sources of gain in psychotherapy. *American Psychologist*, 1962, *17*, 741-747.

Irion, A. L. A survey of the introductory course in psychology. *Teaching of Psychology*, 1976, *3*, 3-8.

Kasschau, R. A., & Wertheimer, M. *Teaching psychology in the secondary schools.* Washington, DC: American Psychological Association, 1974.

Kluckhohn, C., & Murray, H. A. Personality formation: The determinants. In C. Kluckhohn, H. A. Murray, & D. M. Schneider, (Eds.). *Personality in nature, society, and culture* (2nd Ed.). New York: Knopf, 1961.

Latane, B. The psychology of social impact. *American Psychologist*, 1981, *36*, 343-356

Lazarus, R. A. A riddle review. An author speaks. *Teaching of Psychology*, 1974, *1*, 41-42.

Lefton, L. A. A riddle review. A reviewer speaks. *Teaching of Psychology*, 1974, *1*, 41.

Lux, D., & Daniel, R. S. Which courses are most frequently listed by psychology departments? *Teaching of Psychology*, 1978, *5*, 13-16.

Miller, G. Psychology as a means of promoting human welfare. *American Psychologist*, 1969, *24*, 1063-1075.

Neisser, U. Self-knowledge and psychological knowledge: Teaching psychology from the cognitive point of view. *Educational Psychologist*, 1975, *11*, 158-170.

Thompson, R. All together now. A one, and a two. . . An author speaks. *Teaching of Psychology*, 1978, *5*, 224.

Vaughan, E. D. Misconceptions about psychology among introductory students. *Teaching of Psychology*, 1977, *4*, 138-141.

Wrightsman, L. S., & Sigelman, C. K. Take the fifth. The authors speak. *Teaching of Psychology*, 1979, *6*, 246-247.

# An Organizational Framework for the Teaching of Basic Psychology

Richard E. Dimond
*Sangamon State University*
R. J. Senter
*University of Cincinnatil*

The teaching of introductory psychology may be one of the most difficult courses any professor can attempt. In the first place, classes are usually large and are composed of both psychology majors and nonmajors. Consequently, the instructor must provide both a foundation course for future study in the discipline and at the same time deal with students who will perhaps never have another course in the field. To make matters worse, the professor is faced with the task of conveying information about a discipline which is sometimes perceived by students as a conglomeration of discrete topics.

Faced with these problems, how then can the subject be taught? It is the intent of this paper to offer an answer to this question through a proposed reorganization of the topics typically presented in basic psychology courses.

**A Solution Through Reorganization.** The solution to the problems discussed above involves devising a system for teaching basic psychology to students of varying backgrounds and futures. Hopefully, this system would also convey some knowledge about the structure of modern psychology itself, a topic infrequently discussed in basic psychology courses. It is felt that a plausible system for accomplishing these goals would be to organize current psychological information by subsuming the discrete topics now covered under several basic psychological processes. Simultaneously, students may be exposed to the structure of modern psychology by examining these processes from the viewpoint of various psychological subspecialties.

**The Basic Psychological Processes.** Obviously, when attempting to reduce all of psychology into a few basic processes, selectivity and bias occur. However, it is felt that, without enroaching upon the integrity of the discipline, the functions of learning, perception, and motivation may be usefully identified as the basic psychological processes.

In considering this choice of topics, the selection of the learning process as basic must appear logical. From Ebbinghaus to Skinner to behavior modification, it is emphasized both professionally and in most introductory texts and courses. Furthermore, if some thought is given to the matter, many topics currently presented under headings such as personality, social, developmental, cognitive or abnormal psychology may better be presented as examples of the pervasive interest in the learning process in psychology.

Perception may be considered a basic process both by its historical importance to psychology as a discipline and in terms of its necessity for the organism's contact with the environment. Consequently, a good argument may be made for including perception as a basic process of psychology. As is the case with learning, many aspects of psychological investigation may be taught as higher-order perceptual processes rather than as separate functions.

Motivation, broadly conceived of as the energizing function in organisms, seems to complete the triad of basic processes. It seems reasonable that without motivational processes, behavior is drastically reduced and the psychological characteristics currently investigated are greatly altered. Again, as for learning and perception, many current aspects of psychology can be nicely integrated as examples of psychologists asking themselves why individuals behave in certain ways.

**The Structure of Psychology and Psychological Specialties.** Once the basic psychological processes are accepted as unifying themes running through the discipline, the question becomes how to teach psychology from this point of view. A reasonable answer, and one which also conveys some idea as to psychology's structure and its specialty areas, is to present each basic process from the interest of several specialized branches of psychology. This approach permits students to study basic psychology within a unified organization, to familiarize themselves with different types of psychologists, and to learn to appreciate the complexities of the basic processes as they are studied from various approaches.

Conceivably, in selecting specialties to present, a myriad of combinations is possible. However, it would seem that in selecting the areas for study one should consider including enough specialties to encompass most of modern psychology and yet, for simplicity, to simultaneously select a manageable number.

The selection of psychological specialties may be left to individual professors. However, as an example, consider the areas of experimental, developmental, clinical, social, and applied psychology. Basic concepts and methods may be presented under the heading of experimental psychology; information on children and adolescents in developmental sections; and abnormal, personality, and testing issues in the clinical grouping. Social psychology could discuss people in groups while the application of the basic processes may be demonstrated in discussions on applied psychology. This would appear, then, to be a satisfactory selection of specialties.

**The Organization of the Introductory Psychology Course.** Given the notion of emphasizing the basic psychological processes of learning, perception, and motivation, and the integration of subspecialties, the course in basic psychology would consist of three units, one on each of the basic processes. Within each unit, each psychological specialty chosen would be examined in relation to a given process. Consequently, instead of a study of apparently discrete topics, students would have a unified base from which to understand and integrate the discipline. Additionally, they may appreciate that although all psychologists are interested in the basic psychological processes, they may differ greatly in approach and functions.

**Advantages of the Proposed System** Even though arguments may be advanced against this model, the organization suggested does have several advantages over traditional organizations. Some of these advantages have already been implied. These include giving students a more meaningful (and hence more easily recalled?) presentation of psychological information and at the same time an understanding of psychology's diverse structure. These two advantages would appear to be enough in and of themselves. However, there are other strengths to this model.

The proposed system appears to circumvent some of the difficulties in the teaching of introductory psychology. For example, the model serves to deliver basic concepts to all students, certainly a major goal of basic psychology courses no matter what the student's background or future goals. In addition, it provides students with an overall system for integrating psychology's apparently discrete subject matter. For nonmajors, this means that the basic psychology course may be more useful in later life due to its coherence. For psychology majors, they may approach advanced courses with some idea as to their relationship to the entire discipline. They will also possess the ability to identify basic processes among new material. Again, this strategy amplifies the importance of the beginning course of study.

The final strength of the basic process by specialty model is its flexibility and the ease with which it may be adapted to current methods of teaching basic psychology. It is flexible in that the professor may adopt the model in varying levels of difficulty and comprehensiveness. In other words, the three units may include an exhaustive coverage of topics or they may sample topics of special interest without destroying the integrity of the system. Students will still receive the basic organization permitting easy integration of new topics in the future. The system is adaptable in that current texts and lecture notes may be utilized by a simple rearrangement of lecture and reading assignments. Alternatively, professors may emphasize the essential basic process involved in various topics while simply following a more or less standard reading schedule and lecture presentation. All of this would seem to argue in favor of the proposed organization.

**Conclusion.** Psychology is a complex discipline with a varied history which has led to making it a difficult subject to teach at the introductory level. As greater demands are placed upon the introductory psychology professor by his or her students, it seems time to adopt a model of presenting psychology which is more systematic than present methods. The model proposed here would seem to have both logical and pedagogical advantages over traditional techniques. The adoption of this model, therefore, may result in better teaching and comprehension of a difficult subject.

# 2. A VARIETY OF APPROACHES TO THE INTRODUCTORY COURSE

## Designing an Introductory Course for Transfer Students: A Behavioral Systems Approach

Philip N. Chase
*West Virginia University*
Beth Sulzer-Azaroff
and Arnold Well
*University of Massachusetts/Amherst*

Two seemingly different approaches toward solving problems within social organizations have been synthesized recently into a strategy labelled *behavioral systems analysis* (Krapfl, 1975; Maley & Harshbarger, 1974; Malott, 1973). Subsequently, many organizational problem-solvers have applied this combination of systems analysis and behavior analysis successfully (cf. Frederiksen & Johnson, 1981; Maley & Harshbarger, 1974; Noah, Krapfl & Maley, Note 1). However, most of these applications have been in business and mental health organizations. This paper reports a unique application of behavioral systems analysis to a complex problem in the design of instruction: developing an introductory psychology course for students who transfer into a large eclectic department from other institutions. The following briefly outlines the components of behavioral systems analysis and describes in detail the application of this model to the problem of designing an introductory psychology course.

**Behavioral Systems Analysis.** As implied by its name, behavioral systems analysis integrates systems analysis and behavior analysis. Behavioral systems analysis has adopted the systems perspective that social problems require solutions that concentrate on the interactions among the people who comprise a group. This means that representative members of the group must be involved at all levels of problem-solving: defining the problem, collecting information, evaluating any procedures used and maintaining accountability for the whole process. The systems process requires gradual change in individual behavior, redundancy in procedures and reciprocity among individuals, yet it does create lasting and dynamic solutions (Bateson, 1972).

Malott (1973) added a number of behavior analytic components to the basic systems model. He suggested that group problems be analyzed in terms of the environmental contingencies that affect the members of the group (Malott, 1973). These contingencies usually describe the relations between group behavior and its functional antecedents and consequences. For example, at one level of analysis, the antecedents are the events that indicate that a problem exists, the behaviors are the actions that one takes to attempt a solution, and the consequences are the immediate and long range outcomes of the attempts. In order to sequence and operationally define these functional relations, the analyst writes behavioral goals and objectives, then employs solu-

A systems model was used for getting problem information, a behavioral model for analyzing it, and behavioral teaching methods for the solution.

tions based on established principles of behavior. Thus, behavioral systems analysis combines the concentration on groups of people and procedures for gathering and communicating information with clearly specified temporal relations between environmental events, operationally defined procedures and measurable outcomes. This paper reports the application of this model to the problem of designing a special introductory psychology course for transfer students.

**The Problem.** The following issue stimulated the project: how to design an equitable introductory psychology curriculum for transfer students. Frequent complaints voiced by both faculty and transfer students had made the problem apparent to the Director of Undergraduate Studies. In the past, faculty of advanced courses in psychology had complained that transfer students were not prepared for advanced courses because they had not completed introductory course(s) equivalent to the two-course sequence offered in this department. A simple solution had required all transfer students to take the two semester introductory sequence unless they could demonstrate that the course(s) they had taken previously were equivalent to this two semester sequence (i.e., that courses used similar texts covering both Psychology as a Natural Science and Psychology as a Social Science over two semesters). Although this requirement solved the problem for the advanced-level courses, it created new problems. The transfer students and faculty of the introductory courses complained that the solution forced the students through a curriculum that was redundant for many. In addition, because many of these students transferred at the beginning of their junior year, they could not complete the introductory courses, a range of advanced courses and other important activities, such as research, within a four year undergraduate program. Thus, a system of teaching transfer students introductory psychology that would minimize these problems was needed.

A behavioral systems analysis of this problem suggested the following actions: (a) formalize the complaints and other antecedents to the problem by gathering information from all constituencies (input), (b) prepare specific behavioral objectives that when met would potentially solve the problem (objectives), (c) implement the procedures specified in the objectives (procedures), and (d) collect student performance data, and student and faculty satisfaction data to determine the effect of the attempted solution (evaluation).

Methods.    The system studied consisted of 58 faculty members and hundreds of students majoring in psychology at a large state university. Specifically, this study concentrated on the contingencies operating on the behavior of the following people: the Director of Undergraduate Studies, a behavior analyst, 21 faculty who taught introductory psychology courses, 24 faculty who taught advanced undergraduate courses and 84 students who transferred to the department over four semesters.

The behavior analyst conducted meetings and interviews with each of the constituencies of the department: the Director of Undergraduate Studies, the faculty who taught introductory and advanced courses, and both transfer and non-transfer student representatives. Meetings with the faculty revealed that they considered the transfer students' involvement in introductory courses a major problem. A number of those faculty volunteered to assist the behavior analyst to design an introductory curriculum specifically for the transfer students. Some faculty agreed that curriculum guidelines would also help them meet the needs of all students taking introductory psychology, and suggested a partial standardization of the introductory curriculum.

Meetings and interviews with the students revealed concerns similar to those expressed by the faculty. Non-transfer students suggested that the diversity of content taught in different introductory courses provided inadequate preparation for any particular advanced course. Transfer students reiterated their complaints as described above.

The information gathered from these meetings and interviews indicated a general consensus: The department needed a special introductory psychology course for transfer students that identified clearly the concepts students needed to know before entering the advanced courses. The meeting/interview process resulted in the specification of the following six objectives:

1. Given access to current introductory psychology textbooks, the faculty and the analyst will develop a list of topics (concepts and sub-concepts) that are judged to be prerequisites to the advanced courses taught in the Psychology Department at the University of Massachusetts. These topics will be outlined and presented to the current introductory faculty in a form that the faculty can rate as either essential, optional, or not necessary.

2. Given the ratings of the majority of the faculty, the analyst will develop a list of topics that are essential to teach as prerequisites to advanced courses in psychology. This list will be distributed to the department faculty for comment.

3. Given a list of essential topics, a series of meetings and faculty consensus, the faculty will adopt two introductory psychology texts that cover the topics. One text will be used in Psychology as a Natural Science and the other will be used in Psychology as a Social Science. This decision is subject to annual revision.

4. Given the list of essential topics, and the two texts' coverage of these essential topics, the analyst will develop a method for assessing students' knowledge of the prerequisite topics. The method will be evaluated by the students and by the faculty via written course evaluations.

5. Given the list of essential topics, the two selected texts and materials that test for mastery of the essential topics, a course will be developed that is structured around topical modules designed to teach each of the essential topics. These individualized instructional modules will be evalu-

ated continuously by the students taking them and by the faculty who will oversee their development.

6. Given the course materials developed for the essential topics, the faculty will standardize 70% of the introductory material that they teach so that they are consonant with the special modular-based course. These six objectives will be completed within 24 months.

As the project progressed, it became clear that objective six would not be accomplished. Faculty would not agree on a uniform standardization of the regular introductory courses. Therefore, the analyst and Director of Undergraduate Studies decided to eliminate objective six in favor of a single course designed primarily to meet the needs of transfer students. It was assumed that their improved preparations would also reduce the complaints of non-transfer students and faculty of advanced courses.

*Selection of topics and essential concepts.* As a starting point the faculty suggested two texts; one for each of the two emphases. Lists of topics were selected from chapter headings. The analyst then divided the topics into their component concepts according to the following method: A concept was identified if it was featured in a heading or a sub-heading; was a bold-faced printed word; was included within a summary section; or was part of a question within the text material.

The resultant list of concepts was then distributed to all twenty-one faculty of the introductory courses, who were asked to rate each concept as either "E" for essential, "O" for optional or "NN" for not necessary. The questionnaire also asked the faculty to add essential topics and concepts that were not included in the outline.

Then the ten concepts from each chapter that received the highest proportion of essential ratings were analyzed further by identifying their critical features. For example, the concept "reinforcement" was analyzed into its three critical parts: (a) the occurrence of a behavior; (b) that is *followed* by a particular object or event; (c) and the rate of the behavior either increases or maintains over time. In this way, the analyst outlined each topic module.

*Instructional materials and methods.* In order to cover adequately all the concepts identified as essential, chapters were selected from six different texts. Copies of the texts were placed on reserve at the library. These could be taken out overnight or the students could make single copies of the assigned material for their own personal use, as permitted by copyright laws.[2]

Due to the large variability of knowledge and skills among transfer students, it was decided to offer the course according to the Personalized System of Instruction format (Keller, 1968; Johnson & Ruskin, 1977). In addition to permitting flexible enrollments (PSI courses have been offered to just a few or as many as several hundred students at a time), PSI enables students to progress at different rates. The students with advanced repertoires, then, could move rapidly through the content, while those with minimal competence could progress at slower rates. Another advantage of PSI is that it is mastery based. Thus, all transfer students would have to demonstrate a high level of proficiency with the material on completion of this course and would assumedly be prepared adequately for advanced level courses.

Study guides and two forms of quizzes and answer keys were developed for each topic module or "unit." The study guides were designed to prompt a range of responses to the textual material. Questions requested definitions, short essays, original examples, example identifications, and solutions to problems. (See Chase, Sulzer-Azaroff & Johnson, Note 3, for an analysis of an evolving technology for teaching complex concepts.) Quiz questions were similar but not identical. Students were required to demonstrate mastery of each of the 14 units by scoring at least 90%, before being permitted to progress to the next unit.

In addition to these quizzes, the analyst prepared three "review" or "hour exams" consisting of three questions from each unit. Students who took the whole course would take the review tests at the end of each third of the course. Those who wished to test out of taking the course would also take these review tests. A score of 80% or above on all three of these exams and documentation of having passed at least one general psychology course was considered sufficient evidence of preparation in introductory psychology. The remaining procedures were those necessary to implement the course. These procedures followed the standard PSI format as defined by Keller (1968).

Evaluation Methods.    The discrepancy between actual accomplishments and the six original objectives constituted the general evaluation. In addition to the intermittent feedback from the faculty discussed above, several specific evaluation components were also incorporated within the system and applied within the experimental course during each of four semesters.

An item analysis systematically analyzed students' performance on each quiz item to identify problematic items. The question could be examined and revised, if necessary, and the study questions related to that quiz question could be traced to determine if the study guide questions were consistent with the quiz question (Merrill, 1977).

Proctors also kept an *ongoing commentary* on the quiz questions, answer keys and study questions with which the students had reported trouble. Whenever a student challenged the quality of a question, the proctor recorded the problem and, if appropriate, suggested a change. As often as possible the instructor discussed these changes with the proctor. At the end of each semester, two, two-hour sessions were devoted to discussing the suggested revisions with the group of proctors.

The *student feedback forms* were another source of evaluation. These changed throughout the implementation of the course. During all four semesters, a suggestion box and forms were placed at the front of the quiz room. The feedback received ranged from requests to keep the quiz room more quiet to thank-you notes addressed to the proctors—comments too general to provide measurable evaluation data. Another form was added during later semesters to elicit more specific comments regarding curriculum materials (e.g., which questions were too easy, too hard, etc.). Although the suggestion box continued to be used for general feedback, this new form provided data useful for improving the course.[4]

The standard University and Departmental Student Evaluation forms were also used. Although these evaluation forms obtained specific comments from the students, only a few of the questions were applicable to a PSI course. Results of these questions were also used as a basis for revising the course.

Student progress was examined as well. The course would be considered successful only if most students finished within a semester. A final source for assessing the success of the course was whether or not instructors of upper level undergraduate courses complained about the lack of preparation of transfer students after finishing this introductory course. To tap potential complaints, a brief questionnaire was distributed to those faculty asking them whether transfer students were differentially prepared and if they might have any additional comments on the special course for transfers.

Results and Discussion.    As mentioned previously, the project did not achieve objective 6 in the 24-month time period. Additionally, the order of the objectives was rearranged, and the focus of the project narrowed to apply primarily to a special course for transfer students. However, the first five objectives were met within four semesters.

All materials (i.e., texts, quizzes, answer keys and study guides) and course procedures were revised on the basis of student feedback and performance. Ultimately, a single text book was selected, many quiz questions were eliminated or changed and answer keys were rewritten to obtain more reliable scoring of quizzes.

Feedback from students in the PSI course was quite positive. Table 1 displays the results of a few applicable items

#### Table 1. Selected Items from University Student Evaluations

| Item | Spring '79 N[1] | M | SD | Fall '79 N | M | SD | Summer '80 N | M | SD | Fall '80 N | M | SD |
|---|---|---|---|---|---|---|---|---|---|---|---|---|
| The instructor is available to students; has a genuine interest in students and realizes that different students have different needs. | 14 | 6.36[2] | .74 | 17 | 6.06 | .75 | 12 | 6.14 | 1.21 | 18 | 5.89 | 1.37 |
| This course has: | | | | | | | | | | | | |
| Increased my learning, has given me new viewpoints and appreciations, has increased my capacity to think and formulate questions. | 14 | 6.0 | .96 | 17 | 6.06 | .90 | 12 | 6.29 | 1.11 | 18 | 6.39 | .85 |
| Given me extensive knowledge and skills which I expect to be able to put to practical or professional use, and/or to help me deal with and comprehend day-to-day events and phenomena. | 14 | 6.14 | .86 | 17 | 5.82 | .81 | 12 | 5.83 | 1.17 | 18 | 6.11 | .96 |
| I would rate this course in comparison to other courses I have taken at U Mass as: | 14 | 6.14 | .87 | 17 | 6.13 | .83 | 12 | 5.57 | .98 | 18 | 5.81 | 1.05 |

[1]N = number completing questionnaire
[2]1 = hopelessly inadequate—7 = unusually effective

taken from the University Student Evaluation forms. On a scale of one to seven, with 1 being "hopelessly inadequate" and 7 "unusually effective," the scores were quite high for an introductory level course. (Follow-up data taken for the same instructor for an additional semester and with a different instructor for one semester remain outstandingly high.)

Table 2 presents a summary of the students' rates of progress during the first four semesters the experimental course for transfer students was taught. Table 2 also presents review or hour exam performance of these students, demonstrating that quality was not sacrificed for pace.

Table 2. Course Completion Record and Examination Performance in Percents

|  | n | Students | Mean for Hour Exams |
|---|---|---|---|
| Spring 1979 | 19 |  |  |
| Early |  | 62 | 86 |
| On time |  | 19 | 87 |
| Late |  | 19 | 87 |
| Fall 1979 | 24 |  |  |
| Early |  | 54 | 89 |
| On time |  | 38 | 90 |
| Late |  | 8 | 87 |
| Spring 1980 | 14 |  |  |
| Early |  | 57 | 88 |
| On time |  | 29 | 78 |
| Late |  | 14 | 85 |
| Fall 1980 | 27 |  |  |
| Early |  | 48 | 87 |
| On time |  | 44 | 80 |
| Late |  | 8 | 86 |

Early completion is defined as any date before the last day of scheduled classes: On-time is defined as completing between the last day of classes and the last day of the final exam period, and late completion is any date after the last day of exams.

A final version of the course materials was shared with interested faculty, and they were asked to comment on the breadth and depth of the quizzes and study materials. Their feedback permitted further improvements of the course. Subsequent changes will continue to be made to keep up with progress in the field. Student and proctor feedback will continue to be solicited and item analyses conducted. Thus, reciprocity between individuals will continue to produce a dynamic course.

The PSI introductory course for transfer students has continued to be taught since its developer completed his doctoral training and moved elsewhere. In fact, during one semester, a rumor circulated that the course might be abandoned. The organization of undergraduate psychology majors rapidly mobilized to head off the event were it necessary. (Fortunately, it wasn't.) In fact, several instructors have volunteered to take responsibility for coordinating the course for the next several semesters. Instructors have reported that the transfer students continue to complain that they are required to re-take an introductory course, but it seems that they complain less frequently and intensively than previously. Students have also told their instructors that they feel they have learned a good deal and feel better prepared to move on to more advanced material.

Finally, eight of the faculty who teach advanced courses returned the questionnaire on transfer students. Of these eight, none reported any problem with the preparation of transfer students. In fact, they could not discriminate the transfer students from the other students in their courses!

Conclusions. A behavioral system analysis is apparently applicable to the solution of a complex instructional problem involving a substantial number of people. The success we have documented suggests that a behavioral systems approach may be relevant for the solution of various curriculum design problems. However, our experience has suggested that a number of variables should be closely monitored.

First, the success or failure of different components might be attributable to the degree to which the analyst can manage real contingencies for all individuals involved in the system. In this particular project, the analyst had no control over the actions of the faculty. Interestingly, the objectives that were directly related to the faculty were the least successful.

Second, one should always ask whether less costly procedures are potentially available for solving the problem. In order to answer this question, measures of cost effectiveness would need to be designed and several alternative procedures tried.

Third, more valid before and after comparisons could be made if different kinds of data were collected. For example, we suggest adding the criterion of student achievement to the objectives. Specifically, data on achievement by transfer students in both introductory and advanced courses should be collected. If this is done both before and after the program is implemented, a more refined, precise evaluation of the program would be possible.

It should be recalled that the purpose of this paper was to demonstrate how behavioral systems analysis could be used to design a special introductory course for transfer students. The data indicated that the course met the demands of an eclectic department without requiring transfer students to study redundant introductory material. The students who had adequate preparation in all the topic areas could test-out of the course, others could study the topics that had not been covered in previous courses, and finally, those that needed to take the entire course could do so. These results suggested that behavioral systems analysis did provide an organized, dynamic model for effecting changes that influenced a large number of people. It is hoped that this example will foster the use of behavioral systems analysis for approaching similar problems. The authors believe that by concentrating on the issues raised here that behavioral systems analysis can promote long-range instructional innovation and improvement.

## References

Bateson, G. *Steps to an ecology of mind.* New York: Balantine Books, 1972.

Frederiksen, L. W., & Johnson, R. P. Organizational Behavior Management. In M. Hersen, R. M. Eisler & P. M. Miller (Eds.), *Progress in behavior modification* (Vol. 12). New York: Academic Press, 1981.

Johnson, K. R., & Ruskin, R. S. *Behavioral instruction: An evaluative review.* Washington, DC: American Psychological Association, 1977.

Keller, F. S. "Goodbye teacher. . ." *Journal of Applied Behavior Analysis*, 1968, 1, 78-89.

Krapfl, J. Accountability for behavioral engineers. In S. Wood (Ed.), *Issues in evaluating behavior modification. Proceedings of the First Drake Conference on Professional Issues in Behavior Analysis.* Champaign, IL: Research Press, 1975.

Maley, R. F., & Harshbarger, D. The integration of behavior analysis and systems analysis: A look to the future? In D. Harshbarger & R. F. Maley (Eds.), *Behavioral analysis and systems analysis: An integrative approach to mental health problems.* Kalamazoo, MI: Behaviordelia, 1974.

Malott, R. W. *An introduction to behavior modification.* Kalamazoo, MI: Behaviordelia, 1973.

Merrill, M. D., Richards, R. E., Schmidt, R. V., & Wood, N. D. *The instructional strategy diagnostic profile training manual.* Salt Lake City: Coursewares, 1977.

### Notes

1. Noah, J. C., Krapfl, J. E., & Maley, R. F. Behavioral systems analysis: An integration of behavior analysis and systems analysis to meet the demands of accountability. Unpublished manuscript, 1977. (Available from the Psychology Department, West Virginia University, Morgantown, WV 26506).

2. This procedure was used for three of the four semesters described. During the fourth semester the authors found a text that adequately covered ten concepts from each topic area described as being essential by the faculty.

3. Chase, P. M., Sulzer-Azaroff, B., & Johnson, K. R. Verbal behavior and verbal instruction. Are functional classes functionally distinct? Unpublished paper, 1982. (Available from the Psychology Department, West Virginia University, Morgantown, WV 26506.)

4. A copy of this form may be obtained from the first author.

5. Portions of this paper were presented at the Association of Behavior Analysis Conference, Milwaukee, WI, May 1981.

6. The authors wish to thank Thomas Zane and William Tyson for comments on an earlier version of the manuscript, Douglas Lynch for assistance in developing student feedback questionnaires, and the students and faculty of the Department of Psychology who participated in this program.

---

# Teaching a Large Lecture Course in Psychology: Turning Defeat into Victory

Brett Silverstein
*State University of New York at Stony Brook*

This experienced teacher gets students involved, attends to educational basics, and uses many undergraduate TAs to make the large course succeed.

In recent years the task of teaching undergraduate college courses has become more difficult. Class size appears to be increasing while resources are decreasing. Some people believe that incoming college students are less well-prepared than they used to be. If college teachers are to meet these challenges we must increase the attention paid to teaching. This article represents an attempt to stimulate debate about the goals and methods of teaching psychology, and to share the techniques that I have found useful, during the past five years, in trying to provide quality education in an Introductory Psychology course with an enrollment of nearly 1200 students.

**Theoretical Background.** In teaching the course I combine two perspectives on education that have sometimes been conceptualized as being mutually exclusive. The first, which might be called the classical perspective, emphasizes the importance of imparting to students those skills and ideas that are considered to be important for educated people in our society. The ability to write well, to present oneself orally, and to read and understand the ideas of the "great thinkers" broadens and empowers a person regardless of his or her college major or occupation.

The second perspective, which might be called the Freirean or critical consciousness perspective (Freire 1975; Shor 1980) came to prominence after the campus turmoil of the late 1960s. This perspective places emphasis on the process of education in stressing the need to avoid a "banking model" of teaching wherein the teacher does all of the talking and the students simply listen and memorize, as if the teacher were depositing knowledge in the students' minds. The perspective goes beyond a Socratic model in emphasizing true dialogue wherein students play an active role in defining important questions and in applying the material to the world in which they live. The perspective also stresses the need to make course material relevant to the lives of the students.

The narrowest conception of a relevant course is one in which the material is all taken from areas with which students are familiar. Courses on pop music or on the history of the 60s exemplify this approach. But "making a course relevant" can be more broadly conceptualized as connecting the material to the important experiences of people in our society and to the problems faced by the students and faced by people about whom the students are concerned. Thus relevance is not simply a function of the choice of course material but also of the approach to that material. It is my belief that the importance of most (if not all) of the truly great ideas of psychology (and of other disciplines for that matter) lies in their connection to the experiences of people and in their ability to explicate who we are and on how we might solve our problems. Thus, the most effective teaching is that which can bring out the relevant aspects of any important material.

The process might be framed in terms of a Piagetian model of assimilation and accommodation. In bringing out the connections between the course material and the experiences of students, a teacher allows the students to more easily assimilate the material into schemas that are already in existence. At the same time the students are accommodating to the material, broadening their schemas, and in the process, digesting the knowledge of their culture. We might even apply the Piagetian framework to the students' motivation for learning. Students will be more eager, and thus more likely, to learn material that can be assimilated to their lives. At the same time the material will exert a pull on the students, enticing them to want to learn more and broadening their view of what is relevant and interesting.

Goals.  Before discussing the methods used in teaching a course it is important to clearly define its goals. Certainly an Introductory Psychology course must introduce students to the basic facts and findings of psychology with enough breadth so that students who take no other psychology courses will be familiar with the most important aspects of psychology and students who want to take other psychology courses can get some sense as to which other courses they might like to take. As this is the first course taken by psychology majors it is important to focus on how psychologists attack a problem: What questions do we ask? How do we answer them? What kinds of information are supplied by the different areas of psychology—in my course, developmental, social, personality, and clinical psychology? How is the scientific method applied to psychology? This calls for more attention to the concepts of psychology than is given in many introductory courses, which tend to stress the facts. In other words, many teachers believe that given enough of the facts and research findings that constitute the data of psychology, students will eventually understand the concepts (an inductive approach, based perhaps on the philosophy of empiricism and associationism). I believe that unless the theories, assumptions, and concepts underlying the data are given at least equal weight the students will be overwhelmed by a mass of disconnected facts and will quickly forget the material (a deductive approach, rooted more in Kantian philosophy).

But an Introductory Psychology course should do more than just provide an overview of the field of psychology and begin to train young psychologists. The course is one part of a college education and should promote the training of educated adults. This goal is common to all disciplines. Our problem is how to use the subject matter of psychology to provide the ideas, skills, and attitudes that constitute being educated in our society.

To begin, we can teach the ideas of those psychologists such as Freud, Piaget, the Gestaltists, whose work has significantly influenced the way people in the twentieth century interpret their world. In addition, we can relate the "great ideas" of psychology to those provided by other disciplines. In my course students read and relate to the rest of the course the writings of philosophers such as Plato, sociologists such as George Herbert Mead, social theorists such as Karl Marx and Peter Berger and Thomas Luckman, and anthropologists such as Margaret Mead. An educated person must be able to relate the overlapping ideas of different disciplines and to transcend disciplinary boundaries when asking questions about the world. If we do not want to produce narrowly-focused technocrats who are only aware of

the material of their discipline, and if we do want to train researchers who some day may contribute to scientific revolutions by reshaping the boundaries of psychology, we must make students aware of the overlaps that exist between psychology and other disciplines. The transdisciplinary perspective is also less confusing and less atomizing to students who take courses in many departments each semester.

As part of a general education, students must also develop their skills in various areas. One important area is reading. By the time they enter college most students are able to read English sentences but many are unable to read scholarly articles and books with complete comprehension. In order to instill in students the confidence that they can understand works that contain large words and foreign phrases, and to give them practice in reading, they must be asked to read works (preferably primary sources) of varying difficulty. Sometimes they find that if they avoid being overwhelmed by scholarly writing they are able to understand it almost immediately. At other times they need to go over the more complex readings line by line with someone who can explain them. This process must at least begin in the introductory courses if students are to get as much as possible from their college educations.

Writing is another skill that must be mastered by educated people. To this end students must be given some training in how to write well, a lot of practice in writing, and feedback about their strengths and weaknesses in putting together written arguments which are clear, concise, comprehensive, and interesting. All teachers must participate in this process. Relying on Introductory Composition courses to complete the job is naive.

Educated people must also be able to present their ideas orally. Before they are able to do so most students must overcome their inhibitions about speaking in front of an audience and must, again, learn to present material clearly and concisely. Students who are forced to give oral presentations are often afraid at first but most of them eventually find that it is not so difficult as they had thought it would be. Pride, the fear of looking "dumb," and the desire for a good grade usually motivate them to put a lot of time into preparing their presentations so that the presenters as well as the students to whom they present often learn a great deal from oral presentations. Some presenters have no problems while others need help in structuring their material or in overcoming stage fright. If every student in a class must do an oral presentation and if the class discusses how the listeners can make the task of the presenters least frightening, students can receive useful practice in presenting their ideas in a relatively unthreatening situation.

The final skill to be developed is that of dialogue. Students must learn to share their ideas. Shy students must be helped to overcome their inhibitions about participation. The more advanced students must learn how to participate actively without overwhelming their classmates. All of these skills can best be learned by means of discussion, practice, and feedback. Therefore students in my course read many primary sources, write many essays, give oral presentations, and spend much time discussing the course material while receiving feedback about their performance in all of these activities.

Education is also a process of instilling attitudes in

students. I believe that good teachers will consciously choose the attitudes they want to promote and will use methods that promote them rather than promote other attitudes by default. For example, many college courses promote competition among students through the use of grading curves and a stress on working individually. I attempt to promote attitudes of cooperation by using no curves, by having students teach one another, by assigning some projects that are most effectively done in groups, and by allowing students to help each other with their assignments so long as they do not write each other's papers.

Another important attitude is that of critical thinking, the belief that the events that occur in the course of everyday life are not random and are not to be taken for granted; that they can be understood with some effort, so that people can, and must, continually ask questions about themselves and their environment. To promote this critical attitude I use techniques such as projects (see below) and demonstrations that relate the material to the everyday lives of the students. Psychology is a particularly appropriate subject on which to use this approach. Relating the material to the lives of students both increases their motivation to learn and gives them practice for using the material outside of school. It is particularly effective when much of the relating is done by the students in discussion classes rather than for the students in lectures.

**Format.** The format of the course has changed some over the years. At the present time, each week students attend an hour-long lecture (the lecture hall holds about half of the 1100-1200 students enrolled in the course so I give each lecture twice), participate in two hour-long discussion classes (consisting of 15-20 students each), read a few selections from a book of readings, do a short (less than an hour) out-of-class project, and write or rewrite an essay.

**Lecture.** The lecture hall has a stage and a balcony and a microphone that must be used if the lecturer is to be heard. That these are not ideal conditions for education is perhaps best exemplified by one of the students in the class who accidentally walked into my office one day, found he was in the wrong place, turned to leave, and then looked back and asked me if I was Brett Silverstein. When I said that I was he said "Oh, I'm in your class but I didn't recognize you in person."

Even a lecture given to 600 people at a time can be effective in presenting material if it is used correctly. A book presents material in a manner that allows students to learn at their own pace, so most complex material is better learned by reading and by discussion in small groups than in a large lecture. But a live lecturer is more dynamic than a book and a good lecture can excite, involve, and stimulate students. To do so, however, on a stage in a large lecture hall in front of 600 people, some of whom are in a balcony, I have to put on a show. This does not mean that I never simply explain material. It does mean that whenever possible the material is "brought to life." There are many techniques available for doing this. Attention getting experiments, such as the Asch conformity study, can be reenacted. Hypothetical constructs, such as the id, ego, and superego, can become characters that engage in a dialogue. Metaphors, particularly those with a visual component such as Flavell's (1963) depiction of

Piagetian processes of assimilation and accommodation as similar to eating a chicken leg, can be used in explaining abstract concepts. Examples of the psychological processes being discussed can be taken from the lecturer's life or from the lives of the students. For example, to make plausible the notion of unconscious thought I relate how one day when a woman friend with whom I was having a drawn-out breakup after a long romance was visiting my apartment, I found myself humming some music while doing the dishes. After a few moments I was able to remember the words to the music I was humming: "Please release me, let me go, for I don't love you anymore."

Demonstrations of the processes being lectured on that allow the students to experience those processes during the lecture are very effective. Early in the semester I ask the students to help me with a demonstration. They are told to stand, cover one ear with a hand, put the other arm out in front of them and rotate it, and hum. Almost everyone complies with my request. I allow them to continue this ridiculous activity for about a minute, by which time most of them have stopped. I then announce that we are about to deal with the topic "obedience to authority," that is, how, under the right circumstances, people will do almost anything when instructed to do so by an "expert" or "authority figure." Later in the course I ask the students how many of them agree with the statement made by Lenin (or Ayatollah Khomeini or Moammar Qaddafi depending upon who is in the news that week) that "When a government fails to meet the needs of its people it is not only the right of the people but their duty to overthrow that government." Usually from 5-to-25% of the students agree. I later ask them how many agree with the Declaration of Independence. Almost all of them agree. I then point out that I made a slight error and that the original quote actually came from the Declaration of Independence. We then go on to discuss Hovland's work on the effect of the credibility of the communicator on attitude change. One final example: After the students learn about Piaget's conservation studies I show them a rectangle made out of string. I pull slightly on the top of the rectangle while releasing the bottom, turning the figure into a parallelogram and ask the students how the area within the figure has changed. Most students answer that the area is unchanged. I again pull slightly making the top right hand angle of the figure more acute and again ask how the area has changed. I continue pulling and asking until the top of the parallelogram meets the bottom and the area of the figure becomes zero. Sometime in the middle of the process the students realize that the area cannot be unchanged since it is disappearing. The momentary confusion and discomfort they experience is very instructive when I explain how children learn conservation and how schemas change.

Jokes can be used not only to make the lecture entertaining but also to make the material memorable. After seeing the film "Annie Hall" in which Woody Allen introduces his major points by telling two very old, very corny jokes I realized that a well-chosen joke, even if it is not extremely funny, can make material more concrete and easier to remember. For example, I tell the students that for the last month, each morning when I left my house I saw my neighbor throwing salt on his lawn. Finally, my curiosity got the best of me and I went over to him one morning and asked "Mr. _____ (I usually use the name of the President of the university in order to get some cheap laughs) why do you throw salt on your lawn every morning?" "To keep the Soviet army away" he answered. So I told him "There are no Soviet troops within a thousand miles of here." His face lit up with delight as he crowed "You see. It works!" The groans following the corny punchline do not stop the students from repeating the joke to their friends. The joke relaxes everyone, maintains the attention of the audience, serves as an excellent introduction to attribution theory (which focuses upon the rules people use and the errors they make in explaining the causes of behavior) and can be referred to again in introducing the topic of self-fulfilling prophecy. I believe (although I do not yet have any formal evidence) that jokes like these also make the material easier to understand and remember.

I tend to go into a few topics in depth rather than spend a little time on each of many topics. The shotgun approach does expose students to more material but I believe that it is not good for teaching the concepts underlying the material and that it leads to more forgetting. I choose topics that have been important in the field of psychology and that can be used to stimulate thinking about everyday life such as the work on conformity, the development of sex roles, the psychology of aging, situational effects on personality, defense mechanisms, and irrational cognitions. When the topic is complex, like Piaget's theory of cognitive development, I go over it once at moderate speed and allow the teaching assistants to clear up problems in discussion classes.

**Text.** I do not use a typical text book. I find that the available texts contain too little on any one topic, are not conceptual enough, almost never cross disciplinary boundaries, and do not teach reading skills that apply to most material that adults read outside of school. I use a book of readings compiled specifically for the course. There are publishing companies that will obtain copyright permissions and reprint articles or sections from books in the form of a paperback reader if you choose the articles and edit the material. These companies even provide catalogues of popular articles that are easily available. The first edition of my reader (Silverstein, 1978) took quite a bit of time to compile but it allowed me to personalize the course, to include primary sources, to vary the level of difficulty of the reading, and to include relevant readings from other disciplines, some of them in the form of poetry. Each year, based on suggestions from the teaching assistants, I have made small changes in the reader, sometimes including material that I have written. As a supplement I keep some textbooks available in the office for those who feel the need to consult them.

**Discussion Classes.** Most of the learning occurs in discussion classes led by teaching assistants. I would remind those who feel that I am somehow being remiss in my duties by foisting off the teaching on assistants (two discussion classes each week and only one lecture) that (a) people learn best by using, discussing, and questioning material, not by simply listening to it; and (b) that 1/20th of a good TA is better than 1/600th of a professor. The discussion classes are very personal, beginning with communication exercises which are used to reduce inhibitions, stimulate participation, and, as a bonus, teach about humanistic psychology. For example, the students may be asked to introduce themselves by using an

adjective that describes them and that begins with the first letter of their first name (e.g. "I'm Bashful Brett") and then explaining their choice of adjectives, or they may be asked to form a line, one after another making a different bodily movement and a different noise. If some of the exercises may seem silly, they do serve to create a sense of community and to "break the ice."

In the average week the discussion classes are of two different types. One type focuses directly on the lecture and readings. Students ask questions about the material, and discuss their answers to a set of questions that we have written to stimulate thought. The questions, which are printed in the reader, can seldom be answered with a simple word or phrase. They are designed to incite disagreement. The TA uses these questions to start discussion and to diagnose gaps in the student's knowledge, which necessitate mini-lectures by the TAs. During these classes the difficult readings are gone over in depth.

In the other type of discussion class the students discuss their weekly projects. These projects are designed to bring the material alive to the students by demonstrating it at work in their own lives. The projects take little time to do, are fun, and provide the students with shared experiences that they can analyze using the ideas from the lectures and reading. For example, when we are discussing sex roles the students create and perform skits which show typical male-female interactions. They then repeat the skits with the females taking the male roles and vice versa. The skits are fun and they help the students to become more aware of the power and frequency of sex roles. The skits (particularly those involving parents and children) serve as good jumping-off points for a discussion of social learning—modelling and reinforcement—and the development of sex roles. When we discuss behavior modification the students are required to use simple behavior modification techniques to change one of their problem behaviors. TAs are encouraged to design their own projects, and some of the discussion sessions are left open so that they can review material that continues to present problems or discuss topics that are of particular interest to them or to the class. The creativity of some of the TAs has been very impressive and each year we include new projects or demonstrations originally designed by the previous year's TAs.

The teaching assistants lecture only when they must. Usually they stimulate discussions by asking questions or by volunteering anecdotes from their own experience, they promote equal participation, they step in when the discussions of projects becomes too "silly," they constantly connect the discussions of real life to points from the lecture and readings and the discussion of concepts to experiences from real life, they grade discussion classes and essays (see below), they help students to prepare their oral presentations, and they give help outside of class to students with special problems such as poor writing skills, language difficulties, or shyness. Before I discuss how I find and train these wonderful TAs, I would like to briefly describe the grading scheme used in the course.

**Grading.** The grade for the course is based on participation in discussion classes, one oral presentation, and essays written throughout the term. Students write two kinds of essays. Three times during the year they must answer a question made up by their TA which necessitates integrating material from several weeks of class such as "Compare the notion of intelligence used by Piaget with that used to create IQ tests" or "Compare G. H. Mead's theory of the development of the self with Freud's view of the development of the superego." In addition to these three "mandatory" essays students must write some "optional" essays. These essays are optional in that the students get to choose their topics from among the topics that we have covered in the course and they can do as many of them as they want. The essays must integrate the material from one week—the lecture, readings, projects, and discussion. The optional essays are not written in response to questions made up by the TAs, thus forcing the students to learn to pick out the most important points and to ask questions for themselves and allowing the more advanced students to exhibit much creativity. Many students do not like this freedom, so some TAs supply suggested questions in the beginning of the course, but an educated person must be able to do more than answer someone else's questions. Students are allowed to substitute for one optional essay an easy-to-write essay on the scientific method used in experiments in which they have participated. This provides a non-coercive method for promoting participation in experiments (which is also educational).

The TAs provide extensive feedback on the strengths and weaknesses of the essays that are evaluated on both the knowledge of the material they exhibit and the form of presentation they use—including grammar and sentence structure. Only three grades are given on the essays: "Excellent," "Satisfactory," or "Rewrite." The use of only three grades takes some of the emphasis off grading, slightly reduces feelings of competition, and makes grading easier. Students can rewrite any essay. An "R" can become an "S" or an "E" and an "S" can become an "E." Some rewrites necessitate multiple changes and perhaps a complete rethinking of the essay, but others are minor, calling for perhaps a change in one paragraph or a mention of a reading that was ignored. Rewriting turns grading into a learning process, for we know that an effective way to learn is to try to do something, to be corrected, and then to try to improve. It also allows the TAs to have high standards without penalizing the students. Even a good essay can always be improved.

The grade for the course is based on the number of "E"s and "S"s received on discussions (discussion classes are graded twice each semester), essays, and the oral presentation. For example, this year to get an "A" a student must get two "S"s in discussion class plus five "E"s and three "S"s on the essays and the oral presentation. To get a "C" a student must get two "S"s in discussion class plus three "E"s and three "S"s on the essays and the presentation. This grading scheme allows students to get whatever grade they choose to work for. Students who start behind the rest of the class can rewrite as many essays as needed to get "A"s. All guesswork is eliminated and a student who is not completely up on the material on a particular day is not permanently penalized, as occurs when exams are used. Of course, some students do not like to write and would rather take multiple choice tests. I warn these students at the beginning of the semester that my course is not for them and that they might prefer to take a different Introductory Psychology course.

**Teaching Assistants.** A large teaching staff is needed for the course. In order to have discussion classes of 15 to 20 students each, 75 sections are needed. Each teaching assistant teaches two classes: so I use about 40 TAs for the course. The psychology department cannot afford to assign 40 graduate students to teach a single course, so I recruit senior psychology majors as TAs. The use of undergraduates began as a necessary, experimental compromise. I have been so pleased with the results that I now prefer undergraduates to most graduate students.

I recruit them through announcements made in psychology classes, posters, and an ad in the school newspaper that instructs interested students to attend one of the information meetings. At the meetings I explain my philosophy of teaching and, with the help of former TAs, I warn the students about how much work they will have to do. I find that the heavy warning serves as my best selection criterion. Those students who are not dissuaded are highly motivated and not afraid to work. Of the 100 or so students who attend the meetings usually about 70 fill out the application forms that ask them to list the psychology courses they have taken, the courses in related disciplines such as the social sciences, philosophy, or education, and the experiences they have had working with people (such as tutoring, being a camp counselor, or volunteering at a mental hospital). Applicants are also asked to write an essay about teaching that provides us with information about their attitudes as well as a sample of their writing. Each candidate is interviewed by a committee composed of at least two former TAs. When they disagree about the qualifications of a candidate, I interview the candidate a second time.

The 42 candidates that are selected (I choose a few extra because some drop out over the summer) attend a preparatory meeting in the spring during which we get to know each other, we deal with some administrative details, and I assign Ira Shor's book *Critical Teaching and Everyday Life* to be read over the summer.

The day before classes start in the fall semester I meet with the TAs for a day-long orientation session. The session builds a sense of community, prepares them for their first few classes, and accomplishes last-minute business. During the orientation we do the humanistic exercises, we talk about how to prepare for a class (they may do the first project), I and some former TA lead sample discussions, we discuss the philosophy of education while reviewing Shor's book, and we go over the information that students will want about grading, requirements, syllabus, etc.

Each week the TAs attend a three-hour seminar on teaching. They receive credit for attending and I receive credit for teaching it (i.e., it serves as my second course). The TAs are organized into three teams and, along with me, these teams run the seminar. The teaching team collects and disseminates ideas for upcoming discussions and projects and organizes observation and constructive criticism of the teaching of each TA by others. The writing team checks on the feedback and grades given on essays, leads sessions on teaching writing (with help from me and the Shor book), and gives help to students with special writing problems. The coordinating team deals with administrative details including planning course evaluations. I lead discussions on solutions to typical teaching problems (e.g., lack of participation, shyness, cheating), give extra lectures on, and answer questions about, the material that is hardest to understand, and consult with the coordinators of each team (who are allowed to teach one discussion class rather than two) in order to provide guidance as well as to keep track of everything that goes on.

Earlier, I noted that I have come to prefer undergraduate TAs to most graduates. There are several reasons for this preference. When given enough credits the undergraduates have more time to devote to teaching than does the average graduate student. The honor of being chosen and the newness of the experience of being given responsibility motivate the undergraduates to work very hard to do a good job. They are also often able to relate better to freshmen than are graduate students. I worry about exploiting them, but most of them tell me that they enjoy and learn from the experience. Some even call it their best experience as undergraduates. In addition to course credit they benefit from an experience that is more exciting than is a typical class, they learn about teaching and about psychology (which is useful in reviewing for the GREs), they can include the teaching experience on their applications for employment and for graduate school, and they can get a recommendation from me. I also worry that using undergraduates results in exploiting the students who enroll in the class. Most of the TAs, however, receive excellent evaluations from their classes; better, I believe, than those given to the average graduate in other psychology courses, and certainly better than those given to some of the poorly-trained graduates who teach introductory courses in some of the other departments.

There are many problems with this system for teaching Introductory Psychology. If not used properly it is susceptible to exploitation of both students and TAs. Each year one or two of them find that they cannot handle the job and do it poorly. I am concerned that the use of undergraduates may eventually put graduate students and perhaps even professors out of work. I also wonder whether it is good to try to improve teaching in giant lecture courses or whether we might be better off just using our energy to fight against teaching under these conditions. But for now I have decided that the disadvantages and dangers of teaching an introductory psychology course as outlined above are outweighed by the opportunities made available for providing information about psychology, access to important ideas about the world, skills, self-understanding, training in critical thinking, and enjoyment to large numbers of students. I hope that we can increase the attention given to discussions about what constitutes good teaching and the number of attempts made to share ideas about methods that have been used to improve the teaching of psychology.

### References

Flavell, J. H. *The developmental psychology of Jean Piaget.* Princeton, NJ: D. Van Nostrand, 1963.

Freire, P. *Education for critical consciousness.* New York: Seabury, 1975.

Shor, I. *Critical teaching and everyday life.* Boston: South End, 1980.

Silverstein, B. *Introductory psychology reader.* Lexington, MA: Ginn, 1978

# A Different Approach to Teaching Introductory Psychology

Larry D. Walker and Paul W. Inbody
*Oral Roberts University*

"Happy students probably exert
more effort toward
achievement than unhappy ones."

Psychology, which is now enjoying an unprecedented popularity on college campuses (Psychology: Hot Course . ., 1973), probably serves as many students with its beginning courses as any other academic discipline. Therefore, the introductory psychology course should be one of the most interesting and challenging courses on campus. Too often it is not. Student complaints usually include one or more of the following: (a) the classes are too large, (b) the teacher is a poor lecturer and uninterested in the students, (c) the tests are unfair, (d) there is improper feedback to students regarding test performance, (e) course grades are based solely on test performance, etc.

The number and severity of the listed complaints are necessarily aggravated by the circumstances under which many introductory psychology courses are offered. A typical course on university campuses involves large numbers of students being lectured to by one of the following: (a) an academically qualified but uninterested adjunct professor, (b) a full-time professor who is academically qualified but inexperienced, or (c) a graduate assistant who may be minimally qualified but also inexperienced. The large classes alone impose almost insurmountable barriers when it comes to establishing rapport with individual students. The additional problems of uninterested instructors or instructors who have had little training and experience, if in fact any at all, in the art of teaching, can make the almost insurmountable barriers impossible. Although neither large classes nor inexperienced teachers necessarily comprise intolerable situations alone, the combination of both frequently leads to much student disenchantment.

Student criticisms of introductory psychology courses sometimes stem directly from the lecture method used in teaching those courses. The lecture method at best is only moderately acceptable to students (McLeish, 1968, 1970). Inexperienced and uninterested lecturers, as are frequently found in charge of introductory psychology courses, sometimes pass off as lectures a mere reading of key sentences or phrases from the textbook. Very little material from outside the textbook is made a part of their presentations. This type of approach appears to assume audience illiteracy. While practical illiteracy may be a fact with individual students, it is inappropriate to make such a blanket assumption on a college campus. Most college students are capable of reading the textbook for themselves and probably prefer to do so. Whether or not they do read it is an entirely different question.

The frequency with which the discussed problems arise suggests that the traditional approach to teaching introductory psychology is less than satisfactory. It was decided that the Oral Roberts University (ORU) student body, while nothing like as large as that of many state universities, provides too many candidates for an introductory psychology course for the University to continue to think in traditional terms. This was especially true in light of the University's claims to personalize education, capitalizing upon relatively small student-teacher ratios. Consequently the authors have designed what is believed to be a rather unique approach to teaching introductory psychology. While the approach is not totally different than one reported by Ingalls and Moakley (1971) at Northeastern University in Boston, the ORU program has some unique characteristics of its own.

**The ORU Course.** The ORU Learning Resources Center purchased on behalf of the Department of Behavioral Sciences sixteen contemporary films selected to satisfy course objectives set up by the professor. These films were then placed on video-tapes, along with objectives and comments by the professor, for presentation on the University's Dial Access Information Retrieval System (DAIRS). The student's first major learning experience for each week is the retrieval of this information at his convenience from any one of numerous retrieval stations on campus. The student is thus presented vital subject matter via a professional production adapted for local needs that entertains as well as educates. The video tape experience scheduled for each week is supplemented with a rather stringent reading assignment from a widely used textbook of introductory psychology.

A DAIRS presentation of subject matter has at least four distinct advantages over the traditional classroom lecture. (a) The convenience of retrieving information from most anywhere on campus makes the material easily accessible. The dial access retrieval system on the ORU campus allows a student to retrieve the information on a properly installed home television set, thus bringing the material right into his dormitory room. (b) The problem of students' missing lectures is eliminated. While all sixteen video-tapes are not part of the DAIRS program for the entire semester, each tape is shown often enough to accommodate the schedules of all conscientious students. If a student should inadvertently miss a video-tape, he still has two alternatives for getting the material first-hand. The student can request a special scheduling of the video-tape, or check out from the library circulation desk a sound track of the video-tape to be played by himself on one of several audio-tape machines. The audio-tape machines, which are scattered throughout the library, do not disturb other library activities since they are equipped with earphones instead of speakers. (c) The video-tape scripts are professionally prepared to prevent redundancy and the repetition of reading materials, and (d) each section of introductory psychology students is guaranteed a standardized presentation of important subject matter.

A second major learning experience that involves each student each week is participation in a 1-hour discussion of selected topics taken from the week's video-tape and reading assignments. No attempt is made during this small group meeting of twenty or fewer students to repeat material presented in the textbook or video-tape. The already small discussion groups are frequently broken down even further as recommended by Maier (1971). The resulting smaller groups practically compel some input from all class members, thus eliminating a major source of dissatisfaction with traditional introductory psychology courses. No student can argue that he has no opportunity to verbalize his attitudes and opinions because of a few, highly articulate students who tend to dominate large-group discussions. The tasks of the small-group interactions range from discussions of selected materials from the reading assignments and video-tapes to solving hypothetical problems suggested by those materials.

**Laboratory Experience.** A third major learning experience for each student consists of an average of one to two hours per week spent in the department's psychology laboratory. It was assumed that an appropriate laboratory experience would not only introduce the student to scientific methodology, but also provide variety that would be a significant motivating factor. Efforts were made in designing the laboratory part of the course to incorporate the suggestions of Regula (1971) which, in our opinion, have merit. The resulting student interest has, at least to this early stage in the history of the new course, supported the integrity of those suggestions.

Introductory psychology students are introduced to the methodology of scientific psychology by serving as experimenters in a variety of elementary experiments. The traditional approach is for students to serve as subjects in the research of graduate students which, according to student comments and through our own experience, can get quite boring and unchallenging. Oral Roberts University students act as experimenters rather than subjects in their own experiments. Lower animals as well as other human beings are used as subjects, thus giving the students an appreciation for both types of research. Students are allowed to schedule each of the experiments at their convenience during the forty or more hours that the laboratory is open each week. The flexibility in scheduling promotes student cooperation and interest.

A significant limitation of laboratory courses has been the problem of matching "the experimental expertise of the student with the expertise required by the experimental designs" (Regula, 1971, p. 1021). This limitation was minimized by staffing the ORU introductory psychology laboratory with an ample supply of assistants trained in the statistical procedures involved. Each assistant is given the responsibility of aiding a given number of students in meaningfully interpreting the data derived from experiments, thus assuring the student of some personal help in this very frustrating task. The assistants, being senior psychology majors who have satisfactorily completed the department's course in experimental psychology, are adequately prepared to accept this responsibility.

A fringe benefit of the laboratory program is the opportunity it provides for upper-division psychology students to gain experience in operating a laboratory. The assistants, some of whom aspire to be teachers, have had considerable laboratory experience as students. However, the opportunity for them to encounter the day-by-day problems of laboratory operation, such as scheduling students, providing appropriate data forms, and organizing, wiring, and maintaining apparatuses, is considered invaluable. The assistants are given a major share of responsibilities in these areas. Although the professor is always available for consultation, the introductory psychology laboratory is a student-managed and student-operated laboratory. Assistants are given an appropriate number of credit hours for their work instead of cash, thus minimizing the strain on the departmental budget for laboratory operation.

**Student Assessment.** The assistants are also involved in, although not finally responsible for, the evaluation of student performance. Objective tests are used for evaluating student achievement in the reading and video-tape parts of the course. However, an independent evaluation of laboratory performance gives the student an opportunity of showing progress apart from his skill at performing on objective tests. A major criticism of traditional psychology courses has been that evaluation was restricted to performance on objective tests which, according to the critical students, discriminate against them, their personal skills not being measurable by such tests. The ORU introductory psychology course allows a student to earn approximately one-third (31 percent) of his course grade in the laboratory. While student criticisms may not always be valid, it can be argued that happy students probably exert more effort toward achievement than unhappy ones. To the extent that this is true, the ORU program offers some relief in the area of motivating students.

All objective tests are scheduled by the student in advance and on an individual basis during laboratory hours. The laboratory assistant on duty at any given time administers the test to students who have previously scheduled themselves for testing during that time. The tests are then scored, the grades recorded on confidential forms, and the answer sheets filed for future reference by the laboratory assistants. The flexibility of scheduling examinations benefits the students by allowing them to take the examination when they are ready. It benefits the professor by eliminating the need to assemble large groups of students for testing at one time, a procedure that inevitably results in excessive numbers of make-up examinations.

The assistants fill a post-testing role that minimizes a major source of criticism in traditional courses, that of providing needed feedback to students on test performance. To give detailed test feedback to the hundreds of students enrolled in some traditional psychology classes is an impossibility. It would be necessary to go over every test in class in order to avoid going over it numerous times for individual students. This procedure is undesirable for at least two reasons. (a) The time necessary to merely redistribute answer sheets and test forms, aside from the time necessary to go over the tests, would be prohibitive. (b) The time spent in going over tests would be perceived as a waste for students uninterested in such feedback. Consequently many students never receive anything in the way of desired feedback more than a test score. The ORU program makes the laboratory assistants responsible for providing students with test feedback when requested.

**Conclusion.** In conclusion, there is probably no single approach to teaching any course, regardless of how innovative, that will eliminate all student complaints. To attempt to eliminate all student complaints might not be a worthwhile endeavor. However, to minimize complaints while maintaining course quality is considered a worthwhile goal by the ORU faculty. The course designed by the authors for teaching introductory psychology on the ORU campus is approaching this goal. The course incorporates a variety of learning experiences that eliminates material repetition and minimizes student boredom. Most of the learning experiences can be scheduled at will by the student, thus providing some very desirable flexibility. Evaluation procedures, not being restricted to the use of objective tests, offer the students other welcomed alternatives for showing progress. A close interaction between students and a group of select laboratory assistants preserves a rapport between students and professor that probably would be destroyed if the students became lost in a large, traditional class. Although the program is too young at this point for ultimate evaluation, it was felt that almost anything could be a significant improvement over the traditional approach.

### References

Ingalls, R. E., & Moakley, F. X. Systems approach to development of a complete psychology course of study. *Audio Visual Instruction*, 1971, 16(6), 78.

Maier, N. R. Innovation in education. *American Psychologist*, 1971, 26, 722-725.

McLeish, J. The lecture method. *Cambridge Monographs on Teaching Methods*, 1968, 1, 60. *(Psychological Abstracts*, 1971, 45, No. 11040).

McLeish, J. Students' attitudes to teaching methods. *Alberta Journal of Educational Research*, 1970, 16(3), 179-187. *(Psychological Abstracts*, 1971, 45, No. 9025).

Psychology: Hot course on campus. *Newsweek*, 1973 (May 21), p. 105-107.

Regula, C. R. Some suggestions for improving the psychology laboratory course experience. *American Psychologist*, 1971, 26, 1020-1021.

# Effective Teaching: Facilitative vs. Directive Style

Wilbert J. McKeachie, Yi-Guang Lin,
Mary M. Moffett, and Monica Daugherty
*University of Michigan*

Teachers emphasizing the role of facilitator-person produce students with greater interest in psychology.

In a review of research on college teaching methods, McKeachie and Kulik (1975) pointed to the consistency with which methods emphasizing student participation resulted in greater effectiveness as measured by measures of retention, critical thinking, attitudes, and motivation for further learning. Examples are the studies by McKeachie (1951; 1954), Maloney (1956), Dawson, Messé, and Phillips (1972), and Morgan (Note 2).

The present study represented an attempt to integrate this generalization about student-centered teaching with the Mann *et al.* (1970) system of classifying teacher behavior in terms of the roles filled by teachers over the course of a term. Mann *et al.* described a teacher typology which included six identifiable teacher roles. They suggested that teachers may, at different points in the development of a class, emphasize one or another of these roles. Similarly teachers may differ from one another in the degree to which certain roles are dominant over the course of a term. The four roles relevant to our purpose were: Teacher as (a) Expert, (b) Authority, (c) Facilitator, and (d) Person.

We hypothesized that instructors emphasizing the roles of Facilitator and Person would be more effective with respect to measures of student thinking, attitudes, and motivation than instructors emphasizing the roles of Expert and Authority, while the latter instructors would be more effective on measures of student knowledge. Mann suggests (personal communication) that these Expert and Authority roles are likely to be positively correlated across teachers as are the Person and Facilitator roles.

## Method

**Samples.** *Course sample.* The sample was drawn from the three introductory psychology courses given at the University of Michigan. The three courses are: "Psychology as a Natural Science" (170), "Psychology as a Social Science" (171), and "Introduction to Psychology" (172).

*Teacher sample.* The teacher sample was made up of twenty-one teachers: two teachers from Psychology 170, eleven from Psychology 171, and eight from Psychology 172. One teacher was a professor with twenty-seven years of experience, two were senior psychology majors, and the rest were graduate students with none to four terms of teaching experience. Class size ranged from 16 to 31 with the typical class size being 20 to 25 students.

*Student sample.* The student sample was made up of 580 students, 291 of these being female. As one of the educational features of the introductory courses, students participate in research projects for three hours. Each project is screened to insure that the research offers educational benefits to the students. We utilized two hours of the students' time to give the attitudinal measures and criteria tests two weeks before the end of the term.

**Measures.** *Student measures.* The Introductory Psychology Criteria Test (Milholland, 1964) is a multiple-choice test designed to measure six levels of cognitive outcomes of an introductory psychology course: Interpretation, application, analysis of elements, analysis of relationships, derivation of abstract relations, and judgment by external criteria. Forty-eight items were chosen from earlier forms of the test for this study. In addition twenty-five item multiple-choice tests of knowledge were constructed for each of the three courses. Items were selected from the tests previously developed by Dyer (Note 1).

As a measure of motivation for further learning, students checked which of the advanced undergraduate psychology courses offered at the University of Michigan they would like to take. The score was simply the number of courses chosen. An Attitude Toward Psychology scale (Carrier, 1966) with 20 Likert-type items administered at the end of the semester to measure student attitude toward psychology. Student ratings of the value of the course and its impact on their learning were obtained as part of the scale for assessing student perception of teaching.

*Instructor classification.* Six meetings of each class were observed. Three research assistants acted as observers. Because of scheduling conflicts, some teachers were not observed by all of the observers. Instructors were categorized by the two prime observers into three groups: those emphasizing Facilitator-Person roles, those emphasizing Expert-Authority roles, and those falling between these two. Definitions of the roles given by Mann *et al.* were used to define the categories. Reliability of categorization for teachers observed by both observers was 0.9.

## Results

As shown in Table 1, an analysis of variance indicated that instructors classified as Facilitator-Person were more

Table 1
The Effects of Expert-Authoritarian vs. Facilitator-Person
Teacher upon Student Performance

| Group | Number of Psychology Courses | | |
|---|---|---|---|
| | Mean | SD | N |
| Expert-Authoritarian | 14.01 | 10.35 | 134 |
| Middle | 13.88 | 10.17 | 145 |
| Facilitator-Person | 17.10 | 11.90 | 106 |
| *F* | | 3.334 | |
| *P* | | .04 | |

effective than other teachers in terms of student motivation for taking additional psychology courses. Other measures failed to show significant differences except that facilitative teachers also gave higher grades. This led us to suspect that the way to motivate students to take additional courses is to give high grades. At least in this sample, this suspicion is ill-founded. The correlation between mean grades and mean advanced courses over all 23 sections of the course was −.19.

### Discussion

As we indicated in the introduction, this study fits with the theory developed in McKeachie (1954) suggesting that changes in motivation are facilitated by teaching that gives students an opportunity to express their own ideas and feelings. In terms of Lewinian theory, such teaching unfreezes previously held attitudes and allows influences from the group and from the teacher as a model to have an effect. The effect of the teacher as a model is enhanced if the teacher is seen as a person, rather than as an impersonal occupant of an instructional role. Thus instructors em-phasizing person-facilitator role behaviors are particularly likely to affect student motivation.

### References

Carrier, N. A. *Evaluating the introductory psychology course.* Reading, MA: Addison-Wesley, 1966.
Dawson, J. E., Messé, L. A., & Phillips, J. L. Effect of instructor-leader behavior on student performance. *Journal of Applied Psychology,* 1972, *56,* 369-376.
Mann, R. D., Arnold, S. M., Bender, J. L., Cytrynbaum, S., Newman, B. M., Ringwald, B. E., Ringwald, J. W., & Rosenwein, R. *The college classroom.* New York: Wiley, 1970.
McKeachie, W. J. Anxiety in the college classroom. *Journal of Educational Research,* 1951, *45,* 153-160.
McKeachie, W. J. Individual conformity to attitudes of classroom groups. *Journal of Abnormal and Social Psychology,* 1954, *49,* 282-289.
McKeachie, W. J., & Kulik, J. A. Effective college teaching. In F. N. Kerlinger (Ed), *Review of research in education* (Vol. 3). Itasca, IL: Peacock, 1975.
Maloney, R. M. Group learning through group discussion: A group discussion-implementation analysis. *Journal of Social Psychology,* 1956, *43,* 3-9.
Milholland, J. E. Measuring cognitive abilities. In W. J. McKeachie, R. L. Issacson, & J. E. Milholland, *Research on the characteristics of effective college teaching* (Final report: Cooperative Research Project No. SAE 850, United States Office of Education and the University of Michigan). Washington, DC: US Government Printing Office. 1964.

### Notes

1. Dyer, P. J. L. *Psychology 171, an evaluation of pass-fail grading and level of learning.* Unpublished thesis for Education Specialist, University of Michigan, 1970.
2. Morgan, G. *Effects of less prescriptive, student-centered college curriculum on satisfaction, attitudes, and achievement.* Paper presented at the meeting of the American Psychological Association, Honolulu, August 1972.

---

# Teaching Information Processing System (TIPS): Evaluation in a Large Introductory Psychology Class

Hal R. Arkes
*Ohio University*

This evaluation suggests that TIPS improves performance by forcing distributed learning and it is an attractive alternative to PSI.

During the last decade a number of teachers have successfully implemented instructional programs based on contingency management principles (Keller, 1968). Results of such programs have generally been quite positive (Alba & Pennypacker, 1972; Born, Gledhill, & Davis, 1972; Johnson, Zlotlow, Berger, & Croft, 1975). Also during the last decade, computer assisted instruction (CAI) has enjoyed increasing popularity and success. One instructional program which combines some features of both contingency management and CAI is the Teaching Information Processing System (TIPS) (Kelley, 1968), which is presently in use in 150 American universities. Under the TIPS program all students take short weekly multiple-choice quizzes based on the material covered during the prior week. Based on quiz performance, each student gets rapid feedback on his or her strengths and weaknesses plus an assignment designed to eliminate the latter. The feedback and assignment are computer generated, based on simple programming done by the instructor prior to the quiz. The instructor merely needs to have decided what the remediation should be for each possible area of deficiency revealed by the quiz. In addition, special assignments or opportunities may be given to those who need no remediation. Assignments may also be keyed to performance on prior quizzes, the student's interests (for example, math major versus psychology major), or any of a large number of other factors. Item analyses are generated, consisting of a summary of the total number of students choosing each multiple-choice option for each question. The instructor also receives a summary of the number of students at each possible level of performance. If the course is subdivided into discussion sections, each section leader receives a summary of the performance of each student in his or her discussion section along with item analyses for that subset of the class. (The weekly computer cost of this program for us was 90 seconds of c.p.u. time for a class of 383 students.)

Like contingency management, the TIPS system utilizes frequent testing over relatively small course units. Unlike contingency management, it is not necessary to demonstrate mastery before moving on to new material, no proctor assistance is required, and self-pacing is eliminated. Goldwater and Acker (1975) have shown that self-pacing and individualized testing procedures are not needed in order to demonstrate the superiority of contingency management over traditional teaching methods. Goldwater and Acker (1975, p. 155) suggest that the success of their modified program and other more traditional contingency management programs may be due largely to frequent testing which leads to distributed, efficient studying. Since the TIPS system involves such testing but does not involve the more costly features of self-pacing and proctor assistance, it is possible that TIPS would be both a beneficial and economical addition to a traditional teaching program.

I know of no published reports containing an evaluation of TIPS used in any psychology course, so I present our experience with TIPS in a large introductory psychology class. This class enrolled 383 students who met four times per week, three of the times to attend a lecture given by a faculty member and once to attend a discussion section led by a graduate student. The text used was McNeil and Rubin (1977).

The typical weekly schedule was as follows: During the last ten minutes of Wednesday's lecture session, every student attending class was given a ten-item multiple-choice test over the two or three main topics covered during the prior week. The students' answers were analyzed using the TIPS program that evening, and each student's feedback sheet was placed in special mailboxes very early Thursday morning. Since the large majority of discussion sections met on Thursday, students typically picked up their feedback sheets en route to discussion. Feedback sheets were removed from the boxes by the professor if they had not been picked up by the student within six days.

Each feedback sheet consisted of the student's score on the ten-item multiple choice test, the correct answers, and assignments linked to the questions incorrectly answered. These assignments included questions from the text's workbook, questions generated by the instructor, and suggested readings. Students who did these assignments were asked to hand them in to their discussion leaders by Monday. The assignments were not mandatory, and they did not count toward the student's final grade.

The course grade was based on the total number of questions answered correctly on the course's three exami-nations (maximum = 150). No examination questions duplicated or closely approximated any questions used on the weekly TIPS quizzes.

**Method.** On the next-to-last day of class, a questionnaire was handed out. The anonymous questionnaire contained items assessing the evaluation and effects of the TIPS program. On the last day of class the questionnaire was handed out again, but this time the students were asked to fill in their social security number. Knowing each respondent's identity would allow us to correlate each student's performance in the course with his or her evaluation of TIPS. Since it is possible that the lack of anonymity on the second questionnaire would cause distortion in the responses, the group responses on the anonymous questionnaire were compared with the group responses on the questionnaire containing the social security number.

In order to assess the impact of TIPS on student performance, two analyses were performed. First, the number of students who picked up each of the eight TIPS feedback sheets was examined. The median number of sheets picked up was seven. Each person who picked up TIPS feedback sheets eight times was matched on high school graduating class rank ($\pm 3\%$) with a person who picked up TIPS feedback sheets less than seven times. Excluded from this analysis were the large number of students for whom high school rank was unknown and all students who did not attend two or more Wednesday classes, the day on which TIPS quizzes were given. Thus, only students with very high class attendance were included. Sixty-eight such matched pairs were found, 15 from the bottom third of their high school class, 31 from the middle third, and 22 from the upper third. The number of examination questions answered correctly by each high TIPS participator was compared to the number answered correctly by the matched low TIPS participator.

The second analysis consisted merely of a regression analysis examining the relation between the number of TIPS feedback sheets picked up and the number of questions answered correctly on the course's examinations. Again, those students with more than two Wednesday absences were excluded from the analysis.

**Results.** The evaluation of TIPS on the anonymous questionnaire did not differ from the evaluation on the identified one ($t$ (508) = 1.60). Therefore only the results from the latter one will be presented.

On the last day of class, 276 students (72% of the class) were present to fill out the questionnaire. The first question, "What is your evaluation of the TIPS system," was anchored at 1 ("very good") and 7 ("very poor"). The mean response was 2.2. The second item, "Did the TIPS system affect your test performance," was anchored at 1 ("No effect") and 4 ("strong effect"). The mean response was 2.55, approximately midway between "slight effect" and "moderate effect." Students also indicated that on the average they did less than half of the eight homework assignments. Intercorrelations were calculated among these items and the number of TIPS feedback sheets picked up, the number of test questions answered correctly, and high school class rank. The correlation matrix is presented in Table 1.

## Table 1
### Correlation Matrix of TIPS Evaluation Data and Student Characteristics

| Variable | 1 | 2 | 3 | 4 | 5 | 6 |
|---|---|---|---|---|---|---|
| (1) Evaluation of TIPS | | 38** | .13 | .13 | .12 | .11 |
| (2) Rated effect of TIPS on test performance | | | .24** | .13 | .40** | .15 |
| (3) No. of TIPS feedback sheets picked up | | | | .39** | .40** | .21** |
| (4) No. of homework assignments done | | | | | .10 | .18** |
| (5) Total points on exams | | | | | | .49** |
| (6) High school class rank | | | | | | — |

*p < .01    **p < .001

Next, the number of examination questions answered correctly by the high and low TIPS participators was examined. Recall that these are only high class attenders matched on high school class rank. A 2 (TIPS participation) x 3 (third of high school class) ANOVA was performed. Both TIPS participation ($F (1,130) = 11.02$) and high school rank ($F (2,130) = 14.47$) were significant (both $ps < .001$). The data are displayed in Figure 1.

In the third analysis the number of questions answered correctly was regressed on number of TIPS feedback sheets picked up. Again, only high class attenders (317) were included in the analysis. The two variables were correlated +.27 ($p < .001$). The regression equation is: T.Q. = 76.90 + 3.56 TIPS, where T.Q. is the number of test questions answered correctly and TIPS is the number of TIPS feedback sheets picked up.

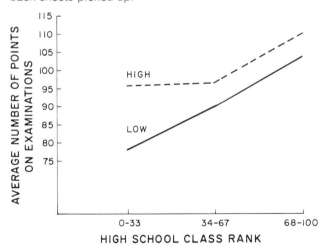

Figure 1. Mean number of examination questions answered correctly by the high and low TIPS participators as a function of high school class rank.

**Discussion.** The questionnaire data indicated that the students both felt quite positive about TIPS and felt it improved their performance. The ANOVA and regression analyses suggested this latter opinion was based upon fact. For each TIPS feedback sheet they picked up, students were able to answer correctly another 3.56 examination questions. Also, the high TIPS participators averaged over ten more test questions correctly answered than their cohort matched for high school class rank. Although the TIPS participation X class rank interaction was not significant, there was a trend for TIPS to be more beneficial to students in the lower third of their high school class. This result has also been found by Kelley (1972).

The present analysis also supports the contention of Goldwater and Acker (1975) that neither self-pacing nor individualized testing are necessary to achieve some gains attributed to traditional contingency management methods. The weekly TIPS quizzes may have forced the distributed studying that Goldwater and Acker believe may be responsible for some of the success of contingency management. It is interesting to note that students handed in only slightly less than half of these weekly assignments to the instructor. However, many students reported that they did far more assignments but did not hand them in because they knew it would not count toward their grade. We decided on the policy of homework not counting toward the grade in order to discourage copying both during the taking of the TIPS test and during the doing of the assignment. Apparently much benefit can be derived from TIPS feedback even if the assignment is not formally handed in to the instructor.

### References

Alba, E., & Pennypacker, H. A multiple change score comparison of traditional and behavioral college teaching procedures. *Journal of Applied Behavior Analysis,* 1972, 5, 121-124.

Born, D. G., Gledhill, S. M., & Davis, M. L. Examination performance in lecture-discussion and personalized instruction courses. *Journal of Applied Behavior Analysis,* 1972, 5, 33-43.

Goldwater, B. C., & Acker, L. E. Instructor-paced, mass-testing for mastery performance in an introductory psychology course. *Teaching of Psychology,* 1975, 2, 152-155.

Johnson, W. G., Zlotlow, S., Berger, J. L., & Croft, R. G. F. A traditional lecture versus a PSI course in personality: some comparisons. *Teaching of Psychology,* 1975, 2, 156-158.

Keller, F. S. "Goodbye, teacher . . ." *Journal of Applied Behavior Analysis,* 1968, 1, 79-89.

Kelley, A. C. An experiment with TIPS: A computer-aided instructional system for undergraduate education. *American Economic Review,* 1968, 58, 446-457.

Kelley, A. C. TIPS and technical change in classroom instruction. *American Economic Review,* 1972, 62, 422-428.

McNeil, E., & Rubin, Z. *The psychology of being human.* New York: Canfield, 1977.

### Note

1. The installation of TIPS at Ohio University was supported by a grant from the Exxon Educational Foundation. I am grateful to Jerry Solamon for his assistance on this project.

# An Individual Differences Model for The Design of Courses in General Psychology

Stephanie I. Splane
*Colorado State University*
and Richard I. Kushner
*University of Redlands*

The model was empirically examined to determine if it has promise for modifying treatments for different student subgroups.

The introductory course is the most frequently offered course in psychology at colleges and universities throughout the nation. The introductory course receives first listing among psychology courses in school catalogs, and the heaviest enrollments of all psychology courses (Kulik, 1973). It gives most students their first formal introduction to psychology. The introductory course must accommodate students definitely committed to the field, students exploring psychology as a possible major, students viewing the field as a possible background for careers in related areas, and those students taking the course merely as an elective. A study conducted by Walker and McKeachie (1967) of students graduating from a typical large state university showed that practically every student enrolls in an introductory psychology course some time during the college career. Considering the present eminence and critical importance of the introductory course, careful scrutiny must be given to the structure and design of such courses.

The introductory course presents particular problems in the area of course design. Because there is great heterogeneity among the students enrolled in the course, one will find individual differences with regard to student abilities and interests. Thus, it becomes important to identify homogeneous subgroups of individuals in terms of their performance on tests tapping cognitive processes demanded for success in the course as well as measures of academic interests. The present study represents the first step in a programmatic approach to applying an individual differences model involving a task-first, aptitude by treatment approach to designing courses in education. Cronbach (1957) first emphasized the value of the aptitude by treatment interaction (ATI) approach for optimizing individual differences in performance. Rhetts (1974) stressed the need to take a "task-first" approach in organism-environment research. A task-first approach to ATI research emphasizes the need to identify treatments and aptitudes which are congruent with the tasks required for success in a course. Thus, the first step in research concerned with designing alternative instructional methods should be the identification of the tasks required of the student in a particular course.

Using a task-first individual difference approach, Forsyth (1977) identified three cognitive ability task factors in a statistics course, and five homogeneous subgroups of students with a different group being selectively weak on each of the three factors. Forsyth stressed the potential value of this model for designing courses in psychology. The purpose of the present study is to determine if this model can be applied to designing a major survey course such as introductory psychology.

**Procedure.** Sixty-two University of Redlands undergraduates enrolled in two sections of a general psychology course served as subjects for the present study. The two sections were taught by the same instructor. A test consisting of 42 evaluation items was administered to all the students in two, 55-minute testing sessions during the last week of the semester. The 42 test items were constructed to represent all cells of a matrix formed by crossing seven course content areas and six cognitive educational objectives. The seven content areas were: research methods, personality theories, abnormal behavior, learning, cognition, social psychology and psychotherapy. The six cognitive educational objectives were those described by Bloom, Engelhart, Hill, Furst and Krathwohl (1956): knowledge, comprehension, application, analysis, synthesis and evaluation. Forsyth (1977) suggests that this method of constructing test items will permit task factors to be identified in terms of content areas, cognitive processes, or their interaction.

**Results.** A principal-components factor analysis of the test item scores resulted in the identification of three process-related task factors accounting for .37, .19 and .16 of the variance respectively. An orthogonal rotation was used to obtain rotated factor loadings on test items and factor scores on students. The three factors were labelled according to which test items had the highest loadings on the factor. The pattern of loadings of the 42 items on these three factors indicated a cognitive process rather than a content area definition of the factors. Factors 1, 2 and 3 were labelled application-evaluation, knowledge-comprehension and analysis, respectively. Items from the application and evaluation rows of the matrix loaded the highest on Factor 1. These items required the student to make use of abstractions in particular and concrete situations, and to make judgments about the value of material and methods for given purposes. Items loading high on Factor 2 were primarily from the knowledge and comprehension rows of the matrix. These items asked the students to recall specific information and to demonstrate the ability to understand and make use of this information. Items loading high on Factor 3 were from the analysis row of the matrix. These items involved the breaking down of communications to get at the constituent parts, and the ability to recognize the relationships between these parts.

The three factor scores for each student indicate the strength of that student's performance on each task factor in z-score form. The factor score for any student reflects his/her performance profile across the three task factors. The subgroups were formed using an H-group analysis (Ward, 1963) based on the Euclidean distance of each student from every other student in a three-dimensional space formed by the three task factors. The subgroups were identified using the criteria of minimal distances between students within a subgroup, maximum distances between students in different subgroups and the stability of the subgroup in the H-group sequential combinations (i.e., how early a subgroup was formed and how long it remained intact before it was combined with other $Ss$ in the analysis). Initially eleven subgroups were identified with this clustering analysis, but only six of these subgroups were of particular interest because they were the most clearly interpretable in terms of the three task factors. The mean factor scores for each of the eleven subgroups are presented in Table 1. The number of students in the subgroups (see table) account for 90 % of the $Ss$. As illustrated in Table 1, Subgroups 2, 6, and 7 were selectively weak on Factors 1, 2, and 3 respectively whereas Subgroups 8, 5, and 11 were selectively strong on Factors 1, 2, and 3 respectively.

## Table 1
## Subgroup Mean Factor Scores on Each Task Factor

| Sub-group | N | Task Factors | | |
|---|---|---|---|---|
| | | 1 | 2 | 3 |
| 1 | 7 | -.84 | .25 | .14 |
| 2 | 4 | -1.18 | -.60 | .56 |
| 3 | 6 | .99 | -.52 | -.30 |
| 4 | 9 | .02 | -.52 | .68 |
| 5 | 3 | -.46 | 1.63 | -.50 |
| 6 | 5 | .07 | -1.56 | -.01 |
| 7 | 3 | .92 | -.51 | -1.21 |
| 8 | 3 | 1.55 | 1.42 | -.26 |
| 9 | 10 | -.38 | .35 | -.66 |
| 10 | 3 | .86 | .15 | .77 |
| 11 | 3 | .004 | 1.01 | 1.88 |

Discussion. The findings of the present study demonstrated (a) that the task factors emerging from the content by process evaluation items were process-related (i.e., application-evaluation, knowledge-comprehension, and analysis); and (b) that strong individual differences in terms of the task factors are present with six of the eleven subgroups being selectively strong or weak on each of the task factors. These findings support those of Forsyth (1977). The present study validated two of the three task factors

identified by Forsyth: knowledge and analysis. The third factor not validated in the present study was a synthesis factor. It is believed that the failure to replicate this factor was a function of particular differences in the testing conditions in the two studies. Forsyth tested students enrolled in an upper division statistics course whereas the present study tested students enrolled in a lower division course. Forsyth used multiple-choice items to evaluate the process objective of synthesis, whereas the current study used an essay format. In the present study a multiple-choice format was used for knowledge, comprehension, application, analysis, and evaluation processes.

The findings of this study present strong implications for implementing Forsyth's (1977) task-by-aptitude-by-treatment interaction design. This would involve: (a) searching for or developing pre-course measures which tap each of the three processes represented by the task factors, and (b) designing special-emphasis treatment conditions, each giving special training on one of the three process-related task factors. Based on the pre-course measures, students would be placed into appropriate groups and assigned to different extra-core workshop sessions selectively emphasizing each of the three task factors. These special emphasis treatment conditions would then need to be crossed with subgroups preselected on the basis of aptitude measures tapping these processes, along with academic interests. This procedure should optimize task factor performances for specific cognitive-processing subgroups by permitting the identification of the optimal treatment for each homogeneous subgroup.

It is becoming increasingly apparent that the "teaching-learning system" must become more responsive to the diverse society which it serves through the development of adaptive environments designed to optimize unique cognitive styles and the development of competence in each individual. If we are to maximize our use of human potential and optimize learning outcomes for each individual, then direct attention must be given to the underlying processes of task performance and the characteristic ways in which different individuals engage in such processes. Such a position has been advocated in many recent articles including Glaser (1972, 1977), Hunt (1975), and McKeachie (1976). Psychologists interested in course design should be developing effective methods of instruction that will maximize the number of individuals able to attain success. Emphasis should be placed on how the processes that contribute to competent performance can be influenced and how the individual's cognitive skills can be improved to make the attainment of competent performance easier and more effective.

The present research suggests the need to use factorial based tests such as Guilford's (1959) measures of intellectual ability to obtain a clear definition of the cognitive factors being tapped with course tests. Future research could also explore the importance of interest as well as ability measures, both as task factors and as a basis for forming homogeneous subgroups at the beginning of a course. The task-first approach represented in the present study has been demonstrated to be of use in both the identification of underlying process-related task factors and in the forming of homogeneous subgroups. Now, the adequacy and effectiveness of this design must be tested through continued attempts at its application.

## References

Bloom, B. S., Engelhart, M. D., Hill, H., Furst, E. J., & Krathwohl, D. R. *Taxonomy of education objectives: Handbook I: Cognitive domain.* New York: David McKay, 1956.

Cronbach, L. J. The two disciplines of scientific psychology. *American Psychologist,* 1957, *12,* 671-684.

Forsyth, G. A. A task-first individual-differences approach to designing a statistics and methodology course. *Teaching of Psychology,* 1977, *4,* 76-78.

Glaser, R. Individuals and learning: The new aptitudes. *Educational Researcher,* 1972, 7, 5-13.

Glaser, R. *Adaptive education: Individual diversity and learning.* New York: Holt, Rinehart and Winston, 1977.

Guilford, J. P. Three faces of intellect. *American Psychologist,* 1959, *14,* 469-479.

Hunt. D. E. Person-environment interaction: A challenge found wanting before it was tried. *Review of Educational Research,* 1975, *25,* 209-230.

Kulik, J. A. *Undergraduate education in psychology.* Washington, DC: American Psychological Association, 1973.

McKeachie, W. J. Psychology in America's bicentennial year. *American Psychologist,* 1976, *31,* 819-831.

Rhetts, J. E. Task, learner, and treatment variables in instructional design. *Journal of Educational Psychology,* 1974, *66,* 339-347.

Walker, E. I., & McKeachie, W. J. *Some thoughts about teaching the beginning course in psychology.* Belmont, California: Brooks/Cole, 1967.

Ward, J. J. Hierarchical grouping to optimize an objective function. *American Statistical Association Journal,* 1963, *58,* 236-244.

## Notes

1. Stephanie Splane is now at the University of California, Irvine.
2. Special thanks to G. Alfred Forsyth for his very helpful comments and suggestions.

---

# Making Students Take a Stand:
# Active Learning In Introductory Psychology

Michael E. Gorman, Anne Law
and Tina Lindegren
*University of New Hampshire*

One of the major goals of education is to foster critical thinking. The information we teach our students in psychology classes may be out of date in twenty years, but not the ability to think and argue. If students can be taught to critically evaluate new ideas, then they will be better prepared to continue learning long after they leave the classroom. To encourage this kind of active learning, we designed a new teaching technique for introductory psychology classes. Specifically, we built into our course a requirement that students take a stand on a major perspective in psychology and then actively defend this position against alternative views. The goal of this technique was threefold: (a) to stimulate critical thinking and evaluate skills in psychology and other areas; (b) to provide an overall framework and organizing structure from which to present basic ideas, empirical research and concepts from the varied topical areas in psychology; and (c) to encourage discussion and student participation in the classroom.

In three sections of introductory psychology (up to fifty students in each class). one taught by each of the authors, we presented three perspectives as representative of the dominant and prevailing approaches to understanding psychological phenomena. The first was termed the biological position, the idea that human behavior is primarily the result of genetic and evolutionary mechanisms. The second was defined as the environmental position, the idea that human behavior is primarily the result of environmental influences. The third perspective was referred to as the humanistic position, the idea that people are free to choose how they will behave. None of these positions alone is adequate to explain "human nature." nor are the three positions necessarily mutually exclusive. But rather than explaining this to students, the goal was for them to discover it for themselves.

These perspectives were discussed and defended in relation to two books selected by the instructors, *Walden Two* by B. F. Skinner and *The Eden Express* by Mark Vonnegut. *Walden Two* was chosen because it is a forceful and controversial statement of the environmental position. In Skinner's utopia, human beings are easily modified by manipulation of their environment. Skinner seems to ignore biological constraints on learning and dismisses the idea that people are in some way free to choose how they will behave and think. As a novel, this book provides no counter-arguments and thus it is an ideal catalyst—it forces students to generate their own criticisms.

In *The Eden Express,* Mark Vonnegut tells the story of his own descent into. and return from, schizophrenia. Because the effective therapy for Mark involved the use of tranquilizers and megavitamins, he believed the root of his madness was biological. However, the book also shows how Mark was caught up in existential dilemmas, family problems, troubles with his girl-friend, etc. There is ammunition for other perspectives: humanists could focus on the tension between Mark's real and ideal selves and environmentalists could focus on changes in his living situation, the way other people treated him, and the hospital environment in which he finally recovered.

At the beginning of the semester, the details of this teaching technique were explained to the students. Each instructor spent the first week of class discussing how each of the three perspectives could be applied to an understanding of aggression. From this, students were able to gain an initial appreciation of each perspective's approach and basic philosophy, *and* had some basis for choosing a position to defend in the subsequent discussions. Students either signed up for a group espousing one of the three positions (biological, humanistic, or environmental), *or* served as members of a separate evaluation group.

The position groups met several times, both in and outside of class, to prepare 10-15 minute presentations of their positions on each of the books. One class period was set aside for presentations with the next class reserved for discussion of all three perspectives. Evaluators listened to each position group's presentation on both books. Their role was to compare and evaluate, in writing, the perspectives and presentations. The *Walden Two* discussion was held approximately one month into the semester; *The Eden Express* discussion was conducted near the end of the semester.

The grading procedures were defined as the following: (a) position groups would receive a group grade based on each of their presentations; (b) members of each position group would write an individual paper describing his/her group's position on each book, encompassing both the pros and cons of their perspective; (c) evaluation group members would write a paper after each group presentation and the following discussion. These evaluation papers were to contain individuals' reactions to the three presentations, the positions they espoused, and the relation of these views to the important issues in each book. (In order to balance the workload, evaluators were also required to write a critique of a book selected from a prepared reading list.)

Evaluation.   To assess the effects of this teaching technique, we distributed questionnaires at several times during the semester. It was our belief that small group discussions would facilitate individual student participation in the generating of ideas to defend their group's position and criticize other positions. After each in-class discussion, all position group members were given a questionnaire designed to assess the students' perception of the usefulness of this position group technique. One question asked students to rate, on a scale from 1 to 7, the extent to which their understanding of their own position has been increased by this group experience. A second question asked students to rate, again on a scale from 1 to 7, their impression of the combined effects of the group presentations and class discussion on understanding all three perspectives. For each question, mean ratings were combined across the three classes (n=76). Results of the questions from the *Walden Two* and *Eden Express* questionnaires are presented in Table 1. Results from the first question suggest that participation in a small group does lead students to perceive an understanding of their own position in relation to the books discussed. Results from the second question show that, overall, students felt this was an important learning experience. These results support our general hypothesis that small group participation is a useful technique to encourage critical thinking and increase general understanding of the issues at hand.

Table 1. Mean Ratings by Combined Classes on Two Evaluation Scales

| Position groups | Scale Item | |
|---|---|---|
| | Understanding of position due to group experience | Understanding of all positions due to presentations and discussion |
| Biological | | |
| Walden Two | 5.62 | 5.90 |
| Eden Express | 5.68 | 5.67 |
| Humanistic | | |
| Walden Two | 5.38 | 5.33 |
| Eden Express | 4.40 | 5.74 |
| Environmental | | |
| Walden Two | 5.48 | 5.30 |
| Eden Express | 5.26 | 5.57 |

N = 76. Rating of 7 = strongest effect.

In general, we were pleased with our attempt to induce an appreciation for the complexity of psychology. We feel that we encouraged students to think critically about issues as opposed to (or in addition to) learning the "content" of introductory psychology. The three perspectives served as three themes that ran through the course. They provided the cohesion that is often lacking in introductory psychology courses, where the instructor feels as though he/she is teaching five courses instead of one.

This technique complements a wide range of teaching styles and approaches. Each of us taught the course somewhat differently, and emphasized different topics. Although we made an attempt to relate each topic to the perspectives, we often found that students were making the connections on their own. This reinforced our observation that the discussion groups were effective.

Many large sections of introductory psychology employ teaching assistants. This technique would lend itself well to that situation, as teaching assistants could run small sections for presentations and discussions. This could be a substantial improvement over traditional discussion sections that often degenerate into arguments over trivial points, or where students end up not knowing what is expected and contribute little to the discussion.

Students in large classes often feel stifled and anonymous. Splitting the class for discussion and assigning each student an active role may relieve some of the lost feeling of being only one of two or three hundred students. Presenting, arguing and questioning are important skills and this technique forces students to go beyond just learning information, to thinking critically about major issues in psychology.

### Note

Order of authors is alphabetical; contribution of the three authors was equal.

# Reciprocal Learning: A Supplemental Tutoring Program For Introductory Psychology

Eileen T. Brown
*Athens, Georgia*
Pamela S. Engram
*State College, Penn.*

With the rapidly increasing enrollment in introductory psychology classes, instructors are being faced with students of increasingly diversified backgrounds. It would seem likely that these students have not been extensively exposed to the standard youth-oriented, middle-class approach taken in the traditional introductory psychology course. Anecdotal evidence also suggests that these students have been disproportionately represented among dropouts. Thus, the professor is faced with a lack of knowledge about the needs of these non-traditional students, and the students have difficulty coping with a traditional approach. The Reciprocal Learning program was designed to meet these dual needs by encouraging two-way communication between tutor and student.

Originally, the program was limited to members of racial minorities, but participation was later opened up to the whole class, and we personally spoke to those students who were enrolled in a remedial program for reading and writing skills. These two procedures helped to recruit other non-traditional students, such as older women returning to school, as well as those students who had trouble with basic skills.

A needs assessment of these non-traditional students was then conducted so that the tutorial program could attempt to meet needs which were not addressed in the classroom.

Because we had an opportunity to learn from the students as well as have the students learn from us, the program was named Reciprocal Learning (RL). Two self-report measures, a questionnaire and a short description of the student's own needs, revealed that the non-traditional student had two major needs: (a) training in study skills, and (b) an understanding of psychological content.

There were two major reasons for including study skills in the RL program. First, it was hoped that by giving the students concrete and explicit instructions on how to improve their modes of study, they would be able to better comprehend and retain the substantive course content. This is supported by a number of study skills manuals (Lindgren, 1969; Morgan & Deese, 1969; Pauk, 1974). Second, a small group situation enabled each student to receive individualized attention for particular skills deficits. It was hoped that the fulfillment of these objectives would help to break the pattern of failure and defeatist attitudes they had experienced in other, traditional courses.

Why not concentrate on study skills? For one thing, psychology is a relatively "new" subject to college freshmen. As such, students lack the familiarity with psychology that they have with more traditional disciplines such as history or math. Psychology is still seen by them as more speculative and less certain. One meets with hypotheses, untested

models, theories that are not as yet full-blown, conflicting sets of evidence, few absolutes, and even fewer clear-cut "rights" and "wrongs." It's substantive content includes intangibles such as cognitions, emotions and motivations, as well as more concrete observable behaviors. In sum, psychology as a subject discipline is in many ways unique. Its features therefore present a challenge to the introductory student and create the additional need to deal with psychology as a focal point for the implementation of effective study skills. However, without a firm grounding in these techniques, the student is further handicapped in making the transition to a new kind of content area.

Students in the RL program met for 1½ hours per week beyond the regularly scheduled lectures. Attendance at these tutoring sessions was voluntary, and although a small, faithful group attended weekly, there was a predictable increase in numbers prior to the course examinations. In spite of the somewhat variable nature of the group, we, as tutors, tried to gear our efforts toward the dual goals of the RL program—emphasizing an overall understanding of the psychological content and introducing new study skills. For example, when working with the chapter on the biological bases of the human nervous system, we tried to emphasize the development of the human brain and compared the regions of the human brain to those of other animals. By giving the students this historical frame of reference, the important features of the human brain stood out more clearly. In order to help the students remember the lobes of the brain we used a mnemonic ("POT"—parietal, occipital, and temporal, with the frontal lobe being in "front").

Another way study skills can be combined with psychological content is by the use of a student's own personal experiences. The differences between a common sense approach and the scientific method of investigation can both hinder and help. On the one hand, personal familiarity with everyday psychological phenomena can breed a false sense of security which may belie the rigors and complexity of psychological knowledge. This caveat particularly applies when dealing with topics such as emotion and motivation. On the other hand, personal experiences can be used as exemplars of concepts grounded in empirical research. In our experience, one young mother who had recently returned to school used experiences with her own children to learn the concepts of reinforcement and punishment.

The presentation and practice of study skills was found to be a key element of the RL program. It became apparent that although basic study skills may be obvious to the sophisticated student, our non-traditional students were hearing about them for the first time. Four major areas of skills were stressed: (a) reading the text, (b) taking notes, (c) studying for exams, and (d) taking exams.

The study skills which were subsequently utilized most frequently by the students seemed to be those which took the least time and/or had the highest payoff in terms of passing the class exams. One such study skill which was especially effective was our suggestion that the students start their reading assignment by looking over the chapter summary, which pointed out the most important points. Another skill utilized was that of taking an exam. We helped our students become more "test-wise" by encouraging them to answer the easiest questions first, to allocate a proportionate amount of time per question, and to develop decision rules on how to choose between two possible alternatives in a multiple choice exam.

The general theme of the study skills which we stressed was that the students take an active vs. a passive approach to their own learning behavior. By stressing that the students should think up examples, explain the concepts in their own words, and in general get involved with the psychological content, we hoped to increase each student's capacity to exert control over their learning behavior. This theme seems especially important in light of the fact that the non-traditional student is often ill-prepared to cope with a traditional curriculum. Thus, the RL program provided an informal, supportive atmosphere in which students were able to begin to exert control over psychological material.

Students reported that they utilized at least some of the study skills on a regular basis. The major practical result was that the student performance did, in fact, improve. All of the regularly attending students remained in their introductory course through its completion. These students passed psychology with grade of C or better. At least as important were two affective by-products of our program: increased student enthusiasm and reduction of anxiety.

### References

Lindgren, H. C. *The psychology of college success.* New York: Wiley, 1969.

Morgan, C. T., & Deese, J. *How to study.* New York: McGraw-Hill, 1969.

Pauk, W. *How to study in college* (2nd Ed.). Boston: Houghton Mifflin, 1974.

### Note

We would like to thank Dr. Barbara Bunker of the State University of New York at Buffalo for her guidance and insights in the development of this program.

# The Relevance Connection: Relating Academic Psychology to Everyday Life

Myron Brender
*Kingsborough-CUNY*

Traditionally the focus of the introductory course in general psychology has been on providing the student with a brief historical account of the development of psychology as a science and a reasonably comprehensive overview of the current state of the discipline. More recently, instructors have been faced with a persistent and rising demand that the subject matter be made more relevant to the daily experiences and concerns of the average student (Lyons & Barrell, 1979, preface).

In response to this demand, I have developed over a period of years (Brender, 1975) a procedure to relate the technical material of academic psychology to the everyday life experience of the student without sacrificing rigor or compromising the scholarly quality of the course content in the process. This is accomplished through the assignment of an optional term paper, an earlier and independently devised variant of a format subsequently described by Hettich (1976, 1980). The paper can be regarded as the logical culmination of the term's work in the introductory course, offering the student an opportunity to demonstrate ability to apply the facts, terms, concepts, principles, and theories of psychology to an analysis and explanation of at least five incidents personally observed and recorded from everyday life.

The optional aspect allows election by any student who wishes to offer a substitute for the lowest score she has earned on any examination given during the semester. The student who consistently scores 90% or higher on all mandatory term examinations is permitted to substitute the term paper for the final examination.

**The Procedure.** At the beginning of each semester, every class is advised that in preparation for the term paper they should begin immediately to keep a log of any events that capture their attention or arouse their interest each day, no matter how ordinary or commonplace these incidents appear to be. They are encouraged to make their accounts of the observations as detailed as possible. They are assured that at or near the midterm they will have completed enough of the course material to have become sufficiently acquainted with the basic technical concepts to be able to translate the important features of the incidents they had collected and recorded into accurate, formal psychological terminology. Moreover, at that time they are sufficiently exposed to psychological theory to formulate some plausible interpretations of the events they compiled. To assist them further, they are also assured that the instructor will periodically demonstrate the kinds of psychological formulations they are to prepare. Furthermore, as they begin to accumulate log entries, they are invited to consult the instructor if they have any doubts about the appropriateness or adequacy of the material they are gathering.

Classroom demonstrations by the instructor of the procedure for describing and analyzing incidents for inclusion in the term paper are conducted in two ways. One approach entails a presentation and analysis of incidents gathered in advance by the instructor. The other consists in the impromptu description and analysis of incidents that occur spontaneously during class and are examined shortly after their occurrence. This is accomplished by my calling attention to the incident, requesting the class to "stop the action" (i.e., to halt the discussion or activity in progress), and to "replay the tape" (i.e., to reconstruct an accurate description of the event). I then guide and support the students in describing the incident; insisting, however, that they take the initiative, as much as possible, in the collaborative recollection. Similarly, simply by strategic questioning, I guide them through the subsequent analysis and explanatory formulations. Eventually, after a few such demonstrations, I merely direct attention to a promising incident and ask students to assume complete responsibility for a description, analysis, and explanation of the event. Students are also encouraged to share with the class any incidents they may notice independently. Having gotten the hang of participant observation, most students seem to prefer to reserve their independent classroom observations for inclusion in their own term papers.

Shortly after the completion of midterm examinations, each class is guided through a summary review of the main facts, concepts, principles, and theories they have become familiar with, and the suggestion is made that it is time for them to begin thinking systematically about how this technical knowledge might be applied to the material they will include in their term papers. As a procedural strategy, it is suggested that they analyze each incident as thoroughly as possible by identifying the emotions, motives, attitudes, beliefs, and values displayed, as well as the respondents, operants, reinforcers, and social models present. Having isolated and identified as many of these components as they can, they will then be in a position to consider which theoretical formulation—behavioristic, dynamic, cognitive-phenomenological, humanistic, or eclectic—seems most suitable as an explanation of each incident in their report. If any of the approaches enumerated have not yet been adequately discussed in class, the students are encouraged to work with whatever has been covered already and to test out new formulations subsequently as they are reviewed during the next quarter of the semester. Around the beginning of the final quarter, if I am not behind schedule, the class has been reasonably well acquainted with the main concepts, principles, and theories they need to know in order to do a creditable job of constructing a psychologically plausible account of the events they will report.

The only modification in the model necessary to adapt it for use in a course in developmental psychology is the requirement that log entries be confined to incidents in which infants, children, or adolescents play a major role. However, even here, an accommodation is made to permit the inclusion of incidents involving the crises or challenges of adulthood, such as marriage, parenthood, divorce, death of a spouse, mid-life career changes, retirement, and old age.

Evaluation. Although no formal evaluation of this exercise has been attempted, reports from colleagues[2] using the procedure confirm my impression that its most obvious value is as a teaching device, a vehicle for concretizing the abstract. Not only does it afford the instructor repeated opportunities to demonstrate the ubiquitous presence of even the most recondite principles of psychology embedded within the fabric of everyday life, it also serves to spur the student to initiate his own search for such in vivo examples. On occasion, the more intellectually involved student will bring to class material that he does not plan to use personally, simply in order to have the instructor use it to model a technical analysis and explanatory formulation for the general benefit of the class.

Whereas the intrinsic interest of the task and the challenge it presents (as well as the degree of gratification derived from its successful completion) probably varies with the individual student, its general value as a reinforcer appears evident from the amount of student participation it generates each semester, despite its status as merely an optional assignment.

Finally, with respect to the quality of student performance, it seems that the above average student is more likely than is the less able one to select and apply accurately those concepts and principles that are most appropriate and useful for the psychological reformulation of the material. This finding contrasts with the one reported by Hettich (1976) who states that ". . .it is not uncommon to find a student who 'tests' at the average or below average level, yet writes a genuinely lucid and insightful journal" (pp. 61-62). In my experience, the poorer student, for example, is typically inclined to confuse the applications of the principles of respondent and operant learning and to misapply or overapply the concepts derived from psychoanalytic psychology. The identification of this kind of error consistency has provided me with invaluable feedback that has been instrumental in preparing me to deal more effectively with such material, both preventively and remedially, whenever it comes under consideration during the term.

### References

Brender, M. An end-term project involving the application of principles of general psychology to the analysis of everyday events. In J. B. Maas & D. A. Kleiber (Eds.), *Directory of teaching innovations in psychology*. Washington, DC: American Psychological Association, 1975.

Hettich P. The journal: An autobiographical approach to learning. *Teaching of Psychology*, 1976, 3, 60-63.

Hettich, P. The journal revisited. *Teaching of Psychology*, 1980, 7, 105-106.

Lyons, J., & Barrell, J. J. *People: An introduction to psychology*. New York: Harper & Row, 1979.

### Notes

1. Adapted from a paper presented at the annual conference of the Eastern Community College Social Science Association in Baltimore, MD, on April 12, 1980.
2. The writer wishes to express his appreciation to Dr. Philip Stander, Chairperson of the Department of Behavioral Sciences and Human Services, Kingsborough Community College of City University of New York, for his enthusiastic adoption and support of this activity.

# 3. TEAM TEACHING APPROACHES

## An Interdisciplinary Approach to the Introductory Psychology Course

Robert V. Levine
*California State University, Fresno*

Professors from four departments developed a model for an interdisciplinary student experience where the whole was greater than the sum of its parts.

Two criticisms commonly made of undergraduate education are: (1) that the course work has no direct connection with practical matters and actual experience and (2) that the various courses are isolated and disconnected from each other. Students often miss the integrated nature of human knowledge and do not see the living consequences of ideas. These problems are particularly clear in the traditional introductory psychology course.

During the Fall Semester, 1975, four instructors, including myself, conducted a 16-credit hour lower division interdisciplinary course entitled "Freedom and Authority." Through team teaching, field trips, small discussion groups, guest lectures and individual projects, we attempted a solution to these criticisms of undergraduate education.

The four instructors represented the departments of psychology, philosophy, political science and English. Students enrolled in this "cluster" course received credit for the introductory courses in each of these disciplines. These credits partially fulfilled their university general education requirements and represented the entire academic program for most of the students and most or all of the teaching workloads for the four instructors during that semester. A total of 29 students enrolled in the course.

The present paper will describe both the organization and content of the course, emphasizing material most relevant to psychology. It will also attempt to evaluate both the positive and negative attributes of our experience for others interested in designing a similar program.

**Course Structure.**  Having committed ourselves in principle to teaching this interdisciplinary course, we set out to design our "innovative" program. After meeting weekly for some nine months we found ourselves on the first day of class prepared with a course schedule encompassing only the first four weeks of the semester. It was decided that, given the uncertainties of this virtually unexplored area, we would finalize the schedule on a month-to-month basis.

We did reach several firm conclusions before beginning the course: (1) We would do a minimum of formal lecturing. This would be supplemented with guest lectures, films, student discussions, simulation games and field trips; (2) Almost all of our teaching would be truly interdisciplinary, i.e., all four instructors would be present and participate in all classroom and field activities; (3) We would attempt to maximize student participation in all phases of the course, including the preparation of course material and field trips; (4) Each instructor would grade students independently in their respective disciplines and would independently decide on their grading methods; (5) Individual student projects would be the major focus of the course during the last few weeks.

Each week, twelve hours of formal classroom meetings were arranged. Six of these hours were devoted to class discussion of readings, field trips, guest lectures, or other material which had been presented at the previous class meeting. The remaining classroom hours were used for guest lectures, films and our lectures.

**Content Areas.**  The first month of the course focused on theories of government and personality and their relationship to the problem of freedom and authority. Students were exposed to behavioral, psychoanalytic and humanistic theories within the context of such classical theorists as Plato, Locke, Rousseau, and Machiavelli. The remainder of the course examined freedom and authority in such substantive areas as government, education, racism and sexism, poverty, revolution, communism and socialism, work, psychotherapy, religion and institutions. Specific topics covered in psychology included social perception, educational psychology, stereotyping and prejudice, alienation and locus of control, self-esteem, biofeedback, learning theory, psychopathology and psychotherapy, aggression and violence, environmental psychology, motivation and emotions. These topics were discussed in relation to whichever content area the course was focusing on at that particular time. Most important, traditional subject matter from our various disciplines did not determine the overall course topic. Rather, we chose our interdisciplinary topic, e.g., revolution, and then searched our disciplines for information pertinent to the issue, e.g., the psychology of aggression. Thus, we sacrificed the coherency and organization of our specific introductory courses for a coherent and organized interdisciplinary series of topics.

**Readings.**  Our choice of required readings was similarly dominated by our motivation to present a coherent overall interdisciplinary course, even if this entailed sacrificing some of the usual comprehensiveness in each specific discipline offered by the individual introductory course. Thus, although some readings were "purely" psychological, most overlapped at least two disciplines. One book (Flacks, 1973) served as a quasi-text for psychology[1], offering readings related to the question of freedom and authority from personality theory, experimental social psychology, sociology, political science and education. Other psychology related readings including several academic works (e.g., Nye, 1975), novels (e.g., Kesey, 1962; Burgess, 1962), and individual articles (e.g., Szasz, 1960). We attempted to analyze all readings assigned by all instructors from the standpoint of each discipline represented in the course.

Field Trips.  Exposing students to "real life" examples of academic concepts was a major focus of the course. This was attempted through field trips and individual student projects. Despite an unanticipated volume of red tape, we were able to arrange two overnight field trips: one to our state capital to observe our state government and meet with various officials and one which included visits to a state prison and a state mental hospital. One-day field trips included first-hand observation of a local high school in the midst of a school busing controversy and a guided tour of local farmland which is the focus of an intense legal struggle between individual and large corporate farmers regarding rights to state funded irrigation water. Aspects of each field trip were later analyzed from the perspectives of psychology, political science and philosophy.

Guest Lecturers and Films.  Guest lecturers and films, as opposed to our own lectures, were used as much as possible. These programs varied in nature from a panel discussion on crimes without victims by a local judge, district attorney and public defender to individual presentations by local citizens, other faculty and prominent authors of books on education and the women of Viet Nam. Speakers and films were always discussed from the viewpoints of each discipline.

Student Projects.  The final month of the semester was largely concerned with student projects and presentations. A major goal of this work was to provide students with the opportunity to either pursue in depth one or more of the social problems they had been exposed to during the semester, and/or to become involved with real-life situations for which they had received academic preparation during the course. Projects varied greatly, ranging from an investigation of the economic and social consequences of small versus large farms to a case study of a transsexual. Some of the better projects included active involvement in an anti-nuclear power plant group, a tense school busing issue, a student group called students for consumers, and the therapeutic program of a state mental institution.

Grading.  Students received separate grades for each of the four courses represented in the cluster. Grades and grading methods were independently formulated by each of the instructors. Psychology grades were assigned on the basis of a series of papers based on readings and lectures most salient to this area and a take-home exam integrating information relating to each of the four disciplines reviewed in the course. It should be noted that this course structure presented the opportunity for considerably more creative graded material than the usual multiple-choice memorization tests one becomes accustomed to in introductory courses (Irion, 1976). In that students in this program were also taking introductory English, they were afforded the opportunity to express their knowledge of psychology concurrently with their writing ability in their papers. Psychology

and English were, thus, integrated for these assignments within the interdisciplinary nature of the overall program. Instructors might wish to consider integrated psychology-English courses in the future. This plan would allow deeper coverage of both the psychological and literary elements of adopted readings that might result from study in either course alone. There are, in fact, several texts now in existence which study psychology through literature (e.g., Fernandez, 1972; Katz, Warrick & Greenberg, 1974).

Evaluation of the Program.  Despite the difficulty of evaluating our innovative course, student evaluation questionnaires and frequent discussions both with students and between faculty led to five conclusions:

1. Our approach to this course resulted in coverage of a body of subject matter which was in no way the sum total of information covered in our usual psychology, philosophy, political science and English courses. We soon became aware that we were not so much integrating the subject matter of our usual courses as we were creating an entirely new body of knowledge, at least for ourselves, based on much of our previous information. None of us felt that we had exposed students to as much of the information covered in our traditional introductory courses as we had in past courses, but all felt we presented students with a total volume of information exceeding what they might receive if they had taken the four courses independently. That is, students learned only a portion of the information covered in a usual introductory psychology textbook, but were exposed to applications to those principles to many areas not usually dealt with in any psychology course.

This observation raises the question of whether students were left at a disadvantage for future advanced courses in our fields. Although we cannot unequivocally answer this question, we do know that our new interdisciplinary body of knowledge may be a step toward the more "relevant" psychology so often demanded by both students and academicians (e.g., Gergen, 1973; Elms, 1972). If this approach leaves our students at a disadvantage in future courses, we may be forced to evaluate the content of these other courses.

2. This interdisciplinary approach often presented difficulties for students. Many felt a need for the coherent organization and specialization usually provided by four fundamentally unrelated textbooks. They were faced, instead, with a volume of information drawn from various authors, guest speakers and field experiences. Only through their own efforts could students both organize this information and distinguish its psychological, philosophical and political components. Although some benefited greatly from this experience, others were often confused by the course.

Related to this point, we often felt a similar course might be of great value to advanced students who have already mastered the fundamental concepts of each discipline. Unfortunately, the degree requirements of most universities presently make it difficult for a college junior, senior or graduate student to devote an entire semester to courses largely outside their major. Similarly, the possibility of presenting the course as a two semester program, the first semester being devoted to the fundamental concepts of each discipline and the second to a more integrated and applied experience, would present practical difficulties for students attempting to meet their degree requirements.

3. The fact that the course constituted almost the entire teaching load for us and classwork for our students led to opportunities for both creativity and spontaneity not usually available. We were able to plan our curriculum, especially in regard to field trips, with no fear of conflicts with other classes. This freedom, however, placed a great deal of pressure on the instructors. Knowing that we were neither limited to classroom hours nor any traditional curriculum led to constant examination and re-examination of the course, and, often, our daily plans. Our excitement often fluctuated with our desire for a good, old-fashioned textbook.

4. Students reaped many social benefits from the course. It allowed incoming freshmen the opportunity for close contact with each other and with professors by virtue of the many hours of shared interaction and a commonality of purpose not usually found in a traditional course program. A successful, student inititated encounter group also emerged at the end of the semester. In a sense, students were afforded many of the benefits of the small college experience in a large university.

5. Finally, the course provided a stimulating educational experience for the instructors. We learned to apply old principles to new problems, to integrate our particular areas of specialty, and were exposed to long forgotten basic principles of other subject areas. Possibly most important, we were given the opportunity to plan a "perfect" general education program. Although only moderately successful in achieving this goal, we now have a better understanding of the limits and potentialities of higher education.

## References

Burgess, A. *A clockwork orange.* New York: Ballantine, 1962.
Elms, A. C. *Social psychology and social relevance.* Boston: Little, Brown, 1972.
Fernandez, R. (Ed.). *Social psychology through literature.* New York: Wiley, 1972.
Flacks, R. *Conformity, resistance, and self-determination: The individual and authority.* Boston: Little, Brown, 1973.
Gergen, K. J. Social psychology as history. *Journal of Personality and Social Psychology,* 1973, *26,* 309-320.
Irion, A. L. A survey of the introductory course in psychology. *Teaching of Psychology,* 1976, *3,* 3-8.
Katz, H., Warrick, P., & Greenberg, M. H. *Introductory psychology through science fiction.* Chicago: Rand McNally, 1974.
Kesey, K. *One flew over the cuckoo's nest.* New York: Signet, 1962.
Nye, I. *Three views of man: Perspectives from Sigmund Freud, B. F. Skinner, and Carl Rogers.* Monterey, CA: Brooks/Cole, 1975.
Szasz, T. S. The myth of mental illness. *American Psychologist,* 1960, *15,* 113-118.

## Notes

1. The complete course reading list may be obtained from the author.
2. This course was partially supported by a grant from California State University.
3. I wish to thank Rendall Mabey, Bernard McGoldrick and H. Ray McKnight, all of whom both participated in the course and provided helpful comments on an earlier version of this manuscript.

# Learning With Gusto in Introductory Psychology

Daniel S. Kirschenbaum and
Sheryl Wetter Riechmann
*University of Cincinnati*

Contract grading plus demonstrations plus team teaching plus group facilitators equals introductory psychology with gusto.

Learning is like eating a great pastrami sandwich. The only real way to consume a great pastrami-on-rye is to devour it with gusto; cautious nibbling leads to little joy and an unfinished sandwich. Similarly, learning with gusto (actively, with involvement) leads to satisfaction and achievement, but cautious and passive learning leads to little joy and little achievement (see McKeachie, 1969, pp. 37-81). Teaching a large introductory course in a traditional lecture-multiple-choice exam format does not allow students to "devour" the subject matter, the teacher, or each other. In this paper we will describe one way to facilitate students' active involvement with psychology, the instructors, and themselves in a large introductory psychology course (135 students).

In brief, the course was a two-quarter (3 credit hours per quarter) course that had three components. These were: (a) a contract grading system, (b) lecture/demonstrations by the instructors once a week, and (c) weekly small group sessions (10-12 students per group) led by undergraduate psychology majors. After describing, in some detail, each of these components and our rationale for using them, course evaluation data and suggestions for improvement of this course design will be presented.

## What We Did and Why

On the first day of class, the instructors passed out and discussed, at length, a long hand-out which described their educational goals and philosophy, the course format, the weekly topics and accompanying reading assignments, and the course requirements.[3] Included in the goals and philosophy section was the following statement:

> Our aim is to provide a course in which a student has the opportunity to take responsibility for his/her own learning, get actively involved with the subject matter, and have a good time while learning.

Consistent with this statement, a contract grading system and small group meetings were built into the course.

**Contract Grading Systems.** Since the class was too large for developing individual contracts between each student and the instructors, the two teachers devised a contract without student input. This contract allowed students to make choices about which grade they wanted to work for and how actively involved they wanted to get with each other and with the subject matter. It also shifted a lot of the responsibility for what got learned from the instructor to the student.

The contracts are outlined below in Table 1. Passing the multiple choice tests meant getting a grade of 70% or better. Students were given 50% of the questions (with answers indicated) a week before each of the tests, so that they would spend more time and effort working on projects and less time worrying about the exams. Exams were used to make a demand on the students to read their textbooks (Psychology Today, 1972). We felt that without exams students would have spent more of their time on their other courses and activities and not enough time reading about general psychology.

As indicated in Table 1, to get a "C," a student had to pass both the mid-term and final exams. To get a "B", a student had to pass a B-project in addition to

Table 1
The Contracts Presented to the Students

| Grade | Mid-term | Final | "B" project | "A" project | Write up | Book Report |
|-------|----------|-------|-------------|-------------|----------|-------------|
| "A" | Pass | Pass | Pass | Pass or | Pass or | Pass |
| "B" | Pass | Pass | Pass | No | No | No |
| "C" | Pass | Pass | No | No | No | No |

passing both exams. The B-project involved 2-4 students working together on a topic which was either chosen from a list of about fifty provided in the hand-out or created by the group members (e.g., Human Instincts: Do they really exist?). Passing a B-project meant compiling a written report, which included a review and discussion of the work done on their topic in the past, a discussion of current research and thinking, and a discussion of the personal relevance of their topic for each member of that B-project group. B-projects also had to be presented, with a one-page handout, in one of the small group sessions. The B-projects were read by a Group Facilitator (GF) and both instructors. If the instructors and the GF thought the project didn't meet the criteria it was returned to the students with suggestions for improvement. The project could be redone and handed back once with no penalty.

We felt that this kind of project would provide students with experience in working cooperatively with a small group of their peers and it might encourage them to seek out the sources within our community for finding out about their topic (e.g., library resources; people resources). Perhaps by doing B-projects they learned a little more about how to be self-directed learners and how to learn from each other.

Since the B-project required a considerable amount of effort and time, we decided to make the next step (toward an "A") a little easier. To get an "A" a student had to pass both exams, a B-project, and some kind of A-report (see Table 1). An A-report required somewhat less research than a B-project and it could have been done

individually. An A-Book Report could be done on one of the fifty books provided on the hand-out or on a book which wasn't on the list but which was something we were studying in class. The criteria for a passable book report included a section on personal relevance and a section on how the material in the book fits in with what the student had been learning about psychology. The Experiment Write-Ups (another type of A-report) were short papers about two psychology experiments in which the student voluntarily participated. These write-ups had to be descriptions of what it felt like to be a subject, what they surmised the experiment was all about, and whether they thought the experiment made sense to them.

As illustrated in Table 1 a student had to do only one type of A-report in an acceptable way, in addition to passing both tests and completing a B-project, and get an "A". The A-reports, like the B-projects, also could be redone if they were judged unacceptable at first. We hoped that all of these choices would provide the students with an opportunity to match their efforts in this course to their own learning styles in an actively involving way (Grasha, 1972).

Team Teaching and Lecturing. Once a week the class was gathered in a large room and one or both instructors lectured, led discussions, conducted experiments with the class, demonstrated something in front of the class, had debates, presented films, and/or told stories relevant to psychology. The purpose of these meetings included: to provide some continuity and perspective (historical, philosophical, scientific, personal) concerning the subject matter; to provide a place in which all of us could talk about the purposes of education and about the structure of this course; to supplement the basic reading material (the text) with current research findings and theorizing; and to make even this kind of learning (learning in a large group) an involving enjoyable experience.

There has been quite a bit written about the pros and cons, the trials and tribulations, and the relative effectiveness of team-teaching (e.g., Johnson & Geoffroy, 1970). By anticipating some of the problems in team-teaching mentioned in the literature, such as the need for a lot of communication and planning, the instructors felt ready for the experience. The instructors hoped that team-teaching would make this course a more enjoyable, simpler, and better learning experience for each of them than it would have been if each of them had taught it alone. They also expected the team approach to provide the students with a greater variety of models, greater stimulation in lectures and discussions, and increased opportunity for personal contact with at least one of the instructors.

Small Groups with Undergraduate Leaders. Using small groups to encourage active and personal involvement in learning has become very popular during the last several years (see Runkel, Harrison, & Runkel, 1972). In our class, small groups provided a place in which students could form their B-project groups, find out about relevant resources in the community (e.g., the types of references available in the medical school library, the activities of researchers at the university) to help them with their projects, and discuss or enact the course material.

We decided to use undergraduates as Group Facilitators (GFs), partially because research on the Keller plan (an instructional system involving self-paced learning facilitated by immediate feedback from proctors), has indicated that students find working with undergraduate proctors to be a very helpful and satisfying experience (Kulik, Kulik, & Carmichael, 1974). Such GFs don't have to be paid, are typically eager to do a good job, and eliminate the problem of having a leader emerge from a group of students who are randomly placed together. This method also affords GFs a good chance to learn more about psychology, small group dynamics, teaching, and about themselves as leaders, teachers, and persons. We hoped that the participants in the small groups might be able to respond more freely and openly if led by one of their peers rather than an older (and wiser?) instructor or graduate student.

As part of their training for their new roles, the GFs took a "guided study" course designed to help them learn how to be effective group facilitators. They received materials on group processes (e.g., leadership; the use of feedback) from two consultants from the Institute for Research and Training in Higher Education (I.R.T.H.E.)[4] which is a university institute which supports and encourages innovative and effective teaching. GFs also received almost immediate feedback from the instructors who "floated" from group to group during the weekly small group sessions. In addition to this type of feedback, the instructors and the consultants met with all of the group leaders once a week for an hour and a half. During this session we all shared ideas on problems in the groups (e.g., non-participative or dominating group members), reviewed the plan for the next small groups session which the instructors had outlined, and exchanged feedback on how the small group sessions and the lecture-class sessions had been going. At the end of the quarter, consultant-instructor pairs held short interviews with each of the students to share feedback and overall feelings about the course.

## Course Evaluation

Students were asked to complete a variety of evaluation forms during the course and these data are discussed below along with the observations of instructors and consultants.

Contract Grading.    The vast majority of students indicated that they very much preferred the contract grading system used in this course to the more usual grading systems (e.g., grades assigned based on a curve). No student liked contract grading *less* than more usual grading and most students greatly preferred contracting. In fact, on evaluation forms asking students to rate various aspects of the course on 9-point Likert scales (with "1" being most positive), to the questions about contracting the modal response was "1" and no student responded with a rating less positive than "4." The reasons for these extremely favorable ratings are probably indicated in some of the comments made by students; they felt that the contract grading system pro-

vided for "more personalized grading," "getting out what you put in," and "working at your own pace."

In addition to liking contracting the students produced many projects of exceptional quality. Reports about brain control techniques and the fallacy of human instincts are examples of some of the topics of the better projects. Approximately one third of the class members were involved with projects worthy of senior psychology honors students. However, these sweet fruits of the course were matched by some rotten apples.

The rotten apples were not the poorer projects because students effectively used their chance to revise projects to increase their quality. Hence, all projects which eventually met the criteria were of good quality. The rotten apples were the problems that some students created by finding loop-holes in the contract through which they could squeeze out unearned high grades. Some students handed in reports late, just barely missed the cut-off on the exam, submitted A-reports but no B-project, and claimed they couldn't find anyone to work with, or failed to present their B-projects. What were the instructors to do with these people? The instructors handled these cases which emerged through the loop-holes, individually, and as fairly as possible. These frustrating and confusing cases forced the instructors into an authoritarian role because they had to make many decisions which seemed quite arbitrary.

Team-Teaching and Lecturing.    Almost all of the students responded favorably to questions in the evaluations about having the course team taught. They enjoyed getting two viewpoints and they especially liked the experiments and the variety of presentations offered in class.

The two instructors met frequently to discuss presentations and the course in general and, although there were some disagreements along with agreements, both thought the experience was very valuable and both plan to team-teach again.

Small Groups with Undergraduate Leaders.    More than 75% of the students liked having the small group sessions and found them valuable; they liked the GFs being at about their level as students and felt they could identify more easily with the GFs than with most instructors.

Attendance at the small group sessions during the first quarter was only about 50% as compared to about 90% at the large sessions. This improved during the second quarter to about 90% at small group and large sessions, possibly because the GFs developed better skills then and were working in pairs rather than working individually.

## Suggestions for Improvement

The students responded favorably to all aspects of this course as indicated in the discussion above, and the instructors and consultants felt good about it also. Still there are improvements which could have been made.

While the contracting system was especially appreciated by the students, some students tried to find loop-holes in the contract to avoid working and learning. Perhaps the rationale for contracting and the importance of sticking to the agreement wasn't clear to many students. Maybe, a more complete statement about why this system was developed, the mechanics of how it works and a more elaborate exchange on "what education is for us" on the first day of class would have helped clarify the contract. Also a written statement and examples in the hand-out of the instructors' expectations concerning the quality of reports, the necessity of fulfilling all aspects of the contract (e.g., punctuality; making presentations), and a statement of clear contingencies for failing to meet criteria might have helped to close some loop-holes (Homme, 1970).

During the first class meeting of the second quarter these changes were instituted. They seemed to help increase two-way communication in addition to reducing unwanted tensions between the instructors and the students (Bolton and Boyer, 1971). The deadlines for submitting reports were moved up two weeks and this seemed to reduce the confusion and the number of attempts to get around, or through, the contract.

Much of the feedback about the instructors' team-teaching and lecturing that was received in formal evaluations, in informal discussions, and in our self-evaluation, helped us design the second quarter of the course. For example, the instructors received many favorable comments about the classroom experiments. Even though many of the experiments did not work out as we expected they were always fun, lively, and very instructional. A brief description of one of these experiments may make this discussion more concrete.

Our demonstration of classical conditioning was a surprise to the class. As one of the instructors introduced the topic he casually mentioned the word "rabbit" as he talked about eyelid conditioning. One of the GFs in the back of the room slammed a large metal pot on the wall as soon as he heard the instructor say "rabbit." The class reacted with the appropriate startle response. The second time "rabbit" was uttered the slamming of the pot was a little too slow and most of the students evidenced no startle response. The instructor was hoping that when he said "rabbit" for the third time students would emit a conditioned emotional response. Unfortunately, or perhaps fortunately, only four of the 135 students reacted as expected. The ensuing discussion of why the experiment failed focussed attention on the importance of inter-stimulus intervals, stimulus intensity, and individual differences in learning.

We conducted even more experiments which involved the class during the second quarter. It seems that the students really liked, and really seemed to learn a lot, from the more experiential or action-based teaching methods that were used (see McKeachie, 1969, pp. 212-228).

Students seemed to particularly enjoy the classes in which both instructors talked about the same topic. Sometimes the instructors presented their views of the same topic and sometimes they divided the topic in units and alternated in presenting the units. Perhaps having two instructors teaching in the same class session varied the stimuli to which students were exposed enough to increase their attending to what was going on.

Improving the small group sessions seems like a more complex task than improving the team-teaching or lecturing aspects of the course. Six possible ways to have made

these sessions more productive and enjoyable for everyone involved are discussed below.

(1) GFs could have been pre-selected to get only people who were very sincerely interested in teaching and learning about small groups involved.

(2) GFs could have team taught so that they could share responsibility and support each other more directly.

(3) A workshop could have been conducted before classes started to establish some effective communication patterns and trust between all staff members.

(4) A contract could have been developed between GFs and instructors. It would probably be helpful to include in that contract a provision for GFs to do some reading and sharing with each other about some theoretical and conceptual issues concerning small groups. Another provision could be a required write-up about what happened in their small group meetings to be shared at the weekly staff meetings. These provisions might help GFs and instructors focus more easily and quickly on the problems that develop in the groups.

(5) Allowing the GFs to plan their own group sessions, rather than having instructors plan the sessions, would probably increase their involvement and enthusiasm for the small group sessions.

(6) Conducting regular (bi-weekly or monthly) individual interviews with each GF might have allowed for increased feedback to be shared and, perhaps, closer relationships to develop.

## Conclusion

A lot of work was required by the instructors and the consultants to make this course work, and perhaps even more work would be required to implement some of the suggestions mentioned above. All of the questionnaire data and the high percentage of "A's" (64% in the first quarter; 86% in the second quarter) achieved by students cannot answer the question: Was it really worth it? We think it was. The students said things like: "I have learned very much." "I have met more people in this class than in any other." "I feel reinforced as a freshman that I have something to give and communicate to others." So many other students have communicated their appreciation for this experience with their smiles and their laughter and their pats on the back.

It was worth it.

## References

Bolton, C. K., & Boyer, R. K. One/way and two/way communication processes in the classroom. *IRTHE*, 1971, *1*, No. 1.

Grasha, A. F. Observations on relating teaching goals to student response styles and classroom methods. *American Psychologist*, 1972, 27, 144-147.

Homme, L. *How to use contingency contracting in the classroom*, Champaign, Ill.: Research Press, 1970.

Johnson, J. C., & Geoffroy, K. E. A subjective appraisal of team teaching. *Improving College and University Teaching*, 1970, *18*, 227-229.

Kulik, J. A., Kulik, C., & Carmichael, K. The Keller plan in science teaching. *Science*, 1974, *83*, 379-383.

McKeachie, W. J. *Teaching tips: A guidebook for the beginning college teacher.* Lexington, Mass.: Heath, 1969.

*Psychology Today: An introduction.* Del Mar, Calif.: CRM Books, 1972.

## Notes

1. The first author, Daniel S. Kirchenbaum, was one of the instructors; many thanks are owed to Bill Epps, the other instructor, for his suggestions in the design of the course and for his enthusiasm and energy used to make the course work.
2. Sheryl Riechmann is presently the Director, Center for Improvement of Instructional Resources, University of Massachusetts at Amherst.
3. The second author, Sheryl Wetter Riechmann, and Bob Francis, whose helpful suggestions about the course were very useful, were the two consultants from I.R.T.H.E. Anthony F. Grasha, Acting Director of I.R.T.H.E., also made several helpful suggestions about the contract system used in the course.

# Team Teaching Introductory Psychology as Pedagogy and for Faculty Development

Mark E. Ware, Louis E. Gardner
and Daniel P. Murphy
*Creighton University*

If you plan to try team teaching, perhaps this experience will provide some helpful hints on values and problems.

The concept of team teaching has been extremely powerful in attracting the attention of American educators in recent years (Schuck, 1970). In addition, the use of the team approach has inspired extensive research efforts to test it against more traditional teaching methods. The bulk of such studies has been carried out in elementary and secondary schools with some research done at the technical college level. As yet, there has been little activity in evaluating the team approach in four year college programs. Perhaps the lack of research on team teaching in college stems from the fact that some educators view the usual college system as a team taught experience in its present form when compared with lower levels of education (Casey, 1966). This perception is realistic when one looks at the typical college experience as a sequence of classes taught by specialists in the various disciplines, and compares this with lower level systems where a single teacher covers several disciplines with the same class. Within particular disciplines the team method in teaching one course would seem to be a deviation from the usual approach. We were stimulated to try the team approach in teaching an introductory psychology course for some of the same reasons that prompted the evolution of the method in elementary education as well as some of our own.

One of the basic advantages of the team approach involves the consequences of maximal use of special competencies of the team members (Singer, 1966). To the competency factor, we added an interest factor based upon the assumption that a teacher who had both expertise and interest in a particular topic could present a better lecture than one who does not have these qualities. We expected that each team member, working in his areas of specialization, would impress the students more favorably than one instructor covering all topics in the course. In this instance, favorable impression is intended to mean the elicitation of a positive attitude toward the course as well as a perceived facilitation of the learning process.

A second interest in our use of the team approach, which would expose students to the personality and teaching style of a greater number of departmental faculty, was also directed at a student benefit. In this case, we thought that these students would have more information in making decisions about selecting psychology as a major, taking other psychology courses, choosing a faculty member for advising purposes, etc.

Finally, we believed we would improve opportunities for faculty development including teaching and research by using the team approach. Joint effort in the development and implementation of the course should provide an environment for learning from each other about the teaching process. Although we would be very busy teaching for shorter periods of time, we anticipated being freer for longer periods of time for scholarly activity and research. This final benefit accruing from the use of team effort seemed to be particularly attractive in a small private college where teaching is emphasized.

In sum, we sought student and faculty evaluation of a team taught course in introductory psychology as a teaching method and an occasion for professional growth.

Method. The participants were 316 students enrolled in the two sections of Introductory Psychology at Creighton University during the fall semester. There were approximately an equal number of students in each section. About 2/3 of the students were in the College of Arts and Sciences with the remainder in the College of Business Administration. Since the course was classified as lower division, 75% of the students were freshmen or sophomores. The distribution by sex consisted of 55% males and 45% females. By the end of the semester, withdrawals from the course were approximately 7%, which is slightly less than the level of attrition found by instructors teaching the same course individually.

The team consisted of three of the four full time faculty in the Department of Psychology. They had been affiliated with the institution for from two to five years when the present course was offered. Each instructor had taught introductory psychology at least once in every semester during his tenure at Creighton University.

During the spring and summer preceding the semester in which the course was team taught, the three faculty members met frequently to design the course. The selection of a text and topics for the course were largely dependent on the areas of specialization and/or interests of the instructors. Although all three persons might be characterized as general-experimental psychologists, it was believed that a representative coverage of the discipline was achieved. The topics selected and the sequence in which they were presented were as follows:

Table 1
Student Responses

Table 1. (continued)

| Item | Percent |
|------|---------|

5. In general, what is your opinion of the team-teaching method used in Introductory Psychology?

| | |
|---|---|
| 1. completely favorable | 20 |
| 2. favorable with reservations | 60 |
| 3. generally unfavorable | 12 |
| 4. unfavorable | 8 |
| | (N = 295) |

16. If you have any positive feelings about this course, (if not leave blank) which one of the following characteristics would you say was *most* influential in the formation of those feelings?

| | |
|---|---|
| 1. variation in instructors | 14 |
| 2. content of course | 46 |
| 3. impartial assignment of grades | 15 |
| 4. treatment of contemporary and relevant issues | 24 |
| | (N = 221) |

15. If you have any negative feelings about this course, (if not leave blank) which one of the following characteristics would you say was *most* influential in the formation of those feelings?

| | |
|---|---|
| 1. class size was too large | 30 |
| 2. variation between tests | 24 |
| 3. variation in instructor methods of presentation | 26 |
| 4. poor student-teacher relationship | 11 |
| 5. the content of the course was not what I expected | 9 |
| | (N = 184) |

1. Disregarding differences in types of tests given, the *variation* of instructors with their different methods of presentation and personality dynamics was such that my learning experience was

| | |
|---|---|
| 1. generally facilitated | 21 |
| 2. somewhat facilitated | 31 |
| 3. neither facilitated nor inhibited | 28 |
| 4. somewhat inhibited | 16 |
| 5. generally inhibited | 4 |
| | (N = 291) |

2. Disregarding differences in types of tests given, the *variation* of instructors with their different methods of presentation and personality dynamics

| | |
|---|---|
| 1. required minor adjustment | 42 |
| 2. required an intermediate degree of adjustment | 35 |
| 3. required considerable adjustment (which was possible in the time provided) | 13 |
| 4. required more adjustment than I could make in the time provided | 9 |
| | (N = 285) |

3. Although other options might be more desirable, which of the following would you choose: (assuming the class size would be the same as it was this semester)

| | |
|---|---|
| 1. team teaching | 75 |
| 2. one instructor you knew nothing about | 25 |
| | (N = 286) |

4. Although other options might be more desirable, which of the following would you choose: assuming the class size would be the same as it was this semester)

| | |
|---|---|
| 1. team teaching | 91 |
| 2. one instructor you had heard was not "very good" | 9 |
| | (N = 289) |

19. Which of the following statements applies to you?

| | |
|---|---|
| 1. I never have had and never will have any desire to major in psychology | 70 |
| 2. I was thinking about majoring in psychology, but this course has caused me to reject this possibility | 9 |
| 3. I was not considering a major in psychology, but this course has caused me to decide upon a major in psychology | 11 |
| 4. I was going to major in psychology before this course and I still intend to major in psychology | 9 |
| | (N = 246) |

Science of Psychology, Statistics, Measurement/Intelligence, Principles of Learning, Human Learning, Development, Motivation, Perception, Attitudes, Emotions, Personality, Behavior Disorders, and Psychotherapy.

As can be seen, 13 chapters were covered. Each instructor was responsible for approximately 1/3 of the chapters. In addition to each chapter in the text, there were assignments which consisted of one of four related articles selected from readings books. Copies of the articles were made available on the reserve shelf in the library.

A 40-item multiple choice type examination was scheduled after every two chapters except that the first exam covered only one chapter. All three instructors primarily relied on the authors' test-item file in an effort to maintain the uniformity of test item content and style. Tests included items on the readings to provide some additional incentive for reading them; however, their weighting was relatively small.

On the first day of class, all three teachers attended both sections of the course. Each introduced himself and described his professional background and interests as well as his experience at Creighton. Students were informed that the course would be taught in a team fashion with each faculty member responsible for specific portions of the course. The goals for team teaching were described as including the following: (a) To enhance students' feelings toward and learning of material in introductory psychology by having the faculty members teach their areas of interest and/or expertise; (b) To assist students to decide on a major or subsequent psychology courses by exposure to personality characteristics and teaching styles of several psychology faculty members in the introductory course.

Each student was provided with a handout which gave course policies and mechanics. The first part of the handout identified specific policies governing attendance, examinations, and grading. The second part consisted of a syllabus including the topics to be covered by each instructor and reading assigments from the text and the articles. Finally, a calendar of events was provided that identified the dates on which each instructor would lecture as well as examination dates and holidays. All questions were thoroughly answered and the first lecture began at the second scheduled meeting of the class. Students were informed that the instructors placed a high priority on class attendance, in part because the requirement for a course evaluation at the end of the semester demanded that they had been exposed to a sufficient number of class periods for each instructor. Thus, students who were absent for more than four class periods were to be dropped from the course. Although no student exceeded the specified number of absences, about 7% of the students withdrew from the course as mentioned above. Of the remaining 295 students, all were administered a copy of the Student Evaluation Form (SEF) at the last class meeting of the semester before the final exam.

The SEF was designed to elicit students' reactions to issues more or less related to the team approach as well as to other facets of the course such as the text, number of exams, class attendance, cheating on exams, grades, etc. In contrast to the more commonly used evaluation form, which provides statements and asks students to respond on a five-point Likert Scale from strongly disagree to strongly agree, the SEF focused on response alternatives to elicit student reaction in specific directions. Thus, sometimes as few as two alternatives were appropriate and at other times as many as five were available. Table 1 contains the pertinent items on the SEF along with the available alternatives. Inspection of the items in Table 1 reveals the type of information used in evaluating the team teaching course. The authors thought that the SEF provided more pertinent and useful information than means and standard deviations derived from a Likert-type scale. Moreover, no assumptions beyond a nominal scale of measurement were necessary with the SEF.

In addition to the more formal evaluation described above, each instructor solicited informal feedback from the class after he completed his portion of the course. Thus, each person was able to assess his own contribution independent of the team teaching approach. Since the structure of the instructor evaluations did not lend itself to comparative evaluation and since it does not relate directly to the question of team teaching, the results are not reported.

After the conclusion of the course, the three instructors met to identify both positive and negative experiences which were related to the team teaching approach and to faculty development.

Results.  Table 1 contains those items relating to the team teaching method, the per cent of the students responding to each of the alternatives and the number of students responding to each item. These results reveal that the students' opinion of the course was favorable in 80% of the cases and unfavorable in only 20% of the cases. From among the 295 students who responded to the SEF, 75% indicated some positive and 62% some negative feelings toward the course (items 16 and 15 respectively). In short, students did not seem to respond only on the basis of a positive or negative halo toward the course, but they were able to distinguish both positive and negative feelings. Among those students who indicated positive or negative feelings toward the course, 14% (option 1, item 16) and 26% (option 3, item 15) respectively identified "variation in instructors" as being the most influential.

Two questions were specifically included to determine students' reactions to "variation of instructors with their different methods of presentation and personality dynamics." The results of Question 1 were that 52% of the students indicated that variation of instructor facilitated learning, 28% of the students indicated that it had neither facilitated nor inhibited, and only 20% reported that their learning had been inhibited. Question 2 indicated that 77% of the students reported that variation of instructor was responsible for minor to intermediate degrees of adjustment, but only 22% reported that variation of instructor required greater adjustment.

Another index of students' reactions to team teaching was revealed in questions asking them to select an alternative to team teaching including "one instructor you knew nothing about" and "one instructor you heard was not 'very good'." In the former instance students chose team teaching by a margin of 3 to 1 and in the latter instance by a margin of about 9 to 1.

Students were asked to indicate which of four statements applied to them regarding their thoughts about majoring in psychology before and after the course, as shown for Question 19. Alternatives one and four reflect no change in attitude with regard to majoring in psychology as a consequence of the course with 9% indicating plans to major and 70% no plans to major. Alternatives two and three reflect a change in selection of a major, with 9% indicating that they had decided not to major and 11% that they had decided to major as a consequence of the course. Thus, student responses indicated a net gain of 2% deciding to major in psychology as a consequence of the course.

Considerable enthusiasm was generated among the instructors in conjunction with the views that they were engaged in an innovative educational activity and that collectively they could offer Introductory Psychology in a way which was different and better than that possible by any one of them. Moreover, they felt a greater sense of departmental unity and cooperation in attempting to realize their educational mission. Among the disadvantages were feelings of not getting to know as many students and of not maintaining the same degree of continuity of material as that of a single instructor. Finally, the initial wave of enthusiasm toward the course was not maintained during the implementation of the plan. An ambivalent reaction was experienced toward the variation in teaching load during the semester. The teaching load for each instructor increased by 100% during that part of the semester when he was responsible for teaching the two sections of the course. Not only did the increased teaching load produce fatigue, but a second lecture on the same material each day was found to produce boredom in the instructor.

Seen as an experience for faculty development, the course offered numerous advantages. Planning and implementation provided a structure for discussion and evaluation of many of the details of teaching, including the selection of a text, the sequence of topics, the assignment of grades, class attendance policy, the inclusion of additional outside readings, the number and types of examinations, etc. Moreover, the instructors developed a greater knowledge of demonstrations, anecdotes, audio-visual materials and teaching techniques which had been found to be effective by the other instructors. Finally, those times during which each instructor was not responsible for teaching the course provided an opportunity for more intensive preparation of his lectures, scholarly activity, and research. However, those larger blocks of free time required deliberate structuring of activities for optimal effectiveness. In sum, team teaching provided many occasions for faculty development which are otherwise difficult or impossible when the course is taught in the more traditional fashion.

Discussion.   Although the student reaction overall to team teaching was favorable, a closer examination of the data revealed no evidence of a halo effect. Students identified both positive and negative feelings toward the course, suggesting discrimination in their reactions. That interpretation was further supported by the ranking given to reasons associated with positive and negative feelings toward the course. Although variation in instructors was not the most influential factor cited for positive feelings, neither was it the most influential factor cited for negative feelings. Indeed the responses to Questions 16 and 15 indicate that students' feelings were contingent on several factors in addition to instructor variability. Thus students' favorable feelings seem to constitute a discerning evaluation.

The preponderance of students reported that learning was facilitated by the team approach without significant adjustments required to changes in instructors. The team teaching approach seemed to generate a sense of having learning enhanced without the expense of major adjustment to changes in instructors. Although not conclusive, the observation of a preference for team teaching over an unknown or not very good instructor suggests that team teaching offers students the possibility of getting a good instructor and/or not being stuck with a poor instructor for more than a portion of the course. The goal of enhancing students' feelings toward and learning of material was largely realized.

Team teaching seemed effective among 80% of the students, but it was not and is not a panacea for eliciting favorable student reaction and a perception of facilitating learning. Team teaching seems to offer promise as a reasonable alternative to the more traditional individually taught course, particularly when evaluated in the context of other factors including assistance in student decision making and faculty development.

Exposure to three out of four departmental faculty members may have been of some assistance in student decision-making. A total of 79% of the students indicated that the course had not had an impact on their decision either to major or not major in psychology, but about 20% were so influenced. Of those who decided to change their plans to major, the authors believed that those deciding not to major may have been well advised, because their prior expectation toward the discipline may have been un-

founded. The early elimination of a possible major can facilitate selecting an area which is more suitable to a student's needs and aspirations. On the other hand, the decision to major in psychology as a consequence of taking the team taught course would seem to support the expectation that early exposure to several instructors can assist students in evaluating their compatibility with the discipline and its faculty. A next step in this research consists of a follow up of students to determine whether plans regarding the selection of a major were translated into action. Finally, the finding of a slight net gain in the number of prospective majors is encouraging in face of competition for majors and projections of an overall decrease in enrollments in the coming years.

The results of team teaching for faculty development offer an optimistic outlook. Our findings indicate that several faculty members can work together to provide a single coherent course, to generate enthusiasm toward teaching, to learn more effective teaching techniques, and to increase the opportunities for scholarly activity and research. The latter finding is perhaps of greater significance in smaller, undergraduate departments where teaching load and university/community service make large time demands. Some caution may be advised with regard to the faculty development dimension, because one requisite for effective achievement of that goal involves the quality of interpersonal relationship which exists or can be developed among the participating members. It is not hard for us to imagine that the faculty development gains we experienced might not be found in departments in which tension and conflict exist among the faculty.

The investigation has revealed that team teaching the introductory course can be advantageous both for students and faculty. Although clearly team teaching is not a singular solution for either pedagogy or faculty development, we have found it to be an alternative worthy of serious consideration.

### References

Casey, V. A.  A summary of team teaching: Its patterns and potentials. In D. W. Beggs (Ed.). *Team teaching*. Bloomington IN: Indiana University Press, 1966.

Schuck, R. F.  A social psychological view of large group instruction. *Psychology in the Schools*, 1970, 7, 296-303.

Singer, I. J.  What team teaching really is. In D. W. Beggs (Ed). *Team teaching*. Bloomington IN: Indiana University Press, 1966.

# 4. PSI, MASTERY, AND OTHER INDIVIDUALIZED APPROACHES

## A Comparison of Student- and Instructor-Paced Formats In the Introductory Psychology Course

Stephen H. Hobbs
*Augusta College*

Instructor pacing does not lower academic performance or student attitudes, and it has some advantages over student pacing.

Considerable evidence has accrued over the last decade to suggest that the personalized system of instruction (PSI) pioneered by Keller (1968) is reliably superior to more traditional course formats in terms of student achievement. PSI, however, is not a unitary instructional package. Among the features which are likely to be present in a given PSI course are small instructional units, mastery of units to an established criterion level, self-pacing, multiple testing with rapid feedback, use of student proctors, and primary dependency upon reading materials as opposed to lectures. Appropriately, then, much of the recent research has focused upon analysis of the relative contributions of the various components of PSI (e.g., Kulik, Jaksa & Kulik, 1978).

One of the PSI components which has received considerable attention is student self pacing. The incorporation of this feature into PSI stems from the recognition that students do not all learn at the same rate, a fact especially obvious when rigid mastery criteria are established for students. Self pacing, however, has been viewed by some as incompatible with the demands of the traditional school calendar. Furthermore, the responsibilities of self pacing may provide adjustment problems for students habituated to group pacing systems. The question which must be raised, then, is whether self pacing is a feature which is necessary to obtain the benefits of PSI. One recent study (Reiser & Sullivan, 1977) found that instructor (as opposed to student) pacing did not reduce student achievement in a political science course. Additionally, the withdrawal rate, which is often high in PSI courses, was substantially less in the instructor-paced course. The present study similarly compared withdrawal rates, attitudes, and test performances of students who were allowed to proceed through an introductory psychology course at their own pace with those kept on an instructor-determined pace.

Method. Two classes of the beginning course, Principles of Psychology, were used, one for each of the course structures. The classes were held during the same school term; and each had the same instructor, student assistants, text (Zimbardo & Ruch, 1971), workbook (Minke & Carlson, 1972), and classroom. In addition, lectures, films and demonstrations were presented as similarly as possible, and test items used during the courses were drawn from the same item pool. The instructor-paced (IP) course had an initial enrollment of 83 and met daily at 9:00 a.m., and the self-paced (SP) class met daily at 1:00 p.m. with an initial enrollment of 46. Total elimination of student self pacing necessarily implies additional modifications of the "system." Therefore, the IP and SP designations should be considered as short-hand references to the differences between the two groups which are described below.

Students in the SP course had a minimum performance criterion of 80% imposed on their 10-item unit recognition tests, with course grades determined at the end of the quarter by the number of units completed. SP students could retest up to three times on a unit to achieve criterion, although this maximum rarely occurred after the first few units. Unit length (as determined by the workbook) was approximately one-half of a chapter. Students in the IP class were forced through the course at the rate of one chapter (two SP units) per week for the 10-week term. Students were given one retest opportunity on the 20-item chapter tests. Course grades were determined by averaging the 10 best scores from each chapter and applying the traditional grade scale of 90% = A, 80% = B, 70% = C, 60% = D, and below 60% = F.

On the first day of class all students except those registering late, were given a recognition test composed of 20 items selected from previous final examinations. A 50-item comprehensive final examination was administered whenever students completed the course. Scores on the examination could be used to improve, but not lower, a student's course grade. Students in both classes were asked to evaluate the course after receiving their course grades using a modification of the instrument regularly administered at this institution. The modification consisted of simply adding to the open-ended portion of the questionnaire the item, "Would you take another course of this type in the future?"

Results. The rate of withdrawal of initially enrolled students was twice as high in the SP class (19.6%) as in the IP (9.6%), but these differences did not reach statistical significance ($\chi^2(1) = 2.15$, $p > .05$). Larger differences between the two classes were obtained on the grade distributions of students who remained in the courses ($\chi^2(4) = 20.54$, $p < .001$). Grades in the SP class were highly skewed, with the greatest percentage of students receiving "As" (A = 46%, B = 5%, C = 27%, D = 8%, F = 14%). A more normal distribution was obtained with the IP class, with "C" being the modal grade (A = 12%, B = 29%, C = 35%, D = 13%, F = 11%).

In comparison, then, the upward shift from the "B" range in the SP course was most notable.

Performance comparisons were made on the 27 students in the SP group and 65 students in the IP group for whom pretest and final examination scores were obtained. The pretest averages for the SP and IP students were 52.4 and 48.2, respectively. These were found not to differ statistically ($t(90) = 1.46, p > .05$). The mean SP final examination score was 71.8 as compared with 77.8 for the IP group, a difference which did reach statistical significance ($t(90) = 2.05$, $p < .05$). Item analyses of the examination suggested that the two groups of students may have been learning material differently and/or approaching the test items differently. Thus, items which were "easy" or "difficult" for one group were frequently not so classifiable for the other.

In contrast to the above findings, little difference was found between the IP and SP classes in terms of attitudes toward their respective courses. The SP students often cited self pacing as the most desirable feature of their course. However, elimination of self pacing had no appreciable effects on the numerical feedback. For example, the two classes each gave generally favorable average ratings (on a 5-point scale) to the courses overall (SP: $M = 4.00$, IP: $M = 3.62$) and the distribution of ratings was found not to differ ($\chi^2(4) = 5.80, p > .05$). Furthermore, when asked if they would take another course of the same type in the future, 82% of the SP students and 88% of the IP students answered in the affirmative.

Discussion. The present results are consonant with those of Reiser and Sullivan (1977) and indicate that the elimination of self pacing from a PSI-like system may not result in concurrent lowering of academic performance or student attitude. In fact, superior performance was obtained from instructor-paced students.

For both academic and pragmatic reasons student attitude, as well as achievement, has become one of the variables typically considered in determining course characteristics. In reviewing the written feedback of SP students in the present study, it became clear that the opportunity to proceed through the course at one's own pace was indeed a popular feature. The multiple testing opportunity for the IP students may have contributed to the finding of no substantial differences in numerical attitude ratings between the two pacing groups regarding their experience. As with most research of this type, the present study is limited by failure to include evaluations by those withdrawing from the course.

Two points might be raised regarding the poorer performance of the SP group. First, some SP students had limited exposure to the last units of text material, possibly lowering their total score. An item analysis revealed, however, that SP students were not substantially better than their IP counterparts even on material which they (the SP students) had most recently covered. This becomes all the more striking if one assumes that the higher withdrawal rate in the SP course might create a selective bias, with fewer low achievers in the self-paced section. Second, the differential grade distributions of the two procedures might have differentially affected preparation for an examination which could not lower the student's grade. A comparison of groups matched for expected grade, however, also showed superior examination performance by IP students.

These findings, nevertheless, must be evaluated cautiously because they represent a very restrictive set of conditions. For example, it could well be argued that different results may have been obtained under an open-term arrangement or if the criterion level of the SP class had been raised to 90% or, better yet, 100%. Yet, an objective view of the value of pacing does appear to be increasingly possible when the present data are examined in conjunction with other research: Recent reviewers of this literature (Glick & Semb, 1978; Kulik, et al., 1978; Williams, 1976) have generally concluded that pacing is not a *critical* feature of PSI in improving student achievement. Even where differences between self- and fixed-pace systems have been found, they are usually small and/or statistically insignificant.

Upon reflection, there appear to be at least two advantages of the fixed-paced system over student self-pacing. First, for whatever reason(s), a greater number of initial enrollees may complete the course. This alone should not be considered sufficient reason to eliminate self pacing inasmuch as there are other procedures for reducing withdrawal rates while retaining some pacing flexibility (e.g., Hochstetter & Caldwell, 1977; Semb, Conyers, Spencer & Sanchez-Sosa, 1975). Second, each student remaining in the course is exposed to all of the material intended to be covered during the term. This factor is obviously not relevant when the possibility exists of interminable course length, and students must complete all units of instruction. Few collegiate settings, however, encourage open-term courses, the reasons for which having been recently discussed (Born & Moore, 1978).

It should be clear from the above discussion that the present study does not dictate that the self-pacing concept should be abandoned. Students do not all learn at the same rate; and, as Glick and Semb (1978) have pointed out, many (if not all) students can benefit from self-determined rates of acquisition. More important, the kind of fixed pacing of the IP group in the present study concurrently eliminates the mastery feature of PSI, probably a more significant component of PSI than self pacing (Kulik, et al., 1978). One challenge, then, would be to find means of keeping the essentials of mastery in situations where complete self pacing may not be possible or desirable. Conversely, it might be more profitable to explore ways to make an early identification of those students who may have difficulties with pacing flexibility, and help them develop better time-management skills (Keenan, Bono & Hursh, 1978; Semb, Glick & Spencer, 1979).

### References

Born, D. G., & Moore, M. C. Some belated thoughts on pacing. *Journal of Personalized Instruction*, 1978, *3*, 33-36.

Glick, D. M., & Semb, G. Effects of pacing contingencies in personalized instruction: A review of the literature. *Journal of Personalized Instruction*, 1978, *3*, 36-42.

Hochstetter, G. T., & Caldwell, E. C. The effects of student-selected mastery levels in a PSI course. *Journal of Personalized Instruction*, 1977, *2*, 162-164.

Keenan, J. B., Bono, S. F., & Hursh, D. F. Shaping time-management skills: Two examples in PSI. *Journal of Personalized Instruction*, 1978, *3*, 46-49.

Keller, F. S. "Good-bye, teacher. . ." *Journal of Applied Behavior Analysis*, 1968, *1*, 79-89.

Kulik, J. A., Jaksa, P., & Kulik, C. C. Research on component features of Keller's personalized system of instruction. *Journal of Personalized Instruction*, 1978, *3*, 2-14.

Minke, K. A., & Carlson, J. G. *Psychology and Life unit mastery system* (Rev. ed.). Glenview, IL: Scott, Foresman, 1972.

Reiser, R. A., Sullivan, H. J. Effects of self pacing and instructor pacing in a PSI course. *Journal of Educational Research*, 1977, *71*, 8-12.

Semb, G., Conyers, D., Spencer, R., & Sanchez-Sosa, J. J. An experimental comparison of four pacing contingencies. In J. M. Johnson (Ed.), *Behavior research and technology in higher education*. Springfield, IL: Charles C Thomas, 1975.

Semb, G., Glick, D. M., & Spencer, R. E. Student withdrawals and delayed work patterns in self-paced psychology courses. *Teaching of Psychology*, 1979, *6*, 23-25.

Williams, R. L. Personalized system of instruction: Future research areas. *Journal of Personalized Instruction*, 1976, *1*, 106-112.

Zimbardo, P. G., & Ruch, F. L. *Psychology and life* (Brief 9th ed.). Glenview, IL: Scott, Foresman, 1971.

---

# A Comparison of Two Mastery Approaches to Teaching Introductory Psychology

Jack R. Nation and
Stephen S. Roop
*Texas A & M University*

Treatment effects are more convincing for weekly quizzes than for examinations, but Programmed Student Achievement looks best in this study.

Much of the work in the area of programmed instruction has been based on fundamental learning principles. The empirical relationships that exist in the laboratory have been known for some time but only recently have they been applied to the development of instructional devices and procedures (e. g., Keller, 1968; McMichael & Cory, 1969; Nation, Knight, Lamberth, & Dyck, 1974). This attachment to known scientific phenomena, in addition to providing theoretical guidelines, allows for greater precision in evaluating teaching methods. The identification of the most efficient techniques of instruction in higher education has become a particularly acute problem for educators because of the rapidly increasing number of new programs being made available (c. f., Whaley & Mallott, 1971). Teachers are faced with countless possibilities, most of which are attractive and have some support from well controlled research projects. How, then, is an individual interested in improving educational practices going to make a decision? The present analysis attempts to answer this question, in part, by directly comparing two popular mastery-based instructional programs, i. e., Programmed Student Achievement (PA) and Total Mastery Learning (TML).

Programmed Student Achievement (PA) is a motivation and reward technique in which the key tool is the testing procedure. In this procedure, multiple choice tests are administered to the students, spaced throughout the semester, on discrete segments of material. Students are required to achieve perfect mastery on these quizzes. Students who initially fail to reach the mastery criterion on a given quiz are required to take further quizzes over the same material until mastery is achieved. It is important to note that only the score the first time the student takes a quiz on a given segment of the assigned material is used in computing the semester quiz average, which counts as 50% of the total semester grade. Quiz performance on additional opportunities to achieve mastery is not involved in determining the grade. The other 50% of the final grade comes from major examinations. Research over the last several years (e. g., Haddad,

Nation, & Williams, 1975; Lamberth & Knight, 1974; Knight, 1973; Nation, et al., 1974) has indicated that PA has been, and continues to be, an effective and reliable method for motivating introductory psychology students.

One of the most recent instructional programs to be developed is the Total Mastery Learning (TML) approach described by Vernon (1974). This experimental package of teaching materials represents the culmination of several years of research on programs involving innovative instruction. Specifically, this procedure states definite performance objectives and allows a person to improve his quiz score by a re-exam over the same material. Unlike the Programmed Student Achievement (PA) procedure outlined previously, the student operating under TML contingencies receives the higher of two test scores, i. e., the original score or the re-exam score. Under these conditions, Vernon was able to demonstrate, on a comprehensive final examination, that the average grade of the mastery students was 21 percent higher than was the average of students in a traditional course. Thus, TML appears to be another significant educational accomplishment of behavioral technology.

Both of the procedures described above are of sufficient worth to make them more attractive than conventional, unimaginative programs. Of central concern in the present investigation, however, is which mastery technique *best* fulfills the basic needs of the student, i. e., which procedure results in the best classroom performance. Regardless of one's theoretical bias, an empirical determination can be made concerning the relative merits of each program and that was precisely the intention of the present experiment.

## Method

**Subjects.** The subjects were 302 students enrolled in three sections of Introductory Psychology during the fall semester of 1974. All sections met Monday through Friday: at 8:00 am (section 1, N=113), 2:00 pm (section 2, N=75), or 3:00 pm (section 3, N=114). Pretest scores were obtained from a comprehensive examination taken from the text manual, administered to all classes during the first meeting of the semester. A total of 24 students across all three sections dropped the course during the semester and their data were not included in the analysis. Of the 24 students who dropped the course, 10 were from section 1, 4 were from section 2, and 10 were from section 3. Each section was randomly assigned to one of three treatment conditions at the beginning of the semester.

**Materials.** The text for the course was *Introductory Psychology: A mastery coursebook with performance objectives* by Walter M. Vernon, 1st edition. This text was used because it was specifically designed for Total Mastery Learning and could be readily adapted to a Programmed Student Achievement course.

**Procedure.** The Programmed Student Achievement (PA) class (section 1) involved a technique which required the student who failed to demonstrate criterion performance on each of five weekly quizzes[1] (100% mastery) to re-take conceptually related quizzes as many times as necessary to reach criterion. If the student had not evidenced 100% mastery by the end of the week he received a grade of "F" for the course. The Total Mastery Learning (TML) class (section 2) involved each student taking one re-exam over each of five weekly quizzes. However, there was no criterion requirement and students merely received the higher of their two test scores made during the week. The Standard Control (S-C) condition (section 3) was required to take the five initial weekly quizzes without the requirement, or opportunity, for re-take examinations. In addition to weekly quizzes, all groups were required to take a mid-term and final examination.

At the beginning of the semester all three classes were told the weekly quizzes (consisting of 10 manual multiple choice items taken from study questions provided at the end of each chapter) would constitute 50% of their total grade and the two major examinations would comprise the other 50% of their total grades. The group required to re-take weekly quizzes until evidencing 100% mastery (i.e., PA class) was given one of two weekly quiz forms on Monday. If criterion performance (100% mastery) was not evidenced on Monday, the student was required to take a second form on Wednesday. The Wednesday form, also consisting of 10 multiple choice items, was composed entirely of new items taken from the same general topics covered on the Monday quiz. Students failing to demonstrate 100% mastery on either the Monday or Wednesday quiz were given unlimited opportunities to reach criterion by taking one of the two forms on Friday. A random schedule was used to determine quiz form assignments to students. The PA students were instructed that only the first attempt on the weekly quizzes would be recorded for credit but they still had to evidence 100% mastery by the end of the week. Group TML could take the Monday and/or Wednesday quiz and were told that the higher of the two quiz scores would be the score recorded for credit. While participation on both quizzes was encouraged, no attempt was made to enforce such a policy. Group S-C took only the Monday quiz.

Identical weekly quizzes were administered to all classes during a given day, i.e., all three classes received exactly the same 10-item quiz on Monday and Groups PA and TML received the same 10-item quiz on Wednesday. On each quiz a detachable section was provided at the bottom of the page to allow the student to copy down his choices by letter and immediately compare them with the correct letters which were posted outside the examination room. In order to avoid transfer of test information to a later class, a different sequence of identical test items was given to each class. The mid-term and final examinations each contained 50 new test items constructed by the authors. Students were told that mid-term and final examination items *would not* be taken directly from study questions.

Three different instructors were randomly assigned to teach one of the three treatment conditions. Since the instructor variable has been shown to have little effect in research related to different instructional techniques, e.g., Nation et al. (1974), all instructors were informed of the experimental design and were involved in student counseling and testing. It should be mentioned that Introductory Psychology is normally run by the coordinator, and the senior author served in that capacity during the present study. Instructors in the program have little control over their assignments and, therefore, there is every reason to believe that the experiment had no influence on the instructors' performance in the classroom.

## Results

**Pretest.** A one-way analysis of variance using mean number correct as the dependent variable was performed on the pretest given to all classes. The analysis revealed a significant difference between Groups, $F(2,236) = 5.80$, $p < .05$. Scheffe's method for *post hoc* comparisons performed on means shown in Table 1 indicated that Group PA was inferior ($p < .05$) to both TML and S-C, which did not differ significantly from each other ($p > .10$). This suggests that students in the PA condition were below the other students regarding their basic understanding of psychological concepts, at least at the beginning of the semester.

### Table 1
Mean Percent Correct for Groups on the Pretest and Major Examinations

| Measure | Groups | | |
|---|---|---|---|
| | PA(N=113) | TML(N-75) | S-C(N=114) |
| Pretest | $33.94_a$ | $38.13_b$ | $37.91_b$ |
| Midterm | $82.17_a$ | $77.42_b$ | $81.25_{ab}$ |
| Final | $74.35_a$ | $74.03_a$ | $72.73_a$ |

*Note.* Row means which do not have the same subscript or a common subscript are significantly different at the .05 level.

**Weekly quizzes.** A 3 (Groups) x 2 (initial vs. block of last 4 quizzes) repeated measures analysis was performed on the weekly quizzes. The mean percent correct across the five weekly quizzes (Monday attempt only) is presented graphically in Figure 1. The results of the analysis revealed a nonsignificant main effect for Groups, F(2,260) = .79, *p* > .10. However, the test for the interaction between groups and quizzes did reach an acceptable level of significance, F(2,260) = 18.73, p < .001. Scheffe's procedure for *post hoc* comparisons indicated that on the block of last 4 quizzes the PA condition was superior (p < .05) to both the TML and S-C conditions, which did not differ from each other (p > .10). This is particularly impressive in view of the fact that the PA group was below the other two groups on the initial quiz. Additionally, the PA class was the only condition to show a significant increase from the initial quiz to later quizzes (p< .01). Further inspection of these data indicated a significant main effect for initial quiz vs. block of last 4 quizzes, F(1,260) = 40.29, p < .001, but the interaction results mentioned above render this finding unimportant.

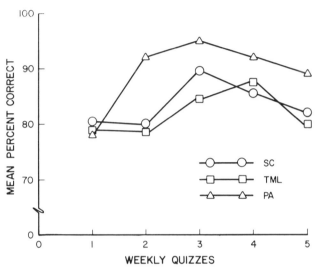

Figure 1. Mean percent correct for each group on the weekly quizzes (Monday attempts).

Since classes TML and PA were the only conditions required to take the Wednesday quiz, t-tests were performed on the quiz means shown in Table 2. The results showed statistical superiority for PA students on quiz 1, *t*(126) = 4.59, *p* < .01, and quiz 2, *t*(89) = 4.06, *p*< .01. The remaining comparisons failed to reach acceptable levels of significance (all *t's* < 1.5).

Table 2
Mean Percent Correct for Groups on the Wednesday Quiz

| Group | Quiz number | | | | |
|---|---|---|---|---|---|
| | 1 | 2 | 3 | 4 | 5 |
| PA | $92.14_a$ | $91.89_a$ | $85.01_a$ | $88.12_a$ | $89.67_a$ |
| TML | $79.98_b$ | $78.97_b$ | $85.43_a$ | $85.97_a$ | $91.86_a$ |

*Note.* Column means not having the same subscript are significantly different at the .05 level.

**Midterm.** Students performance on the mid-term was analyzed for each of the three groups by a one-way analysis

of variance test. Mean percent correct for each group on the mid-term examination is shown in Table 1. The analysis showed a significant effect on Groups, F (2,262) = 4.18 p< .05. *Post hoc* comparisons performed on group means indicated that the PA condition, although not significantly different from Group S-C (p > .05), was statistically superior to Group TML (p < .05). The difference between Groups S-C and TML failed to reach an acceptable level of significance (p > .05). Since the mid-term was drawn from new items (i. e., items not covered in the study questions provided at the end of each chapter), these data suggest students in the PA class were best able to generalize concepts learned earlier in the semester.

**Final.** Table 1 depicts mean student performance on the final examination. A one-way analysis of variance was performed on the final examination using percent correct as the response measure. The analysis failed to show a statistically significant, F (2,257) = .57, ·p >, 10. While this failure of PA students to show differential performance on a major examination is at odds with some data (e. g., Nation, et al., 1974), it is consistent with at least one report (i. e., Haddad et al., 1975).

## Discussion

The evidence indicates a superiority of the PA condition relative to the TML condition on weekly quizzes and the mid-term examination and to the S-C condition on weekly quizzes. These data are particularly impressive in view of the fact that the PA class was significantly inferior to the other classes on the pretest. It appears that the motivational influence of the PA contingency was sufficient to overcome any basic differences that might have existed at the beginning of the semester. One need only inspect the performance on the first two weekly quizzes (first attempts) to see how quickly the PA procedure can result in high achievement (see Figure 1). The fact that PA students were initially below the other groups (a finding consistent with pretest results), and then were 12% higher on the next quiz is certainly a convincing index of enhanced student performance as a result of employing the PA contingency.

Unfortunately, the results were not as favorable for the TML procedure. TML student performance was not significantly different from that of a control on any of the response measures, i. e., the weekly quizzes, the mid-term, or the final. One possible explanation for this unexpected finding is that all the students did not concentrate on a particular quiz. That is, one-half the class may have given their best effort on Monday while the other one-half may have waited until Wednesday to put forth a maximal effort. However, while this explanation might account for poor weekly quiz performance it can not disclaim the significantly inferior performance demonstrated by TML students on the mid-term.

It would be inappropriate, if not erroneous, to suggest that one of the methods compared in the present study is more desirable than the other for all students under all conditions. What can be asserted with some degree of confidence, however, is that the PA condition seems to be better suited to meet student needs when classes are arranged in a manner similar to those involved in the present analysis, e. g., large classrooms, sixteen week semesters, graduate student teachers, etc. The effect on classes structured in another manner may be quite different. The conclusion, as ever, calls for extensive parametric investigation. The present analysis may be of some help in considering and designing such investigations.

## References

Haddad, N. F., Nation, J. R., & Williams, J. D. Programmed student achievement: A Hawthorne effect? *Research in Higher Education,* 1975, in press.

Keller, F. S. "Good-bye, teacher . . ." *Journal of Applied Behavior Analysis,* 1968, *1*, 78-89.

Knight, J. M. The effect of programmed achievement on student performance. *Journal of Educational Research,* 1973, *66,* 291-294.

Lamberth, J., & Knight, J. M. An embarrassment of riches: Effectively teaching and motivating large introductory psychology sections. *Teaching of Psychology,* 1974, *1,* 16-20.

McMichael, J. S., & Corey, J. R. Contingency management in a introductory psychology course produces better learning. *Journal of Applied Behavior Analysis,* 1969, *2,* 79-83.

Nation, J. R., Knight, J. M., Lamberth, J., & Dyck, D. Programmed student achievement: A test of the avoidance hypothesis. *Journal of Experimental Education,* 1974, *42,* 57-61.

Vernon, W. M. *Introductory psychology: A mastery coursebook with performance objectives.* Chicago: Rand McNally, 1974.

Whaley, D. L., & Malott, R. W. *Elementary principles of behavior.* New York: Appleton-Century-Crofts, 1971.

## Notes

1. It should be noted that "weekly quizzes" represents a label used to indicate short quizzes administered during a given week and is not meant to imply that quizzes were given each and every week of the semester.
2. This research was supported by a grant from Research Development, Liberal Arts. The authors would like to thank Robert R. Berg, Director of University Research, and W. David Maxwell, Dean of Liberal Arts, whose valuable contributions made the present research possible. The authors would also like to thank Judy Sears, Arnette Ingram, Paula Long, and Richard Dickenson for their assistance in the conduct and analysis of the experiment.

# Personalizing the Large-Enrollment Course

Michael Terman
*Northeastern University*

Describing a systematic method, with planned
support facilities and materials, to extend
PSI for very large enrollment courses.

The large-enrollment introductory course provides a special set of pedagogical problems. The students form a heterogeneous group with respect to background preparation, professional goals, academic aspirations and aptitude. In standard courses the flow of information in lectures and text assignments is the same for all students, and is presented at the instructor's pace. Exam-score distributions generally dishearten both instructor and students. But, since the student-to-instructor ratio is so large there is little opportunity to confront the study problems of individual students in an attempt to improve performance.

Small-enrollment courses may have a very different character. With a responsive instructor, spontaneous tutorials can occur during and after class. It is possible implicitly to work toward mastery of the material by adjusting the flow of information to students' questions and answers. An intensive laboratory experience is feasible, giving students immediate, moment-to-moment feedback that psychology offers tangible results. But budgetary constraints and logistical problems make this model unfeasible for many large institutions.

In order to confront the large-enrollment problem successfully, our content and our teaching methods must be re-examined. The field is now so large, with many concepts in need of refinement, that we are inclined to emphasize psychology's strongest results and brightest prospects. We surprise students by presenting a science course, and try to show them why this route into the field is intellectually compelling. We hope that they will become objective behavior analysts in a few months, voluntarily rejecting laymen's misconceptions about the field; that they will come to our laboratories and join in research; and that a few at least will dream about becoming Psych I instructors themselves.

With only one instructor and several graduate assistants, such a prospect will remain elusive for thousands of introductory students in the large-enrollment course, unless we can personalize their study. We must acknowledge and confront each student's background and study problems. We must set study objectives that are attainable and yet sophisticated, without compromising the standards set for students who study in more intimate and selective surroundings.

Keller's (1968) guidelines for a personalized system of instruction (PSI) are a starting point: Study is self-paced, in order to accommodate students with varying abilities and time demands; the material is presented in small units, for which the student must show mastery-level performance on quizzes in order to proceed; lectures and demonstrations are not used to present material that will be tested; written performances are the basis for evaluating progress; and fellow undergraduates, trained to serve as tutors, join the instructor in working individually with students on the study objectives, providing immediate discussions of quiz performances and assistance in achieving the mastery criteria.

PSI courses are generally based on standard text units with study guides. A student-to-tutor ratio of 12:1, and a tutor-to-instructor ratio of 10:1 are generally considered practical upper limits (Keller & Sherman, 1974), which suggests that PSI class size should not exceed about 120. Although systematic comparisons of PSI and standard lecture courses almost always show better exam performances with PSI (Kulik, 1976), procedural elaborations seem necessary to implement the model in large-enrollment courses.

The task of tutors in most PSI courses is both administrative (record keeping, quizzing, scoring) and academic (working with students on study problems and course content). Teaching 1000 students at a time (a typical quarterly enrollment in the introductory course at Northeastern) requires modification of tutors' responsibilities so that they can effectively deal with a larger student group. Our solution involves: (1) the development of a Central Instructional Facility, where administrative procedures are overseen by a specialized staff; and (2) a recasting of text content into a interactive videotape format which provides continual feedback for active study responses well before the mastery quiz and tutorial session at the end of a unit.

## Use of the Central Instructional Facility.
The student who thinks he is ready for a mastery quiz comes to Psych Central. A staff assistant pulls a quiz for the unit, first checking the student's progress record (updated daily by computer) to make sure that it is a new quiz form at the appropriate level.

Along with the quiz, the student receives two sheets. The first allows for long-form responses on the back, but is formatted for computer processing on the front. The student writes answers on the back; the staff and tutors make computer code entries. The second sheet contains a "calendar question," in which the student compares his or her progress through the units of the course with respect to the recommended minimum pace, a series of dates which assures completion of the course just before the end of the term. The answer is scored as correct or incorrect, but the student is not criticized for a slow pace. A recent study (Lazar, Soares, & Terman, 1977) indicates that the calendar question assists students in self-pacing their study efficiently: It insures that they always know where they stand, and how much time remains. (A student who has made slow, consistent progress during the quarter, but has not completed all units by final exam week, may sign a formal agreement to complete the course in the early weeks of the next quarter. Any further delay results in a failure.)

After the quiz, the student goes to the scoring desk and waits to meet a tutor. The scorers themselves are not tutors, but staff assistants who are specifically trained to use the answer keys, code errors for computer analysis, and page the tutors when both student and quiz are ready.

When paged by the scorer, the tutor comes out to meet the student and pick up the quiz. Student and tutor then enter the tutorial room. The student is first asked if he or she has any questions about the quiz, thus allowing an opportunity for clarifications. The tutor and student then check for errors. If the student met the mastery criterion (at least 10 of 12 questions correct), a brief tutorial follows based on any questions missed, the two chat informally about the course, and the tutor solicits comments and suggestions. But if there were several errors, an intensive tutorial begins which may last half an hour or longer.

## The Tutorial.
Each tutor uses methods for probing and prompting responses which successively approximate the correct answers. Afterward, the tutor asks further questions based on the same study objective in order to ascertain that he or she did not just teach a specific answer to a specific question. Finally, the student reviews the objectives missed, and leaves for more study before returning for the next attempt at demonstrating mastery.

An elaborate protocol guides the tutorials, discouraging the tutor from lecturing and from ignoring prerequisites that a given student may need to learn before confronting the study objective at hand. Despite the high degree of structure in a tutorial, interactions are as diverse, surprising and clever as any between two fellow students. We know this because all tutors tape-record several tutorials during the term as part of a Teaching Practicum for which they receive academic credit. The instructor analyzes and critiques these both in written reports and in weekly training seminars.

A typical tutorial consists of three components: (1) determining the student's baseline (Is the question read correctly? Is it paraphrased correctly? Do probe questions indicate that the student has the prerequisites needed to answer the question?); (2) shaping the student's behavior by presenting a series of prompts that lead toward answering the question missed; and (3) measuring final performance by asking a series of new questions based on the same study objective as the question missed.

Much of the instructor's time is now spent training tutors and supervising them while they interact with the students. Our Teaching Assistant's Manual for the Personalized System of Instruction (Northeastern University Psychology Department, 1978) describes these functions in more detail. Tactics for training new PSI tutors have been discussed by Lazar, Soares, Goncz, Ott, Terman, & Terman, 1977.

## Interactive Videotapes and Workbook.
Our method relies on a union of videotaped lab and workbook. The content is divided into a frame-by-frame sequence, which keeps the student involved in active study responses throughout each session, with continual confirmation for written responses. The workbook and tapes are called, together, Interact with Psychology (Terman, 1978).

The objectives of the videotape session, and associated programmed materials, differ from standard courses based on lecture and text. We want our students to try their hand at doing some of the things psychologists do in their work: observing behavior, measuring the effects of environmental and physiological manipulations, collecting raw data, reducing it to graphical formats, and drawing conclusions about the functional relations that form the base of the science. We do not want to teach about these functional relations as much as we want the students to discover them for themselves, document them, and apply them to experiences in their own lives. Figure 1 lists a sample of topics in the course. Other topics follow in the second quarter of the sequence, currently taught without the use of videotapes (Sidman & Terman, 1977).

---

Interact With Psychology

Methods to observe and record behavior objectively
Aspects of the environment affecting behavior
Analyses of aggression
Relation of physiological and behavioral functions
Reflex analysis, including recent Russian research on interoceptive functions
Clinical applications of classical conditioning procedures
Shaping operant behavior in humans and animals
Learning and retardation
Schedules of reinforcement
Superstition
Complex behavior: chaining
Stimulus control and the analysis of sensory functions
Control of psychotic verbal behavior
Aversive control of behavior
Anxiety
Physiological methods for psychology experiments
Behavioral control by physiological manipulations

---

Figure 1. Abbreviated Content Outline of "Interact with Psychology."

The interactive videotape method suits PSI courses well, since the study objectives are well-defined and the students know just how they stand at each moment. The mastery quiz/tutorial sequence provides delayed confirmation of study success relative to the programmed feedback; and, indeed, we find that most students are prepared to excel on the formal quizzes without the extensive tutorial assistance and re-testing typical of PSI courses. Thus, we can teach larger groups by PSI, and increase the student-to-tutor ratio without compromising students' success rates.

The workbook is designed to complement the material presented in the videotape sessions. The *Objectives* section lists the study goals, and is accompanied by sample questions to test for understanding of each objective. Some questions ask for the application of a principle to a situation in the laboratory or everyday life, and for prediction of the outcome. Other questions test understanding of technical terms. The *Preparation* section teaches new technical terms and skills that will be used in the videotape session. The student may choose between standard prose and programmed formats, followed by self-tests to determine readiness to attend a videotape session. The *Interaction* section consists mainly of frames formatted for the writing of responses to questions posed on the videotape. The tapes minimize lecturing, and emphasize laboratory experiments and illustrations from the world-at-large. Interactions occur when the student records raw data, constructs data tables and graphs, writes conclusions, and answers questions integral to the teaching sequence. Tapes are shown on a pre-announced schedule throughout the day, with selections geared to the recommended minimum pace, which most students follow. Faster or slower students may request individual videotape sessions if the tape they need is not on the main schedule. After the videotape session, the student continues with a programmed section called *Extensions and*

*Implications,* which expands on the newly introduced concepts and techniques. Often, this section raises broad issues and elicits evaluative judgments meant to spark discussion in tutorials. Finally, most chapters end with a *Source Reading,* a journal selection on the theme of the chapter, accompanied by study questions and a glossary of new technical terms used by each author.

**Opportunity for Personal Contacts.** Critics of PSI have sometimes suggested that the method removes the instructor from routine contact with students because there is no schedule of live appearances, as there is with lectures. Our course in fact increases the frequency and meaningfulness of such contacts. The instructor joins the tutors in Psych Central, supervising, solving problems in difficult tutorials, and tutoring individual students. Students who have not met the mastery criterion after three quiz attempts and three tutorials must sign up to work personally with the instructor or Psych Central supervisor before a fourth attempt is allowed. Every student has frequent personal contact with tutors, at pre- and post-quiz tutorials. Psych Central is staffed throughout the day and evening, so that there is always someone to talk to as problems arise. Further, our Department sponsors a Psychology Roundtable for introductory students. A different faculty member speaks each week on a wide range of professional and scholarly topics, often followed by a lab tour. Students are invited to attend any session of interest, and regular attendees can receive an extra quarter-hour of academic credit by writing a paper on any of the Roundtable topics.

**Applicability to Small-Enrollment Courses.** Our material can also be used for small-group instruction. The Central Instructional Facility, its staff, and computerized record-keeping are then unnecessary. The course has been taught with quizzes and tutorials in classrooms manned during standard hours by an instructor and assistants. For small groups, one videotape playback unit will suffice, but showings must be available at times other than scheduled quiz and tutorial hours (the library can often handle flexible videotape showings). Development costs for our course were considerable, and were justified by the large-enrollment application; however, the materials can be used economically for groups of any size. The system is being tested with a small group outside Northeastern, by Dr. Robert W. Bass at Ohio Dominican College, Columbus.

**Evaluation.** *Student performance.* Our course produces a distribution of final exam scores with the pronounced negative skew typical of PSI courses (Keller, 1968). Most students receive A's and B's, based on demonstrated mastery of the material, and considerable work. The withdrawal rate (students dropping after at least one mastery quiz) averages about 9%; summer quarters (not including freshmen) have gone as low as 2%. We have found that withdrawals correlate with slow self-paced progress as well as with low Scholastic Aptitude Test scores (Brady, Soares & Terman, Note 1), suggesting that prerequisites in mathematics and English, which are often out of the province of our tutorials, may be high priorities for students who do not complete the course. However, it must be noted that many students with low SAT scores have obtained high grades.

The student who studies at the median self-paced rate closely matches the recommended minimum pace. Students who study at faster rates earn, as a group, higher final exam scores (Waranch, Lazar, Soares, & Terman, Note 2). Students who study at slower rates generally require more mastery quiz attempts to proceed through the course. Thus, progress rates, number of mastery quiz attempts, SAT scores and final exam scores are correlated. An advantage of the system is that it is possible to identify students in potential trouble during the first few weeks of the course, based on their entry credentials and early quiz and tutorial performances, thus allowing us to give them extra attention or to refer them to remedial materials.

*Student evaluations.* In anonymous evaluations after completion of the course, 80% of the students say that they would recommend the course to another student; 51% rate their interest in the content as high or very high, as opposed to 36% before the course; the self-pacing procedure is rated as the most attractive feature, and the unit mastery requirement as least attractive; 87% say that they found the tutors helpful most, or all of the time; and 43% say that they would be interested in becoming a tutor in a future quarter.

A sample of comments written to the instructor points out other aspects of student evaluation: "I am a student who has difficulty with multiple choice exams. But I can't help from writing to say how TA's are so valuable in this respect. They have helped me tremendously before exams to reason questions out for myself." "I want to tell you that I got an A. I can honestly say I learned a great deal. Keep on 'fighting' people like me who are basically very lazy students." "I think that because we could do it at our own rate I worked harder at it and didn't slacken off. I also feel it made me more disciplined in my study habits in other subjects."

*Tutors' evaluations.* Among the tutors, 98% would recommend this academic experience to other students. Some representative comments: "It appeals to a vast number of students because of its untraditional ways. With each new quarter it continues to grow toward a more 'perfect' course. Revisions are constantly made to fit the needs of the students." "It teaches a student responsibility, something which I think is not stressed enough in other courses. And the personal one-to-one relationship makes this course more human." "As a result of my experience of being taught in such a course, and then being a TA, I've come to fully understand and appreciate the psychological principles employed in it. I strongly support implementing PSI courses in other fields of study." "My experience as a TA has been my most rewarding and personally satisfying course in five years. I helped some students progress through their education with more understanding and ease than if they had not received my help. These personal relationships are not only helpful to the student, but gratifying to the teacher." "I feel I know the material inside out." "I found I did a great deal of thinking and learning about myself and my attitudes toward teachers. I have a good deal more respect for them now. I found that I put in much more time than I ever anticipated and thoroughly enjoyed stepping out of my narrow world of biology. It was an enlightening learning experience."

## References

Keller, F. S. "Good-bye teacher . . ." *Journal of Applied Behavior Analysis*, 1968, *1*, 78-89.

Keller, F. S., & Sherman, J. G. *The Keller Plan handbook.* Springfield, Mass.: Benjamin, 1974.

Kulik, J. A. PSI: A formative evaluation. In B. A. Green, Jr. (Ed.). *Personalized instruction in higher education.* Washington, DC: Center for Personalized Instruction, Georgetown Univ., 1976.

Lazar, R., & Soares, C. *Teaching assistant manual* (4th ed.). Boston: Northeastern Univ. Psychology Dept., 1975.

Lazar, R., Soares, C., Goncz., R. P., Ott, S., Terman, J. S., & Terman, M. Tutorial training for PSI proctors in the large-enrollment course. *Journal of Personalized Instruction,* 1977, in press.

Northeastern University Psychology Department. *Teaching assistant's manual for the personalized system of instruction* (6th ed.). Boston: Northeastern University Press, 1978, in press.

Sidman, M., & Terman, M. (Eds.) *Interact with psychology* (Vol. 2, 4th ed.) Dubuque, IO: Kendall/Hunt, 1977.

Terman, M. *Interact with psychology* (Vol. 1, 6th ed.). Dubuque, IO: Kendall/Hunt, 1978.

## Notes

1. Brady J., Soares, C., & Terman, M. *Predicting freshman performance in a PSI course.* Unpublished manuscript, 1977.
2. Waranch, H.R., Lazar, R., Soares, C., & Terman, M. *"Fading in" the PSI mastery quiz: a method to reduce procrastination and repeated failures.* Paper presented at National Conference on Personalized Instruction in Higher Education, Washington, D.C., 1974.
3. This paper is based on a presentation at the symposium on Alternatives for the Introductory Course, meeting of the American Psychological Association, Washington, DC, 1976.
4. Course development is supported in part by a grant from the Exxon Education Foundation.
5. Special thanks to my colleagues who have shared in planning this project: Robert W. Bass, John Brady, Mina B. Ghattas, Rita P. Goncz, Harlan Lane, Ronald Lazar, Murray Sidman, Carlos Soares, Jiuan S. Terman, and H. Richard Waranch; and to J. Lee Riccardi, for comments on the manuscript. This paper is dedicated to the memory of F. Andre Favat.

# Systematic Manipulation of Student Pacing, the Perfection Requirement, and Contact with a Teaching Assistant in an Introductory Psychology Course

Peter S. Fernald, Michael J. Chiseri, David W. Lawson,
Gayle F. Scroggs, and Jeanne C. Riddell
*University of New Hampshire*

Which of these three major features of PSI is most responsible for its effectiveness? The answer depends in part upon the criterion of effectiveness employed.

The effectiveness of the Personalized System of Instruction (PSI) is quite well established. Compared to traditional lecture approaches, it produces significantly higher exam performance and more positive attitudes toward the course (Alba & Pennypacker, 1972; Born & Davis, 1974; Born, Gledhill, & Davis, 1972; Cooper & Grenier, 1971; Johnston & Pennypacker 1971; Keller, 1968; Malott & Svinicki, 1969; McMichael & Corey, 1969; Sheppard & MacDermot, 1970; Witters & Kent, 1972). However, since the studies cited treat PSI as a single global factor, they provide little indication as to which PSI factors contribute most to its success. In the present study three instructional variables—student pacing, the perfection requirement, and contact with an undergraduate teaching assistant—were systematically manipulated in an introductory psychology course. These variables were chosen for study because they were considered to be among the most unusual of the PSI factors.

## Method

The subjects were introductory psychology students, mostly freshmen, at the University of New Hampshire. Twenty-five either formally withdrew from or failed to complete the course, leaving 255 students.

**Instructional Procedures.** At the first class meeting the students were informed, both orally and in the course syllabus, about each of the instructional factors to be studied. The description, as it appeared in the syllabus, was as follows:

Each student is assigned to an undergraduate teaching assistant (TA) who will administer as many as three different quizzes for each of the twelve units (chapters) in the text.

Quiz sessions will be held at either 12 or 1 PM every Monday, Wednesday, and Friday. Administration of the ten-item multiple-choice quizzes will vary along three instructional dimensions: teacher versus student pacing, perfection versus no perfection requirement, and much versus little TA contact. *Teacher-paced* students will take the quiz(zes) for the assigned unit (chapter) on specified weeks according to the course calendar, thus spreading the quizzes out evenly over the semester. *Student-paced* individuals, on the other hand, will take the quizzes as rapidly or as slowly as their mood dictates. Hence, they may finish all the quizzes after just two weeks, or they may postpone taking the quizzes until later in the semester.[3]

Students assigned to groups having a *perfection* requirement must obtain at least 9 out of 10 correct on one of the first two quizzes *or* take all three quizzes for the assigned chapter before proceeding to the next chapter. Failure to meet these expectations will result in a score of zero for that particular unit. Students having *no perfection* requirement may proceed to a subsequent chapter whenever satisfied with their performance on the preceding chapter.

The third instructional variable, much versus little TA contact, concerns the amount of social interaction the student has with his TA. In addition to administering and scoring quizzes, the TA employing *much contact,* gets to know the student on a first-name basis, explains difficult concepts to him, and may even rap on topics unrelated to the course. With *little contact,* the TA administers and scores the quizzes and provides page numbers for items answered incorrectly.

Note that this course is actually "two courses," each running for half of the semester and covering six units. Each student will be assigned one set of instructional procedures for the first course and the opposite set of instructional procedures for the second course. For example, if in the first course you have much TA contact, no perfection requirement, and student pacing, then in the second course you will have little TA contact, a perfection requirement, and teacher pacing.

The students were told that the quizzes and exams would not cover lectures, which were entirely optional, that the second exam would cover only the material presented in the second course, and that the final grades would be weighted as follows—quizzes (30%), first exam (30%), second exam (30%), and laboratory experience (10%). The latter relates to a few brief reports which students completed after participating in studies conducted by faculty and graduate students.

Each unit consisted of a chapter from the third edition of *Basic Psychology* (Munn, Fernald, & Fernald, 1972). The *Student Guidebook* (Fernald & Fernald, 1972), which includes both a programmed overview and fifteen self-quiz items with answers for each chapter in the text, also was assigned.

**Teaching Assistants.** The procedures used in selecting and training the undergraduate TAs are described in detail elsewhere (Fernald, 1973), so only a brief account is included here.[4] The TAs were selected according to three criteria—*thorough knowledge of introductory psychology* as indicated by grades in the introductory course, *strong desire to be a TA* as assessed by both the willingness to fill out a long and detailed TA application form and the contents of the completed form, and *personal-social teaching skills* as manifested in an interview. The TAs had earned four semester hours of credit participating as TAs in a similar course the previous semester, but in the present project they received $2.30 per hour for a total of ten hours each week.

In the first course each of the 12 TAs was assigned two groups of 8 to 12 students and told to employ a particular set of instructional procedures with one group and the opposite procedures with the other. For the second course each TA employed different sets of procedures with two other groups of students.

**Dependent Variables.** Three types of dependent variables were observed: (1) quiz and exam performances, (2) preference ratings for the different instructional approaches, and (3) evaluations of the course. The quizzes and exams contained standard multiple-choice items. When more than one quiz was taken for a particular unit, only the highest score was counted. Ratings of the different instructional conditions and the course were obtained from a questionnaire administered at the end of each course. The questionnaire contained several seven-point rating scales, three of which ranged from 1 ("strong preference" for one type of instruction) to 7 ("strong preference" for the other type of instruction). These scales assigned 1 to the conventional method (teacher pacing, little TA contact, or no perfection) and 7 to the PSI method (student pacing, much TA contact, or perfection requirement). Another scale, which assessed how students compared the course to other courses at the University, ranged from 1 ("among the very worst") through 4 ("about average") to 7 ("among the very best").

**Statistical Analysis.** The experimental design was a 2 x 2 x 2 for each course, and the three factors were student pacing versus teaching pacing, perfection requirement versus no perfection requirement, and much contact versus little contact with a TA. The chief statistical procedure was multivariate/univariate analysis of variance (Tatsouka, 1971; Cooley & Lohnes, 1971), although several correlation coefficients also were calculated.

Difference scores, indicating changes in instructional preferences as the students moved to and from the various PSI conditions, were computed and evaluated statistically through a univariate analysis of variance.

Rank-correlation coefficients were calculated to determine the relationship between actual and expected performances on quizzes and exams and between actual and expected course evaluation ratings for the eight different instructional combinations. Assuming each PSI component had a positive and additive effect, the expected rank order for the eight different combinations of instructional conditions was established by noting the number of PSI components present in each. The set of instructional conditions having no PSI components received a rank of 8, the sets having one and two components received the respective ranks of 3 and 6, and the set having all three PSI components received a rank of 1 (See Table 1, right column).

## Results

The data and results of the statistical analyses have been organized around the three dependent variables.

**Performance on Quizzes and Exams.** Mean quiz and exam scores for both courses are shown in Table 1. Multivariate analyses of variance, with each course considered separately, revealed significant ($F = 3.40$ and $3.05$, $df = 2/246$, $p < .05$) effects on combined quiz/exam performance due to the pacing factor and no significant effects due to the perfection or TA contact factors. Univariate analysis, with quizzes and exams considered independently, indicated the quizzes were primarily responsible for discrimination on the pacing factor, where the student-paced groups scored significantly ($F = 6.81$, $df = 1/247$, $p < .01$) higher than the teacher-paced groups. No other significant univariate main effects or interactions were obtained.

Rank-correlation coefficients, indicating the relationship between expected and observed quiz performances, were .60 ($p < .10$) and .80 ($p < .05$) respectively for the first and second courses. Correlations similarly obtained for exam performances were non-significant.

**Preferences for the Different Types of Instruction.** Most students held moderate to strong preferences for much TA contact and student pacing and mixed preferences with regard to the perfection requirement (Table 2). For the two courses combined the mean preference (5.53) for TA contact and the mean preference (5.17) for pacing deviated significantly ($t = 14.70$ and $9.59$, $df = 254$, $p < .0001$) from the assumed null (no preference) value of 4.

## Table 1
### Mean Quiz and Exam Scores and Expected Rank Order for the Various Combinations of Instructional Conditions

| Instructional Combinations | First Course | | | Second Course | | | Expected |
|---|---|---|---|---|---|---|---|
| | Quizzes | Exam | N | Quizzes | Exam | N | Rank Order |
| Much contact, perfection, student pacing | 52.28 | 44.48 | 33 | 53.06 | 48.00 | 32 | 1 |
| Much contact, perfection, teacher pacing | 50.41 | 45.03 | 29 | 53.61 | 50.26 | 35 | 3 |
| Much contact, no perfection, student pacing | 53.82 | 46.03 | 34 | 54.26 | 49.35 | 34 | 3 |
| Much contact, no perfection, teacher pacing | 52.91 | 44.00 | 33 | 51.92 | 49.92 | 25 | 6 |
| Little contact, perfection, student pacing | 52.76 | 45.88 | 25 | 55.52 | 49.52 | 33 | 3 |
| Little contact, perfection, teacher pacing | 50.47 | 45.06 | 34 | 52.29 | 50.26 | 34 | 6 |
| Little contact, no perfection, student pacing | 52.46 | 45.31 | 35 | 51.76 | 47.03 | 29 | 6 |
| Little contact, no perfection, teacher pacing | 49.38 | 43.28 | 32 | 50.52 | 47.27 | 33 | 8 |

## Table 2
## Percentages of Students Indicating Different Ratings
## for the Three Instructional Approaches

| Instructional Component | Ratings | | | | | | |
|---|---|---|---|---|---|---|---|
| | 1 | 2 | 3 | 4 | 5 | 6 | 7 |
| Pacing | 6.0 | 9.0 | 8.6 | 7.6 | 9.4 | 23.0 | 36.4 |
| TA Contact | 2.3 | 5.6 | 3.1 | 11.3 | 14.7 | 22.4 | 40.6 |
| Perfection Requirement | 10.8 | 16.8 | 10.0 | 21.0 | 10.5 | 15.6 | 15.3 |

*Note:* Ratings of 1 indicate strong preferences for conventional methods (teacher pacing, little TA contact, or no perfection requirement), while ratings of 7 indicate strong preferences for PSI methods (student pacing, much TA contact, or the perfection requirement). The percentages are for the two courses combined.

In the first course students who received any of the three PSI methods indicated significantly ($F = 16.45$, 12.61 and 11.94, $df = 1/247$, $p < .01$) stronger preference for this approach than did students who received the conventional method. For the second course these preference differences were not observed. Students who moved *to* a PSI condition modified their preference significantly ($F = 8.65$, $df = 1/763$, $p < .01$) more in the direction of the new instructional condition than did students who moved *from* a PSI condition.

In the second course TA contact interacted significantly with the pacing ($F = 5.81$, $df = 1/247$, $p < .05$) and also with the perfection requirement ($F = 5.19$, $df = 1/247$, $p < .05$). With regard to pacing, students having much TA contact gave similar preference ratings on the pacing scale irrespective of whether they were teacher or student paced, while students having little TA contact gave different ratings depending upon which pacing condition they received. A similar pattern emerged with regard to perfection. Students having much TA contact offered similar ratings on the perfection scale regardless of whether they had a perfection or no perfection requirement, but students having little TA contact gave different ratings depending upon type of perfection requirements received. In both cases, students having little TA contact indicated greater preferences for the pacing and perfection condition opposite to the one received.

**Evaluation of the Course.**  With regard to overall evaluation of the first course, no main effects or interactions were noted for the different instructional variables. For the second course, on the other hand, mean course rating (4.94) of students having much TA contact was significantly ($F = 9.07$, $df = 1/247$, $p < .01$) higher than the mean course rating (4.40) of students having little TA contact, and students who were student-paced gave significantly ($F = 5.19$, $df = 1/247$, $p < .05$) higher course ratings (4.87) than students who were teacher paced (4.47).

Rank correlation coefficients between actual and expected course ratings for the eight instructional combinations were .11 and .70 ($p < .05$) respectively for the first and second courses.

## Discussion

Generally speaking, the findings suggest that student pacing enhanced students' achievement in both courses, that much TA contact and student pacing increased students' evaluations of the second course, and that the perfection requirement produced no effects.

**Performance on Quizzes and Exams.**  With regard to quiz and exam performance, pacing was the important PSI factor, and its effects were more closely tied to quizzes than to exams. Just how student pacing increased performance is not clear, though one explanation is that student-paced individuals were better prepared, as they were not required to take the quizzes until they felt ready to do so. While student pacing improved quiz performance, practically speaking the gain (less than two points out of a total of 60) was not especially impressive.

That the perfection requirement had no effect upon exam performance and especially upon quiz performance was unexpected. A possible reason for this outcome is that the weekly quizzes were not especially difficult for the students whose sole course responsibility, except for the laboratory experience mentioned above, was to master one chapter of the text each week. The mean quiz score (for the six quizzes combined) of 52, which students knew was equivalent to a grade of B/B+, substantiates this view. Had the quiz task been more demanding, the perfection requirement might have influenced quiz and exam performance. Indeed, a previous study suggests this may be the case (Johnston & O'Neill, 1973). The study demonstrated that mastery level, when varied from essentially no mastery criterion to rather stringent criteria of 3.8 correct/0.4 incorrect per minute, influenced performance on recall items. The ratio of 3.8 correct/0.4 incorrect is comparable to the 9 correct/1 incorrect ratio employed in the present study, but the use of recall items and especially the per minute rates requirement probably provided a more difficult task than the untimed multiple-choice (recognition item) quizzes used in the present study. These comparisons may not be valid, since the two courses differ in content and possibly in other ways, yet they suggest that a mastery requirement may influence performance only when the task is difficult enough to yield sufficient variation in performance.

The manipulation of TA contact also did not influence quiz and exam performance. In another study of PSI it was noted that students receiving TA assistance achieved higher exam scores than non-assisted students (Farmer, Lachter, Blaustein, & Cole, 1972). However, teaching assistance was defined in terms of the percentage (0%, 25%, 50%, 75%, and 100%) of units on which each student was tutored. This definition clearly is more task related than the predominantly social definition of TA contact employed in the present study. Most likely the different findings relate to the different definitions of TA contact.

Somewhat surprisingly, instructional factors did not interact, but apparently did combine additively to improve performance. The additive effects are suggested by the close correspondence between performance and number of PSI components employed.

The majority of studies comparing PSI and the conventional lecture approach have shown the former produces superior exam performance, yet the present findings indicate each PSI component by itself has either no effect or only a very slight effect upon quiz and exam performance. Perhaps each PSI component contributes only a small amount to achievement, but the total effect of all PSI factors operating together is substantial. Or, more likely, it may be that the reported success of PSI is due largely to PSI factors not considered here—namely, small units of study, clearly specified objectives, multiple opportunities to demonstrate proficiency, and immediate knowledge of results.

**Preferences for the Different Types of Instruction.** A vast majority of the students preferred student pacing over teacher pacing and much over little contact with a TA. The endorsements of much TA contact is not surprising, as most students and faculty often state the many advantages of small-sized classes and/or tutoring-type relationships where the instructor and students have close contact. What is surprising, at least in terms of traditional college and university practices, is the extremely strong endorsement of student pacing.

Approximately 41 percent of the students preferred the perfection requirement. This figure stands in marked contrast to the virtual absence of perfection (or mastery) requirements in most college and university courses. However, almost an equal percentage (approximately 38%) preferred no perfection requirement. This finding suggests that the positive attitudes toward PSI noted by various investigators are due, at least in part, to student pacing and much TA contact but *not* to the perfection requirement.

In the first course preferences for a PSI method were stronger for students receiving the method than they were for those not receiving the method. One explanation of this finding is that students' preferences for a PSI method are enhanced through experience with it, while another explanation is that students endorse an instructional method just because they received it. Assuming the latter possibility, one would expect all students to show a substantial shift in preferences toward the instructional methods received in the second course. However, the shift is more pronounced for students moving *to* a PSI method than for those moving *from* a PSI condition. This observation supports the view that experience with PSI methods enhances students' preferences for these methods.

The interaction of TA contact with the pacing and with the perfection requirement factors in the second course suggest the importance of TA contact, or more specifically, of *little* TA contact. The effect of the latter was to decrease students' endorsements of the pacing and perfection requirement conditions they received.

**Evaluations of the Course.** Considering the students' very favorable ratings of student pacing and much TA contact, it is not surprising that receiving these instructional procedures resulted in higher evaluations of the second course. Manipulation of the perfection requirement, on the other hand, did not influence course ratings. These findings suggest that much TA contact and student pacing may contribute to the positive attitudes toward PSI noted elsewhere.

The high correlation between number of PSI components and students' evaluations of the second course suggests that the greater the number of PSI components incorporated in the course the better the students liked it. This relationship was not noted for the first course.

**The Cross-Over Design.** All of the significant findings concerning instructional preferences and course evaluations occurred in the second course only. Why? The most plausible explanation seems to be that the students made *comparative* ratings after experiencing the opposite instructional procedures during the first course. This explanation is consistent with scaling research which demonstrates that finer discrimination is possible when a comparison stimulus is presented.

A second explanation concerns the observation that students typically evaluate an instructional method in conjunction with many other course variables, for example, the instructor, textbook, class size, and subject matter, just to mention a few. In view of these circumstances, an evaluation of the instructional method independent of other variables is difficult, if not impossible. With the present cross-over design, however, instructional methods were perhaps more readily identified and evaluated independently of other course variables, because it was chiefly these methods that differentiated the second course from the first. To use a Gestalt analogy, in the second course the new instructional methods stood out as figure in relation to the other course variables which were ground, since they remain unchanged.

Assuming they are valid, these interpretations indicate the value of cross-over designs in which students receive two different instructional methods within the same course. Compared to designs where a student receives only one instructional method, the cross-over design seems to provide more sensitive measures of students' evaluations of an instructional method. See Semb (1973) for a discussion of merits and cautions in the use of this design in instructional research.

**Recommendations for Future Research.** It is reasonable to inquire why groups receiving different instructional approaches, such as those in the present study, show no or only slight differences in exam performance. One obvious possibility is that the different instructional manipulations produced similar effects. Another possibility is that the quiz and exam items were taken exclusively from a textbook, and textbooks may be so powerful as to override differences in instruction (Hilgard, as cited by Dubin & Taveggia, 1968). Both the data collected here and that reported elsewhere (Dubin & Taveggia, 1968; McKeachie, 1969) make this explanation quite plausible. Accordingly, a first recommendation is that investigators pay closer attention to the effects of various instructional methods on textbook study behavior. One recent study has done this (Born & Davis, 1974).

A second recommendation concerns the use of undergraduate TAs for both instructional and research purposes. Several investigators have noted the important contribution undergraduate TAs make to personalized instruction (Farmer, Lachter, Blaustein, & Cole, 1972; Johnston & Pennypacker, 1971; Sheppard & MacDermot, 1970), and similar observations were made in this study. The present authors were impressed by the TAs' ability to implement the different instructional methods. It seems unlikely the authors could have found colleagues or faculty whose teaching schedules and work loads would have allowed them to carry out the prescribed instructional conditions. The use of undergraduate TA's to manipulate instructional conditions may be an important and often overlooked resource for research into instruction.

A third recommendation is for greater use of cross-over designs which allow subjects to compare different instructional methods for the same course. As the present findings indicate, this procedure seems to provide sensitive evaluations of instructional methods. The general lack of cross-over designs in the literature on college instruction may reflect researchers' reluctance to manipulate students, since such manipulations are often construed, and quite legitimately so, as an honest admission that the instructor is not sure which instructional procedures are most effective. However, reviews of the literature concerning different methods of instruction in higher education suggest that one may reasonably take this position (McKeachie, 1969; Dubin & Taveggia, 1969), and moreover, there is precedence for manipulating subjects in even more sensitive areas than college and university instruction, namely in psychotherapy (Moos & MacIntosh, 1970).

An investigator runs the risk of having some students and even faculty contend that manipulating instructional methods over the course of a semester is either "unfair" or lacking in effectiveness. This position seems unreasonable for at least two reasons. First, most of the students seemed to support the use of instructional manipulations for research purposes. Only a small minority objected, and once allowed to voice their objections and listen to the researchers' reactions to their objections, these individuals readily accepted the instructional manipulations. Second, investigators can take steps which minimize instructional inequities, and the present investigation in which student-paced individuals outperformed teacher-paced individuals is a case in point. By using a cross-over procedure with two level factors, it was possible to have all students experience equal amounts of the two pacing procedures and of the other instructional conditions as well. As it happened, there were no significant interactions with regard to quizzes or exam performance, but if there had been, students who received certain combinations of instructions would have had an advantage over those who did not receive these combinations. This did not occur, but if it had, a correction factor could have been included in determining final grades (see Chute, 1974).

As was shown in this study, a student's general reaction to a method of instruction usually represents some sort of additive or interactive combination of different reactions to each component of the method. To determine the effects of the components it was necessary to systematically manipulate each by itself and in various combinations with the other components. A fourth and final recommendation, therefore, is for researchers to manipulate the several components of a general instructional procedure rather than, as is the usual practice, to compare one general instructional approach with another.

## References

Alba, E., & Pennypacker, H. S. A multiple change score comparison of traditional and behavioral college teaching procedures. *Journal of Applied Behavior Analysis*, 1972, 5, 121-124.

Born, D. G. & Davis, M. L. Amount and distribution of study in a personalized instruction course and in a lecture course. *Journal of Applied Behavior Analysis*, 1974, 7, 365-375.

Born, D. G., Gledhill, S. M., & Davis, M. L. Examination performance in lecture-discussion and personalized instruction courses. *Journal of Applied Behavior Analysis*, 1972, 5, 33-34.

Chute, D. L. Innovations in teaching: An ethical paradox. *Teaching of Psychology*, 1974, 1, 85.

Cooley, W. W., & Lohnes, P. R. *Multivariate data analysis*. New York: Wiley, 1971.

Cooper, J. L., & Grenier, J. M. Contingency management in an introductory psychology course produced better retention. *Psychological Record*, 1971, 21, 391-400.

Dubin, R., & Taveggia, T. A. *The teaching-learning paradox*. Eugene, Oregon: University of Oregon Press, 1968.

Farmer, J., Lachter, G. D., Blaustein, J. J., & Cole, B. K. The role of proctoring in personalized instruction. *Journal of Applied Behavior Analysis*, 1972, 5, 401-404.

Fernald, P. S. The selection and training of undergraduate teaching assistants for large personalized instruction course. Division Two (Teaching of Psychology), *Newsletter*, March, 1973, 3-5.

Fernald, P. S., & Fernald, L. D. *Student Guidebook to accompany Basic Psychology* (2nd edition) by Munn, N. L., Fernald, L. D., & Fernald, P. S. Boston: Houghton Mifflin, 1972.

Johnston, J. M. & O'Neill, G. The analysis of performance criteria defining course grades as a determinant of college student academic performance. *Journal of Applied Behavior Analysis*, 1973, 6, 261-268.

Johnston, J. M., & Pennypacker, H. S. A behavior approach to college teaching. *American Psychologist*, 1971, 26, 219-244.

Keller, F. S. "Good-bye, teacher. . ." *Journal of Applied Behavior Analysis*, 1968, 1, 79-80.

Malott, R. W., & Svinicki, J. G. Contingency management in an introductory psychology course for one thousand students. *Psychological Record*, 1969, 19, 545-556.

McKeachie, W. J. *Teaching tips: A guidebook for the beginning college teacher*. Lexington, Mass.: Heath, 1969.

McMichael, J. S., & Corey, J. R. Contingency management in an introductory psychology course produces better learning. *Journal of Applied Behavior Analysis*, 1969, 2, 79-83.

Moos, R. H., & MacIntosh, S. Multivariate study of the patient-therapist system: a replication and extension. *Journal of Consulting and Clinical Psychology*, 1970, 35, 298-307.

Munn, N. L., Fernald, L. D., & Fernald, P. S. *Basic Psychology* (2nd edition). Boston: Houghton Mifflin, 1972.

Semb, G. Research strategies in higher education. Division Two (Teaching of Psychology) *Newsletter*, December 1973, 9-13.

Sheppard, W. C., & MacDermot, H. G. Design and evaluation of a programmed course in introductory psychology. *Journal of Applied Behavior Analysis*, 1970, 3, 5-11.

Tatsuoka, M. M. *Multivariate analysis: Teaching for educational and psychological research*. New York: Wiley, 1971.

Witters, D. R., & Kent, G. W. Teaching without lecturing: Evidence in the case for individualized instruction. *Psychological Record*, 1972, 22, 169-175.

## Notes

1. This investigation was supported in part by the Central University Fund for Teaching, University of New Hampshire, Durham, New Hampshire.
2. Michael J. Chiseri is now at George Mason University.
3. Although permitted to take quizzes at their own rate, student-paced individuals were required to take quizzes according to the assigned chapter sequence and no more than two quizzes for a single chapter on the same day.
4. The authors wish to acknowledge the conscientious efforts and fine performances of the twelve undergraduate teaching assistants who participated in the investigation. They were Diane E. Bucholz, Martha A. Celluci, Janice R. Chadwick, Joseph G. Colby, Ann Colcord, Martha R. Deming, Paul S. Denner, Joanne Merrill, Alan L. Nemetz, Lulu Pompema, Mary P. Rowland and Richard V. Sales.

# Instructor-Paced, Mass-Testing for Mastery Performance in an Introductory Psychology Course

B. C. Goldwater and L. E. Acker
*University of Victoria*

The PSI method of weekly testing with a mastery criterion appears to be sufficient to produce improved learning economically.

In response to the need for more effective teaching techniques, a number of university instructors have experimented with programs of instruction based upon principles of contingency management (Keller, 1968). These programs have typically involved several characteristics: (a) course material is covered in relatively small units; (b) the student must attain a high level of performance ("mastery") in order to gain credit for a given unit and/or advance to further units; (c) the amount which the student covers, and often the rate at which he covers it, is individualized through self-pacing; (d) testing is carried out individually or in small groups through the use of student proctors, and (e) the student is provided with immediate feedback on his test performance. Reports on the application of these methods have claimed an encouraging degree of success (e.g., Alba & Pennypacker, 1972; Born, Gledhill, & Davis, 1972; Ferster, 1968; McMichael & Corey, 1969; Moore, Hauck, & Gagné, 1973; Moore, Mahan, & Ritts, 1969; Sheppard & MacDermott, 1970).

Keller (1968), in his original discussion of these programs, stressed the importance of the ". . .go-at-your-own-pace feature, *which permits the student to move through the course at a speed commensurate with his ability . . .*(p. 83)." The current tendency to refer to the Keller type of program as "individualized" or "personalized" instruction further reflects the importance placed upon self-pacing and the individual testing which necessarily accompanies it. It should be recognized, however, that differences in student ability may not necessitate these features of individual pacing and testing. It is possible that the small units of material usually employed in personalized instruction can also be "mastered" by most students within time limits applied uniformly by the instructor to all students; this would then allow more easily managed mass-testing. In this regard, it is important to note than the self-pacing and individual-testing features of personalized instruction account for the major portion of expense in money, manpower and administration. Thus, in order to permit self-pacing and individual-testing, a team of assistants or proctors is employed, the size of which must increase with the number of students in the course. McMichael and Corey (1969), for example, employed 19 undergraduate assistants for a class of 221 students. Assistants in this case were given academic credit for their work; where this manner of payment is precluded by university regulations, the financial cost of putting such a team of assistants on salary might well be beyond the reach of many hard-pressed budgets. An alternative source of proctors, such as utilizing students *within* the course itself

(Gaynor & Wolking, 1974) might also be precluded either by university regulations which prohibit class self-evaluation and/or by instructor concern over the validity of student judgments.

The aim of the present authors was to design a system which would serve to improve student performance while at the same time obviating the need for proctor-assistance. In order to accomplish this, the self-pacing and individual-testing features of contingency management were excluded. Such an approach is not without precedent; *degree* of self-pacing has been reduced by some investigators, for example, by making completion of course material a requirement for writing of mid-term and final exams (Born, et al., 1972) or by an instructor-imposed minimum rate of progress (Semb, 1974). The present program, however, removed *entirely* the features of individual pacing and testing, while preserving the principles of examining on small units of course material, and setting a "mastery" level of performance which students had to meet in order to gain credit for a given unit. There is evidence that, *within programs of self-pacing and individual-testing,* students' grades are superior when high levels of performance are demanded (Johnston & O'Neill, 1973; Semb, 1974) and when relatively short assignment lengths are employed (Semb, 1974). Thus, we sought to examine the merits of a system of high performance demand ("mastery") and short assignment length, within the context of instructor-pacing and mass-testing.

## Method

Students registering in the Introductory Psychology course at the University of Victoria were offered a choice between two "traditional" lecture sections and the authors' "experimental" class; the general procedures to be followed in each of the three sections were described in a handout made available at the registration desk. Two hundred and thirty-four students (approximately one-third of the total enrollment for the 3 sections of Introductory Psychology) signed up for the experimental section. Half of these were assigned by the instructors to a Mastery Performance (MP) group, while the remaining students were placed in a "Control" group. Assignment was carried out by simply selecting every second name of tne alphabetized class registration list for the MP condition. This assignment was maintained throughout the first term of the year-long course. The conditions of the two groups were reversed in the second term so as to provide each student with exposure to both programs. This eventual exposure of all students to the MP program obviated against ethical concerns arising from unequal student treatment. At the same time, reversal of conditions at the end of the first term introduced a possibility of confounding the second term comparison between MP and Controls by transfer effects. Therefore, the critical comparison between MP and Control conditions should rest upon an analysis of the uncontaminated first term data.

Kendler's *Basic Psychology*, 1968 edition, was employed as the class text. It was divided into 22 units of 20 to 30 pages each; 11 units were covered each term. Students in both MP and Control groups attended a common lecture during the first class hour of the week. The second and third hours of the week for the MP students were each employed to administer a different 10-item quiz (eight multiple choice items and two fill-ins) based on the text unit assigned that week. Quiz items were selected for each quiz so as to sample equally and broadly from the week's unit. Correct answers were announced in class immediately following each quiz so that the student could check his own carbon copy of his answers and determine whether or not he had passed. Details of the testing technique and materials, designed to minimize cheating, are specified elsewhere (Acker & Goldwater, 1973), but essentially involved utilizing a test booklet comprising reduced size printing for presentation of questions, an inkless stylus for invisible recording of answers by the student, and embedded carbon sheets for readable impressions of such answers both for later grading and as a record for the student. MP students were required to pass one of the two weekly quizzes with a score of 8 out of 10 or better (grade of "A") in order to receive credit for the material. A student could take the second quiz without penalty, but could not do so to raise an already passing grade. Tutoring was available for all students from a graduate teaching assistant, or if so requested, from one of the instructors (only two such requests were actually made). Control students were not permitted to write the weekly quiz though approximately every second week they were strongly advised, as a group, to keep up in their readings so as to keep pace with the lectures. Also, the Controls spent a second hour of the week in a small (15 to 25 students) graduate assistant-led discussion section oriented around the Kendler text and Whaley and Surratt's Attitudes of Science (1967). Because the principles of scientific method stressed in Whaley and Surratt were consistent with those emphasized in the Kendler text, and students were encouraged to consider these principles in their reading of the text, it was felt that these discussion meetings were similar, in effect and intent, to laboratories and small seminars or discussion groups frequently employed in conventional lecture courses and would, if anything, give an advantage to the Control group. To assure that Controls' participation in the discussion sections would not detract from their study of the primary course text, no home assignments on Whaley and Surratt were given and the Attitudes of Science workbooks were available only for work in class. A second lecture was offered in the third class hour of the week, which was open to students in the Control group and to any in the MP group who had passed the first weekly quiz. Attendance at both lectures was optional.

At the end of the first term a single final examination, consisting of 100 multiple-choice items, was administered to the entire class under formal examination conditions. Multiple-choice items for all quizzes and final examinations were taken from question pools provided by the publishers, with all items being used only once. A detailed course evaluation questionnaire was attached to the final examination. It was of the Likert type, and consisted of seven points with appropriate descriptors at the anchor points. Selected items from the questionnaire are shown below:

1. Given the opportunity, would you take another course employing the weekly testing-to-80% criterion procedure?
2. In general, did you enjoy this first (second) term as compared to your other large lecture courses?
3. Are you more or less likely to take another psychology course *as a result of your experience in this course since September (Christmas)?*
4. In a typical week, how many hours of study time, outside of class, did you spend on this course in the first (second) term?

Point 1 on each scale was the most favorable. For item 4, the points were labeled in half- or one-hour intervals, ranging from "4 hours or more" at point 1 to "0-½ hour" at point 7.

**Grading.** For the MP group the student's term grade was determined by the final examination (40%) and the weekly quizzes (60%). For the Control group it was determined by the final examination (40%), the mid-term examination, 50 multiple choice items, (30%), and the discussion section tests (30%).

The weekly quiz grades for the MP students were based upon the total number of units passed during the term, with one of the 11 units being dropped without penalty. For those students who had passed nine or more units, the grade was based upon not only the number of units passed but also upon the average score (among scores of 8, 9, or 10) with which they were passed.

Thus the MP group worked under a unit mastery criterion, with two opportunities to pass each unit, in a weekly mass-testing situation with immediate feedback of results. By eliminating individual pacing and testing, it proved possible to restrict the extra expense of the program to the salary of a part-time grader and record-keeper (6 to 10 hours a week of an undergraduate with no special skills or training) and to the nominal costs of preparing the weekly quiz materials. The same procedure was followed in the second term of the course, except that students in the two groups now exchanged programs.

It should be noted that the concept of mastery herein employed differs in one basic respect from prevailing usage of the term. Contingency management programs have typically demanded that the student display mastery of a given unit before proceeding to subsequent units. Such a requirement must result in individualized-pacing. For this reason, and because it was felt that the different chapters in the text were relatively self-contained, mastery-for-advancement was not employed. Thus a student who failed to meet the mastery criterion within the two test sessions allotted received no credit for that material and simply proceeded to the next unit. It is of course possible that such a procedure would be unworkable on texts in which material was very "hierarchically" ordered. However, it should be pointed out that the assumption that a mastery-for-advancement system is necessarily superior under any or all circumstances must ultimately rest on empirical evidence, such as a systematic comparison between coverage of a text in an ordered vs. randomized sequence of chapters. (One might speculate that leaving it up to the student to identify and review that material which is necessary for comprehension of a currently-assigned unit might in fact produce learning which is comparable to a system where the sequencing of assignments renders such behavior unnecessary.)

Standard University of Victoria cut-offs were employed for final exams and were as follows: A = 80% and above, B = 65-79%, C = 55-64%, D = 50-55%, F = less than 50%; all percentages refer to percent of items correct.

## Results

A total of 198 students wrote the final examination for the first term (101 MP's and 97 Controls) and 190 wrote the second term final (94 MP's and 96 Controls). The final examination data from the first term revealed a substantial advantage for the MP students over the Controls (Medians = 66.5 & 55.5 percent respectively, $p < .005$).[1]

The success of the MP program is even more apparent when it is considered that more than half of the MP group

(55%) received grades of A or B on the first term final examination, compared to only 30% of the Controls. On the other end of the scale, 19% of the MP's failed the final examination, compared to 32% of the Controls. First term final exam performance of the Controls was not dissimilar to results obtained in another, traditional section taught by a different instructor utilizing a similar introductory text (median score of the latter section's exam = 57.9%).

Performance on the second term final examination did not distinguish significantly between the two groups (medians: 70.8 and 67.8 percent for MP's and Controls, respectively). This convergence of the groups in the second term might be attributable to one or both of two factors. First, the text material covered in the second term was apparently less difficult than that in the first term, as judged by content (first term topics included statistics, sensation and perception, and biological foundations), and as judged by MP performance on the weekly quizzes (80% passing 8 or more quizzes in the second term compared to 60% in the first term). A second explanation for the lack of a MP superiority in the second term has to do with the possibility, alluded to earlier, that study habits acquired by the MP students in the first term transferred, contaminating their second term behavior as Controls. In fact, many students reported to the instructors that their improved study habits under the first term MP condition has persisted into their second term experience as Controls.

The Mastery Performance program in the first term thus generated not only an immediate benefit as measured by first term final exam performance, but may have had a longer lasting effect on second term study habits as well. It would of course be interesting to inquire whether the MP program had any effects which lasted beyond the course itself. Two types of data bear on this question.

**Retention Effects.** A follow-up was done in the first week of classes in the next school year to test long-term retention of the text material. Eighteen questions were selected, two questions from each of nine chapters, with items being restricted to those which had never appeared on previous exams or quizzes and which covered points of relatively major importance. The resulting test was administered to students in all second year psychology courses who had been in the authors' section the previous year. These students were asked to identify themselves as having been in the MP or Control group during the first and second term. MP students from the first term did significantly better on items from the first term than did those students who were in the Control group in the first term ($\overline{X}$'s = 12.1 and 10.8, respectively; t = 1.89; $p < .05$ for 1-tailed test, $df = 38$). There was, as would be expected, no significant difference in performance on the second term items. Thus, the superiority of the first term MP group over the first term Controls seems to have persisted when measured some nine months later. This long-term persistence of MP superiority is consistent with the similar finding of Moore, et al. (1973).

A second source of data bearing on long-term effects was derived from items on the course evaluation questionnaire which attempted to assess the effect of the MP program upon the students' likelihood of continuing in psychology. In each of the two terms, MP students indicated, on average, a significantly greater probability of taking another Psychology course as a result of their term's experience than did the Controls (questionnaire item #3, median scale values: *First term:* 3.7 and 4.2 for MP and Controls, respectively; $p < .05$). *Second term:* 2.8 and 3.8 for MP and Controls, respectively; $p < .005$). Although these reports are, of course, no more than stated projections, earlier data of the authors suggest that these questionnaire findings do in fact predict subsequent enrollment; comparison of a previous MP class with a traditional lecture class produced not only questionnaire data comparable to that found in the present study (i.e., greater stated likelihood of taking a future psychology course in the MP class), but also follow up data which showed that, in fact, a significantly greater proportion of these MP students did enroll in second year psychology courses. These findings are, again, similar to those of Moore, et al. (1973) regarding mathematics, physics, and engineering students.

## Discussion

The data from the present study suggest that a weekly quiz procedure, coupled with a mastery criterion, is sufficient to generate clear benefits in performance. It seems likely that the major source of this effect is the extra study time which the MP student engages in on a regular weekly basis; the MP students, as compared to Controls, reportedly spent, on average, approximately twice as much time each week in studying the text (questionnaire item #4, median scale values: *First term:* 2.5 hours and 1 hour for MP and Controls, respectively; $p < .001$. *Second term:* 2.5 and 1.5 hours for MP and Controls, respectively; $p < .001$.) Interestingly enough, this extra work investment was not at the cost of the MP students' enjoyment of the course; not only did they report a greater likelihood of enrolling in future psychology courses because of their MP experience (see above), but in fact reported significantly greater enjoyment of the course (questionnaire item #2, median scale values: *First term:* 3.2 and 4.2 for MP and Controls, respectively; $p. < .01$ *Second term:* 3.1 and 4.0 for MP and Controls, respectively; $p. < .001$). Moreover, 80% of the students writing the final exam in the second term indicated that they would take another course employing the Mastery Performance procedure (questionnaire item #1; i.e., 80% with scale ratings of less than 4, "neutral" to "definitely yes").

It should be noted that the present MP system, in its omission of proctor-student interaction, may not develop the verbal skills which could accrue from such interactions. There are other possible benefits of a proctor system, such as the *"marked enhancement of the personal-social aspect of the educational process* (Keller, 1968, p. 83)" which may also be missing from the MP program. Though perhaps not providing such ancillary benefits, the present mass-testing mastery system would seem to compare favorably with more individualized mastery systems; the full grade-point difference between MP and Control groups in the first term (again, the first term being uncontaminated by possible transfer effects) is not unlike advantages over conventional instruction which have been reported for mastery programs utilizing individual pacing and testing.

The possibility that the present system of instruction might, in many respects, be as effective as more individualized systems would seem to suggest a reappraisal of the shortcomings typically ascribed to mass-testing. Moore, et al. (1973) asserted that ". . .traditional testing in which all students take the same test at the same time, assumes that all students learn at a constant rate (p. 335)." By implication, instructor-paced mass-testing places many students at a disadvantage because their need for extra study time may not be met. However, there is logically no necessary and insidious connection between instructor-paced mass-testing *per se* and any assumption of equal learning rates among students. In the MP system, for example, the fact that students are limited to a week of preparation for each test does not mean that all students *must* study for equal periods of time within that week—conceivably, some students may spend more time than others. The important point is not the fact that mass-testing sets a uniform limit to study time for all students, but whether or not the total amount of study time thus available is sufficient for most students. In the present study, almost 70% of the students were able, when under the MP conditions, to study enough within the allotted 7 days to meet the first class criterion on at least 80% of their weekly quizzes; indeed the proportion might have been even higher if students had not been explicitly instructed to study and pass only that number of units necessary for obtaining the grade they desired for the course. Moreover, as already pointed out, even the poorer students benefited from the MP program, with 13% fewer failures under this condition compared to the Controls.

Although most students may in fact be capable of meeting the demands of instructor-paced mass-testing, there are other implications of such systems. Mastery performance demands imposed within the context of mass-testing could, on occasion, conflict with study requirements of other courses. The present instructors, however, received few student complaints to this effect. On the other hand, it also should be recognized that instructor-pacing may have an advantage over self-pacing in that the former may obviate the possibility of the student self-pacing himself into protracted delays. Miller, Weaver and Semb (1974) point to evidence of this weakness in self-pacing.

The basis for the success of mass-testing in the MP condition is likely the fact that in the present program, unlike conventional courses, testing was frequent and involved small units of material along with a mastery performance demand. These features may benefit all students by obviating intense "cramming" of large amounts of material while pacing students into more consistent weekly study habits (as evidenced by questionnaire item #4 discussed above). These considerations, together with the performance and questionnaire results of the present study, suggest (a) that conventional mass-testing systems may fail largely because they involve infrequent testing on large amounts of material, and *not* simply because they demand that students be tested at the same time; and (b) that the essential requirement for *any* effort to improve instruction may be to simply engineer the learning environment in ways that maximize the amount and efficiency of study behaviors in the time allotted. The weekly testing on small units of material with a mastery criterion, as employed in the MP

program, would seem to represent a relatively efficient and economical approach to university instruction.

It should be recognized that the present study made no comparison between a system of weekly testing with and without a mastery criterion. Thus any final conclusion as to the necessity for a mastery criterion in a system of weekly testing must be guarded. There is evidence that weekly testing without a mastery criterion can augment student performance when compared to traditional infrequent examination (Stalling, 1971). Further research is therefore needed to clarify the relative contributions of a mastery criterion and weekly testing in improving student performance.

## References

Acker, L. E. & Goldwater, B. C. A written exam procedure to minimize in-class cheating. *Journal of Applied Behavior Analysis*, 1973, *6*, 540.

Alba, E., & Pennypacker, H. S. A multiple change score comparison of traditional and behavioral college teaching procedures. *Journal of Applied Behavior Analysis*, 1972, *5*, 121-124.

Born, D. G., Gledhill, S. M., & Davis, M. L. Examination performance in lecture-discussion and personalized instruction courses. *Journal of Applied Behavior Analysis*, 1972, *5*, 33-43.

Ferguson, G. A. *Statistical analysis in psychology and education.* New York: McGraw-Hill, 1959.

Ferster, C. B. Individualized instruction in a large introductory psychology college course. *Psychological Record*, 1968, *18*, 521-532.

Gaynor, J. F. & Wolking, W. D. The effectiveness of currently enrolled student proctors in an undergraduate special education course. *Journal of Applied Behavior Analysis*, 1974, *7*, 263-269.

Johnston, J. M. & O'Neill, G. The analysis of performance criteria defining course grades as a determinant of college student academic performance. *Journal of Applied Behavior Analysis*, 1973, *6*, 261-268.

Keller, F. S. "Goodbye teacher. . ." *Journal of Applied Behavior Analysis*, 1968, *1*, 79-89.

McMichael, J. S. & Corey, J. R. Contingency management in an introductory psychology course produces better learning. *Journal of Applied Behavior Analysis*, 1969, *2*, 79-83.

Miller, L. K., Weaver, F. H., & Semb, G. A procedure for maintaining student progress in a personalized university course. *Journal of Applied Behavior Analysis*, 1974, *7*, 87-91.

Moore, J. W., Hauck, W. E., & Gagné, E. D. Acquisition, retention, and transfer in an individualized college physics course. *Journal of Educational Psychology*, 1973, *64*, 335-340.

Moore, J. W., Mahan, J. M. & Ritts, C. A. Continuous progress concept of instruction with university students. *Psychological Reports*, 1969, *25*, 887-892.

Semb, G. The effects of mastery criteria and assignment length on college-student test performance. *Journal of Applied Behavior Analysis*, 1974, *7*, 61-69.

Sheppard, W. C. & MacDermott, H. G. Design and evluation of a programmed course in introductory psychology. *Journal of Applied Behavior Analysis*, 1970, *3*, 5-11.

Stalling, R. B. A one-proctor programmed course procedure for introductory psychology. *Psychological Record*, 1971, *21*, 501-505.

Whaley, D. L. & Surratt, S. L. *Attitudes of science: A program for a student-centered seminar.* Kalamazoo, Michigan: Behaviordelia, 1967.

## Notes

1. Because final examination and questionnaire distributions were skewed, all group statistics are reported in terms of medians and tested for significance by the Median Test (Ferguson, 1959).
2. Supported by a grant for innovations in instruction from the President of the University of Victoria.
3. Authorship is considered equal.

# Student Performance in Introductory Psychology Following Termination of the Programmed Achievement Contingency at Mid-Semester

Jack R. Nation, Phillip Massad,
and Dennis Wilkerson
*Texas A & M University*

A depression of the final examination
score was found to follow withdrawal of
the mastery requirement at mid-semester.

In recent years educators have been under fire for teaching in ways that do not result in adequate learning and retention of subject matter. Some of the criticism reflects a basic lack of understanding of the role of education in our society, but some of it is more valid than many of us would care to admit. With increasing reports of a deteriorating educational product, it becomes more and more difficult to justify the use of traditional methods of teaching. As a result, there have been a substantial number of innovative instructional systems developed over the past several years to assist in the difficult task of teaching survey classes such as introductory psychology. Educational programs such as the Personalized System of Instruction (Keller, 1968), Competency-based instruction (Smith, 1975), and Total Mastery Learning (Vernon, 1974) are examples of teaching approaches, in introductory psychology courses, that offer at least partial solutions to the many problems confronting contemporary educators.

In addition to the above mentioned "classroom intervention" techniques, one other successful method of instruction has been labeled Programmed Achievement (PA). PA, having been used primarily in introductory psychology courses, is a motivation and reward instructional system in which a crucial ingredient is the testing procedure. In this procedure, multiple choice tests are administered to the students, spaced throughout the semester, over discrete segments of material. Students are required to achieve perfect mastery, or nearly perfect mastery, on these quizzes. Students who initially fail to reach a set mastery criterion on a given quiz are required to take further quizzes over the same material until mastery is achieved. It is important to note that only the score the *first* time the student takes a quiz on a given segment of the assigned material is used in computing the semester quiz average, which counts as fifty percent of the total semester grade. Quiz performance on additional opportunities to achieve mastery is not involved in determining the grade. Fifty percent of the final course grade also comes from major examinations. Research over the last several years (e.g., Haddad, Nation, & Williams, 1975; Knight, Williams & Jardon, 1975; Lamberth & Knight, 1974; Nation, Knight, Lamberth & Dyck, 1974; Nation & Roop, 1975) indicates that PA has been, and continues to be, an effective and reliable vehicle for motivating introductory psychology students.

Because Programmed Achievement is thought to have its foundation in and among fundamental principles of learning (see Nation et al. 1974 for a discussion of theoretical mechanisms involved in the effect), the procedure lends itself well to experimental manipulation. Laboratory findings, of course, do not always provide solid support-bases for later applied investigations but when one can gain useful information from modeling such procedures it would seem desirable to do so. Accordingly, the present research project attempted to increase our understanding of Programmed Achievement phenomena by shifting reinforcement contingencies in a manner analogous to reward manipulations often performed in a more "basic" research context. Specifically, the present experiment involved training introductory psychology students the first half of the semester under full PA contingencies and then discontinuing these contingencies the second half of the semester. If PA results indeed occur because of larger positive and negative incentives, as has been suggested (cf. Nation et al. 1974), then removing these added motivational stimuli should be formally analogous to a shift downward in reinforcement magnitude.

Compared to control students who have always operated under lower incentive conditions (i.e., traditional classroom), PA students shifted to traditional contingencies predictably should follow one of these three patterns: First, due to the positive reinforcing effects of high grades, the higher performance scores expected for PA students while under PA contingencies may remain high even after the shift. Second, following the shift, PA student performances may come down and essentially parallel those performances of control students which have been operating under the lower incentive throughout. Third, following the shift, PA students may demonstrate performance scores that are *below* those of control students operating under the lower incentive conditions throughout. Note that this last possibility actually defines a negative contrast or "depression effect." Such reports have been known to occur in the basic learning literature (see Dunham, 1968, for a review) as well as more applied areas (Nation, LeUnes, and Gray, 1976).

## Method

**Subjects.** The subjects were 214 students enrolled in two sections of Introductory Psychology during the spring semester of 1976. Both sections met Monday through Friday: (1) at 11:00 a.m. (N = 133) and (2) 4:00 p.m. (N = 81). A total of 11 students across both sections dropped the course during the semester and their scores were not included in the analysis. Of these 11 students, 5 were from section 1 and 6 were from section 2. Each section was randomly assigned to one of two treatment conditions at the beginning of the semester.

**Materials.** The text for the course was *Psychology* by Lindsey, Hall, and Thompson; first edition. Students did not receive study guides or supplementary materials.

**Procedure.** Two different instructors, both male, were randomly assigned to teach one of the two treatment conditions. Since the instructor variable has been shown to be of little importance in research related to different instructional techniques (see Nation et al. 1974), both instructors were informed of the experimental design and were involved in student counseling and testing. It should be mentioned that Introductory Psychology is normally run by the coordinator and the senior author served in that capacity during the present study. Instructors in the program have little control over their assignments and, therefore, there is every reason to believe that the experiment had no influence on the instructors' performance in the lecture hall.

**Preshift Period.** The preshift period of the experiment lasted for the first eight weeks of the sixteen week semester. During this period the Programmed Achievement (PA) class (section 1) operated under a technique which required the student who failed to demonstrate criterion performance (90% mastery on each of 3 weekly quizzes[1]), to retake conceptually related quizzes as many times as necessary to reach criterion. If the student had not evidenced 90% mastery by the end of the week, he or she received a grade of "F" for the course. In preshift, the Standard Control (S-C) condition (section 2) was required to take the three initial quizzes without the requirement, or opportunity, for retake examinations. In addition to the weekly quizzes during preshift, both groups were required to take a comprehensive mid-term exam. The mid-term exam was administered at the end of the preshift period during the eighth week of classes.

At the beginning of the semester both classes were instructed that the weekly quizzes (consisting of 10 manual multiple choice items selected by the authors) would count as 50% of their grade, and the other 50% would come from major exam performance. The class required to retake weekly quizzes until evidencing 90% mastery (i.e., PA class) was given one of two weekly quiz forms on Monday. If criterion performance (90% mastery) was not evidenced on Monday, the student was required to take a second form on Wednesday. The Wednesday form, also consisting of 10 multiple choice items, was composed entirely of new items taken from the same material covered on the Monday quiz. Students failing to demonstrate 90% mastery on either the Monday or Wednesday quiz were given unlimited opportunities to reach criterion by taking a third quiz on Friday. The Friday quiz was a 10 item multiple choice quiz which had questions taken from the two previous quiz forms. A random schedule was used in the selection of items from the previous quizzes. The PA students were instructed that only Monday attempt (first attempt) would count toward their total grade, but they still had to evidence 90% mastery by the end of the week. Group S-C took only the Monday quiz.

Identical weekly quizzes were administered to both classes during a given day, i.e., both classes received exactly the same 10 item quiz on Monday. On each quiz a detachable section was provided at the bottom of the page to allow the students to copy their choices by letter and immediately compare them with the correct letters which were posted. In order to avoid transfer of test information to the later class, a different sequence of identical test items was given to each class. The mid-term examination contained 50 new multiple choice items selected by the instructors.

**Postshift Period.** During the first regularly scheduled class period of the week following preshift (the first eight weeks of the course), students in the PA class were told that the Programmed Achievement contingencies were being dropped. Specifically, PA students were told that the requirement to retake quizzes until a 90% mastery criterion had been reached was being discontinued. The requirement to take the initial weekly quiz on Monday remained, of course, but PA students no longer took quizzes on Wednesday or Friday of the quiz week. In effect, during the postshift phase of the experiment, the PA students operated under the same contingencies as students in the control condition. Aside from these changes, the procedure for PA students was exactly as was previously described for preshift. There were 3 weekly quizzes (Monday attempts only) given during postshift. Additionally, all PA students were required to take a final exam which was comprehensive over all material covered since the mid-term exam. The final exam was composed of 50 multiple choice items selected by the instructors.

In postshift, as in preshift, the S-C condition continued to receive weekly quizzes with no requirement for mastery. Actually, for S-C students the postshift phase of the experiment was a continuation of preshift contingencies. In postshift, S-C students received the identical 3 weekly quizzes that were administered to the PA class. Also, S-C students were required to take the same 50 item final exam that was given to the PA class.

In terms of final course average, students were instructed that 50% of their total grade would come from the 6 weekly quizzes (3 preshift and 3 postshift) and 50% would come from the 2 major exams (mid-term and final).

**Course Evaluation.** Immediately preceding the administration of the mid-term examination, and again at final exam time, students were asked to rate the overall quality of the course (independently of instructor, which was done separately) on a scale of 0 to 10, with 0 labeled "very poor" and 10 as "very good." Other questions were included to provide detailed information to the instructors. These evaluations were to serve two functions: (a) to allow a comparison between PA and S-C classes, and (b) to allow a within-subjects comparison of introductory psychology as taught under PA contingencies and traditional contingencies.

In addition to the above evaluations, further evaluative data were obtained from PA students. During the last regularly scheduled class period, students were asked to indicate whether they preferred the PA teaching method used the first half of the semester or the traditional method used the last half of the semester. It was felt that this procedure, coupled with reports from the above scales, would give us, for the first time, a fair comparison of PA and traditional class structures by people who had operated under both contingencies.

## Results

**Weekly Quizzes.** A 2 (teaching methods) x 2 (block of three weekly quizzes) repeated measures analysis of variance was performed on the Monday quizzes using mean number correct as the dependent measure. The mean percent correct for each group during preshift (quizzes 1-3) and postshift (quizzes 4-6) are depicted in Table 1. The results of the analysis revealed a significant main effect for teaching method, $F(1,201) = 14.37, p < .001$. This was shown to be a result of the superior performance by the PA students. The main effect of block of three weekly quizzes did not reach an acceptable level of statistical significance, $F(1,201) = .79, p > .05$. Additionally, the teaching methods X blocks interaction was shown to be nonsignificant, $F(1,201) = 1.02, p > .05$.

The finding of a significant main effect for quizzes, coupled with the report of a nonsignificant interaction, indicate that PA students were superior to control students while operating under the PA contingencies (preshift) *and* were still superior even after the contingencies had been terminated (postshift). The superior preshift performance shown by PA students on the initial test over assigned material is consistent with other reports which show elevated student performance scores when students study under the PA course structure (viz., Haddad et al., 1975; Knight, et al., 1975; Nation et al., 1974; Nation & Roop, 1975). The postshift data, of course, are of particular interest as they seem to suggest that the initial separation, which may have been generated by fear of course failure, was sustained by the positive reinforcement of high grades.

**Major Exams.** Student performance on the midterm and final examinations was analyzed with a 2 (teaching methods) x 2 (major exams) repeated measures analysis of variance. Mean percent correct for each of the groups on the midterm and final examinations is shown in Table 1. The analysis

### Table 1
### Mean Percent Correct for Pre- and Post-Shift Quizzes and for Examinations

| Measure | PA (N=128) | S-C (N=75) |
|---|---|---|
| Preshift (Quizzes 1-3) | $85.13_a$ | $81.20_b$ |
| Postshift (Quizzes 4-6) | $85.39_a$ | $80.80_b$ |
| Midterm | $84.80_a$ | $80.16_b$ |
| Final | $77.80_c$ | $82.44_{a,b}$ |

Row and column means within a set (quizzes or exams) which do not have a common subscript are significantly different at the .05 level.

showed a significant teaching methods x major exam interaction, $F(1,201) = 13.17, p < .001$. *Newman Keuls* post hoc tests were performed on means and these analyses revealed that PA students were superior to control students on the midterm ($p < .05$). However, the reverse was the case on the final where it was shown that PA students were inferior to control students ($p < .05$). That this effect was due to a decline in PA student performance, and not elevated control performances, was further revealed by the post hoc comparisons, i.e., PA students dropped significantly from the midterm to the final ($p < .01$) while control students remained at the same level ($p > .05$). A main effect of midterm over final

was also revealed ($F(1,201) = 9.77, p < .002$) but this was most likely a result of the strong interaction effects discussed above and therefore is relatively unimportant. Also, the main effect for teaching method failed to reach an acceptable level of significance, $F < 1$.

Since the midterm was drawn from new items (i.e., items not included previously in weekly quiz forms), these data suggest that students in the PA class, while still operating under the full contingencies of Programmed Achievement, were better able to generalize concepts learned earlier in the semester. Furthermore, the inferiority of PA students on the final, following the removal of Programmed Achievement contingencies at mid-semester, could be taken as evidence for a "depression effect," about which more later.

**Course Evaluations.** Student ratings on the 10-point rating scale revealed a great deal of consistency from the first half of the semester to the last half of the semester. Ratings from PA students averaged 7.30 at mid-semester and 7.27 at the courses' end. S-C students rated the course 6.81 at mid-semester and 6.75 at final exam time. So, though descriptively PA ratings were above S-C ratings, there did not appear to be any change in course evaluations across the semester. It is worth noting that these results follow more closely to the pattern of results obtained with weekly quizzes than obtained with major exams.

Of particular interest in the present study were the within-subject evaluations of PA students regarding course preferences. To the question "Do you prefer the Programmed Achievement method of teaching used the first half of the semester, or the traditional method of teaching used the second half of the semester," 67 percent of the students indicated their choice to be the PA method while 33 percent preferred the traditional method. Thus, Programmed Achievement was preferred by a margin of 2:1.

## Discussion

The findings of this study indicate that Programmed Achievement (PA) contingencies must be maintained throughout the semester in order to obtain optimal results. While it is true that student performance on weekly quizzes remains high following removal of the PA structure, the report that final exam performance, following a shift off of PA, drops below that of control students would certainly suggest that the continuation of PA contingencies throughout the semester is a preferable procedure. The within-subjects evaluation data, where it was shown that PA was the preferred teaching method, would seem to underscore such a position.

The finding that PA student performance remains high on weekly quizzes, even after being shifted to control contingencies, is at least partially consistent with an earlier report by Knight (1973). However, since Knight did not have a post-shift control condition similar to the one in the present investigation, any comparisons would have to be made most cautiously. Moreover, the report of deteriorated performance by PA students on a post-shift final examination is directly in contradiction to data obtained by Knight (1973) where it was shown that students shifted from PA to control contingencies did not significantly decrease in performance on their last major exam. But once again Knight did not have an adequate control group to which to compare post-shift major exam performance. Possibly nothing firm should be stated at this point, but present results do clearly indicate that, compared to control students who have always operated under traditional course requirements, terminating PA at mid-semester results in inferior scholastic achievement. Therefore, termination should not be considered as an alternative to the more complete use of the program.

One of the more intriguing issues in the present study concerns the emergency of a marginal "depression effect" on the final exam. The fact that PA students were below control students on the final could be some evidence of the phenomenon. Depression effects, which are quite reliable, are said to occur when subjects shifted from a high valued incentive to a lower valued incentive perform more poorly than subjects who have experienced the lower valued incentive throughout training (Dunham, 1968). All of the necessary ingredients for such an effect would appear to have been present in this investigation. PA students, as revealed by evaluations and test scores, originally operated under high incentive conditions and subsequently were shifted to a lower incentive condition, all the while being compared against control students who had always operated under the lower incentive condition. The inferior performance shown by PA students on the final exam then may be identified as a "depression effect."

Even though the results of this experiment apparently show a depression effect, an alternative explanation may, at first glance, seem equally defensible. Specifically, motivational variables may have interacted with course progression, mitigating student performance on major exams. That is, at the time of the final exam, three-quarters of the course grade had already been determined for both PA and control students. PA students had done well on the midterm, on quizzes 1-3, and on quizzes 4-6. Therefore, PA students did not need as many final exam points to get a good final course grade and their motivation, and ultimately their final exam scores, were depressed accordingly. However, previous research (e.g., Haddad et al., 1975; Knight et al., 1975; Nation et al., 1974; Nation & Roop, 1975) would seem to discount such a position. In all of these investigations, students operated under PA contingencies throughout the semester. As in the present study, these students, by the time of the final exam, had already demonstrated superior scholastic achievement relative to control students. Yet in all previous investigations PA students have either been equal or superior to control students on the final exam. If high grades following three-quarters course completion were sufficiently strong demotivational instruments in the present study, why have not the same effects been observed in earlier reports where the PA contingency has been maintained? Clearly, the "depression effect" account of the present results, as previously outlined, would seem to be the more tenable explanation of the present data.

There are, as seems to always be the case, alternative theoretical interpretations of such a depression effect (cf. Amsel, 1967; Capaldi, 1974) but those need not concern us here. Rather, of primary interest in the present article is the specification of boundary conditions within which Programmed Achievement functions successfully. Considering the depression effect obtained in the present study, those boundary conditions would appear to exclude the termination of PA at some point during the semester.

In closing, in this paper we have attempted to apply existing knowledge of the learning process to the development of an instructional device known as Programmed Achievement. PA's apparent relationship to scientific underpinnings offers the potential for teaching introductory psychology and other subject matters more effectively than they are being taught at the present time. Programmed Achievement, then, is concerned with the selection and arrangement of educational content based upon what is known about human learning. It is a process of constructing sequences of instructional material in a way that maximizes the rate and depth of learning, fosters understanding, and enhances the motivation of the student. Explicitly, it is what an effective teacher does intuitively.

### References

Amsel, A. Partial reinforcement effects on vigor and persistence. In K. W. Spence and J. T. Spence (Eds.). *The Psychology of learning and motivation: Advances in research and theory.* New York: Academic Press, 1967, Vol. 1, pp. 1-65.

Capaldi, E. J. Partial reward either following or preceding consistent reward: A case of reinforcement level. *Journal of Experimental Psychology*, 1974, *102*, 954-962.

Dunham, P. J. Contrasted conditions of reinforcement: A selective critique. *Psychological Bulletin*, 1968, *69*, 295-315.

Haddad, N. F., Nation, J. R., & Williams, J. D. Programmed Student Achievement: A Hawthorne effect? *Research in Higher Education*, 1975, *3*, 315-322.

Keller, F. S. "Good-bye, teacher..." *Journal of Applied Behavior Analysis*, 1968, *1*, 78-89.

Knight, J. M. The effect of programmed achievement on student performance. *Journal of Educational Research*, 1973, *66*, 291-294.

Knight, J. M., Williams, J. D., & Jardon, M. The effects of contingency avoidance on programmed student achievement. *Research in Higher Education*, 1975, *3*, 11-17.

Lamberth, J., & Knight, J. M. An embarassment of riches: Effectively teaching and motivating large introductory psychology sections. *Teaching of Psychology*, 1974, *1*, 16-20.

Nation, J. R., Knight, J. M., Lamberth, J., & Dyck, D. G. Programmed student achievement: A test of the avoidance hypothesis. *Journal of Experimental Education*, 1974, *42*, 57-61.

Nation, J. R., LeUnes, A. D., & Gray, M. Student evaluations of teachers of psychology as a function of academic rank. *Teaching of Psychology*, 1976, *3*, 186-187.

Nation, J. R., & Roop, S. S. A comparison of two mastery approaches to teaching introductory psychology. *Teaching of Psychology*, 1975, *2*, 108-111.

Smith, M. D. *Educational psychology and its classroom applications.* Boston: Allyn and Bacon, 1975.

Vernon, W. M. *Introductory psychology: A mastery coursebook with performance objectives.* Chicago: Rand McNally, 1974.

### Notes

1. It should be noted that "weekly quizzes" represents a label used to indicate short quizzes administered during a given week, and is not meant to imply that quizzes were given each and every week of the semester.

2. This research was supported by a grant from Research Development, Liberal Arts, Texas A & M University.

3. The authors would like to thank Robert R. Berg, Director of University Research, and W. David Maxwell, Dean of Liberal Arts, whose valuable contributions made the present research possible.

# 5. SELECTING A TEXTBOOK

## Choosing a Text for the Introductory Course

Charles J. Morris
*Denison University*

An identification of objectives, review of texts, assessment of outcomes, and consideration of students are suggested procedures for effective text adoption.

The trend in reviews of introductory textbooks appears to be away from evaluations which fit a prescribed set of criteria. Instead, one finds judgments made, if at all, in terms of the goals set forth by a particular author, apparently in recognition of the different and usually multiple functions served by the introductory course (e.g., see Popplestone, 1975; Rubinstein, 1975). This diversity of purpose renders foolish any effort to pass judgment on what constitutes a good introductory text. On the other hand, in light of the apparent high turnover rate in adoptions, it does seem appropriate to make an evaluation of the process by which texts for the introductory course are selected. That process, from my point of view, is not very commendable in far too many cases.

All too often textbook adoptions appear to be made hastily, without sufficient information, at times selfishly, and, in some instances, on questionable ethical grounds (McKeachie, 1976). One also hears occasional tales about adoptions being made almost exclusively on the basis of some relatively superficial feature of a book (e.g., the pictures, number of chapters), an irrelevant external consideration (e.g., to counter charges of "softheadedness" by colleagues), and even because of some essentially negative aspect of a book (e.g., a text is out of date, thus giving the instructor something to talk about!). Extreme cases of this kind are no doubt few in number but less flagrant practices are not. And even in the absence of hard data, I am willing to suggest that, in general, the process by which texts are selected is far from ideal.

The importance of choosing an appropriate text cannot be overemphasized. A rather sizeable literature has emerged in the past decade which supports the notion that it is the textbook more than the mode of instruction that affects performance in a course (Dubin & Taveggia, 1968; for exceptions, see Kulik & Jaksa, 1977; Taveggia, 1976). Thus one would think that great care would be taken in choosing a text. Moreover, it is the introductory course which is likely to be neglected the most, even though it serves the largest number of students and is generally thought to be the most important course in the curriculum—providing the basis for further study, attracting and/or selecting appropriate majors, and giving many students their only formal experience with the discipline. We are fortunate in that most introductory texts are reasonably good and so probably very few students

suffer from our indiscretions. But we could be doing a better job. At the very least, a more careful approach to choosing a text would lead to the design of a better course, increase the probability of a positive response from students, and perhaps even obviate the need for a hasty, uninformed adoption decision the following quarter, semester, or year.

My task in this paper is to offer some suggestions on how an instructor might go about selecting an introductory text suited to his or her needs. No claim is being made that these suggestions are necessarily better than others which have been or could be tried, but it is hoped that my comments and, indeed, this entire issue of *ToP*, will serve to catalyze a new approach to choosing texts for our courses. Changes appear to be in order.

**Suggestion #1: Identify Your Objectives.** In thinking about textbook decisions, it is important to remember that the choice of a text cannot be divorced from the broader issue of designing a course to meet certain objectives. Thus it almost goes without saying that the most important consideration is that a text be consistent with one's goals for a course. Even those with relatively limited experience in the classroom are probably aware of the confusion and disenchantment which can arise when a text appears irrelevant to the instructor's stated goals or when lectures are critical of, contradict, or even imply the unimportance of the material presented in the text. In such cases students may legitimately wonder why the text was assigned in the first place or why they should bother wasting their time reading it (or their money buying it). Unless one's goal is to confuse, generate hostility, and essentially neutralize the impact of a text (and maybe even the entire course), a text should be selected which is consistent with, and, hopefully, facilitates progress toward, an instructor's goals for the course. This is not to say that a text must reflect the instructor's particular theoretical bias. If, for example, one goal is to help students identify how different views lead to very different questions about, or explanations of, certain phenomena, a text might be chosen that represents views opposing those of the instructor. In this instance, of course, care must be taken to make this purpose clear to the students and to refer to examples of conflict when appropriate. The point is that a text should be chosen with specific objectives in mind; it should be one which lends coherence to the overall structure of the course. The frequent complaint from students that the textbook and lectures seem disjointed or unrelated suggests that more attention should be given to this matter. In one survey of student ratings across a variety of courses, the median response of 31 percent of the classes indicated disagreement or strong disagreement with the statement that "Reading assignments are relevant to what is presented in class," whereas only 13 percent of the classes showed strong agreement with the statement (Note 2). Poor explanation of course objectives may account for some of the low ratings, but it is likely that inappropriate text selection played a major role. The same survey revealed that 30 percent of the classes did not agree that the text made a valuable contribution to the course, with another 45 percent of the classes falling in the "neither agree or disagree" category. Clearly, a closer inspection of potential texts than is typically undertaken will be necessary to correct what appears to be a serious problem.

When viewed within the context of total course objectives, it becomes obvious that choosing a text cannot be considered independently of instructor characteristics, teaching format, and a host of other factors unique to a given course. The inspiring lecturer may not be concerned with the "interest level" of a text; classes heavy on the discussion of basic issues may not need a text with the same emphasis; interesting films may offset the drab appearance of an otherwise excellent text. Whatever the case may be, I am confident that spending time on the development of course objectives, and especially the relationship between text and lectures in achieving these objectives, will lead to the selection of an appropriate text. It will also raise a number of fundamental questions about teaching in general, the resolution of which should produce a better course in all respects.

**Suggestion #2: Why Not Read The Book?**  This recommendation may strike some as a radical step, but if we take seriously the significance of the first course in psychology and the primacy of the text in influencing learning, the time involved to read a few books is not that great and may even be enlightening. The alternative is to rely upon our own quick survey of potential texts, a book representative's pitch, a reviewer's comments, or perhaps a content analysis or measure of readability. However useful these sources of information may be in a general sense, they are not meant to serve as substitutes for a careful reading of a potential adoption. They do not tell us, for instance, how well the text fits into our total course structure, or what changes in other features of the course will be needed in order to use the text and still meet our objectives. As one who has spent many hours going through a text almost line by line for the purpose of developing study questions and self-paced materials, I can say with confidence that taking the time to read a text is worth the effort. The payoff includes not only a good text in most cases, but also a remarkably lightened burden in designing and coordinating other activities (lectures, films, lab, etc.) consistent with one's goals for the course.

Of course, no one individual (except, perhaps, a reviewer) is likely to read most of the texts available for the introductory course. Here is where a cooperative venture of the kind initiated in this issue of ToP plus a reassessment of individual or departmental procedures might be helpful. My own survey of reviews suggests that, if one first identifies a set of objectives for the course, sufficient information is usually available to sort texts into potentially acceptable and unacceptable categories. For example, a brief search located over 30 texts which have been reviewed in the past year or so in Contemporary Psychology and the Teaching of Psychology. By applying different sets of criteria an instructor might use in selecting a text (e.g., survey-eclectic, behavioral, etc.), it was possible to narrow down potential candidates to a manageable number. As few as two books were placed into the potentially acceptable category in several cases and in no instance did more than five books appear in a given category. It might be noted that the criteria used were stated in rather general terms and that, with more care in specifying objectives, the number of candidates could probably be reduced further. This rather surprising finding attests to the quality of the reviews that were consulted, and leads one to believe that more effective use of reviews combined with a careful reading of a few selected texts would reduce the turnover on adoptions. The statements by authors which have appeared in ToP were also helpful and it might be worthwhile to extend this practice to include most authors, even if their books are not reviewed concurrently in the same issue.

Admittedly, the number of texts available is much greater than the sample considered above, so one should expect to find a greater number of texts within a designated category than reported here. But additional tactics are possible. The careful analysis of introductory texts provided by Quereshi and Sackett (1977) in this issue should make the task much easier than one might expect, and reduce the number of candidates to a reasonably manageable size. The burden of reading the texts that remain after the initial screening process will still be heavy in some instances, thus necessitating some additional procedures if those texts are to be read. Some obvious solutions to this problem involve sharing the task with others who teach the course or asking for systematic evaluations from teaching assistants. In undergraduate institutions, it might be possible to make more effective use of advanced undergraduates or perhaps ask the psychology honorary to play a role in the decision making process. Other approaches might be equally fruitful, but the point is that we need to develop selection procedures which are commensurate with the importance we attach to the introductory course.

**Suggestion #3: Assess The Impact On Students.**  In light of the apparent importance of the text in determining course outcomes, it is surprising that we haven't spent more time evaluating textbooks the same way the effects of different instructional methods have been assessed. It is, after all, the effects a text has on students that ultimately determines its worth. Moreover, if the little research available on the issue is to be trusted, inspection of course materials does not always predict their actual effectiveness. In fact, a sizeable negative correlation has been reported in one case between predicted effectiveness of instructional materials and subsequent student performance (Rothkopf, 1963). Although one cannot make any convincing generalizations from this study to conventional forms of instruction, it is equally true that we should not, in the absence of data to the contrary, trust our own judgments too strongly. Careful reading of a text should definitely help, but we also need to collect feedback from students—both in the form of achievement measures and other effects not usually assessed on our exams.

It is indeed a rare book which provides the above kind of information before it comes on the market (for an exception, see Miller, 1975), although more and more authors appear to be making efforts in this direction (e.g., McConnell, 1974). Without intending to endorse any particular text, which may or may not be appropriate for a given course, I welcome a trend toward writing or rewriting texts on the basis of systematically collected information on actual student achievement and/or student feedback—a trend which, by the way, was encouraged some years ago (Emme, 1941). This is not to suggest practices which amount to the "coddling" of students (as some critics have charged). Texts which sacrifice certain objectives for the sole purpose of pleasing students probably do more damage than good in the long run. But a text that focuses entirely upon "cognitive" objectives and ignores the so-called "affective" consequences of instruction may be even worse. Who among us would be satisfied if a substantial percentage of our students left our course feeling that psychology was dull, irrelevant, and unworthy of further study, even though they may have learned a great deal? Certainly we must pay attention to instructional consequences other than those which are measured on our exams—and which, incidentally, may extend well beyond the time when the content of the course is long forgotten. It might be noted in passing that published descriptions of objectives for the introductory course (e.g., McKeachie, 1969) place heavy emphasis upon these "non-cognitive" instructional outcomes.

A rather dramatic example of how a text can influence student attitudes was observed in my introductory course, one segment of which included rather extensive treatment (lectures and labs) of basic principles of learning. Two different supplementary texts had been used to cover the material on separate offerings of the course, one of which was highly readable, humorous, full of interesting pictures, and used examples primarily from human case studies. The other text, while much shorter, more carefully written, and actually containing more information, was also rather dull, unmotivating, and viewed as irrelevant (according to most students) because of the almost excessive use of examples from basic animal research. Exam performance on the material covered by the text and lectures was roughly the same for the two classes (favoring the latter slightly), but subsequent feedback from students revealed enormous attitudinal differences. One (of several) interesting example of these differences came on an item which asked students to express their feelings about behavior modification. Those using the former book tended to be very positive, emphasizing the humanistic nature of the research, whereas the latter book was judged by a majority of the students to be cold and manipulative. How one might make use of this kind of information raises an interesting issue, and yet it does make clear that a text can have important effects of which we may often be unaware. We need to take these effects into account, preferably in advance, but at least (and this may be the only alternative) after we have used the text in our course. Becoming aware of some negative effect of a text we

otherwise value may also permit us to change other aspects of a course in other to counteract the negative effect.

Suggestion #4: Know Your Students.  Most of us are probably willing to argue that instructional methods, including the text, should be geared to the aptitudes and interests of our students. However, the extensive research literature on so-called "attribute-treatment" interactions, while at times provocative, does not permit any simple generalizations on how to design a course (let alone choose a text) appropriate for a given group of students. There is some evidence that different types of students might benefit more or less from a particular instructional approach or teaching style (McKeachie, 1969, 1974), but it is unclear whether similar conclusions can be drawn about different texts. Nonetheless, it certainly makes good sense to give some thought, prior to choosing a text, to the kinds of students you will be teaching.

Having had the opportunity to teach the introductory course at a relatively selective liberal arts college and at a community college, I am reasonably confident in asserting that the same approach cannot be taken in both environments. Either the text or what goes on in the classroom must be different, and I suspect that a change in the text would be the most beneficial. The issue here is primarily one of student heterogeneity; the community college students representing a much greater challenge because of a broader range of talents, academic experience, vocabularies, and reading skills than among liberal arts students. Resolving this problem will depend in large measure on one's goals and educational philosophy; my own preference being (short of the opportunity to individualize the whole process) for a less difficult text and workbook for the community college students— along with the hope that classroom activities can maintain the interest of the brighter students. Alternative solutions readily come to mind but, in any event, it seems foolish not to consider student characteristics in planning a course. For unless we intend to approach our task independently of actual course outcomes, at the very minimum a knowledge of our students should provide hints for selecting a text and/or planning classroom activities which appear to increase the likelihood that our course objectives will be met. Most of the reviews I consulted provided a reasonably clear picture of the type of audience for which a particular text might be appropriate—at least in terms of text difficulty. However, it is probably the individual instructor's own experience with certain types of students that should be the deciding factor. Other than suggesting the obvious by encouraging a match between text difficulty and student preparedness, we are not in a position to offer much more. Student expectations may also be worthy of consideration but it is unclear as to how they might be used in choosing a text. Research is needed on this issue.

In Closing.  When one begins to generate a list of suggestions for improving the manner in which introductory texts are selected, it soon becomes clear that prescriptive statements cannot be altogether avoided. Any further suggestions on my part would be even more biased, apply only to some courses and instructors, and have less empirical support than the already speculative recommendations made here. There is, however, one additional item that deserves comment. I'm referring to the test item files made available by publishers. Those inclined or perhaps almost forced by large classes to make use of test files have a right to expect that performance on these items is a valid measure of student learning. It would be even more helpful to know if the items measure only factual information or include more complex learning outcomes as well. This concern is not merely one of making life easier for the instructor. Instead of being a neutral process as some of us appear to believe (not students, however), testing may have a significant impact on how and what students learn in a course (Milton & Edgerly, 1976). Regrettably, the kinds of information we need are not available, a point made abundantly clear by Colle, Vestewig and Baird (1977) in this issue of *ToP*. We are, therefore, left in almost total ignorance of a factor which might have an important bearing on achieving our course goals. This is one area where collective pressure on our part might force a modification of current practices in textbook publishing.

Any critical view of the process of text selection for the introductory course must be tempered by the obvious popularity of the course among college students. Things are not all that bad in spite of what at times appears to be a very haphazard process, no less so perhaps than in other disciplines, but nonetheless far from ideal. As psychologists, however, we might take the lead in setting high standards for the writing, evaluation, and adoption of all texts. Success on our part in better achieving instructional goals could play a significant role in the general upgrading of undergraduate instruction. It's at least worth a try.

### References

Colle, H. A., Vestewig, R. E., & Baird, R. R. Testing the test files: What do you ask of your publisher? *Teaching of Psychology,* 1977, *4,* 31-35.

Dubin, R., & Taveggia, T. C. *The teaching-learning paradox: A comparative analysis of college teaching methods.* Eugene: University of Oregon, 1968.

Emme, E. E. Content analysis of the nine most recent textbooks in general psychology. *Journal of Psychology,* 1941, *11,* 257-260.

Kulik, J. A., & Jaksa, P. PSI and other educational technologies in college teaching. *Educational Technology,* 1977, in press.

McConnell, J. V. *Understanding human behavior.* New York: Holt, Rinehart & Winston, 1974.

McKeachie, W. J. *Teaching tips: A guidebook for the beginning college teacher.* Lexington, MA: Heath, 1969.

McKeachie, W. J. Instructional psychology. *Annual Review of Psychology,* 1974, *25,* 161-193.

McKeachie, W. J. Textbooks: Problems of publishers and professors. *Teaching of Psychology,* 1976, *3,* 29-30.

Miller, L. K. *Principles of everyday behavior analysis.* Monterey, CA: Brooks/Cole, 1975.

Milton, O., & Edgerly, J. W. *The testing and grading of students.* New Rochelle, NY: Change Magazine, 1976.

Popplestone, J. A. 12 pre-paradigmatic variations on a theme. *Contemporary Psychology,* 1975, *20,* 711-717.

Quereshi, M. Y., & Sackett, P. R. An updated content analysis of introductory psychology textbooks. *Teaching of Psychology,* 1977, *4,* 25-30.

Rothkopf, E. Z. Some observations on predicting instructional effectiveness by simple inspection. *Journal of Programmed Instruction,* 1963, *2,* 19-20.

Rubinstein, J. Introductory potpourri. *Contemporary Psychology,* 1975, *20,* 302-308.

Taveggia, T. C. Personalized instruction: A summary of comparative research, 1967-1974. *American Journal of Physics,* 1976, *44,* 1028-1033.

### Notes

1. I would like to thank Donald R. Brown and James A. Kulik, Center for Research on Learning and Teaching, University of Michigan, for their helpful suggestions and comments on an earlier version of this paper.
2. James A. Kulik, personal communication.

# Textbook Evaluations By Students

Keith W. Jacobs
*Loyola University*

One problem that we all face on a regular basis is the selection of textbooks for use in our courses, along with the related questions of whether there should also be supplemental printed materials (study guides, readings books, and similar supplements) and how the courses should be organized. For a few courses there may be only one ideal textbook, but for the majority of courses the instructor must decide between a large number of possible texts, each of which has some strong points in its favor. It seems that this decision is one of the most important that must be made by the course instructor, not only because of its contribution to course content but because it serves to tell students about the course before the class ever meets.

For the past two years I have systematically involved the course or semester, is to ask those students completing a course to review textbooks that could have been used in the course. The general procedure has been to make examination copies of the possible textbooks available in some central location, such as a table in the departmental office or laboratory, and provide the students with a pre-printed evaluation form. The particular format that I have been following on this form lists the authors and titles of from six to twelve books and asks the students to describe the "strong points" and "weak points" of each book, assign each book a traditional letter grade, and then vote for the ones that they would like to see adopted (by listing up to three of these in order of preference). Of course, I pre-screen these books myself, and try to keep the number of books to some managable number, but when that number is relatively small I also include for comparison a few of the books that I would not seriously consider adopting. I also include the textbook that was used in the course, because I would like to see how they rate the other books in comparison with the one that they have just used.

In those courses where this activity has been planned as a part of the course, with time allotted during the semester for the activity, and it having been initially described in the course syllabus, I have found that about three-fourths of the students voluntarily complete the evaluations. When this activity was first attempted, and was introduced rather spontaneously toward the end of the semester, approximately half of the class participated. I have not made this a mandatory activity, or one which contributes to the course grade, but those practices could potentially produce 100% participation.

It has been my experience that the students will provide several descriptive phrases of both the strong points and weak points of each text. There does appear to be fairly strong agreement among students on the descriptors that they provide for each text, although I have not studied this statistically. Interestingly, they often comment on factors that I did not previously consider or did not expect them to consider important. For example, they may notice the absence of a glossary, confusing figure captions, the use of "ugly brown print," or a difficulty level inconsistent with the particular course. On the positive side, they have noted such factors as good chapter summaries, inclusion of definitions of new terms as they occur, and integration of practical examples into the text. The actual narrative comments seem to be different for different courses; the students seem to value different factors for textbooks in physiological psychology and developmental psychology, for example. These narrative comments provide valuable information about why the students grade each text the way they do, as well as suggesting aspects of the text that they consider important in each course. Some of the more detailed comments suggest that they sometimes give detailed reading to chapters that interest them.

I have used this practice repeatedly in my physiological psychology course, where there is usually a week remaining in the semester after the course material is completed but before the date of the final examination. When the same textbooks have been repeatedly evaluated by different students in different semesters, but for the same course, the narratives of strong and weak points have been very similar across semesters.

When I most recently asked my physiological psychology class to evaluate textbooks, I provided them with eleven texts and found that 26 of the 32 students in the course completed the evaluations (81% of the class). The average grades given each text ranged from a weak "C" (mean = 2.06, SD = .77) to a high "B" (mean = 3.69, SD = .37). The second highest grade, given to the text that I had used in the course, was also a "B" (mean = 3.13, SD = .69). Interestingly, those two texts each received the same number of "votes" for adoption as the text in the course.

It seems reasonable to expect that student populations at different schools would be different in their evaluations and would recommend different texts for the course. For this reason I resisted the temptation to cite the specific textbooks recommended by my students for that specific course. I am not convinced that the findings at one school should weigh heavily in the adoption of a text at a different school. However, I would be willing to provide other teachers of physiological psychology courses with summaries of the evaluations recently completed by my students.

This general concern for student input into course planning has also led me to administer questionnaires to my classes in an attempt to answer questions such as: Should there also be a readings book for the course? Should the course meet on a Tuesday/Thursday or a Monday/Wednesday/ Friday schedule? Should the number or size of outside projects be changed? When I have had only one or two such questions about a specific course I have been able to include those as optional questions in the standard course evaluation instrument. I have also sponsored several projects in which students actually plan and develop proposals for courses they would like to see added to our departmental curriculum. These projects also include a requirement that the students evaluate possible textbooks for use in the course.

My own experiences with having students in my courses provide evaluations of possible textbooks for the course (and other similar information) has been sufficiently encouraging that I will continue the practice. I also propose it as a practice that my colleagues might try as a way to gain student input into one of their important decisions. I believe that students completing a course are in a unique position to provide data that cannot be obtained from any other source. I also believe that the use of these practices contributes to student satisfaction by giving the student a feeling that they have some real control over their own education.

# 6. CONCEPTIONS OF STUDENTS IN INTRODUCTORY PSYCHOLOGY

## Misconceptions About Psychology Among Introductory Psychology Students

Eva D. Vaughan
*University of Pittsburgh*

Common misconceptions about behavior are distressingly resistant to change by text reading and class discussion.

Many students enter an introductory psychology course with considerable "knowledge" of psychology, gleaned from books, the popular media, and the proverbial grandmother's knee. Some of the knowledge is accurate. However, much of it is a collection of half-truths and untruths, supported by popular belief but refuted by psychological research (e.g., "Schizophrenics are people with split personalities," "Dull children often grow up to be bright adults.")

How prevalent are such misconceptions and to what extent are they dispelled by the introductory psychology course? The literature to date is not encouraging. Though McKeachie (1960) reported a significant gain from pre- to post-test on the Northwestern Misconceptions Test at six institutions, the actual mean gain was only 6.6 out of 100 points. Furthermore, few individual items, including those deemed most important by the course instructors, showed any significant gain at all.

One may question whether a misconceptions test is a good way to measure change in knowledge about psychology, or whether indeed a primary function of the introductory course should be to dispel misconceptions at all. Obviously, there is a great deal of important psychological information which is unrelated to most current popular beliefs. Nevertheless, many introductory textbooks mention a few popularly held misconceptions in the first chapter, at least implying that one purpose of the text is to dispel them. Instructors often administer some kind of misconceptions test early in the course, either their own or a published version (e.g., McInish & Coffman, 1970, pp. 110-114). Personally, I believe that *one* of the functions of an introductory psychology course is to dispel common misconceptions. Therefore, it seemed worthwhile to measure the nature and prevalence of common misconceptions among students beginning a course in introductory psychology.

**Developing a Test of Misconceptions.** The following guidelines were developed for assembling a set of misconceptions: (1) Only statements representing fairly common beliefs were to be included; statements about which most people have little or no information or opinion were excluded. (2) Statements were to represent a large number of topics within psychology, so that no one type of misconception would predominate.

For several weeks, I carried a small tablet with me constantly and jotted down misconceptions whenever they occurred to me. Colleagues were asked ("pestered" is a better word) for suggestions. I must have leafed through a record number of introductory psychology texts, searching for possible items. Some of the items in the Northwestern Misconceptions Test (McKeachie, 1960) were used, sometimes in slightly altered form, and some items were taken from the Misconceptions Test in McInish and Coffman (1970). An effort was made to include relatively recent misconceptions (e.g., " 'Behavior modification' refers to the use of aversive stimuli, like shock, to bring about changes in behavior") as well as the old cliches (e.g., "A high forehead is a sign of intelligence."). All the statements were phrased or rephrased as misconceptions, so that they were false as stated. I realized that this form might make them susceptible to response sets such as acquiescence, but the purpose was to state them so that they would sound plausible to people holding the given belief.

A preliminary set of 72 statements was administered to 57 students enrolled in introductory psychology in the University of Pittsburgh External Studies Program in Spring, 1975. A discussion of the items with the students and with colleagues resulted in the elimination of 13 which were either ambiguous or statements of opinion rather than fact. The remaining 59, plus 21 new ones, were combined and scrambled to form a new set of 80 items, which I called the Test of Common Beliefs (TCB). The number of items in the TCB representing each of ten broad topics is as follows: Definition and Scope of Psychology (10), Development (10), Learning and Memory (7), Thinking and Creativity (3), Intelligence (11), Sensation and Perception (6), Motivation and Emotion (11), Personality and Adjustment (8), Abnormal Behavior and Its Treatment (11), Social Behavior (3).

Method. In the Fall and Winter terms, 1975-76, the TCB was administered to 119 students enrolled in four introductory psychology classes through the General Studies Program of the University of Pittsburgh. Three of the classes met once a week and the remaining class met only three times during the term in a marathon, three-hour "workshop." Most General Studies students at the University of Pittsburgh are part-time, their major activity consisting of wage-earning or homemaking or both. They tend to be older (average age in the mid-thirties) than full-time college students, and many of them are not studying for a degree. Thus, they are somewhat more representative of the general adult public to which psychologists like to generalize than are the usual college

sophomores (or pigeons). The textbook used in all classes was by Charles Morris (1973). In addition, the class which met only three times used a Study Guide prepared by the instructor.[1]

The TCB was administered orally during the first meeting of each class. The students were instructed to listen to each statement carefully, to decide whether they agreed with it or not, and to mark "True" or "False" on a machine-scorable answer sheet. They were told not to worry if they seemed to be marking more items true than false or vice versa but to consider each item on its own merits. The test took twenty minutes to half an hour to administer.

Results. The TCB was scored by counting the number of misconceptions (statements marked "true") for each student. Scores ranged from 8 to 64 with a mean of 31.57, median of 30.94, and standard deviation of 9.28. The distribution was approximately symmetrical. A K-R 20 reliability coefficient of .84 indicated a reasonable degree of internal consistency.

The percentage of agreement for individual items ranged from 2 to 92%, with a mean of 39.5%. Table 1 lists the items marked "true" by at least half the students, as well as the

Table 1
Items Marked "True" by More Than Fifty Percent of the Students ($\underline{n}$ = 119)

| Item (topic) | % "True" Responses | Item (topic) | % "True" Responses |
|---|---|---|---|
| 20. To change people's behavior toward members of ethnic minority groups, we must first change their attitudes. (Social Behavior) | 92 | 4. Unlike man, the lower animals are motivated only by their bodily needs—hunger, thirst, sex, etc. (Motivation and Emotion) | 69 |
| 11. Memory can be likened to a storage chest in the brain into which we deposit material and from which we can withdraw it later if needed. Occasionally, something gets lost from the "chest," and then we say we have forgotten. (Learning and Memory) | 87 | 34. Psychiatrists are defined as medical people who use psychoanalysis. (Definition and Scope) | (59)* 67 |
| 10. Personality tests reveal your basic motives, including those you may not be aware of. (Personality and Adjustment) | 85 | 32. Children memorize much more easily than adults. (Learning and Memory) | (63)* 66 |
| 42. The basis of the baby's love for his mother is the fact that his mother fills his physiological needs for food, etc. (Motivation and Emotion) | 84 | 7. The ability of blind people to avoid obstacles is due to a special sense which develops in compensation for their absence of vision. (Sensation and Perception) | 65 |
| 79. By feeling people's faces, blind people can visualize how they look in their minds. (Sensation and Perception) | 83 | 22. Boys and girls exhibit no behavioral differences until environmental influences begin to produce such differences. (Developmental) | 61 |
| 9. The more highly motivated you are, the better you will do at solving a complex problem. (Thinking and Creativity) | 80 | 58. "The study of the mind" is the best brief definition of psychology today. (Definition and Scope) | 57 |
| 30. The best way to ensure that a desired behavior will persist after training is completed is to reward the behavior every single time it occurs throughout training (rather than intermittently). (Learning and Memory) | 77 | 78. Genius is closely akin to insanity. (Intelligence) | 53 |
| | | 5. The weight of evidence suggests that the major factor in forgetting is the decay of memory traces with time. (Learning and Memory) | 52 |
| 41. A schizophrenic is someone with a split personality. (Abnormal Behavior and its Treatment) | 77 | 64. The unstructured interview is the most valid method for assessing someone's personality. (Personality and Adjustment) | 52 |
| 25. Blind people have unusually sensitive organs of touch. (Sensation and Perception) | 76 | 66. Under hypnosis, people can perform feats of physical strength which they could never do otherwise. (Abnormal Behavior and Its Treatment) | 51 |
| 80. Fortunately for babies, human beings have a strong maternal instinct. (Motivation and Emotion) | 73 | 45. The more you memorize by rote (for example, poems) the better you will become at memorizing. (Learning and Memory) | 50 |
| 49. Biologists study the body; psychologists study the mind. (Definition and Scope) | 71 | 6. Children's IQ scores have very little relationship with how well they do in school. (Intelligence) | 50 |

*Data from McKeachie (1960) on the same item.

topics these items represent. Obviously, no particular psychological topic was more subject to misconception than any other. For those items identical with ones used by McKeachie in 1960, Table 1 also shows the percentage of agreement in his sample.

A principal components factor analysis was performed on the item intercorrelations. The 38 factors extracted accounted for less than half the total variance, indicating a high degree of specific variance and/or error for most the items. Only one factor (Factor I) contributed more than five percent of the total variance. Sixteen items had a loading ≥ .30 on Factor I. Of these, ten represented two topics: Intelligence, and Abnormal Behavior and Its Treatment. Three others seem related to the same topics. Therefore, Factor I might be regarded as a kind of "Individual Differences" factor. However, this interpretation must be regarded as tentative, because the three remaining items represent other topics, and since fourteen items about intelligence or abnormal behavior and its treatment loaded high on other factors. Factor II, in fact, seems to involve the prediction of school and adult success from childhood intelligence test scores. However, Factor II accounted for only 2.5% of the total variance. The remaining factors account for even less and seem inconsistently related to any particular topic. Therefore, no further discussion of the factor analysis seems warranted. It appears that students beginning introductory psychology are heterogeneous in the way they organize their "knowledge" about psychology, and there is no indication that they organize it along our traditional topical lines.

I had originally hoped to administer the TCB again at the end of the course to all the students. However, in three of the classes, the instructor used the TCB as a springboard for discussion immediately after the first administration—a use which I would ordinarily approve as sound instructional practice, but which made re-administration impossible (a nice illustration of how an effective instructional strategy can foul up a carefully planned experimental design). The TCB was re-administered in the one remaining class, but neither the TCB nor attendance being required, posttest scores were obtained for only 17 students. The course was offered again in the following term, so additional data were collected, yielding a total of 30 students for whom both pretest and posttest TCB scores were available. For this combined group, the mean posttest score of 29.17 was significantly lower than the pretest mean of 33.57, $t (29) = -3.97, p < .01$, suggesting some reduction in the number of misconceptions held. However, note that the percentage change is only 5.5% of the 80 items, not very different from the 6.6% reported by McKeachie in 1960. It appears that, in 1977 as in 1960, students leave the introductory course with almost the same number of misconceptions as they held when they entered.

An item-by-item analysis of change scores, limited to the items listed in Table 1, was undertaken. Reductions of 50% or more in frequency of "true" responses occurred on only three items (items 6, 9, and 30), with reductions of 25 to 49% on three more (items 41, 78, and 80). All but one of these (item 78) were explicitly discussed in the course reading materials. These particular misconceptions, then, seem to have been effectively dispelled in this group of students. However, 15 of the 23 items showed little change in either direction (24% or less), despite the fact that most of them

referred to material dealt with in the book. Items 4 and 45 were marked "true" more frequently on the posttest than on the pretest, with changes of 23% and 17%, respectively. There was no discernible relation between the amount or direction of change and the topic represented by that item.

Finally, I examined the relationship between the TCB and performance in the course. It makes sense to predict that students with high TCB scores will do worse, since they presumably have more misinformation to unlearn. Pretest TCB scores and summed scores on the course examinations were significantly correlated in one of the four classes, $r (25) = -.510, p < .01$, but not the other three, $r (27) = -.083, p > .10; r (39) = .172, p > .10.$[2] Why TCB performance predicted course grades in one class and not the others is not clear, but could reflect different instructors, different instructional methods, or other variables differentiating the classes.

**A Case Study in the Dynamics of Belief.** Item 42 (See Table 1) was one of the items explicitly refuted in the course reading materials yet accepted as true by most students both before and after the course. Let me relate an interesting experience with this item in another introductory psychology class not included in this study. On the first of three workshops, I originally scheduled the TCB to be administered first, to be followed by the film *Mother Love* (CBS, 1960), about Harlow's studies of infant monkeys reared with surrogate mothers. However, since the projectionist had to leave early, we viewed the film first. Now, if there is one message that *Mother Love* drives home, it is that the infant's love for his mother is based on contact comfort, not on physiological need fulfillment. Therefore, when the students took the TCB immediately after the film, they should all have declared item 42 "false." Right? Wrong! Of the 35 students, a whopping 23 (66%) chose "true"; their faith in the power of nursing unshaken.

Does this mean that the movie had no effect? To answer this question, I compared the responses to item 42 in another class which had not viewed the film, finding that, in that class, 34 of 37 students (92%) chose "true." The difference between the two classes was significant, $\chi^2 (1) = 4.85, p < .05$. Apparently, *Mother Love* induced some students to change their answers. But the fact remains that the majority did not. Perhaps they failed to see the relevance of the film to the item on the TCB. More likely, this belief is so deeply rooted in people's ideas about the basic causes of human behavior that a single film is unlikely to have much effect.

**Discussion.** Apparently, students enter the introductory psychology course with a wide variety of misconceptions. The number of misconceptions they hold seems to have little effect on their performance in the course. And, like McKeachie, I must conclude that the course has little influence on their erroneous beliefs. Some misconceptions are effectively dispelled, particularly if they refer to topics explicitly discussed in the reading materials. However, there is little evidence for a generally heightened skepticism, which might lead students to question statements about which they have received no additional information; for the most part, such statements are agreed with as readily at the end of the course as at the beginning. In fact, some misconceptions are maintained in the face of contrary evidence presented during the course.

I am afraid we must resign ourselves to the fact that a single psychology course is unlikely to affect beliefs deeply rooted in conceptions of human nature, beliefs which concern what it means to be human and the wellsprings of human behavior, beliefs closely tied to people's value systems. Contrary evidence will be either ignored or perceived as irrelevant to the central issue. The student who firmly believes that love is based on physiological need will not be convinced by Harlow's studies, done in the "artificial" environment of the laboratory and using non-human subjects. The student who truly believes that only humans can think may correctly answer a question about problem solving in chimps on an exam; but deep down inside, he *knows* that isn't really thinking. The student deeply committed to a belief in human maternal instincts will perceive non-loving mothers as at least aberrant and possibly even not quite human.

However, there are many misconceptions about psychology resulting not from some deep-seated view of human nature but simply from lack of information or from misinformation. I believe these can and should be identified, using instruments such as the TCB. Once identified, they can be refuted, through textbooks, lectures, and the popular media. The introductory psychology course, which reaches so many students, both majors and non-majors, seems an obvious place to begin.

## References

Columbia Broadcasting System Television Network. *Mother Love.* New York: Carousel Films, 1960. (Film)

McInish, J. R., & Coffman, B. *Evaluating the introductory psychology course: A test booklet designed to accompany Psychology* (2nd edition, by W. J. McKeachie & C. L. Doyle). Reading, MA: Addison-Wesley, 1970.

McKeachie, W. J. Changes in scores on the Northwestern Misconceptions Test in six elementary psychology courses. *Journal of Educational Psychology*, 1960, *51*, 240-244.

Morris, C. G. *Psychology: An introduction.* Englewood Cliffs, NJ: Prentice-Hall, 1973.

## Notes

1. Vaughan, E. Psychology 780: Introduction to psychology. Unpublished study guide, 1975. (Available from University External Studies Program, 3808 Forbes Avenue, University of Pittsburgh, Pittsburgh, PA, 15260).
2. In cases where two or more classes were taught by the same instructor and used the same syllabus and examinations, their scores were combined for the purpose of analysis. A few students in each class were omitted because examination scores were not available.
3. The factor analysis discussed in this paper was performed with the assistance of the University of Pittsburgh Computer Center.

---

# College Students' Common Beliefs About Psychology

P. A. Lamal
*University of North Carolina at Charlotte*

An extension of Vaughan's study verifies that student beliefs change very little, even those teachers believe they have corrected.

The introductory psychology course is considered to be important because it is the first formal exposure to psychology for all but a small percentage of students enrolled in the course. It will be the only formal exposure to psychology for many of them.

Students come to introductory psychology with notions about what psychology is and what psychologists do, as well as notions about various topics or areas of psychology. Many of these notions would be considered by many, if not all, psychologists to be erroneous. It can be argued, then, that a major objective of any introductory psychology course should be the dispelling of misconceptions about psychology. The little evidence available indicates, however, that there is a good deal of room for improvement in this sphere.

In 1960, McKeachie reported the results of the administration of the Northwestern Misconceptions Test (Holley & Buxton, 1950) in the introductory psychology classes at six schools. Although the pretest-posttest gains were statistically significant at all of the schools, the results provided little basis for self-satisfaction, because students at the end of these courses typically retained about 85% of their original misconceptions. In addition, it was found that on the eight items regarded as most important by the instructors, the pre-post gain was negligible (from 80.5% correct to 82.0% correct).

Vaughan (1977) compiled a Test of Common Beliefs by using misconceptions generated by herself and colleagues, as well as drawing upon introductory psychology texts, the Northwestern Misconceptions Test and the Misconceptions Test in McInish and Coffman (1970). Her Test of Common Beliefs (TCB) consisted of 80 items which were phrased so that they were all false as stated. The following ten topics or areas of psychology were represented in the TCB: Definition and Scope of Psychology, Development, Learning and Memory, Thinking and Creativity, Intelligence, Sensation and Perception, Motivation and Emotion, Personality and Adjustment, Abnormal Behavior and its Treatment, and Social Behavior.

The TCB was administered at the beginning and end of two introductory psychology courses with both pretest and posttest data being obtained for 30 students. Although there was a statistically significant reduction in the number of misconceptions held, the percentage change was only 5.5% of the 80 items, which was close to the small change reported by McKeachie (1960).

The present study is both similar to, and different from, both the McKeachie (1960) and Vaughan (1977) studies. It is similar to the former in that data were collected at a number of schools and instructors' ratings of each item of the instrument were also obtained. It differs from the McKeachie (1960) study in many of the items comprising the instrument, and in that the present study includes information about the structure of, and materials used in, the different introductory sections.

The present study is similar to the Vaughan (1977) study in terms of the instrument used. It differs in that Vaughan did not obtain instructors' ratings of the items, and that Vaughan obtained both pretest and posttest data in only two sections at one school, for a small number of subjects.

The purpose of the present study, then, was to extend the work of Vaughan (1977) by obtaining data from a number of introductory psychology classes at three schools. In addition, a comparison was made between the pretest and posttest performance of introductory psychology students and the performance of students enrolled in senior psychology courses at one of the schools.

**Method.** Four items were deleted from Vaughan's (1977) Test of Common Beliefs, the result being an instrument of 76 items. As with Vaughan's original TCB all of the items in this Shorter TCB (STCB) were phrased so that they were false as stated.

The STCB was administered in eight introductory psychology courses during the first week of classes at three schools, and was readministered during the last week of classes in seven of the introductory courses, and during the penultimate week of classes in the other course. The pretest and posttest data were collected by the author in all of the courses except one, where the posttest data were collected by the course instructor.

In addition, the STCB was administered by the author in four senior level psychology courses (three Senior Seminars and one History & Systems course) at one of the schools during the first two weeks of classes.

The experimenter told the students that they did not have to participate, but that their participation would be appreciated. One of the three schools was a state university (8500 students) located in an urban area. The psychology department included 19 full-time faculty; it did not offer an advanced degree. Both pre and post data were collected from 57 students enrolled in three sections of introductory psychology at this school. The sections, one of which was an evening class, were taught by different instructors. The data from senior psychology majors were also collected at this university. The second school was a four-year state college (4300 students) located in an adjacent state. The psychology department included eight full-time faculty and offered a master's degree in school psychology. Pre and post data were collected from 66 students enrolled in three sections of introductory psychology at this school. Two of the sections were taught by the same instructor; the third section was an evening class. The third school was a two-year community college (2400 students) located in a semirural/suburban setting. The psychology department included three full-time faculty. Pre and post data were collected from 39 students enrolled in two sections of introductory psychology which were taught by different instructors.

The instructors of all the introductory psychology courses from which data were obtained rated each of the items of the STCB in accordance with the following instructions and rating scale:

> Please write your name and that of your school on the appropriate lines on the answer sheet. Your students have been instructed to indicate whether or not they agree with each of the items on the accompanying instrument. According to the key, each of the statements on the instrument is false. Please rate each statement on the following scale:
> A. I disagree with the key; I do *not* think that the statement is false.
> B. I don't care how many students answer.
> C. I'd be mildly unhappy if my students missed this.
> D. I'd be quite unhappy if my students missed this.

The rating scale was from McKeachie (1960). These instructor ratings were obtained after the collection of the posttest data in the instructors' respective classes.

All of the introductory psychology courses followed a lecture discussion format. The greatest difference in the mechanics of the courses was in the number of examinations that students took. The range was from three exams (three courses) to twelve exams (one course). The course involving twelve exams also featured an undergraduate proctor who provided students with their exams, graded them, clarified the reading material, and kept track of students' course progress. Also in this course, students were allowed three exams on any of the twelve units. In another course, students making less than a "C+" on a test could take an alternate test to reach a maximum of "C+".

The following texts were used in the various classes; the number in parentheses after each title indicates the number of classes in which it was used: Bourne and Ekstrand (1976) plus the accompanying workbook (2), Hilgard, Atkinson, & Atkinson (1975) (2), Kagan and Havemann (1976) (1),

Krech, Crutchfield, Livson, & Krech (1976) (1), Zimbardo and Ruch (1976) (2). The Bourne and Ekstrand text was used by the two instructors at the two year college.

**Results.** The Kuder Richardson reliability values for the Shorter Test of Common Beliefs were .85 for the pretest and 83 for the posttest.

Only three of the 76 items were marked "True" by ten percent or less of the students when they first responded to the STCB. The three items, with the percentage of those answering "True" in parentheses, are: "A high forehead is a sign of intelligence" (6%); "If children are well protected from frustration, they will be better equipped to tolerate frustration as adults" (9%); "There is little that psychology can do for the normal person" (5%).

Twenty-two of the items were marked "True" by more than fifty percent of the students on the pretest. Table 1 presents the pretest and posttest results for these items, as well as the results of the pretest from Vaughan (1977). Also presented is the number of faculty rating each of the 22 items as "D" ("I'd be quite unhappy if my students missed this.").

Table 1
Items Marked "True" by More Than Fifty Percent
of the Students on Pre-Test (n = 156)

| Item | % "True" | Item | % "True" |
|---|---|---|---|
| 19. To change people's behavior toward members of ethnic minority groups, we must first change their attitudes. | 91[a] 89[b] 92[c] (2)[d] | 60. The unstructured interview is the most valid method for assessing someone's personality. | 63 64 52 (4) |
| 23. Blind people have unusually sensitive organs of touch. | 87 86 76 (1) | 42. The more you memorize by rote (for example, poems), the better you will become at memorizing. | 62 65 50 (1) |
| 10. Memory can be likened to a storage chest in the brain, into which we deposit material and from which we can withdraw it later if needed. Occasionally, something gets lost from the "chest," and then we say we have forgotten. | 82 89 87 (3) | 4. The weight of evidence suggests that the major factor in forgetting is the decay of memory traces with time. | 58 63 52 (2) |
| 75. By feeling people's faces, blind people can visualize how they look in their minds. | 78 77 83 (2) | 31. Psychiatrists are defined as medical people who use psychoanalysis. | 57 43 67 (1) |
| 39. The basis of the baby's love for his mother is the fact that his mother fills his physiological needs, for food, etc. | 77 82 84 (3) | 74. Genius is closely akin to insanity. | 56 51 53 (5) |
| 38. A schizophrenic is someone with a split personality. | 75 57 77 (6) | 45. The high correlation between cigarette smoking and lung cancer proves that smoking causes lung cancer. | 55 42 <50 (5) |
| 46. Biologists study the body; psychologists study the mind. | 72 75 71 (5) | 54. "The study of the mind" is the best brief definition of psychology today. | 54 50 57 (4) |
| 28. The best way to ensure that a desired behavior will persist after training is completed is to reward the behavior every single time it occurs throughout training (rather than intermittently). | 70 42 77 (7) | 21. Psychologists psychoanalyze people. | 54 35 <50 (5) |
| 29. Children memorize much more easily than adults. | 68 68 66 (1) | 50. Because of their training, psychologists are better than most people at "seeing into your mind" and telling what you are thinking and feeling. | 54 48 <50 (3) |
| 61. Psychotherapy has its greatest success in the treatment of psychotic patients who have lost contact with reality. | 67 60 <50 (6) | 3. Unlike man, the lower animals are motivated only by their bodily needs—hunger, thirst, sex, etc. | 53 71 69 (3) |
| 65. By giving a young baby lots of extra stimulation (like mobiles and musical toys), we can markedly increase his intelligence. | 65 74 <50 (2) | 9. Pencil-and-paper personality tests reveal your basic motives, including those you may not be aware of. | 51 48 <50 (3) |

[a]Pretest; [b]Posttest; [c]Vaughan's data (1977); [d]Number of faculty rating the item "D" (n = 7).

The pretest and posttest means and standard deviations of the STCB scores at each of the schools are presented in Table 2. There was a significant main effect for the variable of Pretest/Posttest, $F(1, 146) = 8.28$, $p<.004$, indicating overall statistically superior performance on the posttest.

### Table 2
### Pre and Post Means and Standard Deviations at Each School

| School | Pre | Post |
|---|---|---|
| 1 | M 43.80 | M 46.94* |
|   | SD 10.54 | SD 8.29 |
| 2 | M 43.01 | M 45.89* |
|   | SD 8.04 | SD 7.71 |
| 3 (two-year) | M 44.59 | M 42.58 |
|   | SD 8.98 | SD 7.98 |

*$p<.05$

There was also a significant School X Pretest/Posttest interaction, $F(2, 146) = 6.01$, $p<.003$. Scheffe tests yielded identical results for tests of the pretest-posttest difference at both of the four-year schools: $F(1, 46) = 8.82$, $p<.05$. The pretest-posttest difference at the two-year school was not significant. A comparison was also made of the STCB scores of senior psychology majors at the larger of the four-year schools with the pretest and posttest scores of the sample of introductory psychology students at that school. Data were obtained from 44 senior psychology majors in four classes. Since there was a significant effect, $F(2, 151) = 18.39$, $p<.0001$, Scheffe tests were also conducted. The seniors' scores ($M = 55.31$, $SD = 6.56$) were significantly higher, $F(1, 51) = 35.65$, $p<.01$, than the introductory students' pretest scores ($M = 43.80$, SD = 10.54). They were also significantly higher, $F(1, 151) = 17.75$, $p<.01$, than the introductory students' posttest scores ($M = 46.94$, SD = 8.29).

Discussion. The results of the present study were in agreement with those reported by McKeachie (1960) and Vaughan (1977) to the extent that they indicated that an introductory course in psychology seems to have little effect, in a practical sense, on some common beliefs about psychology which are widely held by students. Although two of the pretest-posttest changes were statistically significant, they were changes of only three points on a 76-point instrument. Many of the beliefs which were widely held by students in the present study were also reported to be widely held by Vaughan's (1977) students. An examination of Table 1 reveals that the majority of these beliefs are resistant to change in the "right" direction. Indeed, on the posttest there was an increase for eight of the items in the percent of students marking them as "True." However, the differences between the pretest and posttest scores of the introductory psychology students and the scores of the senior psychology majors could certainly be claimed to be practically as well as statistically significant.

It is noteworthy that 6 of the 8 items for which increased belief was evidenced, were rated "D" by three or fewer of the instructors (n = 7). The one item (#28) which was

marked "True" by more than fifty percent of the students (70%), and which was also rated "D" by all of the instructors, dropped to a 42% belief level on the posttest.

These findings are related to the fact that only two of the 76 items were rated "D" by all of the instructors. The item so rated other than #28 was #47: "'Behavior modification' refers to the use of painful stimuli, like shock, to bring about changes in behavior." This lack of consensus among instructors regarding the importance of various beliefs was also noted by McKeachie (1960), who reported that only one item out of a 100-item instrument was rated "D" by all eleven instructors in his sample. There was, however, consensus among the instructors about the "truth" of the items. Only two of the items were rated "A" ("I disagree with the key; I do *not* think that the statement is false.") by two instructors; seven were so rated by one instructor. None of the remaining 67 items was rated "A" by any of the seven instructors.

The lack of consensus among psychology faculty about what is important for students to know is not surprising if one agrees with the view that psychology is "preparadigmatic" in the sense in which Kuhn (1962) used the term "paradigm." Thus there is no consensus among psychologists concerning the definition of psychology, or about what questions and problems are most important for the field. What in effect this means is that there is no single discipline of psychology, instead there are "psychologies." Add to this the fact that students in introductory psychology courses already have relatively long histories of exposure to widely held beliefs about psychology via the mass media, parents, and peers and it is not surprising that a one-term course results in little change in such beliefs.

### References

Bourne, L. E., & Ekstrand, B. R. *Psychology: Its principles and meanings* (2nd ed.). New York: Holt, Rinehart, & Winston, 1976.

Hilgard, E. R., Atkinson, R. C., & Atkinson, R. L. *Introduction to psychology* (6th ed.). New York: Harcourt, Brace, Jovanovich, 1975.

Holley, J., & Buxton, C. A factorial study of beliefs. *Educational and Psychological Measurement*, 1950, *10*, 400-410.

Kagan, J., & Havemann, E. *Psychology: An introduction* (3rd ed.). New York: Harcourt, Brace, Jovanovich, 1976.

Krech, D., Crutchfield, R. S., Livson, N., & Krech, H. *Psychology: A basic course*. New York: Knopf, 1976.

Kuhn, T. S. *The structure of scientific revolutions*. Chicago: University of Chicago Press, 1962.

McInish, J. R., & Coffman, B. Evaluating the introductory psychology course: A test booklet designed to accompany *Psychology*, (2nd edition, by W. J. McKeachie & C. L. Doyle). Reading, MA: Addison-Wesley, 1970.

McKeachie, W. J. Changes in scores on the Northwestern Misconceptions Test in six elementary psychology courses. *Journal of Educational Psychology*, 1960, *51*, 240-244.

Vaughan, E. D. Misconceptions about psychology among introductory psychology students. *Teaching of Psychology*, 1977, *4*, 138-141.

Zimbardo, P. G., & Ruch, F. L. *Psychology and life, Brief 9th Ed.* Glenview, Ill.: Scott, Foresman, 1976.

### Note

1. The author thanks the instructors who allowed him to collect data in their classes, and Paula Goolkasian for assistance in the data analysis.

# Misconceptions of Psychology and Performance In the Introductory Course

Arthur Gutman
*Georgia State University*

Again misbeliefs are found to change little by course exposure, but there is an intriguing relationship with student performance.

Periodic reports across a 25-30 year interval suggest that students enter the introductory psychology course with far too many misbeliefs (Holley & Buxton, 1950; McKeachie, 1960; Vaughan, 1977). Moreover, it appears that the course is only minimally effective in dispelling misbeliefs. For example, despite differences in such factors as institution(s) sampled, year of administration, composition and structure of test items, and format of test administration, both McKeachie (1960) and Vaughan (1977) found only a 5-6.5% reduction in misbeliefs as a function of the introductory course.

In addition to the pretest-posttest manipulation, Vaughan also related pretest misbelief score with course performance (i.e., exam average), but with mixed results. Specifically, a significant correlation between these two factors was obtained in only one of four class sections. Vaughan's conclusion was (a) that pre-course misbeliefs have little effect on course performance; and (b) that the course has little effect on misbeliefs.

The purpose of the present study was to examine further the relationship between misbelief and performance. The decision to do so was based on pilot data collected using Vaughan's "Test of Common Beliefs" (TCB). I had acquired the TCB from Vaughan a week or so prior to the Winter Quarter of the 1977-78 academic year and decided to use it as a didactic tool. Thus I administered it much like she did, but, since this was not a study, I immediately began a lecture on the topic of misbelief. In other words, any posttest data in this situation would have been seriously confounded. Interestingly, after the course, while computing grades, I found a fairly strong relationship between the TCB and course performance, particularly as a predictor of A/B vs. D/F grades (it did not do well in differentiating the C grade from either B or D grades).

These pilot results suggested that Vaughan's first conclusion (i.e., that pre-course misbeliefs and course performance are not related) is questionable. Moreover, if so, it makes sense to question the generality of her second conclusion (i.e., that the course has little effect on misbeliefs). A relationship between misbelief and performance, if it exists, suggests that pretest-posttest differences should vary with level of performance. Thus the A student should change more erroneous beliefs than the F student. However, neither McKeachie nor Vaughan tested for this possibility. In short, it is conceivable that the 5-6.5% decrease in misbeliefs as a function of the introductory course seriously underestimates the effect of the course on good students, and seriously overestimates its effect on poor students. The present study was designed to investigate this possibility.

Method. The subjects were 311 of 411 students enrolled in nine sections of introductory psychology at Georgia State University during the Spring Quarter of the 1977-78 academic year. Of the 100 students who did not participate, 41 dropped the course, 22 received incompletes, and 37 refused to take the posttest. Unfortunately, many of the students who did not take the posttest were in the D/F grade range, thus diluting this category.

Four sections (N=171) were taught by faculty and five sections (N=130) by graduate assistants (GA's). Each section used the text *Psychology: Understanding Behavior*, by Baron, Byrne, and Kantowitz (1st Ed.). Despite variations in number of exams per section, all instructors pulled approximately 80% of their exam items from a common test bank and each used the same grading scale (i.e., A=>90%, B=80-90%, C=70-79%, D=60-69%, F=<60%).

The TCB served as the pre and post-course measure of misbelief. It is an 80 item true/false test wherein each item is false as stated. It was devised by Vaughan and used in the present study in unadulterated form. However, unlike Vaughan, who administered the TCB orally, I used the more standard paper-and-pencil format. The reason for doing so was quite simple. According to some of my students, I was incapable of keeping the same facial expression across all items during pilot testing.

The pretest was administered at the first scheduled class meeting before any lecture was given. Students were told that the TCB is only a measure of belief and that it had no bearing on course grade. They were also told to "scribble" their names on the answer sheet for clerical purposes (e.g., subject-pool credit). All questions regarding items on the TCB were deferred until "later." The posttest was administered after the final exam, an unfortunate decision since several students in the F-range either failed to take the final or simply walked out without taking the TCB.

To control for a possible pretest x treatment interaction (McKeachie, 1960), some sections received both pre and post-course TCB measurement, whereas others received only post-course measurement. Also, this control was instituted separately among faculty and GA sections. Originally,

85

our departmental schedule called for five faculty and four GA sections. Thus, the design called for 3 vs. 2 faculty sections and 2 vs. 2 GA sections in the *pre-post* and *post only* conditions. However, there were two unfortunate developments, both involving faculty sections in the *pre-post* condition. First, one of these sections was reassigned to a GA *after* the first day of classes. Secondly, because of a breakdown in communications, one of my colleagues on the faculty could not find, and hence, could not administer, the posttest. Consequently, there were four faculty sections, one *pre only,* two *post only,* and one *pre-post,* and five GA sections, two *post only* and three *pre-post.*

**Results.** The TCB was computer-scored by counting the number of correct (i.e., false) items. Of the 311 participants, 28 took the TCB *pre-only,* 153 *post-only,* and 130 *pre-post.* Comparison of posttest scores for subjects in the *pre-post* ($M=50.1$) and *post-only* ($M=51.0$) conditions revealed no differences ($t<1.0$). In other words, as in McKeachie's study, there was no pretest x treatment interaction.

Using the entire sample, the mean pretest and posttest scores were 45.5 and 50.5, respectively, for a net difference of 5.0 items, or 6.3%. For those in the *pre-post* condition, these means were 45.3 and 50.0, for a net gain of 4.7 items, or 5.9%. This gain was statistically reliable ($t(129)=56.6$, $p<.01$). Moreover, these figures virtually duplicated Vaughan's, which were 46.4 and 50.8, respectively, for a net gain of 4.4 items, or 5.5%.

The relationships between TCB and grade were examined using Pearson-r correlation coefficients and one-way ANOVAs. Preliminary analyses revealed no difference between *D* and *F* grades in any single comparison. Consequently, these two categories were pooled. For statistical purposes, letter grades were assigned numerical values (i.e., $A=4, B=3, C=2, D=1, F=0$). In the case of the pooled *D/F* category, the value assigned to each subject was between zero and one, depending upon the proportion of D's to F's in a given sub-sample.

The correlation between pretest and grade was positive and statistically reliable for the entire sample ($r(156)=.345$; $p<.01$), as it was for both faculty ($r(77)=.365$, $p<.01$) and GA's ($r(77)=.338$). Comparison of faculty vs. GA relationships revealed no reliable differences. Thus, these data were pooled and a one-way ANOVA on pretest x grade was computed. Table 1A depicts the breakdown by grade of mean pretest score. The ANOVA resulted in a significant main effect ($F3.154=7.55$; $p<.01$), and subsequent comparisons made via Tukey-HSD tests revealed reliable differences in pretest scores between *A vs. B* and *B vs. C* grades ($t(44)=3.91$ and $2.84$; $p<.01$), but not between *C vs. D/F* grades.

The correlation between posttest and grade was positive and reliable for the entire sample ($r(281)=.410$, $p<.01$) and larger for faculty ($r(151)=.471$, $p<.01$) than GA's ($r(128)=.428$, $p<.01$). Table 1B depicts breakdowns by grade of mean posttest scores for both faculty and GA's. Interestingly, for faculty, there were reliable differences in posttest scores between *A vs. B* and *C vs. D/F* grades ($t(43)=5.68$ and $3.68$, $p<.01$), but not between *B vs. C* grades. For GA's, the only reliable difference between successive grades was between *A vs. B* ($t(37)=6.23$, $p<.01$).

Table 1
Scores, Difference Scores, and Vincentized Percent Difference Scores by Group and Grades

| Group | Student Letter Grades | | | |
| | A | B | C | D-F |
| --- | --- | --- | --- | --- |
| | A. Pretest Scores | | | |
| Pooled Sample | 51.6(31)[a] | 46.5(55) | 42.8(49) | 40.8(23) |
| | B. Post Test Scores | | | |
| Faculty Taught | 62.0(28) | 53.2(47) | 50.5(42) | 44.8(36) |
| GA Taught | 56.6(35) | 47.2(48) | 44.9(36) | 42.6(11) |
| | C. Pre-Post Difference Scores | | | |
| Faculty Taught | 10.7(13) | 7.6(25) | 6.6(15) | −1.2(9) |
| GA Taught | 6.6(11) | 2.9(23) | 1.7(26) | 1.1(8) |
| | D. Mean Vincentized % for Diff. Scores | | | |
| Faculty Taught | 39.6(13) | 22.2(25) | 17.2(15) | −1.6(9) |
| GA Taught | 21.8(11) | 9.1(23) | 5.4(26) | −1.3(8) |

[a]The N is shown in parentheses.

To examine these relationships further, pretest-posttest differences in TCB score were computed for each subject in the *pre-post* condition, and breakdowns of this measure by grade are depicted for faculty and GA's in Table 1C. For convenience of exposition, I will call this measure *DIF.*

Table 1C reveals two general findings. First, the mean absolute gain, or *DIF* score was greater for higher grades; and secondly, the gain in the *A-C* grade range was greater for faculty than for GA's. For faculty, there was no reliable difference in *DIF* score between any two successive grades in the *A-C* range. However, *DIF* score was greater for *A vs. C* grades ($t(17)=1.81$, $p<.05$) as well as *A, B,* and *C vs. D/F* grades (e.g., for *C vs. D/F: t(17)=3.44$, $p<.01$). For GA's, *DIF* score was greater for *A vs. B* grades ($t(19)=2.36$, $p<.01$), but did not differ among *B, C,* and *D/F* grades.

One interesting aspect of these comparisons is that absolute differences in pretest vs. posttest TCB score is biased against the higher grades. This follows because of the positive relationship between pretest score and grade—relative to the upper limit (i.e., all 80 correct), the student with a higher grade has less room for improvement. To ameliorate this difficulty, individual *DIF* scores were Vincentized by dividing them by the number of incorrect items (i.e., posttest-pretest/# of incorrect on pretest). In cases where students scored lower on posttests than pretests, the *DIF* score was divided by the pretest score (i.e., posttest-pretest/# correct on pretest). For convenience of exposition, I will call this measure *R-DIF* (i.e., to denote relative difference). Breakdowns by grade of *R-DIF* percentages are depicted for faculty and GA's in Table 1D.

Table 1D reveals differences comparable to those observed in Table 1C. That is, *R-DIF* score increased with grade, and the increases in the *A-C* grade range were greater for faculty than for GA's. Indeed, *R-DIF* percentage for *A* grades was nearly twice as large for faculty, and the percentage for faculty *C* grades approached the percentage for GA *A* grades. The only comparable level for faculty and GA's was in the *D/F* grade range. In terms of statistical comparisons, for faculty *A vs. B, A vs. C,* and *C vs. D/F* differences were reliable ($t(17)=2.76$, $3.56$, and $2.98$, $p<.01$), but the *B vs. C* difference was not. For GA's, the *A vs. B* ($t(19)=3.54$, $p<.01$) and *C vs. D/F* ($t(19)=1.87$, $p<.05$) differences were reliable, but the *B vs. C* difference was not.

Discussion. The present findings are consistent with McKeachie's (1960) and Vaughan's (1977) in showing a mean loss of 5-7% of misbeliefs as a function of the introductory course. When looked at in this fashion, the course has a reliable but minuscule effect on misbeliefs. However, the present findings also show that A/B students start out with fewer misbeliefs than D/F students, and that A/B students tend to change many of these misbeliefs, whereas D/F students do not. Thus, by considering only the group average in pretest-posttest difference scores, one underestimates the effect of the course on achievers and overestimates its effect on nonachievers.

Now it may be argued that the correlations and pretest-posttest gains were still not nearly as large as they could be. However, such an argument, even if true, does not bear as directly on the nature of the course as it does on the variability of the measurements taken. For example, for the present sample as a whole, the correlation between pretest and grade, though reliable, was small ($r(128) = .345$). However, if we compare this to the more standard predictors, this particular value is rather good. Thus, in our present sample, the correlations between verbal and math SAT and grade were $r(241) = .3177$ and $r(241) = .3188$, respectively. Moreover, with institutional data I have collected previously, the best predictor of grade has been grade-point average (GPA). In the present study, the correlation between GPA and grade was $r(256) = .5707$. Interestingly, the correlations between verbal and math SAT and GPA were $r(210) = .3728$ and $r(210) = .2775$, respectively, whereas the correlation between pretest and GPA was $r(128) = .3882$. It should be noted that in prior quarters, I have typically found stronger relationships between verbal and grade than math and grade. Also, the correlation between GPA and grade obtained for this sample is the lowest I have yet seen. However, this does not detract from the main point, which is, that the pretest score on the TCB is very comparable to the SAT scores in its ability to predict achievement in our introductory course.

Regarding Vaughan's data, she found a reliable relationship between pretest and course average in only one of four classes. At face value, this would seem to be inconsistent with much of what was implied above. However, her sample size per class was small, and as she indicated, variability across the four sections "could reflect different instructors, different instructional methods, or other variables differentiating the classes" (p. 140). In other words, it is not clear what the relationship would have been had Vaughan pooled her data, whether the dependent measure (course average) represented a common measure for the four sections, and/or if the instructor variable had an effect as it did in the present study.

Conclusions. The main findings in the present study suggest that misbelief can predict course performance and that the course has a differential effect on misbeliefs of achievers vs. nonachievers. This raises the question why do nonachievers fail to achieve? Although it is fair to say that traditional academic factors are important, we must also look past the traditional remedial procedures in counseling our poorer students. These procedures are important, of course. However, in addition, the present data suggest that attitudes also affect performance. In this regard, Vaughan notes that a student may change a belief on a posttest, but that this may reflect merely learning of a response desired by the instructor. Thus, the pretest-posttest difference is only a beginning. It is also important to determine the ontogeny of these beliefs (e.g., mass media?), and what differences other than the traditional academic ones predispose students to change or fail to change their misbeliefs (e.g., cognitive styles?).

Finally, it should be noted that such research is not futile. Vaughan's study, to my knowledge, was the first of its kind in 17 years. In it, she took psychology instructors to task for not realizing how important misbeliefs are. She pointed out how most introductory textbooks mention misbeliefs. Interestingly, at least one major text, presently in revision, has responded by listing in tabular form those misbeliefs which Vaughan found most difficult to alter. Clearly, then, such research is not futile. If the textbook writers are paying attention, it is probable that this will ultimately filter down to the classroom, thus fulfilling the mission of this journal.

### References

Baron, R. A., Byrne, D., & Kantowitz, B. H. *Psychology: Understanding Behavior,* Philadelphia: Saunders, 1977.

Holley, J., & Buxton, C. A. Factorial study of beliefs. *Educational and Psychological Measurement,* 1950, *10,* 400-410.

McKeachie, W. J. Changes in score on the Northwestern Misconceptions Test in six elementary psychology courses. *Journal of Educational Psychology,* 1960, *51,* 240-244.

Vaughan, E. Misconceptions about psychology among introductory psychology students. *Teaching of Psychology,* 1977, *4,* 138-141.

### Note

1. I would like to thank Eva Vaughan for supplying a copy of the TCB, and Gwen Bate, Rex Karger, May Kennedy, Linda Makahon, Jim Pate, Celine Payne, and Gerald Weeks for their help in administering it.

# Some More Misconceptions About Psychology Among Introductory Psychology Students

Larry T. Brown
*Oklahoma State University*

The author uses a unique investigative approach to show that students do not have as much misconception as supposed.

As all teachers of psychology know, introductory students don't enter the classroom with blank slates. They enter with a knowledge of psychology resulting from at least 18 years of observing humans and other animals behave. And what they haven't observed, they've read, seen on TV, or been told by others. The teacher obviously can't start from scratch; he or she must build upon an already existent foundation of lay psychology. Often the foundation is helpful, as when it provides examples of psychological phenomena. But because it sometimes contains beliefs that are at odds with the data of more systematic observation, it can also be a stumbling block. When this is the case, the teacher of psychology must rebuild.

Rebuilding the student's knowledge of psychology is no easy chore. For one thing, many of the student's misconceptions are resistant to change (e.g., McKeachie, 1960; Vaughan, 1977). Stemming as they do from a folklore that embodies and summarizes the efforts of countless generations to explain and predict behavior, this shouldn't really be surprising (Vaughan, 1977). Cultural tradition is hard to budge.

A second problem facing the rebuilder is knowing what the misconceptions of lay psychology are. Vaughan (1977) presented 80 possible misconceptions to introductory psychology students and found that 23 of the items were endorsed by 50% or more of the students. The 80 items were either constructed by Vaughan and her colleagues or borrowed from the work of others, including McKeachie (1960). Lamal (1979) gave 76 of Vaughan's items to introductory psychology students and senior psychology majors at three colleges and found that 22 of the items were endorsed by more than 50% of the students. Of the 22, 16 were the same as those endorsed by Vaughan's students, 6 were unique to Lamal's subjects. Using the 50%-belief criterion for labeling an item a misconception, Vaughan and Lamal together identified 29 (23 + 6) misconceptions. This is not a large number, especially given the scope of Vaughan's efforts to identify candidates. The difficulty in uncovering misconceptions was recently underscored by Panek (1982), who found that, out of 10 suspected misconceptions about the psychology of aging, only 2 were believed by the majority of his introductory psychology students.

The purpose of the present study was to uncover more of the misconceptions that characterize lay psychology, at least the lay psychology of the introductory psychology student. Lengthening the list of misconceptions should be of value to teachers of psychology, and would provide a larger pool for researchers interested in the correlates and other aspects of misconception belief (e.g., Gardner & Hund, 1983; Gutman, 1979).

**Method.** The search for more misconceptions took two directions. First, an effort was made to collect a set of false statements about psychological phenomena. Four criteria were used in selecting the statements: (a) knowledge of the falsity of the statement could not depend on knowledge of specialized vocabulary; (b) the statement could not overlap with any of the misconceptions identified by Vaughan or Lamal; (c) the statement had to be refutable by data, not inference or suspicion; and (d) the data refuting the statement had to be based on more than just a single study. Some of the statements were taken from lists of possible misconceptions compiled by Gardner (1980) and Kimble, Garmezy, and Zigler (1980). Others were written by myself, usually in consultation with colleagues. Yet others were taken from discussions of possible misconceptions in various articles and textbooks (e.g., Birren, Kinney, Schaie, & Woodruff, 1981; Loftus, 1980; McKenzie, 1980; Peplau & Perlman, 1982; Wagstaff, 1981).

Thirty-seven statements meeting the selection criteria were identified. Eighteen of the statements were reworded to make them true; the remaining ones retained their original wording and, hence, were false. Selection of statements to be true or false was determined by the flip of a coin. Twenty-one of the statements were typed and distributed as a "True/False Test of Psychology" to a section ($n = 79$) of the introductory course at Oklahoma State University. The "test" was given during the first week of classes. The remaining 16 items were similarly presented to another section ($n = 140$) of the same course the following semester.

The second approach in the search for misconceptions involved examining the distributions of responses to multiple-choice items used in regularly scheduled class quizzes and exams. Items were selected that met four criteria: (a) the item had to be missed by at least 50% of the class, (b) the item had to be a nonvocabulary item, (c) the item could not overlap with any of Vaughan or Lamal's 29 misconceptions, and (d) the item had to address the findings of more than one study.

The choice of the first criterion represented something of a compromise. Because endorsement by 50% or more of the class was used to declare the wrong answer a misconception in a true/false item (see below), consistency would seem to require that endorsement by 25% or more of the class be used to declare a wrong answer a misconception in a four-alternative multiple-choice item. The 25% criterion by itself, however, is probably overly lenient. For example, if for a given item 60% of the class chose the correct alternative "a," and 25%, 10%, and 5% chose the incorrect alternatives "b," "c," and "d," respectively, the use of the 25% criterion would result in labeling "b," one of the incorrect alternatives, a misconception. Yet this despite the fact that the majority of the class got the item right. This would seem to be an inappropriate use of the term "misconception." At the same time, the use of a 50% criterion for individual incorrect alternatives in a four-alternative item would appear overly stringent. Consequently, the decision was made to select items that were missed by at least 50% of the students, and then to label as a misconception any incorrect alternative receiving 25% or more of the choices.

The response distributions were for multiple-choice items used in the introductory psychology course at three Midwestern and Southwestern state universities.[5] Data were obtained for 28 classes (the numbers of classes for the three universities were 7, 1, and 20) taught during the 1980-81 and 1981-82 academic years. The classes ranged in size from about 30 to over 350 students. The total number of multiple-choice items for which data were available was 2885 (the separate totals for the universities were 979, 106, and 1800), and the total number of students for whom data were obtained was 1818 (the separate *n*'s were 680, 356, and 782). The tests themselves ranged from short quizzes to final exams.

In all cases the items covered material that had been presented in class and/or discussed in the assigned reading. Some of the items were constructed by the class instructors, but the majority were taken from the test-item files accompanying the course texts. Several textbooks were used for the various classes, but the majority of the students were assigned either *Psychology* (Lefrancois, 1980) or *Introduction to Psychology* (Brown & Weiner, 1979).

**Results.** Of the 37 true/false items, 19 were missed by at least 50% of the students. These are presented in the list below. Each item is indicated as true (T) or false (F), followed by the total number of students and the percent who expressed belief.

1. Everything we learn is permanently stored in the mind, although sometimes particular details are not accessible. With hypnosis, or other special techniques, these inaccessible details could eventually be recovered.[1] (F), 79, 87%
2. Claustrophobia can be used to explain the morbid fear many people have of being suffocated in confined places. (F), 79, 86%
3. People who are weak in some academic subjects are usually good in others. (F), 140, 84%
4. Behaviors and characteristics which are presumed to reflect an ideal standard of mental health for the mature adult are meant primarily for men, less so for women. (T), 79, 82%
5. Males and females show equal attention to auditory information; both sexes also show an equal interest in visual stimuli. (T), 140, 77%
6. Girls and boys tend to be about equal in achievement motivation. (T), 140, 77%
7. Psychologists and psychiatrists have dissimilar educational backgrounds. (T), 79, 76%
8. The human being has five senses (vision, hearing, taste, smell, and touch). (F), 140, 76%
9. Depressed people are more objective about their lives than non-depressed people. (T), 140, 69%
10. Women are more likely than men to say they are lonely. (F), 140, 68%

11. We can learn while we are asleep although it is not a very efficient technique. (F), 79, 68%
12. Greater social activity is an ineffective solution to loneliness. (T), 140, 67%
13. Peptic ulcers tend to occur in people who are basically nonaggressive. (T), 140, 66%
14. Hypnosis is usually ineffective in stopping smoking. (T), 79, 65%
15. The "only" child is no more spoiled, selfish, or likely to suffer later emotional problems than the child from a two-child or larger family. (T), 79, 63%
16. Homosexual males are more effeminate than heterosexual males. (F), 140, 60%
17. Subliminal perception—the influencing of behavior by presenting the stimulus so rapidly that it cannot be consciously perceived—can be used to control our behavior. (F), 79, 59%
18. A psychosis is an extreme form of neurosis. (F), 79, 56%
19. Older people are just as afraid of dying as younger people. (T), 140, 53%

From the 2885 multiple-choice items examined only 40 met the four selection criteria. Whereas the majority of the items failed on the first criterion (missed by 50% of the students), most of the rest were rejected on the second criterion (the item had to be a nonvocabulary item). Eight of the 40 items meeting the criteria were dropped for being inaccurate or too closely related to one of the other items. The remaining 32 items were converted to single-sentence statements. In some cases the statement was simply the alternative favored by the most students; in most other cases the wording of the stem of the question was combined with the wording of the favored alternative. In one case (item #32 below) all of the alternatives were correct, and the correct answer was "All of the above." "All of the above" was rejected by the majority of students, however, and two of the three other alternatives were favored. The alternative that was shunned was chosen by less than 6% of the class. On the assumption that the shunned alternative probably touched upon a misconception, the alternative was worded to be false and used as the statement. The 32 statements are given in the list below, with the number of students and the percent who expressed belief.

1. The coefficient of correlation is a measure that proves cause and effect relationships between two variables. 93, 78%
2. Loss of consciousness is a scientifically useful definition of sleep. 75, 71%
3. Catharsis has been shown to be an effective method in reducing subsequent acts of aggression. 66, 66%
4. When a person is in a deep hypnotic state, heart rate and blood pressure decrease as during a sleeping state. 356, 62%
5. Research has shown that in general some form of therapy is no more effective than no therapy at all. 239, 60%
6. The farther you are from an object, the smaller it will appear subjectively. 54, 59%
7. Most studies of sex differences support the commonly held belief that girls are more dependent and affiliative than boys. 224, 55%[2]
8. Masters and Johnson's sex therapy concentrates almost entirely on changing how couples respond to one another physically. 254, 54%[2]
9. Each receptor in the skin is specialized for one of four sensations: warmth, cold, pain, or pressure. 80, 51%
10. Depression is a Freudian defense mechanism. 81, 51%
11. The nose is the primary olfactory organ.[3] 88, 48%
12. Children with high achievement motivation tend to be high risk takers. 408, 47%[2]
13. Puberty precedes the adolescent growth spurt. 90, 47%[2]
14. Science has verified the belief held by many theorists that birth is a highly traumatic experience. 187, 46%
15. Freudian defense mechanisms are conscious attempts to reduce anxiety. 286, 46%

16. In terms of important values, children are most like their parents in early childhood and more like their friends in adolescence. 80, 43%
17. Electroconvulsive therapy and insight therapy are widely used in the treatment of schizophrenia. 167, 43%
18. Extremely high levels of arousal typically lead to moderately or extremely effective levels of performance. 226, 42%
19. About 15 to 25% of the elderly live in nursing homes and similar institutions. 189, 42%
20. If projective tests are better than objective tests in getting at "hidden" motives it is because of the informal setting of the projective test. 66, 39%
21. Associations between responses and the consequences they produce come about through classical conditioning. 507, 39%
22. The Russian physiologist, Ivan Pavlov, discovered classical conditioning. 192, 39%
23. The psychoanalytic model is the one that would hold that intense fear of partridges is abnormal.[4] 284, 39%
24. Opium is a hallucinogen. 454, 37%
25. LSD is a physiologically addictive hallucinogenic. 462, 37%
26. An optimistic understanding of oneself and the surrounding social environment is the major component of most definitions of psychological health. 69, 35%
27. If all members of a species exhibit the same behavior, it follows that the behavior is an instinct. 237, 34%
28. Hypnotized subjects cannot be made to engage in acts they might not otherwise ordinarily perform. 461, 33%
29. Most psychologists agree that behavior results primarily from dispositions. 182, 32%
30. Most adolescents have extremely high expectations about how long they will live and about how they will die. 80, 29%
31. Exaggeration of reflexes would not be expected if the spinal cord were severed. 356, 25%
32. Most people experience a great deal of trouble and turmoil during adolescence. (See text)

When an item was used in two or more classes and/or for two or more semesters, all data for the item were combined. This explains the large *n*'s for some of the items. (It should be noted, however, that such items were counted only once in arriving at the total, 2885, for the number of items examined).

The percentages given above are in most cases the percentages of students choosing the statement listed. In a few cases the percentages reflect the percentages of students selecting the statement *plus* the percentages selecting "All of the above." The assumption was made that selecting "All of the above" implied endorsement of the statement in question as well as the other alternatives.

Discussion. Kendler (1965) has suggested that a great part of lay psychology is valid, though perhaps in need of polishing. The relatively small number of misconceptions emerging in the present study is consistent with Kendler's view. Of the 37 items in the true/false quizzes only slightly over half (51%) were missed by the majority of the students, and hence labeled misconceptions. The original items were suspects to begin with, derived as they were from the accumulated observations of a number of experienced teachers of psychology, so 51% is not particularly impressive. It will be remembered that, of Vaughan's (1977) 80 suspected misconceptions, only 29 (36%) were missed by 50% or more of her or Lamal's (1979) subjects. And only 2 of Panek's (1982) 10 suspects met the 50% criterion.

Relatively little evidence of misconceptions was also found in the data for the multiple-choice questions. Of the 2885 items examined, only 40 (1.4%) appeared to reveal the presence of a misconception. And when 8 of these were dropped because of inaccuracy or overlap with other items,

the number fell to 32. It is very probably the case that such a small number underestimates the number that students actually bring with them when entering the introductory course. The multiple-choice exams were taken after classroom and/or text coverage of the material. Furthermore, students are certain to be "on guard" when taking an exam and can be expected to avoid alternatives that they personally prefer in favor of those that the instructor is perceived as "wanting." Nevertheless, the fact remains that very few suspected misconceptions surfaced and that, even if it be assumed that the students entered their study of psychology with large numbers of misconceptions, the coursework has apparently been successful at either dispelling or suppressing most of them.

The fact that only 32 suspected misconceptions could be gleaned from student responses to over 2500 multiple-choice questions certainly doesn't mean that the questions were mostly easy ones. As indicated above, many of the questions were difficult ones but failed on the nonvocabulary criterion. The emphasis on vocabulary in the introductory psychology course, and the multiple-choice test in particular, was underscored by the overall paucity of difficult questions for which knowledge of the correct answer didn't depend on knowledge of one or more psychological terms. Even the difficulty level of some of the items assembled in the lists above was doubtless due, at least in part, to ignorance of psychological terms, and this despite the effort to exclude vocabulary items. For example, multiple-choice item #21 was probably chosen by many students simply because they confused the terms "operant conditioning" and "classical conditioning."

Few would argue that the introductory psychology course, whether taught for the major or as a general education course, shouldn't build the student's vocabulary. What is important to note, however, is that so many of the multiple-choice items missed by students owe their difficulty to the psychologist's vocabulary, not to the complexity of the subject matter or to a lay psychology riddled with misconceptions.

The psychology that beginning students bring with them to the classroom does of course contain some misconceptions. This has been shown in the present study as well as the studies of others. Further, we know that many of the misconceptions are stubbornly resistant to instructional intervention (Gutman, 1979; Lamal, 1979; McKeachie, 1960; Vaughan, 1977), although this appears to be much truer for the poor than the good student (Gutman, 1979). However, when viewed in conjunction with the work of others, the present findings suggest that student misbeliefs may be far from plentiful. Many of the misconceptions that teachers suspect are widely shared are in fact rejected by the majority of students. And when student knowledge of psychology in general is examined, it turns out that widely shared misconceptions are rare indeed.

### References

Birren, J. E., Kinney, D. K., Schaie, K. W., & Woodruff, D. S. *Developmental psychology; A life-span approach.* Boston: Houghton Mifflin, 1981.

Brown, L. T., & Weiner, E. A. *Introduction to psychology.* Cambridge, MA: Winthrop, 1979.

Gardner, R. M. *Exercises for general psychology.* Minneapolis: Burgess, 1980.

Gardner, R. M., & Hund, R. M. Misconceptions of psychology among academicians. *Teaching of Psychology*, 1983, *10*, 20-22.

Gutman, A. Misconceptions of psychology and performance in the introductory course. *Teaching of Psychology*, 1979, 6 159-161.

Kendler, H. H. Motivation and behavior. In D. Levine (Ed.), *Nebraska Symposium on Motivation* (Vol. 13). Lincoln: University of Nebraska Press, 1965.

Kimble, G. A., Garmezy, N., & Zigler, E. *Instructor's resource manual for principles of general psychology* (5th edition). New York: Wiley, 1980.

Lamal, P. A. College students' common beliefs about psychology. *Teaching of Psychology* 1979, 6, 155-158.

Lefrancois, G.R. *Psychology*. Belmont, CA: Wadsworth, 1980.

Loftus, E. Memory: Surprising new insights into how we remember and why we forget. Reading, MA: Addison-Wesley, 1980.

McKeachie, W. J. Changes in scores on the Northwestern Misconceptions Test in six elementary psychology courses. *Journal of Educational Psychology*, 1960, *51*, 240-244.

McKenzie, S. C. Aging and old age. Glenview, IL: Scott, Foresman, 1980.

Panek, P. E. Do beginning psychology of aging students believe 10 common myths of aging? *Teaching of Psychology*, 1982, *9*, 104-105.

Peplau, L. A., & Perlman, D. (Eds.). *Loneliness: A sourcebook of current theory, research and therapy*. New York: Wiley, 1982.

Vaughan, E. D. Misconceptions about psychology among introductory psychology students. *Teaching of Psychology*, 1977, *4*, 138-141.

Wagstaff, G. F. *Hypnosis, compliance and belief*. New York: St. Martin's Press, 1981.

### Notes

1. Quoted from Loftus (1980, p. 43).
2. Includes students selecting "all of the above."
3. The correct alternative gives the olfactory epithelium.
4. The correct alternative gives the statistical model.
5. The author wishes to thank David S. Holmes, J. Michael Knight, Gary Nickell, and Diane Williams for their willingness to compile and share these data.

# What the Consumer Thinks Is Important In the Introductory Psychology Course

Larry T. Brown
*Oklahoma State University*

Teachers may want to approach different objectives in different ways, depending upon their outcome in this consumer study.

Selecting among topics for in-depth coverage in class is rarely easy, especially for the introductory psychology course. A wide range of topics is typically covered by the introductory textbook, and it can therefore be hoped that the student will receive at least brief exposure to the major areas of psychology. The problem arises when the instructor must decide on those topics to expand upon in class. Although the instructor is certain to select those topics which he or she believes to be of greatest importance, input from the course's consumers as to what they feel is important might at times contribute in a helpful way to the selection process. At the very least, such input should be helpful to the instructor in approaching topics which the consumer does not initially feel are important, and contrariwise, in skirting topics which the consumer feels are very important.

The present study was therefore designed to determine which topics the student and those who frequently finance his or her education, the parents, believe should be covered in an introductory psychology course. Secondary purposes of the study were to look for topics which are regarded as important by the student but not by the parent, and vice versa, and to determine to what extent topics selected as important by the student who has not studied psychology differ from those of the student who has.

**Survey Instrument.** Topics were selected by screening the learning objectives listed in the study guides accompanying introductory texts by Baron, Byrne, and Kantowitz (1977); Brown and Weiner (1979); Hilgard, Atkinson, and Atkinson (1975); Lindzey, Hall, and Thompson (1978); and McConnell (1977). With few exceptions only objectives were selected which were listed by at least two guides. Consequently, objectives relating to relatively specific areas of research (e.g., "Specify the types of behavior which develop in fatherless males and females.") were excluded. Many of the objectives were reworded in an effort to make them grammatically parallel and as similar in length as possible. The final list contained 128 objectives.

The objectives were grouped by topic area (e.g., Memory, Motivation, Abnormal Psychology) and reproduced in 550 booklets of 7 pages each.[1] Half of the booklets (275) bore a cover letter with the greeting, "Dear Parent/Relative/Guardian," and half a letter with the greeting, "Dear Student." The letters explained the author's desire to learn more about what students and their families believe should receive major emphasis in an introductory psychology course. The critical paragraph of the "Parent" letter read as follows:

I would be very grateful . . . if you might take a few minutes to glance over the attached learning objectives and check those *10* which you would most like to see your son or daughter (or niece, nephew, grandchild, ward, etc.) satisfy. It will be especially helpful if you read over them before you begin making your decisions. Obviously there are no "right" or "wrong" answers, as each of these objectives is regarded as important

91

by most psychologists. Please do not be concerned if you find you are unfamiliar with some of the objectives; given the increasingly complex and technical nature of psychology, few people can be expected to be familiar with the many subareas of the discipline.

The critical paragraph of the "Student" letter was identical except that the phrase "your son or daughter (or niece, nephew, grandchild, ward, etc.)" was replaced by "the student (including yourself)."

The last page of the Parent booklet requested the printed name of the respondent, relation to the student, address, and signature; the last page of the Student booklet requested the printed name of the respondent, telephone number, signature, and a check indicating whether or not the respondent had ever had a psychology course. Names, addresses, telephone numbers, and signatures were requested in an effort to discourage introductory psychology students overly zealous to earn extra credit points by fabricating responses (see below).

A Parent and a Student booklet were distributed to 275 students enrolled in the introductory psychology course at Oklahoma State University. The booklets were distributed immediately before spring recess in order to make it possible for students to deliver the Parent booklet to their parents in person. Attached to each booklet were the following instructions:

> Attached are two letters with accompanying questionnaires. Give the letter with the greeting "Dear Parent/Relative/Guardian" to your mother or father, one of your grandparents, an aunt or uncle, or legal guardian. Select your mother or father if possible. Give the letter with the greeting "Dear Student" to any friend, acquaintance, roommate, etc., presently atending O.S.U. who is *not* presently enrolled in Psychology 1113.
>
> Please make sure that both of the people you select give their names and sign the questionnaire and that the student also give his/her telephone number and indicate whether or not he/she has ever taken a psychology course. It is important that this information be accurately completed, as we will want to contact some of the respondents for further information.
>
> Please return the completed questionnaires to your instructor as soon after Spring Recess as possible.

The request that student respondents not be "presently enrolled in Psychology 1113" was made because the introductory students were midway through the course and might therefore have been biased by their greater familiarity with the more "basic" areas of psychology which form the first half of the course. The students were promised extra credit for their participation in the project.

Results and Discussion.  Of the 275 Parent booklets, 164 (60%) were completed and returned; of these, 142 were retained for analysis (22 were rejected because the respondents checked more than 10 objectives). Of the 275 Student booklets, 165 (60%) were completed and returned; of these 136 were retained and 29 rejected. The 136 Student booklets were further divided into those completed by students who had had at least one psychology course (85) and those completed by students who had never had a psychology course (51).

The "parent" respondents included 81.5 mothers (one booklet was completed by both parents working together),

45.5 fathers, and 15 mothers-in-law, stepfathers, uncles, fraternity mothers, etc. A spot check of the Student booklets indicated that the names and telephone numbers written on the backs matched listings in the campus and local telephone directories—there was, in other words, no obvious evidence that respondents had been "manufactured."

Dunn's (1961) method was used to control the Type I error rate for the 128 tests performed for each of the three groups of subjects. Critical values were obtained from a computer program that generated upper-tail probabilities for the binominal distributions, with $p = .078$ (10/128) and $n = 142$, 85, or 51, depending on the group examined.[2] Twenty-five learning objectives were identified as having been chosen with above-chance frequency by at least one of the groups; these are listed in Table 1, along with their frequencies of choice. To enable comparisons among groups, a Chi Square test of homogeneity of distributions ($df = 2$) was performed for each of these objectives (see right-hand column of table).

Inspection of the table indicates that the "parents" were more homogeneous in their preferences than were the students. Of the 25 objectives listed, 21 were checked with above-chance frequency by the parents, but only 8 were checked by students who had studied psychology, and 3 by students who had never studied psychology.

The objectives selected by the parents, and to a lesser extent the students, referenced several topics of basic psychology (e.g., forms of learning, memory storage, attitudes and their acquisition), along with several with applied overtones (e.g., drugs and their effects, effects of punishment, mnemonic devices, obesity, characteristics of good mental health). Strong interest was shown in the field of emotion (objectives 60, 61, and 62), especially in the area of anxiety.

The parents showed more interest than the students in knowledge about current fields of specialization in psychology (#4), modes of problem-solving (#40), achievement motivation (#59), I.Q. tests (#76), creativity (#84), personality (#86), and the use of statistics to deceive (#128). It is interesting that four of these—problem-solving, achievement motivation, I.Q. tests, and creativity—center on processes and attributes that bear in one way or another on academic and vocational success. In contrast, the students showed more interest than the parents in sleep and dreaming (#50). Students with psychology differed from students without psychology in preferring topics concerned with schedules of reinforcement (#30), information processing (#43), anxiety (#62), and sexual stereotypes and sex differences (#70).

It was in principle possible for the parents and the two groups of students to differ in their preferences for a learning objective even in the absence of an above-chance selection of the objective on the part of any group. The Chi Square test was therefore used to compare the three groups on each of the remaining 103 objectives. As can be seen in Table 2, the groups showed significant differences in their responses to seven of these.

In general, the data in Table 2 suggest that, relative to one or both of the student groups, the parents were uninterested in the ability to design an experiment on sensory sensitivity (#16), transcendental meditation (#26), conditioning (#29), sexual motivation and development (#56 and 71), and group hostility (#118). Students who had studied psychology were

Table 1. Frequency of Selection of Learning Objectives by Parents and/or Students

| Objective | Group | | | $\chi^2$ |
|---|---|---|---|---|
| | Parents (n=142) | Students (psych.) (n=85) | Students (no psych.) (n=51) | |
| 2. Be able to design a simple psychological experiment and specify the dependent, independent, and controlled variables | 14 | 16* | 9 | 4.22 |
| 4. Be familiar with current fields of specialization within psychology. | 33*** | 8 | 9 | 6.90* |
| 5. Be familiar with the different parts of the central nervous system and their functions. | 27*** | 8 | 7 | 3.92 |
| 12. Be able to define and discuss sociobiology (the study of the biological basis of social behavior) | 24* | 6 | 6 | 4.65 |
| 14. Be able to distinguish among stimulants, depressants, and psychedelics in terms of their behavioral effects. | 29*** | 16* | 10 | 0.09 |
| 28. Be able to describe and compare the several forms of learning, including habituation and sensitization, and explain how each can be adaptive. | 26** | 16* | 6 | 1.33 |
| 30. Know the various schedules of reinforcement and their effects on learning. | 10 | 16* | 4 | 8.23* |
| 32. Know the effects, positive and negative, of punishment. | 39*** | 27*** | 13** | 0.75 |
| 40. Be able to describe and compare the major modes of problem-solving. | 37*** | 11 | 7 | 7.21* |
| 43. Know the processes whereby information is committed to memory (incl. sensory, short-term, and long-term stores). | 31*** | 26*** | 7 | 5.35 |
| 45. Know some of the mnemonic devices employed to improve memory and how they work. | 27*** | 22*** | 9 | 1.91 |
| 49. Be familiar with the mechanisms that control hunger and thirst and be able to discuss the current theories of obesity. | 24* | 10 | 6 | 1.49 |
| 50. Be able to describe the stages of sleep and their relationship to dreaming. | 23* | 26*** | 16*** | 8.37* |
| 59. Know how achievement motivation develops and how it affects behavior. | 35*** | 10 | 2 | 13.78** |
| 60. Be able to describe the research and problems in the identification of emotions in oneself and others. | 30*** | 9 | 10 | 4.24 |
| 61. Be familiar with the physiological changes that occur during emotion. | 29*** | 15 | 6 | 1.92 |
| 62. Know how anxiety affects the performance of individuals on tasks and tests. | 35*** | 31*** | 12 | 4.32 |
| 70. Know how children acquire a sexual identity and be able to discuss sexual stereotyping and research on sex differences. | 16 | 18** | 8 | 4.09 |
| 76. Be able to discuss why or why not IQ tests are reliable and valid measures of intelligence. | 24* | 9 | 4 | 6.58* |
| 84. Be able to discuss the characteristics of the creative person and the factors that inhibit or facilitate creative thinking. | 26** | 5 | 5 | 7.83* |
| 86. Be familiar with the various approaches to the study of human personality (e.g., trait, learning-theory, existential). | 30*** | 8 | 7 | 5.66 |
| 91. Know the criteria that enter the definition of abnormality as well as the characteristics that are considered indicative of good mental health. | 29*** | 15 | 6 | 1.92 |
| 100. Know the various causes and effects of drug abuse (incl. alcohol). | 26** | 17 | 10 | 0.11 |
| 107. Know what attitudes are and how they are acquired. | 32*** | 13 | 13** | 2.50 |
| 128. Know the different ways statistics can be used to mislead or deceive. | 24* | 6 | 1 | 10.52* |

*$p <.05$; **$p <.01$; ***$p <.001$.

uninterested in identity formation (#72), and students who had never studied psychology were uninterested in conditioning (#29) and group hostility (#118).

Taken together, the data reported in Tables 1 and 2 suggest several conclusions regarding the views of parents and students on what should be stressed in the introductory psychology course:

First, parents appear to be more homogeneous in what they think is important than are students. Whether or not they've ever had a course in psychology, students show little agreement on what they regard as important. Perhaps in the present survey the students took the task less seriously than the parents and, hence, hurried through the pages of the booklet checking objectives on a hit-or-miss basis. If so, more careful assessment of the students' opinions might have revealed more areas of agreement.

Second, parents tend to favor (a) topics falling within the areas of biological psychology, learning and memory, personality, social psychology, and especially, emotion; and (b) topics of an applied nature (e.g., mnemonic devices) and/or current public concern (e.g., drug abuse).

Third, parents are more interested than students in achievement motivation and topics relating to the higher mental processes (creativity, problem-solving, intelligence). Here there may be some evidence for a "generation gap," with parents more overtly concerned than students about topics correlated with college- and career-related success. It is also possible that students feel threatened by these topics (it has been my own experience that these topics arouse little general interest in the classroom).

Fourth, students show more concern than parents for topics of an experiential nature (sleep and dreaming, transcendental meditation) and topics in the area of human sexuality (sexual stereotyping and sex differences, determinants of sexual arousal). In addition, students who have studied psychology tend to favor topics concerned with basic learning and memory phenomena (including classical and operant conditioning, schedules of reinforcement) more than do parents and/or students who have never studied psychology. The latter finding may reflect the influence of instruction in psychology, as basic learning and memory processes play an important role in most psychology curricula.

Fifth, parents and students alike believe that the topics of anxiety and punishment should receive major emphasis in the introductory course.

Table 2. Nonpreferred Learning Objectives Differentially Selected by Parents and Students

| Objective | Group | | | $\chi^2$ |
|---|---|---|---|---|
| | Parents<br>*(n=142)* | Student<br>(psych.)<br>*(n=85)* | Students<br>(no psych.)<br>*(n=51)* | |
| 16. Be able to design an experiment to measure some aspect of sensory sensitivity (e.g., visual acuity). | 1 | 4 | 6 | 12.26*** |
| 26. Be able to discuss transcendental meditation as an altered psychological and physiological state. | 2 | 12 | 6 | 14.82**** |
| 29. Be able to illustrate the principles of classical and operant conditioning using your own personal experiences as examples. | 5 | 11 | 3 | 7.50* |
| 56. Know the factors involved in the control of sexual arousal in both males and females. | 11 | 15 | 10 | 7.08* |
| 71. Be able to discuss the stages of psychosexual development proposed by Freud. | 0 | 4 | 1 | 6.68* |
| 72. Be able to discuss the process of identity formation. | 15 | 4 | 10 | 7.58* |
| 118. Be able to discuss the experimental evidence on the factors affecting the formation of ingroups and outgroups and the development and reduction of hostility between ingroups and outgroups. | 1 | 5 | 0 | 8.13** |

*$p$ <.05; ** <.02; *** <.01; **** <.001.

Finally, parents and students assign relatively little importance to topics concerned with the history of psychology, sensory psychology, perception and attention, developmental psychology, psychotherapy, and comparative psychology and ethology.

Although the purposes of this survey were concerned with identifying topics of psychology judged to be important by the consumer of the introductory course, the rating task was certain to serve an educational function as well, especially for the students and parents who had never studied psychology. Class projects which call for the participation of nonpsychology students can only broaden the base of general education. And class projects which call for the participation of parents help bring the interests, concerns, and goals of the psychologist to the attention of an important segment of the public. Judging from the comments of their children, and, in some cases, notes written directly on the survey booklet, many of the parents in the present study learned "a lot about psychology"—and enjoyed it. This was gratifying.

### References

Baron, R. A., Byrne, D., & Kantowitz, B. H. *Psychology: Understanding behavior*. Philadelphia: Saunders, 1977.

Brown, L. T., & Weiner, E. A. *Introduction to psychology*. Cambridge, MA: Winthrop, 1979.

Dunn, O. J. Multiple comparisons among means. *Journal of the American Statistical Association*, 1961, *56*, 52-64.

Hilgard, E. R., Atkinson, R. C., & Atkinson, R. L. *Introduction to psychology* (6th ed.). New York: Harcourt Brace Jovanovich, 1975.

Lindzey, G., Hall, C. S., & Thompson, R. F. *Psychology* (2nd ed.). New York: Worth, 1978.

McConnell, J. V. *Understanding human behavior* (2nd ed.). New York: Holt, Rinehart and Winston, 1977.

### Notes

1. Copies of the booklet may be obtained by writing the author.
2. The author wishes to express his gratitude to James M. Price and Kevin R. Loomis for their advice on and help with the statistical analysis.

# 7. MOTIVATING STUDENTS IN INTRODUCTORY PSYCHOLOGY

## An Embarrassment of Riches: Effectively Teaching and Motivating Large Introductory Psychology Sections

John Lamberth, *Temple University,* and
John M. Knight, *University of Oklahoma*

How to influence students to study
the way they have always been advised to,
and still stay within your budget.

One of the most difficult problems of mass education is keeping the quality of education high while instructing large numbers of students. This has become a particularly acute problem for psychology departments because of the burgeoning popularity of the subject as reflected by the fact that Psychology ranks high as a major in many Arts and Sciences Colleges. The wealth of riches in the form of students may quickly become a massive headache. The present paper is aimed at describing a method of effectively handling huge numbers of students in an introductory course, while maintaining high academic standards, and substantially improving the quality of education.

Aside from those involving budgets, the problems associated with teaching introductory psychology on a large scale may be classified as instructor and student problems. On the instructor side, the course is difficult to teach because of its broad scope. In addition, there is often a reluctance on the part of faculty to teach the course. In many universities those lowest in the power structure of a department, i.e. graduate students, instructors or assistant professors, mixed with a small group of more senior faculty who like teaching the course, often are assigned to teach introductory psychology.

The student problem can be broken into two categories. The first of these is the desire of students to have a regular faculty member as their instructor as opposed to a graduate assistant. In an informal survey conducted at the University of Oklahoma, our students wanted faculty-taught sections of introductory psychology with 25 to 30 students in each section. This, of course, would require 50 to 60 sections of the course each semester which would be economically unfeasible.

Student Motivation. A far more serious student problem and the one this paper will primarily deal with, is the motivational component. In most universities, a vast majority of students in introductory psychology are capable of mastering the material in the course. Again, however, because of the difficulty of handling large numbers of students, grades typically follow the ubiquitous normal curve. At the University of Oklahoma grades had been assigned in the past on the basis of approximately 10% A's, 20% B's, 40% C's, 20% D's and 10% F's. Typically the distribution of scores was such that grades were not forced into this distribution; examination scores actually closely approximated a normal curve. This scheme, however assumes that 70% of the students in the course receive a grade of C or lower.

Whaley and Malott (1971) argued that students in introductory psychology are capable of achieving at a higher level than the grades in the average course would indicate. They introduced what they called a "Doomsday Contingency." Daily quizzes were given over discrete units of material and the student had a specified length of time to achieve a criterion of 100% mastery of each quiz or he failed the course. The grades which were recorded were the terminal quiz scores, i.e., 100% on the quiz or failure in the course. No major exams were given and 98% of the students received A's and 2% dropped the course or received F's. Obviously, the results were predetermined by the method of handling the grading, all grades would be either A or F. This study did not include a control group handled in the usual way, i.e., two or three major exams during the semester.

A series of investigations (Knight, 1972, 1973; Williams & Knight, 1972; Nation, Knight, Lamberth, & Dyck, 1973) has attempted to extend and refine the methodology of Whaley and Malott. Much of the research to be described used basically similar methodology. For purposes of clarity, that methodology will be outlined. Students were required to retake 10-item multiple-choice weekly quizzes until 100% mastery was evidenced. Immediately after the first in-class quiz was administered the quizzes and the answers to the quizzes were posted in a convenient location. The quiz was retaken during the next class period by those who did not achieve 100% mastery. Virtually unlimited opportunities to retake the quizzes were given outside of class to students who failed to achieve the mastery criterion on either of the first two administrations of a quiz. These quizzes were the basis for 50% of the student's grade, with the initial score, i.e. the score earned the first time the test was taken, being recorded. Fifty percent of the grade came from major exams, usually two in number. Fifty percent of the items on the major exams were items that had appeared on the weekly quizzes (old items), while 50% of the items were new to the students.

Three early concerns in research were the use of control groups, a less severe contingency for failure to achieve mastery on the quizzes, and fewer short quizzes. Knight (1972) compared groups which (a) took weekly

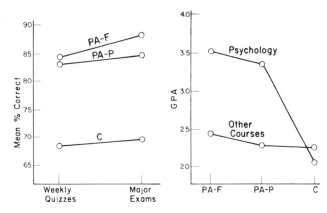

Figure 1 (A) Student performance under conditions with varying avoidance contingencies either PA-F, course failure; PA-P, loss of a letter grade; or C, the absence of
a contingency requirement, (Knight, 1972).
(B) Student performance in Introductory Psychology
using a PA procedure as compared to their performance in other courses taken concurrently
(Williams & Knight, 1972).

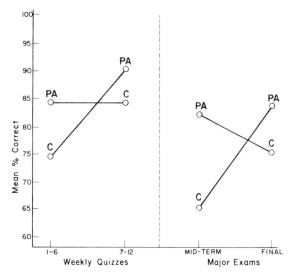

Figure 2 Weekly quiz and major exam performance under the
PA and control conditions (Knight, 1973).

quizzes and had to achieve 100% mastery or fail the
course; (b) took weekly quizzes and had to achieve 100%
mastery or lose a letter grade and; (c) a control group
which did not have to achieve 100% mastery on the weekly
quizzes. Figure 1A gives Knight's results. Since initial
rather than terminal grades were used as the basis for 50%
of the student's final grade, there were significantly fewer
A's than reported by Whaley and Malott. However, the
large percentage of students who did significantly better
in the programmed student achievement (PA) groups than
in the control group made the procedure potentially appealing. Williams and Knight (1972) investigated performance in other classes during the semester that the students took psychology under the PA contingency. They
found no differences between the control group and the
PA groups in grade-point average in other courses, as
depicted in Figure 1B. One experience with PA does not
seem to generalize to other courses, nor is it so time
consuming that performance in other courses suffers.

One criticism of these studies received from anonymous reviewers is that students have not been randomly
assigned to experimental conditions, i.e., whole classes
are assigned to specific treatments. In most universities
it is impossible to assign students randomly to sections, a
student must work in the course when his schedule permits. Knight (1973) addressed this problem in a somewhat
unique way. Using two classes, he started the semester
with one class serving as a control group and the other
class under the PA contingency. Halfway through the semester he shifted contingencies, i.e., the original control
group was now under the PA contingency while the original PA group had the contingency removed. Figure 2 presents the results graphically. There is little decrease in
performance when shifted off of PA but a dramatic increase in performance when shifted to the PA contingency.
There is, however, enough of a drop in major exam performance when students were shifted off of PA that it is
probably important to keep the contingency in effect
throughout the semester.

Another flaw in the research described to date was
that the instructor(s) in each of the studies described
above were aware of the PA contingencies and could very
well have influenced the outcomes. Nation, Knight, Lamberth, and Dyck (1973) ran four groups (2 PA groups
and 2 control groups) with the instructors "blind," and all
testing in the course handled by individuals who were not
teaching the class. To insure the comparability of the four
groups, all test items were taken from the text. Additionally, each student was given a series of study questions (50 for each chapter upon which the test items were
based.) During the eight-week summer term, seven
quizzes were given. This is equivalent to giving bi-weekly
quizzes during a regular semester. The PA groups again
showed the significantly improved performance over the
control groups. This indicated that it was possible to reduce the number of quizzes which are time consuming
and costly when classes are large.

As has been indicated, the research described
above, with the exception of the Whaley and Malott study,
graded on the basis of both the weekly quizzes and major
exams, 50% coming from each. Initial scores on the
weekly quizzes were used to determine grades, even
though students had to achieve mastery if they were in a
PA group. The major exams contained 50% items which
the students had seen on the weekly quizzes and 50% new
items. Figure 3A shows the performance of four groups
from the Nation, et al. (1973) study on old items and new
items on the final exam. It is apparent that a more severe
PA contingency (course failure) was no more effective
than a less severe (loss of a letter grade) contingency. The
Standard Control group took weekly quizzes with no mastery criterion while the Normal Control did not have weekly
quizzes. It is observed from Figure 3A that the mere use of
weekly quizzes without the mastery criterion was not effective in increasing performance.

Two weeks after the mid-term exam in the Nation, et al.
experiment, an unannounced retention test was given. The
midterm exam was given again along with an equal num-

ber of new items from the test manual which were chosen because they appeared to be extremely difficult. The results are shown in Figure 3B. There were no differences between the two PA groups, nor between the two Control groups, while the PA groups performed significantly better.

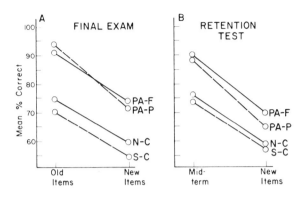

Figure 3 Student performance with varying avoidance contingencies, from Nation, Knight, Lamberth, and Dyck (1973).

**Summary of Research.** The research on PA to this point has indicated several things about the procedure:

1) Weekly quizzes without a mastery criterion are not effective. The PA effect is dependent upon the student retaking the quizzes and the presumed restudying of material which has been missed on quizzes.

2) The knowledge of the PA contingency by the instructor does not account for the superior performance of those students in the PA groups.

3) Students who were faced with losing a letter grade if 100% mastery was not achieved on the quizzes performed as well as students faced with failure in the course.

4) Bi-weekly quizzes are probably as effective as more frequent quizzes in increasing performance. This conclusion was tentative since fewer quizzes in PA research had been investigated in a summer semester which was obviously shorter than a regular semester.

With this information, it seemed possible to proceed with the use of PA in a large introductory section. In the previous research on PA, small sections of approximately 30 to 50 students had been utilized. The Spring semester of 1973 was chosen to initiate PA on a large scale at the University of Oklahoma because the enrollment drops to approximately 900 students each Spring, a number which our resources permitted us to handle.

**Instruction of Introductory Psychology.** To reach a compromise with what students wanted in introductory psychology (small, faculty-taught sections) and what was economically feasible, large lecture sections taught by faculty members twice a week supplemented by small discussion sections meeting once a week and led by graduate assistants were utilized. Three faculty members team-taught the course. One instructor was responsible for three large lecture sections for a third of the semester, when another lecturer took over. In this way faculty members taught only their broad specialties for a third of the semester. By assigning this effort as one course in their teaching load,

faculty members lecture a great deal for one third of the semester, but were compensated by a reduced load for two-thirds of the semester. The major problem with this approach is that there is the possibility of having, in essence, three distinct courses. This problem can be alleviated by careful selection of the team-members to teach the course, by the continuity provided by the graduate assistants in the discussion sections, and by careful coordination of the course by a faculty coordinator.

**Implementing PA with 900 Students.** Even though quizzes were scheduled on a bi-weekly basis, there was a great deal of work involved in implementing PA. Three separate forms of each weekly quiz (10 multiple choice items) had to be constructed. One of the elements of PA is that students are given immediate feedback on their performance. The correct answer sequence was written on the blackboard after students had turned in their quizzes. Each student wrote his answer sequence down and compared it to the correct sequence. If he had not correctly answered all 10 questions, he immediately knew he had to retake the quiz at the next class meeting. The quizzes were then immediately posted.

Six bi-weekly quizzes were utilized with students given the chance to achieve 100% mastery during the last 10 minutes of the two lecture sections during each quiz week. Students who did not achieve mastery in their first two chances came in on Friday between 8:00 a.m. and 5:00 p.m. and were given unlimited opportunities within that time period to achieve 100% mastery. Students who did not evidence 100% mastery on all the quizzes lost a letter grade.[3]

Three major examinations were given, one after each lecturer had completed his section of the course. Half of the questions on the major exams had appeared on one of the three forms of the weekly quizzes, while half of the items were new items. Seventy percent of the questions on both weekly quizzes and major exams were from the textbook and 30% from lectures. Because all students in introductory psychology were under the PA contingency, assignment of grades was somewhat of a problem. The average cutting points for the introductory psychology course at the University of Oklahoma for the previous five years were determined and used as the cutting points for the classes taking the course under PA. The cutting points were announced to the students during the first week of class. Fifty percent of their grade came from the initial scores on the weekly quizzes and 50% from the major exams.

One sensitive area is in explaining the program to students. When they are told that they must evidence 100% mastery of any amount of material, panic sets in. It is important to emphasize to the students that the quiz upon which they must evidence 100% mastery is posted with the correct answers indicated. Additionally, they have virtually unlimited opportunities to retake the quizzes. Thus, a motivational variable is being manipulated.

**Results.** In a sentence, the results of the present use of PA did not differ to any great degree from the results of previous studies. The predetermined criterion for an A was achieved by 56.75%, 29.98% received B's, while only

9.9%, 2.8% and .5% received C's, D's, and F's, respectively. Figure 4 shows the comparison for distribution of grades for both the semester immediately preceeding the introduction of PA and the semester being described here

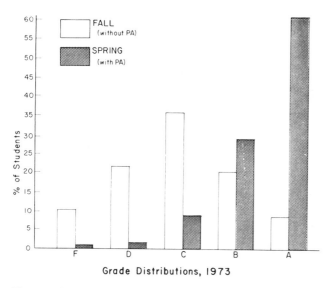

Grade Distributions, 1973

Figure 4   Grade distributions for Introductory Psychology at the University of Oklahoma with and without a PA procedure.

with PA. One further element of interest has to do with the students who failed the course in the preceeding semester and retook it under the PA contingency. Of the 23 students involved, 52.17% made A's, 39.1% made B's and 8.7% made C's. There were no D's or F's. Making a similar comparison when a student has failed and retaken the course without the PA contingency is revealing. Going back one semester, there were 14 students who had failed the course and retook it under our old system. Of these, 7.1% made A's, 7.1% made B's, 47.85% made C's, 21.4% made D's and 21.4% made F's. PA is obviously an excellent method of motivating even those students who have previously failed the course. One of the striking aspects of the results of the use of PA with a large group is that students are willing to do what they have to do and little or no more. For example there was a large grouping of individuals who received A's but who scored between 80 and 85%, just enough to get that A. Anecdotal evidence for the hypothesis that students are willing to do only what they have to do comes from the numbers retaking the weekly quizzes on Friday. To do this they had to come in on their own time and it did not affect their grade unless they failed to achieve 100% mastery. On the average Friday, approximately 200 students retook the quiz to achieve 100% mastery. On the Friday before Spring vacation, when retaking the quiz would have kept them from leaving early for the break, only 13 had not achieved the 100% mastery criteria before Friday.

Just prior to the last major exam, a course evaluation form was filled out by each student. Obviously there was a great deal of information available about the student's grade, but the final grade was not yet known. The evaluation encompassed a number of issues, but two are of general interest to the student's overall evaluation of the course. The first of these questions was: "Generally speaking what was your overall reaction to the course?" Responses were 1) very favorable, much better than other survey classes I have had in the past, 2) favorable, 3) unfavorable, and 4) very unfavorable. Forty-eight percent of those responding chose number 1, 36% selected number 2, while only 6% and 3% chose options 3 and 4 respectively. The next question asked "If you had the option would you prefer taking psychology using the present procedure or would you prefer the old system where only two or three exams were given and you didn't have to worry about mastery of the material (i.e., retaking quizzes). Eighty-two percent of those responding favored the present system while only 9% favored the old system.

Discussion.   Whatever else may be said about PA, it does increase academic performance. The exact nature of the effect is not fully understood. Whaley and Malott hypothesized that the PA task is analogous to an avoidance task, with the student avoiding failure if he evidences 100% mastery on each quiz. The evidence that the severity of the penalty for failing to evidence 100% mastery does not affect performance (Knight, 1972; Nation, et al., 1973) seems to dispute the avoidance hypothesis. It is however possible that students did not discriminate between the severity of failing the course and losing a letter grade (the two penalties imposed for failing to evidence 100% mastery), i.e., perhaps they were equally noxious.

One of the serendipitous statements which constantly recur in oral and written evaluations by students is that even though PA has made them work hard, they are better prepared for major exams. Concomitant with this change in study behavior is a reported reduction in anxiety at taking exams. Practically, students are forced to study small, discrete units of material until they have achieved 100% mastery. This spaced practice proves to be superior for the retention of the material two weeks after a major exam (Nation, et al., 1973). This, of course, is consistent with research in other areas, particularly when the material to be learned is extremely difficult or involves competing responses on a performance test (e.g., Underwood, Keppel, & Schulz, 1962; Underwood, 1961).

In unpublished research, PA has been used in courses other than Introductory Psychology, i.e., Personality and Statistics.[4] In these courses and in Introductory Psychology courses, diverse instructors using various methods of teaching the course and different textbooks[5] have uniformly reported increased academic performance under PA contingencies.

One course utilized a 90% mastery criterion rather than a 100% mastery criterion. Results were analogous to the use of a 100% criterion. It is possible that an even lower criterion of mastery may be effective. Research is continuing into (a) the effects of severity of the penalty for failing to evidence mastery, (b) the number of quizzes necessary to achieve the PA effect and (c) the level of mastery necessary. Obviously a less severe penalty and a lower level of mastery affect the anxiety of students taking the course. The number of quizzes involved affects the expense in implementing PA.

The most probable explanation for the effect of PA is that students are forced to do what they have been told to do for years, i.e., study small amounts of material throughout the semester rather than cram the night before the exam. Thus, it seems that PA reinforces appropriate study behavior. Although it may be appropriate to force good study habits for the introductory courses by using PA, the technique is probably inappropriate for advanced courses. At some point it must be decided how long it is appropriate to provide a motivational crutch to students. In addition, higher level courses do not lend themselves to multiple choice exams as readily as the more basic courses.

A more effective method of handling PA would be to use computerized teaching machines. This, of course, is expensive and we preferred to expend our limited funds in a way which would support graduate students. Our PA[6] team dubbed themselves the "Poorman's Teaching Machine." Our experience is that it takes approximately one graduate assistant to each 400 students if all work on the weekly quizzes is done by the assistants. As more services are handled by computer, such as scoring of tests, a decrease in the number of assistants would be possible. At any rate, the expense of the program is relatively low for the benefits gained.

Obviously, as more and more universities have been faced with growing enrollments several methods of meeting instructional problems have been developed. One such method with intuitive appeal has been the self-paced approach. The philosophy behind PA is quite different from such a self-paced system. Reports of completely self-paced instruction at the lower division undergraduate level which have reached us have indicated that many students need some sort of push to complete the course. This, of course, results in many students not finishing the course when it is self-paced.

A particularly good system of semi-self-paced instruction has been developed by Keller (1968). In this system each student is interviewed by his peers over discrete units of material and must complete a certain number of interviews successfully, as well as pass exams. This system has been successfully used in smaller classes, but the administration and record-keeping for all of the interviews as well as the number of assistants necessary becomes unwieldy with large classes.

In short, PA has been demonstrated to be a method of affecting study behavior, of increasing student academic performance, and of increasing their liking of the introductory psychology course, while still being economically feasible for extremely large sections. As such, it should prove valuable to others who would like to motivate their Introductory Psychology students.

## References

Keller, F. S. Good-bye, teacher . . . *Journal of Applied Behavior Analysis*, 1968, 1(1), 79-89.

Knight, J. M. Two varieties of Programmed Student Achievement. Paper presented at the meeting of the Southwestern Psychological Association, Oklahoma City, April, 1972.

Knight, J. M. The effect of Programmed Achievement on Student Performance. *Journal of Educational Research*, 1973, 66(7), 291-294.

Nation, J. R., Knight, J. M., Lamberth, J. & Dyck, D. G. Programmed student achievement: A test of the Avoidance Hypothesis. *Journal of Experimental Education*, 1973, in press.

Underwood, B. J. Ten years of massed practice on distributed practice. *Psychological Review*, 1961, *68*, 229-247.

Underwood, B. J., Keppel, G., & Schulz, K. W. Studies of distributed practice: XXII. Some conditions which enhance retention. *Journal of Experimental Psychology*, 1962, *64*, 355-363.

Whaley, D. L. & Malott, R. W. *Elementary Principles of Behavior.* New York, Appleton-Century-Crofts, 1971.

Williams, J. D. & Knight, J. M. The effect of Programmed Achievement in a General Psychology course on Student Performance in other courses. Paper presented at the meeting of the Southwestern Psychological Association, Oklahoma City, April 1972.

## Notes

1. We would like to express our appreciation to Dean John S. Ezell of the College of Arts and Sciences, University of Oklahoma, who provided the financial support for the research reported here. Perhaps even more important was Dean Ezell's position that he would be pleased to see all Introductory Psychology students receive a grade of A providing, of course, that academic standards were maintained.

2. To date in our research and use of PA, it has not been necessary to actually use the penalty for failing to achieve mastery. Medical excuses are obviously accepted and make-ups are allowed for legitimate reasons. Other than these exceptions, students have achieved mastery in the allotted time.

3. We would like to express our thanks to Professor Larry E. Toothaker for making data available to us from his statistics course taught using PA.

4. Introductory Psychology textbooks used with PA have been McMahon, F. B., *Psychology the Hybrid Science*, Englewood Cliffs, New Jersey, Prentice-Hall, 1972; Munn, N. L., Fernald, L. D., Jr., & Fernald, P. S. *Introduction to Psychology*, 2nd edition. Boston, Houghton-Mifflin, 1969; Whaley, D. L., & Malott, R. W. *Elementary Principles of Behavior*. New York, Appleton-Century-Crofts, 1971; Kimble, G. A. & Garmezy, N. *Principles of General Psychology*, New York, Ronald, 1968; Hutt, M. L., Isaacson, R. L., & Blum, M. L. *Psychology, The Science of Interpersonal Behavior*, New York, Harper & Row, 1966. One caution should be noted concerning the selection of a text. PA utilizes a great many multiple-choice questions and some teacher's manuals which accompany texts have an insufficient number of questions or questions which are poorly done. This latter point has been driven home to us by more than one irate student who has shown us that one of the "distractors" for a question was indeed correct. If he has failed to achieve mastery on the quiz solely because of that question, his irritation could border on pugnaciousness.

5. Thanks are due to Nabil Haddad, John Haller, Marianne Hunnicutt, Jack Nation, and Jerry Williams who served as either part-time or full-time graduate assistants on the PA project.

# Arousing Intrinsic Motivation as a Goal for Introductory Classes: A Case Study

C. Daniel Batson and Alan Johnson
*University of Kansas*

A quasi-experimental study shows that students perceived a motivation-oriented course as equal or superior to information-oriented courses.

The goal of introductory psychology courses is generally assumed to be information acquisition. Students must learn the ABC's of what we know about perception, learning, memory, motivation, etc., to prepare them for more advanced courses in these areas. There is, of course, difference of opinion about how such information is best acquired. Many instructors rely upon a lecture-discussion approach. "Small" discussion sections of from 20-50 students are used to supplement and personalize material presented in mass lectures. A widely-acclaimed alternative is the performance-based (PSI) approach suggested by Fred Keller (1968; note 1). The Keller plan focuses on self-paced learning of informational units that are hierarchially ordered, each unit building on the preceding ones. Performance-based courses frequently involve no lectures and no examinations other than individually administered unit quizzes.

Controversy over the relative merits of the lecture-discussion and performance-based formats has been spirited (e.g., Ruskin & Bono, 1975). But advocates of each approach seem to agree that information acquisition is the basic goal of introductory courses. We wish to take issue with this assumption. Many educators suggest that student motivation should be the focus of introductory education (Bruner, 1966; Dewey, 1916; Hunt, 1971; Moore, 1966; Schroder, Karlins & Phares, 1973). The student needs first to develop a desire to learn material in a given area; he needs to be intrinsically motivated (Deci, 1975).

In introductory college courses, students often appear confused about why they are learning what they are learning. Unable to see the personal relevance of the information presented, they may conclude that they are learning only for the extrinsic rewards of grade, credit, and diploma. Intrinsic motivation is undermined (Lepper, Green & Nisbett, 1973), and education becomes little more than a game. Although performance-based courses tend to be more popular with students than traditional lecture-discussion courses (Ferster, 1968; McMichael & Corey, 1969), they may actually encourage students to view education as a game. In performance-based courses the extrinsic factors of points, credits, and "getting through" are made particularly salient.

Examples of motivation-oriented educational programs are rare. One especially worthy of note is the adult literacy program of Brazilian educator Paulo Freire (1970; 1973). Freire succeeded at the difficult task of teaching adult peasants to read by basing reading materials on important issues in his students' lives, arousing their motivation to learn. Working within a carefully prepared context of emotional support, academic information was used to expose contradictions and errors in students' understandings of themselves and their society. Freire found that once students lost confidence in their present understanding of some personally relevant issue, they were motivated to seek new information in order to establish a more comprehensive, defensible position. Information was by no means unimportant, but neither was it presented as an end in itself to be learned in the abstract. It was used to challenge students to reexamine their present understanding and to provide a base for a reformulated understanding.

## Constructing a Motivation-Oriented Introductory Class

During the 1972-1973 academic year an attempt was made at the University of Kansas to develop an introductory social psychology course that would incorporate Freire's motivation-arousing elements. Five key structural elements were employed.

1. Reading material was carefully selected to address issues and concerns that were live for the students (e.g. aggression, competition, prejudice, interpersonal attraction, deviance). There was no attempt to give students a comprehensive or exhaustive treatment of these topics. Rather, students were exposed to some major theoretical models and research relevant to each.

2. Lectures were used to sharpen the practical implications of research on a particular issue. The lecturer sought to accomplish this by taking a stand based on available research on the issue, a stand that would differ at least in part from that of the majority of students. For example, during the 1972 presidential campaign it was suggested that the McGovern candidacy, which was supported by a majority of the students, might inadvertently work to strengthen political conservatism due to an inoculation effect (McGuire, 1969). The lecturer emphasized that the position presented was not necessarily correct, but was a position against which students should feel free to react and argue.

3. The idea of unitizing material was borrowed from Keller (1968) but was used toward a different end. Mastery of information was not the major goal of the course; it was instead a necessary condition for the intelligent reevaluation

of one's stance. Reading and lecture material were broken up into weekly units consisting of a several hour reading assignment and two lectures. Brief quizzes (approximately seven short-answer questions and a short essay) over the reading and lectures for the unit were an integral part of each week's discussion section. Mastery was the criterion set for quizzes. If a student missed more than one or two of the ten points on the quiz, he was required to do further study and retake the quiz at a later discussion section. Essays were oriented toward integration and application of the material to aspects of contemporary social life. They served as a springboard to discussion.

4. The discussion period allowed the student to try out his emerging stance on issues considered in the unit. This setting was organized to have several facilitating features: (a) small size; (b) non-threatening peer leadership; (c) assurance via the mastery quizzes that other participants had at least a basic grasp of the material; and (d) the student's own desire for closure and/or rebuttal on unresolved issues raised by reading, lectures, and other students.

5. Each discussion section was under the leadership of an advanced undergraduate or graduate student. Use of undergraduate "Aides" made it possible to have discussion sections of not more than fifteen students despite an enrollment of 400 or more. It should be noted that the responsibilities of our discussion Aides were far greater than those of undergraduate assistants in performance-based courses. Aides not only handled quizzing but also directed discussion of the personal implications of material covered in reading and lectures. They had to create a relaxed environment that encouraged exploration of personally relevant and significant issues, to be able to arbitrate when arguments broke out, and to encourage students' tentative, developing thinking.

Could undergraduates handle such a task? Would it not require faculty or at least graduate students? Perhaps; but undergraduates seemed to have certain qualifications that neither graduate students nor the instructor possessed. First, the Aides were relatively new to the material themselves and, therefore, might be more sensitive to difficulties that introductory students would encounter. Second, since the Aides were close to the age of the introductory students, they were more aware of the particular issues in students' lives to which the material would be most relevant. Finally, the Aides might be expected to generate more enthusiasm for the task than either graduate students or faculty, for the introductory material was not "old hat" for them. These unique qualifications did not, of course, mean that undergraduate Aides could or should be turned loose on discussion groups without guidance. To equip the Aides better for their role, seminar meetings were held once a week. In addition to reviewing material for the week's unit, Aides talked over discussion ideas and ways to facilitate learning.

To summarize, an attempt was made to create two conditions deemed necessary to arouse students' extrinsic motivation to learn social psychology. First, the student's current understanding of himself and society was challenged, using material available from the discipline. Readings and lectures were developed with this intent in mind. Unitization was employed to insure that students had the necessary background to raise meaningful questions. Second, a supportive context was provided in which students could explore new ways to interpret personal and social issues in the light of empirical research. Peer-led small discussion groups provided this context.

## Evaluation

The motivation-oriented course described above was offered experimentally and evaluated for two semesters (Fall and Spring, 1972-1973). The evaluation was designed to answer three questions:

1. Did students perceive the motivation-oriented course to be better, the same, or worse than information-oriented courses as a learning experience?
2. Did the motivation-oriented course achieve its goal of arousing interest in the discipline?
3. Could undergraduates perform satisfactorily as Aides (and how did they perform relative to graduate students)?

We collected data relevant to each of these questions. It must be admitted, however, that the data collected represent a compromise. Had we been willing to risk students' learning in the interest of hypothesis testing, we could have set up separate sections of the course oriented toward information acquisition and motivation, covered the same material in each section, had a common final evaluation procedure, and randomly assigned students to one of the sections. But students had not contracted to be in an experiment, so we chose instead to compare examples of the different educational approaches as they occurred naturally. This quasi-experimental approach introduced a number of confounding variables: the different educational approaches were represented by different courses, taught by different instructors, and sometimes even in different fields. Therefore, only tentative conclusions should be drawn from our comparative data.

Method. Of the 896 students who took the motivation-oriented course during the 1972-1973 academic year (primarily sophomores and juniors), 736 (82%) completed the University of Kansas anonymous course evaluation form, the Curriculum and Instruction Survey (277 of 391 students responded in the fall semester; 459 of 505 responded in the spring). Responses of these 736 students were compared with Survey responses in four information-oriented courses. Courses selected for comparison included three lecture-discussion courses and one performance-based course. The lecture-discussion courses selected were: (a) the same introductory social psychology course before it was restructured along motivational lines (Spring, 1972: 173 of 445 students responded to the Survey); (b) an economics course (Spring, 1973: 126 of 211 students responded), and a biology course (Spring, 1973: 129 of 239 students responded). The latter two were selected because they were non-psychology life science courses with enrollment approaching that of the social psychology course. Data from these two courses were pooled for comparison. The performance-based course was an introductory course in human development (Spring, 1973: 488 of 708 students responded). This course, described in detail by Spencer, Conyers, Sanchez-Sosa, and Semb (1975), included a variety of performance-based methods. It was the only large performance-based introductory course in the University.

Three questions asked on the Survey were selected as relevant for comparative analysis: "For me, the subject matter of this course was. . ." (Of Little Value-1, Valuable-3, Extremely Valuable-5); "All in all, this course as a learning experience was. . ." (Of Little Value-1, Valuable-3, Extremely Valuable-5), "I think that the students in this course made..." (Little Attempt to Learn-1, A Reasonable Attempt to Learn-3, An Outstanding Attempt to Learn-5).

Data relevant to the goal of arousing intrinsic motivation were obtained from an anonymous evaluation questionnaire prepared for and administered in the motivation-oriented course. This questionnaire was completed by 765 students during the 1972-1973 academic year. Students were presented with four statements relevant to the goal of arousing intrinsic motivation; rating each using a 5-point scale (Disagree 1, Agree 5).

1. Generally, I was prepared for each class session.
2. This course aroused my intellectual curiosity.
3. I made an honest effort to learn in this course.
4. The subject matter of this course seemed unimportant and insignificant to me.

As a more direct measure of the effect of the course on interest in social psychology as a discipline, in the spring semester an item was added to the evaluation questionnaire. Students were asked to rate their interest in the field of social psychology prior to taking the course and at the semester's end. Ratings were on a 4-point scale from not at all interest (1) to extremely interested (4).

Finally, performance of the undergraduate Aides was assessed both by student ratings and by final exam performance. On the evaluation questionnaire students were asked to rate: "The overall value of the discussion section" (Unsatisfactory 1, Satisfactory 3, Excellent 5); "The value of the discussion section for your learning of social psychology" (No value 1, Average 3, Great value 5).

Results and Discussion. 1. *Comparison of information-oriented and motivation-oriented approaches.* Table 1 presents students' mean ratings on the three questions from the University-wide survey. The first column presents student evaluations of the introductory social psychology course when it had a lecture-discussion format. The second column presents combined evaluations of two other large introductory courses in the life sciences using a lecture-discussion format. The third column presents evaluations of the performance-based course, and the last column presents evaluations of the revised motivational-oriented introductory social psychology course.

As can be seen from Table 1, both the performance-based and the motivational-oriented courses received significantly higher ratings on the three items selected for evaluation than did the lecture-discussion courses. (Similar differences existed on items not selected for comparison.) There was little difference between the performance-based and motivational-oriented courses on the first two items, but there was a small, significant difference ($p < .05$) in favor of the performance-based course when students evaluated their attempts to learn. Across the courses compared, both the performance-based and motivational approaches appeared superior in presenting the subject matter in a way that was perceived as valuable, in providing a learning experience that was perceived as valuable, and in generating a genuine effort on the part of students to learn. Although differences between these two formats were slight, the one significant difference favored the performance-based approach.

Two comments should be made about these results. First, the Survey provided no information on students' evaluations of the amount of information acquired or increased or decreased interest in the area, questions of central concern in evaluating the relative success of the information- and motivation-oriented approaches in achieving their stated goals. Goal-relevant data were collected for the motivational course and will be discussed shortly, but no comparative data were available.

Second, there was a major change in the structure of the motivation-oriented course from the fall to the spring semester, one which seems relevant for interpreting students' evaluations of the motivation and performance-based approaches. In the fall semester no final exam was given in the motivational course; in the spring one was. As a result, the grade distribution changed dramatically. In the fall semester 69% of the students received A's, 26% B's, and 3% C's. In the spring 35% received A's, 53% B's, and 6% C's. Table 2 presents a breakdown by semester for the motivation-oriented course on the three items presented in Table 1. One

## Table 1
### Mean Student Ratings of Large Introductory Courses With Information or Motivation Orientation

| Item | Course Orientation | | | |
|------|------|------|------|------|
| | Information-oriented | | | Motivation-oriented |
| | Lecture-discussion | | Per-formance-based | |
| | Social Psych. (n=173) | Other (n=255) | (n=488) | Social Psych. (n=736) |
| Value of subject matter | $2.24_a$ | $3.11_b$ | $3.53_c$ | $3.54_c$ |
| Value as a learning experience | $2.05_a$ | $3.02_b$ | $3.49_c$ | $3.54_c$ |
| Students attempt to learn | $2.45_a$ | $3.09_b$ | $3.56_c$ | $3.41_c$ |

For a given row, means not sharing the same subscript differ significantly, $p < .01$.

## Table 2
### Student Rating of Motivational Course in Semesters With and Without Final Exam

| Item | Semester | | |
|------|------|------|------|
| | Fall: Without Final Exam (n = 277) | Spring: With Final Exam (n = 459) | t |
| Value of subject matter | 3.84 | 3.37 | 6.44* |
| Value as a learning experience | 3.81 | 3.37 | 6.20* |
| Students attempt to learn | 3.57 | 3.34 | 3.97* |

*$p < .001$

can see that the course was rated significantly higher by students in the fall, when grades were higher.[2] Further, comparison of the motivational course without a final exam (fall) to the performance-based course (which had 70% A's, 20% B's and 7% C's) reveals that under these parallel conditions students evaluated the motivation-oriented course more highly. Although many factors might account for this pattern of results, it raises a general question deserving further investigation: To what extent is student enthusiasm for performance-based courses an artifact of the higher grades obtained?

2. *The goal of arousing interest in the discipline.* Results reported thus far suggest that the motivation-oriented course was rated by students as generally comparable if not superior to both lecture-discussion and performance-based courses (when matched on grade distribution). But one must still ask whether the course successfully achieved its stated goal of arousing increased interest in the discipline of social psychology. Students were presented with four items relevant to this goal on the evaluation questionnaire. Pooled across semesters, students' responses indicated that they considered themselves to have been well prepared for each class (mean rating, 4.34 on a 5-point scale), felt the course aroused their intellectual curiosity (4.08), felt they made an honest effort to learn (4.52), and felt the subject matter was neither unimportant nor insignificant (1.63).

Although this pattern of results appears quite consistent with the goals of the motivational approach, none of these items asked directly about an increase or decrease of interest generated by the course. Students in the spring rated their interest in the field of social psychology prior to taking the course and at the semester's end. They reported a significant increase in interest during the semester: The mean rating for initial interest was 2.65, and after the course was 3.19, $t$ (451) = 10.1, $p$ < .001. Because both interest ratings were made at the end of the semester, they should not be taken as an objective assessment of interest at each point. The ratings do, however, provide important data on students' perceptions of how their interest changed as a result of the course. This perception may be as important as an objective change in leading the student to pursue further studies in the discipline.

3. *Pros and cons of using undergraduate discussion leaders.* Several sources of data were available for evaluating the effectiveness of the undergraduate Aides. First, two items concerning the value of the discussion section appeared on the evaluation questionnaire. As is apparent from the results in Table 3, discussion sections during both

semesters were rated quite positively. Students seemed very pleased with discussion as a structural component of the course.

But how did undergraduate Aides compare with graduate students as discussion leaders? If the assumptions undergirding the use of undergraduate Aides were correct, they should have been more effective than graduate students. Consistent with this assumption, discussion sections led by undergraduates were rated as having more overall value, $t$ (64) = 3.73, $p$ < .001, and greater value for students' learning of social psychology, $t$ (64) = 2.63, $p$ < .01, than discussion sections led by graduate students. Further, undergraduate Aides were rated as being more capable of clarifying readings and lectures, encouraging student participation and raising questions than graduate students (data available on request).

But before one concludes that undergraduates were more effective, an additional question must be asked. Did students in undergraduate-led discussion sections actually learn more? Comparison of scores on the final exam given in the spring semester allows a partial answer to this question. Of the 130 possible points on the final, the mean score for discussion sections with graduate student Aides was 97.13, while undergraduate-led sections averaged 91.18, $t$ (38) = 3.52, $p$ < .002. Although students indicated they were learning more when led by an undergraduate, they showed less learning on the exam.

Two general classes of explanation for this discrepancy between students' subjective evaluations and objective performance seem plausible. First, students may have artificially inflated their ratings of undergraduate Aides. This might result from a shift in their evaluation standards ("He's doing a fine job. . .for an undergraduate."), increased empathy with another undergraduate, or novelty of the situation (the well-known Hawthorne effect). Any of these possibilities could lead to an artificially high student evaluation of the undergraduate Aides.

A second possibility is that students may indeed have learned more in the undergraduate-led sections, although not the sort of learning measured by an exam. The primary goal of the motivational approach is to generate personally relevant learning, which is difficult if not impossible to assess by examination.

## Conclusions

Although necessarily tentative, due to the quasi-experimental methods employed, the results of this evaluation of an introductory social psychology course oriented toward arousing intrinsic motivation seem encouraging. Student ratings indicated that the motivation-oriented course was perceived as equal or superior to large introductory information-oriented courses. Further, there was evidence that the course did what it was intended to do, arouse student interest in social psychology as an area for personally relevant learning. Finally, data suggested that undergraduates were capable of serving as discussion leaders; indeed, they were preferred to graduate students. But their students did not perform as well on an information-oriented examination. The last finding points to the need for further consideration of appropriate assessment procedures in motivation-oriented introductory classes.

Table 3
Student Ratings of Discussion Sections Led by
Undergraduate and Graduate Students

| Item | Section Leadership | | |
| | Undergraduate (n=583) | Graduate (n=182) | t |
|---|---|---|---|
| Overall value of discussion | 4.09 | 3.78 | 3.73* |
| Value of discussion to learning social psychology | 3.92 | 3.61 | 2.63* |

*p < .01

103

## References

Bruner, J. S. *Toward a theory of instruction.* Cambridge, MA: Harvard University Press, 1966.

Deci, E. *Intrinsic motivation.* New York: Plenum, 1975.

Dewey, J. *Democracy and education.* New York: MacMillan, 1916.

Ferster, C. B. Individualized instruction in a large introductory psychology course. *Psychological Record,* 1968, *18,* 521-532.

Freire, P. *Pedagogy of the oppressed.* New York: Herder & Herder, 1970.

Freire, P. *Education for critical consciousness.* New York: Seabury Press, 1973.

Hunt, J. McV. Intrinsic motivation and psychological development. In H. M. Schroder & P. Suefeld (Eds.). *Personality theory and information processing.* New York: Ronald, 1971.

Keller, F. S. "Good-by teacher. . . ." *Journal of Applied Behavior Analysis,* 1968, *1,* 79-89.

Lepper, M. R., Greene, D., & Nisbett, R. E. Undermining children's intrinsic interest with extrinsic rewards: A test of the "overjustification" hypothesis. *Journal of Personality and Social Psychology,* 1973, *28,* 129-137.

McGuire, W. The nature of attitudes and attitude change. In G. Lindzey & E. Aronson (Eds.). *The handbook of social psychology* (Vol. 3). Reading, MA: Addison-Wesley, 1969.

McMichael, J., & Corey, J. R. Contingency management in introductory psychology course produces better learning. *Journal of Applied Behavior Analysis,* 1969, *2,* 79-83.

Moore, O. K. Autotelic responsive environments and exceptional children. In O. J. Harvey (Ed.). *Experience, structure and adaptability.* New York: Springer, 1966.

Ruskin, R., & Bono, S. (Eds.). *Personalized instruction in higher education.* Washington, DC: Center for Personalized Instruction, Georgetown University, 1975.

Schroder, H. M., Karlins, M., & Phares, J. *Education for freedom.* New York: Wiley, 1973.

Spencer, R., Conyers, D., Sanchez-Sosa, J. J., & Semb, G. An experimental comparison of two forms of personalized instruction, a discussion procedure, and independent study procedure. In R. Ruskin & S. Bono (Eds.). *Personalized instruction in higher education.* Washington, DC: Center for Personalized Instruction, Georgetown University, 1975, 11-20.

## Notes

1. Keller, F. S. A programmed system of instruction. Address given at Autumn Conference of the Pacific Northwest Association for College Physics, October, 1969.

2. Grading differences cannot fully account for student ratings of the motivation-oriented course, however, for in the spring semester, 1974, when only 19% of the 332 students received A's, 45% B's, and 30% C's, mean ratings on the three questions reported in Table 3 rose to 3.6, 3.6, and 3.5, respectively.

3. This research was made possible by Educational Innovation Grant #71-2294 from the Endowment Association of the University of Kansas, C. Daniel Batson, principal investigator. The authors gratefully acknowledge the assistance of John M. Darley, Princeton University, in developing the proposed course structure, and of the staff of the Curriculum and Instruction Survey, University of Kansas, in evaluating it. C. R. Snyder and Dennis Embry made helpful comments on drafts of the manuscript.

# The Two-Point System: A Method for Encouraging Students To Read Assigned Material Before Class

Paul R. Solomon
*Williams College*

A simple substitute for daily quizzes increases incidence and criticality of reading and frequency of class discussion.

A successful lecture or discussion usually requires the student to be somewhat familiar with the material being covered. In some cases the student gains this familiarity by taking a prerequisite course, but more often the student acquires the necessary information by doing the assigned readings before the class. Unfortunately, in many classroom situations there is no incentive to read the assigned material prior to the class in which it will be covered. Rather, the contingencies are such that the student may actually fare better by doing the readings shortly before examinations. This strategy is problematic to the instructor who assumes a common background among students prior to teaching a particular subject matter. Thus it would be useful to have a technique to assure the instructor that the student had read the assigned material prior to the day in which it was discussed.

One way to accomplish this is to test students on the material at the beginning of each class. This is typically done in the format of a short quiz. Although there are data to suggest that this method is successful (e.g., Malott & Suinicki, 1969), it is not without drawbacks. The daily-quiz method can be quite time consuming both in terms of quiz preparation and grading, and in terms of class time spent taking the quiz. The daily-quiz method also assumes that the student has understood the material and can answer specific questions pertaining to it. Finally, the method of giving quizzes has its negative overtones (see Rogers, 1969; Skinner, 1968).

During the past two years I have used a technique which has been effective in motivating students to read the assigned material prior to attending class, but at the same time circumventing the problems inherent in quizzes. The method, which I call the "Two-Point System" rewards students who have read the material and has no consequences for those who have not.

**The Two-Point System.** At the beginning of the term I tell the students that I would like them to do the assigned readings before they come to class. I also tell them that from time to time at the beginning of a class, I will ask them to write a paragraph or two critiquing the reading assignment. I point out that merely outlining the chapter or article will not suffice; rather, to receive credit they will have to indicate that they have not only read the material, but have some insight into it. Specifically, I tell them not to summarize the entire chapter, but only to select a few salient points and indicate how these points relate to the topic of the day, or to material previously covered in the course. If more than one chapter or article is assigned, they are asked to integrate the two. As an incentive for doing this, I inform the students that for each successful critique, they will receive two points on their next exam. In a typical course I might do this, on a random basis, 6 to 9 times a semester.

To test the success of this method I have collected data from two different sections of a course in The Psychology of Learning. Both sections were periodically asked to submit a critique of the reading, but only one section received two points for each successful attempt.

**Method** The subjects were 57 students taking the course during the summer semester. Prior to the first class meeting, each student selected the section they would attend. The instructor, subject matter, and reading materials were the same for each section. Students in the section that met at 12:00 noon served as the two-point group (Group 2-PT), whereas students in the 10:00 A.M. class served as controls (Group CON).

On the first day of class I explained the two-point system to students in the 2-PT Group. Students in the CON Group were told that from time to time they would be asked to write a critical description of what they had read, that this would in no way affect their grade, and that they should not put their name on their papers. Instead, they should use an alias or a number. This was so the papers of each student could be grouped at the end of the semester.

The semester lasted 6 weeks with classes meeting 4 days per week. Once a week, for the first 5 weeks, students in both groups were asked to write a critical discussion of what they had read. The day in which this occurred was selected at random and was the same for both classes.

The critiques were read by the instructor without knowledge as to which critiques came from which class. Specifically, both groups were asked to place their names or identifying numbers on the opposite side of the page on which the critique appeared. The critiques were then mixed and graded (2 points, or not acceptable) and only then were they separated into groups for data tabulation. Students in the 2-PT group got their critiques back during the next class whereas students in the control condition did not get any feedback.

At the end of the semester both classes were asked to fill out a course evaluation which included questions on what percentage of the reading they did in this course and others before the classes to which they pertained.

**Results.** The data were analyzed in terms of percentage of successful critiques per student over the five opportunities and in terms of percentage of successful critiques per class for each of the five opportunities. The percentage per student was calculated by dividing the number of successful critiques by the number of classes the students attended in which critiques were required. Similarly, the percentage per class was found by dividing the number of successful critiques by the number of students in class that day. It is possible that not counting absentee students inflates the percentage of successful critiques (perhaps students who do not read do not attend class), but this seems unlikely for two reasons. First, there were no negative consequences for not completing the critiques, and second, the absentee rate was relatively low, and more important, there was no difference between the 2-PT and CON groups (mean percent attending: Group 2-PT = 89, Group CON = 90).

The mean percent of students with passing (2-PT) critiques over the five week period is shown in Figure 1. In general, students in the two point condition started out at a higher level than the control group and this difference increased as the term progressed. The mean percentage of successful critiques for students in the 2-PT condition over all 5 opportunities was 75.4, whereas the mean percentage of successful critiques for students in the CON condition was 45.8. A $t$ test indicated that this difference was highly reliable, $t(55) = 4.13$, $p < .001$.

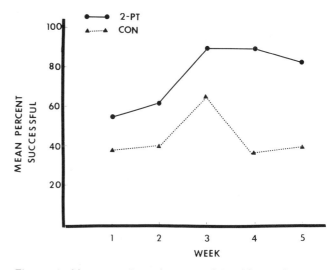

Figure 1. Mean number of successful critiques for students in both conditions over all five testing sessions.

A series of $\chi^2$ tests indicated that although there was no significant difference between the 2-PT and CON conditions on Day 1, $\chi^2(1) = 3.10$, $p > .05$, the difference between the two groups on Day 5 was reliable, $\chi^2(1) = 15.28$, $p < .001$. Furthermore, as suggested by Figure 1, there was no increase in percentage of passing critiques between the first and fifth session in the control group, $\chi^2(1) < 1$, $p > .05$, but the 2-PT group showed a "learning curve" with significantly more successful critiques on Day 5 than Day 1, $\chi^2(1) = 5.32$, $p < .025$.

To determine if the 2-PT system affected test scores, I analyzed the final exam performance for the two conditions.[2] Although the 2-PT group did slightly better than the CON group (Group 2-PT = 82.6%, Group CON = 80.50%), this difference was not significant, $t(55) < 1$, $p > .05$. Similarly, there was no relationship between final exam scores and percentage of successful critiques in Group 2-PT, Rho(34) = 0.06, $p > .05$.

Table 1 shows the student response to 4 questions which pertain to completion of assigned readings. The response to the first question indicates that students in the 2-PT group reported doing more reading before coming to class than students in the control group. This, of course, is consistent with the analysis of the critiques. Interestingly, when students are asked what percentage of the readings were performed before the exams (Question 2), there is essentially no difference between the two groups. Questions 3 and 4 ask for the same information as the first two questions, but refer to other courses. A comparison of the results of Question 1 and

## Table 1
## Student Responses to a Questionnaire on the Amount of Assigned Readings Completed

| Percent of Readings of Completed | Percent of Students Responding in Each Category | | | | | | | |
|---|---|---|---|---|---|---|---|---|
| | Q.1 | | Q.2 | | Q.3 | | Q.4 | |
| | 2-PT | CON | 2-PT | CON | 2-PT | CON | 2-PT | CON |
| 81-100 | 56 | 23 | 88 | 86 | 16 | 19 | 66 | 90 |
| 61-80 | 28 | 18 | 3 | 9 | 38 | 24 | 25 | 5 |
| 41-60 | 9 | 23 | 0 | 5 | 22 | 38 | 3 | 5 |
| 21-40 | 3 | 18 | 3 | 0 | 22 | 10 | 3 | 0 |
| 0-20 | 3 | 18 | 6 | 0 | 3 | 10 | 3 | 0 |

Questions:
1. What percentage of the readings did you do before you came to class?
2. What percentage of the readings did you do before the material was included on an exam?
3. In other classes that you have taken, what percentage of the readings did you do before the material was covered in class?
4. In other classes that you have taken, what percentage of the readings did you do before the material was included on an exam?

Question 3 suggests that students in the 2-PT group exhibit different behavior when the 2-PT system is in effect, that is, they tend to read more before coming to class.

To determine if there was any difference in students' participation between the 2-PT and CON conditions, I asked students to respond to the question: "Compared to other classes I have taken, the number of times that I participated in this class was:" The result showed that 87% of the 2-PT Group answered "considerably" or "somewhat" higher, whereas only 44% of the CON Group did so.

Discussion. The data from this study indicate that the two-point system accomplishes its goal of encouraging students to read the assigned material before attending the class in which it is covered. During the last half of the semester approximately 85% of the students in the 2-PT group read before attending class. These data seem especially encouraging in view of the performance of the control condition. Only 45% of the students in this group read before coming to class during the second half of the semester. Whether the control condition in this study is representative of all courses is an open empirical question. But, if they are, and the response to Question 3 in Table 1 suggests that this is the case, the data indicate that relatively few students read the assigned material before the day it is covered without some incentive to do so.

It is interesting that Figure 1 shows a "learning curve" for the 2-PT group. This is probably caused not only by the students receiving credit for successful critiques (critiques were always returned at the beginning of the next class), but also social pressure. In classes where critiques were requested, students who had not done the reading generally sat and did nothing during the 5-minute period during which the remainder of the class wrote. A number of students indicated that they were embarrassed by this and several turned in sheets stating they had not done the reading but they did not want to sit idly while the others wrote. Figure 1 also shows an increase in the CON group during Week 3. It is interesting to note that this comparatively high level occurred 3 days before the mid-term exam.

The final exam data indicate that the 2-PT system does not improve final exam scores. Perhaps this should be expected since the response to Question 2 in Table 1 indicates that both groups did about the same amount of reading before the final. Nevertheless, the data did show that the 2-PT system facilitated classroom discussion. Similarly, my perception was that both the quality of the discussion and the number of students participating was higher in the 2-PT class. These data, however, are based on self reports; they need to be verified by actually having an objective measure of the number of students participating in each condition.

Although daily quizzes or other similar forms of incentive (see Johnson & Ruskin, 1977, for a review) might accomplish the same ends as the 2-PT system, the latter method seems to have several advantages. First, it encourages students to read the material critically rather than to read for detail (reading for detail can be done prior to exams after the material has been discussed in class). Critiques were only acceptable if the student actually discussed some aspect of the reading. Often the discussion ranged from applying a principle discussed in the reading to an "everyday" situation to a statement such as: "this topic was not presented very clearly in the book," followed by a description of what specific points needed clarification. Statements like these not only indicate the student is reading critically, but they are also useful to the instructor in evaluating the text and planning subsequent lectures.

A second advantage to the 2-PT system is that students seem to prefer it to quizzes. I asked students in the 2-PT group to respond to the question: "I prefer the 2-Point system to periodic quizzes on the material." Sixty-eight percent responded strongly agree, 20 percent agreed, whereas the remaining 12-percent were either neutral or disagreed (no one strongly disagreed).

It is possible that the advantages of the two-point system may be incorporated into a quiz format. For example, rather than asking specific questions on a quiz, open-ended questions could be used. Coupled with a procedure which would reward only students who achieved a certain level of proficiency on each quiz while having no explicit consequences for those who didn't, might be one way to combine the two methods.

The data from the present study do not indicate whether the awarding of two points or simply indicating to the student whether or not their critique was successful was the critical factor in encouraging students to read the assigned material. Subsequent studies might investigate this by giving feedback to students without awarding two points to determine if feedback alone is sufficient to produce increased reading.

### References

Johnson, K. R., & Ruskin, R. S. Behavioral instruction: An evaluative review. Washington, DC: American Psychological Association, 1977.

Malott, R. W., & Suinicki, J. G. Contingency management in an introductory psychology course for one thousand students. Psychological Record, 1969, 19, 545-556.

Rogers, C. R. Freedom to learn. Columbus, OH: Merrill, 1969.

Skinner, B. F. The technology of teaching. Englewood Cliffs, NJ: Prentice Hall, 1968.

## Notes

1. Parts of this research were supported by a faculty research grant from Williams College. I am grateful to Nancy L. Van Duyne for her assistance in tabulating the questionnaire data and to Andrew Crider for his critical comments on an earlier version of the paper.

2. The final exam scores for the two-point group did not include additional points for successful critiques.

# Incentive Preferences of Introductory Psychology Students

Muriel J. Bebeau, James L. Eubanks
and Howard J. Sullivan
*Arizona State University*

Students' expressed evaluations of incentives used to promote learning may not agree with teachers' choices.

The effects of incentives on student learning in instructional settings appear to be closely related to student perceptions of the desirability of the incentives being offered. The experimental literature generally indicates that the use of a performance-contingent incentive results in improved learning (*cf.* Lipe & Jung, 1971). Yet, a number of studies have been reported in which incentives have either failed to facilitate learning or actually have had a decremental effect (Sullivan, Baker, & Schutz, 1967; Frase, Patrick, & Schumer, 1970; Wolk & Du Cette, 1974); and a recent series of studies by Eubanks, 1976). The variable effects of different incentives are apparent from the research of Sullivan, *et al.* (1967; 1971), who failed to obtain a facilitative effect when using a monetary incentive in instruction of university ROTC cadets, but subsequently obtained significant learning improvements by offering cadets release from 7:30 a.m. close-order drill as an incentive.

University instructors use a variety of incentives in efforts to promote student learning in their courses. The incentives they select may not be those that are most preferred by students. Currently, there is no body of information indicating student perceptions of the desirability of various incentives commonly available for use in university courses. The present study was conducted, therefore, to determine the preferences of introductory psychology students for incentives that are normally under the control of the course instructor.

## Method

**Subjects.** The total sample included 369 college students, 156 male and 213 female, enrolled in four sections of the introductory psychology course at Arizona State University. The first semester sample included 76 males and 114 females; the second semester sample included 80 males and 99 females.

**Instrument Development.** A list of incentives available for regular use in university classes was developed through discussion with instructors and groups of students. The list then was submitted to three instructors who revised and edited it until consensus was reached on the wording of nine incentives. Those selected were considered by the judges to be among the most common incentives normally under the control of a course instructor. A tenth category was added to represent a "no incentive" situation. The list was as follows: (1) release from taking a final examination, (2) release from attending future class sessions, (3) receiving a letter grade indicating the quality of work, (4) receiving points toward a course grade, (5) having work recognized in department publications, (6) assisting the instructor as proctor, (7) receiving positive comments from the instructor, (8) participating in a group discussion with an authority on a class topic, (9) participating in course-related field trips, and (10) no reward at all.

A two-part incentive preference scale was devised. The paired-comparison method (Edwards, 1957) was used for the first part. Each incentive was paired with every other incentive to create 45 items. The 45 items were arranged on three pages so that each incentive appeared no more than three times on each page. Order of the incentives within each pair was randomly determined. The student selected the incentive most preferred for each item in response to the following directions:

> Your instructor has identified a number of possible rewards that he/she might use to encourage you to do your best work in his/her class. Each item below lists two such rewards. Check the item in each pair which you would most prefer as a reward for doing good work.
> BE SURE TO CHECK ONE REWARD FOR EACH PAIR.

On the second part of the scale, students were asked to rate each incentive on a seven-point scale in response to these directions:

> Beside each item below, circle the number which represents how you would feel if each method described were used to motivate you to do your best in a course. Use the scale below. (A Likert-type, 7-point scale, with end points and midpoint

labelled "very favorable," "neutral," and "very unfavorable" was shown.)

Subjects also indicated their sex, age group, and cumulative college grade-point average. Complete anonymity for all subjects was verbally assured.

An initial tryout of the Incentive Preference Scale was conducted with a sample of 40 students to identify potential problems with its use. Several students reported that they felt they had responded to many identical items in the paired-comparison section of the instrument. Consequently, brief oral directions were prepared to explain the pairings to students immediately before the scale was administered.

**Procedures.** The scale was administered to intact groups of students during the regularly scheduled class period. All students present in each session voluntarily completed the questionnaire in approximately 10 minutes. This sequence occurred for two separate introductory psychology sections during both the fall and spring semester. The fall semester sample (190 students) completed the scale during the week preceding final examinations. The spring semester sample (177 students) completed the scale at mid-semester.

## Results

**Paired Comparison.** Table 1 shows the percentage of preference of each of the 10 incentives over each of the remaining nine. Scale values were determined according to the Case V model of Edwards (1957, pp. 31-40) by (1) converting these preference percentages to z-scores from a standard table, (2) summing and averaging each column, (3) converting each of the 10 means to a scale value by adding a positive constant equal to the largest negative value. Thus, the scale values are in terms of deviation units above the least preferred option.

As shown in the table, "Release from final examination" was by far the most preferred incentive with a mean scale value of 1.86. "No reward at all" was least preferred, and "assisting the instructor as proctor" ranked ninth. "Points toward course grade" ranked second at 1.25, whereas "Discussion with authority" (.73) and "recognition in publication" (.66) were low in preference. The remainder of the items were bunched in the middle of the scale (.95 to 1.06).

The between-subject consistency of paired-comparison ratings—i.e., the degree to which subjects showed the same preference pattern—is indicated by $u$, the coefficient of agreement. Kendall's Test was employed to test the obtained coefficient of .2393 for significance. The resulting $\chi^2$ of 2124.5, $df = 46$, $p < .0000$ revealed that the agreement among raters was highly significant.

The within subject consistency of ratings is indicated by the percentage of subjects who obtained significant coefficients of consistency (zeta). Eighty-five percent of the subjects had zeta values greater than .80, $p < .0005$, and only two percent had values less than .45, $p < .05$. Within-subject ratings on the paired comparisons, therefore, were highly consistent.

Pearson product-moment correlations for the two administrations of the instrument and for within-sample categories were as follows: Time$_1$ (mid-semester)/Time$_2$ (week preceding final exam): $r = .98$; Male/Female: $r = .98$; High GPA/Low GPA: $r = .92$; and Age 18-20/Age 21 and above: $r = .94$.

**Scale Ratings.** The mean ratings for each of the 10 incentives on the seven-point rating scale are also shown in Table 1. "Release from final examination" was again the most preferred, with a mean rating of 2.11. "No reward at all" and "assisting the instructor as proctor" were again least preferred. The Pearson product-moment correlation between

### Table 1
### Preferences by Paired Comparison and by Rating Scale

| Incentive | 1 | 2 | 3 | 4 | 5 | 6 | 7 | 8 | 9 | 10 |
|---|---|---|---|---|---|---|---|---|---|---|
| | Paired Comparison: % of Students Preferring | | | | | | | | | |
| 1 Release from final exam | — | .10 | .17 | .25 | .13 | .10 | .20 | .14 | .18 | .05 |
| 2 Release from class attendance | .89 | — | .51 | .60 | .38 | .28 | .48 | .40 | .40 | .17 |
| 3 Letter grade indicating quality | .82 | .49 | — | .60 | .29 | .19 | .54 | .34 | .47 | .13 |
| 4 Points toward course grade | .75 | .40 | .40 | — | .23 | .21 | .37 | .33 | .40 | .08 |
| 5 Recognition in publications | .87 | .62 | .71 | .77 | — | .33 | .63 | .54 | .51 | .26 |
| 6 Assisting the instructor as proctor | .90 | .72 | .87 | .79 | .67 | — | .79 | .73 | .77 | .43 |
| 7 Positive comments from instructor | .80 | .52 | .46 | .63 | .37 | .21 | — | .38 | .50 | .08 |
| 8 Discussion with authority | .86 | .60 | .66 | .67 | .46 | .27 | .62 | — | .66 | .26 |
| 9 Course-related field trips | .82 | .60 | .53 | .60 | .49 | .23 | .50 | .34 | — | .17 |
| 10 No reward | .95 | .83 | .87 | .92 | .74 | .57 | .92 | .74 | .83 | — |
| Sums | 7.66 | 4.88 | 5.19 | 5.83 | 3.76 | 2.39 | 5.05 | 3.94 | 4.72 | 1.63 |
| Scale Values | 1.86 | .95 | 1.05 | 1.25 | .66 | .28 | 1.06 | .73 | .95 | .00 |
| Rank Order | 1 | 5 | 3 | 2 | 8 | 9 | 4 | 7 | 6 | 10 |
| | Mean Values on a 7-Point Rating Scale | | | | | | | | | |
| Mean Ratings | 2.11 | 3.13 | 2.99 | 2.71 | 3.37 | 4.13 | 2.78 | 3.44 | 3.01 | 5.41 |
| Rank Order | 1 | 6 | 4 | 2 | 7 | 9 | 3 | 8 | 5 | 10 |

*The data show the proportion of times that the column incentive was preferred to the row incentive. For example, .89 in Column 1, Row 2 indicates that release from final examination was selected over release from future class sessions by 89% of the subjects. The scale value of 1.86 and rank order of 1 in Column 1 apply to incentive 1, Release from final examination.

the scale values of the 10 incentives obtained from the paired-comparison preferences and from the mean ratings on the seven-point scale was .94, indicating high consistency between preferences as assessed by the paired-comparison and rating-scale methods.

## Discussion

Scale values obtained from student responses to paired-comparison items and from student ratings indicate a consistent pattern of preferences across the 10 incentives rated in this study. "Release from final examination" was the most preferred incentive. The high degree of consistency between mid-semester and end-of-semester samples indicates that this preference was stable and was not simply a function of the imminence of final examinations at the end-of-semester period.

The present data provide an initial base for use by instructors in selecting incentives for use in their classes. On the basis of student preferences, it appears that the opportunity to earn release from the course final examination is one potentially effective incentive for motivating students to perform well during the course. The second most preferred incentive—"points toward the course grade"—is one that could easily be used in conjunction with release from the final examination.

Student attitudes toward assisting the instructor as a proctor are of interest because of the common use of undergraduate students as proctors in personalized system of instruction (PSI) courses in psychology and other disciplines (Keller, 1968; 1974). "Assisting the instructor as proctor" was the least preferred of the nine incentives (excluding "no reward at all") rated in the study, and "no reward" was preferred to "assisting the instructor as proctor" by 43 percent of the students. Although skilled instructors in PSI courses may be very successful in developing student willingness or desire to serve as proctors, data from this study indicate that students do not generally value this activity.

The present research was concerned only with student preferences for incentives and not with the crucial issue of the effects of performance-contingent incentives on student learning. However, data and methodology from the study should facilitate the selection and use of student-preferred incentives in instruction and, more importantly, in experimental research on incentive effects. In turn, the use of preferred incentives, either selected on the basis of group preferences or varied within a group according to individual preferences, should maximize the potential for obtaining positive effects.

## References

Edwards, A. L. *Techniques of attitude scale construction.* New York: Appleton-Century-Crofts, 1957.

Eubanks, J. L. *Differential incentive effects under varying instruction conditions* (Interim Report, Air Force Contract No. F41609-75-C0028). Tempe, Arizona: Arizona State University, 1976. (NTIS No. AD-A028 477/8GI)

Frase, L. T., Patrick, E., & Schumer, H. Effect of question position and frequency upon learning from text under different levels of incentive. *Journal of Educational Psychology*, 1970, *61*, 52-56.

Keller, F. S. "Goodbye, teacher..." *Journal of Applied Behavior Analysis*, 1968, *1*, 79-89.

Keller, F. S. Ten years of personalized instruction. *Teaching of Psychology*, 1974, *1*, 4-9.

Lipe, D., & Jung, S. Manipulating incentives to enhance school learning. *Review of Educational Research*, 1971, *41*, 249-280.

Sullivan, H. J., Baker, R. L., & Schutz, R. E. Effects of intrinsic reinforcement contingencies on learner performance. *Journal of Educational Psychology*, 1967, *58*, 165-169.

Sullivan, H. J., Schutz, R. E., & Baker, R. L. Effects of systematic variations in reinforcement contingencies on learner performance. *American Educational Research Journal*, 1971, *8*, 135-142.

Wolk, S., & Du Cette, J. Monetary incentive effects upon incidental learning during an instructional task. *Journal of Educational Psychology*, 1974, *66*, 90-95.

## Note

1. This research was supported by the Flying Training Division, Air Force Human Resources Laboratory, Williams AFB, under contract No. F41609-75-C0028.

# 8. USE OF STUDENT TEACHING ASSISTANTS

## Undergraduate-Taught "Minicourses" in Conjunction with an Introductory Lecture Course

Camille B. Wortman and Jay W. Hillis
*Northwestern University*

A contract-option educational experience designed and presented by selected upperclass students for introductory students is highly rated by both.

In many universities and colleges, the typical introductory psychology course is one in which a teacher with a microphone confronts several hundred students in a large lecture hall. For years, investigators have been pointing out the learning problems faced by students enrolled in classes with this structure (see, e.g., Maier, 1971; Diamond, 1972). Perhaps the most serious drawback of this approach is that there is little opportunity for students to discuss their ideas, to receive feedback on them, or to become actively involved in the learning process. A second problem is that students enroll in introductory psychology courses for a variety of reasons, and differ in their interests, their needs, and their ability to assimilate the material. With large lecture classes, it is difficult to devise a course in which students can pursue their individual interests and progress at their own rates. Finally, many people have pointed out that students enrolled in such courses spend an inordinate amount of time learning facts and definitions rather than thinking about important issues (see, e.g., McCollom, 1971). This is especially true when evaluation of students' progress stems solely from grades on an objective midterm and final; yet practical considerations often make it impossible to employ forms of evaluation which encourage and stimulate critical thinking (e.g., essay exams or papers).

In recent years some admirable efforts have been made to overcome these problems. Several instructors have experimented with the use of undergraduate discussion leaders in order to involve students in the material and provide a climate for the exchange of ideas (see, e.g., Maas, Note 1; Diamond, 1971; McKenna, Note 2). For example, McKenna structured his course so that small groups of students would meet weekly with an advanced undergraduate who would be responsible for involving them in the material. On the basis of such criteria as student evaluations (McKenna, Note 2; Diamond, 1971), these groups appear to be very successful. In order to individualize the teaching of introductory psychology, Keller (1968) has advocated the now well-known PSI system in which students read the course material at their own rate, take tests when they feel prepared to do so, and retake the tests as often as they like until they pass. Keller has recommended that these tests be administered by advanced undergraduate proctors. Presumably, the proctor-student relationship will permit a marked enhancement of personal and social aspects of the educational process.

An attempt was made to structure a large, several-hundred-person introductory psychology course at Northwestern University so as to incorporate the advantages of both of these methods—to provide opportunities for discussion of the material and to permit students to progress at their own rates. In addition, the course was arranged so students would have a great deal of freedom concerning the particular topics they would pursue.

**Overview of the Course.** More than 75% of the students enrolled in the course were not psychology majors. Because this course may be their only formal exposure to psychology, it seems important to let students explore topics that are likely to be meaningful for them. A premed student may wish to concentrate on biological psychology; a journalism major may be particularly interested in persuasion and attitude change; a speech major might wish to focus on psycholinguistics. We believe that ideally a course structure should be flexible enough to permit this type of exploration. In order to provide students with the freedom to pursue psychological phenomena of interest to them, a variety of options was made available. Students received a prescribed number of points toward their grade for each option completed successfully. The number of points necessary for grades of A, B, C, and D were specified early in the course, so students could decide what grade they wanted and plan which options they would complete to earn the grade. Options included reading chapters of a textbook and taking objective exams, reading articles from a book of readings and taking essay exams, reading paperback books and writing short papers, attending lectures and movies, attending special seminars, and working on an independent study project.[3] Students could choose the specific chapters, articles, or lectures which they preferred.

In order to provide the opportunity for discussion of

course material and for some forms of evaluation that would stimulate critical thinking, approximately 40 advanced undergraduate students were recruited and enrolled in a parallel course entitled "Special problems in psychology." Recruitment for this course was accomplished primarily through circulation of course description sheets. This announcement informed potential participants that only highly qualified students, with recommendations from their professors, could be selected to serve as "resource people" for the Introductory Psychology course. In this way, applicants, in effect, "screened" themselves, because those who knew they could not meet the requirements would be unlikely to apply. The instructor interviewed each applicant, and asked her colleagues about the applicants that she did not know. As it turned out, all applicants to the "special problems" course were accepted and became "resource people."

"Minicourse" seminars. These advanced undergraduates read and evaluated the introductory students' essay examinations and papers, and were available to discuss the books and articles or to supervise independent study projects. The most important responsibility entrusted to these "resource people" was for each to develop and teach a two week "minicourse" on a topic of choice to a small group of Introductory Psychology students. These minicourses were scheduled to begin near the middle of the quarter, and they qualified as one type of option for the introductory students. Early in the quarter, resource people were instructed to choose a topic for their minicourse seminar and to begin looking for interesting reading materials. It was stressed that the topic selected could be either broad (e.g., personality theory, mental illness) or narrow (e.g., biofeedback, psychological testing), and could either overlap or complement the other materials used in the course. Every week each resource person was required to hand in a tentative syllabus in which the topic to be covered, proposed readings, and plans for the use of class time were described. The course instructor commented on each syllabus, and made suggestions for revision. The instructor met with these advanced students weekly and made specific suggestions concerning how the minicourses might be run. For example, she conveyed McKenna's (1970) finding that student-led discussion groups tend to be more successful if the students are actively engaged in the material, and if the leaders refrain from lecturing. Thus, it was recommended that the resource people try to design class activities in which students could learn while becoming actively involved (e.g., taking a psychological test before discussing I.Q. testing; visiting a home for autistic children and discussing various treatment strategies with the personnel). It was also suggested that students might wish to locate "experts" from the university or the community and persuade these experts to attend a class session.

Decisions concerning what readings would be used, how class time would be spent, where and when classes would meet, and whether or how to "grade" participants were left up to the resource person. Of course, these issues (e.g., whether to make grades contingent on performance) were actively discussed during the weekly meetings and the course instructor offered suggestions about how best to conduct minicourses. Near the middle of the quarter, resource people were required to submit final course syllabi which contained descriptions of the minicourses and information advising prospective students on how to enroll. These syllabi were posted so that introductory students could examine the available options.

Minicourse topics included behavior modification (3 seminars), depression (2 seminars), the self (2 seminars), mental institutions (2 seminars), personality, autism, psychosurgery, animal behavior and training, psychological testing, hypnosis, group decision-making, attitude change, sex roles, nonverbal communication, sleep and dreams, sexual behavior, psychology and management, schizophrenia, brain waves, political psychology, laboratory experimentation, group problem solving, psychology applied to sports, child and adolescent suicide, transcendental meditation, drugs, group interactions and therapy, and the psychology of imprisonment. If two or more resource people were interested in offering seminars on a particular topic, the instructor did not attempt to dissuade them. It was reasoned that if a topic were popular among the resource people, it would also generate interest among the introductory students. Furthermore, most seminars given on the same topic took different approaches to that topic. Of the three seminars offered on behavior modification, for example, one was geared to improving study habits, another focused primarily on treatment for phobias, and a third compared behavior modification to insight therapies.

Of course, some of the minicourse topics were more popular than others. Some were filled immediately, while others never attracted a large number of students. The decision concerning how many students to admit was left to the resource persons, although the instructor recommended that class size be held to about 12. Several minicourse leaders had the familiar experience of acceding to students who were quite persistent in their efforts to enroll in the course, and consequently admitted more students than they wanted. Most of the seminars met twice weekly for two weeks, although there were exceptions (e.g., the leader of a minicourse on group decision-making arranged to meet less frequently but for longer periods of time). Approximately 80% of the students enrolled in Introductory Psychology decided to take minicourses. Because most of the seminars met concurrently, the majority of students enrolled in only one minicourse.

Readings were put on reserve in the University library. Details about assignments were included on the posted syllabi so that students could come to the first class period prepared to discuss the material. From all indications, resource people used very good judgment in planning how class time would be spent. They appeared to be successful at involving the students in the material. They displayed a great deal of energy in planning class activities, bringing in experts and arranging educational trips for students in the class. For example, the resource person teaching a seminar on behavior modification vs. insight therapy invited two faculty members, one from each persuasion, to discuss how they would treat the same patient. Needless to say, the discussion was lively and controversial.

An ex-offender was invited to attend the class on the psychology of imprisonment. He not only discussed life in contemporary prisons, but had a unique perspective on the problems faced by ex-offenders seeking employment. The leader of the minicourse on mental illness arranged a bus trip to Elgin State Hospital, where the students were permitted to tour the facilities. The leader for the seminar on animal training and behavior took his students to the Shedd Aquarium for a demonstration of the training program there.

Faculty members and graduate students were very helpful to the advanced undergraduates offering minicourses. They seemed pleased to be consulted for advice concerning appropriate readings and films, and were also gracious about visiting a seminar meeting and sharing their insights and experiences. For example, a faculty member in physiological psychology helped a student organize a demonstration on electrical stimulation of the brain, and an advanced graduate student demonstrated deep muscle relaxation techniques for students in one of the behavior modification seminars. Apparently, the contexts in which faculty members were sought out (to provide advice or help on their area of speciality) was one that the faculty found acceptable and in many cases enjoyable.

"Minicourses" Evaluation Results.    On the final day that the minicourse seminars met, participants were asked to evaluate the minicourse seminars. The evaluation forms were anonymous. It was repeatedly and strongly stressed that individual resource people would not be penalized by low ratings, and that participants should therefore respond as honestly as possible when making their evaluations. The specific questions asked, as well as the mean responses, are presented in Table 1. On the basis of the participants' ratings, a separate evaluation was prepared for each minicourse seminar. The second column on Table 1 portrays the range of responses — the ratings of the minicourse rated lowest and that of the one rated highest. The third, fourth, and fifth columns indicate the percentage of minicourse seminars that were rated on the upper half, on the upper third, and on the upper quarter of the scale.

As can be seen from Table 1, the ratings of the mini-

courses were generally positive. For example, on a five point scale with endpoints of "strongly disagree" and "strongly agree," subjects were asked whether the leader did a good job of organizing and planning the seminar. The mean ratings by the 519 students was 4.25. Interestingly, students did not agree that the minicourse would be more effective with a faculty leader ($\overline{X} = 1.91$).

On almost all of the dependent measures, the majority of the minicourses received ratings in the upper fourth of the scale. Even the lowest rated of the 35 minicourses received respectable ratings for each question. Recall that the screening system used by the instructor was informal and unsystematic: she merely chatted with each student, and questioned her colleagues about students she did not know personally. The instructor was initially apprehensive that no matter what screening system she used, one or two of the leaders might turn out to be inept or unqualified, and provide an unsatisfactory experience for the introductory students. Happily, this did not turn out to be the case. The results suggest that if an instructor uses reasonable care in selecting leaders, he or she can expect that most or all of them will perform well.

In order to analyze factors that might contribute to high overall ratings of the minicourse seminars (see Table 1, question 11), rank order correlations were computed between the ratings of overall value and all other items. There were significant positive correlations ($p<.001$) for all of the items except whether the minicourses would be more effective if taught by a faculty member, which correlated negatively ($p < .001$), and whether the workload was heavy, which did not correlate with overall value of the minicourse ($r = .08$).

Prior to the end of the quarter, resource people were required to write a paper discussing how their minicourse had gone and how they would change it if they were to offer it again. On the final day of class, they were asked to complete an evaluation of their experiences during the quarter. Again, the evaluations were anonymous, and the need for honest responding was stressed. The specific questions asked, as well as the mean responses, are presented in Table 2. The results reveal that resource people reacted favorably toward their role. For example, when

Table 1
Student Evaluations of the Minicourse Seminars

| Measure | Overall $\overline{X}$ (N = 519) | Range | % of responses ≥3.000[a] | % of responses ≥3.667[a] | % of responses ≥4.000[a] |
|---|---|---|---|---|---|
| 1. Leader did a good job of organizing & planning the seminar | 4.25 | 3.17 - 4.81 | 100.00 | 88.24 | 82.35 |
| 2. Leader comunicated ideas effectively | 4.09 | 3.22 - 4.87 | 100.00 | 88.24 | 64.71 |
| 3. Leader genuinely interested in helping students | 4.34 | 3.16 - 4.85 | 100.00 | 91.18 | 85.29 |
| 4. Grading procedure fair | 4.40 | 3.36 - 4.82 | 100.00 | 97.06 | 85.29 |
| 5. Work load heavy | 2.00 | 1.30 - 2.88 | | | |
| 6. Readings valuable and worthwhile | 4.14 | 2.89 - 4.75 | 97.06 | 88.24 | 67.65 |
| 7. Would minicourse be more effective with faculty leader? | 1.91 | 1.33 - 2.83 | | | |
| 8. Minicourse has had positive influence on my attitude toward psychology | 3.81 | 3.21 - 4.50 | 100.00 | 76.47 | 41.18 |
| 9. Minicourse should extend for more sessions | 3.53 | 2.77 - 4.57 | | | |
| 10. Students should be able to take more than one minicourse | 4.20 | 3.71 - 5.00 | | | |
| 11. Overall, minicourse experience was valuable | 3.80 | 3.22 - 4.50 | 100.00 | 76.47 | 32.35 |

Note. All ratings were made on five point scales with endpoints of 1 ("strongly disagree") and 5 ("strongly agree")
a. Percentages were calculated for the major evaluative items only.

## Table 2
## Resource Persons' Evaluations of the
## Minicourse Teaching Experience

| Measure | $\bar{X}$ (N = 33) |
|---|---|
| 1. How valuable an experience was it to prepare and teach a minicourse? | 4.48 |
| 2. Did teaching a minicourse alter your attitudes toward psychology? | 3.72 |
| 3. If so, are you less interested or more interested in teaching as a result of this experience? | 3.64 |
| 4. To what extent did teaching a minicourse provide a vehicle for you to increase your understanding of an area of psychology? | 3.94 |
| 5. In general, are you glad you enrolled in this course? | 4.76 |

Note. All responses were made on 5-point scales with endpoints of 1 and 5. The higher the rating, the more favorable was the indicated response.

asked how valuable an experience it was to prepare and teach a minicourse, students responded with a mean of 4.48 on a 5-point scale going from "not at all valuable" to "extremely valuable." When asked whether they were glad they had enrolled in the parallel course, they responded with a mean of 4.76 on a 5-point scale ranging from "not at all glad" to "extremely glad." As the responses in Table 2 suggest, the experience of leading a minicourse seminar altered many of the students' opinions concerning teaching. Some students were disillusioned by the amount of busy-work involved in teaching (e.g., getting articles duplicated), and by the fact that students seemed concerned only about grades; others found the experience of providing an intellectual climate exhilarating, and "could not wait" for an opportunity to be in a teaching role again.

Of course, these data are only preliminary. We will need more research with undergraduate resource people before this approach can be recommended unconditionally. But the present results imply that employing such students in a large lecture class may be extremely beneficial both for introductory psychology students and for the resource people themselves.

### References

Diamond, M. J. Improving the undergraduate lecture class by use of student-led discussion groups. *American Psychologist*, 1972, *27*, 978-981.

Keller, F.S. "Goodbye, teacher. . ." *Journal of Applied Behavior Analysis*, 1968, *1*, 78-89.

Maier, N. R. F. Innovation in education. *American Psychologist*, 1971, *26*, 722-725.

McCollom, I. N. Psychological thrillers: Psychology books students read when given freedom of choice. *American Psychologist*, 1971, *26*, 921-927.

### Notes

1. Maas, J. B. (Chm.). Using undergraduates as teaching assistants in introductory psychology. A symposium presented at the meetings of the American Psychological Association, Washington, D. C., September 1, 1969.
2. McKenna, V. V. Undergraduates as laboratory-discussion leaders in an introductory course emphasizing concepts: A preliminary report. Background material for "different approaches to student-led discussion groups." A symposium presented at the meetings of the American Psychological Association, Miami, Florida, September 6, 1970.
3. More detailed information about the course is available from the first author.
4. This research was supported by Biomedical Sciences Support Grant FR 7028-05 from the National Institute of Health.

# Peer Leadership of Small Research Teams in Two Introductory Psychology Classes

William J. Gnagey
*Illinois State University*

Elected peer leaders are high achievers and producers of group cohesion, but they show some unexpected personality traits.

Our earlier studies have shown that small, face-to-face groups of students can learn psychology effectively without the presence of a teacher (Gnagey, 1963). We later found that, although psychology students prefer some small-group activities, they also value some aspects of the large lecture approach (Gnagey et al., Note1). We subsequently reported the development of a "laboratory team method" for teaching introductory psychology that combines the two approaches, making use of eight-member, peer-chaired "research" teams as adjuncts to a large auditorium lecture class (Gnagey & Girmscheid, Note 2).

This article presents the results of two projects that focus on the elected leaders of these small teams. The data reveal a number of differences between leaders and non-leaders, some interesting relationships between leader behavior and team success, and an apparent contradiction between the personality traits associated with being elected and those related to team effectiveness.

## Study One

Procedure. The general psychology class chosen for this project consisted of 319 students (134 males and 185 females) who were scheduled to meet in a large auditorium on Monday, Wednesday and Friday at 1:00 p.m. The first day was spent introducing the course and explaining the procedures outlined on the course description sheet. Each student filled out a 3″ x 5″ card with his or her name, identification number, home town, campus address, and phone number.

Using these data, we organized six- to eight-member laboratory teams that were balanced for the sexes and made up of students from the same campus residence areas. Students who lived off campus were randomly assigned to teams whose other members lived in dorms. After the team functions had been explained, the groups were convened for the first time to choose their own meeting sites. Most of these sites were dormitory social rooms and lounges. We discovered that such places were rarely used by others during the day, so we avoided what would otherwise have been a mammoth scheduling and space problem.

Thereafter, the teams, chaired temporarily by their youngest members, met every Wednesday during the regular class time. Their assignments were to produce two research projects and to help each other learn the concepts in the text. After several meetings, each team elected its own leader, who was subsequently "paid" ten extra points for submitting a weekly report that contained a list of members present, a brief summary of the meeting, and a list of questions or problems that needed the instructor's attention. Periodically, the instructor met with the team leaders to talk over problems that arose.

Essay-type study guides for each chapter were handed out to every student on Monday of each week. Lectures delivered on Monday and Friday were carefully organized around the study questions. Before a team carried out a research study, it submitted a proposal which the instructor approved and handed back with suggestions. Teams received 25 points for each acceptable lab study completed. They were allowed to rewrite substandard reports until they reached a level of acceptability. Bonus points were awarded to students whose team leader rated their contribution to the research projects as average, good, or excellent, as an attempt to secure better participation on the team projects. Team leaders were awarded bonus points (over and above their flat rate of ten) on the basis of their ratings on a team sociogram. This was to compensate leaders who may have assumed more than their share of responsibility.

**Measurement of Variables.** Each leader's power was measured by a team sociogram in which all members listed three persons in their group that they would "take along" if new teams were to be formed. A leader's power ratio was computed by dividing the number of sociometric choices he/she got by the number of team members who completed the sociogram. Group cohesion was measured by asking all students to check whether they would elect to spend the remainder of the semester with the same or another team. A team cohesion ratio was computed by dividing the number of members marking "same" by the total members who responded.

The course was evaluated at the end of the semester by an eight-item, five-choice Final Course Rating Scale. Mean course evaluations were computed for each team. The laboratory team aspect of the course was also rated by a five-

choice Team Experience Rating Scale item which accompanied the sociogram. Means were computed for each team.

**Results.** Of the 29 elected leaders, 22 were women and 7 were men. This is a significantly higher proportion of women than we would expect from the sex composition of the class ($X^2 = 4.18$, $df = 1$, $p < .05$). A comparison of the mean test scores of team leaders with those of a random sample of 50 non-leaders showed that the team leaders scored higher on all 13 quizzes and the final examination. A sign test revealed that the differences were significant at better than the .01 level.

Pearson product-moment correlation coefficients were computed in order to get a picture of the relationships between the group evaluations of their team experience and several other variables. A significant positive relationship was found between the Team Experience Rating Scale (TERC) scores and the leaders' final exam score ($r = .40$, $p < .05$). A stronger relationship was found between the TERC and the team cohesion ratio ($r = .72$, $p < .01$). A third significant positive correlation was found between the leaders' mean quiz scores and the teams' evaluation of the whole course ($r = .46$, $p < .05$).

Apparently, laboratory teams tend to elect female leaders who are relatively high achievers in psychology. The leader's achievement seems to be positively related to the team's evaluation of the course. Evidently, leaders who can promote high group cohesion can influence their team's positive appraisal of introductory psychology.

### Study Two

**Procedure.** A general psychology class with an initial enrollment of 341 students was chosen for the second study. At the close of the semester when the criterion measures were taken, only 324 remained (146 males and 178 females). This class met on Tuesdays and Thursdays from 5:30-6:45 p.m. in a large auditorium. Each week a new chapter from a general psychology text was assigned. All students were provided with a set of essay-type questions which alerted them to the key aspects of the material. Two short lectures were presented each week, designed to arouse interest and explain difficult concepts in the chapter.

During the first week of class, the students were divided into 34 groups by starting at the beginning of an alphabetical class list and partitioning off sequential sets of ten names until every student was assigned to a group. A temporary convener (the youngest person) was indicated for the first three meetings so that group members would have a chance to size each other up before they were asked to elect their team leader. At the third meeting of the class, the teams were assigned to smaller rooms and instructed to "make a circle of chairs and copy down each other's names, addresses and phone numbers." They were then asked to submit written reports containing their answers to several questions about a simple research study that had been presented in the auditorium. The teams met for one hour each of the next two weeks and produced written reports of similar problems intended to bring out the elements of psychological research.

During the fifth week, the groups met and elected a permanent team leader. Thereafter, the elected team leader assisted the group to propose, carry out and report two research projects using human subjects. Several times the instructor met with the team leaders as a group to clarify the research process and help them increase the involvement of their group members. In addition to their research responsibilities, the team leaders kept track of attendance at group meetings, submitted written minutes, and filled out team leader evaluation forms at the end of the course. For these responsibilities, each leader was awarded 15 extra points which was equivalent to one perfect chapter quiz.

Measurement of Variables. Near the end of the semester, Cattell's *Sixteen Personality Factors Questionnaire* (1962) was administered to the 36 elected team leaders and a random sample of equal size of non-leaders in the class. At the close of the semester, an anonymous course evaluation form was administered to measure leader power, cohesion, and team effectiveness. Leader power was assessed by an item which asked, "If you had it to do over, would you elect the same team leader?" The number of team members answering "yes" was divided by the total number of reporting team members. This produced the *leader power index*. The team effectiveness scores were means computed from the reporting members' responses to the following five-point rating scale in the final evaluation.

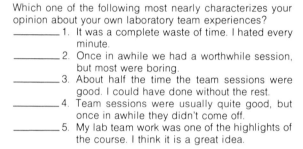

Which one of the following most nearly characterizes your opinion about your own laboratory team experiences?
_____ 1. It was a complete waste of time. I hated every minute.
_____ 2. Once in awhile we had a worthwhile session, but most were boring.
_____ 3. About half the time the team sessions were good. I could have done without the rest.
_____ 4. Team sessions were usually quite good, but once in awhile they didn't come off.
_____ 5. My lab team work was one of the highlights of the course. I think it is a great idea.

Results. In order to ascertain which of Cattell's sixteen personality factors differentiated between our team leaders and non-leaders, a one-way ANOVA was computed between the scores of the two groups on each of the sixteen factors. Because some of the responses had to be disqualified on account of incomplete records, the results are based upon the data produced by the 33 elected leaders and 34 non-leaders remaining. Only Factors I and M revealed differences at the .05 level of significance. The mean Factor I scores for the 33 team leaders was 7.18 but the 34 non-leaders averaged only 5.68. This means that the students who were elected as team leaders appeared to be significantly more sensitive and effeminate and less tough and realistic than the non-leaders. The mean Factor M scores averaged 6.88 for the 33 elected leaders and 5.88 for the 34 non-leaders. Apparently, team members voted for people who were more introverted and imaginative and less practical than non-leaders.

In order to determine which of the two discriminating factors was associated with group success, product-moment correlations were computed between the scores for each factor and the leader power indices, the team cohesion indices, and the team effectiveness ratings (see Table 1). Although Factor M was not significantly related to any of the three indices of group success, Factor I showed a modest

Table 1
Product Moment Correlations Between 33 Leaders'
16 PF Scores and Their Teams' Ratings of Leader
Power, Cohesion and Effectiveness

| | Personality factor | Team Ratings | | |
|---|---|---|---|---|
| | | Leader power | Team cohesion | Team effectiveness |
| A | (outgoing) | −.053 | −.037 | .048 |
| B | (intelligent) | −.401** | −.262 | −.245 |
| C | (emotionally stable) | .393** | .147 | .145 |
| E | (dominant) | −.218 | −.165 | .035 |
| F | (happy-go-lucky) | .019 | −.191 | −.192 |
| G | (conscientious) | .397** | −.057 | .068 |
| H | (venturesome) | −.002 | −.279 | −.003 |
| I* | (sensitive) | .051 | −.115 | −.395** |
| L | (suspicious) | −.023 | .256 | .009 |
| M* | (imaginative) | −.129 | .098 | .050 |
| N | (shrewd) | −.513*** | −.234 | −.036 |
| O | (apprehensive) | .152 | −.111 | −.299 |
| Q₁ | (experimenting) | −.099 | −.018 | .166 |
| Q₂ | (self-sufficient) | .227 | .058 | .088 |
| Q₃ | (controlled) | −.219 | −.199 | .117 |
| Q₄ | (tense) | .194 | .015 | −.218 |

*These factors discriminated between leaders and non-leaders at the .05 level.
**These coefficients are significant at the .05 level.
***This coefficient is significant at the .01 level.

relationship to team effectiveness ($r = -.395$, $p < .05$). Ironically, the correlation was negative. Evidently the characteristics which are associated with being elected a team leader are either not pertinent or counterproductive to the success of the team.

There were a few non-discriminating personality factors that seemed related to one of the indices of group success. Table 1 shows that Factors B ($r = .401$, $p < .05$), C ($r = .393$, $p < .05$), G ($r = .397$, $p < .05$), and N ($r = -.513$, $p < .01$) are all significantly related to our indices of leader power. Apparently, the team leaders with the higher power indices tended to be less intelligent, more emotionally stable, more conscientious, but less shrewd than those who received the lower power indices.

Since the personality factors associated with being elected a team leader seem to be essentially different from those associated with our indices of group success, it may be more efficient to appoint laboratory team leaders who score high on Factors C and G and low on Factors B, N and I.

### References

Cattell, R. B., & Eber, H. W. *Sixteen personality factor questionnaire* (2nd ed.). Champaign, IL: Institute for Personality and Ability Testing, 1962.
Gnagey, W. J. The comparative effects of small group vs. teacher-led discussion sessions upon student achievement and perception of educational psychology. *Journal of Educational Research*, 1963, 56, 24-32.

### Notes

1. Gnagey, W. J., Chesebro, P. M., & Johnson, J. J. Student evaluations of two methods of presenting educational psychology and the actual effects upon their achievement, retention and professional attitudes. Paper read before the American Psychological Association, San Francisco, September, 1968.
2. Gnagey, W. J., & Girmscheid, D. Laboratory team leaders in a general psychology class. Paper read at the annual meeting of the American Educational Research Association, New Orleans, February, 1973.

# An Introductory Demonstration Laboratory Produced Entirely by Undergraduates

Art Kohn and
Max Brill
*Oakland University*

This hands-on program features no-cost, use
by several courses, and enthusiastic student
involvement in organization and administration.

In the Winter Semester of the 1978-79 school year, an Introductory Demonstration Laboratory (IDL), for the introductory psychology courses, was planned and produced almost entirely by undergraduate students. We discuss the situation which inspired the IDL, and the plan as it was developed, with six major features characteristic of the IDL (with at least some of these features being, we believe, unique), how it worked out, and the results as indicated by the students who attended IDL sessions and the student-staff who put them on. We conclude with some suggestions as to how we think IDLs of this sort might be produced at other universities, with fewer problems, and with more positive features than we were able to realize in this first attempt.

## The Situation

Introductory Demonstration Laboratories (IDL) have not been conspicuously successful as adjuncts to introductory psychology courses. At least they have not been successful enough to inspire any large number of psychology departments to insist on including them in their programs. None of the best known universities in our state (University of Michigan, Michigan State, and Wayne State) produce IDL's nor has our own Oakland University since ". . . back in the sixties" (according to the vague memories of two senior faculty members). Western Michigan has the rather famous Skinnerian lab attached to its gigantic introductory course, but it is not really one of the type that is being referred to here; it is not a *general* psychology lab as most of us would think of one. Some of the other universities in Michigan *do* produce IDLs, most do not. Michigan universities, in this regard, are probably more like those of the other 49 states than not.

Oakland University is a medium sized university (11,000 students) located in a suburb north of Detroit. During the typical Winter Semester, there are about 400 students enrolled in the three introductory psychology courses. These courses have been taught almost entirely in the traditional lecture style. There has been little opportunity for the students to profit from individual or small group instruction except where there have been special teaching-assistant-run meetings. Generally, these have been concerned with priming students to pass imminent quizzes.

The project started among several undergraduate psychology majors (including A. K., then a student, since graduated) who had been teaching assistants during the preceding Fall Semester, in one of the introductory psychology courses (that of M. B.).[1] They were interested in psychology, and in teaching, and they felt that Oakland's introductory psychology courses would be improved if IDL's were added.

With undergraduate enthusiasm, the originating group of students decided to enlist peer help and themselves produce an IDL that would be available to all students enrolled in any of the introductory psychology courses, or, for that matter, in any other lower level courses where there might be interest.

Their goals were not particularly novel. They wanted to provide additional learning opportunities for themselves, to have a chance to teach, and to have fun doing it. More altruistically, they wanted to help their fellow students to a better understanding of some of the basic concepts of psychology, and thereby to encourage in them a more active interest in course mateial and in the field itself.

## The Plan

If the student goals were ordinary, the IDL plan arrived at had several features which were probably unique, or at least worth additional comment. *Features:* (a) The IDL was to be student-planned, student-staffed, and student-run; (b) It was to be put on essentially without funding; (c) It was to be available on a voluntary attendance basis to students who were enrolled in any of several courses, each taught by a different regular faculty member; (d) It was to be an IDL with different multiple "sessions" for each major psychological topic and multiple "stations" in each session, giving it cafeteria-choice features; (e) There was to be a pre-lab statement of the points being made and post-lab quizzes covering these points; and (f) It was to be evaluated purely in terms of what the students thought about what was important and what had gone on; not in terms of what faculty thought or might have measured.

It did not all turn out as planned, but it worked out remarkably well for a first effort. It is worth looking at each of these planned features, and at what happened when the plan was realized.

**Feature #1: Student-Planned, Student-Staffed, and Student-Run.** The entire project was indeed planned and pulled off by undergraduate students. We think that this is a unique (and wondrous?) feature of what was done.

Before anything more than talk and planning could be accomplished, departmental permission to proceed had to be obtained. This proved to be surprisingly easy, as the idea was supported by the chairman of the department and by the three faculty members who were teaching the introductory psychology courses that semester. It helped that virtually nothing was added to the faculty teaching burden. It also helped that some preliminary laboratory demonstrations had been successfully produced during the preceding semester, for the students of one of the courses (that of M. B.) Not only was permission granted, but the student-staff members were reinforced by being given upper-level Psychology credits for their semester's work on the project.

The faculty's only role, besides approving credit for the student-staff members, was to offer an extra credit grade point or two to those of their students who attended the IDL sessions, to give clearance to proposed lab demonstrations which might in some way be controversial or unethical, and to offer occasional suggestions for additional interesting demonstrations.

A "student-staff" was recruited. It was composed of 16 undergraduate students. Of these, five were upper-class psychology majors, seven others were beginning psychology majors but had previously taken only an introductory psychology course, and four were non-psychology majors who had taken introductory psychology plus a variety of other psychology courses. They met regularly to plan and discuss the project and to assure that assigned responsibilities were being carried out.

## Feature #2: Produced Without Funding.

The IDL for the semester was not, as we had hoped, produced for nothing. But the entire IDL cost was less than $100.00, which is about as close to nothing as one can get these days.

Because the lab added little to the faculty teaching load, and the student-staff worked for love and for course credit, there were no salaries to pay. There were only a few miscellaneous clerical and supply costs. The major expense was for the purchase and keep of six albino rats which were used in some of the lab demonstrations. The necessary demonstration equipment was acquired through the "beg, borrow, and fix-up" method. As many departments must, ours had a messy storeroom full of equipment that had been long ignored. Much of this was put into reasonable working order, and used. Other pieces of equipment (e.g., finger mazes, reaction times measures, photographs, cognitive devices, etc.) were produced from scraps and ingenuity.

## Feature #3: Available on a Voluntary Basis to Students in Different Courses.

The IDLs were administratively independent of any of the regular Psychology Department courses. They were designed to serve all of the students in any course where the professor was interested. The professors teaching the three *Introductory Psychology* courses showed interest. as did the professor teaching *Introduction to Social Psychology*, and the one teaching *Introduction to Research Design*. The students who attended the IDLs ("student-attendees"), therefore, came from five different courses. They came voluntarily. after having signed up the week before.

## Feature #4: A Multiple Station IDL.

The student-staff decided to produce a number of IDL "sessions," each of which would be devoted to a different psychological topic, and each of which would be composed of a number of demonstration "stations."

A different topic was covered in each week's sessions, eight different topics in all. They were, in order of presentation, Sensation and Perception, Learning, Memory, Motivation, Emotion, Cognitive/Developmental, Abnormal/Personality, and Social. This was an order which, with a few compromises, was a reasonable approximation of that which the three faculty members were using in their introductory courses. The student-staff also produced some lab sessions which they called "IDL's Greatest Hits," the title hinting at the varied content.

Each IDL session was composed of seven to ten stations. Each station was meant to feature an experiment or demonstration that exemplified an area of research within the week's IDL topic. It was in coming up with plausible, interesting, and informative stations that the student-staff was most taxed. Special efforts were made to design the stations in a way which would require active student-attendee participation wherever possible. As it turned out, better than two thirds of them involved the active collection of data for treatment and analysis.

Some of the stations produced were "old chestnuts." Others were original and showed a pleasant ingenuity. Typical of the more popular stations used are these five:

(1) *Classically conditioned eye blink*. A wooden panel was mounted on a table. The student-attendee looked through an opening in the panel at a fixation point on the wall several feet away. A small diameter plastic hose was mounted on the wooden panel, on the side away from the student, so that one end was available to the experimenter and the other end opened toward the subject's eye. The experimenter snapped a toy "cricket" (the conditioned stimulus) and immediately blew a puff of air through the hose at the subject's eye (unconditioned stimulus). Classical conditioning of the eye blink to the cricket noise was easily and dramatically demonstrated. With some student-attendees, the eye blink response was "extinguished" by sounding the cricket a number of times without the puff of air. Other student-attendees were not directly extinguished but were allowed to "forget" the CR. They attended other stations of the IDL directly after having been conditioned. At the end of the session, all of the students were tested again and none of them still showed the CR. The two reasons for the loss of the conditioned response, extinction and forgetting, were compared.

(2) *Weber's Law*. This was demonstrated with a weight discrimination task. Student-attendees tried to place in the correct order 20 little Kodak film canisters, each of which contained a measured weight of BBs, and which formed an ascending scale of weights. The weights differed, one from the other, by exactly equal increments. Student-attendees were presented with the canisters in a random order and attempted to arrange them correctly. It was easy to show that the difficulty of the discriminations, as measured by the number of errors, increased markedly as the canisters got heavier. Weber's Law was discussed in its historical context, and was offered as an explanation of the results obtained.

(3) *Developing cognitive strategies*. A set of 24 drawings was available on 1½" x 1½" pieces of paper. These were sketches which could easily be put into four categories: "transportation," "animals," "home furnishings," and "clothing." Student-attendees were shown the drawings one at a time, each one being placed face up on the table in a random

arrangement. Subjects were allowed three minutes to attempt to memorize them. Some of the students physically rearranged the drawings on the table according to the categories, some did not. The students who grouped them according to the categories were shown to remember more of the drawings correctly than those who had not done so. Organization aids memory.

(4) *Lie detection.* Student-attendees selected a playing card and attempted to conceal its suit by lying when questioned about it. Both an old GSR apparatus and a new Hagar Voice Analyzer were used in the lie detection.

(5) *Halo effect.* Student-attendees were shown six photographs of persons of the opposite sex. Unknown to the student-attendees, these photographed persons had previously been rated, by the student-staff, as either "unattractive," "moderately attractive," or "very attractive." The student-attendees rated each of the six persons on a number of perceived characteristics. The "very attractive" persons were seen as highest on "kindness," "sociability," and "sexual responsiveness," but lowest on "future prospects as a spouse" or "as a parent." The "unattractive" persons were rated differently. The "moderately attractive" were rated somewhere in between.

Each student-staff was made a co-chief responsible for one of the IDL topics that was covered. The co-chiefs, working with the student-staff leaders, determined the content of the lab. They gathered the required equipment, found space, scheduled the IDL sessions, and handled the promotion necessary to induce introductory students to attend these sessions.

Each IDL session was scheduled to last two hours and to be repeated 11 times during the week, Saturdays included. Most were given for just one week. Student-attendees signed up the week before for one of the upcoming sessions. Each session was open to a maximum of ten students. Ordinarily, 12 or 13 signees had to be obtained in order to have 9-11 actually attend. Once that discovery was made, the student-staff played to full houses thenceforth. Several of the sessions were repeated at odd times to accommodate students who were unable to attend the labs as they were originally scheduled.

The stations were physically scattered within a large classroom, or a lounge, or whatever room was available at the scheduled time. As it worked out, the IDL was as "floating" as any crap game. The stations were managed by student-staff members who were expected to be physically present at at least five IDL sessions per week. An attempt was made to give all of the student-staff members experience managing each of the many stations through the semester.

The typical session was introduced by a student-staff member who explained how this week's topic fell within the overall field of Psychology, and what was to be found at each of the stations. They also mentioned some of the major points which the IDL was designed to get across, and it was explained that a post-lab quiz would be given and that it would have to be passed for IDL credit to be given.

After the opening remarks, the student-staff members took charge of the stations which were assigned to them. They introduced the station to the student-attendees, directed the activities there, and answered questions. Student-attendees were expected to go to each of the available stations and to take part in the activities. In actuality, they tended to prefer some stations to others, lingered at these, and sometimes returned to them after having done the

circuit. At any particular station, the student-attendee might take the role of passive observer, subject, or experimenter. Often, as it turned out, they added the role of student-staff member. The regular staff member did no more than explain the station to the first student-attendee who approached it. Then that student-attendee explained the station and discussed it with those who came after.

About 90 minutes were allowed for the students to attend all of the stations. The entire group was then reconvened for the "wrap-up." This was designed to help the student-attendees to develop some kind of encompassing picture, and to fit what they had observed into that picture. Each student-staff member was given a short time to review and explain what had gone on at his or her station. Where data had been collected at a station, the results were looked at and explained. Open discussions were encouraged, and these usually turned out to be lively and long.

At the close of the session, which was almost always determined by the pressures of time rather than by the lack of interest or sense that all that could be said had been said, the student-attendees were read a list of questions from which the post-lab quiz, given later, was selected.

**Feature #5: Pre-Lab Statements and Post-Lab Quizzes.** The post-lab quizzes were, of course, intended to measure whether anything that had been "taught" had been "learned." The student-staff made special attempts to be clear in all of their statements of the principal points being made. A list of seven or eight short-essay questions had been read to the student-attendees as the last act of each session. They were reasonably demanding questions and to answer them correctly required some genuine understanding of what the IDL session had been about.

The quiz itself was, whenever possible, given immediately following the next meeting of the students' regular class. This was usually within three or four days after the IDL session they had attended. The quiz consisted of two or three questions selected from the list that had been read to the students at the close of the IDL session. The quiz rarely took more than five minutes to complete and it was graded by staff members on an S/N basis. All student-attendees were required to take and pass the appropriate post-lab quiz before they were given extra credit by the professors involved.

**Feature #6: Effectiveness Measured in Terms of What Students Thought.** The effectiveness of the lab was measured in three ways; (a) by the performance on the post-lab quizzes, (b) by a questionnaire survey of the student-attendees, and (c) by a questionnaire filled out by the student-staff. We would like to have some kind of measure of the IDL as seen by faculty, but frankly, no one thought of it at the time. The student-staff was, as they say, "student oriented."

## Results

**Post-Lab Quiz Performance.** Over 98% of the post-lab quizzes were graded "satisfactory." Such a satisfactory pass rate indicated, we believed, that something worthwhile had happened in the IDL sessions. Casual observatiohs of students who took one or more of the quizzes have reinforced our idea that something was well learned. One student-attendee, for example, four months after he attended the IDL Memory session, was able to state the main point for six of the seven stations he had encountered.

Student-Attendee Survey.   A student-attendee survey was distributed at the end of the semester to all of the introductory psychology students who were available (about 350); those who had attended the IDL sessions and those who had not. Of these questionnaires, 220 were returned, 129 of which were from students who had attended at least one IDL session. Twenty-one had attended only one, 85 had been to two, 19 had been to three, and four had been to four or more. A check was made of some of the more obvious variables, (age, sex, introductory professor, G.P.A., etc.) and those who attended the sessions were not found to be noticeably different from those who had not. It was clear, from what they wrote, that most of those who had not attended any of the sessions had other time obligations, such as outside jobs, families waiting with baby-sitters, etc., which precluded attendance.

Seven questions were asked, all using a one to seven scale, with one being very positive and seven very negative. The actual labels used varied: One was either "very much" or "strongly agree," while seven was either "not at all" or "strongly disagree." (Whatever subtle differences there appeared to be in this phrasing at that time do not seem to be there now.) The questions and the tabulated answers are in Table 1A. It is obvious that everything is clearly skewed in the desirable direction.

The student-attendees also indicated, in their free comments, their approval or disapproval of various aspects of the IDL. As Table 1 results would lead us to predict, mostly it was approval. For example: "The staff was closer to the students in the lab. I never felt intimidated by anyone and, as a result, I was more willing to get involved in the experiments." "I like this way of learning; superior to lectures." ("Perhaps," says M. B.) "I was always eager to discuss any questions with the students running the lab . . . the discussion gave me a much better understanding of the course material and an overall better liking for the course." It is interesting to note that 18 of

our respondees after attending IDL sessions expressed great interest in becoming members of the student-staff. And about one-fifth of the students attended more than two sessions even though there was no extra grade credit for going beyond two. If the student survey is to be credited, it is clear that the IDL was a happy success.

Student-Staff Survey:   A student-staff survey (anonymous) was distributed at the end of the semester to the 14 (of our 16) staff members who could be reached. Ten of the 14 questionnaires were returned.

Seven questions were asked, all using a one to seven scale, with one being either "very much," or "strongly agree" and seven being either "not at all" or "strongly disagree." The questions and the tabulated answers appear in Table 1B. It also clearly shows that everything is skewed in the desirable direction.

The only question where the responses were not markedly skewed in the good direction was an eighth question which asked about the "degree of organization" of the IDL itself. The one to seven scale ranged from "very organized" to "very disorganized." The modal response (N = 5) was three. Evidently, the student-staff perceived the IDL as lacking something in the way of administrative organization.

There were also some free comments which conveyed the same positive attitude that the rating scales indicated. One student-staff member wrote: "The lab gave me a view of all of Psychology. I finally see where different kinds of research fit in." Another wrote: "I enjoyed working with the staff and I got a big thrill when the students got involved in the labs." Another: "The IDL gave me a way to discuss with others what I am interested in. I don't just mean with students either. I mean with friends, relatives, etc. If my statements were questioned, I could back them up." And another: "The staff got along very well and worked well together. If there had been an easier way to learn the stations (a project booklet), then the lab would have run smoother. But for a first year staff, things went pretty well." Finally, one student-staff member expressed it best: "I learned that it is possible to develop an atmosphere which not only aids in the learning of psychology but that can make it enjoyable as well . . . I feel that it was a tremendous

Table 1. Frequency of Survey Responses by Scale Value

| Item | Scale Value | | | | | | |
|---|---|---|---|---|---|---|---|
| | 1 | 2 | 3 | 4 | 5 | 6 | 7 |
| A. Student Attendees (N = 129) | | | | | | | |
| The labs increased my interest in Psychology. | 18 | 31 | 36 | 21 | 12 | 6 | 5 |
| The labs increased my understanding of the course material. | 19 | 33 | 38 | 17 | 10 | 8 | 4 |
| The lab increased my interest in the course material. | 23 | 22 | 40 | 22 | 9 | 9 | 4 |
| I found the lab to be informative and interesting. | 42 | 43 | 29 | 8 | 2 | 4 | 1 |
| The "station" approach is a good way to organize the lab. | 41 | 51 | 16 | 13 | 2 | 5 | 1 |
| I enjoyed the lab. | 58 | 38 | 17 | 8 | 4 | 3 | 1 |
| I enjoyed having an undergraduate as a teacher. | 68 | 32 | 11 | 12 | 1 | 4 | 1 |
| B. Student-Staff (N=10) | | | | | | | |
| The lab increased my understanding of Psychology. | 6 | 2 | 2 | 0 | 0 | 0 | 0 |
| The lab increased my interest in Psychology. | 3 | 5 | 2 | 0 | 0 | 0 | 0 |
| The lab caused me to want to study more Psychology. | 3 | 4 | 1 | 2 | 0 | 0 | 0 |
| As a result of the lab, my teaching skills have improved. | 3 | 5 | 2 | 0 | 0 | 0 | 0 |
| Compared to other Social Science classes, I retained more from the IDL. | 4 | 4 | 1 | 0 | 1 | 0 | 0 |
| The lab gave me a broader perspective on Psychology. | 7 | 3 | 0 | 0 | 0 | 0 | 0 |
| I enjoyed working in the IDL. | 10 | 0 | 0 | 0 | 0 | 0 | 0 |

opportunity for undergraduates to staff the IDL and I believe that we proved that it could be done effectively. Right on undergraduates!"

### Suggestions

It is always a pleasure to make suggestions to those who might follow; giving advice is easy. The student staff went through the IDL semester aware of many things that might have been better. They spent many hours discussing what was wrong and why, and how it might have been improved. Since then we have given the matter additional thought. In capsule form the suggestions are: (a) Better administration, (b) Better preparation of the student-staff, (c) More and better stations, (d) More student-attendees at more sessions, (e) Better distribution of station explanatory information to the student-attendees, and (f) A permanent location.

**Better Administration.** There were clearly recognized problems in the way the whole thing was run. Student-staff members often yearned for faculty guidance, but there was little available. The direction within the student-staff itself was based almost entirely upon the personality interactions among its members. Some were explicitly or implicitly recognized as leaders, others regularly and willingly followed, others balked at times. Some handled every responsibility, but others let too much slide. Some were frequently unprepared, some came late to too many sessions, etc. The student-staff leaders had no way to assure the performance of the others of the student-staff, except persuasion. This sometimes failed.

Having a faculty member directly involved would almost certainly help. An interested faculty member might assume overall responsibility for the lab, and offer a regular course called something like "IDL Staff Participation." Faculty administrative involvement would probably go far toward reducing student-staff "goof-offs." As a bonus, it would probably make information gathering, student-staff recruiting, equipment purchasing, room scheduling, etc. much easier.

We are thinking of some sort of faculty-student-staff hierarchy, and a semester-to-semester continuity. New groups of interested students might be invited to join the IDL student-staff and to move upward in the hierarchy. The first semester student-staff members would spend most of their time studying and running stations. Second semester student-staff members would study and run stations, but would also be in charge of designing IDL topic sessions and seeing that it all came off well. One or two of the most capable students, who had already had one or two semesters in the IDL, and perhaps some TA experience, would then be made student-staff leaders with overall IDL supervision, subject to guidance by the faculty member involved.

We think it important that the IDL still be mostly student planned and student run. Faculty skill would be tested in giving just the right amount of guidance and leeway to the student-staff.

The semester to semester continuity would be the basis for an accumulation of interesting stations and for the development of improved techniques for getting things across. This leads to our second suggestion.

**Better Preparation of the Student-Staff.** Student-staff members were often inadequately prepared for running the stations; the time and the means for instructing them were simply not available. Some of the student-staff members felt acutely their lack of relevant background knowledge. It is revealing, however, that few of the student-attendees perceived the student-staff to be unprepared. ("You can fool some of the people, some of the time . . .").

The problem of preparation is one that something positive can be done about. We think that it is important that information notebooks be prepared for the student-staff to study. These notebooks should contain introductory discussions of the various session topics, plus descriptions and explanations of each of the stations. They might also contain references for suggested further reading. Student-staff accounts of their experiences running stations might also be added from semester to semester. This would make the notebooks more entertaining to read, and have motivational and informational value as well. New station ideas would be added to the notebooks as they were thought of, and pertinent information would be developed over time. The notebooks might be reviewed periodically by the faculty member in charge, or by other faculty members who might have special relevant knowledge or information. Part of the semester's grading of student-staff members might be based on their demonstrated knowledge of the contents of these notebooks, and on their contributions to the notebook itself.

**More and Better Stations.** A greater variety of stations should be developed. The suggestions made above (better administration, and information notebooks) would almost certainly open the IDL sessions, and the stations themselves, to continuing critical review. We feel that this review would lead to the development of more interesting and challenging stations. Some of those of the first attempt turned out to hold little interest for some of the student-attendees, some held little challenge. Designing a few of the stations for competition and others for cooperative student performances might help. We also see that the student-attendee should be made into the "experimenter" more often. And some kind of "write-up" experience might well be incorporated into the IDL's. It could start with very simple partial write-ups and gradually work toward a final full scale one. This suggestion assumes, of course, that the student-attendee would be coming to each of the labs during the semester. As you might have guessed, this leads to another suggestion.

**More Attendees at More Sessions.** It is the nature of projects, when they are perceived by those involved as having been successful, to expand. We must admit that we have had speculations in that direction. Our introductory students attended purely on a voluntary basis. Most student-attendees came to one or two sessions. A dream would be to have all of the potential attendees attend a session for every topic. Whether the logistics of the situation (facilities, time, energy, etc.) would allow for such an enlarged project is a problem that each department contemplating an IDL would have to tackle. A suggestion that we have played with is to make the lab sessions daylong and continuous. Student-attendees could then attend any time that they wished during the week of a particular topic. Quizzing would then be done more formally, with the introductory professors adding a selection of the handout questions to their regular quizzes, or quizzing in some other way as they saw fit.

**Better Information to Student-Attendees.** Handouts should be prepared and distributed to each student-attendee at every station. These handouts should contain the obvious descriptions and explanations. They might also contain blank charts and tables of the type generally found in laboratory workbooks. Finally, the handouts should contain three or four questions about the station. The post-lab quizzes would then, of course, consist of a selection of these questions taken from all of the handouts of a given IDL session.

**Permanent Location.** It would be nice, and it would make things easier, if there were a permanent lab room set aside for the IDL. Permanently set up stations, with self-explanatory directions, could be part of the lab. This might help to deemphasize the role of the student-staff members as operatives of stations; student-attendees could work many of the stations themselves with minimal student-staff guidance.

### Conclusion

It is clear that something of value was added to the teaching of our introductory psychology students by other students working pretty much on their own initiative, and with few funds expended. The added value was to the student-attendees who came as consumers to the Introductory Demonstration Laboratory sessions, and especially to the student-staff who put on the whole thing. What was added for both groups seems to have been a better understanding of the realities involved in the accumulation and development of the facts and theories which go to make up psychology. Among the student-staff in particular, there was added some appreciation of the problems involved in getting material across, and much enthusiasm and self-confidence derived from the fact that they had individually and collectively created something so obviously worthwhile.

We believe that any psychology department which would institutionalize an IDL of the type described and suggested would accumulate a corps of highly enthusiastic and involved psychology students—that would, in this world of so much talk of apathy, be nice.

### Notes

1. M.B. has become involved in this write up as a second author. The fact is that he contributed relatively little to the actual production of the IDL. This makes it, at times, somewhat awkward for us to use the term "we" while telling the story. It is a bit awkward, but we are doing it in lieu of a better idea.
2. The authors want to offer a special thank you to the following people who helped to make the I.D.L. possible: Bill Dobreff, Jean Crews, Robyn Stevens, Kathy Soditch, Michelle Scheuern, Bohdan Hrecznyj, and Lynn Yadach. We also thank the other members of the student staff; Gary Forbes, Rene Hinkle, Bob Kreigh, Tina MacKintosh, Sue Parka, Katie Royce, Alison Spear, Kevin Takacs, Nina Warrick, Jodi Wolozynski, and Gary Wylin—we did it!

---

# Undergraduate and Graduate Students As Discussion Section Leaders

Kathleen M. White
and Robert G. Kolber
*Boston University*

> Teachers should not assume that their undergraduate TAs will be less successful than graduate TAs.

Current research in the field of educational psychology has revealed a strong interest in the evaluation of university teaching and the improvement of the undergraduate experience. One of the classic concerns of educators and researchers has been the impact of large lecture classes on undergraduates (Keller, 1968; Rogers, 1967, 1969). A typical assumption is that large lecture courses contribute to the impersonalization of education and the alienation of students from their faculty. Ferster (1968) argues that small classes (about 17 students) are far superior to large lectures. He reports improved grades and better student participation in the smaller groups.

One type of attempt to deal with the presumed impersonality of the large lecture course has been to supplement it with small discussion groups, typically led by graduate student "teaching fellows." Recent research has investigated the notion that undergraduates can also be effective teaching assistants (Boeding & Vattano, 1976; Diamond, 1972; Janssen, 1976; Keller, 1968). In the attempt to facilitate student-centered education, Rogers (1967) has argued for years that undergraduates can be effective leaders of intellectual pursuits with other students.

One question that arises is how students feel about the adequacy of an undergraduate teaching assistant as a discussion leader. Although there is little direct evidence, Rayder (1968) found that less experienced instructors received higher ratings than older, more educated and more experienced instructors. A study by Adams (1973) confirmed these findings and, indicated that the younger the instructor, the higher the ratings. On the other hand, in a review of 62 studies on the characteristics and relationships of selected criteria for evaluating teacher effectiveness, Dwyer (1973) concluded that there are no significant relationships between the evaluations of a professor or course and such variables as teaching experience, age of instructor, class size, or sex of instructor. However, there was evidence that low ratings were given to instructors who dwelled on the obvious, didn't prepare their lectures, or were authoritarian or sarcastic. While these variables may not be related in any consistent way to teaching experience, it seems unlikely that undergraduates who volunteer and are accepted as teaching assistants generally are characterized by such traits.

Another variable which has received some attention is sex of the instructor. As early as 1936, Heilman and Armentrout stated that sex of the instructor has no significant effect upon ratings. However, in a pioneer study, Joesting and Joesting (1972) argue that female instructors enhance the self-image of women students and also influence feelings of belongingness. This finding raises the possibility that female personality characteristics may be especially conducive to a discussion-oriented atmosphere, making females better facilitators of group participation.

In the traditional sex-role literature, men have been described as more achievement oriented, more independent, and more aggressive than females (Bennet & Cohen, 1959; Roessler, 1971). Females are warmer, less aggressive, more nurturant, more cooperative and better socialized than males of comparable ages (Bennet & Cohen, 1959; Bronfenbrenner, 1961; Roessler, 1971). In more recent sex-role literature, a new dimension to sex-role development has been proposed—that of androgyny (Bem, 1974). Individuals who can combine both masculine and feminine characteristics (as traditionally defined) are labeled "androgynous" by Bem. Bem found that highly sex-typed scores do not reflect a general tendency to respond in a socially desirable direction, but rather a specific tendency to describe oneself in accordance with sex-typed standards of desirable behavior for men and women.

It is Bem's belief that the androgynous person will come to define a more human standard of psychological health which focuses upon the behavioral and societal consequences of more flexible sex-role self-concepts. The androgynous person, by definition, bridges the gap between the sexes and widens the scope of societal behavior. It seems reasonable to speculate that an androgynous person, combining both "masculine" achievement and "feminine"

nurturance might make a more effective instructor than a sex-typed person.

The present study was designed to investigate the relationship between evaluations of the teaching effectiveness of discussion group leaders and (a) teaching status (undergraduate or graduate), (b) sex of section leader, and (c) sex-typing. One prediction was that undergraduate teaching assistants would receive higher ratings than graduate teaching fellows. The possibility that women might receive higher ratings than men or that androgynous persons might receive higher ratings than sex-typed persons also was investigated. Because it was thought that there might be some sort of "halo" effect, with assistants for professors who were rated highly receiving high ratings, and vice versa, ratings for each teaching assistant and teaching fellow were correlated with the ratings of the professor he or she assisted.

## Method

**Subjects.** The subjects were 15 graduate teaching fellows and 33 undergraduate teaching assistants. Teaching assistants conducted only one discussion section, but teaching fellows led as many as three discussion sections. Each section was in an undergraduate psychology course at a private metropolitan university.

Discussion sections ranged in size from 10 to 35 undergraduate students and were formed on the basis of time-scheduling needs. Both undergraduate teaching assistants and graduate teaching fellows chose their section(s) according to their particular academic schedules. Thus the sections were not randomly assigned to graduate or undergraduate leaders, and students were not assigned randomly to sections. The students were permitted to change sections if their time schedule allowed, or if for any reason they did not want a particular discussion leader. In a few cases students did make changes to avoid having an undergraduate teaching assistant.

The 15 graduate teaching fellows and the 33 undergraduate teaching assistants ranged in age from 19 to 28 years. Seven of the teaching fellows were men and eight were women. Comparable figures for the teaching assistants were 18 and 15 respectively. The two groups of discussion leaders were enrolled in either a graduate or an undergraduate level seminar on the psychology of teaching.

**Procedure.** All subjects were given the Bem Sex Role Inventory (Bem, 1974) at the onset of the term. Masculinity,

Table 1
Ratings on Teaching Goals as a Function of Teaching Status, Sex, and Sex Role

| Goal | Teaching Status | | Signif. | Sex | | Sex Role Status | | | | |
|---|---|---|---|---|---|---|---|---|---|---|
| | Undergrad | Grad. | | Males | Females | M++ | M+ | A | F+ | F++ |
| 1. Clarifies lectures | 5.06 | 3.04 | p <.001 | 3.83 | 4.91 | 4.25 | 2.84 | 4.53 | 4.69 | 4.77 |
| 2. Encourages discussion | 5.80 | 3.84 | p <.005 | 4.75 | 5.47 | 4.50 | 3.43 | 5.54 | 5.28 | 5.64 |
| 3. Helps skill development | 5.11 | 3.41 | p <.007 | 3.93 | 5.10 | 4.13 | 3.23 | 4.74 | 4.69 | 4.91 |
| 4. Facilitates examination of concepts | 5.29 | 3.19 | p <.001 | 4.20 | 4.94 | 4.55 | 2.84 | 4.74 | 4.80 | 5.16 |
| 5. Facilitates application of concepts | 4.66 | 2.76 | p <.001 | 3.63 | 4.40 | 3.68 | 2.77 | 4.13 | 4.19 | 4.49 |
| Average score | 5.18 | 3.25 | p <.001 | 4.07 | 4.96 | 4.22 | 3.02 | 4.74 | 4.73 | 4.99 |

There were no significant differences in the sex or the sex-role comparisons.

femininity and androgyny scores were derived from this instrument. The scores were classified into five categories according to Bem's derivation: (a) $F^{++}$, or sex-typed females; (b) $F^+$, or slightly-typed females; (c) A, or androgynous; (d) $M^+$, or slightly-typed males; and (e) $M^{++}$, or sex-typed males.

At the completion of the course all subjects gave teacher evaluation forms to their sections. On this form, discussion section participants were asked to rate statements on a 7-point scale, depending on how well each statement describes (a) the section leader, and (b) the professor for the course. All of the student ratings for each statement were averaged, as was the total evaluation score, for each teaching assistant or teaching fellow. Section 1 of the form, "Discussion Section Goals," was developed in the undergraduate teaching seminar in accordance with the suggestion of Grasha (1972), that teaching methods be evaluated only in relationship to explicit teaching goals. Section 2 was adapted from Doyle (1975), and included 26 items like "stimulated curiosity about the subject matter," to which students responded on a 5-point rating scale ranging from "always" to "never."

## Results

A one-way analysis of variance revealed that there were significant differences between undergraduate and graduate section leaders on each goal, and on the average of goals. As can be seen in Table 1, the ratings· of the undergraduate section leaders were higher than the ratings of the graduate student section leaders.

A second one-way analysis of variance revealed no sex differences in ratings on each of the section leader goals or on the average of goals.

Goal scores by each of the Bem Sex Types on each of the teaching assistant goals separately, as well as on the average goal score, are also shown in Table 1. A one-way analysis of variance indicated that none of the differences were statistically significant. The correlation between average teaching skill scores for professors and their section leaders was very high ($r = .96$, $df = 47$, $p < .01$).

## Discussion

In this study of evaluations of psychology discussion leaders as a function of the leader's teaching status, sex and sex-typing, only teaching status emerged as a statistically significant predictor. Although Dwyer (1973) reports no significant differences in teaching evaluations as a function of teaching experience or age of instructor, we found that undergraduates received significantly higher evaluations than graduate section leaders.

These results are consistent with those of Rayder (1968), who found that less experienced instructors had higher ratings than older, more educated and more experienced instructors. Many of the teaching fellows used as subjects in this study were more experienced teachers than the undergraduates. They also had more education and generally were older. Also consistent with our data are Adams' (1973) findings that younger instructors are rated more highly than older instructors.

According to the student ratings in our study, undergraduate teaching assistants are respected and successful section leaders. The closeness in age and status between undergraduate teaching assistants and their students seems to be an asset. It may be that students find it easier to relate to someone closer to their age, and as a result there is greater participation.

Another possible explanation of our findings is that these advanced and self-selected undergraduate assistants spend a great deal of time preparing their discussion sections to create a high interest level on the part of the students. This idea is consistent with Dwyer's (1973) report that lower ratings have been given to instructors who dwelt on the obvious or who didn't prepare their lectures. It is also consistent with Rogers' (1967) assertion that undergraduates can be effective leaders of intellectual pursuits with other students, and with reports on the success of undergraduates as section leaders (Boeding & Vattano, 1976; Janssen, 1976).

We found no significant differences in teaching evaluations as a function either of sex or sex-typing classifications. The lack of sex differences is consistent with the findings of Dwyer (1973) and Heilman and Armentrout (1936), but inconsistent with the findings of Joesting and Joesting (1972). Such inconsistencies provide support for Crawford and Bradshaw's (1968) argument that student evaluations can be interpreted only in relation to the particular students who are doing the evaluating. Each student has personal expectations of an instructor and these may be related to the sex of the instructor. It seems equally likely that comparisons across evaluation studies must take account of the particular evaluation used. The form used in the current study was composed largely of skill items such as: presents or allows various points of view, organized lectures well, and has an interesting style of presentation. These measure the instructor in terms of specific teaching capabilities as a presenter rather than personality characteristics, where the greater warmth, nurturance, and cooperation found in females (Bennet & Cohen, 1959; Roessler, 1971) may not be clearly reflected.

Finally, the highly significant correlation between ratings of course professor and ratings of discussion leaders cannot be ignored. There may have been a selection effect operating. That is, professors who take on the responsibility of using and supervising undergraduate teaching assistants as well as a graduate teaching fellow may be seen as better teachers than professors who do not take on this responsibility. Moreover, if there is any halo effect, it may be operating on the professors rather than on the section leaders. Most professors used both undergraduate and graduate section leaders. It is quite possible that the same professor was rated more highly by students who had an undergraduate leader than by those who had a graduate teaching fellow.

At any rate, the evidence seems clear that professors who use undergraduate teaching assistants should not be fearful that these undergraduates will be seen as any less successful at teaching than graduate students. Given the increasing use of undergraduates as section leaders, these are encouraging findings.

## References

Adams, H. L. Favorable student evaluation as a function of instructor's age. *Improving College and University Teaching*, 1973, *21*, 72.

Bem, S. L.   The measurement of psychological androgyny. *Journal of Consulting and Clinical Psychology*, 1974, *42*, 155-162.

Bennet, E., & Cohen, L.   Men and women: Personality patterns and contrasts. *Genetic Psychological Monographs*, 1959, *59*, 101-155.

Boeding, C. H., & Vattano, F. J.   Undergraduates as teaching assistants: A comparison of two discussion methods. *Teaching of Psychology*, 1976, *3*, 55-59.

Bronfenbrenner, U.   The changing American child: A speculative analysis. *Journal of Social Issues*, 1961, *17*, 6-18.

Crawford, P. L., & Bradshaw, H. L.   Perceptions of characteristics of effective university teachers: A scaling analysis. *Educational and Psychological Measurement*, 1968, *28*, 1029-1085.

Diamond, M. J.   Improving the undergraduate lecture class by use of student-led discussion groups. *American Psychologist*, 1972, *27*, 978-981.

Doyle, K. O.   *Student evaluation of instruction.* Lexington, MA: Heath, 1975.

Dwyer, F. M.   Selected criteria for evaluating teacher effectiveness. *Improving College and University Teaching*, 1973, *21*, 51-52.

Ferster, C. B.   Individualized instruction in a large introductory psychology course. *Psychological Record*, 1968, *18*, 521-532.

Grasha, A. F.   Principles and models for assessing faculty performance. *IRTHE Teaching-Learning Monograph*, 1972, *1*, #2.

Heilman, J. D., & Armentrout, W. D.   The rating of college teachers on ten traits by their students. *Journal of Educational Psychology*, 1936, *27*, 197-216.

Janssen, P.   With a little help from their friends. *Change Magazine*, March 1976, *8*(2), 50-53.

Joesting, J., & Joesting, R.   Sex differences in group belongingness as influenced by instructor's sex. *Psychological Reports*, 1972, *31*, 717-718.

Keller, F. S.   "Good-bye, teacher . . ." *Journal of Applied Behavior Analysis*, 1968, *1*, 79-89.

Rayder, N. F.   College student ratings of instructors. *The Journal of Experimental Education*, 1968, *37*, 76-81.

Roessler, R. T.   Sexuality and identity: Masculine differentiation and feminine constancy. *Adolescence*, 1971, *6*, 187-196.

Rogers, C. R.   A plan for self-direct change in an educational system. *Educational Leader*, 1967, *24*, 717-731.

Rogers, C. R.   *Freedom to learn.* Columbus, OH: Charles E. Merrill, 1969.

## Notes

1. An earlier version of this paper was presented at the Undergraduate Psychology Conference at Brandeis University, 1976.
2. Our thanks go to John Houlihan for his help with the data analysis and to Freda Rebelsky for her comments on an earlier draft of the manuscript.

# 9. TESTING IN THE INTRODUCTORY COURSE

## True-False Tests That Measure and Promote Structural Understanding

George M. Diekhoff
*Midwestern State University*

When students ask before an exam, "What kind of test is this going to be? True-False? Multiple-choice? Essay? Do we have to work any problems?" their questions do not reflect idle curiosity. They are trying to determine through these questions what they should study and how they should go about studying it. Studying for examinations that cover factual information—names, dates, definitions, etc.—requires different thought processes than do exams that focus on applications, integration, synthesis, and going beyond the information given. Because students tend to learn only what they must learn in order to do well on examinations, these examinations, as much as teaching, influence what students learn from our courses (Doak, 1970; Ladd & Anderson, 1970; Willson, 1973).

We can bemoan students' lack of motivation to learn all that they can, regardless of exam content and grades, or we can see the situation in a more positive light. Because students learn in accordance with anticipated exam formats, we can control the types of learning in which they engage by manipulating the types of exams we use. Testing is as much a part of the educational process as is the delivery of a lecture. This is fortunate, because some knowledge is difficult to *teach* and must instead be *learned*.

Structural knowledge, the knowledge of how concepts within a domain are interrelated in a semantic network of ideas (e.g., Collins & Loftus, 1975), cannot easily be communicated through standard lecture/text teaching methods, because language is sequential and presents ideas in a linear string. Teaching that ideas found early in a course are related to ideas following in the middle and end of a course is thus difficult, although the importance of this kind of teaching has been stressed and ways of accomplishing it have been suggested (Bell, 1981; Diekhoff, 1982; Diekhoff & Diekhoff, 1982; Diekhoff & Wigginton, 1982). Study methods that students can use to build integrated knowledge structures have also been developed (Dansereau et al, 1979a, b; Diekhoff, Brown & Dansereau, 1982), but unless students anticipate being tested over structural-level information, they are unlikely to retain structural information presented in class or to use learning strategies that promote structural knowledge acquisition.

Developing practical methods of testing structural knowledge in large classes, however, has proven difficult. Essay exams of the "compare-and-contrast" or "discuss the ways in which *x* and *y* are related" varieties possess obvious face validity as measures of structural knowledge, but, in addition to problems that stem from the subjectivity in scoring essay responses, the time required to evaluate essays of even moderate length makes essay testing impractical for use outside of relatively small classes. Other methods of testing at the structural level, such as those based on word-association and graph-construction techniques (Johnson, 1967, 1969; Preece, 1976; Shavelson, 1972, 1973, 1974), methods involving the evaluation of recall order and pause times in free recall (Reitman & Reuter, 1980), and methods based on the analysis of students' numerical judgments of concept interrelatedness through multidimensional scaling (Fenker, 1975; Johnson, Cox, & Curran, 1970; Stanners & Brown, 1982; Weiner & Kaye, 1974), or other methods of analysis (Diekhoff, 1983), have also proven impractical for the same reason; i.e., lengthy scoring time. In the present study I sought to develop and evaluate a method of generating true-false test items that could be scored quickly and easily and would clearly assess knowledge of relationships between concepts.

**Method.** Nineteen students enrolled in an undergraduate perception and cognition course served as subjects in this research. All students were juniors or seniors and were enrolled in the course as an elective toward a major or minor in psychology.

Students completed four unit exams and a comprehensive final exam during the semester (although five graduating seniors were excused from taking the final exam). Each of the four unit exams consisted of two parts: first, a traditional, 50-item true-false (TF) section which contributed 75% toward the exam grade and which focused on factual information presented in class (e.g., "Echoic storage may last as long as two seconds"; and second, a relational knowledge section (REL) which contributed 25% toward the exam grade. The 30-item REL tests were also presented in a true-false format, but assessed knowledge of interrelationships between ideas that were often presented in very different contexts and at different times. The nature of these REL tests is discussed below. The final exam contained only TF items taken from previous tests and modified for the final. No REL items were included on the final. Means and standard deviations for scores on all exams are presented in Table 1.

In constructing REL items for a given unit, the instructor listed 30-40 key concepts discussed in that unit, pared this list down to 25-30 of the most important concepts, and formed all possible pairs of these concepts. These concept-pairs were examined for strength-of-relationship (generally defined as the degree to which one would tend to talk about the two concepts in terms of each other) and the instructor selected 15 concept-pairs judged to be of high relationship and 15 pairs judged to be of low relationship. Pairs of intermediate relationship were dropped from further consideration. The selected list was always re-examined after two or three days to ensure that the instructor's original perceptions of relatedness were consistent. (They always were.) The selected concept-pairs were then presented to students with the following instructions:

> On each of the following items, answer "true" if you think the two concepts are moderately to strongly related. Answer

## Table 1. Means, Standard Deviations and Correlations For All Course Examinations

| Item | Exam 1 (N = 19) | | Exam 2 (N = 19) | | Exam 3 (N = 19) | | Exam 4 (N = 19) | | Final (N = 15) | |
|---|---|---|---|---|---|---|---|---|---|---|
| | TF | REL | TF | REL | TF | REL | TF | REL | TF | REL |
| M | 72.95 | 74.89 | 79.74 | 79.47 | 88.63 | 82.58 | 88.00 | 78.63 | 76.00 | N/A |
| SD | 8.80 | 10.55 | 7.77 | 8.32 | 4.55 | 6.93 | 6.80 | 13.59 | 11.07 | N/A |
| Correlations | | | | | | | | | | |
| TF-REL | .62 | | .48 | | .30 | | .77 | | | |
| p< | .005 | | .01 | | .10 | | .001 | | | |

"false" if you think the two concepts have little or no relationship. Two concepts are related to the extent that one can be discussed in terms of the other. Remember that your decision as to whether or not a given pair of concepts is related should be based not only on the concepts in that pair, but also on the entire set of concepts included in this test. There are an equal number of related and unrelated items.

Sample items follow:

*From the "Sensory Processes" Unit:*
ADAPTATION LEVEL THEORY—FIGURAL AFTEREFFECTS (Answer: True)
OPPONENT-PROCESS CELLS—PARTIAL REPORT METHOD (Answer: False)

*From the "Pattern Recognition" Unit:*
PHONEMIC RESTORATION—FURST EFFECT (Answer: True)
PERCEPTUAL READINESS—SEGMENTATION (Answer: False)

*From the "Attention and Concentration" Unit:*
CAPACITY ALLOCATION RULES—PREATTENTIVE STAGE (Answer: True)
YERKES-DODSON LAW—RECEPTOR ORIENTATIONS (Answer: False)

*From the "Memory Systems" Unit:*
ACOUSTIC ENCODING—INTRALIST INHIBITION (Answer: True)
PROACTIVE INHIBITION—PRIMACY EFFECT (Answer: False)

Scores on both TF and REL tests consisted of the percentage of items answered correctly (i.e., in the same manner as the instructor).

**Results and Conclusions.** Objective and subjective observations support two conclusions from this study: First, REL tests possess favorable psychometric qualities; second, REL tests alter the ways students think and study in ways that promote acquisition of structural knowledge.

REL tests possess strong face validity as a means of measuring knowledge of structural interrelationships. In addition, scores on REL tests showed moderately strong correlations to TF scores on corresponding examinations (see Table 1). Finally, students' REL scores on the four unit examinations were as predictive of the all-TF, comprehensive final exam scores ($R = .81$, $F (4, 9) = 4.15$, $p < .05$) as were their TF scores from the four unit exams ($R = .84$, $F (4, 9) = 5.43$, $p < .05$).

There is no direct evidence in this study (aside from face validity) that the REL tests used measured a different kind of knowledge (structural) than was measured by TF tests (definitional). However, other research (e.g., Diekhoff, 1983) has shown that students' judgments of concept interrelatedness do carry information concerning structural knowledge. In addition, comments from students in this study indicated

that the use of REL tests in the course led them to think more about similarities between theories and principles presented in the course, rather than simply trying to remember the theories singly. Students regularly asked if REL testing would be included in upcoming exams and occasionally asked for clarification of how various concepts might be seen to be related to each other. These kinds of questions suggest that students were thinking relationally, largely because of REL testing.

It is important that students be tested at the structural level if we wish them to acquire knowledge at that level. The true-false testing method described here provides a quick, easy, and thorough means of testing structural knowledge and causes students to think about relationships among concepts as they study.

## References

Bell, M. E. A systematic instructional design strategy derived from information-processing theory. *Educational Technology*, 1981, 1981, *21*, 32-35.

Collins, A., & Loftus, E. A spreading-activation theory of semantic processing. *Psychological Review*, 1975, *82*, 407-428.

Dansereau, D. F., Collins, K., McDonald, B., Holly, C., Garland, J., Diekhoff, G. M., & Evans, S. H. Development and evaluation of a learning strategy training program. *Journal of Educational Psychology*, 1979, *71*, 64-73.(a)

Dansereau, D. F., McDonald, B., Collins, K., Garland, J., Holly, C., Diekhoff, G. M., & Evans, S. H. Evaluation of a learning strategy system. In H. F. O'Neil, Jr., & C. D. Spielberger (Eds.), *Cognitive and affective learning strategies*. New York: Academic Press, 1979.(b)

Diekhoff, G. M. Cognitive maps as a way of presenting the dimensions of comparison within the history of psychology. *Teaching of Psychology*, 1982, *9*, 115-116.

Diekhoff, G. M. Relationship judgments in the evaluation of structural understanding. *Journal of Educational Psychology*, 1983, *75*, 227-233.

Diekhoff, G. M., & Diekhoff, K. B. Cognitive maps as a tool in communicating structural knowledge. *Educational Technology*, 1982, *22*, 28-30.

Diekhoff, G. M., Brown, P. J., & Dansereau, D. F. A prose learning strategy training program based on network and depth-of-processing models. *Journal of Experimental Education*, 1982, *50*, 180-184.

Diekhoff, G. M., & Wigginton, P. K. Using multidimensional scaling-produced maps to facilitate the communication of structural knowledge. Paper presented at the annual meeting of the Southwestern Psychological Association, Dallas, April, 1982. (ERIC Document Reproduction Service No. ED 218 245.)

Doak, E. D. Evaluating levels of thinking. *School & Society*, 1970, *98*, 177-178.

Fenker, R. M. The organization of conceptual materials: A methodology for measuring ideal and actual cognitive structures. *Instructional Science*, 1975, *4*, 33-57.

Johnson, P. E. Some psychological aspects of subject-matter structure. *Journal of Educational Psychology*, 1967, *58*, 75-83.

Johnson, P. E. On the communication of concepts in science. *Journal of Educational Psychology*, 1969, 60, 32-40.

Johnson, P. E., Cox, D. L., & Curran, T. Psychological reality of physical concepts. *Psychonomic Science*, 1970, *19*, 245-246.

Ladd, G. T., & Anderson, H. O. Determining the level of inquiry in teachers' questions. *Journal of Research in Science Teaching*, 1970, *7*, 395-400.

Preece, P. F. Mapping cognitive structure: A comparison of methods. *Journal of Educational Psychology*, 1976, *68*, 1-8.

Reitman, J., & Reuter, H. Organization revealed by recall orders and confirmed by pauses. *Cognitive Psychology*, 1980, *12*, 554-581.

Shavelson, R. J. Some aspects of the correspondence between content structure and cognitive structure in physics instruction. *Journal of Educational Psychology*, 1972, *63*, 225-234.

Shavelson, R. J. Learning from physics instruction. *Journal of Research in Science Training*, 1973, *10*, 101-111.

Shavelson, R. J. Methods for examining representations of a subject matter structure in a student's memory. *Journal of Research in Science Teaching*, 1974, *11*, 231-249.

Stanners, R. F., & Brown, L. T. Conceptual interrelationships based on learning in introductory psychology. *Teaching of Psychology*, 1982, *9*, 74-77.

Weiner, H., & Kaye, K. Multidimensional scaling of concept learning in an introductory course. *Journal of Educational Psychology*, 1974, *66*, 591-598.

Willson, I. A. Changes in mean levels of thinking in grades 1-8 through use of an interaction analysis system based on Bloom's taxonomy. *Journal of Educational Research*, 1973, *66*, 423-429.

# Effects of Competing Activities on Test Performance In Large Introductory Courses in Psychology

Richard Lore
*Douglass College, Rutgers University*

> Next time students ask to take a make-up examination for a questionable reason, request that they read this paper.

Every teacher is regularly confronted with anguished students pleading that they be allowed to postpone the forthcoming examination or paper deadline. A small minority of the students who make these requests do so regularly and seem to take a perverse delight in delaying as much work as they can for as long as possible. But, in my experience, most students who request delays honestly feel overwhelmed by their work schedule and are convinced that postponement is their only salvation.

Not surprisingly, requests for a delay—particularly for the postponement of scheduled tests—also represent a predicament for the teacher. If a delay is granted, the teacher is violating an important psychometric principle: Accurate performance comparisons can be made only if the work is performed under entirely comparable conditions. Moreover, if the make-up exam is identical or even similar to the regularly-scheduled exam, the possibility of cheating exists. On the other hand, if the instructor goes to the trouble of constructing completely different make-up exams, the alternate versions may not be comparable in difficulty, grading takes more time and departmental secretaries resent the additional work associated with typing multiple versions of the same test and, in many cases, bearing the responsibility for administering make-up exams.

Instructors adopt a variety of strategies in coping with exam schedules and requests for delays. An informal survey of some of my colleagues at Rutgers indicates that some teachers readily grant delays in taking tests or handing in a paper, whereas others do so only rarely. Permission for postponement is most often granted for personal illness or a family emergency. However, many students request and are granted delays because the exam schedule conflicts with a favorite extracurricular activity, a job, or—perhaps most often—simply because the student is convinced that he or she will not have time for adequate preparation. One partial solution to the latter problem involves an attempt to schedule exams in your course so that they do not conflict with exam schedules in other courses. I have had little success with this method. No matter how early or how late in the term the exam is scheduled, a good percentage of the students still have competing assignments.

Students and many faculty members assume that academic performance will be seriously impaired if more than one scheduled test or paper deadline occurs during a given time period. Of course, the criterion for declaring a state of academic emergency varies from person to person. For some, requests for postponement will be made if the student faces more than one hurdle a week. Others are more conservative and request a delay only if two or three exams are scheduled on the same or adjacent days. In any event, the education/learning literature provides no direct information on the effects of reported amounts of competing work on test performance and thus I decided to subject the assumption to a field test in two large sections of Introductory Psychology.

**Method.** Participants were 585 undergraduate students enrolled in two sections of Introductory Psychology at

Douglass College in the fall semester of the 1976/77 academic year. Approximately 81% of the students were females (Douglass is a woman's college). However, both males and females from other coeducational divisions of Rutgers take this course. Most students were either freshmen (43%) or sophomores (36%). Less than 4% were part-time students. Both sections were taught by the author.

Two hourly tests and a final examination were given in both sections. The final was similar to the hourly in length (50 multiple-choice questions) and amount of material covered and each of the three tests contributed equally to the final grade. The second examination was given on Tuesday just prior to the Thanksgiving recess that began with the last class on Wednesday of the same week. At the next class meeting on the following Tuesday, each student was asked to complete a short questionnaire indicating the number of tests taken and papers (including laboratory reports) due and completed during the three-day Thanksgiving week. A total of 441 students in both sections completed and signed the questionnaires for a return rate of 75%. Two weeks after the questionnaires were completed, both sections were informed of the study's purpose and the results were discussed in class.

Results.   The results for each section were analyzed separately. Each student was assigned to one of four groups: those with 0, 1, 2, or 3 or more tests taken and papers due during the three-day Thanksgiving week. The mean scores for both sections on the second test are presented in Table 1. In both sections, students who reported one or two competing assignments during the three-day period actu-

Table 1
Mean Scores on the Second Test of Students in Both Psychology Sections
Who Reported 0, 1, 2, or 3 or More Competing Assignments at the Time They Took the Second Test

| Section | Measure | Number of Tests and Papers Due | | | |
|---------|---------|------|------|------|-----------|
| | | 0 | 1 | 2 | 3 or more |
| I | N | 43 | 73 | 51 | 28 |
| | Mean score | 37.13 | 37.92 | 37.65 | 36.98 |
| II | N | 56 | 93 | 69 | 28 |
| | Mean score | 37.64 | 37.87 | 38.02 | 37.74 |

ally earned slightly higher grades on the test than those reporting zero competing activities. Section II students with three or more competing assignments performed somewhat better than students with zero competing assignments but Section I students with three or more assignments tended to score slightly lower than those with zero assignments. However, analyses of variance indicated that there were no differences among work loads in either Section I, $F (3, 194) = 1.86$, $P > .10$, or Section II, $F (3,245) = .76$, $P > .10$.

Effects of competing activities were also analyzed by subtracting the score on the first test from the score on the second test for each student. Use of these difference scores as the unit of analysis is based on the assumption that the

work assignments of the students were essentially random on the first test and thus the procedure controls for any possible group differences in initial ability level. Again, analyses of variance of the difference scores in both Section I, $F (3,194) = 1.41$, $P > .10$, and Section II, $F (3,245 = .15$, $P > .10$, were not significant. The latter result indicates that the performance of students on the Second Test—relative to their performance on the First Test—was not influenced by the reported number of competing assignments on Test Two.

Discussion.   The results provide no evidence for the assumption that test performance in a college course is adversely affected by the number of competing assignments during a limited time period. Indeed, in both sections performance on the psychology exam tended to be somewhat better if students had a moderate amount of competing work, and even the performance of the group reporting the heaviest concurrent workloads did not suffer appreciably. In light of these findings, instructors should not feel compelled to grant postponements solely on the basis of a reported heavy workload.

A complementary study in the same two sections supports the above conclusion and merits discussion. The first test was given on a Tuesday, the day after Yom Kippur. In both sections, 54 students reported that they had actively observed Yom Kippur and several had requested (unsuccessfully) that they be allowed to postpone the first test. Scores of these 54 students on the second test were matched with those of 54 students (both Jewish and non-Jewish) who reported no observance of Yom Kippur. The score on the first test was subtracted from the score on the second test for each student in both groups. Thus if participation in religious activities on the previous day adversely influenced performance on the first test, then the mean of the difference scores for the religious group should be greater. But the mean difference scores of the groups were virtually identical (+1.86 for the group observing Yom Kippur; +1.83 for those matched students who did not).

The evidence presented here indicates that students are capable of dealing with the usual variations in workload that are so characteristic of academia. Still, the anxiety of students faced with a week of exams is quite real. Some methods that I employ to reduce this anxiety—and at the same time discourage requests for work delays—seem to help. Most important, the ground rules, class requirements, and test schedule should be available at the beginning of the course, preferably on the first day. Criteria for taking tests either early or late should be clear. In my courses, only personal illness or family emergencies qualify. If more than one test is delayed or if the makeup test is taken after the regularly scheduled test has been graded, returned, and reviewed in class, students are required to take a 30-40 minute oral exam. Grades on makeup tests are not counted if the student's score is unusually high or low (plus or minus 15%) relative to his or her performance on other tests. Finally, I give short "practice tests" that are taken outside of class to encourage students to begin to read the assigned material early and to familiarize the class with the kind of questions they will be expected to answer. Occasionally, I include a question from the practice test on the hourly in order to determine if students are taking the practice tests. Invariably, these questions have the lowest error rates on the exam.

To my knowledge, no comparable data on the effects of academic workloads exist. Perhaps test performance on essay exams or tests in other disciplines might decrease with increasing workloads. The point here is that college teachers receive virtually no formal training in their craft and—despite their research training—do too little research on classroom policies and procedures. Consequently, teaching strategies in institutions of higher education are based largely on personal whimsy, superstition or tradition. Surely, college teaching merits more research attention than it receives.

---

# Effects of Exam Frequency on Student Performance, Evaluations of Instructor, and Text Anxiety

Frank E. Fulkerson, *Western Illinois University*
and Glen Martin, *Virginia Commonwealth University*

All dependent measures except final exam scores showed a positive effect of more frequent student testing.

The number of tests students will be given in a traditional lecture course is a decision that some educators seem to feel is a minor one. Often, the decision as to when the students will be tested is made after considering how much material the instructor wants to cover between tests or the time at which one topic will be finished and another started, and where the vacations fall during the semester. Of course, all these must be considered but it seems that the important "number of tests" factor is often overlooked.

Previous studies (Dustin, 1971; Keys, 1934) indicate that students perform better on frequent short tests than on less frequent, long tests; furthermore, frequent testing facilitates retention so that frequently tested students perform better on unannounced retention tests than students that have taken fewer tests (Dustin, 1971; Keys, 1934). However, the evidence concerning the effects of frequent testing on the performance of students on announced retention tests such as comprehensive final exams is mixed. According to Kulp (1933) and Turney (1931) frequent testing facilitates such performance. According to Keys (1934) and Marso (1970), it does not.

It is interesting to note that the studies that compare students taught under the Keller plan (or Personalized System of Instruction) (e.g., Born, Gledhill, & David, 1972; Keller, 1968), to students taught in the conventional lecture method can be viewed somewhat as studies comparing groups of frequently and less frequently tested students. This is true in that a component of the PSI methods of teaching is very frequent testing. The obvious differences between these studies and the Dustin and Keys paradigms are that each group is taught by a different method, and the frequently tested group is required to earn a near perfect score on a test before going on to new material. Certainly these are major differences, but comparisons can still be made.

According to Keys (1934) and Marso (1970) when both frequently and non-frequently tested groups are given an opportunity to prepare for a retention test, the groups should perform equally well. However that is not the case in the Keller and Born et al. studies. In these studies, the frequently tested groups consistently perform better than the less

frequently tested groups on announced retention tests, thereby giving limited, but additional support to Kulp's and Turney's conclusions that frequent testing facilitates retention of course material.

The major purpose of the present study was to investigate further the effects of exam frequency on student performance during an introductory psychology course and on an announced final exam in the same course. In addition, the experiment was designed to investigate relationships between exam frequency and (a) the students' evaluation of their instructor as well as (b) student test anxiety.

In the present study, one section of a course in introductory psychology was given one objective 25-item test every two weeks; a second section was given an objective 50-item test identical to the two combined 25-item tests every four weeks. This testing procedure was the same throughout the duration of the course. The two sections met at different times, but were taught by the same instructor presenting the same lectures to each group and using the same text. A comprehensive final exam (identical in the two groups) served as the announced retention test. Near the end of the quarter, the attitudes of the students toward the instructor were assessed and the test anxiety levels of the students in both sections were measured.

Method. The subjects for this study were Western Illinois University students who enrolled in Introductory Psychology during a Fall quarter for Section 2 (N=203) and for Section 4 (N=202). Although no attempt was made to measure the overall intelligence or knowledge of psychology of the two groups, there is no reason to assume that two groups of students as large as these differed in initial knowledge or ability. Analyses of two sets of students similar to these taught by the same instructor the previous Spring and the following Fall revealed no significant differences in performance. For purposes of this experiment Section 2 will be referred to as the Control Group and Section 4 as the Experimental Group.

Kagan and Havemann's *Psychology: An introduction*

(2nd ed.) was the textbook used in both groups. Both groups read and were tested on the same 15 out of 16 chapters in the text. Eight separate 25-item tests were constructed from the Kagan and Havemann test manuals and from lecture materials for use in the Experimental Group. Four separate 50-item tests made up of the same questions were constructed for use in the Control Group. A 60-item final exam consisting of questions only from the Kagan and Havemann test manuals (i.e., covering only the book) was constructed. None of these questions were questions that had been used on previous exams. Final grades were determined by the total number of points earned during the quarter.

A 15-item Course Evaluation Survey developed by the Psychology Department at Western Illinois University was used to assess the attitudes of students toward the instructor of the course. The Test Anxiety Scale developed by Mandler and Sarason (1952) was used to measure the test anxiety of the students in both sections.

Section 2 was randomly assigned to the 4-test Control condition and Section 4 to the 8-test Experimental condition. On the days when the students in the Experimental Group took their second, fourth, sixth, and eighth 25-item exams, the students in the Control Group took their four 50-item exams. On the days when the students in the Experimental Group took their first, third, fifth, and seventh exams, the students in the Control Group saw a film on which they were not tested, reviewed their first, second, and third exam, and took the Test Anxiety Scale, respectively. The students in the Experimental Group were allowed to review their previous exams after completing each of their 25-item exams. Otherwise, both sections received the same lectures from the same instructor, met the same amount of time, and took the same final exam.

On the day on which the students in the Experimental Group took their seventh exam, the students in the Control Group who were present on that day all took the 37-item Test Anxiety Scale and were dismissed. The students in the Experimental group took their seventh 25-item exam, and then also completed the 37-item Test Anxiety Scale. Finally, both groups of students completed the Course Evaluation Survey, which was administered by TAs.

Results. The means and standard deviations for all exam comparisons made are presented in Table 1. As assessed by $t$ tests for independent groups, the Experimental Group (N=174) scored significantly higher ($ps < .001$) than the Control Group (N=169) on all comparisons except for

Comparison F (Final exam) where $t$ was less than 1.00. Only students who took all exams when scheduled were included in these comparisons.

A total of 154 students in the Experimental Group and 158 students in the Control Group rated the instructor on the Course Evaluation Survey. On this scale the #1 represented the "good" end of the scale and the #5 represented the "bad" end of the scale. Mean scores and standard deviations were calculated for each of the 15 questions on the scale. The mean of the means for the Experimental Group was 1.89 and the standard deviation was .48. The mean of the means for the Control Group was 2.41 and the standard deviation was .65. A $t$ test for independent samples indicated that the difference between these means was significant, $t(28) = 2.50$, $p < .02$. It is also interesting to note that the Experimental Group rated the instructor better than the Control Group on every question on the scale.

One hundred ninety students completed the Test Anxiety Scale in the Experimental Group and 160 students did so in the Control Group. The means and standard deviations were 17.00 and 7.03 for the Experimental Group and 18.89 and 6.46 for the Control Group. A $t$ test for independent samples indicated that the Control students were significantly more anxious than the Experimental students, $t(340) = 3.63$, $p < .001$.

Intercorrelations were also computed for both the Experimental and Control groups between anxiety scores, performance scores (tests 1-8 and 1-4, respectively), final exam scores, and total points (all tests, including the final exam). These correlations are presented in Table 2. As can be seen, significant negative correlations were found in the Experimental Group between anxiety and performance on tests 1-8, and between anxiety and total points earned. The correlation between anxiety and final exam scores, although negative, was not statistically significant. Extremely high significant positive correlations were obtained between performance on tests 1-8 and final exam scores, between performance on tests 1-8 and total points, and between final exam scores and total points.

As can be seen also from Table 2, significant negative correlations were obtained in the Control Group between anxiety and performance on tests 1-4, and between anxiety and total points earned. The negative correlation between anxiety and final exam scores was also statistically significant. In addition, there were high significant positive correlations between performance on tests 1-4 and final exam scores, between performance on tests 1-4 and total points, and between final exam scores and total points.

Other comparisons were made between and within the most highly anxious subjects (defined as having an anxiety score of 25 or greater) and the least anxious subjects (defined as having an anxiety score of 9 or less) in the Experimental and Control groups. The means and standard deviations involved in these comparisons are presented in Table 3.

The most highly anxious subjects in the Experimental Group (N=27) performed significantly better than the most highly anxious subjects in the Control Group (N=29) on Comparison E (Questions 1-200), $t(54) = 2.56$, $p < .02$. However, there was no significant difference between these two groups on Comparison F (Final exam) scores ($t < 1.00$).

Table 1. Means and Standard Deviations for Exam Scores of Experimental and Control Groups

| Exam Items | Experimental Group | | Control Group | |
|---|---|---|---|---|
| | Mean | SD | Mean | SD |
| A. (1-50 | 38.61 | 5.85 | 35.00 | 6.44 |
| B. (51-100 | 38.34 | 6.13 | 35.49 | 6.51 |
| C. (101-150 | 39.50 | 6.26 | 35.67 | 6.92 |
| D. (151-200 | 37.35 | 6.89 | 35.21 | 5.81 |
| E. (1-200 | 154.34 | 21.17 | 141.46 | 21.42 |
| F. Final-60 | 46.09 | 7.65 | 45.57 | 7.36 |
| Total | 200.44 | 27.47 | 186.73 | 27.69 |

| Variable | Anxiety | | Tests 1-8 | | Final Exam | |
|---|---|---|---|---|---|---|
| | E | C | E | C | E | C |
| Anxiety | | | | | | |
| Tests 1-8 | −.34 | −.33 | | | | |
| Final Exam | −.20 | −.25 | .77 | .79 | | |
| Total Points | −.31 | −.33 | .98 | .98 | .87 | .88 |

Note: Data are from those students who took all exams on schedule and who were present when the *Test Anxiety Scale* was administered (N = 166 for the E Group and 137 for the C Group). Significance levels corrected for number of variables are as follows: $r \geq .27$, $p<.01$; $r \geq .22$, $p<.05$ for the E Group and $r \geq .29$, $p<.01$; $r \geq .25$, $p<.05$ for the C Group.

Those subjects showing the lowest amount of anxiety in the Experimental Group (N = 27) did not differ from the equivalent subjects in the Control Group (N = 15) on either Comparison E or Comparison F ($ts<1.00$). As would be expected from the correlation data, within the Experimental Group the low anxious subjects performed significantly better than the high anxious subjects on Comparison E, $t(52) = 3.68$, $p<.001$, and on Comparison F, $t(52) = 2.40$, $p<.05$. Within the Control Group the same results occurred on Comparison E, $t(42) = 4.27$, $p<.001$, and on Comparison F, $t(42) = 2.41$, $p<.02$.

Discussion. It is obvious from the examination data that the frequent, shorter tests over smaller amounts of material in the Experimental Group led to significantly better test-by-test performance than the less frequent, longer tests over larger amounts of material in the Control Group. This finding is congruent with previous research on this topic (e.g., Dustin, 1971; Keys, 1934). It is also equally apparent that the number of tests taken during the quarter had absolutely no effect on performance on the announced final exam where the mean scores of the two groups were almost identical, replicating previous findings by Keys (1934) and Marso (1970).

These findings are also consistent with those of a recent study by Badia, Harsh, & Stutts (1978) who conducted a comprehensive study covering 18 sections of an introductory psychology course wherein a personalized system of instruction (PSI) was compared with a lecture method having frequencies of three, five, or nine exams. Badia et al. found that subjects in PSI sections did better than subjects in lecture sections who took only three or five exams. However, the test performance of subjects in the lecture sections who took nine exams was comparable to that of subjects in the PSI sections. Badia et al. concluded that it is conceivable

that frequency of testing may be the basis for the superior performance of the PSI students, although they stated that it was unlikely because of other differences found when they contrasted PSI and lecture sections. For example, the variability of the students in their PSI sections was significantly less than for students in their lecture sections. Other evidence in their study indicated that the higher mean exam scores and reduced variability for students in their PSI sections resulted from higher levels of performance by students with lower ability levels and poorer study habits. Students with high scores on these measures did equally well in PSI and lecture sections. Unfortunately, however, Badia et al. did not include a comprehensive final exam in their study.

In the present study, the students in the Experimental Group also had a much higher opinion of their instructor than the students in the Control Group. This finding is probably related to the fact that the most frequent negative comment of the Control students on the open-ended portion of the Course Evaluation Survey was that the instructor was treating them unfairly by making them take longer tests over more material. Although none of the students were aware of the fact that a study was being conducted, it was obvious from student statements on the Course Evaluation Survey that it was general knowledge that the two groups were being tested differently. It is also somewhat informative that a negative impression characteristic of the Control Group can influence student ratings of their instructor on all sorts of competencies other than fairness to students. For comparative purposes, since the instructor taught two large sections of introductory psychology during quarters preceding and following the experiment, he also looked at his student ratings on the Course Evaluation Survey for those terms. The mean ratings for the previous Spring quarter were 1.88 and 1.84, respectively for the earlier and later sections. For the following Fall quarter the mean student ratings were 1.96 and 1.95, respectively, for the earlier and later sections. These differences are not nearly as large as the difference between 2.41 and 1.89 found in the current study.

The results of the Test Anxiety Scale, while interesting, are rather difficult to interpret. Although the Control Group was significantly more anxious than the Experimental Group, the absolute difference of 1.89 between the mean scores (18.89 vs. 17.00) was not very large. It is difficult to conclude whether fewer tests cause more test anxiety or whether the fact that the Experimental students took the Test Anxiety Scale immediately after completing their seventh exam might have led to a "relief syndrome" compared to the Control students who took only the Test Anxiety Scale on that day. Nevertheless, the fact that the most highly anxious subjects in the Experimental Group did significantly better

Table 3. Means and Standard Deviations for Exam Scores of High and Low Anxious Subjects

| Group | High Anxious Ss | | | | Low Anxious Ss | | | |
|---|---|---|---|---|---|---|---|---|
| | Material E (Questions 1-200) | | Material F (Final Exam) | | Material E (Questions 1-200) | | Material F (Final Exam) | |
| | Mean | SD | Mean | SD | Mean | SD | Mean | SD |
| Experimental | 141.89 | 21.29 | 43.74 | 7.99 | 162.33 | 19.53 | 48.04 | 7.04 |
| Control | 128.24 | 18.87 | 42.24 | 7.43 | 156.20 | 23.60 | 48.13 | 8.11 |

than the most highly anxious subjects in the Control Group on Comparison E supports the notion that frequent testing may aid the performance of highly anxious subjects. In addition, the present results are consistent with findings by Dustin (1971) whose frequently tested subjects showed less anxiety than his control subjects at the end of six weeks.

The fact that there was no significant difference between the most highly anxious subjects in the Experimental and Control Groups on Comparison F (Final Exam) is consistent with previous findings by Marso (1970). Marso's analysis of test performance on two post-test measures indicated that, although subjects in general achieved more from frequent graded unit tests followed by feedback, variations of these conditions did not influence the final exam performance of his high test-anxious subjects. In other words, his high anxious subjects did more poorly on the final exams than his low anxious subjects regardless of the number of unit tests, as was the case in the present experiment.

In conclusion, it appears that frequent testing helps students to perform better on a test-by-test basis, but this advantage disappears on an announced final exam when, presumably, cramming can equalize knowledge of course material. Students definitely favor frequent tests over infrequent tests as indicated by both objective ratings of their instructor as well as by subjective comments. In addition, high anxious subjects do better on short frequent tests than on longer infrequent ones, although they still perform below the level of equivalent low anxious subjects on either kind of test. Finally, the relative improvement of high anxious subjects on short frequent tests does not carry over to their performance on an announced final exam.

## References

Badia, P., Harsh, J., & Stutts, C. An assessment of instruction and measures of ability. *Journal of Personalized Instruction*, 1978, *3*, 69-75.

Born, D. G., Gledhill, S. M., & Davis, M. L. Examination performance in lecture-discussion and personalized instruction courses. *Journal of Applied Behavioral Analysis*, 1972, *5*, 33-43.

Dustin, D. Some effects of exam frequency. *The Psychological Record*, 1971, *21*, 409-414.

Kagan, J., & Havemann, E. *Psychology: An introduction* (2nd Ed.). New York: Harcourt, 1971.

Keller, F. S. "Good-bye teacher . . ." *Journal of Applied Behavior Analysis*, 1968, *1*, 79-98.

Keys, N. The influence on learning and retention of weekly as opposed to monthly tests. *Journal of Educational Psychology*, 1934, *25*, 427-436.

Kulp, D. H. Weekly tests for graduate students? *School and Society*, 1933, *38*, 157-159.

Mandler, G., & Sarason, S. B. A study of anxiety and learning. *Journal of Abnormal and Social Psychology*, 1952, *47*, 166-173.

Marso, R. N. Classroom testing procedures, test anxiety, and achievement. *Journal of Experimental Education*, 1970, *38*, 54-58.

Turney, A. H. The effects of frequent and short objective tests upon the achievement of college students in educational psychology. *School and Society*, 1931, *33*, 760-762.

# INSTA-EXAM: A Card-Based Exam Preparation System that Eliminates Repeated Typing and Proofreading

Robert T. Tauber
*Pennsylvania State University, Erie*

Today, more than ever before, all aspects of education need to be alert to the wachwords *efficiency* and *effectiveness*. Exam preparation is a good target for such efforts. What is needed is a system that solves the following problems: (a) How can we speed up the preparation of exams when we want to reuse the questions at a later time or when we need several versions of the same exam?; (b) How can we prepare exams that require little, if any, proofreading?; and (c) How can we prepare exams without monopolizing skilled secretaries' time and keeping them from more important projects (typing manuscripts and grant proposals)?

The solution is a system of exam preparation I call INSTA-EXAM. It is a card-based system that rivals today's computer-based exam preparation systems. A specific comparison follows later in the paper. As was described by Mershon (1982), such card-based exam preparation systems make several assumptions. First, for various reasons (from time constraints to the relative permanence of the content of introductory courses) faculty who teach undergraduates do *reuse* examination questions. Second, exam questions must be stored in an exam "bank" (for later manipulation and retrieval). Methods of storage range from cards, marks in Instructor Guides, to circles on "old exams." Third, exam questions must be typed and proofread the *first* time no matter what system is being used.

The INSTA-EXAM system consists of two parts, INSTA-EXAM cards and a plastic Card Aligner.[2] Exam questions, of any test format, are placed one per card, on INSTA-EXAM cards. The INSTA-EXAM cards are 4½" x 8" index weight cards with faint gray orienting lines that disappear when photocopied and a single ¾" line of reproducing ink in the upper left hand corner. This line has three purposes. First, it marks the upper line of the examination question. Second, the end of this line marks the left-hand margin for the typed question. Third, the line provides a space (on the later photocopy) in which a question number may be inserted. Along the left-hand margin of the card is a series of holes of uniform size and spacing (¼" holes on ½" centers). These holes allow the cards to be placed on the Card Aligner. The plastic Card Aligner comes in two pieces (to facilitate storage) and when snapped together resembles a ruler 15" long and 1" wide with a series of ¼" pins, also on ½" centers, along the side to accept the INSTA-EXAM cards. The pins provide a good "grip" to positively align or register the INSTA-EXAM cards (a problem highlighted in Mershon's method) yet are sufficiently small to permit easy attachment and removal of the cards.

The front side (along the bottom edge) of each INSTA-

EXAM card also contains, in non-reproducing ink, spaces which act as "prompts" for the instructor's data collection—including "correct answer," "chapter," and "textbook." The back side of each card contains more elaborate prompts to encourage instructors to do an item analysis, columns to record several years worth of data, space to outline essay answers, and a set of typing and exam preparation instructions for the INSTA-EXAM system.

Steps in Using the INSTA-EXAM system. 1. Type exam questions, one per INSTA-EXAM card. Cards accommodate any question format—multiple-choice, true/false, matching, essay, word problems, etc. Exam questions have to be typed, whether on INSTA-EXAM cards or on a stencil master. Why not do it just once for those questions you plan to use again? Questions can be typed on INSTA-EXAM cards before they are needed, for example, during less demanding time periods. The end result is a "bank" of test questions on INSTA-EXAM cards, easily stored, catalogued, retrieved, added to, changed, or deleted. The 4½" height of the cards permits common 5" x 8" index cards to be used as topic dividers.

2. Form an exam by selecting INSTA-EXAM cards and placing them, in an overlapping or shingling fashion, on the plastic Card Aligner. For multiple-choice and true/false questions squeeze as many cards as you can on the Aligner. This is easy with Aligner pins only ½" apart. For short answer and essay questions leave as much space as is needed for the answer between questions. For questions incorporating a chart or table that you plan to use over again, place the chart or table on the Aligner first *and then* have the questions relating to the diagram follow on separate INSTA-EXAM cards. Cut out complicated graphs/diagrams from other sources and then tape them on INSTA-EXAM cards (the tape will not show when photocopied), again with exam-specific questions following on separate cards. Thus, one really detailed graph (taking a good deal of instructor preparation time) can be used over and over again with different sets of exam-specific questions. To temporarily alter (highlight/change) a diagram that is on an INSTA-EXAM card, use a piece of overhead transparency acetate with ¼" holes down the left margin. Place this on top of your INSTA-EXAM card, write your change on the transparency with a grease pencil, and instantly, when photocopied, your diagram is temporarily altered. This step results in the formation of a "page" of the exam made up of a series of instructor selected INSTA-EXAM cards shingled (like shingles on a roof) one over the other. The Card Aligner accepts cards for standard 8½" wide paper and anywhere up to 14" long paper. Using several plastic Card Aligners permits the preparer to format the entire exam before tying up the busy photocopier (next step).

3. Using the Card Aligner(s) to align (register) and hold the instructor selected INSTA-EXAM cards in place, make a photocopy of each "page" of the exam. Using several Aligners permits the preparer to have the entire exam ready for photocopying at one time. The gray orienting lines on the face of the cards, used as an assist in typing, have all disappeared. Any notes written at the bottom of the cards have been covered by succeeding cards. This gives you a photocopy, or master, of each page of the exam that looks as if it were an original, just-typed copy.

4. If you are satisfied with the quality of the page(s) generated in step #3, number the exam questions by placing the numbers immediately above the dark horizontal line (upper left hand corner) that survived the photocopying process. (Note, do not number the actual INSTA-EXAM cards prior to photocopying as they will occupy different spots on different exams.) At this point, after 4 steps, the INSTA-EXAM process is complete. You have a master ready for duplicating in required quantities—by using the photocopier, by cutting a mimeograph stencil, or by forming a ditto master. Getting to this point, though, takes just a *fraction of the time usually required!* (See comparison study.) The result is a numbered photocopy of each page of the exam suitable for duplication. For a 2nd or 3rd version of the exam, peel the cards off the Aligner, shuffle them, replace them, and make your photocopy.

5. Using the numbered photocopies of the exam, run off required copies.

Evaluation. A study was done to compare the INSTA-EXAM preparation system with a more traditional exam preparation method—typing directly on a mimeograph stencil. A skilled college secretary prepared a 50-item multiple-choice exam using both systems. The 50 exam items were taken directly from published Instructor Guides. Four of the questions contained simple sketches.

The secretary was given the 50 items in the best possible form, each question already typed on individual INSTA-EXAM cards. She was given the following instructions. "Type the exam as quickly as you can but at the same time remember you must proofread it and correct any errors. We are after both speed and accuracy." Nine stencils and 22 corrected errors later the "test" was ready for duplicating. It took 2 hours and 18 minutes to type, 32 minutes to proofread, and 25 minutes to draw the sketches for a total of 3 hours and 17 minutes.

The secretary was given the same 50 questions on INSTA-EXAM cards, a set of plastic Card Aligners, and instructions as to how to put the cards on the Aligners, make the photocopy, and number the pages. In addition the secretary was given the same caution (shown above) to stress both speed and accuracy. Nine photocopies and *no errors* later the exam was ready for duplicating. It took a total of only 18 minutes! the INSTA-EXAM system of exam preparation was *10 times faster* than the more traditional, labor intensive method of typing directly on stencil masters.

INSTA-EXAM vs. Computerized Testing Services. Lately textbook publishers have been offering a computerized testing service to those who adopt a given text. Basically, the service consists of a file of test questions accessible to a faculty member by the use of a toll free number (during business hours) or by the submission of an order form. In either case, test questions are identified by number and within 48 hours in-house time a master of some sort is forwarded to the instructor.

The INSTA-EXAM is not nearly as technologically sophisticated, but it does compare favorably. Specifically, users of the INSTA-EXAM system are *not limited* to any particular publisher's test question file. Instructors can build their personal "test banks" on INSTA-EXAM cards by creating their own questions and by using or altering publisher provided questions. Content validity is increased. INSTA-EXAM users have no limits as to how many exams or quizzes they may have generated (computerized systems often do). Lead-time is less of a worry for INSTA-EXAM users. Exams can be prepared, even by less skilled secretarial help, closer to the time when the exam is to be administered. Compare this to computerized systems requiring 48 hours in-house processing time *plus* mailing time. INSTA-EXAM users are better able to test what has been taught rather than having to teach for that last week what has already been submitted for the exam. Finally, computerized exams are not yet (perhaps never will be for smaller markets) available for all textbooks. The INSTA-EXAM system adapts to all disciplines and to any textbook—big seller or not.

Most recently, publishers have begun to provide instructors with floppy disks containing test questions to accompany textbooks adoptions from which exams can be generated via an institution's microcomputer facilities. Although I am a believer in the use of microcomputers (this manuscript is being prepared on an Apple IIe), I do not believe that their use has overcome any of the problems highlighted above, except perhaps that of lead-time. In fact, an additional problem, the requirement for instructors and/or secretaries to interact directly with microcomputer hardware and software (assuming they have it available), has been created.

**Additional Uses for the System.** The INSTA-EXAM's ability to quickly and efficiently change, update, and delete information (especially in the form of lists) adapts it to other uses. Consider its use for creating phone directories, class rosters, intramural team rosters, instructor vitae, inventory lists, and more.

The INSTA-EXAM system is not designed to supplant any exam preparation methods that are more efficient and more effective—only those that are less so. I believe the INSTA-EXAM system fills the void between more traditional exam preparation methods and the as yet unreached potential of computerized methods. It is a method that has had to wait until good photocopying devices were widely available. It is a simple, yet flexible, cost effective system that produces high quality results and gives its user a feeling of direct control. The INSTA-EXAM system solves, for a large segment of the educational community, many of the most basic problems of exam preparation.

### Reference

Mershon, D. H. An inexpensive system for producing examinations with minimal typing and proofreading. *Teaching of Psychology*, 1982, 9, 108-109.

### Note

1. INSTA-EXAM materials, the INSTA-EXAM cards and plastic Card Aligner, are available from TTK Communication Products, 3892 Gay Road, Erie, PA 16510. Card Aligners are $2.50 each or 5 for $10.00. INSTA-EXAM cards are approximately $0.04 each in lots of 500.

---

# Test Administration In Large Lectures:
# An Alternative to the Paper Chase

J. Gregory Carroll
*University of Pennsylvania*
R. J. Senter
*University of Cincinnati*

For instructors conducting traditional large lectures, the logistics of administering an examination can be overwhelming. The amount of materials and labor expended can be dramatically reduced with one simple and straightforward technique. Instead of printing test items on paper, project them on a screen using 35mm slides. This technique has worked well for several years in an introductory psychology course at the University of Cincinnati. The course consists of two separate lecture sessions, each with about 800 students.

Before this technique was used, the administration of a test was truly an awesome task. The initial trouble was the manufacture of the tests. On the average our examinations contained six pages. This meant that we had to produce about 1600 copies, or a total of 9,600 sheets for each test.

Once the individual pages had been produced there came the problem of collating, assembling, and stapling them. Finally, these 19 reams of paper had to be transported to the lecture hall, handed out to individual students, and collected at the end of the hour.

In these days of necessary emphasis on ecology and energy conservation, this procedure of traditional test administration to "mega-classes" becomes almost disgracefully wasteful. In our own class, for instance, we ordinarily give four tests during each quarter. We calculate that we were using about 115,200 individual sheets of paper per year—a number verging on an *eighth of a million*!

**Description of the New Testing Technique.** With some modification our procedure can be used in any classroom equipped with an ordinary 35mm slide projector and screen. The room in which our classes meet has three large rear-projection screens mounted high above the floor of the stage. In the beginning of a test session, students receive standard IBM answer sheets. Half of the sheets are marked "Form A," and the other half are marked "Form B" in large letters applied with a mimeograph machine. Students in alternate seats are issued the alternately marked answer sheets.

The students are instructed that the test questions for Form A will appear on the left-hand screen and the questions for Form B will appear on the right-hand screen. The center screen contains a set of answer alternatives tailored to go with *both* of the questions appearing on the side screens. All students holding Form A answer sheets direct their attention to the left-hand screen to read the items projected there; then they choose from the multiple-choice alternatives shown on the center screen. Form B holders read their questions from the right-hand screen and then choose the appropriate answer from the same set of choices being projected on the center screen. A little ingenuity and thought are necessary in the generation of items so the same set of alternatives will comprise reasonable answers for both questions being projected, as in the example below.

| Form A | | Form B |
|---|---|---|
| Destruction of tissue in the ventromedial nuclei of the hypothalamus of the rat produces: | A. Nocturnal isomorphism <br> B. Dermatomycosis <br> C. Rats which refuse to eat <br> D. Fat rats | Destruction of tissue in the lateral nuclei of the hypothalamus of the rat produces: |

Items are projected for 40 seconds each, and then another set is projected. The 40-second time limit was decided upon only after considerable "piloting." A full minute was much too long. Students were noticeably bored and impatient to get on with the next item. Thirty seconds was not enough time. A large segment of the student group would shout and jeer when the test item slides were changed at 30-second intervals. At 40 seconds there are, sometimes, a few students who begin to show their impatience by whistling or clapping between slides but very few ever complain about 40 seconds being too little time.

The original materials which we photograph are produced on ordinary white paper with an IBM Selectric typewriter using a carbon ribbon. Any typewriter will do and the carbon ribbon is not absolutely necessary, but it does make much better copy. We have produced the best slides with Kodalith film, which is a high-contrast, black-and-white, negative film, producing brilliant white letters on a very dense black background when properly exposed.

Discussion. The advantages of this testing technique in terms of expense, time, and logistic simplification are obvious. There is one additional advantage which is not so immediately obvious, i.e., test security. No printed examinations are handed out to the students to find their way into various test files commonly kept by student organizations. If one uses the same textbook and changes one's lecture notes moderately from year to year, one can use a large proportion of the test slides for several years with little fear that these items are "out." It is then easier to edit and improve one's test file from year to year.

The disadvantages of this method, aside from those normally encountered with any large scale testing, are very few. The main difficulty arises with students who have visual problems which preclude their seeing the screens or language problems which prevent their reading English fast enough to keep up. Special arrangements have been made

for these students, but their number has been quite small. Similarly, make-up examinations are scheduled separately for students who miss more than one test during the quarter, but students rarely miss more than one test. (Every student is required to take three of the four tests each quarter; if four tests are completed, the lowest score is dropped.)

Similar testing procedures have been mentioned elsewhere (Kennedy, 1969; Maslow, 1969), but we have not found any published reports of empirical research on the topic. The distributions of our test scores for the projected method reveal nothing dramatic. The means run on the order of mid- to high 30s for 50-item tests. There is a slight ceiling effect with a few students "topping out," and there is a rather characteristic negative skew generated by a few students who score little better than chance. This is about what our test distributions have always looked like.

How have students reacted to the "automated" test? To be perfectly honest we thought that when we announced this testing procedure the students would attack the stage and string us up from one of the trees we are trying to save. But this did not happen—on the contrary the acceptance was remarkably high. There was some grumbling, of course, with the chief complaint being that there was no opportunity to go back and reconsider items which had been answered previously. The students in our course have been quite responsive to the argument that everyone is working under the same conditions so that their relative position in the class, hence, their "curved" letter grades, would not suffer.

At the end of the first quarter of the 1976-77 academic year we administered a course evaluation questionnaire prepared by the University of Cincinnati Faculty Resource Center. Imbedded in this questionnaire were items specifically designed to tap the students' reaction to some aspects of our testing procedure. To the questionnaire item, "I perform better on paper and pencil tests," 43% of the students agreed, 31% were neutral, and 26% disagreed. In spite of the substantial number of students who felt that they would have done better with the paper-pencil format, only 15% of the students reported that they thought the use of slide tests was unfair, with 60% disagreeing with the "unfair" statement. To the item, "Enough time was allowed for the tests," 81% indicated that they thought the 40-second per item time limit was adequate, 6% were neutral and only 13% felt that the time limit was too short.

Many intriguing questions about this method of testing are yet to be answered. How does the method affect students' test performance? Would variable time intervals between test items be preferable to the fixed 40-second interval? Could the multiple screens be better utilized by projecting additional items simultaneously so that each student could better control the time he or she devotes to a given item? If an opportunity to review all the items were provided at the end of the test session, would test scores improve? Does the method deter or facilitate cheating? At this point we feel that the method certainly deserves further study, and our own experience indicates that its advantages will far outweigh the disadvantages. If the procedure were to be adopted on a large scale, substantial savings would be achieved in preparation time, natural resources, and energy. One rather striking point: consider that if our procedure were to be used in seven other courses of comparable size, a savings of almost one million sheets of paper, which are ordinarily expended in total redundancy and ultimately thrown away, could be achieved annually.

## References

Kennedy, C. A. *Teaching Asian thought and culture via television: A pilot study. Final report.* Washington, DC: US Department of Health, Education, and Welfare, Office of Education, 1969. (ERIC Document Reproduction Service No. ED 031 098)

Maslow, R. *The one course class load:A first step for teaching general psychology in community colleges.* Paper presented at the annual meetings of the American Psychological Association, Washington, DC, September 1969. (ERIC Document Reproduction Service No. ED 032 881)

# Section II
# Demonstrations and Activities in Introductory Psychology

# 10. GENERAL

# The Journal: An Autobiographical Approach to Learning

Paul Hettich
*Barat College*

*If your student evaluations are weak on "stimulus to thinking outside of the classroom," you may wish to try The Journal.*

This article describes an autobiographical technique of learning wherein students relate course material to their thoughts and experiences. The literature on this topic is sparse. Allport (1942) discussed at length the uses of personal documents (e.g. as a diagnostic supplement; as a method for studying religious experiences, adolescent behavior, historical personalities, and creativity) and their forms (e.g. autobiographies, letters, diaries, literary and artistic creations). In his analysis of the role of autobiography in personality development, Jung (1972) noted that during the 1920s and 1930s attention was given to the use of personal documents in the study of personality. However, questions concerning validity, reliability, subjectivity, and verifiability produced doubts about the value of this technique. Gestwicki's description (Note 1) of journal writing in a college religion class was the sole written account of this autobiographical technique located by the writer.

**What Is the Journal?**   The journal is neither a diary (i.e. a continuous, intimate, spontaneous outpouring of important events) nor a log (i.e. an account or record of events). Rather, according to Allport, it is a topical autobiography: a short discontinuous personal document which represents the excerpting from an individual's life of a special class of events—in this case, events constituting a psychology course.

**Journal Writing Procedures.**   The aim of the journal is to partially individualize the undergraduate psychology course. It is described to students as a means of connecting the knowledge, concepts, and ideas which they acquire from the course to their past and present experiences, thoughts, work. self-reflections; books or articles read; and other courses.

Students are asked to write at least two entries each week in a notebook. The length of entries has ranged from one sentence to four pages, the average entry containing about five sentences. To encourage spontaneity and the development of a personal writing style the writer accepts any entry which is anchored directly to course-based material. Journal entries represent *examples* of psychological concepts, *evaluations* or *analyses* of ideas, *applications* of principles, or (on occasion) new ideas. Unedited sample entries written for four different psychology courses are shown below.

*Introductory Psychology*
1. There is a small boy around school. One day he called me "Lulu." I was very surprised because I do not know him. Later, I learned that there is another Chinese girl around school by that name and he knew her. So whenever he sees other Chinese girls, he calls them "Lulu". I think this would be an example of *stimulus generalization*. This little boy has associated the name "Lulu" with certain looks and features of a Chinese girl and he tends to generalize to all Chinese girls. J.C. (Comprehension)

2. Another form of aggression which I have experienced myself occurs when I am frustrated by the outcome on a test which I thought I had studied for very well and then I find out I didn't study the right things. This *displaced* aggression usually transfers from the original cause of frustration (myself) to another thing related to the task. Such things could be blaming the teacher for making up too difficult a test, or blaming one's friends for making too much noise during study periods. This seems to be a form of conflict reduction when one tries to reduce the conflicts within oneself for doing poorly on a task by blaming something else for the outcome. This aggression constantly occurs in learning when I am faced with an overload of material to be learned for a particular class and have to study one less or both less in order to grasp any concept. Thus, if I do poorly on succeeding tests, I tend to blame the instructor somewhat for my poorer grades for assignment overloads. N.E. (Analysis)

*Experimental Psychology*
1. I'm making a definite effort to look at research on a much more critical note than I was previously. I'm trying to decide if certain points were valid, and if experimental method was relevant to the study. In my Social Psych. class, I find myself mentally critiquing Aronson's research techniques. I hope this will provide a sounder base for my next examination. S.F. (Analysis)

2. The Article on Demand Characteristics fit in well with experimentation. It was good to read it after our group experiment because it stated so clearly many things we were feeling and experiencing doing the experiments—the desire to do well was expressed by all participants, the inquiry into what the experiment was about, the deliberate attempt to memorize the letters even though we were counting, the personality inter-

jection, even the control was felt. I remember getting tired of counting and wished it would end - but still kept trying as long as Brenda kept saying letters. This happened in the 2nd experiment also. The degree of frustration the problems created could almost be felt (and was verbally expressed occasionally) yet the subject kept trying to finish. Another reason I found this interesting was last semester in Psych. of Personality—Ullman and Krasner went into quite a bit of detail on experimental biases. They emphasized one fact of experimenter and subject influencing and being influenced by each other. All experimentation has to be viewed with this in mind. B.S. (Comprehension, Analysis)

*Psychology of Learning*
1. When I was in high school I did not enjoy schoolwork that much. It was a chore rather than a satisfying experience, as it is now. My father thought he would help me enjoy this work more if he reinforced good grades on my report cards. He would give me $1.00 for every A, 50¢ for every B and a quarter for every C. D's and F's were not positively reinforced. This system of giving money for good grades was an example of token reinforcement which was based on a fixed interval schedule. The reason this reinforcement was on a fixed interval schedule is that grades are delivered periodically after a standard interval of time. L.A. (Comprehension)

2. I was struck by a similarity between the generative theory of language of Chomsky and Jung's personality theory. Chomsky holds that a universal language structure exists in all men. A child is born with this native equipment for producing language. It is an innate deep structure of universal syntax. Jung's theory of personality involves the idea of the collective unconscious, which is also universal and inherited. Jung's archetypes are like pre-dispositions to perceive or act in a certain way. Although it may be stretching a point, I think that Chomsky's universal syntax could be looked on as a sort of language archetype. T.M. (Analysis-synthesis)

*Cognition*
1. Sapir's idea of word length being related to or a cue to the age of a word is an interesting thought. In studying Chaucer this semester one can trace the word "called" (Modern English) to "yclep" (Middle English) and "clepan" (Old English); or the modern term ride from "ridan" (O.E.) and "ridin" (M.E.). Tokenyng (M.E.) has been shortened to token; and portrays (M.E.) to draw or paint. I think the language took a turn of shortness in that period, and that modern words of length now are "new" words, such as astronaut or discrimination. The classic example of a long modern word is antidisestablishmentarianism. It's going to be interesting to see if that one even survives. I think that usage or colloquial use play a major role, as television, a common household item these days, is shortened to TV (a classic example!). J.V.L. (Comprehension)

2. Serial position effect: subjects presented with a list of nonsense syllables or other material to be learned have found the material in the middle of the list to be the most difficult. In a classroom situation, Johnson and Calhoun (1969) found the serial position phenomenon when utilizing meaningful lecture material. They found that material at the beginning of the lecture was most easily learned. Therefore, teachers should consider the most important and crucial concepts at the beginning of the instruction period. The middle portion of the period could be used for elaboration and pupil discussion of the concepts. The final minutes of a period could then be used to summarize and synthesize. C.L. (Analysis)

Because autobiographical learning is a new experience for most students, guidelines and sample entries are distributed during the first week of class. During the third week and again during the last week of class, journals are collected, read and returned with comments. As autobiographical learning is a supplement to the course, standard texts are used and tests are administered regularly. The criteria employed for evaluating journals include depth of thinking, accuracy (when appropriate), types of entries (e.g. examples, evaluations, analyses), and number of entries written.

**Problems Encountered.** The problems that arise in using this autobiographical technique concern the students, teacher, and the journal. Nearly all students can write a journal of satisfactory (or better) quality, although less than 15% have had prior experience with it. Some students report difficulty in beginning the journal — a problem which is exacerbated by the tendency of authors to begin texts with discussions of definition, theory, and scientific method. Similarly, some students find it challenging to relate and apply psychological concepts to their experiences. Finally, a few report that they sometimes forget the subject of an entry before they have the opportunity to record it.

The procrastinator, a student who delays journal writing until shortly before it is collected, is a problem facing both instructor and students. "Cramming" reduces a student's spontaneity and the opportunity to observe improvement. The solution to cramming—collecting and reading journals more frequently—requires additional time, another limitation. It has been the writer's experience that class sizes of 35 to 40 students represent the maximum permissible for using the journal, without teaching assistance.

In his critical analysis of personal documents, Allport identifies two weaknesses that pertain to journals. First, the journal is a subjective measure of learning: entries cannot be verified, memories can become distorted. Second, as the journal constitutes about 15% of the final grade, the opportunity for, and likelihood of, deception is substantial. For instance, it is not usually possible to determine if demonstrations have been performed or if insights, analyses and criticisms are original. However valid the arguments of subjectivity and deception, their significance is diminished because the journal is a supplementary, not a primary, measure of learning.

**Results: Teacher Perceptions.** First, the journal provides an element of individualized instruction to a predominantly lecture type course. Consequently, students enhance their understanding of many abstract psychological concepts and forge their thoughts on broader issues, using their own words and experiences as tools. Thus, psychological concepts become anchored to the student's cognitive framework, not just to examples provided by the textbook and teacher. Second, the journal provides the teacher with additional information for understanding and evaluating the student. It is not uncommon to find a student who "tests" at the average or below average level, yet writes a genuinely lucid and insightful journal. Third, the journal extends the student's contact time with the course from the class and study periods to other points in the student's life. A few students have indicated that they *search* for daily events which relate to course material. Thus, in so far as education is intended for "life" beyond the classroom, the journal can assist in the process of transfer by teaching the student to connect life to course experiences. Fourth, the journal provides an opportunity for active involvement in the learning process, increased motivation, and self-produced feedback, factors considered by McKeachie (1963) as critical for effective learning.

**Results: Student Perceptions.** Table 1 summarizes the responses given to seven questions (part of a questionnaire) by 109 students: 60 enrolled in learning, experimental or cognition courses at Barat College, and 49 enrolled in Introductory courses at the College of Lake County. Opinions were recorded on a seven point scale, with 7 denoting "very much" and 1 indicating "not at all." Students tend to regard the journal as a valid measure of learning ($\bar{x}=5.08$), as a source of feedback ($\bar{x}=5.75$), as a means of stimulating critical thinking ($\bar{x}=5.84$), and as a way of permitting self-expression ($\bar{x}=5.69$). They view the journal more as a supplement than as a substitute for examinations ($\bar{x}=5.11$ versus $\bar{x}=3.53$). However, journal writing is not generally regarded as a strong source of motivation for learning course material ($\bar{x}=4.95$). A Chi Square One Sample test, comparing the expected with the observed distribution of ratings to the seven categories, was performed on the data produced by each of the seven items listed in Table 1. All Chi Square values were found significant (df=6, p<.01), indicating that the distributions of ratings were not random.

The first five questionnaire items presented in Table 1 may be regarded, collectively, as a crude index of student opinion toward the journal. Summed, the values for each of the five items produce an Opinion Score for each student, and a basis for comparing the classes in which the journal was used. Using this index, means of 6.12, 5.91, 5.33, and 4.86 were obtained for the cognition, learning, introductory,

and experimental courses respectively. Higher Ns for the cognition and experimental courses could yield different values. The means suggest that the journal is an apparently (no tests of significance were calculated) successful technique in the cognition, learning, and introductory courses, but less successful in the experimental course. Considering the abstractness of most experimental psychology concepts, and the amount of work demanded by the writer in this course, it was not surprising to find students in that course less enthusiastic about relating courses and life experiences.

When asked about their preference for writing a journal or a term paper, 95% of the 102 respondents selected the journal because: (a) it deals with more and broader topics than a term paper; (b) it represents a personal application of psychology; (c) entries are written throughout the course; or (d) journals are more interesting and stimulating than term papers. Many students remark that the journal would be appropriate in child, social and abnormal psychology courses. Data from the writer's consumer, industrial and physiological courses are forthcoming.

**The Journal and Bloom's Taxonomy.** The types of entries (examples, applications, evaluations, analyses, and new ideas) parallel in part, Bloom's Taxonomy of Educational Objectives for the Cognitive Domain (Bloom, 1956). Bloom's six levels include: knowledge, comprehension, application, analysis, synthesis, and evaluation, respectively. In the journal, examples of concepts correspond to Bloom's comprehension level, demonstrations to the application level, analyses to analysis, new ideas to synthesis, and evaluations to evaluation. Below each entry at the beginning of this article, the corresponding level or levels of the taxonomy have been identified. To date, most entries have been written at the comprehension and application level. A smaller number are analyses or evaluations of ideas, and an occasional entry exemplifies synthesis. Assuming the validity of the taxonomy, it would seem appropriate to examine the extent to which journal entries fit one or more of Bloom's categories. (Some entries are difficult to catego-

Table 1.
Student Ratings of the Journal in Four Courses

| Questionnaire item | | Introductory N=49 | Learning N=34 | Experimental N=21 | Cognition N=5 | Total N=109 |
|---|---|---|---|---|---|---|
| To what extent: | | | | | | |
| Is the journal a valid measure of learning? | Mean | 5.04 | 5.51 | 4.38 | 5.40 | 5.08 |
| | S.D. | 1.59 | 1.02 | 1.86 | 1.20 | 1.53 |
| Is the journal a source of feedback about your learning? | Mean | 5.73 | 6.18 | 4.95 | 6.40 | 5.75 |
| | S.D. | 1.20 | 1.15 | 1.86 | .80 | 1.40 |
| Does the journal stimulate critical thinking? | Mean | 5.85 | 6.00 | 5.38 | 6.60 | 5.84 |
| | S.D. | 1.55 | 1.24 | 1.59 | .49 | 1.46 |
| Does the journal assist in the self-directed expression of learning? | Mean | 5.31 | 6.38 | 5.29 | 6.20 | 5.69 |
| | S.D. | 1.36 | .73 | 1.67 | .98 | 1.35 |
| Was the journal a source of motivation to learn? | Mean | 4.76 | 5.50 | 4.29 | 6.00 | 4.95 |
| | S.D. | 1.45 | 1.29 | 1.75 | 1.26 | 1.54 |
| Is the journal a supplement to exams? | Mean | 4.96 | 5.76 | 4.19 | 6.60 | 5.11 |
| | S.D. | 1.58 | 1.52 | 1.94 | .49 | 1.72 |
| Is the journal a substitute for exams? | Mean | 3.22 | 4.19 | 3.14 | 3.60 | 3.53 |
| | S.D. | 1.57 | 1.73 | 1.75 | 1.02 | 1.71 |

rize.) Furthermore, it may be valuable to teach students to *think* (thus write) at Bloom's levels, through the journal. Essentially, perhaps Bloom's taxonomy could become a teaching device incorporated into journal writing.

A number of questions suggest further investigation of the journal technique. For example, to what extent could the journal become an influential, perhaps predominant, measure of learning? What is the correlation between skill in journal writing and course grades? and test performance? How does journal writing affect learning in subsequent courses? The data of this study, and the questions posed by the findings warrant further examination of this potentially valuable technique.

### References

Allport, G. W. *The use of personal documents in psychological Science.* New York: Social Science Research Council, 1942.

Bloom, B. S. (Ed.). *Taxonomy of educational objectives.* New York: Longmans-Green, 1956.

Jung, J. Autobiographies of college students as a teaching and research tool in the study of personality development. *American Psychologist,* 1972, *27,* 779-783.

McKeachie, W. J. Research on teaching at the college and university level. In N. L. Gage (Ed.). *Handbook of Research on Teaching,* Chicago: Rand-McNally, 1963.

### Notes

1. Gestwicki, R. Autobiographical journals and beyond. Paper presented at the meeting of the American Academy of Religion, Chicago, November 1973.
2. The author thanks Drs. Joseph Rizzo and John Cotton for critically reading this paper and Ms. Mary Janeczek for assisting in the data analysis.

# Sherlock Holmes and the Educational Process

Richard L. Kellogg
*State University of New York,*
*Agricultural and Technical College*

More interest and enthusiasm may be generated for basic psychological concepts if the teacher engages the famous detective as a consultant.

Picture yourself for a moment in a small London flat during the late 1800's. Rain is beating against the window-panes and a strong wind is howling through the streets of the city. Suddenly a candle flickers out of the darkness and a tall, thin man emerges from a bedroom. He walks slowly across the room and gently taps the shoulder of a man sleeping on the sofa. He says sharply, "Come, Watson, come! The game is afoot."

If the previous scene generated pleasant memories from the past, you may be familiar with the magic and mystery of the Holmes legend. The adventures of the great detective, Sherlock Holmes, and his close friend and associate, Dr. John Watson, have provided countless hours of entertainment for generations of readers. The stories which comprise the Canon (four novels and fifty-six short stories) are still popular today, and are frequently presented on the stage, motion picture screen, and television.

Probably the current upsurge of interest in the intrepid investigator stems from the best-seller by Meyer (1975), in which Holmes is united with Sigmund Freud on a bizarre case involving crime and psychopathology in Vienna. In the 1960s, a biography of Holmes assembled by Baring-Gould (1962) also inspired readers to review the original tales of suspense written by Doyle (1930).

When the enigmatic detective first appeared in "A Study in Scarlet" in 1887, few realized that the genius of Arthur Conan Doyle had created one of the most durable and recognizable characters in all of fiction. The public clamored for more stories about the brilliant sleuth and Doyle was quick to oblige. As new adventures flowed from Doyle's pen, fans around the world learned to associate the pipe, cape, deerstalker cap, magnifying lens, and violin with the fascinating personality of Sherlock Holmes.

Doyle, having grown weary of Holmes and aspiring to write on other topics, had Holmes plunge to his death at Reichenbach Falls during the final struggle with his arch-enemy, Professor Moriarty. The reading public was outraged that the author would allow its hero to be destroyed at the height of his career. Doyle finally relented (perhaps good Dr. Watson, who sometimes became confused, had hallucinated Holmes' death) and revived the popular detective for a series of new exploits. Some fans contended that Sherlock was never as formidable in subsequent stories after his fall from the cliff. Nevertheless, he was back at 221B Baker Street to practice his profession as the world's first unofficial consulting detective for a total of twenty three years. For seventeen of those years, Watson assisted Holmes on his investigations and chronicled the more singular cases for his enthusiastic followers.

For both Baker Street Irregulars and the casual reader, Holmes has become almost a real person rather than just another imaginary character. How do we account for the phenomenal popularity of this man over so many years? Other fictional detectives have not received as much critical analysis or captured as large an audience.

To shed light on the man and his mystique, let us review the ideas, methods, and principles which directed his investigations. In particular, we will concentrate on concepts of learning and problem solving which enabled Holmes to solve mysteries which had baffled representatives of Scotland Yard. His approach to resolving difficult cases is relevant for assisting contemporary educators to facilitate the teaching-learning process.

**Relevance to Education.** Since Holmes was neither psychologist nor educator, it may seem ironic to link his investigative strategies to the field of education. However, the detective was a keen student of all human behavior and he developed sophisticated insights into such topics as problem solving, creativity, motivation, perception, and learning. His unexcelled abilities in observation and deduction, employed brilliantly in his criminal investigations, can be used as a model for directing students in their learning experiences.

Holmes enjoyed playing the role of instructor in his relationships with others. He frequently was professorial in his detailed explanations of how he solved particular cases. In one adventure, Watson states that Holmes "began to lecture with the air of a professor addressing his class" (Doyle, 1930, p. 511). In another adventure, police inspector Hopkins "professed the admiration and respect of a pupil for the scientific methods of the famous amateur" (Doyle, 1930, p. 560). Throughout the tales of the Canon, Holmes seems to relish presenting educational demonstrations on his methods of detection to Watson and others.

Holmes had great respect for education and for the necessity of academic preparation. This is illustrated by a revealing conversation between Holmes and Watson while aboard a London-bound train. When Watson noted that the English boarding schools looked sordid in appearance, Holmes became agitated and referred to such schools as "Capsules, with hundreds of bright little seeds in each, out of which will spring the wiser, better England of the future" (Doyle, 1930, p. 456). Holmes was well-educated himself and his statement suggests how strongly he felt about the importance of academic training.

Let us examine some of the significant factors in the teaching-learning process which appear in the Holmes literature. As these factors are explored, it is well to keep these words of the great detective in mind, "Education never ends, Watson. It is a series of lessons with the greatest for the last" (Doyle, 1930, p. 907).

Factors in the Teaching-Learning Process. Each person who peruses the adventures of Sherlock Holmes can assemble a different list of factors which relate to education. The subjectivity of such a task is inevitable. Realizing how imperfect this structure is, I have outlined seven factors in learning which may be of interest to both instructors and students. It is hoped that some readers will delve into the Holmes literature and discover seven (or seventy) more factors of their own.

Deduction. Holmes delighted in shocking his clients by making accurate observations and then drawing bold inferences from his data. Few detectives would have the audacity to glance at a client and declare that he was obviously a manual laborer, used snuff, was a Freemason, had been in China, and had done a considerable amount of writing. To Holmes, of course, such deductions were "elementary." Watson was always amazed at how his friend could analyze his clients and solve the most complex mysteries through a series of rapid, brilliant deductions.

While deduction can be defined in several ways, it involves reasoning from the known to the unknown through knowledge of general principles. Holmes maintained that it was possible to establish a single fact and then, by deductive procedures, to hypothesize the total chain of events which led up to it and which followed from it. He compared his technique to the method whereby Cuvier could describe an entire animal through the analysis of a single bone from the skeleton.

Holmes considered it a mistake to establish theories before making the necessary observations. He felt that premature theorizing causes the investigator to misinterpret the facts in order to fit the theories. It was better to approach each problem with an open mind and let the evidence decide which of the possibilities to pursue. Holmes was fond of saying that "when you have excluded the impossible, whatever remains, however improbable, must be the truth" (Doyle, 1930, p. 315).

Examples of deduction abound in Holmes' exploits. For instance, Dr. Watson once purchased a medical practice next to the house of another physician. Holmes, who knew both houses were built at the same time, casually remarked that Watson had the better practice of the two. When Watson wondered how his friend could possibly know that, Holmes noted that his front steps were worn three inches deeper than those of his neighbor.

Holmes felt that his powers of deduction resulted from heredity as well as from training and experience. He thought this because his older brother, the portly Mycroft, had even greater abilities in this area than his own. Whether deductive ability stemmed from genetics or environment, Holmes realized the limits of logic. The detective, who suffered from personal problems such as drug addiction and depression, once asked Watson, "What object is served by this circle of misery and violence and fear" (Doyle, 1930, p. 901)? It was the investigator's melancholy conclusion that human knowledge has been unable to fathom many of the perennial problems of living.

Memory. Memorization ability often helped Holmes in determining the correct approach to an inquiry. He had extensive knowledge of past criminal activities which could be utilized to solve new crimes. As for the criminal world, Holmes pointed out that "There is nothing new under the sun. It has all been done before" (Doyle, 1930, p. 29). The main implication is that thorough knowledge of past events is essential for successful learning and problem solving in the present.

Holmes occasionally commented on the dangers of retroactive inhibition. He compared man's brain to a little empty attic which could contain only so much furniture. He cautioned that "there comes a time when for every addition of knowledge you forget something that you knew before" (Doyle, 1930, p. 21). Therefore, he thought it crucial that the individual not acquire useless facts which might crowd out more valuable information.

Since memory is limited and fallible, Holmes felt it should be supplemented by the judicious use of reference materials. His early cases indicate that the investigator found it invaluable to consult the Bible, the American Encyclopedia, the Continental Gazetteer, Lloyds Registers, and a variety of professional journals. Standard reference sources often provided him with information which was needed for a particular investigation.

In addition, Holmes compiled a wealth of data on past and present criminal activities from magazines and newspapers. Although Watson thought their lodgings were cluttered with boxes of clippings, he conceded that his associate could quickly furnish information on almost any subject or individual. This large collection of data was necessary since Holmes recognized the impossibility of remembering all the facts which were pertinent to a specific problem.

*Perception.* Perceptual ability concerns the capacity to attach meaning to the sensations that we experience. Holmes attempted to develop his perceptual powers to the degree that he could detect things overlooked by others. He felt that heightened perception was a key to successful problem-solving.

The detective paid attention to the minute details of each investigation and, through extensive interviewing, tried to ascertain every fact from his clients. After all, it was one "trivial" fact unperceived by others which might open up a completely new line of inquiry.

Dr. Watson was sometimes criticized by his companion for not being more perceptive. In one incident, Holmes inquired of Watson as to how many steps there were from the street to their lodgings. When Watson admitted that he didn't know, Holmes informed him that there were seventeen and curtly added, "You have not observed. And yet you have seen. That is just my point" (Doyle, 1930, p. 162).

The perception of a seemingly insignificant event served as a major clue in a famous case involving a stolen horse. When Holmes discovered that a dog did not bark during the alleged abduction of the horse, he suggested to the police inspector that he should pay attention to "the curious incident of the dog in the night-time." When the bewildered officer said that the dog hadn't done anything, Sherlock retorted, "That was the curious incident" (Doyle, 1930, p. 347). Holmes was trying to demonstrate to the inspector that perception of a non-event may be as important as that of an event.

Ability to perceive and interpret body language is another aspect of the Holmesian method. The detective asserted that it was possible to understand the emotions and motives of others through the study of bodily movements and facial expressions. To illustrate this factor, Holmes once startled Watson by reading some of his inner thoughts. The detective then explained to his friend that "The features are given to man as the means by which he shall express his emotions, and yours are faithful servants" (Doyle, 1930, p. 423). Since Holmes recognized that his more intelligent adversaries might use their knowledge of body language against him, he frequently wore elaborate disguises while on their trail.

The use of empathy is also an aspect of effective perception. As Holmes described this technique to a police officer, "You'll get results, Inspector, by always putting yourself in the other fellow's place, and thinking what you would do yourself" (Doyle, 1930, p. 1121). The investigator realized that development of empathy required a lot of imagination and insight. However, it was a valuable tool for probing the thoughts and emotions of others.

*Specialized Knowledge.* In addition to expertise in the areas of deduction, memory, and perception, Holmes stressed the importance of acquiring specialized knowledge in one's own profession. In his own training, Holmes was a product of the English boarding schools and had several years of university education. It is unlikely, however,

that he completed his studies and received a degree. Much of his knowledge in the field of chemistry came from research conducted at St. Bartholomew's Hospital ("Bart's") in London. He also completed extensive independent study in the Reading Room of the British Museum. The result of this training was an individual with knowledge of those disciplines which he considered essential for a private detective to acquire.

To locate concrete examples of Holmes' specialized knowledge, an excellent source is the listing of his writings compiled by Baring-Gould (1962, p. 326). A prolific writer, Holmes wrote a number of technical monographs during periods of leisure between his cases. He wrote on such topics as the dating of documents, the identification of tobacco types, the deciphering of secret codes, the variability of human ears, and the use of plaster of paris to preserve impressions. He also authored a number of brief articles relating to chemistry and music. Holmes began but apparently never completed "The Whole Art of Detection," a definitive volume which would summarize his methods of investigation.

The detective considered specialized knowledge of little value unless it was accompanied by hard work and self-discipline. Observance of the Puritan work-ethic helped Holmes succeed in situations where official police agencies had failed. Records of his cases suggest that he suffered at least two collapses from exhaustion because of overwork and lack of sleep. He would work for weeks at a time without adequate food and rest until the investigations were concluded.

*Emotional Control.* Holmes was aware that emotions play a major role in the areas of learning and problem solving. In fact, he abhorred any sort of emotional involvement when engrossed in a problem. He felt that emotional arousal was a hindrance to the objectivity required for precise reasoning. His position was summarized well in his statement that "whatever is emotional is opposed to that true cold reason which I place above all things" (Doyle, 1930, p. 157).

Holmes had a cold, calculated approach to life which bothered acquaintances and annoyed Dr. Watson. A bachelor all his life, he had few friends while attending university and expressed a mild interest in only one woman, opera singer Irene Adler. Regardless of how his undemonstrative personality was perceived by others, he maintained that strong emotional control was required for the processes of productive thinking.

The unfortunate aspect is that Holmes suppressed his emotions too strongly for his psychological health. Watson worried about his friend's intemperate use of cocaine and tobacco. Holmes was subject to deep depressions when not occupied with an investigation. Finally, elements of conceit, sarcasm, and cynicism were often evident in the personality structure of the great detective.

While Holmes was correct that the cognitive processes are adversely affected by excessive emotional arousal, it was unhealthy that he concealed his feelings so completely. Only once in the years of their relationship did Watson see the inner Holmes. This happened in a situation where Watson was wounded by a bullet and Holmes feared for his companion's life. In a very moving passage, Watson reported that "The clear, hard eyes were dimmed for a moment, and the firm lips were shaking. For the one and only time I caught a glimpse of a great heart as well as of a great brain" (Doyle, 1930, p. 1053). The kindly physician then wrote that all his years of dedicated service to Holmes culminated in that moment of revelation.

*Incubation Periods.* Another point of the Holmes approach concerns an incubation period which precedes creative insight into the solution of a problem. This period is an interval of relatively limited progress before mental inspiration is achieved. During these stretches, Holmes smoked his pipe, listened to music, and played his violin.

In the incubation period, the preferred strategy is to stop thinking about the problem and to focus on other matters for a while before returning to it. Watson has stated that "Sherlock Holmes had, in a very remarkable degree, the power of detaching his mind at will" (Doyle, 1930, p. 692). This statement suggests that the detective was able to switch his attention to a rest period or change of activity when stymied by a complex puzzle.

As for hobbies, Holmes enjoyed such activities as boxing, fencing, reading, and bee-keeping. In addition, he was a composer of considerable ability as well as a virtuoso on his Stradivarius violin. These varied pursuits allowed the chance to escape temporarily from his problems and to restore his mental powers.

In brief, Holmes believed that intervals of rest and recreation, especially when taken during the incubation period, enhanced the capacity for learning and problem solving.

*Divergent Thinking.* The final factor in the Holmes model is divergent thinking ability, or the talent for generating multiple responses to a problem. The detective cultivated this ability to analyze many alternatives to a problem rather than allowing circumstantial evidence to dictate the one correct solution. The need to consider a number of different strategies was once indicated when Holmes wished to gain secret access to a telegram. Instead of taking the most direct approach, the investigator noted that he "had seven different schemes for getting a glimpse of that telegram" (Doyle, 1930, p. 628). He then balanced each alternative against the others and determined which had the greatest probability of success.

Along with divergent thinking, Holmes realized the importance of keeping a flexible viewpoint and an open mind. He repeatedly cautioned against the construction of theories before all the factual evidence was collected and studied. Theories could result in a rigid mental set and the inability to perceive facts which might indicate other explanations.

The need to evaluate every possible alternative to a problem is illustrated by a comment of Holmes that "It may well be that several explanations remain, in which case one tries test after test until one of them has a convincing amount of support" (Doyle, 1930, p. 1011). He felt that the individual must use imagination in a creative way and consider all possibilities before selecting the most suitable

approach. Productive reasoning of this type helped Holmes unravel the mysteries which were submitted to him.

**Instructional Implications.** A review of the adventures of Sherlock Holmes reveals numerous concepts which relate to instruction and the teaching-learning interaction. Although he had neither time nor interest to formulate a complete learning paradigm, specific factors which relate to education can be gleaned from the records of his investigations.

To summarize the model, the following points about the Holmesian approach have instructional significance:

1. Deduction, the ability to draw inferences from detailed observations, is an important ability for the learner to acquire.
2. Memorization ability can be developed and is an essential component of learning and problem solving.
3. Perceptual skills are necessary for effective learning and they encompass such areas as body language and empathy.
4. Specialized training in one's career field, accompanied with a propensity for hard work, increases the probability of professional success.
5. An excessive degree of emotional arousal makes learning and problem solving more difficult to achieve.
6. Creative insight into a problem is more likely when an individual learns to use rest periods, hobbies, and recreational pursuits wisely.
7. Divergent thinking and a flexible viewpoint improve the quality of problem-solving strategies.

It is common for educators to encounter negative reactions when presenting students with theories and research studies which concern human learning. More interest is generated when lectures and discussions on this topic are supplemented with exposure to the Master of Baker Street. Excerpts from the fictional material serve as an excellent vehicle for introducing and illustrating such learning processes as deduction, memory, perception, problem solving, creativity, and divergent thinking.

It is likely that a number of students (and their instructors) will concur with Dr. Watson who, after the apparent death of his companion, sadly remembered Sherlock Holmes as "the best and the wisest man whom I have ever known" (Doyle, 1930, p. 480).

### References

Baring-Gould, W. S. Sherlock Holmes of Baker Street: A life of the world's first consulting detective. New York: Clarkson N. Potter, 1962.

Doyle, A. C. The complete Sherlock Holmes. New York: Doubleday, 1930.

Meyer, N. The seven-per-cent solution. New York: Balantine, 1975.

# Tying it All Together: Research, Concepts, and Fiction in an Introductory Psychology Course

Lita Linzer Schwartz
*Pennsylvania State University*
*Ogontz Campus*

After I was assigned to teach the Introductory Psychology course for the first time in ten years, I sought ways to make it an experience that would have lasting impact on the students. The goal was not original, nor were many of the supplemental aids such as films, handouts, paper-and-pencil activities, and discussions (in a class that began with more than one hundred freshmen and sophomores). Concurrent with the course planning, however, I was (and continue to be) involved in a study of conversion techniques, particularly as they have been used by contemporary cult groups. The possibility of tying this research to the course seemed to be an effective yet low-key method of uniting instructor interest and course content. It also offered an opportunity to make students aware of some of the characteristics of cult groups without preaching to them. The specific mechanism to be used was a report on Ehrlich's novel, *The Cult* (1979).

A traditional introductory text was assigned as basic reading for the course (Belkin/Skydell, 1979), with students encouraged to use the accompanying Study Guide as well. Four quizzes, each based on three chapters of the book, were scheduled. A report on *The Cult* was the fifth component to be considered in determining the student's grade. The report was focused on identifying the application of a number of psychological concepts in the novel. Although students were aware from the opening day of the course that they would have the report to write, specific instructions for the paper were not distributed until half-way through the 10-week course. I thought that by then the students would be less anxious about the terminology used. The instructions read:

> In Psy 2, we have studied many principles and concepts that are demonstrated in this novel. From the list below, select a minimum of five (5) principles or concepts, and write a brief paragraph or two *for each* describing how it is applied in the cult situation. Cite specific examples and page references from Ehrlich's book.
> Altered states of consciousness
> Attitude change and cognitive dissonance theory
> Behavioral modification
> Conformity: compliance and internalization
> Deindividuation
> Effects of sleep and diet deprivation
> Leadership and leader-follower relations
> Motives for becoming involved with groups such as "the cult" (i.e., what needs are satisfied in this type of group?)

Students were referred to the text for definitions of the terms, particularly those not yet discussed in class.

Every student was able to select appropriate applications of at least four concepts, most found one or more examples for five concepts, and a few reached for six concepts. Verification of the knowledge gained from reading the novel as well as the text was sought in the error rate on the dozen final quiz questions (out of 50) that dealt with several of these same ideas.

The last three chapters of the Belkin/Skydell text, on which the final quiz was based, included psychotherapies, social behavior, and group processes. Principal ideas of each chapter were discussed in lecture, supplemented by a film. The only differences between the content of 38 of the questions and the remaining dozen, which were scattered throughout the quiz, were that the latter had also been involved in the novel and the paper based on it. To determine whether this activity had any effect on reinforcing certain concepts, analysis of error rates for the two groups of questions was made.

An initial inspection of the data revealed that students made 1-27 errors on the total quiz, with both the median and mode at 11 errors, or a 22% error rate. The mean was 11.58 errors, or a 23% error rate. The number of errors on the 12 questions relevant to the concepts emphasized in *The Cult* ranged from one to 9, with nine of the 81 students (11%) making more than three errors, or an error rate in excess of 25 per cent. On the remaining 38 questions, the number of errors ranged from one to 18. Ten or more errors would exceed the expected 25% error rate. Forty students of the 81, or almost 50%, had error rates above what was expected. The significance of the difference in error rates was analyzed using the Wilcoxon matched-pairs signed-ranks test formula for large samples, for which $z = -5.94$, which is significant beyond any tabled value. This statistically significant result suggests that learning was enhanced for those concepts demonstrated in the additional reading assignment.

As noted earlier, there was another goal in the assignment. As a result of the author's research and discussions with cult-involved young adults and their families, there was genuine concern that these students, most of whom have not been away from home independently, should have enough information about cult-type groups to be able to make an informed decision on whether or not to accept an invitation to visit such a group. That the goal was attained was apparent in many verbal comments even before the reports were submitted. In the papers themselves, there were also several comments that reflected the hoped-for awareness:

> Personally I would like to add that I found reading *The Cult* to be an eye-opening experience. I had been in some doubt about cults in general. However, after reading Ehrlich's book I regard them in a new light. It is my opinion that cults are not true religions or churches and they are mentally harmful to those people who choose to join them.

> I feel this book was very informative. I have been interested in fraudulent cults for two years, realizing the increasing international problem. I have come in contact with

many devotees in the city collecting "for orphanages and old age homes" (I have never contributed a cent). I truly hope more young people become informed on this evilness than just the 106 people in this class.

Ehrlich's book has left me with a sharpened awareness of a fascinating yet petrifying phenomenon. *The Cult* has brought me to realize that in this world people must be wary with whom they associate. While reading the book, it induced me to think about all the people I come in contact with and question how well I really know them. *The Cult* shows how belief in an authority figure, such as Rev. Hodges of the SFJ, can be carried to a frightening extreme.

I liked this book very much. It was intriguing to read, and very unsettling at times. My advice to anyone who comes in contact with one of those groups is to just keep walking. Don't stop to talk or buy a pamphlet. Pretend that they are not there.

(*Note:* Class members were also sharing their information and opinions with other students on campus, a "bonus" as far as I was concerned, because students in my other courses told me that they'd heard about or even borrowed the book to read. Although this feedback was rewarding, there was an allied reaction that was also very unexpected. In common with many other colleges and universities, we have a student body that rarely reads for pleasure. That fact made the following comment all the more gratifying: "I read the book from cover to cover without once putting it down. For me that's probably the first time.")

Although the choice of novel in this instance was dictated by the instructor's research activities, it would seem that there are at least two other novels that might be equally effective as teaching instruments. These are Huxley's *Brave New World* (1932) and Orwell's *1984* (1949). Both demonstrate the use of psychological principles in manipulating human behavior and life-styles. Although they lack the timeliness of *The Cult* in terms of a current problem, there are aspects of each that can be tied to contemporary events. That the use of the novel as part of the required reading for the introductory course is worthwhile is evident from the reinforcement of information as determined by the significantly lower error rate on novel-related questions.

## References

Belkin, G. S., & Skydell, R. H. *Foundations of psychology.* Boston: Houghton Mifflin, 1979.
Ehrlich, M. *The cult.* New York: Bantam Books, 1979.
Huxley, A. *Brave new world.* New York: Harper, 1932.
Orwell, G. *1984.* New York: Harcourt, Brace, 1949.

## Note

1. Appreciation is extended to Diane Winnemore for performing the calculations for the Wilcoxon test, and to Dr. Jeanne L. Smith of the Ogontz Campus, Pennsylvania State University, for her assistance.

# A Relatively Painless Method of Introduction To the Psychological Literature Search

Louis E. Gardner
*Creighton University*

It would seem that one of the earliest considerations in an experimental psychology course ought to revolve around the literature search. This seems particularly important in the experimental or methodology courses where original individual or group research projects are a part of the requirements. Where this is the case, the most obvious method of introducing the idea of a literature search involves waiting until the students have developed hypotheses and then direct them to the various available sources of information on that particular topic. Another frequently used method is found in assigning various traditional topics and requiring students to write term papers gleaned from the literature. Although both of these procedures ensure some exposure to the literature and the mechanisms for search, they do have some drawbacks.

First, on the subjective side, students report that they find the exercise of writing just another term paper to be distasteful and boring. Objectively, from the instructor's point of view, this kind of activity usually fails to produce a very extensive or creative literature search. As a result, the students really don't gain much additional knowledge of the literature or search techniques from another term paper. Having students use their self-developed hypotheses as starting points for literature searches works somewhat better than the term paper because they have some investment in the problem. However, the development of hypotheses for individual projects usually means that the literature search takes place in a hurried fashion sometime near the end of the course, or even in some cases after the data have been collected. As a result, at a time in the course when students should be concentrating on the development of methodological and reporting skills, they are still stumbling around in an unrewarding literature search. A much more satisfactory approach is to get them involved with the literature and help them develop search skills early in an experimental or methodology course so that this tool is available when needed. In addition, it seems desirable to do this in an atmosphere which fosters ingenuity, creativity, and breadth in carrying out their search for existing knowledge. The method described below appears to do these things.

**Description of the Method.** The concept of a literature search is introduced on the first day of class as are the early steps in the development of a psychological experiment. By way of introduction, the usual sources are explained to the students with particular reference to the way in which the *Psychological Abstracts* are organized and used. At the second class meeting, the students are given an assignment requiring that they experience a literature search.

At the basis of this assignment is a list of clichés and old sayings. Part of that list is reproduced here, and of course, there are many others available. Like father like son. Chip off the old block. One bad apple spoils the barrel. Can't teach an old dog new tricks. Where there is a will there is a way. Let sleeping dogs lie. You can't fight city hall. Birds of a feather flock together. Opposites attract. You can't change a leopard's spots. Politics make strange bedfellows. Better late than never. The early bird catches the worm. Out of sight out of mind. Absence makes the heart grow fonder. Sly as a fox. More fun than a barrelfull of monkeys. Blood is thicker than water. Once a thief always a thief. Too many cooks spoil the broth. Laughing on the outside, crying on the inside. To err is human, to forgive, divine. After his own heart. As mad as a March hare. Tired Nature's sweet restorer, sleep. The course of true love never runs smooth. While there is life there is hope. Virtue is her own reward. Old as the hills. Music hath charms to soothe a savage beast. Men talk only to conceal their minds. Good breeding is the blossom of good sense. Coming events cast their shadows before. Brevity is the soul of wit.

One notes that most of these phrases have a component related to behavior and the students are instructed to treat these sayings as hypotheses. Next, after selecting at least two of the sayings from the list, each student is required to find empirical evidence which would contribute to either the support or rejection of the hypothesis implied by the saying. Finally, they are required to submit abstracts of the studies indicating how they support or refute a saying and to defend their position before the class.

**Results.** The responses of the students over several years have reinforced the use of this method of initial exposure to the psychological literature. The students appear to be challenged by the assignment and go about the successful completion of it with a high degree of enthusiasm.

Quantitative assessments of the method have been made only over the last three years the course has been taught. During this period, the method was employed in teaching 26 Junior and Senior students in an Advanced Experimental Psychology course, and the following data are based upon measures taken with these students. One estimate of the utility of a method such as this can be gained by simply asking if students can successfully complete the assignment. The answer is found in looking at the successful completion rate. That is, the proportion of studies reported by students that do realistically serve as evidence for or against the sayings. The result of this analysis indicated that 85% of the reported studies were relevant to the hypothesis implicit in the sayings chosen by the students. This result would seem to indicate that the students were able to use the psychological literature successfully and thus achieve the primary objective of this exercise. A second major objective

in designing this particular method was to present a challenging assignment which students would enjoy. Assessment of the attainment of this objective was possible through analysis of the students' responses on the course evaluation. Again, using data based upon the responses of 26 students over the last three years that the course was taught, it was indicated that 77% of the students found the work to be challenging and yet maintained a positive attitude in regard to the assignment.

Part of the instructor's verve for using this method stems from the frequent instances of ingenuity and creativity displayed by the students in translating the sayings into behavioral terms and then fitting those to the empirical studies in the literature. Some insight into their behaviors can be gained by looking at some selected titles of studies presented along with the related sayings:

Maruthi (1966) "The impact of genetic propensity and environmental modifiability of human behavior"; Wohlford (1970) "Initiation of cigarette smoking: Is it related to parental smoking behavior?" (Like father, like son.)

Davids, et al. (1961) "Anxiety, pregnancy, and childbirth abnormalities." (Coming events cast their shadow before.)

Darley and Latané (1968) "When will people help in a crisis?" (Too many cooks spoil the broth.)

Kogan and Wallach (1969) "Risk taking behavior in small decision groups."; Connoly (1969) "The social facilitation of preening behavior in *Drosophila melanogaster.*" (Two heads are better than one.)

Byrne, et al. (1967) "Attraction and similarity of personality characteristics." (Opposites attract.)

These kinds of responses to the assignment, together with the interaction and debate initiated by the defense of the evidence have proved valuable as more than just an introduction to the literature search. That is, the process and outcomes of this procedure serve as natural leads to the discussion of central concepts in experimental psychology such as operational definitions and conflicting evidence. In addition, many students find that their ideas for their individual projects later in the semester are germinated during this assignment.

In conclusion, this method achieves its primary objective of introducing students to the idea and process of a literature search in a novel and effective manner. Also, there are secondary gains which are important to other portions of the course. These conclusions are based upon student reports, specific student behaviors in doing the work, and the instructor's subjective evaluation over the past six years. The end result is that both students and instructor find the procedure to be a practical, enjoyable, and challenging learning experience.

### References

Byrne, D., Griffitt, W., & Stefaniek, D. Attraction and similarity of personality characteristics. *Journal of Personality and Social Psychology,* 1967, *51,* 82-90.

Connoly, K. The social facilitation of preening behavior in *Drosophila melanogaster. Animal Behavior,* 1968, *16,* 11-19.

Darley, J., & Latané, B. When will people help in a crisis? *Psychology Today,* June 1968, *2,* 54-57; 70-71.

Davids, A., DeVault, S., & Talmadge, M. Anxiety, pregnancy and childbirth abnormalities. *Journal of Consulting Psychology*, 1961, *25*, 74-77.

Kogan, N., & Wallach, M. Risk taking behavior in small decision groups. *Bulletin du C.E.R.P.*, 1967, *16*, 363-375.

Maruthi, G. The impact of genetic propensity and environmental modifiability of human behavior. *Psychology Annual*, 1966-67, *1*, 54-58.

Wohlford, P. Initiation of cigarette smoking: Is it related to parental smoking behavior? *Journal of Consulting and Clinical Psychology*, 1970, *34*, 148-151.

---

# Some "Thrilling" Short Articles for Use in An Introductory Psychology Class

Camille B. Wortman
and Jay W. Hillis
*Northwestern University*

Because many introductory psychology textbooks are characterized by low levels of readability and human interest (see, e.g., Anderson, 1956; Gillen, 1973), instructors are often eager to supplement a textbook with additional materials. Recently McCollom (1971) provided a list of paperback books which received favorable ratings by students when used as supplemental reading. The purpose of the present writing is to introduce 15 short articles which cover important psychological phenomena and which were highly rated by students.

A very large number of reprints, offprints, and books of readings are available for use in introductory psychology classes. An instructor who is teaching Introductory Psychology is likely to feel overwhelmed by the possibilities, especially if (s)he is teaching the course for the first time. As a step toward aiding instructors in their selection of supplemental readings, we obtained evaluations for 30 short articles from students enrolled in a large Introductory Psychology course at Northwestern' University. We had judged all of them to be important in conveying psychological principles in an interesting and readable style. In the Introductory course in which the ratings were made, students were presented with a variety of options including reading textbook chapters and taking short objective tests, reading the short articles and taking essay tests, reading paperback books and writing papers, and attending lectures, films, and seminars. Students received a prearranged number of points toward their grade for each option they completed. The 30 short articles were roughly divided into areas of biological psychology, learning, social psychology, and clinical-developmental psychology. There were four essay test days, with a separate testing day for the 7 or 8 articles in each area. Students were asked to rate the articles they had read at the end of each of these testing sessions. Although the evaluations were optional, their importance for purposes of improving the course in the future was stressed. Students were asked to rate each article on a 1- to 5-point scale with endpoints of "very poor" and "excellent." All ratings were anonymous, and students were encouraged to be as candid and honest as possible in their ratings. Since students were able to exercise freedom of choice concerning the articles they would read, the number reading and evaluating each article fluctuated from a low of 181 to a high of 327.

Half of the articles received mean ratings of 3.67 or higher, or in the upper third of the scale. These articles are listed in Table 1 in the order in which they were rated by the students. The table indicates the broad area of psychology into which each article falls, as well as the specific subject covered in the article.

Upon examining this table, one is struck by the diversity of the articles that received high ratings by the students. They come from many fields of psychology. Some are journal articles written by researchers; others are magazine articles in which research findings are summarized by journalists. Some are primarily factual; others present opinions. Students responded just as favorably to traditional articles (e.g., those on memory and imprinting) as they did to those of more contemporary interest. In fact, articles on several "flashy" topics (e.g., women's liberation, transactional analysis, encounter groups) received ratings too low to be included on this list. Certainly, an instructor will want to consider such factors as the content of an article, the extent to which the article overlaps with or complements material in the textbook or lectures, etc. But within these constraints, we feel that student ratings provide highly useful information. We realize, of course, that not all areas of psychology are adequately represented by the titles in Table 1. It is our hope that this writing will encourage instructors to search out interesting and involving reading materials, to obtain data concerning student evaluation of these materials, and to make such data available for all of us to draw upon in our efforts to improve the teaching of introductory psychology.

## References

Anastasi, A. Subliminal perception. From *Fields of applied psychology* by A. Anastasi (McGraw-Hill, 1964) as published in Guthrie, R. V., *Psychology in the world today* (second edition). Addison-Wesley, 1971, chapter 22, pages 183-185.

Anderson, W. Readability of readers. *American Psychologist*, 1956, *11*, 147-148.

Bettelheim, B. Joey: A "mechanical boy." *Scientific American*, March, 1959, *200*, 116-127, (offprint #439).

Elkind, D. Giant in the nursery — Jean Piaget. *New York Times Magazine*, May 26, 1968, 25. (Available in Rubinstein, J., et al. *Annual editions: Readings in psychology 75/76*, Dushkin, 1975).

Gillen, B. Readability and human interest scores of thirty-four

## Table 1
## Short Articles Receiving Favorable Student Ratings

| Author | Mean Rating | N | Broad Area | Focus |
|---|---|---|---|---|
| Meyer (1970) | 4.32 | 278 | Social | Milgram's research |
| Rorvik (1972) | 4.30 | 314 | Biological | Cognitive control of involuntary processes |
| Holt (1971) | 4.18 | 313 | Learning | Education |
| Morris (1969) | 4.10 | 327 | Biological | Imprinting |
| Bettelheim (1959) | 4.06 | 220 | Clinical | Autism and childhood schizophrenia |
| Rosenthal & Jacobson (1968) | 3.98 | 280 | Social | Self-fulfilling prophecy |
| Elkind (1968) | 3.90 | 208 | Developmental | Piaget |
| Gresham (1949) | 3.84 | 230 | Personality | Reinforcement of self-concept |
| Jensen/McClelland (1972) | 3.82 | 252 | Individual differences | IQ/heredity versus environment |
| Lifton (1972) | 3.82 | 253 | Social | Deindividuation and technological warfare |
| Rosenhan (1973) | 3.80 | 181 | Clinical | Mental illness |
| Luce & Peper (1971) | 3.80 | 296 | Biological | Biofeedback |
| Anastasi (1964) | 3.79 | 300 | Learning | Subliminal perception |
| Underwood (1964) | 3.76 | 275 | Learning | Forgetting |
| Luria (1968) | 3.73 | 290 | Learning | Mnemonics |

current introductory texts. *American Psychologist*, 1973, *28*, 1010-1011.

Gresham, W. L. Fortune tellers never starve. *Esquire*, November, 1949, *32*, 59. (Available in Edwards, D. C. *Study guide and readings for general psychology* (Second Edition). Macmillan, 1972).

Holt, J. I oppose testing, marking, and grading. *Today's Education*, March, 1971, *60*, 28.

Jensen, A., & McClelland, D. Intelligence and heredity: A symposium. From *Saturday Evening Post*, Summer, 1972, *244*, 8, as published in Zimbardo, P., & Maslach, C. *Psychology for our times*. Scott, Foresman, 1973, 128-137.

Lifton, R. J. The "Gook Syndrome" and "Numbed Warfare." *Saturday Review*, December, 1972, *55*, 66.

Luce, G., & Peper, E. Mind over body, mind over mind. *New York Times Magazine*, September 12, 1971, 34. (Available in Rubinstein, J., et al. *Annual editions: Readings in psychology 75/76*, Dushkin, 1975).

Luria, A. R. The mind of a mnemonist. From Chapter 3, "His Memory," in *The mind of a mnemonist: A little book about vast memory* by A. R. Luria, translated by L. Solotaroff (Basic Books, 1968), as published in Zimbardo, P., & Maslach, C. *Psychology for our times*. Scott, Foresman, 1973, 98-105.

McCollom, I. N. Psychological thriller: Psychology books students read when given freedom of choice. *American Psychologist*, 1971, *26*, 921-927.

Meyer, P. If Hitler asked you to electrocute a stranger, would you? *Esquire*, February, 1970, *73*, 72. (Available in Rubinstein, J., et al. *Annual Editions: Readings in Psychology 75/76*, Dushkin, 1975).

Morris, D. Imprinting and mal-imprinting. From D. Morris *The Human Zoo* (McGraw-Hill, 1969), chapter 5, as published in Edwards, D. C. *Study guide and readings for general psychology* (Second Edition). Macmillan, 1972, 175-186.

Rorvik, D. M. Jack Schwarz feels no pain. *Esquire*, December, 1972, *78*, 209.

Rosenhan, D. L. On being sane in insane places. From *Science*, 1973, *179*, 250-258, as published in Zimbardo, P., & Maslach, C. *Psychology for our times*. Scott, Foresman, 1973, 256-268.

Rosenthal, R., & Jacobson, L. F. Teacher expectations for the disadvantaged. *Scientific American*, April, 1968, *218*, 19-23, (offprint #514).

Underwood, B. J. Forgetting. *Scientific American*, March, 1964, *210*, 91-99, (offprint #482).

### Note

This research was supported by Biomedical Sciences Support Grant FR 7028-05 from the National Institutes of Health.

# Increasing the Relevance of the Media to Psychology Courses

**James L. Sorensen**
*Bowling Green State University*

I suspect that students and educators are less influenced by professional publications than they are by the popular media (newspapers, magazines, television, and radio). Although most psychologists subscribe to at least one professional publication, and many graduate students do likewise, many more of us subscribe to a newspaper or a magazine. Moreover, a more important question might be how often do we read our magazines compared with reading our professional journals? Obviously, *Newsweek* wins hands down over *American Psychologist*.

I wish to share a technique that I have found to increase the relevance of psychology courses to the information sources that students view regularly. The technique—for lack of a better label, the "media project"—involves a student search of the popular media for items applicable to the course and then rating these items on relevant dimensions.

Some time well into the course students are asked "How many of you read a newspaper or a magazine regularly?" The "ayes" comprise about 60 percent of the class. Those remaining are asked if they listen to radio or watch television. Virtually all do. Then we discuss the relevance, or lack of it, of the course to the things students hear about in the media. Usually some students are aware of news items dealing with public services, but the majority of the class is not aware of "psychological" items that appear in the popular press.

Each student then monitors one kind of popular media for a week, in search of items that relate to the course. Magazines are read for one issue and newspapers for a week, with the exception of the Sunday paper, which is assigned as a separate item. Television and radio are divided into news, programming, and commercials. Typically, a class of 20 students monitors news magazines, daily and weekly papers, sports magazines, homemakers' publications, radio, and television.

At the week's end students bring in copies of all articles or advertisements that they saw as applicable to the course work, while "soft media" people bring in written diaries of the television and radio items that they found to be relevant. In a class discussion they share their newly acquired knowledge. Individuals have found anywhere from 3 to 114 items of relevance, ranging from the appearance of a psychologist on "Kojak" to the use of "psychological" coercion in a deodorant commercial. The student is surprised by the amount that the media and course content overlap.

But how relevant is the media to the course work? How central was the course content to the main thrust of items? Was the psychologist, program, or concept misrepresented? Do topics deal with the mainstream of society or only with a fringe group, e.g., a report of an annual convention of faith healers?

The media project addresses these questions by rating a sample of the items for their relevance, centrality, and degree of misrepresentation. In addition, depending upon the course, other items may be included. For example, in a community psychology course students rated items on the degree to which they reflected a preventive vs a medical model of mental illness, and the amount that they focused on systems change vs person centered conceptualizations. The rating scale, two media items per student, is completed in about twenty minutes of class time. Sample scales are available from the author. When the results are tabulated the students have an overview of the content of items, source,

centrality, representativeness, and other issues of interest.

Student response to this method has been enthusiastic. Some students invented variants of the project spontaneously, including measuring the proportion of local and national television news that is spent on mental health issues and tallying the number of neurotic characters appearing in television's "soap operas." In course evaluations students have made such favorable statements as "fun and enlightening," "made the course more practical and enjoyable," and "pointed out the relevance of psychology to the real world." Finally, in a four month follow-up of a community psychology course the nineteen undergraduate participants received a survey dealing with the media project. Nine anonymously completed questionnaires were returned (47% return rate). The data are summarized in Table I, indicating that the lasting impression of the project is quite favorable.

Although to date I have tried this project with only three easily applied courses—community psychology, abnormal behavior and clinical program evaluation—this technique might be helpful in courses on psychological testing, introductory psychology, and adjustment. Additionally, the method might add a concrete foundation to such theoretical courses as statistics ("four out of five dentists recommend sugarless gum for their patients who chew gum") and personality theory.

In the end, such an approach may not only increase the relevance of specific courses to the personal lives of students, but also it may have a more permanent effect. Students typically shelve or sell their texts after completing a course, but they continue to view the media. By encouraging students to regard their typically consumed media sources in a new light, the educator gives students a perceptual set to discover psychology in their daily lives, and soon students find that many things they read are psychological.

## Note

1. The author appreciates the assistance of Mr. William Alexander and Mr. Sung Kim in conceptualizing this project and evaluating its outcome.

## Table 1
## Results of the Follow-up Survey

| Item | Student Evaluation Mean (N=9) | S.D. |
|---|---|---|
| I. General Evaluation | | |
| The media project was worthwhile. | 4.0 | 0.5 |
| The media project was a waste of class time. | 1.9 | 1.1 |
| The use of such projects makes psychology more relevant to students' personal lives. | 4.1 | 0.7 |
| The project increased my awareness of the degree to which the media dealt with the coursework. | 4.3 | 1.2 |
| Through the project I was able to relate better to the course. | 3.1 | 1.0 |
| I notice relevant items in the media more frequently now than before the course began. | 4.0 | 0.7 |
| The project helped me apply my "academic knowledge" to my outside life. | 3.9 | 1.0 |
| Involvement with the media through such projects should be included in other psychology courses. | 4.0 | 1.0 |
| II. Evaluation of the specific elements of the project. | | |
| Searching a media source for relevant items was valuable. | 4.2 | .8 |
| Discussing media items and issues in class was valuable. | 4.1 | 1.0 |
| Rating the media items was valuable. | 3.1 | 1.3 |
| Receiving feedback on the ratings was valuable. | 3.3 | 1.3 |

Scale: 1 Strongly disagree, 2 Disagree, 3 Neutral, 4 Agree, 5 Strongly Agree

# Microcomputers in the Introductory Laboratory

John K. Bare
*Carleton College*

The use of microcomputers is growing and there have appeared on the market the necessary interfaces for use with laboratory equipment; together these components may very well replace much of the current timing, recording, and equipment control devices used in teaching laboratories as well as in research. The purpose of this paper is to describe two successful uses of such a computer system in the laboratory for the first course.

The study of cognitive processes has emphasized one of psychology's earliest measures—reaction time. The computer system employed had the capacity for measuring reaction time on sixteen separate inputs, storing the values for 32 trials, and giving hard copy of the data. For a number of pedagogical reasons we chose to use that capacity to replicate, in slightly modified form, Sternberg's 1966 study of retrieval from short term memory. We used memory sets of one, three, and six digits and a single probe. Five "yes" and five "no" trials were conducted for each memory set length, and thus the design was a three-by-two factorial for three set lengths and two conditions (yes/no).

Each subject had two push button switches labelled "yes" and "no." The sets and probes were put onto slides and projected on a screen at the front of the room. A trial consisted of a "ready" slide followed by the memory set and then the probe. The position of the probe in sets of three and six digits was distributed throughout the set. Reaction times were recorded in a virtual array file in the buffer and then called up from that file.

The statistic employed was the factorial design with repeated measures on both factors, and the analysis was performed by the computer when the data had been collected. The results of the analysis were thus immediately available.

Two hypotheses can be tested, one by each of the factors: Retrieval is by serial search rather than by parallel search; and if one uses a serial search, the process is self-terminating rather than exhaustive. We point out to the students that even if we have no awareness of this rapid search, it would be counter-intuitive for it to be exhaustive in the "yes" case. The data from 13 subjects are displayed in Figure 1.

Memory set size had a significant effect $F(2,12) = 36.91$ ($p < .001$), and neither the difference between the "yes" and "no" means nor the interaction was significant. We could conclude that the retrieval process appeared to be serial and not parallel, and the students are always tempted to conclude that it is exhaustive rather than self-terminating because of the similarities of the reaction time values for the "yes" and "no" trials at all set lengths.

At this point we always examine the question of whether the failure to reject the null hypothesis can support an hypothesis. We then raise the question of whether an experiment can ever prove an hypothesis or only disprove

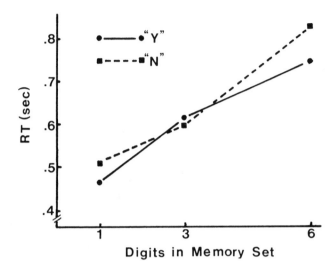

Figure 1. Reaction time as a function of the number of digits in the memory set for a single probe.

one. The discussion is very likely to lead to the decision to test the self-terminating hypothesis.

Logic and a little friendly persuasion lead us to a second test patterned after the study of Wingfield and Bolt (1970), in which memory sets were three and six digits long but *three* probes were provided. The students were instructed to respond with "yes" if any *one* of the three probes were in the memory set. The data, presented in Figure 2, can only be described as very satisfying.

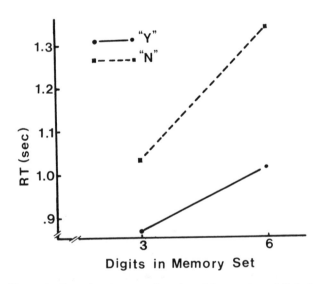

Figure 2. Reaction time as a function of the number of digits in the memory set for a three-digit probe.

The same kind of analysis of variance shows set size to be a significant variable, $F (1,12) = 39.01$ ($p < .001$), the reaction time to be longer for "no" than for "yes" cases, $F (1,12) = 22.42$ ($p < .001$), and the interaction between the two variables is also significant, $F (1,12) = 4.97$ ($p < .05$). A comparison of the ordinates of Figures 1 and 2 shows that the reaction times are longer in the second study, as might be expected. The hypothesis that the search is exhaustive is not supported, but one finds no reason for rejecting the conclusion that it is self-terminating. The significance of the interaction serves as a springboard for further class discussion.

A second experiment exploited the computer's capability for precise timing in the control of equipment. The study chosen was a replication of one of those in the now classic paper by Sperling (1960) on sensory (or iconic) memory.

Slides of three-by-three matrices of consonants were prepared and presented by a projector and a photo-cell operated shutter. The exposure duration was 100 msec. For the uncued trials, the subjects were provided an answer sheet with blank matrices for each trial and were instructed to put the consonants in their proper position. In the partially cued trials, the computer was programmed to pause after sending the "operate" signal to the projector, that pause of such a length that the "operate" signal to the three sound sources occurred 50 msec after the slide had disappeared. For the cued trials, the subjects were provided answer sheets with rows of three cells in which they were to put the

consonants in their proper places. With 30 uncued trials designated the "A" condition and 30 cued trials the "B" condition, 120 trials in an ABBA order were presented.

With an N of eight, the demonstration appears to be almost fail-proof. Because the subjects are unpracticed compared with those of Sperling, the recall is somewhat less under both conditions than he reports, but for a related measures $t$, the $p$ values range in the various sections of the laboratory between .05 and .01. For an N of 25, $t (24) = 9.45$ ($p < .001$, two-tailed test).

The uses of microcomputers in the future in laboratories for the first course may be limited only by our imaginations and by our ability to convince colleagues in our departments that microcomputers are not only for research.

### References

Sperling, G. The information available in brief visual presentations. *Psychological Monographs*, 1960, *74* (Whole No. 498)

Sternberg, S. High speed scanning in human memory. *Science*, 1966, *153*, 652-654.

Wingfield, A., & Bolt, R. A. Memory search for multiple targets. *Journal of Experimental Psychology*, 1970, *85*, 45-50.

### Note

1. The purchase of the computer was made possible by NSF Cause Grant SER77-06304 to Carleton College.

# Individualized Reading for Introductory Psychology

David Winzenz
and Marilyn Winzenz
*California State University*

Over the years, reading research has investigated the nature of certain relationships between reader interest and reading comprehension. According to Shnayer (1969) and Estes and Vaughan (1973) strong relationships can exist between reader interest and reading comprehension at various reading levels. Fader and McNeil (1975) have developed an educational program based on a saturation of the student's environment with high interest materials which they report enhances student attitude, interest, and reading comprehension. A university level approach to capitalizing on student interests was developed by McCollom (1971) who presented students with a list of "psychological thrillers" from which to select books for their course reading in introductory psychology.

Using a revision of McCollom's reading list and a modification of his instructional technique, we also offered individualized reading opportunities for introductory psychology students. During the first class meeting each student was given a detailed outline of the semester's lectures with notations regarding which books correlated with each day's lectures. Each student chose five selections

from the list to be read during the semester and, using the outline, could choose to read a given book during the time that related discussion was occurring in class.

Before reading each selection, students were encouraged to (a) skim the book, (b) predict what the book would be about, (c) formulate a variety of written comprehension questions of their own to guide their reading, and (d) predict the relationship of the book to the corresponding lecture. After reading each book the students then prepared for individual conferences by jotting down on a file card salient information of a psychological nature that they felt they had learned from the book. Each conference was ten minutes long, was graded credit/no credit, and was an opportunity to discuss psychology in a relaxed, one-to-one context where the student and instructor could share insights on the book.

Each conference was structured in part by the student's notations on the file card and in part by the instructor's questions, which were intended to relate the book to other course material. For example, two concepts were stressed in the discussion of *The Oxbow Incident* by W. Clark. First, the behavior of the mob and its influences on individuals both before and after the lynching was considered in relation to studies of obedience and conformity. In addition, students analyzed the level of moral development of several main characters in the book, using Kohlberg's (1968) theory of moral development. The paired selections *I Never Promised You a Rose Garden* by H. Green and *One Flew Over the Cuckoo's Nest* by K. Kesey were used to expose students to the experience of madness and the experience of mental institutions. Schizophrenic language was oftentimes singled out for discussion and both books provided a background for a lively discussion of Rosenhan's (1973) research on being sane in insane places. Each selection on the list was carefully considered in this way for its topical integration into the course material.

A record of reading interests and ease of comprehension was established for each student to allow the instructor to aid in the selection of readings and in the formulation of appropriate goals in the reading program. The records were also useful in planning instruction to develop such reading/thinking skills as the abilities to compare and contrast, to generalize, and to apply a theoretical notion to a specific situation.

In these ways the reading list with individual conferences has been used both with a standard course text and as sole reading material for the course with equal success. Variations on this approach to individualize reading for introductory psychology are certainly possible to provide for individual differences in learning styles, interests, and abilities.

## References

Estes, T., & Vaughan, J. Reading interest and comprehension: Implications. *The Reading Teacher*, 1973, *27*, 149-153.

Fader, D., & McNeil, E. *Hooked on books.* New York: Berkeley Publishing Corporation, 1975.

Kohlberg, L. The child as a moral philosopher. *Psychology Today,* 1968, 2(4), 25-30.

McCollom, I. Psychological thrillers: Psychology books students read when given freedom of choice. *American Psychologist,* 1971, *26*, 921-927.

Rosenhan, D. On being sane in insane places. *Science,* 1973, *179*, 250-258.

Shnayer, S. Relationships between reading interest and reading comprehension. In J. A. Figurel (Ed.). *Reading and realism.* Newark: International Reading Association, 1969, 698-702.

# Panel Discussions in the Classroom

Berthold Berg
*University of Dayton*

As most readers know, a panel discussion begins with the choice by several students of a relevant topic. Students then research the topic, organize their findings, and finally present their findings to the class as a whole. The experience is valuable for several reasons. The systematic oral presentation of research findings develops skills in a way that the casual questions or comments during lectures do not. It offers insight if not appreciation of the demanding role assumed by instructors. Finally, learning as a group is a departure from competitive forms of learning; planning a presentation as a group draws upon organizational resources not normally required in other aspects of coursework. After several years of experience with this method, by trial and error I have developed several guidelines which maximize the educational impact of such discussions.

**Topic Controversy.** The instructor should offer a choice from among several controversial topics. Every content area is filled with controversial issues but many of these are too esoteric to arouse some emotional commitment from students. It is best to select topics on which students have already reached an opinion, however uninformed. Issues in the news, or of an ethical nature, are particularly appealing. Some examples of issues used in a course titled Abnormal Child Psychology are: (a) Should children have the same legal rights as adults? (b) Does the working mother impair the psychological development of her child? (c) Should children be routinely tested for intellectual ability? (d) Should we chemically treat the hyperactive child?

**Debate.** The most successful discussions are those where participants have used an adversary method. Panels where individual participants chose to present both points of view on a sub-area of an issue have worked less well. Members of the audience report that they have been more involved with the topic when they could identify a position with an individual.

At a minimum, sufficient time should be allowed for questions and answers. It is better to allow audience participation throughout the debate. Assessing pre and post debate audience attitudes toward the issue also does much to increase audience participation.

**Evaluation.** Probably nothing is a greater source of student dissatisfaction than the sense that they have been unfairly evaluated. Fairness in evaluation is of course of considerable concern to instructors as well. My philosophy is to evaluate the panel as a whole rather than assign grades based upon individual contributions. To evaluate individual contributions fosters competition in a basically cooperative venture. I have not yet encountered a student who disagrees with this reasoning.

Another evaluation principle worth observing is to allow the audience to evaluate the panel. Since the discussion is for the benefit of the audience and not the instructor, such an approach appears reasonable. The instructor will, however, encounter difficulties if he or she merely asks the audience to assign a letter grade to the panel. In my experience, grade inflation will occur. While some of this may be due to anticipated reciprocity, much of the tendency can be attributed to uncertainty regarding the criteria for evaluation. When in doubt, assign the higher grade. The problem can be overcome by asking the audience to evaluate the panel on a standardized evaluation form. I use a form with five statements which are endorsed (strongly agree to strongly disagree) using a five-point Likert scale. The statements read: (a) The relevant material was thoroughly covered; (b) Different points of view were well represented; (c) Presentations were clear and concise; (d) Presentations were well organized; (e) The panel enhanced my knowledge of the subject considerably. I then determine the mean rating (across dimensions and evaluators), and assign the corresponding letter grade. This method has had a significant impact both in increasing the range of grades assigned and decreasing the mean. The assigned grades using this method also appear more valid, assuming that correlation with test grades can be regarded as a measure of validity.

Course evaluations at the end of the term indicate that the technique has considerable appeal. Panel discussions, both in method and content, are frequently cited as the most interesting aspect of the course. In brief, when certain guidelines are observed the panel discussion is an effective learning method easily adaptable to most courses and teaching formats.

---

# A Brief Structured Activity Model to Facilitate Group Learning in the Classroom

Bruce A. Baldwin
*University of North Carolina*

Structured learning activities to facilitate classroom learning at the university level have become increasingly popular. They provide students with a framework for discussion, exploration and (ultimately) internalization of meaningful information (Alschuler & Ivey, 1973). This learning model blends aspects of both experiential (affective) and cognitive styles of learning to maximize the strengths of each mode. The problems of a purely cognitive (lecture) approach are avoided by helping students to relate material to themselves. An opportunity to conceptualize material generated by students alleviates the major weakness of a solely affective or experiential approach.

This brief Structured Activity Model is designed for time-limited[1] classroom learning at the university level and is adaptable to a variety of learning contexts and content areas. It is particularly helpful when material is controversial or personally threatening to students and there is anticipated difficulty in "opening up" meaningful discussion. This model can be used in classes of 30 or more students, although somewhat fewer students is probably optimal.

**The Learning Activity Model.** This Structured Activity Model has three major stages and each step in the three stages is discussed with an example included for clarification.

*Activity Focusing.* The emphasis in the three parts of this stage is to narrow the scope of the activity and to help students focus on relevant material by defining a clear theme for the activity.

(a) *Premise Statement.* The first step in Activity Focusing is to formulate a premise statement; a single basic question or thematic statement around which the activity is designed. The premise statement is kept as concise and as behaviorally specific as possible.

*Title:* "Proverbs/Sayings and Sexual Values"

Proverbs/sayings related to children during developmental years often represent parental sexual values that are indirectly learned in this form.

(b) *Goal Statement.* The next step is preparation of a goal statement (concise and specific) that describes the outcome expected if the learning activity is successful. By defining the "product" of the activity, the framework for the design of the activity is further clarified.

> The activity goal is to help students to become more aware of sexual values inherent in commonly heard proverbs/sayings in our culture, to understand how sexual values are communicated indirectly in this form, and to become more aware of personal sexual values learned indirectly through development.

(c) *Orientation Remarks.* The orientation remarks are a series of informal and brief (3-5 minutes) statements to help students define the theme and purpose of the activity. The remarks are geared to students' level of sophistication and are related directly to their experience through examples of thought-provoking questions.

> At students' level of understanding, comments emphasize the following points: (1) Parents impart values to children throughout development, both by direct means and by indirect means (*e.g.*, modeling, relating personal experiences, proverbs/sayings). (2) Sexual values are often taught indirectly by parents and may be communicated through commonly heard proverbs/sayings. (3) By examining the sex-related values in commonly heard proverbs/sayings, the influence of these indirectly taught values on development can be explored and better understood. Examples: "A woman's place is in the home." "All you have is your reputation." "Sow your wild oats while you are young."

*Generating Data.* In the second activity stage, data are generated by each student using a structured format. Students assume the responsibility for generating data for discussion that is "theirs" as part of personal experience. There are two parts in this activity stage.

(a) *Task Instructions.* Students receive instructions on how to generate data and to prepare (summarize) this material for later presentation to the group. Students are asked to examine themselves or their experience individually[2] to develop data relevant to the activity theme. Any materials needed are provided to students.

> Students are asked to separate from one another and to recall a proverb/saying heard from parents (or others) during development that was sex-related. On provided 8 x 11 sheets, students are asked to write the following: 1) the proverb/saying, 2) the sexual value inherent in that proverb/saying, and 3) whether that value would be taught to their children when they became parents (why or why not).

(b) *Task Involvement.* As students become involved in generating individual data, leader(s) circulate to provide help, to clarify the task, and to give support. Several minutes warning is given prior to closure.

> As students work, leader(s) circulate to facilitate development of appropriate material with five minutes warning given before ending.

*Data Processing.* In the last activity stage, students systematically present their data to the group for discussion. Through discussion and exploration of the material presented, students are exposed to a variety of different experiences, viewpoints, attitudes, and values. Extending the data beyond direct student experience provides a broader context for conceptualizing the material and studying its implications.

(a) *Reporting Out.* After reassembling, students present their data to the group using a structured framework (*e.g.,* in "round-robin" fashion, by spokespersons from subgroups, etc.). Written material may be posted before the group or summarized on the blackboard (or newsprint sheets) for more visual availability of data. Discussion and exploration of material as presented by each student is encouraged.

> The group is reassembled in a circle and in "round-robin" fashion each student posts his/her data sheet before the group and describes the material on it. Group members are encouraged to clarify, to explore, and to raise questions about proverbs/sayings and related materials as presented in sequence.

(b) *Extending/Conceptualizing the Data.* When all student material has been presented, the data are extended in specific relevant directions and emphasis is placed on conceptualizing broader implications and meanings of the material.

> After students present their data, discussion is guided by leader(s) into the following related areas during time remaining: (1) Relate sexual values defined to male/female sex role stereotyping in our culture and discuss how these values "fit" current sex roles. (2) Examine sexual values presented as positive or negative (*i.e.,* as prescriptive or proscriptive) and

why. (3) Explore other ways that sexual values are learned indirectly throughout development.

Use of outlines listing each of the activity steps in this model is encouraged to guide conduct of the activity and to make notes for improving the activity. A list of materials required for the activity is part of the outline.

**Concluding Remarks.** This brief Structured Activity Model provides an effective alternative to a classroom "lecture" format that involves students, helps them to conceptualize material, and facilitates the internalization process by relating data to their personal experience. Designing this type of learning activity is both a creative challenge and helps to ensure that learning is directed to the particular needs of a particular class at a particular time. The variety of activities that can be designed using this model is limited only by the imagination and ingenuity of the professor *cum* activity leader.

Mastery of this model is not difficult and is but one option for combining cognitive and experiential elements of a particular content area into an effective classroom learning format (see Baldwin, 1972; DeVoge & Varble, 1976). The teaching of psychology is uniquely suitable for use of this model as students are helped to integrate conceptual material and personal experience with enhanced learning as the result.

### References

Alschuler, A. S. & Ivey, A. E. Internalization: The outcome of psychological education. *Personnel and Guidance Journal,* 1973, *51,* 607-610.

Baldwin, B. A. Personality dynamics: Ideographic and nomothetic data in the classroom. *Counselor Education and Supervision,* 1972, *12,* 75-78.

Baldwin, B. A. A Structured Activity Model (SAM) for personal exploration and discussion groups. *Journal of College Student Personnel,* 1976, *17,* 431-436.

DeVoge, S., & Varble, D. L. The joint use of experiential and cognitive learning in the classroom: Teaching with personal relevance. *Teaching of Psychology,* 1976, *3,* 168-171.

### Notes

1. When an extended period of time is available (2-3 hours), a more complex Structured Activity Model can be used (see Baldwin, 1976).
2. Two basic types of techniques are used in designing structured group learning activities: (1) Individually-oriented techniques require material to be generated by participants working alone (e.g., making associations, incomplete sentences), and (2) Interpersonal-oriented techniques use an interaction between or among participants as the basis for generating data (e.g., role-playing, fish-bowling).

# A Strategy for Increasing Class Participation

Michael F. Flanagan
*Florida State University*

In many undergraduate courses class participation is minimal, but increasing the participation can become a challenging and worthwhile goal. Therefore, I would like to describe a strategy that I have been working with for increasing class participation at the beginning of a course and for promoting participation from more than the same few students who typically dominate the discussion.

The basic strategy involves a paper and pencil exercise. The class members are presented with a description of a problem situation and a list of questions they are to answer. After the students have finished answering the questions, they discuss them, with the instructor moderating. An integrative summary by the instructor high-lighting the purpose of each question, relevant course concepts, and feasible answers closes the exercise.

I started using this strategy in a small group psychology course to develop a participation norm. On the first day of class, each student was presented with a brief description of an armed robbery as reconstructed from data in a newspaper article. The students were to assume the role of the defense lawyer and answer three questions based upon this information. First, what type of jurors should be selected to obtain an acquittal for the defendant? Then, what size jury would be most likely to acquit the defendant; six person or twelve person? The third question asked if a unanimous agreement decision rule or a majority agreement decision rule would be most likely to lead to an acquittal. Once all of the students had finished answering the questions, each one was discussed by the class. This particular exercise was also used to introduce the class to several small group concepts such as group composition and group size.

There is a set of design guidelines I follow when developing problem-solving exercises. The exercise must involve a problem-solving situation with which students are familiar and one about which they are likely to have an opinion. The instructor needs to be able to identify such issues or controversies. Usually, current university issues work best. Students themselves are frequently the best source of ideas for these exercises. Also, the problem-solving exercise must relate to a central concept or theory in the course. This strategy aids the learning of the concept or theory through its emphasis on active involvement of the student. Another guideline followed is to keep the problem simple and the questions limited in number (i.e., three or four at most) so that the exercise, including discussion and summary, can be completed in a 50-minute class period. Writing the exercise clearly enough to avoid ambiguity and confusion is important. Even when it is written clearly, students often want more information about the problem situation than is given. Consequently, they are instructed to answer the questions the best they can with the limited information available.

I also follow several procedural guidelines. One is to make sure the students understand that the exercise is anonymous—no name is to be put on their sheet. The anonymity encourages them to try out an answer even if unsure of its appropriateness. It also minimizes evaluation apprehension because they know that if the papers are collected, I will not be able to identify the person responsible for a particular answer. I always ask for a written explanation of their answers, even when the format requires them to select one of several alternative answers for a question. This forces the students to think about the reasons behind their answer and to write more than a yes, no, or don't know. Finally, at times, too much participation can occur, extending the exercise into the next class period, thereby preventing complete feedback and closure. If this occurs at the start of a course, I usually entertain all the questions at the risk of not completing the exercise that period, so students will understand that participation is desirable. However, if there are too many comments and class participation has been good up to this point in the course, I do not call on all the students and, instead, try to complete the exercise in one class period.

This strategy has major advantages for the students. The most important is that each student has enough time to think of answers to the questions. The pressure to reply quickly is minimized because students are given sufficient time to generate answers. Also, this reduces the possibility of very verbal students dominating a discussion due to their ability to generate answers more quickly than deliberate, slow-thinkers. Secondly, students can compare their answers against those of their peers and the instructor without fear of appearing dumb, since they do not have to respond verbally unless they choose to do so. However, because they do have answers written down, they are more likely to want to participate than in a traditional lecture situation. Another advantage for the student is that the exercise serves as an interesting diversion from the lecture routine, especially in large classes of several hundred students where frequent discussion is less feasible. Lastly, all students, even if they have not participated in the discussion, receive immediate feedback on the appropriateness of their answers.

Numerous advantages also exist for the instructor. Probably the most important one is that all the students participate mentally in the exercise and many participate verbally. This strategy requires the students to become involved, thereby developing a participation norm when used at the start of a course or reinforcing the norm throughout the course. Another advantage is that feedback can be obtained on how well the class understands a concept or issue as well as obtaining data on misunderstandings that need to be clarified. This is possible because the students' responses can be collected and reviewed after class.

This strategy has some practical advantages for the instructor. For example, no special training or skills are required to be successful with it. Preparation of problem-solving exercises is not time consuming. With practice, they usually can be designed in less than an hour. The cost for administering one is minimal, one sheet of paper per student, and no equipment is necessary. The strategy can be used with practically any course and with large classes just as easily as small classes. In fact, I have used this strategy with classes of up to 250 students.

In conclusion, this is a simple but powerful technique for increasing class participation. Furthermore, it integrates course concepts with practical issues and thus shows how theory can apply to everyday life. Finally, both the verbal and written replies of the students can be used to assess their understanding of course concepts. Simply stated, I have found this strategy useful and hope others will also.

# 11. PHYSIOLOGICAL PSYCHOLOGY

## Mass Reaction Time: Measurement of the Speed of the Nerve Impulse and the Duration of Mental Processes in Class

Paul Rozin
*University of Pennsylvania*
John Jonides
*University of Michigan*

The "reaction time" subtraction technique is of both historical and current importance in psychology. It was used by Helmholtz in 1850 to demonstrate the speed of the nerve impulse, and it is a major tool of modern research in cognitive psychology. In-class or at-home reaction time demonstrations are typically difficult to arrange because they require use of reliable millisecond timers, and they require many trials in order to stabilize and reduce the variability of individual reaction times. We propose here two new variants of the reaction time technique which overcome these problems. They take advantage of the fact that summing over a series of reaction times, each less than a second, yields a time interval that can be measured easily with a stop watch or wristwatch. Because this total reaction time is summed over a large number of component times, the variability of the resulting value is lower than the variability of the individual times.

The basic procedure for in-class use is to chain a group of people (ideally 20 or so) together so that they must perform some task in sequence. When person n completes the task, he signals person n+1 who then completes the task, and so on. An alternative procedure that can be used in the student's home involves chaining tasks together (e.g. Neisser, 1963). In this way, instead of having to deal with the short times for a particular mental process, one can determine the time needed to complete this process n times.

### Measurement of the Speed of the Nerve Impulse

**In-class Form.** The logic of this demonstration follows directly from Helmholtz's 1850 experiment. Simple reaction time to a pinch of the ankle is compared to simple reaction time to a pinch of the shoulder. The difference between these times should be an estimate of the time for the nerve impulse to traverse the equivalent of the distance between the ankle and the shoulder. Between ten and twenty students are needed for this experiment. Each student grasps the ankle of his neighbor (this can be arranged with a minimum of acrobatics if the person at the end of a row of seats links with the person in front of him). Subjects are instructed to close their eyes and to simply squeeze their neighbor's ankle as soon as their own ankle is squeezed. The last person in the

series is instructed to yell "Stop" when he feels squeezed. The experimenter starts the series by tapping the ankle of the first subject with the starting pin of a stop watch, thus starting the stop watch and the squeeze simultaneously. The experimenter stops the watch on the agreed signal from the last person (i.e., the "Stop" signal). The same sequence of events must be then repeated several times, until the mass reaction time decreases and stabilizes. In our experience, six to ten trials suffice. Following this, the same procedure is repeated with shoulder squeezing. (These initial practice trials provide useful data from which the instructor can plot a learning curve [see Figure 1].) Two ankle and two shoulder trials can then be run in a counterbalanced order (e.g. ankle, shoulder, shoulder, ankle). Appropriate divisions and subtractions yield an ankle vs. shoulder mean time difference for a typical subject, which is divided into an estimate of the average ankle to shoulder distance for the subjects.

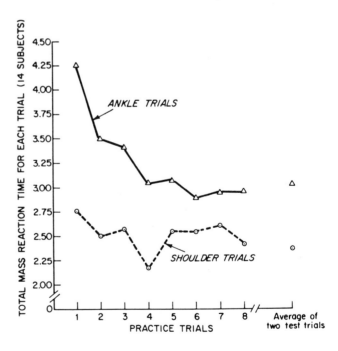

Figure 1. Total mass reaction time for shoulder and ankle trials during practice and test trials of the speed-of-nerve-impulse demonstration. The procedure included eight ankle practice trials followed by eight shoulder practice trials. Following this, test trials were run in the order ankle, shoulder, shoulder, ankle.

We have performed this experiment on eight separate occasions, resulting in values between 15 and 50 meters/second on each occasion (the expected range would be about 6 to 122 meters/second [Milner, 1970]). Figure 1 shows both the learning curves and final test measurements of one such demonstration. It should be noted that because each measurement takes less than ten seconds to obtain, the total of 12-25 measurements needed does not take a great deal of class time.

**At-home Form.** The at-home version of this experiment requires only six students: five participants and one experimenter. The logic of the experiment is the same as that described above, but easily measurable time values are obtained by cycling four times around the five participants. That is, each participant grasps his neighbor's ankle or shoulder (depending on the type of trial), forming a circle. The squeezing is initiated by the experimenter, as in the in-class version. The fifth person in the cycle is instructed to signal "Stop" the fourth time he is squeezed. This procedure was used in an at-home experiment with a class of introductory psychology students and their roommates or other friends. Students were instructed to carry through a series of five practice trials and then to run four critical tests as described above. The mean estimate of nerve impulse speed for the fifteen participating groups was 32.7 meters/second (within the expected range) with a standard deviation of 17.4 meters/second. One group reported an unreasonably slow rate of below 6 meters/second (none were negative). On the high end, the maximum value was 83.2 meters/second, again within the normal range.

### Measuring the Time for More Complex Mental Processes

**In-class Form.** The basic nerve-impulse-speed design can be extended to measure more complex mental processes with one modification. Many reaction time experiments of cognitive processes require subjects to choose between two (or sometimes more) response alternatives. To perform such experiments using the mass reaction time technique, one must provide each subject in the chain with a method of choosing between at least two alternative responses. We illustrate this technique with an experiment that measures the time it takes subjects to scan through a memorized list of target letters in order to determine if a probe stimulus letter is a member of that set (e.g. Sternberg, 1966). Before each trial, subjects are told two, three, or four randomly chosen target letters which they must hold in memory. They close their eyes, and a large stimulus letter is written on the blackboard in front of them. On a signal from his neighbor, a subject opens his eyes, determines whether the letter on the board is in the target set, and signals his neighbor in the following way: Each subject is instructed to hold his index and middle finger above the forearm of his neighbor, and to poke the neighbor's arm with his index finger if the stimulus is in the target set, or with his middle finger if it is not. Because the fingers are not actually touching the neighbor's skin before each trial, the neighbor has no way of knowing which decision his predecessor made when he is touched. The experimenter can observe the response which each subject makes and thus can ensure that no errors are made (subjects should be exhorted to make no errors, and trials with more

than one error should be excluded). A trial is initiated by the experimenter who signals the first subject to open his eyes, and who simultaneously starts a timer. It ends when the last subject yells "Stop." This procedure, when used with ten to twenty subjects, results in an easily measurable time interval.

We performed this experiment in class with a group of twenty-one subjects in the chain. The critical test trials of the experiment were preceded by thirty practice trials, ten each with a different target set size. These practice trials were followed by twenty-five test trials; for fifteen of these (five for each memory set size), the stimulus letter was a member of the target set. For ten trials, it was not. These latter negative trials were discarded in the data analysis. The negative trials are needed minimally to keep the students honest—that is, to keep them from consistently responding with their index fingers. Once the fifteen critical positive mass reaction times are collected, they are divided into three groups, according to the size of the memory set. The five reaction times within each group are averaged and this average is then divided by the number of people in the chain. These overall means are graphed in Figure 2 below, as a function of memory set size.

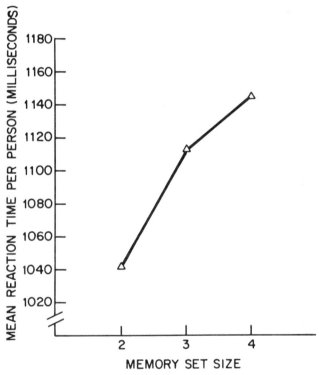

Figure 2. Mean reaction time as a function of memory set size for memory scanning demonstration.

Clearly, there is an increase in mean reaction time as a function of number of items in the memory set. Furthermore, this increase appears to be roughly linear, agreeing quite well with Sternberg's (1966) findings. We have calculated that the search rate in our experiment is approximately 52 msec. per item in the memory set (Sternberg's better controlled experiments give a typical value of 38 msec. per item).

Note that although a fair number of trials (55 in all) is required in this experiment, the actual time occupied by the experiment is not great. Each trial takes no more than 20 seconds so that the whole experiment can be completed in approximately 25 minutes.

**At-home form.** We have applied the same logic to at-home experiments of cognitive processes. In one case, we had our students replicate the Shepard and Metzler (1971) mental rotation experiment.[1] In this experiment, subjects are asked to judge whether two block figures are actually the same figure in different orientations, or whether they are two different figures. This task occupies some considerable time, and it is almost within the range of accurate timing on a wristwatch. However, to make it more appropriate for at-home experimentation, we had subjects obtain mass reaction times from successive judgments about three pairs of block figures. Each subject was presented with a set of three pairs of figures on each page of a mimeographed handout (see Figure 3 for an example of a sheet of this handout). He was instructed to determine whether the members of each pair were identical (except for rotation) or whether they were different from one another. After making this determination

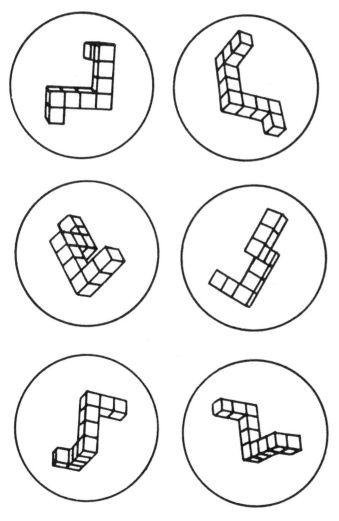

Figure 3. A typical triplet of pairs of block figures used in at-home demonstration of mental rotation effect. The members of each pair in this example are identical to one another, but differ by a rotation of 160°.

for the first pair, the subject proceeded to the next pair, and then to the final pair of the three. At this point, he determined (with a wristwatch) how much time elapsed for all three decisions. He wrote down his responses for all three pairs, and then proceeded to the next triplet of pairs. Most of the triplets of pairs included in the task contained pairs all of which were identical, although subjects were not informed of this beforehand. As with the memory scanning experiment, negative instances (in this case, different pairs), were occasionally inserted to keep subjects honest, but the triplets which contained a different pair were not included in the data analysis. We constructed the all-identical triplets so that the disparity in rotation between the pairs in any triplet was the same: some triplets contained pairs which all differed by a 40° rotation, others by 80°, others by 120°, and finally, others by 160°. In all, there were eight such critical trials in the experiment, two at each of the four degrees of rotation.

Subjects performed all the calculations in this experiment based on instructions provided in a handout which they read after they produced the data. First they identified the eight triplets which contained pairs whose members were identical to one another. Then they determined whether their responses to these triplets were correct. Any triplet in which an incorrect response was made was excluded from data analysis. For any given degree of rotation, (40, 80, 120 or 160) subjects computed the average time taken to respond "identical" to a pair by adding together the reaction times for the two triplets representing that degree of rotation and dividing by six (the total number of pairs contained in both triplets).

One hundred-twenty-two subjects performed this experiment. Though there were many perturbations in the individual data, the group data for all subjects were quite interesting, as one can see by examining Table 1. Across

Table 1
Mean Times for Mental Rotation
(Sec., Averaged Across 122 Subjects)

|       | 40°  | 80°   | 120°  | 160°  |
|-------|------|-------|-------|-------|
| Mean  | 6.42 | 8.92  | 10.73 | 12.98 |
| S.D.  | 7.06 | 12.24 | 17.37 | 23.35 |

subjects there is a roughly linear increase in time with degree of rotation. The slope of the linear function best fit to these data is 18.6 degrees per second, compared to the value of 55-60° that was reported by Metzler and Shepard (1974). In view of the fact that so few trials were run in the present experiment, and that subjects were not pre-selected according to spatial ability (as were subjects used by Shepard & Metzler), this difference is not unreasonable.

Of the 122 individual data reports, 42 showed completely consistent data; that is, time increased as rotation degree increased across all three transitions (40-80, 80-120, 120-160). No subject showed the reverse pattern.

The mass reaction time technique here described thus appears to be a useful tool in demonstrating both measurement of the speed of the nerve impulse, and measurement of the durations of various cognitive processes.

### References

Metzler, J., & Shepard, R. N. Transformational studies of the internal representation of three-dimensional objects. In R. L. Solso (ed.). *Theories of cognitive psychology: The Loyola symposium.* Potomac, MD: Erlbaum Associates, 1974.

Milner, P. M. *Physiological psychology.* New York: Holt, Rinehart & Winston, 1970.

Neisser, U. Decision time without reaction time: Experiments in visual scanning. *American Journal of Psychology,* 1963, *76,* 376-385.

Shepard, R. N., & Metzler, J. Mental rotation of three-dimensional objects. *Science,* 1971, *171,* 701-703.

Sternberg, S. High-speed scanning in human memory. *Science,* 1966, *153,* 652-654.

### Notes

1. We thank Dr. Roger Shepard for supplying us with the stimulus materials used in his experiments.

---

# Should a Psychology Student Have a Brain of Clay?

Craig E. Daniels
*University of Hartford*

Ideally, teaching aids should motivate students and facilitate learning both in the classroom and later when the student studies the material on his own. A variety of teaching aids is often used when teaching brain structure to introductory psychology students, but few seem to meet all three criteria. For example, I have found demonstrations using actual human brains that students can handle if they wish (although relatively few wish to), are surefire "attention-grabbers." Along with slides and movies, such demonstrations pique a student's interest and can be quite useful classroom teaching aids but are of limited value to a student studying in his room for an exam. Diagrammatic handouts and topic outlines or summaries, on the other hand, are available for home study and can be very useful for already motivated students, but in my experience do not themselves motivate students and in a few cases may even be a motivational handicap (the all-you-have-to-do-is-memorize-the-handouts syndrome).

Are there any inexpensive teaching aids that, in this area, meet all three criteria? My suggestion is to give your students 1.5 pounds of air-dry clay and have them model a three-dimensional hemi-section of the human brain. (The technique requires no more artistic talent on the part of either the instructor or the students than a paint-by-numbers set.)

I have used and refined the clay brain exercise over the past three semesters and informal and formal feedback suggests that introductory psychology students find the task "interesting" and "useful." Formal student evaluations are conducted each semester throughout the college and in response to an open-ended question on what the instructor has done especially well, each semester several students write comments such as the clay brains are "a great idea," "fun," "good study aid," "very helpful," "I enjoyed making it."

However, in order to more specifically assess student perception at the time when they would be maximally sensitive to the utility of the clay brain, the following questions are asked anonymously of all students at the end of the course exam covering brain structure and function: "How helpful was making the clay brain in learning brain struc-tures?" (options: very helpful, helpful, slightly helpful, not helpful); "Would you recommend that the clay brain be used next semester as part of this course?" (options: yes, no). More than 90% of the students who made a clay brain indicated that it was "very helpful" or "helpful" and virtually 100% recommend that it be used the next semester.

The task requires approximately 75 minutes of class time, costs about 80¢ per student and, based on student feedback, appears to be well worth the time, money and effort.

**Procedure.** At the class session prior to the one scheduled for the making of the models, students are given self-adhesive unprinted mailing labels together with a list of names of brain structures/areas. Students are instructed to cut each mailing label into smaller labels and write the name of the structures on these in pencil (ink smudges). The list of names indicates the approximate size for each label which range from approximately 3 x 6 mm for the pituitary and amygdala to 9 x 15 (mm) for the temporal lobe and cerebellum. It is much easier if the student removes the mailing label from the backing paper, cuts it into the desired number of small labels, and then resticks these small labels to the backing paper. This way the labels are easily removed in class and applied to the clay model as it is constructed.

When students arrive at the next class, they are given the following materials: a plastic bag containing approximately 1.5 pounds of grey self-hardening clay; an old file folder or piece of plastic to use as a work surface; paper towels for clean-up; two printed diagrams as shown below; a straight pin (colored head dressmakers pins are ideal), a sharpened pencil, a 4-inch piece of multistrand string, a 5-inch piece of colored yarn, and a plastic fork (optional).

Students begin by placing approximately 2/3 of their clay (1 pound) on the outline of the cerebral cortex (Diagram A). Using primarily the fingertips, they should mound up the clay (adding or subtracting clay if necessary) until it approximates the shape of the cerebral cortex. It is important that the final mound of clay conform to the outline on the sheet as closely as possible, and students should lift the edge of the clay from the diagram to check the outline periodically. Once the desired shape is achieved, the student should etch in the central and lateral fissures with the pencil and insert the appropriate label on the side of each fissure. To find the

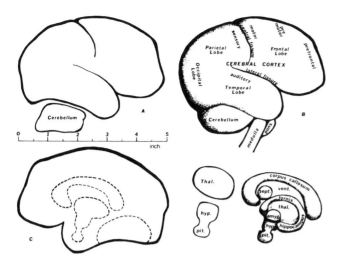

Figure 1. Student handout for construction of clay brain.

correct position for the central and lateral fissures, the student can lift the clay off the diagram slightly, and at this point the student should make sure the outline of the clay cortex corresponds to the outline on the diagram. Labels for the outside of the cerebral cortex can now be attached (frontal lobe, parietal lobe, motor area, auditory area, etc.), and random fissures marked in the clay between the labels.

Next the student should take a medium-sized ball of the remaining clay, and using the outline on the diagram, model the cerebellum in the same way as the cerebral cortex. The height of the cerebellum should approximate that of the cerebrum. The cerebellum can now be moved into position and attached to the cerebrum. Small pieces of plastic coffee stirrers or wooden matchsticks inserted halfway into each piece will give added structural rigidity—these pegs should be used when joining any two pieces of clay. In addition, the separate pieces must be firmly pressed together and the edges sealed with the side of the pencil tip so that the parts do not separate as the clay dries. Stria can now be made on the cerebellum using either the pencil or a plastic fork and the appropriate labels attached.

Similarly, the medulla and pons should be made by rolling and attaching a small cylinder and mound of clay respectively. Once these structures have been attached and labeled, the model should be carefully removed from the diagram, held gently in the hand (curved side down), and the flat surface (medial plane) smoothed. Using Diagram C as a template, the student should mark the position of the corpus callosum, the thalamus-hypothalamus-pituitary complex, and the boundary of the cerebellum by a series of pinholes through the dotted lines on the diagram into the clay (roughly cutting out Diagram C will aid in positioning the template, but is not necessary). After removing the template (Diagram C), the outline of the corpus callosum and the cerebellum should be etched in with the pencil. (The thalamus-hypothalamus-pituitary complex should not be outlined—the pinholes are position guides.) The corpus callosum can then be stippled in with the tip of the pencil to make it stand out clearly and the foliation of the cerebellum etched in (draw a diagram of the foliation on the blackboard). The hindbrain structures, corpus callosum, and areas of the cerebral cortex should now be labeled. Actually the model is not a true hemi-section but

a medial sagittal section with attached contralateral thalamus and portions of the limbic system. Therefore, the student should refer to the handout for size and shape and make a small "pigeon egg" thalamus with attached hypothalamus and pituitary. (The infundibulum on the handout was exaggerated so that if modeled completely from clay the pituitary does not separate as the model dries; however, an alternative method would be to use a wood/plastic peg to simulate the infundibulum and attach the pituitary to the hypothalamus.) This complex should then be attached (with hidden pegs) in the proper position (pinholes in clay). At this point, the anterior end of the lateral ventricle can be added by making an indentation with the end of the pencil between the thalamus and the corpus callosum. The corpus callosum, lateral ventricle, thalamus, hypothalamus, and pituitary should now be labeled. Finally, the major portion of the limbic system (septal area/fornix, hippocampus, and amygdala) should be modeled by rolling a strip of clay into a "long worm," doubling the end back on itself, and pinching the clay at each end into a round ball, as shown on the diagram. This complex can then be fastened into position around the thalamus, and the septal and amygdaloid areas offset slightly. These structures should then be labeled, and at this point the basic model is complete.

Several additional systems/pathways, however, can easily be added. For example, the reticular activating system (RAS) can be represented by a piece of string as follows: Separate the string into individual strands; Knot the strands together about 1" from one end; Press the knot into the pons and fasten in place (a small U of wire is useful); Fan out the individual strands and, using the pencil tip, embed each strand in the clay cortex and cut off any excess string; Embed the short ends of the strands as a bundle into the medulla; Label the pontine nucleus of the RAS (knot) and the RAS.

The pyramidal system can also be easily represented by embedding one end of the piece of yarn in the motor cortex, tacking the center of the yarn in place with a wire U on the side of the thalamus, and embedding the other end in the posterior medulla.

Because the clay dries rapidly on exposure to air, students should be careful to keep the unused clay in the plastic bag until they are ready to use it. By the end of the 75-minute period, the clay will have begun to harden, and although it can be kept in plastic and finished at a later time, it is better to complete the model, including labeling, in one session. Left exposed to the air, the clay will dry in 1-2 days and will last indefinitely if handled carefully and not exposed to water.

# Perception, Illusion, and Magic

Paul R. Solomon
*Williams College*

A little legerdemain can help you in teaching introductory, perception, and statistics courses, and you will be in good company.

The study of illusion has played a central role in psychology for over 100 years. The first psychological treatment of an illusion is usually credited to J. J. Oppel (1854) and since Oppel's paper there have been well over 1,000 articles published on the nature of illusion. It also seems likely that illusion played a role in prompting Wundt to study psychology as a discipline separate from physiology and physics (Coren & Girgus, 1978). The interest in illusion by psychologists still seems to be present. This is perhaps best indicated by the presence of sections on perception and illusion in virtually all introductory texts (Quereshi & Sackett, 1977).

Visual illusions have clearly attracted the most interest from researchers, although more recently psychologists have begun to examine auditory (e.g., Deutsch, 1975; Warren & Warren, 1970), tactile (Geldard, 1972) and gustatory (see McBurney, 1978) illusions. One class of illusions, relatively neglected by psychologists, however, is magical illusions. In this paper I will briefly argue that magical illusions are worthy of study and then describe how we have used magical illusions as a pedagogical tool for teaching the principles of sensation and perception.

**The Psychology of Magical Illusions: A Brief History.** The most comprehensive treatment of the psychology of magic by a psychologist was that of Triplett in 1900. In this paper entitled "The Psychology of Conjuring Illusions" Triplett first reviews the origins of conjuring (a term which he defines as "the performance of wonderful and miraculous deeds of any sort under the pretense of other than ordinary human agency") and then proceeds to make the case that conjuring tricks contain a good deal of material that is potentially valuable to the psychologist. In addition to cataloging several hundred magical illusions, Triplett discusses how certain phenomena such as attention, perception, association, and suggestion can be studied through the use of magical illusion.

Soon after the publication of Triplett's article, Jastrow (1901) published a similar paper called "The Psychology of Deception." Jastrow, of course, had published earlier papers on visual illusions (e.g., Jastrow, 1892) and in the 1901 paper he argued that magical illusions may be governed by many of the same rules as other types of "deception."

It is noteworthy that what appears to be the first treatment of magic by a psychologist was by Alfred Binet in 1894. Unfortunately, Binet's article, "The Psychology of Prestidigitation" has never been translated from French. Karelis (Note 1), however, has provided a summary which suggests that Binet makes many of the points subsequently raised by Triplett and Jastrow.

The German philosopher Dessoir (1893) was also well aware of the role of psychological factors in magical illusions and in his paper, "The Psychology of Legerdemain" Dessoir states "that which makes prestidigitation an art of deception is not its technical appliances, but its psychological kernel." Dessoir then discusses how memory (the past experiences of the observer), association, and expectations all play an important part in magic.

A more recent treatment of the psychology of magic was presented by Ceillier (1922). In this paper, Ceillier argued that there are two basic types of illusions, the psychological and the technical. Ceillier defines psychological illusions as those which rely on the "impressionability of the observer" whereas technical illusions are "rigorously undiscoverable by the senses." Thus Ceillier seems to be making a distinction between sensory and cognitive illusions. It is interesting that in their recent treatment of visual illusions Coren and Girgus (1978) make a similar distinction.

Although psychologists have not written extensively on the subject of magic, others have. Magicians are prolific writers and almost all books on magic contain sections on the psychology of conjuring. Perhaps the most elegant treatment of the topic by a non-psychologist was by Robert-Houdin (from whom Houdini took his stage name). As Jastrow (1901) pointed out "Robert-Houdin, often termed the King of the conjurers, was a man of remarkable ingenuity and insight. His autobiography is throughout interesting and psychologically valuable, and his conjuring precepts abound in points of importance to the psychologist." This is still true nearly 80 years later.

Despite the sometimes elegant treatment of the psychology of magic by early psychologists, philosophers, and magicians, magic has been all but ignored by contemporary psychologists. Nevertheless, it seems that magic may be worthy of study in its own right and, as the rest of this article will indicate, magic may be an interesting method for teaching the principles of sensation and perception.

**Perception, Illusion and Magic: Course Description.** The course was team taught by a psychologist and a philosopher. Both of us are amateur magicians with an interest in illusion. The course was offered during the Winter Study period, during which students take one course for a four-week period. There were 20 students in the class and we met four times a week for between two and two and one-half hours. Each class consisted of a one-hour lecture, usually on some aspects of illusion, followed by a workshop. During these workshops we helped students learn to perform magical illusions. My lectures covered various aspects of sensation and perception with special reference to illusion and magical illusion. Since a majority of the students had never taken a psychology course, these lectures were at the introductory level. The remaining lectures addressed the philosophical aspects of perceiving and knowing, again with special reference to magical illusion.

The main requirement of the course from the students' point of view was two-fold: first, to become familiar with the literature on illusion from several different perspectives (e.g., psychological, philosophical, historical, magical) and second, to become reasonably proficient at performing one illusion (this is not a task which is easily accomplished in one month's time). To demonstrate that they had accomplished this, each student was responsible for a presentation at the end of the month. During this presentation the student performed a magical illusion and then presented an analysis of the illusion in terms of the psychological principles involved. The students also tried to relate the magical illusions to other types of illusions. At the end of the course, each student submitted a paper based on their presentation.

The Use of Magical Illusions as a Pedagogical Tool. Although magical illusions proved to be an interesting topic for a Winter Study course, it seems unlikely that most instructors could justify devoting an entire semester to this topic. Nevertheless, there are many aspects of magical illusion that can be incorporated into other courses. Courses in sensation and perception and the corresponding parts of the introductory course would be the most obvious settings, but with some ingenuity it seems that magic could be incorporated into several other areas (e.g., research methods and philosophy of science). To give an indication of how magical illusion can be used as a teaching method, I will describe several illusions that we presented in our course and their possible applications.

Past Experiences and the Basic Vanishes. One of the basic tenets of virtually all models of perception is that present perception is built on past experience (see, e.g., McCleary, 1970). Although many phenomena such as sensory deprivation, visual stimuli present during development, and cultural influences may all fall under the category of past experience, magicians have simplified (perhaps oversimplified) matters somewhat by combining these factors under the heading: "We See What We Expect To See." Expectation, of course, can be influenced by any combination of the factors discussed above. There are many excellent examples of the role of expectation on perception that are non-magical in nature (e.g., Bruner's 1957 demonstration of perceptual readiness with a deck of playing cards), but there are also a number of magical illusions that nicely make this point.

The main asset of a good sleight of hand magician is mastery of the basic vanishes. There are literally dozens of

vanishes but they all attempt to accomplish the same end: to give the illusion that an object has been passed, for example, from the left hand to the right hand when in fact the object is retained by the left hand. The magician will typically perform the move and then show the right hand empty, implying that the magician has vanished the object (Figure 1). All books on magic which teach vanishes stress the importance of the vanish appearing "natural" to the

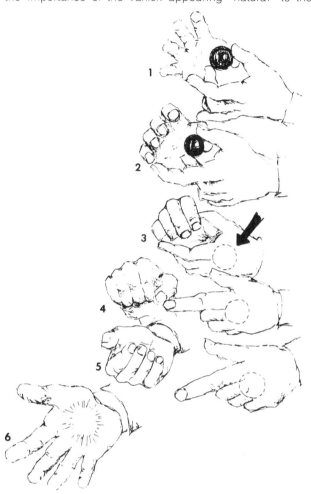

Figure 1. Basic Billiard Ball Vanish. The ball is held in the left hand (1). The right hand approaches the left (2) and while the right hand covers the ball, the ball is dropped into the left palm (3). The closed right hand, which is kept slightly puffed as if actually holding the ball, moves away from the left (4) and turns over (5). The magician then opens the left hand completing the vanish. As is the case with most vanishes, the move should be performed slowly.

audience (Ganson, 1976). That is, all parts of the action of supposedly passing a ball, coin or other object from the left to the right hand must be the same as if the object were actually passed. The only difference is that the left hand actually retains (palms) the object. We would argue (as have many others) that this illusion works because the audience, based on past experience, expects the magician to pass the object from one hand to the other. This expectation is reinforced by the natural moves, and if this is practiced often enough (magicians often practice in front of a mirror), the deceptive or guilty move of retaining the object is not detectable. The new magician can learn this move in a few hours (Tarr, 1976, 1978) and it makes an excellent classroom demonstration and starting point for discussion of the role of experience in perception and illusion.

Set and Perception and the Chinese Linking Rings. There are a number of experiments which show the importance of cognitive set on perception (Murch, 1973) and there are many non-magical demonstrations of this phenomenon which are appropriate in the classroom. Most of these rely upon perception of ambiguous figures (e.g., Leeper's, 1935, old woman/young woman drawing).

There are several magical illusions which also rely on the principle of the effects of cognitive set on perception; perhaps the best example is the Chinese Linking Rings. In this illusion (actually a series of illusions which comprise a long routine), solid rings, which are passed out for inspection, are separated and linked together. The illusion is performed with eight rings and the key to its success is to convince the spectator that there are eight separate and solid rings. In fact, there are only two separate, solid rings. There is also a set of two permanently joined rings and a set of three permanently joined rings as well as a split (key) ring. The actual linking rings routine is too complex to detail in this paper (see Ganson, 1976, for an excellent discussion). But the beginning of the routine is germane to the idea of set and perception as it is here that the notion or cognitive set of eight solid and separate rings is established.

Briefly, the magician begins by holding all eight rings in one hand in a manner such that the closed hand conceals the linked parts of the permanently joined rings as well as the split in the key ring. The magician then passes out the two solid separate rings for inspection and thus establishes the cognitive set of solid, separate rings. The conjurer then asks a spectator to link the two rings. The person, of course, is not able to do this. While the spectator is still trying to link the two separate rings, the magician takes the two linked rings, carefully concealing the place where they are joined with his hand, and proceeds to apparently join them (usually by blowing on them). These are then passed out for inspection. The magician may then take one of the established solid, separate rings and join it to the key (split) ring. The routine can continue in this way for several minutes, but the key to its success is to continually pass out the solid and separate rings for inspection to maintain the cognitive set. Again, this is a fairly simple magical illusion to perform, and can be performed credibly in front of a class after a few hours of practice.

The Laws of Perceptual Organization and the "Popeye Pips." Another topic which is typically covered in courses in perception as well as introductory psychology is the principles of perceptual organization. Central to any discussion of these principles is the work of the Gestalt psychologists. Maas (1967) in his slide set for introductory psychology has summarized these principles by providing several examples. A magical illusion which we have used to

demonstrate some of the Gestalt principles is the "Popeye Pips." This illusion is comprised of an oversized playing card with movable pips (diamonds) on both sides (Figure 2). Thus one side of the card (designated Front) may appear to be the One, Two or Three of Diamonds, whereas the back

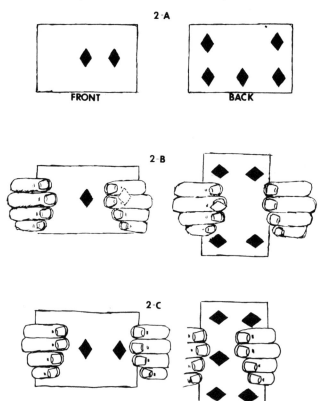

Figure 2. Popeye Pips. Figure 2A shows the playing card as it initially appears. The dotted lines in Figure 2B represent diamonds that are covered by the fingers. In Figure 2C the fingers actually cover the areas where diamonds would normally appear on a standard playing card.

of the card can be anything from the Four to the Eight of Diamonds. There are a number of illusions that can be performed with this card, but it is the basic illusion that is best used to demonstrate the Gestalt principle of closure.

The magician begins with the configuration in Figure 2A. The conjurer then shows the front of the card to the class with the hands positioned as in Figure 2B-Front and says "This side is the One of Diamonds." The magician then reverses the card (Figure 2B-Back) and shows the Four of Diamonds on the back. Next, the magician turns the card back over (Figure 2C) and indicates that it is now the Three of Diamonds on the front (the spectators assume that the third diamond is under the hand) and then quickly turns the card over to show that it is now the Six of Diamonds on the back (Figure 2C). There are a number of variations of this illusion, but the basic deceptions all rely on the same principles.

It appears that this illusion takes advantage of several rules of perceptual organization which generally come under the heading of good figure (Koffka, 1935). For example, the principle of closure indicates that parts of a figure not present will be filled in by the observer in order to complete the picture. This appears to be one mechanism involved in the portion of the Pips shown in Figure 2C. We could also argue that illusion could not work if the spectators were not familiar with how playing cards are supposed to appear. Thus the role of past experience also enters into this illusion.

We have indicated to our students that the principle of closure may also be a factor in the linking rings. When the hand covers the split in the key ring, the audience assumes the key ring is complete. This, of course, is suggested by passing out solid rings for examination before showing the key ring. Other illusions that we have used to illustrate the principles of perceptual organization are rope illusions such as the Cut and Restored Rope and the Professor's Nightmare (see Resource List).

**Auditory Illusions and the Multiple Coin Vanish.** Most of the work on illusions, and sensation and perception in general, concerns visual phenomena. Nevertheless, a number of investigators have recently begun to investigate auditory illusions and there are several magical illusions which rely, at least in part, on "deceiving" the auditory system. One example of this which can be performed with a minimum of practice is the multiple coin vanish (Tarr, 1976). In this illusion, four quarters are placed in the palm of the right hand. The right hand then appears to drop the coins into the left hand while actually retaining them in the right (Figure 3). The magician then holds the left hand in front of the body and drops the right hand to the side. The spectator assumes that the coins have been passed to the left hand (for the same reason that other vanishes work), but what makes the illusion particularly believable is when the magician shakes the left hand and the coins rattle. To accomplish this illusion the magician shakes the right hand (which is now out of view) simultaneously. This auditory deception works because the spectators are in front of the performer and have difficulty in localizing the source of the sound. This illusion is relatively easy to perform and provides an interesting starting off point for discussing sound localization and auditory illusions.

**ESP and "Mental Magic."** ESP is a topic which particularly interests students. Nevertheless it is a difficult topic to teach. This is probably because it is difficult to get the beginning student to appreciate some of the problems inherent in studying ESP (see McConnell, 1969, for a discussion). One of these problems is fraud. This particular problem is not attributable to researchers, who take great care to assure that fraud or subject cheating does not contribute to their results; rather, the problem is perpetuated by those who claim to be psychics, many of whom are well versed in mental magic (i.e., "mind reading" and predicting future events) and sleight of hand.

This problem has not gone unnoticed by scientists. In fact, interested scientists and philosophers have begun to debunk the claims of the psychics in a magazine called *The Zetetic* (Greek for skeptic). Similarly, Persi Diaconis (Diaconis, 1978), who is both a statistician and a magician, and who has been called on to debunk psychics including Ted Serios and Uri Geller, has recently indicated how psychics have demonstrated their powers by using magical

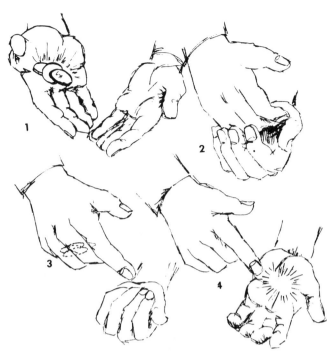

Figure 3. Multiple Coin Vanish. The right hand which contains 3 or 4 coins approaches the left (1). The right hand then turns over and appears to toss the coins into the left (2). Actually, the right hand catches the coins in the cupped fingertips, making a loud clanking noise. The right hand then palms the coins as the left hand closes (3). The magician can then drop the right hand to the side (out of sight) and shake both hands simultaneously, suggesting the coins are in the left hand (see text). The magician then opens the left hand completing the vanish (4).

illusions and sleight of hand. Jastrow (1901) was also aware of this possibility, and one of his primary concerns in studying magic was to stop this sort of deception.

There are many magical illusions which can be used to demonstrate that magic can produce phenomena which can easily be mistaken for psychic events, but one which is particularly convincing is "Intuition" (Garcia & Schindler, 1975).

Prior to conducting this illusion we ask for a volunteer who does not believe he or she has any psychic powers. We then indicate to the person that we intend to show that they are wrong. We next ask the person to go through a deck of cards and select all the spades and hearts (actually any two suits can be used). The selected cards are thoroughly shuffled and then one by one the magician holds cards next to the forehead such that the back is to the volunteer and then asks the person to guess the suit of the card. The magician then places the card in one of two piles depending upon the volunteer's guess. The volunteer gets no feedback, but much to the person's disbelief, the conjurer constantly reassures them that they have guessed every card correctly. After the volunteer has made a guess for every card, the magician turns up both piles to show that the spades pile has all spades and the hearts pile has all hearts; that is, the subject had been correct on every card. After completing the illusion, we argue that the only explanation is clairvoyant powers and it is then relatively easy to get into some of the issues surrounding ESP research.[3]

**Research and Magic.** One final aspect of the use of magic in classroom situations seems worthy of mention. Triplett (1900) described an illusion in which the magician apparently throws a ball straight up in the air, only to have it vanish. This is a standard illusion, but what makes it notable is that Triplett used this illusion to conduct research on magic. In Triplett's experiment, in which 165 school children (no age was reported) served as subjects, the operator (magician) sat behind a teacher's desk, threw the ball 3 feet into the air, and then caught it and let the hands drop behind the desk. The second toss was 4 or 5 feet high and on return the hands were again dropped behind the desk. On the third throw, the hands went up with a regular throwing motion, but the ball was not tossed. The operator then waited for the ball to return.

Triplett reported that whereas 60% of the girls were deceived, that is, they reported seeing the ball go up on the third toss but not come down, only 40% of the boys reported seeing the illusion. Based on this observation, as well as previous work on non-magical illusions, he argued that there may be sex differences in regard to susceptibility to magical illusions. Triplett also reported that in other investigations of the same phenomena, he found the illusion to be more deceptive under dim illumination.

Using Triplett's early work as an example, we have encouraged students to begin to investigate what factors influence susceptibility to various magical illusions. We have pointed out that this has been a fruitful line of research in the study of visual illusion (e.g., Coren & Girgus, 1978), and suggested that it might be an interesting way to approach magical illusion.

**Magical or More Traditional Illusions?** I have described how we have used magical illusions as a framework for teaching some of the principles of sensation and perception. Because our institution has a Winter Term, we were given the luxury of devoting an entire four-week course to these topics; consequently, we were able to consider a variety of topics in detail. But as I have tried to indicate in this paper, the use of these techniques need not be limited to this type of situation. In addition to using magical illusion in the Winter Study Course, I have used these illusions as part of an introductory psychology lecture on perception. I have also used sleight of hand techniques in order to produce some very unlikely events (e.g., selecting 4 aces, apparently at random, from a deck of cards; Garcia & Schindler, 1975) as a demonstration in my statistics course. This is quite useful in getting the class to discuss at what point are they unwilling to accept that something has occurred due to chance, and thereby leads to a discussion of the logic of the null and alternative hypothesis and Type I and Type II errors.

Clearly, there are other demonstrations which will accomplish similar ends, but it has been our experience that magical illusions not only convey material which is similar to that presented in more traditional demonstrations, but that they also have the advantage of creating a high degree of interest and enthusiasm among the students.

Table 1
Basic Illusions and the Principles They Can Be
Used to Demonstrate

| Principles | Illusions | Sources |
| --- | --- | --- |
| Past Experience Perception | Billiard Ball Vanish Sponge Ball Vanish | Tarr (1976, 1978) Ganson, Part II (1976) Tarr (1976) |
| Set and Perception | Chinese Linking Rings Cups and Balls | Ganson, Part I (1976) Tarr (1976) |
| Perceptual Organization | Popeye Pips | See Tannen's Catalog |
| | Cut and Restored Rope | Tarr (1976) |
| | Professor's Nightmare | See Tannen's Catalog |
| | Multiplying Billiard Balls | Tarr (1976) |
| Auditory Illusion, Sound Localization | Multiple Coin Vanish | Tarr (1976) |
| | Hand to Hand Coins | Tarr (1976) |
| | Coin Box | Tarr (1978) |
| ESP | Intuition | Garcia and Schindler (1975) |

### List of Resources for Preparing Demonstrations

Tarr, W. *Now You See It Now You Don't.* New York: Vintage Press, 1976. A beginners guide to sleight of hand; this book describes the basic vanishes with coins and billiard balls. The illustrations are excellent.

Tarr, W. *The Second Now You See It Now You Don't.* New York: Vintage Press, 1978. Much like the first volume, but with an emphasis on cards and coins.

Garcia, F., and Schindler, G. *Magic With Cards.* New York: Reiss Graves, Inc., 1975. An excellent series of tricks on "mental magic" with cards; many of which are applicable to demonstrations of ESP.

Ganson, L. *Routined Manipulation* (Parts I and II). New York: Tannen, 1976. A sophisticated analysis of many illusions including the Chinese Linking Rings and basic billiard ball vanishes (available through Tannen's Catalog).

Tannen's Catalog. The official catalog of Louis Tannen's Magic Shop. The illusions discussed in this paper, as well as most other illusions are available from Tannen's Catalog.

### References

Bruner, J. S. On perceptual readiness. *Psychological Review,* 1957, *64,* 123-152.

Ceillier, R. The psychological and technical problems of illusionism. *General Psychologique Bulletin,* 1922, No. 4-6, 1-42.

Coren, S., & Girgus, J. S. *Seeing is deceiving: The psychology of visual illusions.* Hillsdale, NJ: Erlbaum, 1978.

Deutsch, D. Musical illusions. *Scientific American,* Oct. 1975, *233,* 92-104.

Dessoir, M. The psychology of legerdemain. *The Open Court,* 1893, *12,* 3599-3634.

Diaconis, P. Statistical problems in ESP research. *Science,* 1978, *201,* 131-136.

Geldard, F. A. *The human senses* (2nd ed.). New York: Wiley, 1972.

Jastrow, J. On the judgment of angles and positions of lines. *American Journal of Psychology*, 1892, *5*, 214-221.

Jastrow, J. The psychology of deception, 1901. Reprinted in J. Jastrow (Ed.), *Fact and fable in psychology*. Freeport, NY: Books for Libraries Press, 1971.

Koffka, K. *The principles of Gestalt psychology*. New York: Harcourt, Brace, 1935.

Leeper, R. A study of a neglected portion of the field of learning. *Journal of Genetic Psychology*, 1935, *46*, 41-75.

Maas, J. B. *Slide group for general psychology*. New York: McGraw-Hill, 1967.

McBurney, D. A. Psychological dimensions and perceptual analysis of taste. In E. C. Carterette & M. P. Friedman (Eds.), *Handbook of perception* (Vol. VI A). New York: Academic Press, 1978.

McCleary, R. A. *Genetic and experiential factors in perception*. Glenview, IL: Scott Foresman, 1970.

McConnell, R. A. ESP and credibility in science. *American Psychologist*, 1969, *24*, 531-538.

Murch, G. M. *Visual and auditory perception*. Indianapolis: Bobbs-Merrill, 1973.

Oppel, J. J. Ueber geometrisch-optische Tauschangen. *Jah resb richt des Frankfurter. Vereins*, 1854-1855, 37-47.

Quereshi, M. Y., & Sackett, P. R. An updated content analysis of introductory psychology textbooks. *Teaching of Psychology*, 1977, *4*, 25-30.

Triplett, N. The psychology of conjuring deceptions. *The American Journal of Psychology*, 1900, *11*, 439-510.

Warren, R. M., & Warren, R. P. Auditory illusions and confusions. *Scientific American*, Dec. 1970, *223*, 30-36.

## Notes

1. Karelis, C. C. Personal Communication, May 1978.
2. I am grateful to Andrew Crider, Charles Karelis, David Morse and Richard O. Rouse for their helpful comments on an earlier version of this paper. I am especially grateful to Charles Karelis for providing copies of many of the papers discussed in the section on the history of magical illusions as well as for many provocative discussions on the psychology of magic. I would also like to thank Susan Marchant for drawing the figures.
3. Magicians generally subscribe to a code of ethics whereby they reveal the mechanisms of the illusions they perform only in trade publications. In this paper I have divulged the principles involved in several standard illusions. The illusion "Intuition," however, is a new illusion and it would be a breach of ethics to indicate how it works. Nevertheless, this information is available in Garcia and Schindler (1975).

# A Novel Experiment for Introductory Psychology Courses: Psychophysical Assessment of Olfactory Adaptation

J. Russell Mason
*Monell Chemical Senses Center*

Experimental psychology courses often include laboratory exercises in human psychophysics. These exercises tend to stress psychophysical methods such as the method of limits, the method of constant stimuli and the method of adjustment, at the expense of other newer methods such as the method of magnitude estimation. Also, visual or auditory stimuli typically are used instead of olfactory or gustatory stimuli. The exclusive use of visual or auditory stimuli is unfortunate given recent and increasing professional interest in olfaction and gustation and the inexpensiveness of generating olfactory and gustatory stimuli as compared to common methods of generating visual or auditory stimuli. The present report describes a simple experiment using the method of magnitude estimation to scale odorant intensities: (a) when the subject is in a non-adapted state; (b) when the subject is in an adapted state; and (c) when the subject is in a cross-adapted state. In addition to becoming familiar with the useful psychophysical technique of magnitude estimation, the student is introduced to the phenomenon of adaptation which is believed to reveal something about the nature of the olfactory stimulus and the olfactory receptor (Cain, 1970; Moncrieff, 1957).

The results of this experiment are likely to be robust even when collected in crowded classroom settings and can be interpreted by students with no special background in statistics. All of the materials necessary to perform the experiment are usually accessible in a chemistry storeroom.

Adaptation, i.e., reduced sensitivity as the result of prior stimulation, is a well-known sensory phenomenon which reliably occurs when the olfactory system is exposed to stimulation (Berglund, Berglund, & Lindvall, 1978; Cheesman & Mayne, 1953). It generally is believed to reflect changes at the receptor level rather than changes in more central neural locations and is relatively stimulus-specific. Adaptation to one odorant does not necessarily hamper the perception of another odorant. To explain this specificity, one may assume that there are a number of different and relatively independent receptor mechanisms whose sensitivity can be influenced separately or at least to a different degree by adaptation to different stimuli (Cain, 1970).

Olfactory self-adaptation, that is, the reduction in sensitivity to an odorant as the result of previous stimulation by that odorant, and cross-adaptation, that is, the reduction in sensitivity to one odorant as the result of previous stimulation by another odorant, are believed to result from stimulation of the same receptor mechanisms by both odorant presentations. This belief has led to groupings of odorants on the basis of common influence (i.e., the extent of self- and cross-adaptation) on the same receptor mechanisms (Moncrieff, 1956).

**Method.** The stimuli are five concentrations of butyl acetate and five concentrations of propyl acetate diluted with propylene glycol. Each succeeding concentration should be ten times as dilute as the previous concentration. A convenient set of dilutions might begin with 1 ml of pure butyl acetate (Eastman Kodak, AR grade) or propyl acetate (Eastman Kodak, AR grade) diluted with 9 ml of propylene glycol (Mallinckrodt, AR grade). Subsequent dilutions can be produced by adding 9 ml quantities of propylene glycol. These odorant dilutions are easily kept over long periods in small glass test tubes or glass vials stoppered with teflon plugs (Kimble). Teflon plugs are preferable to rubber or cork plugs since the latter have slight odors.

*Non-adapted intensity estimates.* Initially, the subjects will make magnitude estimates of the perceived intensities of the five concentrations of butyl acetate and the five concentrations of propyl acetate using one three-second sniff of the headspace above each odorant concentration in its container. The subject may assign any number to represent the perceived intensity of the odorant vapor (for discussion of the method of magnitude estimation, see Engen, 1972, pp. 73-79). The inter-trial interval should be at least 90 seconds to permit full recovery of olfactory sensitivity and to minimize the effects of initial trials on subsequent ones.

The first odorant concentration presented to subjects should be the middle (i.e., third) concentration. Subjects may assign whatever number they deem appropriate to this intermediate concentration. Then, subjects should be presented with the other odorant concentrations in a random order and asked to judge the intensity of each in relation to the perceived intensity of the intermediate concentration.

*Self-adapted intensity estimates.* First, subjects should make a non-adapted intensity estimate of the intermediate concentration of butyl acetate; this intensity estimate will serve as a standard for subsequent trials. Then subjects should make magnitude estimates of the perceived intensities of the five butyl acetate concentrations after self-adaptation. Each self-adaptation trial should consist of sniffing the high (or low) concentration of butyl acetate followed immediately by sniffing one of the five butyl acetate concentrations. The subject should make a magnitude estimate of the second of the pair of stimuli in relation to the perceived intensity of the standard stimulus. A ninety second interval should be allowed before the next trial to permit full recovery of olfactory sensitivity and to minimize the effects of initial trials on subsequent ones. Different concentrations of butyl acetate should be presented on successive self-adaptation trials.

*Cross-adapted intensity estimates.* First, subjects should make a non-adapted estimate of the intermediate concentration of butyl acetate; as previously, this intensity estimate will serve as a standard. Then subjects should make magnitude estimates of the perceived intensities of the five butyl acetate concentrations after cross-adaptation. Each cross-adaptation trial should consist of sniffing the high (or low) concentration of propyl acetate followed immediately by sniffing one of the five butyl acetate concentrations. The subject should make a magnitude estimate of the second pair of stimuli in relation to the perceived intensity of the standard stimulus. A ninety second interval should be allowed before the next trial to permit full recovery of olfactory sensitivity and to minimize the effects of initial trials on subsequent ones. Different concentrations of butyl acetate should be presented on successive trials.

Results and Discussion. For each sort of intensity estimate (i.e., non-adapted, self-adapted, cross-adapted), the subject's estimates should be transformed to a scale of ten. This will permit comparisons among all of the sorts of intensity estimate using the same scale. Thus, for example, if the subject assigned "50" as the intensity of the middle concentration of butyl acetate in the self-adapted series, all magnitude estimates in that series would be multiplied by

"0.2". If the subject had assigned "1" to the middle concentration, all magnitude estimates would be multiplied by "10.0" (Cain, 1970).

The geometric mean for intensity estimates for each concentration of butyl acetate in each series (i.e., non-adapted, self-adapted, cross-adapted) should be calculated. This descriptive statistic is commonly used in olfactory psychophysics because it is less sensitive to extreme scores than is the arithmetic mean. In addition, the geometric mean is commonly used with the method of magnitude estimation because magnitude estimation has a true zero point, unlike some other psychophysical methods (See Engen, 1972, pp. 73-79).

The medians of the geometric means for the entire class (i.e., all subjects) can be used to summarize the data. For example, medians could be plotted and the plots readily compared with figures in a variety of current research journals usually available in college collections. Also, differences between medians of the geometric means of magnitude estimates in each condition can be assessed using a simple modification of the sign test (Lehmann, 1975, pp. 162-163).

Figure 1 shows sample results of the present experiment collected by college students during a laboratory exercise. Differences between medians of the geometric means of

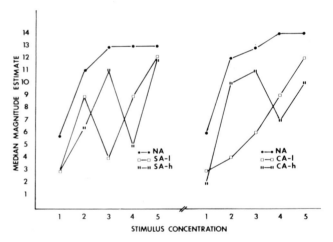

Figure 1. Medians of geometric means of magnitude estimates during non-adaptation (NA), self-adaptation with a low concentration of adapting stimulus (SA-l), self-adaptation with a high concentration of adapting stimulus (SA-h), cross-adaptation with a low concentration of adapting stimulus (CA-l), and cross-adaptation with a high concentration of adapting stimulus (CA-h)

magnitude estimates were assessed using the sign test ($p < .05$). Magnitude estimates of butyl acetate increased reliably with higher stimulus concentrations regardless of the adaptation condition. Also, both self-adaptation with butyl acetate and cross-adaptation with propyl acetate decreased magnitude estimates relative to estimates collected in the non-adapted condition. Within the self-adapted condition, both high and low concentrations of adapting stimulus produced about the same decrement in magnitude estimates. Within the cross-adapted condition, high or low concentrations of adapting stimulus produced different decrements in magnitude estimates. These decrements were dependent upon the concentration of butyl acetate to be judged. These sample findings are readily comparable with findings published by others (e.g., Cain, 1970; Engen, 1963) and are representative of the findings typically obtained using the present design.

## References

Berglund, B., Berglund, B. & Lindvall, T. Olfactory self- and cross-adaptation: Effects of time of adaptation on perceived odor intensity. *Sensory Processes*, 1978, *2*, 191-197.

Cain, W. S. Odor intensity after self-adaptation and cross-adaptation. *Perception and Psychophysics*, 1970, *7*, 271-275.

Cheesman, G. H., & Mayne, S. The influence of adaptation on absolute threshold measurements of olfactory stimuli. *Quarterly Journal of Experimental Psychology*, 1953, *5*, 22-30.

Engen, T. Cross-adaptation to the aliphatic alcohols. *American Journal of Psychology*, 1963, *76*, 96-102.

Engen, T. Psychophysics II: Scaling methods. In J. W. Kling & L. A. Riggs (Eds.), *Experimental psychology*, New York: Holt, Rinehart & Winston, 1972, pp. 73-79.

Lehmann, E. L. *Nonparametrics: Statistical methods based on ranks.* San Francisco: Holden-Day, 1975. pp. 162-163.

Moncrieff, R. W. Olfactory adaptation and odor likeness. *Journal of Physiology*, 1956, *133*, 301-315.

Moncrieff, R. W. Olfactory adaptation and odor intensity. *American Journal of Psychology*, 1957, *70*, 1-20.

---

# Perceptual Demonstrations—Or, What To Do With an Equipment Budget of $75

Ludy T. Benjamin, Jr.
*Nebraska Wesleyan University*

As a scientific enterprise, many areas of research in psychology require little or no expensive laboratory equipment. However, in some fields equipment can contribute significantly to the quality of instruction through class demonstrations and experiments. In truth, it may be redundant to attach the adjective "expensive" to laboratory equipment. Because of the high costs of these materials, even the less expensive items are beyond the equipment budgets of many undergraduate psychology programs. Fortunately, for the psychologist in this position there is a feasible alternative — build it yourself!

The present paper offers some ideas for equipment and visual materials for use in a course in perception, although their use is certainly not restricted to that course alone. These materials can be easily and inexpensively assembled, requiring no special skills. In a few cases however, minimal carpentry skills are helpful.

In addition to equipment ideas, this paper includes references which describe some of the experiments and/or demonstrations in which these materials can be used. These references are in no way meant to be exhaustive of the utility of the materials, rather they represent a starting point for ideas.

A course in perception should involve some real experience in perceiving, yet often the perceptual experiences come solely from diagrams in a textbook. Films can extend the reality of these experiences beyond the means of a textbook, but even films are not "real." Watching a trapezoidal window oscillate in a film does not provide the same kind of perceptual experience one gets from a live demonstration. These "live" demonstrations are indispensable in presenting the psychology of perception as an interesting and intriguing area of study. It is hoped that the ideas presented here will encourage that kind of course offering.

**Displacement Goggles.** Displacement goggles similar to those used in studies of perceptual adaptation to distorted vision can be made from welding safety goggles. These goggles are inexpensive (usually under $5) and are especially advantageous in that they permit the subject to wear prescription glasses when the goggles are in place. Select the kind of goggles with a rectangular faceplate and no center dividing bridge. Remove the safety glass lenses and replace them with a clear piece of one-eighth inch plexiglas. The triangular prisms (two) can be cut from one-inch plexiglas. Begin by measuring the dimensions of the exposed surface of the front side of the faceplate. Cut two pieces identical in size from the one-inch plexiglas and completely cover the exposed faceplate surface. Ideal prism angle should be between 20° and 30° (which provides 10° to 15° of actual visual displacement). Polish the two large faces of each prism and then cover those faces with masking tape. Spray the three exposed edges with a flat black paint to prevent light from entering those surfaces. Finally, after the paint is dry, remove the masking tape and attach the prisms to the plexiglas faceplate using a plexiglas glue such as ethylene dichloride. The prism bases should be mounted to the right or the left if vision is to be displaced in a lateral direction. In most welding goggles the faceplate is removable, thus the direction of the displacement can be reversed by reversing the faceplate. For other perceptual effects, the prisms can be mounted on the faceplate in a variety of orientations.

Harris, C. S. Perceptual adaptation to inverted, reversed, and displaced vision. *Psychological Review*, 1965, *72*, 419-444.

Kohler, I. Experiments with goggles. *Scientific American*, May 1962, *206*, 62-72.

Weinstein, S., Sersen, E. A., Fisher, L., & Weisinger, M. Is reafference necessary for visual adaptation? *Perceptual and Motor Skills*, 1964, *18*, 641-648.

**Visual Cliff.** A visual cliff for use with small animals such as rats and kittens can be constructed from masonite, plexiglas, and contact paper. The dimensions of the apparatus may vary depending upon the subjects you plan to use. A cliff that is 30 in. by 30 in. by 30 in. can be constructed from two sheets of one-fourth inch masonite (4' by 8'). The basic unit is a square box with floor and a center wall extending from the floor to within 6 in. of the top of the box. A section of masonite from the top edge of this center wall to one edge of the box forms the base of the shallow side of the cliff. The masonite should be used so that the smooth surface is always part of the interior of the box.

Handles for carrying the unit should be attached with screws from the inside and countersunk flush with the surface of the interior walls. The cliff can be painted in the traditional checkerboard pattern or a more convenient method is to use contact paper of a checkerboard design. This can usually be found in discount or department stores and has an adhesive backing for easy mounting. Line all exposed interior surfaces and the surface of the shallow side. A sheet of clear one-fourth inch plexiglas should be used to cover the shallow and deep sides of the box. This sheet should rest on the surface of the shallow side and on several plexiglas stops on the deep side walls for support. The center walkway in the cliff can be made from wood and either painted or covered with the contact paper. For the visual cliff described here, the walkway should be approximately six inches wide, with a height of two to three inches above the surface of the plexiglas.

Gibson, E. J., & Walk, R. D.   The "visual cliff". *Scientific American*, April 1960, *202*, 64-71.
Somervill, J. W.   Motion parallax in the visual cliff situation. *Perceptual and Motor Skills*, 1971, *32*, 43-53.
Walk, R. D., Gibson, E. J., & Tighe, T. J.   Behavior of light-and dark-reared rats on a visual cliff. *Science*, 1957, *126*, 80-81.
Walk, R. D., & Walters, C. P.   Importance of texture-density preferences and motion parallax for visual depth discrimination by rats and chicks. *Journal of Comparative and Physiological Psychology*, 1974, *86*, 309-315.

**Pulfrich Apparatus.**   The Pulfrich phenomenon is one of the most effective demonstrations in visual perception and one of the easiest to prepare. The subject views an object swinging back and forth at eye level in a plane perpendicular to the subject's line of vision. Viewing is binocular. However, one of the subject's eyes is covered with a sunglass lens (or some other form of light filter). The swinging object appears to be moving in an elliptical or circular orbit rather than in a straight line. The object will be seen to orbit in a clockwise or counterclockwise direction, dependent upon which eye is covered by the filter.

The simplest way to demonstrate the Pulfrich effect is to attach a string to the ceiling with a weight tied to the free end. The weight should be about the size of a flashlight battery or nine-volt transistor radio battery. (In fact either of those objects will work quite well.) The major problem with this technique is that you must continually restart the pendulum action when the arc begins to decrease. If motion of the object at a constant speed is important for your purposes (e.g., research) then you should consider attaching the pendulum to a motor. You could manufacture a motor and cam system that would supply the appropriate movement (an arc of 70° to 90°), however, that would be very difficult to construct. One solution is to find a motor which is designed for that kind of motion. For example, many motors that are used in window display advertising are often geared to moving an object back and forth. These motors are usually light duty so the shaft of the pendulum and the pendulum bob must be light in weight. A ping pong ball, painted some dark color so that it contrasts well with light colored walls, makes an excellent bob. The shaft can be made of some thin metal rod such as aluminum. It should be light enough not to induce undue strain on the motor, yet heavy enough to remain rigid in the pendulum motion. In demonstrating this phenomenon the background is a critical variable. There should be ample distance (six to ten feet) between the path of the swinging object and any adjacent walls, otherwise the magnitude of the effect will be diminished.

Diamond, A. L.   Simultaneous contrast and the Pulfrich phenomenon. *Journal of Optical Society of America*, 1958, *48*, 887-890.
Lit, A.   The magnitude of the Pulfrich stereophenomenon as a function of binocular differences of intensity at various levels of illumination. *American Journal of Psychology*, 1949, *62*, 159-181.
Rock, M. L., & Fox, B. H.   Two aspects of the Pulfrich phenomenon. *American Journal of Psychology*, 1949, *62*, 279-284.
Standing, L. G., Dodwell, P. C., & Lang, D.   Dark adaptation and the Pulfrich effect. *Perception and Psychophysics*, 1968, *4*, 118-120.

**Distorted Room, Trapezoidal Window.**   A number of extremely effective demonstrations in perception originated with the Transactional group of psychologists at Princeton University. Undoubtedly the best known of these demonstrations are the distorted room and the trapezoidal window. The distorted room can be constructed in a range of sizes from one small enough to hold in your hands to one large enough to accommodate the presence of human adults. Cardboard can be used for the construction of the smaller models, while wood is required for the larger ones.

Similarly, the trapezoidal window can be made in a number of sizes and from a variety of materials including cardboard, wood, and sheet metal. The window should be mounted on a vertical shaft for rotation purposes. Rotation can be accomplished by motor or by a manual crank and gear system. The motor is usually the more desirable alternative as it provides a more constant rate of rotation.

Complete detailed construction plans for the distorted room and trapezoidal window (as well as eighteen other perceptual demonstrations) can be found in W. H. Ittelson's book, *The Ames demonstrations in perception: A guide to their construction and use* (Princeton University Press, 1952).

Epstein, W.   A test of two interpretations of the apparent size effects in a distorted room. *Journal of Experimental Psychology*, 1962, *63*, 124-128.
Gerace, T. A., & Caldwell, W. E.   Perceptual distortion as a function of stimulus objects, sex, naiveté, and trials, using a portable model of the Ames distorted room. *Genetic Psychology Monographs*, 1971, *84*, 3-33.
Haber, R. N.   Limited modification of the trapezoidal illusion with experience. *American Journal of Psychology*, 1965, *78*, 651-655.
Zegers, R. T.   The reversal illusion of the Ames trapezoid. *Transactions of the New York Academy of Sciences*, 1964, *26*, 377-400.

**Classical Psychophysics.**   A Müller-Lyer apparatus which consists of a stationary line and an adjustable line is particularly suited to the method of average error (method of adjustment). Plans for this apparatus which is made of wood and cardboard can be found on page 422 of the 1954 edition of *Experimental psychology* by R. S. Woodworth and H. Schlosberg (Holt, Rinehart, and Winston, Publishers).

A weight set for demonstrating the method of constant stimuli can be made from a collection of uniform containers. The small cannisters used for 35mm roll film are particularly well suited for this task. These containers are usually readily available at no charge from film processing shops, and may be filled with sand, small metal pellets, or similar heavy substances.

Engen, T. Psychophysics 1. Discrimination and detection. In Kling, J. W., & Riggs, L. A. (Eds.). *Woodworth and Schlosberg's experimental psychology* (third edition), New York: Holt, Rinehart, and Winston, 1971. (pp. 11-46)

Townsend, J. C. *Introduction to experimental method.* New York: McGraw-Hill, 1953. (pp. 69-83)

**Overhead Transparencies and Slides.** Numerous demonstrations and experiments in perception require only a projector and visual materials. These are especially desirable for presenting visual illusions, cues for depth perception, shapes, patterns, and words for recognition studies.

Any material which can be produced on paper can be converted to transparencies for overhead projection by means of a Thermo-Fax copier (or similar reproduction process). Slides (35mm) can be made in a similar manner. Material transferred to a transparency can be cut and mounted in cardboard slide mounts (which are commercially available) by sealing them with an ordinary clothes iron.

Attneave, F. Multistability in perception. *Scientific American,* December 1971, *225,* 62-71.

Gregory, R. L. Visual illusions. *Scientific American,* November 1968, *219,* 66-76.

Gregory, R. L. *Eye and brain* (second edition). New York: McGraw-Hill, 1973.

Tolansky, S. *Optical illusions.* New York: Pergamon Press, 1964.

# The Light Box: A Simple Way of Generating Complex Color Demonstrations

Barney Beins
*Thomas More College*

Most undergraduates find the process of color vision interesting, but hard to comprehend without concrete examples. Further, unless one is equipped with demonstrational apparatus, examples of color phenomena are severely limited. In order to enhance the discussion of color vision in our Sensation and Perception course at a reasonable cost, we generated an independent project for one of our undergraduates to construct a "light box" that would provide color demonstrations. Under faculty supervision, he assembled the necessary components, wired the electrical apparatus and constructed the wood housing. In the classroom, it generated some surprising and interesting color effects.

**Apparatus.** The rationale for building the light box was to design something that could, with minimal expense, generate several different effects. Consequently, we wired the equipment to hold four light bulbs of different colors, each controlled by a dimmer switch that would allow adjustment of illumination level for various demonstrations.

The design of the equipment was relatively simple. It consisted of four ceramic sockets to be used for holding three different General Electric colored party bulbs and one regular white bulb. General Electric manufactures four differently colored bulbs: red, green, blue and yellow. They come in two varieties, clear and frosted. Depending on the stimuli to be used with the lights, different bulbs will be preferred. We chose the clear red and blue and the frosted yellow bulbs.[1]

We wired four ceramic bulb sockets in parallel, each attached to its own dimmer switch, in order to control brightness independently. Dimmer switches with the so-called infinite level controls are preferable to the two or three position dimmers. Care should also be taken not to exceed to voltage limitations specified for each dimmer; in general, the 25-watt party bulbs pose no problems.

In addition to wiring the apparatus, we constructed the housing, which measured 5" x 8" x 24". A single 4' x 4' piece of quarter-inch plywood was cut to the appropriate dimensions. The top was hinged; the rest of the body was constructed with screws.

A 1½ inch hole cutter can be affixed to a power drill to make holes in order to attach the sockets to the top of the housing; the dimmer switches can also be attached to the housing after a hole for the body of the dimmer is made. The hinged top allows periodic examination of the wiring should any contacts loosen. Electrical tape can be used to connect the wires although shrink tubing can be a convenient substitution on some connections. (It should be mentioned that some knowledge of electricity is required to make the box, and that an electrician should inspect the apparatus to attest to its safety.) The total cost was less than $35.00.

**Demonstrations.** In order to illustrate the fact that colored surfaces absorb most wavelengths, the colored lights can be turned on individually and students can be induced to guess the color of a stimulus placed next to the light. One striking effect is that a green object appears jet black under red illumination.

In addition, we used artist's colors and felt-tipped markers to draw individual letters on large (175 x 300 mm) pieces of cardboard. Under illumination by different bulbs, the same letter changes appearance. This apparent variability seemed to capture students' interest effectively.

Through the use of stimuli like pseudo-isochromatic plates (i.e., hidden figures) in which, for example, green colored dots form a pattern among red colored dots, color anomalies or color blindness can be illustrated. By viewing these figures under a single colored light, the student can be rendered temporarily "color blind" or "color anomalous."

To show that color is a function of intensity as well as of wavelength, students can view objects of a given color under slowly increasing illumination. We have found that a yellow stimulus will go through a broad range of phenomenal colors by turning on yellow light (the stimulus appears white) and then slowly adding red light (to produce orange). When red is at maximum, turn yellow off and slowly begin to add blue light, at which time the stimulus will become successively blue and then green (with these bulbs). This demonstration can be used to explain color additivity.

Demonstration of rod versus cone vision is relatively easy to simulate although with even a 25-watt white bulb, any object within ten to fifteen feet is sufficiently illuminated as to activate the cones. With distance viewing, the falloff in brightness permits achromatic vision. Within closer range, the dimmest settings of red permit essentially achromatic viewing although the color shift with longer wavelengths distorts the brightness of many objects with normally short wavelength coloration.

Evaluation.   After the segment on color vision had been completed, students filled out an open-ended questionnaire concerning the apparatus. Of the 18 respondents, all were positive in responding to the question "Are there any advantages to using the light box for learning about color vision?" In spite of this leading question, the students later made favorable comments about their impressions of the sessions. Typical comments (14 of 18 students) suggested that the demonstrations made the abstractions more concrete, thus easier to understand. An extreme, but consistent statement by one of the students was that "by using the light box, we are forced into believing what you have said. Without it (the light box), it would be hard to believe that something yellow could look white." Many of the students often specifically asserted surprise that a single stimulus could change color as they watched (10 of 18 students). They were much more impressed with the effects under red illumination, presumably because of its narrower spectrum relative to blue. In fact, there were 32 general comments concerning the effectiveness of the apparatus: 27 were positive and four of the remaining five negative comments mentioned the less dramatic appearance changes under blue illumination.

In order to see whether students actually became more aware of the mechanisms of color additivity, I administered a pre-test and an identical post-test to the students, asking them to name the "real" color of the letters held up before them. For illumination under red light, students improved significantly from pre-test to post-test, $t(16) = 2.36$, $p < .05$. It is also true that students experienced less compelling color shifts under blue illumination, as evidenced by a lack of change in their accuracy in pre- and post-test situations, $t(16) = -0.61$, $p > .05$.

With red illumination, the initial guesses of the students seemed to be just that—guesses. On the 15-item pre-test, students initially averaged over six guesses of either black, white or gray. This dropped to just over three guesses on the identical post-test after they had been exposed to the light box demonstrations, $t(16) = 7.06$, $p < .001$. (There were actually two white stimuli among the others.) The increase in student accuracy is actually more impressive than the mean number correct suggests because in many cases, students responded that an item was blue when it was actually green; green and blue appeared very similar when viewed under red lights.

The students were initially wrong often enough to convince us that the demonstrations did not introduce trivial effects, but actually illustrated more complex psychological phenomena. From the comments on the questionnaires and from the reactions in class, the students seemed not only to learn about color processes, but also to enjoy the experience.

### Notes

1. The spectral ranges for our bulbs are as follows: clear red bulb, 587-685 nm; clear yellow bulb, 487-662 nm; frosted yellow, 526-652 nm; clear blue bulb, 425-562 nm. A spokesperson for General Electric noted that different bulbs will show somewhat different ranges.
2. I would like to thank Jack Wells of the Thomas More Physics Department for his assistance in measuring the spectra of the various bulbs.

# Creating Illusions of Movement by an Overhead Projector

Thaddeus M. Cowan
*Kansas State University*

An overhead projector can be used to demonstrate illusions of movement by employing a principle incorporated by Michotte (1946, 1958) in his classical experiments on perceptual causality. Michotte made use of the fact that when a line is moved across a second stationary line with which it intersects, then the point of intersection will also move in a well defined direction and a determinable speed.[1]

In Michotte's case the moving line was a painted line and the stationary line was a slit. In the descriptions presented here, both the moving line and the stationary line are slits or apertures. Specifically, if two opaque sheets containing different slit patterns are placed on an overhead projector, various movements of points of light are produced when one sheet is moved across the other.

There are a number of positive things that can be said about this procedure. For one, the equipment is simple and not costly. The items needed are an overhead projector, two pieces of construction paper, and a single edged razor blade. Furthermore, precision of construction need not be a concern, and the slit patterns can be made quickly so that spontaneous experimentation in the classroom is possible. Moreover, since these demonstrations appear in large scale on a projection screen, they can be shown to large audiences and are clearly visible to everyone.

What follows are the descriptions of eight visual effects of interest in a discussion of perception. Some illusions of movement are too complex to produce in a simple way. Yet with prior preparation even these can be shown by an overhead projector. The final description in this report describes one of these preparations.

## Simple Constructions

**Phi Phenomenon.** Figure 1a shows how a simple phi phenomenon can be demonstrated. The stationary sheet has two holes placed at a reasonable distance apart. The sliding sheet has a slit cut as shown. The sliding sheet should have a stop placed appropriately on each slide to avoid over-shooting. Variations in the stimulus and inter-stimulus durations can be induced by changing the widths of the slit and the holes. Thus, Korte's laws can easily be demonstrated.

In Figure 1b, the moving slits are crossed, and the crossed slits are passed over a row of evenly spaced holes on the stationary sheet. If the movement is slow, the two end dots of light seem to move to the center then bounce apart. If the speed of the motion is increased the two end lights move to the center, then appear to pass through one another.

**Michotte's Demonstrations.** The patterns for Michotte's perceptual causality are shown in Figure 1c. The perceptual effect is one of A hitting B causing B to continue along A's path while A remains at B's initial location.

Figures 1d and 1e give the slot patterns for Michotte's "transporting" and "tunneling" effects. In the case of the former, A appears to meet B then carry it to the end of the path. With the latter, the spot of light disappears at B, then reappears at C giving the impression that it entered and emerged from a tunnel.

**The Fujii and Johannson Illusions.** Fujii (1943) found that when a dot moves with constant velocity along a square path, then, depending on the speed, the dot appears to follow either a four-cusped hypocycloid path or a path which overshoots at the corners then quickly returns to the original line. A good description of these effects can be found in Festinger and Montague (1974).

Only half of the Fujii illusion can be shown in a simple way. A diagonal line passed over an L-shaped slit in the manner indicated in Figure 1f will produce an illusory distortion of the second line (the vertical line in Figure 1f) which the diagonal intersects.

Johannson's illusion (Johannson, 1950; Kolers, 1964) is created by orienting the moving diagonal slit in the opposite direction so that the point of first contact is either at the apex of the L-slit or the free ends of the vertical and horizontal lines (Figure 1g). A compound motion is established where the two dots move diagonally toward each other, while at the same time this pair of diagonally moving dots slides along the other diagonal. It should be noted that not everyone sees this compound motion (Kolers, 1964).

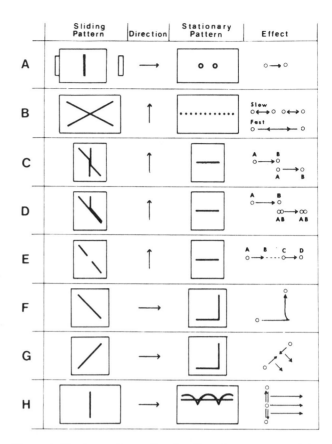

Figure 1. The two patterns, the direction of movement and the perceptual effects for the following phenomena: (a) Simple phi phenomenon (b) Complex phi phenomenon (c) Michotte's perceptual causality (d) Michotte's "transporting" effect (e) Michotte's "tunneling" effect (f) Fujii's illusion (partial) (g) Johannson's illusion (h) Modified cycloid illusion.

**Cycloid Illusion.** Any point on the rim of a wheel describes a cycloid curve as the wheel moves across a surface, and a light on the rim will be seen to trace a cycloid path. However, if a second light is placed at the hub, the rim light appears to move in a circular path around the hub and its cycloid characteristics are lost.[2]

This illusion is complex and cannot be produced in a simple way. However, a related effect can be created easily as shown in Figure 1h. A vertical slit is passed over a series of cycloid curves (here semicircles will do) which are bisected by a straight horizontal line. The effect one sees is an up and down motion of one point of light (on the rim line) passing through a second point of light moving horizontally along the hub line. The rim light in the absence of the hub light is seen to follow a cycloid (or semicircular) path. This effect has not been previously described in the literature, and it is similar to the compound motion of Johannson's illusion. Unlike the Johannson illusion, however, the compound motion produced in this way is readily seen.

## Complex Constructions

A true cycloid illusion requires some preparation and polaroid filters are needed to produce it. In the preparation of this illusion these steps should be followed:

1. Construct a cycloid of at least two cycles. See Riggs

(1910) for a simple way of constructing this curve.

2. Bisect the cycloid horizontally with a hub line. Mark this line off in equal segments. Mark points on the cycloid by using each segment mark as a center and the radius of the generating circle (wheel) as a radius. Connect each cycloid point and its hub line segment mark with a straight line (see Figure 2a).

3. Place a piece of tracing paper over the figure so that the cycloid shows through at the bottom. Trace the first two points to the left which are connected by a line. Move the tracing paper down some predetermined (arbitrary) distance, and mark the second two points connected by a line. Keep moving the paper downward and perpendicularly across the cycloid at a constant distance each time and mark successive pairs of points until the last pair of points on the right has been traced (see Figure 2b). The two paths described by the points on the tracing paper should resemble the cycloid curve in Figure 2a; they will also appear slanted.

4. The two patterns shown in Figure 2b (the original and traced paths) are the figures that will be placed on the overhead projector. The projection figures can be made by placing thin strips of tape on two transparencies in the same pattern as the configuration of lines on the two sheets in Figure 2b. The transparencies are then spray-painted and the tape removed.

5. As one pattern is passed downward and perpendicularly across the other, four dots will appear. These are the hub line and cycloid line of the top pattern intersecting the hub and cycloid lines of the bottom pattern. It is necessary that only the intersection of the two cycloid lines and the intersection of the two hub lines allow the passage of light. This is most easily accomplished by cross-polarization as shown in Figure 2c. Thin strips cut from polarized plastic sheets can be used here.

One figure is passed across the other with the same direction of movement used during the drawing of the patterns (see Figure 2b). The rim light is seen to describe a clear circular path around the hub light. If a polaroid strip of the right orientation is placed across either hub line to eliminate the hub light, the cycloid path described by the rim light can be observed. The effects are very realistic and startling in spite of the fact that the spots of light are rhomboid in shape. Interesting effects can be created by shifting the top sheet to the left or right before passing it across the bottom sheet; the rim light appears to roll like an oval rather than a circle.

The more complicated constructions suffer from a loss of simplicity and ease with which the simpler effects can be made. Even with their complexities, however, they are far less bulky and less expensive than electronic equipment, and the advantage that these illusions can be shown to a large audience still remains.

## References

Festinger, L., & Montague, A. E. Inferences about the efferent system based on a perceptual illusion produced by eye movements. *Psychological Review*, 1974, *81*, 44-58.

Fujii, E. Forming a figure by movement of a luminous point. *Japanese Journal of Psychology*, 1943, *18*, 196-232.

Johannson, G. *Configurations in event perception*, Uppsala, Sweden: Almquist and Wicksell, 1950.

Kolers, P. The illusion of movement. *Scientific American*, October 1964, *211*, 98-108.

Michotte, A. *La perception de la causalite*. Louvain, Belgium: Editions "Erasme," Publications Universitaires De Louvain, 1946.

Michotte, A. Causality and Activity. In Beardsley and Wertheimer (Eds.) *Readings in perception*. Princeton: D. Van Nostrand Company, Inc., 1958.

Riggs, N. C. *Analytic geometry*, New York; Macmillan, 1910.

von Fieandt, K. *The world of perception*. Homewood, Illinois: Homewood Press, 1966.

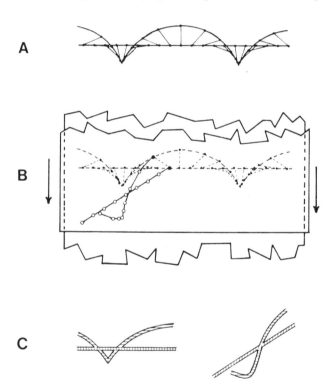

A

B

C

Figure 2. (a) Cycloid curve with points along the curve connected to the center of their generating circles. (b) The construction of the sliding pattern for the cycloid illusion. The broken line pattern is on the bottom sheet and shows through the tracing paper (the top sheet). The patterns formed by tracing appear in large open circles connected by solid lines. (c) Polarization of the slots in the sliding and stationary patterns for the cycloid illusion.

## Notes

1. The fact that this is a degenerate case of a moire pattern should not go unnoted.
2. It is said that Galileo was motivated to investigate the properties of the cycloid curve as a result of observing the paradoxes of this illusion (von Fieandt, 1966).

# Additive (and Subtractive) Color Mixtures With A Single Slide Projector

Donald H. Mershon
*North Carolina State University*

The following suggestion is made under the assumption that both introductory and advanced discussions about perception can benefit from providing active demonstrations of perceptual processes. Reading about or hearing about various phenomena is fine but such information is much more meaningful if it can be associated with direct personal experience. Providing such experiences within a tightly limited (or non-existent) course budget is sometimes difficult. Although a 2 X 2 slide projector is basic, and is usually available, some demonstrations seem to demand two projectors. Additive color mixtures are such demonstrations. The following note describes how one may accomplish good demonstrations of additive color mixing without having to find a second projector.

Additive mixtures of colors, of course, involve the new color experiences created by superimposing lights from two (or more) independent sources on the retina (or, equivalently, on a projection screen). Such a situation is standard in the experimental study of color mixture and understanding its basic rules is important for any appreciation of color vision. Unfortunately, the only type of color mixture with which a majority of students are familiar is subtractive mixture (the process involved in the mixture of paints). Even though it is possible to point out verbally that the rules for predicting additive and subtractive mixtures are different, and colored diagrams are shown in many textbooks to support the distinction, it is more effective to provide an immediate demonstration. It is necessary, therefore, to be able to superimpose at least two spots of projected light (one of each of the colors to be mixed).

The superimposition of two spots of light, say a red and a green, is simple with two projectors. Slides may be made using commercially available frames (with or without glass). A standard office hole punch and a small square of aluminum foil are used to create the "spot" for mounting in the slide frame. A piece of red (or green) filter material from the camera store, school supply house, or Edmund Scientific Co. (see Note 1) provides a well-saturated colored light.

Modifying the two-projector demonstration to a one-projector demonstration requires that both spots be punched in a single piece of foil and that the red and green filters be mounted (one for each spot) in the same frame. For convenience, a vertical positioning of one spot above the other is helpful and will be assumed in the following directions. Finally, one needs a moderately large right-angle prism such as can be obtained from Edmund Scientific Co. for less than $10.[1]

To demonstrate additive mixtures of the two chosen colors, project the slide as usual in a darkened room. The prism is now placed with its long axis perpendicular to the projection beam and slightly in front of, but below, the lens. By slowly raising the prism into the beam of light, some of the rays are captured by the prism and diverted to a new location on the screen, thus producing a double projection of each colored spot. By careful manipulation of the prism's orientation, the "extra" spots can be positioned to superimpose either of the original ones, creating the conditions for an additive mix. If a red spot is superimposed on a green, for example, a clearly yellow area appears. This is much more striking than being told that red plus green equals yellow.

The above demonstration has an additional advantage over any kind of static display of the same situation. The prism can be continuously adjusted, to show the result of changes in the relative proportions of red and green light. This manipulation is accomplished by slightly raising or lowering the prism in the projector beam, leaving the same two spots superimposed. As one lowers the prism, it intercepts less of the light and the "extra" image is reduced in intensity. As one raises the prism to intercept more of the beam, the extra image is enhanced while the contribution of the original fades. Thus, one can vary the "yellow" mixture from quite a green-yellow to a very strong orange. With a little practice at moving the prism, these manipulations are all readily accomplished.

Given the availability of the proper gelatin or acetate filters, one can proceed to prepare any two-color mixture one wishes. The red-green mix is recommended, however, because of the greater availability of suitable filters. (Any filters appearing to be pure green and pure red will do; one need not be concerned with the particular transmission characteristics.) It is usually good to note to the class that actual color vision experiments make use of monochromatic stimuli which the slides are definitely not.

For comparison of additive and subtractive mixtures, one can take small scraps of the same filters as were used to create the additive slide and bind them together in another mounting. One portion of each filter should be visible alone and another portion overlapped with the second filter. Some of the slide area should be left unfiltered to show how (in the subtractive situation) one or both filters remove portions of the original white light.

With a little imagination, a variety of color mixture effects can be produced in such a way that meaning is given to what are otherwise often confusing ideas to the new student of perception.

## Note

We have used a "giant" silvered right-angle prism (base = 54 mm wide X 146 mm long; height of each face = 38 mm). Edmund Scientific Company (Edscorp Building, Barrington, N. J. 08007) lists such a prism as No. 800. If other prisms are available, they might be tried first since the basic requirement is simply the sufficient control of a secondary image to allow the spots to be superimposed. (Edmund Scientific also sells a variety of colored filters).

# A Laboratory Exercise Demonstrating the Relation of Projected Size to Distance

Ernest A. Lumsden
*University of North Carolina at Greensboro*

This exercise demonstrates the idea which Leonardo da Vinci reportedly utilized in one of the first systematic studies of linear perspective. The basic notion is that by viewing the environment through a transparent frontal parallel plane, one can study the relationship of projected size to distance. In this manner, many other cues to distance based on this geometric relationship can be appreciated as well. The instructions are:

1. Clamp a large piece of plexiglas (or framed glass) in a vertical position with the top edge at a height of 5 feet from the floor. The transparent material should be at least 16 inches in width and 12 inches in height.

2. In order to assure that the observer's head will remain relatively stationary throughout the experiment, one can either require that the observer view through a very small hole in a reduction screen or place his head in a head holder. We successfully utilized a reduction screen with a hole $\frac{3}{8}$" in diameter. This screen should be secured in place by clamps in a fronto-parallel position 14 inches from the vertical plexiglass with the center of the viewing hole at a height of 5 feet from the floor, even with the top of the plexiglas. This point in space at which the observer's eye is to be located is hereafter referred to as the point of observation.

3. Several meter sticks (yard sticks or any other objects of uniform length could be utilized) should be placed on the floor at equal intervals from the point of observation. The first meter stick should be placed in a fronto-parallel position to the observer at a distance of 6 feet from the observation point. Because the distance from the observation point to the floor directly beneath it is 5 feet, the distance from this point on the floor to the first meter stick is 3.32 feet. The Pythagorean theory was utilized in the determination of the distances on the floor that will effect equal increments of 4 feet from the observation point. Specifically, the first distance was determined by considering the 6-foot distance from the observation point to the first meter stick as the hypotenuse of a right triangle, "c," the height of the observation point from the ground as the altitude of that right triangle, "a," and the distance on the ground to the first meter stick can be considered as the base of the right triangle, "b." For any viewing distance, c, the floor distance, b, can be determined in the following manner: $b^3 = c^2 - a^2$, with the altitude of the right triangle, a, remaining equal to 5 feet throughout the experiment. In this way, the distances on the ground producing distances from the observation point of 6 feet with increments of 4 feet were determined and are provided in Table 1. The meter sticks should be aligned in a fronto-parallel position to the observer, as are the plexiglas and reduction screen.

**Table 1**

**Variable Dimensions Related to Viewing Six Meter Sticks from an Observation Point 5 feet Above Floor Level**

| Distance from Observation Point to Successive Meter Sticks | Distance from point on floor directly below observation point | Horizontal length of projection on plexiglass of successive meter sticks |
|---|---|---|
| 6' | 3.32' | 7.95" |
| 10' | 8.66' | 3.88" |
| 14' | 13.08' | 2.57" |
| 18' | 17.29' | 1.98" |
| 22' | 21.42' | 1.64" |
| 26' | 25.51' | 1.35" |

4. While holding the head very still and using only one eye, the observer traces the projection of the meter sticks onto the surface of the plexiglas with a black grease pencil. In order to ascertain that the viewing eye is at the same precise point in space when all the edges are being traced, the observer should always check to assure that the lines that have already been traced on the plexiglas overlap perfectly with those meter sticks in the visual field before proceeding to trace any additional edges. The observer proceeds in this manner until all of the meter sticks are traced.

5. Remove the plexiglas and measure very carefully the horizontal length of the projection of each of the meter sticks on the plexiglas. Prepare a data sheet, writing this measurement beside the distance from which it was viewed (6 feet, 10 feet, 14 feet, etc.).

6. Plot a graph showing the projected horizontal length (dependent variable) of each meter stick as a function of the distance (independent variable) from which it was viewed.

The function in Figure 1 was obtained by plotting the means from 18 students, although each of the individual curves (as called for in step 6) approximated this figure very closely.

This demonstration permits the students to study the stimulus information in the retinal projection that corresponds to increased distance. It was very gratifying to hear the comments of the students relating how surprised they were to find that the decrease in projected size is as drastic as it is, particularly over the first 10-15 feet. At the conclusion of the semester, in the context of course evaluation, I solicited anonymous comments on the various demonstrations that had been utilized during the course. The following comments are some of those that were volunteered regarding this particular demonstration as described here:

"The experiment done in lab on projected visual angle was, in my opinion, a very negative way of demonstrating what had previously seemed an almost impossible notion (naive realist here!). Seeing and trying to comprehend this idea through the use of graphs and verbal explanations

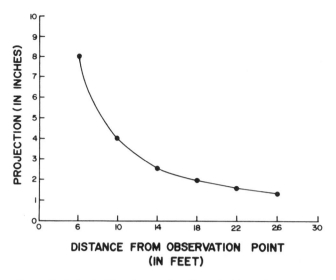

Figure 1. Projected length as a function of object distance.

can't possibly be as effective as demonstrating it for one's self, as was done in lab. Not only were we able to "draw" these different projections, but also took the measurements and made our own graphs—comparisons made of these graphs we did ourselves and those studied earlier made believers out of more than a few of us."

"I felt the use of the plexiglas was very important. It was very surprising to see how the lines got so small as you drew them on the surface. I felt it had a great impact and should be used more extensively."

"I found it very helpful to transfer the 3-D to the 2-D. In taking the meter sticks out of the visual background and examining them in isolation was helpful."

"It was more easily understood, to me, after having drawn the images on plexiglas than when explained to me on the board. It is easier to understand because the finished product eliminates other cues."

"Enjoyed the plexiglas experiment. Helped me to understand constancy—excellent visual aid to point out how extreme the differences are between what is there and how I perceive it."

My own experience with this exercise and such student comments as these convince me that use of this exercise permits an appreciation of the size-distance relationship well beyond that afforded by the more traditional expository approaches alone.

With no further modification in the procedure described, one can also measure and plot the decrease in the vertical distance between the projection of the successive meter sticks on the plexiglas. I have found this relationship to be a decreasing negatively-accelerated function of distance also but asymptoting at a distance slightly less than does the function relating horizontal projection to distance. This method also, of course, permits the study of the relationship of distance to linear perspective, relative size, texture gradient, as well as the vertical position of the visual field just alluded to. Furthermore, the same basic procedure can readily be modified for the study of motion parallax and binocular disparity.

The phenomenon of size constancy can be discussed more meaningfully following this demonstration of the size-distance relationship. The data generated in Figure 1 reflect a decreasing, negatively-accelerated projection of increased distance. Needless to say, size constancy is not phenomenologically in accord with this decreased projection.

# 13. LEARNING

## Words vs Records: A Practical Behavior Recording Exercise for Psychology Courses

Joseph S. Edwards
*University of Missouri-Kansas City*

Teaching students both verbal and performance knowledge of behavioral principles has become a major teaching strategy in psychology. I have found informally through tests and direct observation of student work with children the ease with which "parrots" rather than users of behavioral principles are generated. I also find that even advanced students frequently fail to discriminate the difference and advantages of a quantified description of behavior over a narrative account. This has been especially true when human behavior is at issue. A sound understanding of behavior recording principles (e.g., pinpointing specific types of behaviors and recording frequency) appears to me to be prerequisite to a full understanding (knowing about and using) of principles that describe behavior relationships derived from such data.

Because precise recording is perhaps the most characteristic dimension of the sciences, its utility as a source of more precise information about oneself and other people has become a major teaching target in my junior level child psychology course. The rationale underlying this instructional objective is that the extent and completeness of our knowledge of behavior largely hinges on our measurement or recording procedures. Research in our own discipline (Skinner, 1938; Lindsley, 1962; Edwards & Edwards, 1970a) as well as in other disciplines (Whitney, A., et al., 1973; Guilleminault, C., et al., 1973) validates this position.

The importance of taking self behavior records has been repeatedly emphasized by Lindsley (Note 1) as a more objective source of: (a) obtaining information for self monitoring and decision making (e.g., Hoon & Lindsley, 1974); and (b) self management. Since psychologists and apprentices are supposed to be knowledgeable about behavior, two simple class projects were designed to ascertain the extent of this knowledge.

### Project I: Accuracy of Self and Other Predicted Behavior Rates

**Subjects.** The project involved three undergraduate psychology classes (Ns = Class A, 40; class B, 54; class C, 37) consisting of students with no experience in recording human behavior, and one graduate seminar (n = 11) of students with a minimum of one year's experience in recording human behavior.

**Apparatus.** Wrist counters, tally boards, or paper and pencil were used to record self and other behaviors in field settings.

**Procedure.** Before this project was initiated two class sessions were spent discussing how to record frequency and compute behavior rates. The focus of this discussion was on pinpointing and recording the behavior, i.e., describing the behavior in such a way that it could be counted. Overhead transparencies of the rates of different human behaviors were presented, described and discussed. Larger behavioral units, such as cigarettes smoked rather that puffs per cigarette were encouraged. The project was designed to challenge directly the student's idea of how often people engage in a specific behavior under a specifiable set of circumstances (prediction) with how often people actually engage in those behaviors (record).

In this project students compared predictions of a specific behavior with a record of how often they actually engaged in that behavior. The same procedure was used on a close friend, spouse, etc. The recordings on the other person were not announced until after the data were collected. The project consisted of making a prediction and recording for thirty minutes on oneself and the other person for three consecutive days. Two of the undergraduate classes and the advanced seminar recorded the same behavior on themselves as on the other person; the other class recorded different behaviors that they considered to be most "typical" of themselves and the other person.

The criterion for an inaccurate prediction was a 30 percent difference between what was predicted and what was actually recorded. The data from the first recording session was used to analyze "behavior knowledge" and changes across the three recording sessions were analyzed to determine potential interactive effects of the predictions and recording of the behavior of interest.

**Results.** Table 1 summarizes the major findings of this project. All four classes, in spite of differences in training, more accurately predicted the behavior (65% to 100%) of the other person than the behavior recorded on themselves. This finding occurred in spite of wide differences in the behaviors recorded. The students with the most training showed this result most vividly in that every member of the class predicted the behavior of the other person more accurately than his or her own behavior. The highest percentage of students approximating an accurate prediction of self and other behavior ranged from 0 to 18%. Across the three

## Table 1
### Percent of Students Making Accurate Predictions

| Group | N | % Reaching ±30% criterion | Most Accurate Prediction on: (%) | | | % Showing Improvement on: | |
|---|---|---|---|---|---|---|---|
| | | | Self | Others | No Diff. | Self | Others |
| Untrained Class A | 40 | 1 | 25 | 65 | 10 | 55 | 40 |
| Untrained Class B | 54 | 10 | 19 | 69 | 12 | 22 | 66 |
| Untrained Class C | 37 | 18 | 20 | 72 | 8 | 65 | 25 |
| Trained Class D | 11 | 0 | 0 | 100 | 0 | 75 | 65 |

recording sessions the majority of students in all four classes improved in their predictions of self and other behaviors.

## Project II. Parent Predictions of Child Behavior Rates

In this project, teams of 2 students spend 25 half hour, reliability checked, free play recording sessions of young children in their home environments. Standard recording forms emphasizing early motor, social and language development were used to study children who were in the process of acquiring specific behaviors related to these areas of development. Each team was responsible for one child. After reliable recording (80% agreement) had been obtained, the team interviewed the parent. Parents were asked to predict how often they thought their children engaged in specific behaviors during the half hour period over which the recordings were taken. Every attempt was made to record the child during his or her most active time of the day. If the parent did not understand the name of the behavior being recorded it was pointed out or explained verbally.

**Subjects.** Fifteen children and their mothers participated. The children ranged in age from 14-24 months.

**Apparatus.** Standard behavior recording sheets that reflect developmental changes in the function of speech were utilized (e.g., Edwards & Edwards, 1970b).

**Procedure.** After 6-10 recording sessions (one per day) of the rates of different speech usage behaviors (requests; response to commands; statements initiated; labels; etc.) the parents were interviewed to obtain predicted behavior rates. The students were instructed to ask the parents, "How many times during the ½ hour we observe your child would you guess that he/she..." The students interviewing the parents were instructed to present this task as a game and not as a means to determine "their knowledge of their child's development" or anything of the sort. The predictions were compared to the observed behavior rates in that day's recording period.

**Results.** More parents overestimated rates (40%) than underestimated them (34%) and 26% of the behaviors recorded were predicted accurately (± 30%). The parents were more accurate in predicting behavior rates of their children than undergraduate and graduate students were in predicting their own behavior.

It was interesting to note that only one parent of the fifteen grossly underestimated the speech rates of her child. Six of the seven behaviors that were applicable to her child were grossly underestimated (60% or more). The other 14 parents overestimated more behaviors (median was 6) than they underestimated (median of 3). The team which took the recording of the "underestimating" parent's child terminated their project a week following the interview because of consistent verbal abuse exhibited toward the child by the parent, parent complaints about the students "interrupting the parents' social schedule."

## Discussion

The most frequently asked question from these projects was: "Doesn't knowledge of the behavior to be recorded and the recording of it have an effect on how often we engage in those behaviors?" A partial answer is, "Perhaps this is the most important lesson from the procedure." Awareness of one's own behavior, especially the rate and its consequences, is apparently not an obvious matter. This is specifically the case with rate. The data from this exercise show that self knowledge of behavior rates is deficient in both untrained and trained behavior recorders. In a real sense we are more able to comprehend and know another person's behavior than our own. The influence of prediction over one's behavior was reported by the majority of students, even those reporting that they were not interested in altering the rate of the behavior they recorded. Identical results have been obtained with two trained professionals who had an average of six years experience in recording behavior in laboratory and field research.

In addition to student reports about their own behavior they reported that the level of accuracy and the nature of behavior recorded in the other person could not be appreciated until after they had recorded the behavior and its relationship to the environmental setting. Taking a behavior record appears to expedite understanding of behavior.

Goldiamond (1965) earlier reported on the transitory effects of self recording by patients who stuttered. More recently, Lindsley (in Edwards, 1972) reported that 15% to 30% of adults and children who wish to change a behavior show appropriate increases or decreases in that behavior across time merely as a function of self recording. Thus, the person can directly validate "what he thinks" vs "what he does." Such subtle behavior effects need exploration. In field settings such a finding can serve as a distinct advantage in attempting to alter behavior rates.

The procedure described in this paper focuses on externalizing individual awareness by self recording. Perhaps the most obvious implication from the data is that professional experience without the use of tools such as behavior measurement methods, may remain at the same level or even decrease below that of untrained persons with regard to our knowledge of behavior rate information. In other words, our predictions about behavior are inaccurate in the absence of records.

The direct and unexplained exposure of students to the exercises described in this paper changed the tenor of class discussions about behavior. This change occurred as a function of experiences by the students, rather than as a function of convincing arguments by their professor. For the first time questions centered around the use of psychological terms to describe behavior and methods for studying and changing behavior, rather than focusing on unsolicited theoretical interpretations, etc. This change was related to three discoveries experienced through participation in the exercises. First, although students were not instructed to record behaviors that were personally "irritating" the vast majority did so. Statements such as: "My mother never smiles at me"; "My boyfriend never initiates conversation"; "My brother has the filthiest mouth"; and "Fred smokes incessantly" were found upon direct inspection to be false. Secondly, when the behavior was recorded, students found it to be directly related to specific environmental events. And thirdly, as a result of participation in the predict-record exercise, students began to see how their ideas, thoughts, and accusations about behavior were interpretative and irrelevant. This effect was further amplified for the students by the discovery that the "abusive" behavior of the "underestimating" parent toward her child was not directly related to the child's behavior but to other variables. These discoveries occurred as a function of recording behavior. Of particular importance was the predictive component of the exercises. Verbal and performance knowledge of behavioral principles was accomplished through the predict-record exercises in a dramatic and efficient manner.

The criterion of 30% accuracy as used here could lead to gross errors in applied settings. These findings, although not derived from the rigor of the laboratory, are suggestive of important research which directly focusses on the interaction of verbal and nonverbal behavior performance systems.

### References

Edwards, D. D. (Ed.). *The experimental analysis of behavior.* New York: Simon and Schuster, 1970.

Edwards, D. D., & Edwards, J. S. Fetal movement: Development and time course. *Science,* 1970, *169,* 95-97. (a)

Edwards, J. S., & Edwards, D. D. Rate of behavior development: Direct and continuous measurement. *Perceptual and Motor Skills,* 1970, *31,* 633-634. (b)

Goldiamond, I. Stuttering and fluency as manipulatable operant response classes. In L. Krasner and L. P. Ullman (Eds.). *Research in behavior modification,* New York: Holt, Rinehart and Winston, 1965, 106-156.

Guilleminault, C., Eldridge, F. L., & Dement, W. C. Insomnia with sleep apnea: A new syndrome. *Science,* 1973, *181,* 856-858.

Hoon, P., & Lindsley, O. R. A comparison of behavior and traditional therapy publication activity. *American Psychologist,* 1974, *29,* 694-697.

Lindsley, O. R. Operant conditioning methods in diagnosis. In J. H. Nadine and J. H. Moyer (Eds.). *Psychosomatic medicine: The first symposium.* Philadelphia: Lea and Fabiger, 1962, 41-54.

Skinner, B. F. *The behavior of organisms.* New York: Appleton-Century-Crofts, 1938.

Whitney, A. R., et al. Quasars revisited: Rapid time variations observed via very long baseline interferometer. *Science,* 1971, *173,* 225-229.

### Note

1. Lindsley, O. R. Should we decelerate urges or actions? Thou shalt not covet. Paper presented at the meetings of the American Psychological Association, Washington, DC, September 1969.

---

# Constraints on Learning: A Useful Undergraduate Experiment

Ernest D. Kemble and
Kathleen M. Phillips
*University of Minnesota, Morris*

Although the topic of biological constraints on learning is attracting increased attention in psychology texts, the selection of experiments in this area that are appropriate for undergraduate participation poses a number of problems. The classic demonstrations of constraints may require the administration of toxic substances (often traumatic for student and subject alike), considerable experimental sophistication, prolonged testing, or somewhat elaborate instrumentation. We would like to describe an experiment that is simple to instrument, can be conducted within a single week, yields highly reliable results, and raises a number of interesting theoretical and methodological issues.

Since Shettleworth (1972) has demonstrated that responses are one important source of constraints on learning, we chose to compare the acquisition rate of a food reinforced lever press response to that of a rearing response. Rearing is an extremely common behavior of many rodent species in both the laboratory and field that apparently has considerable adaptive significance. It might be expected then that the ease of acquisition of such a response would differ substantially from the presumably less "natural" lever-press response.

**Apparatus and Procedure.** The testing apparatus was a 29 x 29 x 11 cm chamber constructed of clear Plexiglas with a floor of 0.5 cm diameter steel rods spaced 1.6 cm apart. A 3.0 $cm^2$ food cup was placed in the center of one wall, and a 4.0 x 2.0 cm lever requiring 19 g pressure and approximately 0.5 cm excursion was placed 20 cm from the food cup along one of the side walls. The hole through which the lever projected was sufficiently large to allow 1.0—2.0 cm adjustment of the lever toward or away from the food cup. A photoelectric system (Veritas, Model V-942) was mounted outside the end walls of the testing chamber with the photobeam 23 cm above the floor. The photocell units were suspended on threaded steel rods that were inserted through small Plexiglass platforms extending beyond each end of the apparatus at roof level. The rods were secured by wing nuts that permitted continuous adjustment of photobeam height. Both lever and photobeam relays were connected to separate banks of four Sodeco counters and a recycling 5-min timer. Toggle switches allowed the activation of a pellet dispenser by either rearing or lever pressing, or bypassed the dispenser entirely for recording of operant (baseline) rates of the two responses. The testing compartment was housed in a sound attenuating chamber with all programming equipment located in an adjacent cubicle. Observations were carried out through a one-way vision screen.

Prior to the experiment, the rate of both unreinforced rearing and lever pressing was recorded for eight pilot rats. During these sessions, the height of the photobeam and position of the lever were adjusted until (a) the operant rates of the two responses were similar and (b) the manipulanda (lever and photobeam) were equidistant from the food cup. (We assumed that nonreinforced rears, on the average, would occur at the midpoint of the chamber.) A photobeam height of 23.0 cm and a 20 cm lever to food cup distance produced the desired results. The experimenters were 19 undergraduate students enrolled in an introductory course in research methods. They had little or no previous animal research experience. The subjects for the experiment proper were 19 female albino rats (Holtzman Company) weighing 273-322 g. Prior to student assignment, the rats were habituated to the chamber for 20 minutes, were food deprived (23.5 hrs), and then received five consecutive daily periods of magazine training. Forty 45 mg Noyes food pellets were delivered during each session with care being taken never to reinforce either rearing or lever pressing. After habituation and magazine training, each experimenter was assigned one rat that was weighed and food deprived on the first day of the experiment.

On the following day, each rat was placed into the apparatus and the number of unreinforced rears and lever presses was recorded for a single 20-min session. The baseline response levels were then used to assign rats to either rearing ($N = 10$) or lever pressing ($N = 9$) groups which were virtually identical (M = 55.0 and 57.2, respectively) in the unreinforced rates of their assigned operant responses. The rats then received nine daily 20-min acquisition sessions during which the designated operant response was reinforced on a CR schedule. No shaping was necessary for either response. Body weights were maintained at 80-90% of *ad libitum* values by limited feeding after each session.

**Results.** The results are summarized in Figure 1. It can be seen that while the operant (baseline) levels of the two responses were nearly identical, striking group differences emerged during the first day of acquisition [$U$ (9, 10) = 20, $p$ = .05] and that the rearing group responded at a higher level throughout acquisition [$F$ (1, 17) = 6.75, $p < .025$]. It should be noted that these group differences occurred despite the considerable inter-subject variability which was due in part to the use of multiple experimenters. Although acquisition was continued for nine days, it can also be seen that response rates were asymtotic and group differences clearly

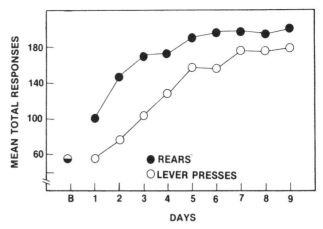

Figure 1. Mean total daily responses during baseline testing (B) and acquisition.

established within five days [$F$ (1, 17) = 7.70, $p < .025$]. Even with this brief period of training, the experiment seems to provide a clear demonstration of constraints on learning with most potentially confounding variables reasonably well controlled.

The immediacy of group differences in acquisition, however, may well cause more able or advanced students to be skeptical. It is possible, for example, that the similarities in baseline responding during the 20-min test masked group differences in the temporal patterning of the responses. If rearing responses were emitted rapidly early in the session but decreased below a steady rate of lever pressing, then the rearing response would be favored early in acquisition. To examine this possibility, we compared the intrasession baseline responding of the two groups. Although the response levels declined steadily during this session [$F$ (3, 51) = 7.53, $p < .001$], there was neither a reliable group difference nor a groups by intervals interaction ($Fs < 1.0$). Thus, temporal patterning of baseline responding does not seem to account for the overall group difference. In contrast, group comparisons of intra-session responding during the first day of acquisition reveal significantly higher response rates by the Rearing Group during the first 5 min of training [$U$ (9, 10) = 17, $p < .05$] and throughout this session [$F$ (1,

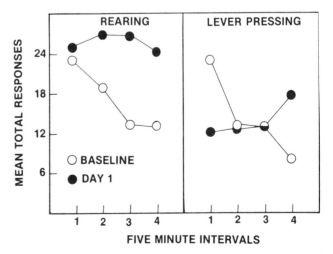

Figure 2. A comparison of intrasession baseline and first day of acquisition responding by rearing and lever pressing rats.

17) = 4.43, $p < .05$]. There were no changes over intervals nor groups by intervals interaction ($Fs < 1.10$).

Comparison of intrasession responding on these two days is presented in Figure 2. It can be seen that while the Rearing Group exceeded its own baseline throughout the first day of acquisition, this did not occur until the final 5 min for the Lever-Press Group. Although the rearing response did seem to be more rapidly acquired, the group differences were exaggerated by the initial depression of lever-pressing. Why did the introduction of food reinforcement inhibit lever-pressing? Observations suggest that the design of the apparatus required the rats that lever pressed (but not those that reared) to turn away from the food cup to make the operant response. In essence, we may have presented the rats that lever pressed with an umweg problem described many years ago by gestalt psychologists (Köhler, 1925).

If that feature of the experiment were removed by minor apparatus alteration, this seemingly clear demonstration of constraints might disappear. Inasmuch as this experiment can be conducted within a single week, suitable follow-up experiments could easily be conducted in more advanced courses. In any case, the experiment certainly highlights some of the methodological problems in investigating constraints on learning. This feature, combined with relative simplicity and robustness of the effect, suggests that the experiment would be a useful undergraduate laboratory project.

### References

Köhler, W. *The mentality of apes.* New York: Harcourt, Brace, 1925.
Shettleworth, S. J. Constraints on learning. In Lehrman, D. S., Hinde, R. A., & Shaw, E. *Advances in the study of behavior* (Vol. 4). Academic Press: New York, 1972, pp. 1-68.

### Note

1. The authors would like to thank Dr. W. Miles Cox for his helpful comments on an earlier version of this report.

# Demonstration Experiments in Learned Taste Aversions

J. W. Kling
*Brown University*

Demonstration experiments or laboratory exercises for undergraduate courses should produce robust effects with relatively simple apparatus and procedures. Furthermore, they should not involve methods that cause physical or emotional distress for the students or the subjects. There are many examples of operant conditioning that fit these requirements, but few suitable demonstrations of classical conditioning seem to be available for undergraduate courses. At various times, we have tried conditioning human eye lid closure, finger withdrawal, and knee jerk. None of these produced consistently successful and orderly results. We have avoided conditioned suppression procedures with rats or pigeons on the grounds that strong aversive stimulation raises too many ethical and safety problems to warrant its use in lower-level undergraduate courses.

Fortunately, learned taste aversions provide a simple and convenient way to demonstrate principles of classical conditioning. In addition, this topic encourages the experimental study of such interesting problems as biological constraints and preparedness, neophobia, learned safety, and the relations between conditioning and physiological variables. The existence of annotated bibliographies (e.g., Riley & Clarke, 1977) related to learned taste aversion publications is a major asset for the instructor.

The learned taste aversion procedure usually involves the creation of some degree of gastrointestinal upset in the experimental subject. Ionizing radiation, or introduction of toxins through esophageal intubation or intraperitoneal injection, are the common ways of producing such illness in the laboratory. Each of these methods has obvious drawbacks for use by beginners.

This report describes a convenient and completely safe way to produce mild malaise and generate robust and reliable conditioned taste aversions without producing noticeable distress in the animal. The technique relies upon the relative inability of animals to distinguish the taste of safe sodium chloride (NaCl) from that of poisonous lithium chloride (LiCl). To illustrate the procedure, one experiment done in an undergraduate course will be described. (Some practical suggestions for organizing and implementing the conduct of such experiments are offered in the Appendix.) In this experiment, the students were led (on the basis of readings and class discussions) to ask whether familiarization and novelty effects had their expected consequences when a complex taste substance was encountered. Typically, flavors that have been met previously will be approached more readily than novel flavors, illustrating the decline in neophobia (Barnett, 1958). If a familiar food is poisoned, rats that recover tend to return to it more readily than if the food has been novel (Rzoska, 1953). If novel and familiar foods are both present and illness occurs, conditioned taste aversions are more likely to occur to the novel food (Revusky & Berdarf, 1967). But what would happen if the food that immediately precedes the onset of the illness is a unique combination of flavors that includes one or more familiar elements? As one student described the problem, "If a person has always enjoyed hot dogs, but becomes ill after his very first chili dog, will he later have an aversion to chili but continue to eat hot dogs?"

In the experiment designed to examine this problem, NaCl was the familiar flavor; NaCl in sodium saccharin (NaSacc) solution was the new compound taste for the Control Group, and LiCl in NaSacc was the new compound for the Experimental Group. Later, each rat would be tested with NaCl, NaSacc, and the mixture of the two.

**Method.** Twenty male albino rats of the Charles River CD strain were used. They had previously served in several operant conditioning experiments in the undergraduate laboratory, and had been mildly food deprived. Prior to starting the present experiment, they were kept on ad lib. food and water for 10 days. The rats were housed in a small room within the undergraduate lab area. The lights were off from 10 pm to 8 am.

Water bottles were removed from the cages, and 24 hrs later the food was removed. The rat in his individual cage was carried to an adjacent test area where a drinking opportunity was provided. After drinking, the rat in his cage was returned to the cage rack. After 10-20 min, water bottles were placed on each cage for a 20-min supplemental drink. The bottles then were removed, and the food returned to the cages. During preconditioning and conditioning sessions, the drinking opportunity lasted 10 min; during post-conditioning testing, each of the three test solutions was presented for 5 min.

All rats were given water in the drinking situation on the first two days, and then were given 0.15 M NaCl solutions for the next six days. On Day 9, a mixture of 0.15 M Nacl in 0.01 M NaSacc was presented to the Control Group rats; the Experimental Group animals received 0.15 M LiCl in 0.01 M NaSacc. On the next two days, the rats remained on the cage rack and received 30 min of "supplemental" watering. On Day 12, each rat was offered 0.15 M NaCl, 0.01 M NaSacc, or the compound of the two. A 5-min pause was inserted between each test taste, and midway in the pause the rat was allowed to take about 10 laps from the spout of a water bottle (to "rinse the mouth").

Drinking tests were conducted by sliding the rat's cage up to a stainless steel drinking spout inserted into a 50 ml burette, and the resulting intake was measured to the nearest 0.1 ml. Supplemental drinking was measured by weighing the water bottles to the nearest 1.0 g before and after use. All solutions were mixed from reagent grade chemicals and distilled water, and were presented at room temperature.

Animals were ranked according to their intakes of NaCl on Days 6-8 and one of each adjacent pair was assigned at random to the Experimental Group. The order of presentation of the test solutions was varied across pairs of rats. Spouts and burettes were used for one solution only, and were thoroughly cleansed between animals.

**Results.** Pre-conditioning intakes of NaCl were vigorous, as would be expected from the finding (Ernits & Corbit, 1973) that 0.15 M is the preferred concentration for mildly thirsty rats. On the last 3 days of NaCl familiarization, the mean intake was 15.2 ml (SD = 1.0 ml). On the Conditioning Day, the rats had their first exposure to the compound containing saccharin. The mean intake in 10 min. was 12.2 ml (SD = 5.8 ml) for the Control Group and 5.36 ml (SD = 3.6) for the Experimental Group. For Control Group rats, the change from NaCl (on Day 8) to NaCl + NaSacc (on Day 9) produced a small decrease in drinking ("neophobia") that was not statistically significant ($p < .10$); for the Experimental Group rats, the change from NaCl to LiCl + NaSacc was significant ($p < .001$, t for paired measures, one-tailed).

Most rats in the Experimental Group drank rapidly for 2-3 min; a few continued for 5 min, but none drank throughout the 10 min period. No rat displayed the overt symptoms (cf. Barker, Smith & Suarez, 1977) of severe lithium poisoning (complete inaction, gagging, diarrhea); all rats drank as soon as the water bottles were placed on the cages.

On the Test Day, rats in the Control Group took approximately equal amounts of each of the three solutions. Rats in the Experimental Group drank large amounts of the familiar NaCl, but took very little NaSacc and NaSacc + NaCl compound. ANOVA revealed significant effects for illness, for test solution, and for their interaction (all $p < .01$). The results are summarized in Figure 1.

**Discussion.** The results illustrate several well-established phenomena of learned taste aversions that have important implications for classical conditioning. For example, preconditioning familiarization with a stimulus decreases the strength of the conditioning to that stimulus. This effect has been ascribed to such processes as habituation of the novel-stimulus reaction (Carlton & Vogel, 1967); to learned safety (Kalat & Rozin, 1973); and to latent inhibition (Lubow, 1965; Best, 1975).

Next, the data show the conditioning of a strong aversion to a novel taste stimulus (the compound) on the basis of a single experience. Such results are typical in learned taste aversions, and are one of the reasons for the widespread acceptance of such principles as "preparedness" (Seligman & Hager, 1972) and "stimulus relevance" (McFarland, 1973). The view that only relative differences exist between taste aversion learning and other examples of conditioning (i.e., "general process theory") has been explored in papers by Krane and Wagner (1975) and Bitterman (1975), among others.

Finally, the data also show that the rat responds to the saccharin taste as if it were a novel element that had been included within the compound, suggesting that taste mixtures can be analyzed by the rat into their taste elements (cf. Rescorla & Cunningham, 1978). But note that the experimental design does not allow us to reject the possibility that a new taste (like the NaSacc) presented for the first time after an illness, might be avoided even if it had not been present

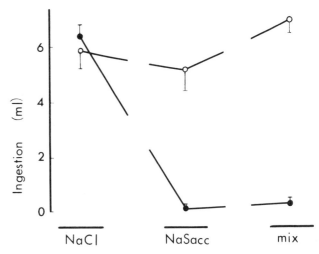

Figure 1. Amount ingested on test day. Filled circles: Experimental Group. Open circles: Control Group. Vertical lines = 1 Standard Error.

on the conditioning day. (Based on experimental analysis of nonassociative novelty effects by Best and Batson, 1977, it would seem unlikely that so strong a reaction to NaSacc would be seen, but an appropriate control group would have strengthened our confidence that the aversion to NaSacc is a conditioned one.)

Human learned taste aversions are thought to be frequent, durable, and based on specific experiences early in life (Garb & Stunkard, 1974). Loss of appetite by cancer patients that continues long after the immediate effects of chemotherapy have subsided, seem to be due, in at least some proportion of the instances, to learned taste aversions (Bernstein, 1978). And it has been suggested (Garcia, 1979) that anorexia nervosa might have its origins in learned taste aversions in some cases. For many students, the potential for dealing with such practical problems validates the efforts invested in animal behavior investigations and provides a useful bridge between the discussions of basic research and applied technology.

Appendix. Animals need not be handled by students. If each rat already is housed in an individual cage, it is convenient to remove the cage and place it on a flat board or small tray for ease of carrying. (The plastic trays measuring 27 x 35 cm that are used by lunch counters and fast-food outlets are an ideal size.) Place a paper towel on the tray to minimize clean-up problems. The open top of the individual cage requires a lid: a piece of 1/4 inch plywood with L-shaped molding glued around 3 edges slides on the cage and provides a secure closure. In the drinking situation, the calibrated tube is positioned so that the drinking spout will be approximately 3 cm above the floor of the cage, and when ready, the tray and cage can be moved forward until the spout passes through the cage mesh and is within reach of the rat. At the end of the interval, sliding the tray and cage away from the spout stops drinking without incurring spillage.

Supplemental drinking is monitored to insure an adequate daily fluid supply. Weighing the animal's water bottle to the nearest 1 g before and after the supplemental drinking provides adequate accuracy. Food should be absent during all drinking opportunities to eliminate prandial drinking. When fluid is available once a day while food is absent, rats lose about 5% of their body weights over the first day or two, but they recover quickly and start slow weight gains again.

During drinking tests, measurements of intake should be accurate to at least 0.5 ml. Weighing fluid containers ordinarily is unsatisfactory because of spillage. Volumetric readings are convenient, and some calibrated containers can be obtained at relatively little cost. Burettes allow measurement to the nearest 0.1 ml but are expensive. In undergraduate chemistry labs, 50 ml burettes broken at the stopcock end are fairly common. Ask your chemistry colleagues to save these for you, have the glassblower cut off that end, and use a 00 rubber stopper to seal the open end. A standard stainless steel drinking spout will fit snugly into the newly cut end if a piece of gum rubber tubing is used instead of a stopper. This arrangement places the numbers on the burette in the upright position for easy reading. Be sure to borrow a burette brush for convenience in cleansing the tubes. Burette clamps that fit on ringstands also provide convenient and stable mounts for the tubes. If burettes are

not available, calibrated centrifuge tubes or graduated cylinders may be substituted, or plastic syringes can be adapted to this purpose (Robbins, 1977). On the test day, each solution must be pre-loaded in a tube. Color coding the tubes and stoppers helps minimize errors and avoid taste contaminations. Standard stainless steel drinking spouts vary considerably in the size of aperture; for drinking tests, select spouts that are of uniform size.

Most of the taste aversion literature specifies taste solutions in percent-by-weight terms, while most studies of taste sensitivity use molar concentration specifications. There are some advantages to the latter, not the least of which is that the instructor does not appear to be ignorant of physical science techniques. Dispensing fluids when students are milling about can be messy: a neat way of filling burettes is provided by a gallon jug (ask your colleagues to save their empties . . .) equipped with a siphoning tube ending in a hose clamp and a short pipette (as a nozzle). These work as well as the more expensive Lister Bottles that can be had from apparatus supply sources. In mixing compounds, the aim is to maintain the concentration of each of the elements. For example, 0.15 M NaCl requires 8.76 g of salt plus enough water to bring the solution to one liter; 0.01 M NaSacc requires 2.41 g plus the water; a compound of NaCl + NaSacc would be made with 8.76 g NaCl plus 2.41 g NaSacc plus enough water to total one liter. To the human observer, each of the tastes is present, although careful analysis suggests that each is somewhat weakened or "compressed" in its intensity by the mixture (Bartoshuk, 1977).

The apparatus and procedures are those that have worked well for rats, but they probably could be adapted for the use with mice (Kimmeldorf, Garcia, & Rudadeau, 1960; Robbins, 1979) guinea pigs (Bravemen, 1974), or other animals that are readily available.

## References

Barker, L. M., Smith, J. C., & Suarez, E. M. "Sickness" and the backward conditioning of taste aversions. In L. M. Barker, M. R. Best, and M. Domjan (Eds.), *Learning mechanisms in food selection*. Waco, TX: Baylor University Press, 1977.

Barnett, S. A. Experiments on "neophobia" in wild and laboratory rats. *British Journal of Psychology*, 1958, *49*, 195-201.

Bartoshuk, L. M. Psychophysical studies of taste mixtures. In J. LeMagnen & P. MacLeod (Eds.), *Olfaction and taste VI*. London: Information Retrieval, 1977.

Bernstein, I. L. Learned taste aversions in children receiving chemotherapy. *Science*, 1978, *200*, 1302-1303.

Best, M. R. Conditioned and latent inhibition in taste-aversion learning: Clarifying the role of learned safety. *Journal of Experimental Psychology: Animal Behavior Processes*, 1975, *1*, 97-113.

Best, M. R., & Batson, J. D. Enhancing the expression of flavor neophobia: Some effects of the ingestion-illness contingency. *Journal of Experimental Psychology: Animal Behavior Processes*, 1977, *3*, 132-143.

Bitterman, M. E. The comparative analysis of learning: Are the laws of learning the same in all animals? *Science*, 1975, *188*, 699-709.

Bravemen, N. S. Poison-based avoidance learning with flavored or colored water in guinea pigs. *Learning and Motivation*, 1974, *5*, 182-194.

Carlton, P. L., & Vogel, J. R. Habituation and conditioning. *Journal of Comparative and Physiological Psychology*, 1967, *63*, 348-351.

Ernits, T., & Corbit, J. D. Taste as a dipsogenic stimulus. *Journal of Comparative and Physiological Psychology*, 1973, *83*, 27-31.

Garb, J. L., & Stunkard, A. J. Taste aversions in man. *American*

*Journal of Psychiatry*, 1974, *131*, 1204-1207.

Garcia, J. Discussion. In M. B. Kare & O. Maller (Eds.), *The chemical senses and nutrition*. New York: Academic Press, 1979, p. 290.

Kalat, J. W., & Rozin, P. "Learned safety" as a mechanism in long-delay taste-aversion learning in rats. *Journal of Comparative and Physiological Psychology*, 1973, *83*, 198-207.

Kimmeldorf, D. J., Garcia, J., & Rudadeau, D. O. Radiation-induced conditioned avoidance behavior in rats, mice, and cats. *Radiation Research*, 1960, *12*, 710-718.

Krane, R. V., & Wagner, A. R. Taste aversion learning with a delayed shock US: Implications for the "generality of the laws of learning." *Journal of Comparative and Physiological Psychology*, 1975, *88*, 882-889.

Lubow, R. E. Latent inhibition: Effects of frequency of nonreinforced preexposure of the CS. *Journal of Comparative and Physiological Psychology*, 1965, *60*, 454-459.

McFarland, D. J. Stimulus relevance and homeostasis. In R. Hinde & J. Stevenson-Hinde (Eds.), *Constraints on Learning*. London: Academic Press, 1973, 141-155.

Rescorla, R. A., & Cunningham, C. L. Within-compound flavor associations. *Journal of Experimental Psychology: Animal Behavior Processes*, 1978, *4*, 267-275.

Revusky, S., & Bedarf, E. W. Association of illness with ingestion of novel foods. *Science*, 1967, *155*, 219-220.

Riley, A. L., & Clarke, C. M. Conditioned taste aversions: A bibliography. In L. M. Barker, M. R. Best, and M. Domjan (Eds.), *Learning Mechanisms in Food Selection*. Waco, TX: Baylor University Press, 1977.

Robbins, R. J. An accurate, inexpensive, calibrated drinking tube. *Laboratory Animal Science*, 1977, *27*, 1038-1039.

Robbins, R. J. The effect of flavor preexposure upon the acquisition and retention of poison-based taste aversions in deer mice: Latent inhibition or partial reinforcement? *Behavioral and Neural Biology*, 1979, *25*, 387-397.

Rzoska, J. Bait shyness: A study in rat behavior. *The British Journal of Animal Behavior*, 1953, *1*, 128-135.

Seligman, M. E. P., & Hager, J. L. *Biological boundaries of learning*. New York: Appleton-Century-Crofts, 1972.

# Making Classical Conditioning Understandable Through A Demonstration Technique

Gerald D. Gibb
*Eastern Illinois University*

An inevitable part of all introduction to psychology courses are the principles of classical conditioning (Pavlov, 1927). Students often display a wide variety of symptoms of confusion ranging from repeatedly asking for clarification of the material, to showing a wide eyed look of bewilderment on their faces. Typically the concepts of acquisition, generalization, discrimination, spontaneous recovery, and extinction, of classically conditioned behaviors are introduced via Pavlov's dogs and their lust for meat powder. The purpose of this article is to give instructors of psychology a more innovative and enjoyable approach in presenting this material to students. The approach described is also advantageous in that it relates classical conditioning to human behavior.

**Method.** One lemon (as the CS), an assortment of other fruits and vegetables (apple, orange, lime, banana, cucumber, etc.), a tennis ball, and a Galvanic Skin Response (GSR) meter to provide a measurable CR are needed. A GSR meter manufactured by Lafayette Electronics Corp., model number 77026, is especially useful because the front and rear coverings are made with a clear plastic, enabling an instructor to project the GSR readings on a screen by using an overhead projector. A block of wood or a small hammer, and a hard surface such as a table top, will also be required to create a sharp noise to serve as the UCS.

Explain the function of the GSR meter and the activity it measures. Students also find it interesting to know that GSR is one of the measures used as part of a polygraph test. Invite a student to participate in the demonstration, assuring the student repeatedly that there is no pain or electric shock involved. This is critical, as anticipation of shock will cause increased GSR from the volunteer. The volunteer should sit comfortably in a chair while facing the class, taking care to instruct them that normal breathing and little movement is important to the success of the demonstration. After attaching the volunteer's fingers to the electrodes of the apparatus, instruct the students to remain silent, and allow at least 3 minutes to establish a baseline GSR reading for the volunteer.

After the GSR reading has become stabilized, present the lemon at eye level to the volunteer for a period of 1 second. The GSR meter may register some upward activity at this point. Repeat this process for 3 or 4 additional trials until the volunteer does not react to the presence of the lemon. With the volunteer still facing the class, create a loud noise (UCS) behind them using a hammer, or block of wood, and the surface of a table. A startle reaction and a dramatic increase in GSR will result if the UCS is of sufficient strength. While waiting for the volunteer's GSR to again stabilize to baseline, inform the students of other unconditioned responses in humans (leg flexion, salivary response, finger retraction, pupil dilation). It is also useful to have students record the GSR reading after each trial from this point on. A good practice to use is to have the students record the highest level of GSR activity after a trial.

To begin conditioning, present the CS, lemon, at eye level for about 1 sec., followed by the UCS, sound delivered behind the volunteer. It is crucial that the volunteer can not see, nor anticipate, the start of each conditioning trial. Repeat this procedure for 10 to 15 trials allowing a 15 to 20 second interval between trials.

To demonstrate the classically conditioned response of GSR to the newly conditioned stimulus (lemon), present the lemon alone for 6 trials using a 15 second interval between trials. The first 2 trials will show a dramatic increase in GSR, and the remaining trials will clearly demonstrate the concept of extinction, as the GSR readings will steadily decline.

In demonstrating the concepts of discrimination and generalization, repeat pairing the lemon and the loud noise as before for an additional 6 trials. On the seventh and eighth trials try using one of the other objects as a new stimulus. Stimuli such as the tennis ball and the lime will invariably cause a high GSR activity because of their relative similarity with the original conditioned stimulus. In order to try a variety of new stimuli the instructor will have to re-establish the conditioned response to the lemon over the course of an additional 6 trials.

On the following class day demonstrate spontaneous recovery by once again attaching the same volunteer to the GSR apparatus and presenting the lemon alone. The first two trials will usually reveal some spontaneous recovery of the galvanic skin response, after which extinction will again occur.

The concepts of time interval effects and stimulus order may also be explored by using the same procedure with new volunteers. By increasing the time interval to 2 seconds and 5 seconds it can be easily demonstrated how important a role temporal variations play in classical conditioning.

**Evaluation.** The effectiveness of the technique was measured by comparing exam scores from a semester using the standard lecture format to cover the material, with exam scores from a semester using the new classical conditioning demonstration technique. For the purpose of this evaluation, only exam items which pertained directly to classical conditioning were considered. During the Fall 1981 semester in which the standard lecture format was used, 20 multiple choice items met this criteria. The demonstration technique was introduced in the Spring 1982 semester, and again, only 20 multiple choice test items met this criteria and were used for the analysis. The test items from each semester were comparable and the instructor, course, and classroom were held constant. For each semester, the first 100 scores of alphabetically listed students who were administered the exam at its regularly scheduled time were used for the analysis.

The means were 74.40 and 68.75, for demonstration technique format and lecture format, respectively. An analysis of variance between the exam scores of the two groups yielded an $F = 8.32, (df 1,198)$ which is significant beyond the .005 level.

### Reference

Pavlov, I. P. *Conditioned reflexes* (Translated by G. V. Anrep), London: Oxford University Press, 1927.

---

# Inexpensive Animal Learning Exercises for Huge Introductory Laboratory Classes

Albert N. Katz
*University of Western Ontario*

In the psychology department at the University of Western Ontario, the introductory course consists of 12 laboratory exercises in addition to the traditional lecture experience. In order to accommodate the 2300 or so students who annually take the course, 76 laboratory sections are scheduled, each meeting every other week for two hours. The laboratories cover a wide range of experimental topics, such as physiological (brain asymmetry), perception (psychophysical techniques), memory (effect of filled delay on the serial position effect), behaviour modification (building a hierarchy for use in systematic desensitization) and group processes (the risky shift phenomenon). The sheer number of people taking the laboratories has forced us to depend to a large extent on paper-and-pencil tasks. Such an option was not deemed advisable for the teaching of basic learning principles inasmuch as such tasks are not representative of the techniques used in learning research and would not allow the student to observe or interact with animals.

The option of using animals in traditional classical or instrumental learning tasks is, however, prohibitively expensive. Consider the cost of employing rats in the cheapest of learning chambers for the 2300 students we must serve. We estimated a minimum of $10,000 initial investment and $3000 per year operating expenses. We have overcome the problems of expense, space and maintenance by employing the planaria *Dugesia Dorotocephala* as our experimental subjects, and by building a cheap, yet effective, learning chamber. The net economic saving has been considerable. The capital outlay in building the chambers was only $375.00, and the operating costs (for 1500 organisms) was under $200.00. Furthermore, employing planaria in our learning chambers has proved to be a useful introduction to selected topics in learning theory, experimental control, ethology, psychobiology and behavioral approaches to mental "illness."

***Dugesia Dorotocephala* and the Conditioning Apparatus.** We have found that the planarian *D. Dorotocephala* can be successfully employed in both classical and instrumental conditioning paradigms. This animal is small (20 mm), easy to caretake, harmless and inexpensive (approximately 10 cents each).[1] In addition the animal is placed in a unique position in the evolutionary scale—it is the first bilaterally symmetrical animal, it is the first animal to have true synaptic nerve conduction and it also has a protobrain (a mass of ganglia located in the anterior region). Thus the demonstration that this animal is capable of *true* learning not only is fascinating in its own right but permits the instructor to introduce questions about the minimal physiological properties needed to produce learning, and how this learning might be represented in the nervous system.

The conditioning chambers which we constructed[2] for the learning laboratories serves for both classical and instrumental conditioning, is inexpensive, flexible and solid. The chamber consists of a clear plastic petri dish which rests within a hole cut in a wooden base. The petri dish can thus be easily removed for cleaning and for the transport of the planaria. When testing occurs the dish is filled 2/3 with water. The base supports a 25-watt light which is mounted 6 inches above the petri dish, as well as two electrodes which extend into the petri dish. Electricity is provided from a regular wall socket, which is connected to a power box (schematically depicted in Figure 1). When one switch is closed the light (conditioned stimulus) is turned on; the closure of the second switch powers the electrodes after having passed through a transformer and bridge. The resultant unconditioned stimulus is 40-volts of direct current with an intensity of 1 to 2 milliamps. This intensity was found to be the minimum level that elicited a vigorous turning response (unconditioned response), and is of a much lower level than typically employed in such experiments. The cost of the whole unit, including transformer, switches, bridge and plugs was about $15.00.

This apparatus is used for both classical and instrumental conditioning exercises. The classical conditioning followed closely from the original Thompson and McConnell (1955) experiment, and consists of pairing the onset of light with electric shock until light onset alone can produce the turning response. The instrumental conditioning exercise employed a punishment training procedure and, although not based on a specific experiment, was suggested by the work of Best and Rubinstein (1962), Corning (1964) and Crawford (1968). The following procedure was used (see Katz, 1976, pp. 39-48). A cardboard was placed underneath the petri dish; half the cardboard was painted black while the other half was white. Directly in the middle of the cardboard a circle was drawn to represent a start box. The planaria was placed in the petri dish so that it was located in the start box and the number of times it moved into the black (and white) side was recorded for 10 two-minute periods. After each period the animal was replaced in the start box. Following these 10 baseline periods, the same procedure was followed excepting now a shock was delivered every time the animal entered the side which, according to baseline, it preferred. The task was to see if the animal learned to avoid the punished side. Avoidance invariably occurred within 30 minutes.

Whereas the laboratories "worked," from a purely technical perspective, we were worried that the students might not find them enjoyable, relative to our other laboratory exercises. These worries were elicited by the dislike some students appeared to take to the planaria (which are, afterall, neither furry nor huggable) and to the hesitations expressed about shocking the animals. Finally, we were worried that the relatively more detailed coverage given learning in the textbook may have made the conditioning labs more redundant and less informative than the other labs. Evaluative data on these concerns were obtained from a questionnaire made available to students at end of term.

The survey addressed questions about the course in general, the text, performance of lab assistants, etc. There was a voluntary supplementary section in which the students were asked to rank-order the 12 laboratory exercises in terms of how enjoyable they were, and in terms of how much they felt they learned from each. Not unexpectedly, the rankings differed considerably. For example the lab on methodology and statistics was overwhelmingly ranked the least enjoyable but was considered to be among the most informative; the lab on systematic desensitization was generally enjoyed but was felt to have taught little. The two learning labs were above the median on both rankings (N = 227 voluntary returns). The classical conditioning lab was ranked between fourth and fifth in both hierarchies (mean enjoyability = 4.6, mean learning = 4.9) while the instrumental conditioning lab was ranked slightly lower (mean = 4.9 and 5.4 respectively). On the basis of unsolicited written comments by some students on their questionnaire it appears that the major factors affecting the enjoyment ranking positively were use of animals and of the equipment, while the major negative contributors were use of worms, use of shock, and the repetitive nature of the procedure.

The factors which underlie the learning-value rankings also appear to be complex, with some students commenting that the exercise helped them better understand the concepts and procedures discussed in the text, but others thought the labs too redundant with the text material. Finally, in an attempt to get a rough index of the effectiveness of the conditioning labs, I examined test performance for questions pertaining to conditioning relative to other topics, for both of the sections which I taught (total N = 500). In both sections students' performance was about one SD above the mean for questions related to classical conditioning ($z$ scores = +0.94, and +1.2) and just at the mean for those questions dealing with instrumental conditioning ($z$ scores = +0.16, and -0.04). In summary then, relative to their other labs, the exercises on conditioning were perceived as relatively enjoyable and informative and, as measured in a subsequent test, were as well or better learned than the other lab materials.

**Some Limitations and Some Further Didactic Uses of the Planaria and Learning Chamber.** It must be emphasized that use of the chamber, and of planaria, have definite financial gain for only certain learning conditions and that they should not be considered omnifarious tools. For example, the chamber does not allow manipulation of shock intensity nor have the capability to present a substantially different form of conditioned stimulus. Thus exercises dealing with discrimination learning or higher-order conditioning can not be performed on the equipment. Some of these limitations can doubtless be overcome with additional expenditures (for example, by setting the dish on a bell and using vibration as a second conditioned stimulus), but the very nature of the apparatus and organism probably make other limitations insurmountable. The apparatus has no capability to provide a non-aversive stimulus and thus labs to demonstrate positive reinforcement and schedules of reinforcement appear to be eliminated. Moreover, the simple repertoire of the organism does not readily permit demonstration of common phenomena like shaping, and

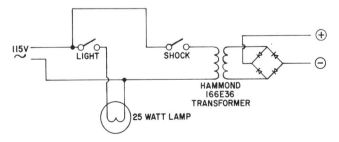

Figure 1. Circuitry of Conditioning Apparatus.

precludes more complex phenomena like chaining.

Despite these shortcomings, the apparatus and organism can still be used to demonstrate selected phenomena of general interest. Some of the more useful applications are listed below.

*To demonstrate general principles of experimental control.* It is often somewhat difficult to ascertain whether the planaria has contracted or not, i.e., whether it exhibited the conditioned response. Thus at least two independent observers are required to rate the animals performance. This procedure is an ideal lead-in to questions regarding the construction of rating scales, to reliability, and to double-blind procedures.

The use of planaria also has special relevance to control questions pertinent to the study of learning inasmuch as the demonstration of classical conditioning in planaria (Thompson & McConnell, 1955) has been questioned on methodological grounds (James & Halas, 1964). The controversy permits the introduction of the problem of pseudo-conditioning and of sensitization, and the need to control for procedure artifacts in order to demonstrate true learning.

*To demonstrate general questions of psychology and ethology.* Observation of the planaria swimming in the petri dishes can be used to demonstrate some ethological concepts such as phototropic and geotropic movements. Such observations were built into the instrumental learning laboratory in that data were collected concerning whether the dark or light side of the dish was preferred by the planaria. (Because planaria are negatively phototropic a dark side preference can be expected).

The demonstration of true learning in planaria is especially exciting since this learning occurs in such a simple organism. The question arises as to how learning is physiologically represented. The presence of true synaptic transmission in these animals permits an ideal introduction to theories of learning which depend on changes at the synapse (Hebb, 1972). Finally, the classical conditioning of planaria has been used as the first step in studying the biochemistry of memory (McConnell, 1962; McConnell, Jacobson, & Kimble, 1959). The laboratory demonstration can thus be extended in that direction, especially if the introductory text being used is biologically oriented (e.g., Krech, Crutchfield & Livson, 1974, pp. 416-442; McConnell, 1977, pp. 368-383).

*To demonstrate the behavioral approach to maladaptive activities.* When shocked repeatedly the animal becomes lethargic, an effect which Best (1963) discussed in terms of an emotional, frustration response. The manifestation of this phenomenon has proven to be a useful introduction to learned helplessness, and hence to one learning explanation of depression. It also serves as a peg for questions related to consciousness, the need to postulate inner mental states, and to behaviourism.

## References

Best, J. B. Protopsychology. *Scientific American*, February 1963, *208*, 54-62.

Best J., & Rubinstein I. Maze learning and associated behavior in planaria. *Journal of Comparative and Physiological Psychology*, 1962, *55*, 560-566.

Corning, W. Evidence of right-left discrimination in planaria. *Journal of Psychology*, 1964, *58*, 131-139.

Crawford, F. T. Operant rate of planarians as a function of photic stimulation. *Psychonomic Science*, 1968, *11*, 257-258.

Hebb, D. O. *Textbook of psychology* (3rd ed.). Philadelphia: Saunders, 1972.

James, R., & Halas, E. No difference in extinction behavior in planaria following various types and amounts of training. *Psychological Record*, 1964, *14*, 1-11.

Katz, A. N. (Ed.). *A laboratory manual for an introduction to psychology* (Volume 1). London, Ontario: University of Western Ontario, 1976, pp. 39-48.

Krech, D., Crutchfield, R., & Livson, N. *Elements of psychology*, New York: Knopf, 1974.

McConnell, J. Memory transfer through cannibalism in planarians. *Journal of Neuropsychiatry*, 1962, *3*, supplement 1, S42-S-48.

McConnell, J. *Understanding human behavior.* New York: Holt, Rinehart and Winston, 1977.

McConnell, J., Jacobson, A., & Kimble, D. The effects of regeneration upon retention of a conditioned response in the planarian. *Journal of Comparative and Physiological Psychology*, 1959, *52*, 1-5.

Thompson, R., & McConnell, J. Classical conditioning in the planarian, Dugesia dorotocephala. *Journal of Comparative and Physiological Psychology*, 1955, *48*, 65-68.

## Notes

1. The planaria were obtained from Boreal Laboratories, 1820 Mattawa Avenue, Mississauga, Ontario, Canada. The care of the animals is best outlined in a special edition of the *Journal of Biological Psychology*, January 1967.
2. The person most responsible for translating my descriptions into a working model was D. Pulham. Thanks are also due J. Orphan and D. Garrod.

# The Gerbil Jar: A Basic Home Experience in Operant Conditioning

Larry Plant
*Niagara County Community College*

For several years I have sought a method of making the experience of the fundamental techniques of operant conditioning accessible to large numbers of students taking classes in introductory psychology. Of high priority in thinking about this objective, is that the system must be: (a) interesting and educationally beneficial to students; (b) relatively inexpensive; and (c) something the students are able to do on their own time.

The advantages of using Mongolian Gerbils in the undergraduate operant laboratory have been detailed elsewhere (Hunt & Shields, 1978). In my classes at Niagara County Community College, students are introduced to conditioning concepts through standard textbook assignments and class lecture presentations. As an optional experience students elect to view a videotaped demonstration of shaping a gerbil to perform various simple operant tasks, i.e., lever pressing or bell ringing, (the videotape is placed on closed reserve at the Library Learning Center). They are then given a gerbil and an operant conditioning chamber to take home to explore these processes on their own.

The operant chamber is a modified glass gallon pickle or olive jar (plastic containers are unsatisfactory as gnawing gerbils will quickly chew an escape). The large jars are readily available from local restaurants who seem willing to save them upon request. The essential process in the rather simple modification of the jar is the capacity to drill various holes in the side for installation of a food magazine, water, and ventilation. This is accomplished with a carbide drill bit specifically designed for drilling glass. Because the gerbils are so small, conventional rat chambers are unsatisfactory and would have to be modified. A gallon pickle jar is an ideal substitute in terms of size, visibility, convenience and cost.

Shelled raw sunflower seed is the reinforcer of choice in my experience with gerbils. The standard beginning exercise is for students to train the gerbil to ring a bell which is suspended on a string from the top of the jar.

Shaping, extinction, generalization, discrimination and various schedules of reinforcement are all explorable on an independent (home) study basis. The student is provided with a mimeographed handout which explains these concepts as well as deprivation schedules, and gives further details and hints as to their specific application. Enthusiastic students have advanced to more difficult operant tasks for their gerbils such as back flips and lifting and carrying various small objects. Coupled with selected readings on behavior modification, the introductory student through his experiences with the "gerbil jar" achieves a firm experiential understanding of both the process and relevance of operant conditioning. Feedback from students indicates that the gerbil training experience is positively reinforcing for them as well as the gerbil.

The costs are insignificant especially when compared to commercial operant chambers which range from sixty to several hundred dollars. Large numbers of "gerbil jars" can be prepared in a few hours for pennies each. To provide a continuous supply of naive gerbils at NCCC, we maintain a small breeding colony at a total cost of approximately $300 per year. For those colleges without the facilities to maintain a gerbil colony, students might be encouraged to purchase a gerbil from a local pet store.

Specific jar modification details are available upon request.

### Reference

Hunt, K., & Shields, R., Using gerbils in the undergraduate operant laboratory. *Teaching of Psychology*, 1978, 5, 210-211

# 14. MEMORY AND COGNITION

## A Classroom Demonstration of Depth of Processing

Roger Chaffin
*Trenton State College*
and Douglas J. Herrmann
*Hamilton College*

When people have to memorize something they often repeat the material to themselves as a way of remembering it. The common sense view that long-term retention is aided by repetition of the material found expression in the late 1960s in what will be referred to as the "standard view" of memory (Shiffrin & Atkinson, 1969; Waugh & Norman, 1965). The standard view still provides the framework used to introduce students to the topic of memory in most textbooks. According to the standard view, repeating information both maintains the information in short-term memory (STM) and increases the chances that the information will be transferred to long-term memory (LTM).

In the demonstration to be described below students find that when they can repeat material their memories are, paradoxically, poorer than when they are prevented from repeating the material. The paradox is explained by the depth of processing approach to memory which maintains that long-term retention depends on how elaborately the information is processed (Craik & Lockhart, 1972; Craik & Watkins, 1973; Glanzer, 1978; Jacoby, 1973). According to this view, simply repeating information, although it maintains information in an acoustic form, will not improve long-term retention.

The standard position was initially supported by studies that demonstrated a relationship between the number of times a word was rehearsed and the probability of later recall (e.g., Rundus, 1971). Later studies showed that the nature of the rehearsal was critical. Thinking about the meaning of a word improved its long-term retention, but merely repeating it did not, as maintained by the depth of processing position (Jacoby, 1973; Lichtenstein, Note 1; Meunier, Ritz & Meunier, 1972; Modigliani & Seamon, 1974).

The present demonstration, which is derived from these studies, is an elaborate one that lays one paradox on another while illustrating many of the main concepts covered in an introductory unit on human memory.

Five-word lists are read to the class. After each list one of two interpolated tasks is performed and is followed by an immediate recall test. The interpolated tasks are to repeat the list rapidly over and over, or to say "hello" rapidly for 15 seconds. When all the lists have been presented, an unexpected delayed recall test is given, followed by a recognition test. Immediate recall is, of course, better for the repeat than for the hello lists. The first paradox comes with the delayed recall. Common sense, the standard position, and the results for immediate recall lead the student to expect better recall for the "repeat" lists. Instead recall is better for the

"hello" lists (Lichtenstein, Note 1). The students now expect the same result for the recognition test. Again they are surprised; for recognition there is no difference. The results can be explained in terms of the distinctions between short and long-term memory, maintenance and elaborative rehearsal, recall and recognition.

The procedure has been used as a demonstration in learning and as a class experiment in lab courses. As a demonstration the data are collected by a show of hands, the recognition test is omitted, and the procedure requires 30 minutes. As a lab 75 minutes are needed to complete the tabulation of the data. The equipment needed includes a tape recorder, a tape of the instructions and stimulus lists, copies of the stimulus lists, recognition test and key for each student, and 14 file cards. Numerous variations in the procedure have been used; the version described below was used recently in an experimental lab section at Trenton State College. A copy of the tape, stimulus lists, recognition test and key can be obtained from the first author.

**Procedure.** Twelve lists of 5 words were selected from among 110 high frequency, high imagability words selected from the Paivio, Yuille and Madigan (1968) norms. Two lists were used for practice, ten for the experimental lists. The remaining 50 words served as new items on the recognition test.

Instructions and word lists were presented on a tape recorder. The procedure was described to the class; to overcome self-consciousness the students practiced covering their ears while doing the hello and repeat interpolated tasks with two practice lists. Individuals were coached as necessary to ignore other class members, and to speak audibly but quietly. Additional coaching was giving during the two warm-up trials. The instructions emphasized that, although it was hard to recall 5 words after saying "hello" for 15 seconds, it was possible and it was up to the students to devise a mnemonic strategy to do it.

Words were read at a 2-second rate. At the end of each list the class was instructed to "repeat" or to "say hello." The two tasks were alternated. After 15 seconds of this interpolated task the class was instructed to write down the five words. Fifteen seconds were allowed for this and then the class was told to prepare for the next list and reminded of the task to be done after the list. While each list was read, the instructor held up a card listing the five words and the task to be done. After all of the lists had been presented, the class was instructed to turn over the paper on which they had been writing and to relax. After one minute the class was asked to write down all the words they could recall from all of the lists. When everyone had finished writing (about 5 minutes), a recognition test was distributed. The 50 words from the experimental lists were randomly interspersed with the 50 words not presented. The students were instructed to check those words that had been on the lists. Finally each student was given the stimulus lists and a key for the recognition test and asked to score the number of words correct from the repeat and hello lists for immediate recall, delayed recall, and recognition. Warm-up lists were not included. There were 15 students in the class.

Results. The mean scores are given in Table 1 as percentages. Immediate recall was higher for repeat than for hello lists, $t(14) = 2.99$, $p < .05$; this is predicted by both the

Table 1. Mean Recall and Correct Recognitions as Percentages for the Repeat and Hello Conditions.

| | Condition | |
|---|---|---|
| Retention Type | Repeat | Hello |
| Immediate Recall | 95.5 | 86.4 |
| Delayed Recall | 21.3 | 43.2 |
| Recognition | 76.4 | 75.6 |

standard and the depth of processing views. For delayed recall, performance was better for the hello than for the repeat lists, $t(14) = 5.10$, $p < .01$. This result supports the depth of processing position and is inconsistent with the standard view. On the recognition test there was no difference between the two conditions, $t(14) = .24$. (The results for the recognition test are reported in terms of correct recognitions as there were only 3 incorrect recognitions.)

Discussion. For the immediate recall test performance for the repeat lists was almost perfect; mere unthinking repetition was effective in maintaining acoustic information for immediate recall. Immediate recall was poorer for the hello lists because STM storage was impaired by the hello task. In order to recall the list it was necessary to create an elaborated representation—an image or story—involving the five concepts, as they were presented. This elaborative rehearsal had transferred much of the information from STM to LTM. As a result delayed recall was better for the hello lists than for the repeat lists. For the repeat lists little information had been transferred to LTM. Maintenance rehearsal of the acoustic information had been adequate for the immediate task, but produced poor delayed recall. Recognition, in contrast, was not affected by the level of processing. Recognition requires only the knowledge that a word has been heard recently. This information was equally available for words from the hello and repeat lists, because the memory representation for both sets of words had been activated when the words were presented (Glenberg, Smith & Green, 1977). Although retrieval was improved by more elaborate processing, recognition was not (Jacoby, 1973).

The effects are robust. The direction of the differences is always the same. The size of the effect for delayed recall is sensitive to subject strategies and sometimes fails to reach

significance. Three aspects of the procedure are important for maximizing the effect. First, the instructions should make clear that the students must devise a way to do well on immediate recall for the hello lists and that this will require some ingenuity on their part. If the students are not familiar with standard mnemonic strategies, explicit suggestions should be made. Second, practice trials with each task must be given to overcome self-consciousness and allow the development of effective strategies. Third, the lists should follow one another without delay to prevent boredom and thus discourage elaborative rehearsal of the repeat lists.

The appeal of the procedure for classroom use comes from the apparent conflict between the results obtained for the three measures of memory. After the commonsensical result has been obtained for immediate recall, each of the succeeding results for delayed recall and then recognition becomes paradoxical. The unfolding of the results can be made very dramatic. The procedure requires a considerable investment of class time but it presents in concrete and memorable form some of the main concepts that must be conveyed in an introduction to human memory.

### References

Craik, F. I. M., & Lockhart, R. S. Levels of processing: A framework for memory research. *Journal of Verbal Learning and Verbal Behavior*, 1972, *11*, 671-684.

Craik, F. I. M., & Watkins, M. J. The role of rehearsal in short-term memory. *Journal of Verbal Learning and Verbal Behavior*, 1973, *12*, 599-607.

Glanzer, M. Commentary on "Storage mechanisms in recall." In G. M. Bower, (Ed.), *Human Memory: Basic Processes*. New York: Academic Press, 1978.

Glenberg, A., Smith, S. M., & Green, C. Type I rehearsal: Maintenance and more. *Journal of Verbal Learning and Verbal Behavior*, 1977, *16*, 339-352.

Jacoby, L. L. Encoding processes, rehearsal, and recall requirements. *Journal of Verbal Learning and Verbal Behavior*, 1973, *12*, 302-310.

Meunier, G. F., Ritz, D., & Meunier, J. A. Rehearsal of individual items in short-term memory. *Journal of Experimental Psychology*, 1972, *95*, 465-467.

Modigliani, V., & Seamon, J. G. Transfer of information from short to long-term memory. *Journal of Experimental Psychology*, 1974, *102*, 768-772.

Paivio, A., Yuille, J. C., & Madigan, S. H. Concreteness, imagery, and meaningfulness values for 925 nouns. *Journal of Experimental Psychology*, Monograph Supplement, 1968, *76*, (No. 1, Part 2), 1-25.

Rundus, D. Analysis of rehearsal processes in free recall. *Journal of Experimental Psychology*, 1971, *89*, 63-77.

Shiffrin, R. M. & Atkinson, R. C. Storage and retrieval processes in long-term memory. *Psychological Review*, 1969, *76*, 179-193.

Waugh, M. C., & Norman, D. A. Primary memory. *Psychological Review*, 1965, *72*, 89-104.

### Note

1. Lichtenstein, E. K. Effects of central and peripheral rehearsal on sentence memory. Unpublished manuscript, University of Illinois, 1972.

# Demonstrating Semantic Memory in the Teaching Laboratory with a Paper-and-Pencil Task

Albert N. Katz
*University of Western Ontario*

Although reaction-time procedures and data have assumed prominent importance in the study of cognitive processes, the individual testing and need for sophisticated (and expensive) equipment required to produce reliable reaction-times has made it difficult to use this technique in the teaching laboratory. The present report describes a paper-and-pencil method for producing reliable reaction-time data suitable for group situations and, as such, can be considered a variant of techniques originally outlined by Rozin and Jonides (1977). In the present exposition the technique was specially constructed to contrast the two traditional theoretical approaches to semantic memory, although the technique itself can be directly applied to other questions of interest to cognitive psychology.

The technique itself only needs the use of prepared test booklets and a stop-watch. The critical component is in the construction of the booklet. Each page of the booklet consists of a homogeneous set of problems or questions. Participants can indicate their answers in several ways. For example, if the problem involves judging or choosing between paired alternatives, they can check the member of each pair which they prefer. Alternatively, if the problem involves solving for truth-value of a statement, the participant can circle a T (for True) or F (for False) printed beside each statement. The task itself is also simple. The participants are given orienting instructions. When a signal is given they turn to the first page of the booklet and go down the page responding to as many of the problems as they can. When a second signal occurs they turn to the next page and repeat on those problems. The logic of this procedure is that one can estimate the time taken to respond to each homogeneous problem-set page by determining the number of items from each homogeneous set (page) which was answered in a set time by the formula:

$$RT = \frac{\text{Time Allocated to page}}{\text{Number of Correct Responses}}$$

Thus, if on one page a person correctly responded to 15 questions in a 20 second period, the average reaction-time would be 20 seconds/15 responses or an average of 1333 milliseconds per response.

In order to examine alternative models of cognitive processes or to demonstrate basic phenomena, one need only vary the relationship found from page to page in the booklet. Consider, for instance, the so-called "symbolic distance effect" in which people respond more quickly to items which are symbolically distant than to those more close. Using Moyer and Landauer's (1967) initial demonstration of this phenomenon as an example, one would transcribe their individual technique to a group procedure useful for the classroom by constructing booklets as follows. One page would consist of a set of paired digits that differed in value only by one digit (i.e., pairs such as 5 4; 8 9). Another page would consist of pairs differing by 3 digits

(5 8; 6 9), and a third page would consist of pairs differing by, let's say, 5 digits in value. Naturally one would ensure that the larger digit appeared equally often on the right and left, and that the order in which the pages appeared in the booklet were counterbalanced. In the task itself, the participants would, on signal, start at the first page of their booklet and, within a given amount of time on each page, choose the digit with the larger value. To replicate the classic findings of Moyer and Landauer (1967) one would expect that the average RT should be fastest for the page in which the pairs differed by 5, and slowest for items differing only by 1 digit.

One could apply the basic technique to many other phenomena of interest. For example, mental rotation (e.g., Shepard & Metzler, 1971) could be demonstrated by presenting booklets in which pairs of figures are presented. The manipulation here would be to vary the degree to which the objects differ in rotation (e.g., 20°, 40°, 60°) from page to page in the booklet. Similarly, differences in processing sentences with varying grammatical meaning (e.g., Clark & Chase, 1972) could be demonstrated by presenting simple pictures and beside each picture a descriptive phrase. In this case each page of the booklet would differ in the nature of the phrase employed (for example, whether the phrase is in positive or negative form such as "star is above cross" or "cross is not above cross"). Responding here could be indexed by having participants choose a T if the phrase was a true description of the picture or an F if otherwise.

A detailed example of the technique, and some data on its comparability to data obtained by the typical individual testing technique is provided below. The technique was specially constructed to contrast two influential models of semantic memory. In very recent years (e.g., Collins & Loftus, 1975) data based distinctions between these two models have narrowed. Nonetheless, I find that detailing the earlier distinctions, and the data that were brought to bear on these distinctions, make current models much easier to understand. The comparability of the group data to the original individual based data will be examined by three independent indicators: the pattern of reaction-time across different conditions, error data, and absolute reaction-time values.

**Models of Semantic Memory and Reaction Time Data.** Semantic memory is assumed to embody the knowledge we have about the world. It can be considered a mental thesaurus wherein knowledge about words, concepts, their meanings and relationships, and rules for their manipulation is stored. Historically, two broad classes of theories have proven most successful in describing the structure of semantic memory. One such class is the *network* model and is best exemplified by the work of Collins and Quillian (1969). This model assumes that the elements of knowledge are organized in an hierarchical arranged network. Moreover the *time* it takes to answer a semantic memory question is assumed to reflect the network structure. Thus to answer the question "is a collie an animal?" requires progression through the inferences, a collie is a dog, a dog is a mammal, a mammal is an animal. Thus three steps are required, whereas to answer, "is a collie a dog?" requires only one step. The prediction of this model is very clear: it should take less time to answer the second question (which involves the time required for one step) than the first (three step) question. Collins and Quillian (1969) provided impressive experimental support for this prediction.

The second class of theories, and best exemplified by the work of Rips, Shoben and Smith (1973), assume that concepts consist of a set of distinctive attributes of features and that one concept can share no, some, or many attributes with another concept. According to these models, people evaluate whether or not two or more semantic concepts belong together by comparing the degree to which they share features in common. Presumably if two concepts share many defining features in common it will be easier (and hence quicker) to decide they belong together. For positive answers, this model makes the same prediction as a network model since items closely related also tend to share more defining features in common.

The two models do make an additional, differentiating prediction however. Consider the following two questions: Is a fish a mammal? Is a fish a chair? According to the network models, items close in the network (fish-mammal) should require fewer steps to find the relevant information and hence should be associated with faster decision times to negate than are more distant items (fish-chair). Set-theoretic models make the complete opposite prediction. Since items such as fish and mammal share more features in common than do fish and chair it should be more difficult (and hence take longer) to decide they don't belong together. Experiments which test the different predictions have favoured the set-theoretic over the basic network approach (Schaeffer & Wallace, 1970; Rips, et al., 1973) although recent network models have been modified to overcome this shortcoming. The paper-and-pencil technique described below was constructed to contrast the basic network and feature models.

The Group Procedure. Booklets were constructed. On each page of the booklet was a series of 25 statements of the form: A _____ is a(n) _____. For example, two such relationships would be: (1) A shark is a piano; (2) A dog is an animal. Beside each statement were the letters "T" (for True) and "F" (for False). The booklets consisted of four pages. On each page there were 5 items meant to keep the subject "honest." These distractor items will be described in more detail later. The 20 non-distractor items were of four types, with each type defining a different page of the booklet. Two pages consisted of relationships for which the correct answer was TRUE. One such page consisted of items in which the semantic relationship was close (e.g., a dog is a mammal) whereas in the other page the relationship is more distant (e.g., a dog is a living thing). The other two pages consisted of items for which the correct answer was FALSE. Again, one of these pages consisted of semantically close relationships (e.g., a shark is a mammal) with the other page consisting of more distant relationships (e.g., a shark is a piano). The criteria for designating a relationship as either close or distant were as follows. For true relationships distance was determined by position in a superordinate hierarchy. Thus, given 'dog'

as the subject of the sentence, the concepts 'mammal', 'animal' and 'living thing' would represent systematically more distant true relationships. For false relationship, semantic distance was manipulated by violating the animate-inanimate distinction, a technique successfully employed by Rips, et al. (1973). For example, the distance involved in the sentence "A robin is a fish," in which both the subject and object are animate, is considered smaller than the distance involved in the sentence "A robin is a bedroom."

In order to keep subjects honest, five distractor relationships were interspersed on each page (in lines 3, 7, 8, 13, 18). For the true-close and true-remote pages, the distractors consisted of items which were false, and for the two "false" question pages, the distractors were true statements. The exact same distractors, placed in the same positions were employed for the two positive sheets. The two negative sheets were similarly treated. The order of the pages in the booklet were randomly assigned, thus eliminating order effects.

The 32 members of my second year laboratory course in Cognition served as subjects. They were instructed to turn to the first page of their booklet and, when a signal was given, to go down the page sequentially and answer as many of the questions as possible. Both speed and accuracy were stressed. When a second signal was given they were instructed to turn to the next page and repeat the procedure. The students were given 20 seconds on each page.

Results and Discussion. These results were evaluated with respect to three criteria. First, in accordance with predictions concerning the pattern of reaction-times, it was quicker to confirm (by 650 msec.) true-close than true-remote relationships, $t(31) = 5.66$, $p < .01$. Thus, as predicted by both network and feature models, people, on the average, correctly answered statements such as "a robin is a bird" more quickly than more remote questions of the form "a robin is an animal." Moreover, consistent again with the literature (e.g., Rips, et al., 1973), people were faster (by 160 msec.) at disconfirming remote statements (of the form "a robin is a bedroom") than those less remote (e.g., "a robin is a fish"), $t(31) = 2.38$, $p < .025$. Thus, the group procedure exactly replicated the expected pattern of result obtained initially by individual testing on sophisticated equipment.

Second, the examination of my error data was completely in line with data obtained with the single subject technique. Our overall error rate of 6.7% was comparable, for example, to the 5.8% errors observed by Schaeffer and Wallace (1970) or the 8% observed by Collins and Quillian (1969). The examination of error data is an important extension of Rozin and Jonides (1977) technique for two reasons. It permits examination of issues critical to the interpretation of reaction-time data. With respect to one such aspect of the present data, error rate increased with reaction-time, confirming that the present findings did not reflect a trade-off between speed and accuracy. Also, with the Rozin and Jonides technique an error trial disrupts performance, at least when the RT chain is of an insufficient length. The present technique does not have this problem.

Finally, the absolute value of the observed reaction-time for false statements (from 1540 msec. to 1700 msec.) is comparable to the 1308 - 1582 msecs. range reported by Rips, et al. (1973). Similarly, for true statements, my observed values (of 1414 - 2058 msec.) although larger than those reported earlier (Collins & Quillian, 1969: 1180 - 1240 msec.; Rips, et al. 1973: 1315 - 1373) are still relatively similar. Rozin and Jonides also examined absolute RT; the present validation extends this comparison to more complex cognitive activities.

**Concluding Remarks.** One of our responsibilities as teachers should be to keep our students abreast of techniques, theories and experimentation current in the literature. The present technique affords the student all of these experiences. I have used the group procedure discussed above to introduce the logic of reaction time as a dependent measure, weaknesses in such a usage, and its application to the study of cognitive processes. With respect to semantic memory, it has permitted me to introduce basic models and empirical phenomena. One assigned "thinking" task which directly follows from these labs has been to attempt to modify the basic network model to try to incorporate the apparently inconsistent data. This assignment has proven to be a most useful means of introducing current models, such as that proposed by Collins and Loftus (1975) and, in a more general sense, has sharpened the students' appreciation of the role of experimentation in theory building.

## References

Clark, H., & Chase, W. On the process of comparing sentences against pictures. *Cognitive Psychology*, 1972, *3*, 472-517.

Collins, A., & Loftus, E. A spreading-activation theory of semantic processing. *Psychological Review*, 1975, *82*, 407-428.

Collins, A., & Quillian, M. Retrieval time from semantic memory. *Journal of Verbal Learning and Verbal Behavior*, 1969, *8*, 240-248.

Moyer, R. S., & Landauer, T. K. Time required for judgments of numerical inequality. *Nature*, 1967, *215*, 1519-1520.

Rips, L., Shoben, E., & Smith, E. Semantic distance and the verification of semantic relations. *Journal of Verbal Learning and Verbal Behavior*, 1973, *12*, 1-20.

Rozin, P., & Jonides, J. Mass reaction time: Measurement of the speed of the nerve impulse and the duration of mental processes in class. *Teaching of Psychology*, 1977, *4*, 91-94.

Schaeffer, B., & Wallace, R. The comparison of word meanings. *Journal of Experimental Psychology*, 1970, *86*, 144-152.

Shepard, R., & Metzler, J. Mental rotation of three-dimensional objects. *Science*, 1971, *171*, 701-703.

---

# Hamilton's Marbles or Jevon's Beans:
# A Demonstration of Miller's Magical Number Seven

Leigh S. Shaffer
*West Chester State College*

The widespread acceptance and influence of cognitive psychology has resulted in the formal consideration of that perspective in introductory psychology textbooks. It is now the task of pedagogy to assess which features of the perspective would be heuristic to teach to an introductory class. Textbooks have frequently started with the computer as a metaphor for human information processing (see, for example, Hilgard, Atkinson & Atkinson, 1979; Lindzey & Norman, 1977). There are two problems with the metaphor that I have repeatedly encountered. First, students do not know much about a computer, especially its mathematical character; for example, Weizenbaum (1976) has cataloged many of the common misconceptions of the computer's ability to process natural language. Second, the computer metaphor suggests to the students such a mechanistic view of humans that using the metaphor risks alienating a large number of humanistically-oriented students before they can appreciate the insights of the cognitive approach. Therefore I found myself searching for a means of introducing cognitive psychology that would be less likely to invoke the cultural misperceptions or apprehensions that students often bring to an introductory course. I found what I consider to be such an approach in considering two "classic" papers by George Miller (Miller, 1956a, 1956b).

Many textbooks (for example McNeil & Rubin, 1977) introduce information processing by explicating Miller's famous "magical number seven" concept of the limitation of sensory capacity for processing information (Miller, 1956a). I discovered that the intellectual predecessors of Miller's work were William Hamilton and William Stanley Jevons, who described the results of primitive experiments (with marbles and beans, respectively) that demonstrated the limits of visual information processing; these demonstrations are reported in Miller (1956a) and more extensively in Woodworth's (1938) *Experimental Psychology*. Hamilton asserted that after throwing marbles on the floor, an observer would find it difficult to view more than "six, or seven at the most, without confusion" (quoted in Miller, 1956a). Woodworth (1938) noted that Hamilton's data were taken informally and probably never recorded, but indicated that Jevons carefully performed a similar experiment on himself in 1871 by throwing beans into a box, and Woodworth's edition reports Jevons' procedures and data (Woodworth, 1938, pp. 685-687). Jevons reported that without counting he could determine that there were three or four beans without mistake, that he was sometimes wrong if the number was five, that he was accurate only 43% of the time when the number was ten, and was wrong on 82% of the trials when the number reached 15. Being somewhat literal-minded myself, I found a box, pitched various numbers of pennies into the box, and roughly verified those findings.

It occurred to me that reviving Hamilton's marbles or Jevon's beans would make for an excellent classroom demonstration of a concept which I had previously covered too abstractly for most of my students to follow. Instead of trying to define information, the value of a bit, the notion of channel capacity, and so forth, I took my box and my pennies to the classroom. My only "refinements" were done in an effort to facilitate the demonstration and avoid some obvious "demand characteristics."

I used a table of random numbers to prepare in advance an order for the number of coins used on each trial. I chose a student confederate to play the role of experimenter and "pitch pennies" for each subject. I chose a box with a lid so that the experimenter could exercise some control over the viewing time by using the lid as a shutter. I set a two second exposure as a reasonable exposure time that would preclude obvious counting and allowed the experimenter to estimate the interval of exposure. Finally, I had the experimenter instruct the subject to try to determine the number of pennies in the box "only by observation," and instructed the subject to "avoid counting" the pennies. The demonstration was then conducted by having the experimenter follow the predetermined sequence in putting pennies into the box for each trial, allowing the subject to look into the box for approximately two seconds, having the subjects report the number of pennies they thought they saw, and having another confederate record the responses and privately record "correct or incorrect" for each trial (subjects were not given any feedback about the accuracy of the judgments).

When several subjects had attempted the task, the results were tabulated and presented to the class on the chalkboard as a frequency distribution of the number of correct responses as a function of the number of pennies viewed. The results each time I have performed the demonstration have clearly followed the predicted pattern, as would be expected of such a robust phenomenon. I have never seen an error for as many as four pennies, I have seen occasional errors at five

pennies, the plotted curve most often decelerates with eight pennies, and with ten or more pennies the frequency of correct responses is so low as to easily be attributed to guessing. (Indeed, to minimize spuriously high frequencies of correct guesses, I have avoided telling subjects the maximum number of pennies to expect.)

I have found this demonstration to be extremely useful. It is based on a robust phenomenon, so it is unlikely to go awry. It is easy to comprehend the limits to information processing in this demonstration, and it focuses on a *human* phenomenon which will be congenial even to students with a bias against mechanistic views of behavior. It is also, of course, highly portable so that it can be used impromptu—even at a playground marble game or on the floor of a country store! It is also adaptable for use with large groups, with some technological support. I have prepared flash cards with varying numbers of dots on them; these need only to be randomly ordered prior to their use, and then everyone in a lecture class can be a subject. A cleaner version of the latter approach merely involves the advance preparation and ordering of the same stimuli to be presented as slides by a carousel projector, especially a projector with a tachistoscopic mechanism. But whether it is done with technological sophistication or not, I highly recommend the use of this demonstration that was first performed over a century ago. It represents a simple, interesting, and non-threatening introduction to cognitive psychology.

## References

Hilgard, E. R., Atkinson, R. L., & Atkinson, R. C. *Introduction to psychology* (7th ed.). New York: Harcourt, Brace, Jovanovich, 1979.

Lindzey, P. H., & Norman, D. A. *Human information processing: An introduction to psychology* (2nd ed.). New York: Academic Press, 1977.

McNeil, E. B., & Rubin, Z. *The psychology of being human* (2nd ed.). San Francisco: Canfield Press, 1977.

Miller, G. A. Information and memory. *Scientific American*, 1956, *195*, 2-6. (a)

Miller, G. A. The magical number seven, plus or minus two: Some limits on our capacity for information processing. *Psychological Review*, 1956, *63*, 81-97. (b)

Weizenbaum, J. *Computer power and human reason: From judgement to calculation.* San Francisco: Freeman, 1976.

Woodworth, R. S. *Experimental psychology.* New York: Holt, 1938.

# 15. DEVELOPMENTAL PSYCHOLOGY

## Think Old: Twenty-five Classroom Exercises For Courses in Aging

Kathleen M. Hynek Dillon
and Sara Goodman
*Western New England College*

Use of this annotated resource guide surely will increase student learning through participation, and may also change attitudes.

As the number of old and very old increases in our population, so does the need for those involved in services for the aged. Although the need is increasing, interest in working with the aged is not. Butler (1975) discusses the reluctance of psychotherapists to work with the aged, known as the YAVIS syndrome—the tendency to treat only Young, Attractive, Verbal, Intelligent, and Successful clientele. In one study of psychiatrists reviewed by Butler, less than 2% of psychiatric time (or less than one hour per week) was spent with elderly patients even though those over age 65 have by far the highest occurrence of new cases of psychopathology. Using data from a questionnaire responded to by 69 graduate students in social work, law, and medicine, Geiger (1978) demonstrated that the YAVIS syndrome is being perpetuated among future professionals. Although many students believed that there were more old people in this country than there actually are (from 44-53 million compared to the actual 22 million), not one person registered a first choice for working with the elderly in their future career. Out of the four age categories, 74% of social work students chose the old as third or fourth preference, and 88% of medical students considered working with old people only as a last resort.

Both Butler and Geiger blame this attitude in part on the failure of the educational system to offer or require courses and experience in working with the aged. As Developmental Psychology finally comes of age with the realization that life does not end in adolescence, the number of courses of at least an elective nature in adulthood and aging is beginning to increase. Many students who elect to take these courses, however, will not be of the age cohort on which the courses focus, and many students will probably bring with them ageism and gerontophobic attitudes from our culture. It becomes the task of the educator then to find ways to bridge the cohort gap in the most stimulating manner possible.

Six hundred fourteen colleges and universities responded to a questionnaire sponsored by the American Psychological Association in order to determine the kinds of programs offered in Psychology. "In talks with students and faculty members, and in our questionnaires to departments, one area emerged as uniquely important in teaching psychology—student involvement in learning activities. It is a widely shared belief in psychology that students learn most when they are active in learning situations" (Kulik et al., p. 206).

The 25 learning exercises we have selected and will review here have the potential to increase student motivation, involvement, and satisfaction, to reinforce and clarify concepts covered in reading and lectures, and to combat aging stereotypes while increasing empathy and understanding. The exercises come from many sources including research studies, course outlines, and popular magazines. Some of the references were intended as classroom exercises; others were not, but any necessary modification is suggested in the summaries. We have arbitrarily divided the exercises into three related categories—the Biology of Aging, the Psychology of Aging, and the Sociology of Aging, although many exercises fit into more than one area. Where possible the summaries were written using words of the authors to describe the intent of the exercise. In the case where a reference would be unavailable from a journal or textbook, we have included an address where it may be obtained.

All of these exercises have been used successfully by one or both of us in either our courses in Adulthood and Aging, Psychosocial Perspectives on Aging, Death and Dying, Developmental Psychology, and Introductory Psychology, or in workshops given by us to staff of long term care facilities for the aged. You will undoubtedly need to personally validate the use of these exercises because success will depend on many factors such as the specific expertise and background of the teacher, the nature of the course, and the type of students enrolled. We do not endorse the use of these exercises as research tools (although some have been used for this purpose) nor do we recommend that these exercises be used in lieu of lectures and reading material; they are intended to complement, not substitute for, traditional learning material.

We hope you find these exercises as helpful and interesting as we have, and that you will be rewarded with many students who become interested in a career in aging.

### Biology of Aging

1. Palmore, E. Facts on aging: A short quiz. *Gerontologist*, 1977, *17*, 315-320.

   A 25-item true-false quiz designed by the author to stimulate group discussions, measure and compare different groups' level of information on aging, identify the most frequently held misconceptions about aging, and indirectly measure bias toward the aging. Palmore also provides comparative data for undergraduate students, graduate students, and faculty.

2. Vickery, D. M. How long will you live? *Family Health*, January 1979, 29-32. (Also in Vickery, D. M. *Life plan for your health*. Cambridge, MA: Addison Wesley, 1979.)

Illustrates how your habits and health history affect the probability of good health and how these factors can be used to estimate your life expectancy (assuming you do not suffer from a serious chronic condition). This test includes not only the more obvious variables as exercise, weight, diet, smoking and drinking habits, but also the use of seat belts, contraceptives, and the Holmes Scale for Stress.

3. Shore, H. Designing a training program for understanding sensory losses in aging. *Gerontologist*, 1976, *16*, 157-165.

Stimulation exercises that review visual, auditory, tactile, olfactory, gustatory, and kinesthetic losses sometimes associated with aging. These exercises provide a useful method for gaining insight and understanding of the difficulties of coping with distorted environmental feedback resulting from sensory losses in order for those working with the elderly to enhance their functioning, independence, and satisfaction.

4. Hulicka, I. M., & Whitbourne, S. K. Teaching undergraduate courses in adult development and aging. Preconvention Workshop, American Psychological Association, Toronto, August 27, 1978. (Obtain from the author, State University of New York College, Buffalo, NY 14627)

Simulation exercises of physical disabilities which affect many older people, including paralysis of fingers and limbs, coordination problems, loss of voice, and constant itching; also role playing exercises of various experiences the aged may encounter in our society. These exercises are designed to foster insight into the difficulties encountered by a handicapped person, and to increase awareness of the experiences of the aged.

5. Farquhar, J. W. Test your heart attack and stroke potential. *Family Circle*, October 23, 1978, 100; 104; 110.

Calculates your risk of heart attack (the leading cause of death) and stroke (the third leading cause of death, but the first in overall costs) by scoring you on such related variables as smoking habits, body weight, physical activity and stress. This article not only tests your potential, but also provides you with a ten step plan to reduce the risk.

6. 60+ and physically fit: Suggested exercises for older people. Hartford, CT: Connecticut Department on Aging's Physical Fitness Committee, (90 Washington St., Room 3123, Hartford, CT 06115), 1977.

Provides simple exercises for both ambulatory and nonambulatory aged to prevent or combat physiological losses that appear to result more from inactivity than from old age. The committee recommends that the exercises be discussed with a physician to decide which would be the most beneficial. Students could try and then discuss the benefits of a regular program of these exercises. A discussion of DeVries' (1977) studies with young men experiencing decreased activity in the form of three weeks of bed rest with resulting losses in physiological functioning similar to those found in the aged might be of interest to the younger student here.

## Psychology of Aging

7. Kastenbaum, R. Age: Getting there ahead of time. *Psychology Today*, December, 1971, 52-54; 82-84.

Stimulation and discussion exercises designed for young persons to pre-experience themselves as old, including trying to work at a pace faster than their normal tempo, and being placed in an environment that makes one feel disregarded and ineffective.

8. Pocs, O., Godwin, J., Tolone, W. L., & Walsh, R. H. Is there sex after 40? *Psychology Today*, June 1977, 54-56; 87.

Provides questions for students to answer anonymously about their parents' sexual activity and known statistics to compare. Usually students are much more conservative in their estimates than facts warrant. Discussion might follow concerning sexual stereotypes of the aged, and their effects on the aged themselves.

9. Wechsler, D. *Wechsler Adult Intelligence Scale*. New York: The Psychological Corporation, 1955.

Two exercises to provide comparative data for the concepts of fluid intelligence (that which is presumed to increase, plateau, and then decline) and crystallized intelligence (that which is presumed to grow throughout the developmental cycle). The digit symbol test taps fluid intelligence whereas the vocabulary test represents crystallized intelligence. To avoid contaminating the validity of this test we recommend you substitute your own symbols and vocabulary words for these exercises.

10. Albert, W. C., & Zarit, S. H. Income and health care of the aging. In S. H. Zarit (ed.). *Readings in aging and death: Contemporary perspectives*. New York: Harper and Row, 1977.
Schaubaum G. Winning the money game. *NTRA* [National Retired Teachers Association] *Journal*, November-December 1978, 14-16.

First article provides a plan to figure an estimated minimum monthly benefit for an older person living alone including food, housing, utilities, clothing, and medical costs. Students could first figure what they would need for a minimum, then compare this figure to minimum Social Security allotments to become conscious of difficulties of living on a minimum income. Second article plans your retirement income, taking inflation into account to see if you will have enough money to live on when you retire, and if not, how to make adjustments now before it is too late. Students could work on a hypothetical problem or use their own parents' income and savings.

11. Bellak, L., & Bellak, S. S. *The Senior Apperception Technique* (S.A.T.). Larchmont, NY: C. P. S., Inc., 1973. (Obtain from publisher, P.O. Box 83, zip 10538.)

Sixteen pictures providing stimuli which permit ascription of themes of loneliness, illness, and other vicissitudes or reflections of happy sentiments such as joy in grandchildren, or ambiguous stimuli which could be interpreted as either happy or as a reflection of difficulties. Students could be shown pictures and asked to discuss what kinds of themes might be elicited.

12. Neale, R. E. Threats to my old age. (Can be obtained from the author, 606 W. 122nd St., New York, NY 10027)

A sometimes difficult exercise asking participants to decide personally what would be the major threats of loss of their body, self, and social environment, and major threats of restraint to their body, self, and social environment as they age.

13. Alpaugh, P., & Haney, M. *Counseling the older adult: A training manual.* Los Angeles: University of Southern California Press, 1978. (Ethel Percy Andrus Gerontology Center, University Park, Los Angeles, CA 90007.)

A workbook providing many informational and skill exercises related to communication skills necessary for knowing and helping the older adult.

14. Neugarten, B. I., Havighurst, R. J., & Tobin, S. S. The measurement of life satisfaction. *Gerontology,* 1961, *16,* 134-143.
Neugarten, B. I. Grow old along with me, the best is yet to be. *Psychology Today,* December 1971, 45-46; 48; 79; 81.

The first article provides a 20-item measure of life satisfaction designed as part of a larger research study of psychological and social factors involved in aging. The second article discusses four major personality types and their likelihood of feeling satisfied with life. Although the life satisfaction scale is primarily designed for those over 65, students could be asked to take the scale and see how to predict which style of aging they thought they would be most likely to adopt and to see if indeed those with the integrated style, for example, were the most likely to have had the highest scores on the life satisfaction scale.

15. Hartford, M. E. Self inventory for planning to maximize my potential in aging. In B. O'Brien. *Aging: Today's research and you: A lecture series.* Los Angeles: University of Southern California Press, 1978. (Obtain from Ethel Percy Andrus Gerontology Center, University Park, Los Angeles, CA 90007.)

Asks you to reflect upon things you enjoyed or considered important first as a child, then a youth, then in young adulthood (and middle years and older, if appropriate), then to look over the lists for common ideas, activities, ambitions, interests, and relationships. Finally, you are asked to examine how your current life fulfills these dreams and expectations and what you can do in the future to accomplish these goals.

16. Neale, R. E. *The art of dying.* New York: Harper and Row, 1971.

Book of reflective exercises and ideas designed to help you explore yourself and your attitudes toward dying.

## Sociology of Aging

17. Hartman, A. Diagrammatic assessment of family relationships. *Social Casework,* October 1978, 465-476.

Acknowledging the importance of the family, this article discusses two methods to diagrammatically assess family relationships, and suggests how these techniques can be used as tools in the life review process found helpful in organizing and putting into perspective the past events in the life of an older person and in assessing ongoing family relationships. Students could then diagram their own family relationships, or that of a hypothetical family. Students could also discuss other tools for assisting in a life review process.

18. Coons, D. H., & Bykowski, J. *Brookside Manor: A gerontological simulation.* Ann Arbor, MI: Institute of Gerontology, 1975. (520 East Liberty, Ann Arbor, MI 48108.)

A simulation exercise illustrating the sometimes conflicting needs of staff and patients in long term care facilities for the aged.

19. Metzelaar, L. *A collection of cartoons: A way of experiencing practices in a treatment setting.* Ann Arbor, MI: Institute of Gerontology, 1975. (See address above.)

Thirty eight cartoons designed as discussion aids for staff of long term care facilities for the aged to explore negative attitudes toward the aged as portrayed in non-therapeutic practices by staff. These cartoons provide a good backdrop for students to discuss the potential for physical and psychological abuses in such facilities.

20. Hickey, T. H., Rakowski, W., Kafer, R., & Lachman, M. Aging opinion survey: Developmental data. Paper presented at the annual meeting of the Gerontological Society, Dallas, TX, November 1978. (Rudolph Kafer, S-110 Human Development, University Park, PA 16802.)

Separately measures attitudes toward aging of friends and known others, attitudes toward one's own aging, and attitudes toward aging people in general, using a Likert scale response to 45 statements.

21. Davies, L. Attitudes toward old age and aging as shown by humor. *Gerontologist,* 1977, *17,* 220-226.
Palmore, E. Attitudes toward aging as shown by humor. *Gerontologist,* 1971, *3,* 181-186.
Richman, J. The foolishness and wisdom of age: Attitudes toward the elderly as reflected in jokes. *Gerontologist,* 1977, *17,* 210-219.

Three sources of many jokes about aging and the aged. Class can discuss the intent and meaning of the joke, whether it is based on stereotypes and whether this type of humor should be discouraged. Students can also be asked to find and contribute their own examples.

22. *The myth and reality of aging in America.* Washington, DC: National Council on Aging, 1975. (1828 L St. NW, Suite 504, zip 20036.)

Provides data showing that a recent Harris poll found that most TV watchers feel that TV presents a fair picture of older people, but that TV commercials do not necessarily. Ask your class to find examples of TV shows and commercials or magazine material and to analyze what role the older person is playing in the example.

23. Cautela, J. R., & Wisocki, P. A. The use of imagery in the modification of attitudes toward the elderly: A preliminary report. *Journal of Psychology,* 1969, *73,* 193-199.

Participants are asked to imagine a specific scene read to them in which an elderly man comes to their aid in a crisis situation. Empirical data are provided to show that the use of this imagery task showed a positive increase in attitudes toward the aged.

24. LaMonica, E. L. The aging process: Positive attitudinal development through an existential approach. Paper presented at the American Psychological Association meetings, Toronto, 1978. (Obtain from the author, Department of Nursing Education, Teachers College, Columbia University, New York, NY.)

A personal learning experience conducted in a group setting in which participants are asked to imagine themselves to be the protagonist in a parable about living, growing, and dying. Participants are then asked to share their reactions and feelings.

25. Kogan, N. A sentence completion procedure for assessing attitudes toward old people. *Journal of Gerontology,* 1959, *14,* 355-363.

Provides a projective technique of eliciting attitudes toward old people compared to attitudes toward people in general. Twenty-five pairs of incomplete statements (one of each pair being distinguished only by the presence of the modifier "old") are given. Give half of your class the list without the modifier "old" and half the list with the modifier "old" and compare responses.

## References

Butler, R. N. *Why survive? Being old in America.* New York: Harper and Row, 1975.

DeVries, H. A. Physiology of exercise and aging. In S. H. Zarit (ed.). *Readings in aging and death: Contemporary perspectives.* New York: Harper and Row, 1977.

Geiger, D. L. Note: How future professionals view the elderly: A comparative analysis of social work, law, and medical students perceptions. *Gerontologist,* 1978, *18,* 591-594.

Kulik, J. A., Brown, D. R., Vesterwig, R. E., & Wright, J. *Undergraduate education in psychology.* Washington, DC: American Psychological Association, 1973.

# The Developmental Psychology Library Search: Can a Nonsense Assignment Make Sense?

Arnold D. LeUnes
*Texas A & M University*

It is obvious that the creation of a positive learning environment is essential in getting one's point across in any subject matter area. Further, getting the attention of the subjects to be taught is conducive to effective learning. In an attempt to accomplish both of these goals, a library assignment was created for a junior-level course in developmental psychology. The students were handed a list of 24 questions on the first day of class to be completed and discussed on the third day. The assignment was designed to: (a) get the students into the library, and (b) acquaint them with the subjective reflections and objective data that make up the rather huge area of our discipline known as developmental psychology. In the process, it was hoped that the assignment would arouse some interest on the part of the students in selected aspects of the area, would alert them to topics to be covered during the term, and would provide a basis for understanding of the overlap and interrelationships within the area.

Initial student reaction was subdued but polite humor. "You've got to be kidding" type responses were occasionally heard and often sensed. Some feeling that there might be some method to the professor's madness was equally sensed. In any case, the 70 students left with the feeling that they would give it the old college try.

If there is in fact some sense to the assignment, I believed that it could serve as an attention-getter in my class in developmental psychology. It could also be adapted to fit a variety of topic areas within psychology.

A sample of the 24 questions/statements and a brief rationale for them are as follows:

1. *Name eight educational/psychological journals that deal with studies on development of children.* Though the list is somewhat endless and the rationale reasonably self-evident, it was maintained that little student exposure to these materials had been required in earlier courses.

2. *Name four journals that deal exclusively with mental retardation.* Familiarity with journals in retardation was deemed useful for several reasons. One, of course, is the prevalence of retardation. Second, the class make-up (primarily Psychology, Education, Pre-Medicine, and Physical Therapy majors) was such that the topic was judged to be of considerable interest.

3. *What book did John Watson write in 1928 pertaining to child development?* This was an opportunity to discuss one of the most influential historical figures in psychology. Further, it created an opening for a discussion of his not-so-popular 1928 dissertation on child rearing.

4. *Name the presidents of the United States who were first-born children.* This one served as a means for introducing birth-order effects into the developmental menu.

5. *How would Dr. Spock handle the problem of the toddler who won't stay in the crib?* Some mention of the Spock influence on child-rearing practices is warranted, and this provides an introduction to his ideas.

6. *Who is the editor of the American Journal of Mental Deficiency?* This was just another device for creating an awareness of the literature on mental retardation. It could well be the first time that many have ever taken the time to read about such things as editorial policy and other matters pertinent to the publication of a professional journal.

7. *Reference: Archives of General Psychiatry, 1972, 27, 711. What topic is discussed?* This is an advertisement for a leading anti-anxiety drug. It serves as an introduction to the use of prescription drugs with young people, particularly but not exclusively the hyperactive child.

8. *What famous developmental psychologist is listed on page 616 of the Manhattan phone book, 1972-73?* This was an attempt to see if the name of Haim Ginott was easily recognized. The opportunity to elaborate on his ideas about children was most welcomed.

9. *Name two fictional books on childhood schizophrenia and/or childhood autism.* This was designed to alert the students to the topic of behavioral disorders of children.

10. *How many children did Sigmund Freud have? How tall was he?* An awareness of Freud as a person was the intent of these questions. They also led to lengthy discussion of his contributions to our understanding of behavior, with particular emphasis on childhood concerns.

11. *Who is Gloria Strauss?* This was a fun question in that the answer was as near as the students' elbows, for Strauss was one of the authors of the course text (Liebert, Poulos, and Strauss, 1974).

It is obvious that there is substantial topical overlap among the various questions. This is intentional and serves to highlight the interrelationships that exist in developmental psychology.

Though no objective data were gathered with respect to the success of the assignment, it seemed to be an educationally profitable venture. It may be that a fair assessment of its success would be hard to make in that its purpose was to plant seeds of awareness in the minds of unsophisticated subjects (with regard to expertise in developmental psychology, at least). As any teacher can testify, whether or not one is planting ideas in the minds of his students is an argumentative and elusive question.

Finally, there is nothing magic about the sample questions presented here. They could be easily altered to fit other subject matter areas within psychology. This exercise is intended to serve only as a general model for the development of alternative assignments for classroom use. Its apparent success in the present case leads me to believe that it is applicable in a broader context.

### Reference

Liebert, R. Poulos, R., & Strauss, G. *Developmental psychology.* Englewood Cliffs, NJ: Prentice Hall, 1974.

# Simulated Parent-Child Interaction in an Undergraduate Child Psychology Course

Stephen J. Dollinger
and Dale F. Brown
*Southern Illinois University*

Simulation can be a useful technique in teaching undergraduate child psychology courses. Recently we used simulated parent-child interactions in a unit on child behavior management and discipline. Our objectives involved (a) illustrating the types of discipline used, and (b) integrating the students' everyday knowledge (or "implicit psychology") of children with research and theory. As a secondary benefit, the simulation illustrated the concept of factorial design in experiments.

Because the simulation took place in December, the context selected for the parent-child interaction was Christmas shopping in a department store. The child's demands for an expensive toy provided the conflict situation that the students role-played.

The 45 students were asked to arrange themselves into triads, consisting of a parent, child, and observer. Each participant received an instruction sheet describing the context, their role, and some suggestions for how they might respond. "Parents" received suggestions for a wide variety of disciplinary practices and were urged to "see what works with your child." In addition, half of the "parents" were given a reminder that they felt embarrassed by the child's behavior, wanted to avoid "creating a scene," and had a long shopping list to get through. These additional instructions were given to lower their tolerance of the "child's" disruptiveness.

Students playing the role of the child were given suggestions on a variety of manipulative techniques to persuade their "parent." Instructions for half of the children also suggested that they "back down" if it seemed that their parent was getting angry or "if it seems that parent no longer loves you." These instructions established the "good child"

group. By way of contrast, the other half of the "children" were given egocentric instructions which emphasized (a) that their sense of being loved depended on whether the parent bought the toy for them; and (b) that they could use this in the interaction (e.g., "you never loved me").

Observers were instructed to keep notes on the interaction. It was also suggested that the observers watch for four types of parenting statements: reason-oriented discipline (explaining why he/she would not buy the toy); power-assertion (pulling rank); guilt-inducing discipline (making the child feel naughty or guilty); and evasive discipline (avoiding the issue).

The two types of parent and child instructions were combined to make four types of triads: tolerant parent-good child; tolerant parent-egocentric child; intolerant parent-good child; and intolerant parent-egocentric child. With 45 students participating, there were 15 triads, 3 of the first type, and 4 of the other types.

The interaction in all groups began with the "child's" request for the parent to buy an expensive toy, followed by the "parent's" refusal. Following this, the students improvised for 5-10 minutes. At the end of the interaction, the "parent" and "child" answered questions on their instruction form, and the observer briefly interviewed them about their feelings. Then the observers reported to the class on how their interaction went, and what types of discipline were used. Also, the "parent" and "child" ratings were collected and the results were presented in the next class period.

While the results were not amenable to statistical analyses, there were some interesting trends which in many cases parallel what likely would be found in the "real world." First, all groups used reason-oriented discipline (generally this was tried first). Power-assertion was most likely within the intolerant parent-good child groups (3 of the 4 groups), but was never used within the tolerant parent-egocentric child groups. Guilt-inducing discipline was only used within the intolerant parent-egocentric child groups (2 of the 4 groups), and evasive discipline was used most in the two egocentric child groups (6 of the 8 egocentric groups vs. 3 of 7 non-egocentric groups). In none of the groups did the "parent" resort to spanking, a result partly attributable to the instruction that "parents" should say "now I would spank you" rather than actually use punishment. Ratings of satisfaction with the outcome of the interaction showed that the "parents" were more satisfied when their "child" was good rather than egocentric, and "children" were more satisfied when their "parents" were tolerant rather than intolerant. Additionally, "parents" overall were more satisfied than "children," a result which is not surprising since the "child" received the toy in only 1 of the 15 groups.

The results suggest that, much as in the "real world," the "parents" accommodated their discipline to the special characteristics of their "children", and "children" accommodated to their "parents." The findings which are suspect in this regard, are the high frequency of reason-oriented discipline (100%), the low frequency of physical punishment (0%), and the low frequency of cases where the "child" was successful in getting the toy (7%). However, these results might be expected within the context of a group of university students who have elected a course in child psychology, most of whom are not yet parents.

On teacher evaluation questionnaires completed at the end of the semester, the students were given an opportunity to comment on the usefulness of the simulation and to give ratings from 0 to 9. Forty-five percent gave a rating of 8 or 9 indicating very favorable attitudes, 23% had mildly favorable attitudes (ratings of 6 or 7), 16% had neutral ratings (4 or 5), and 16% had mildly unfavorable ratings (2 or 3). Comments generally reflected attitudes expressed in the ratings: "fun!" "it was great!" "thought it was worthless" and "good idea." Other students suggested that there be more use of simulations in class. Negative comments generally addressed the issue of people being "too shy" to participate.

When ratings were grouped according to the students' major courses of study, it appeared that the most favorable ratings came from students in psychology, social welfare, and special education. Since students in these majors have probably had more opportunities for role-playing in class, they may have felt fewer reservations about participating.

Several concerns prior to using the simulation were that students would have difficulty taking the "child" role, that most students would be reluctant to participate, and that the contrived nature of the simulation would have no relationship to the "real world." These concerns appear to have been unfounded. In summary, the use of simulated parent-child interaction has promise as an instructional and motivational aid in teaching undergraduate child psychology.

# 16. PERSONALITY

## A Class Exercise in Personality and Psychological Assessment

Ludy T. Benjamin, Jr.
*Texas A&M University*

Our course in introductory psychology provides two kinds of classes for the students: a large lecture section of approximately 240 students that meets twice a week and a small group class (20-30 students) that meets once a week for each student. Thus each large lecture class is subdivided into 8-12 smaller groups. Activities vary in these small groups but they have in common an attempt to take advantage of the small class size and thus to do things that could not be handled in the large lecture section. Some small group sessions involve demonstrations, others experiments, and still others are discussion oriented. This article describes a two-week exercise that focuses on personality and psychological assessment. That is, it is a two-part activity conducted in successive weeks in conjunction with lecture material on personality the first week and psychological assessment in the second week. These small groups are staffed by graduate students who have completed (or are currently enrolled in) a graduate course on the teaching of psychology.

Procedure.   The personality activity begins with the instructor making some introductory remarks about the nature of personality as a construct and the difficulty psychologists have in defining it. The students are then asked to call out terms that they feel are part of the construct of personality. The instructor merely serves as a recorder at this time, writing each of the terms on the chalkboard. Usually in 5-10 minutes there are 25 to 30 terms on the board including such things as sense of humor, sociability, friendliness, honesty, sincerity, leadership, and so forth. At this point, the instructor tells the students that they are going to participate in the construction of a personality test. To do this they need to narrow their list of terms to the *eight* that they feel are major components of personality. (There is nothing magical about the number eight, more or fewer terms could be used.) In this part of the exercise the instructor takes a more active role in the process by encouraging students to eliminate most terms from the list, otherwise the class will spend the entire hour in debate without reducing the number of terms. Some terms can be eliminated quickly because most students will agree that they are of lesser importance. In other cases terms can be combined, for example, sociability and friendliness, or honesty and trustworthiness. We have found that the final list of eight terms is usually agreed upon by about 20-25 minutes after the start of class.

Quickly the instructor divides the class into eight groups, each composed of 2-4 students. This can be done easily by forming groups where students are seated so that they do not have to move around. Next, one of the terms is assigned to each of the eight groups and each group informed that they have 10-15 minutes to jointly write two items that they believe will measure that particular characteristic of person-

ality. In order to ensure uniformity in the format of the items, several examples are provided for the students, typically using one of the terms that was not included in their final eight. For example, suppose that leadership is a term that the class did not select. The instructor might give them sample items such as "when I join clubs, I like to assume one of the officer positions in the club" or "people usually seek my opinion when they are having problems." Students are made to understand that the questions need to be written so that they can be answered "true" or "false."

If there is time at the end of the class, several of the groups are asked to read one or more of the items they have written. Someone in each group should have the responsibility of recording all the items on a single sheet. These sheets are collected and students are given instructions about the rest of the exercise. They are told that their items will be used to construct a personality test made up of 16 questions, that is, the two items they generated for each of the eight terms the class selected. (Poorly written items may be included since the results they are likely to produce will lead to interesting discussion.) These questionnaires will be coded with a number corresponding to each class so that students will not use the questionnaire generated by some other class. The tests are typed and copies made available a day or so after the class meeting. They are placed in an envelope marked with the class number and can be picked up at the office of the graduate student in charge of that class section. Students are told to take one copy of their test and administer it to two students (preferably one male and one female) who are not enrolled in the introductory psychology classes. The test contains a disclaimer which indicates that it has no validity and is being used solely for instructional purposes. Answer sheets contain only the number code for the particular form of the test and the sex of the person answering the questions. Students in the small group classes are told to bring those responses to class with them the following week.

Analysis.   The class session in the second week is begun by placing the numbers 1 through 16 on the chalkboard and listing the number of "true" responses for each item by sex. This tallying procedure is accomplished easily by having the students "vote" by a show of hands. The instructor might begin with responses from males, starting with item 1, by asking for a show of hands on "true" responses. Students who had not tested any males obviously would not vote at that time. Other students would hold up one hand, both hands, or no hands, depending upon the responses of their male subjects. The response frequencies for female subjects are then recorded in the same manner. It is also important to note the total number of female and male subjects in the survey to provide a context for evaluating the data. Students in the class will need to have their copy of the survey in front of them so that the discussion that follows is meaningful. The recording of these responses on the board usually takes no more than 10 minutes.

We usually focus the discussion on three kinds of findings. First, are there any items that show major sex differences in terms of the frequency of responses? Typically one or two items will show such differences and the students are asked to speculate on the reasons for the different response patterns. Second, we look at the pairs of items (which are not adjacent in the test since the items are randomly distributed prior to typing) that are supposed to be measuring the same characteristic. It is common to find that one member of the pair of items will produce a response pattern that is quite different from the other member of the pair. Such a result makes for an interesting discussion about what the two items may be measuring. Third, we look at the items to see if any seem not to discriminate, that is, items which nearly everyone answered either true or false. In addition, we give the students a handout showing the various sets of eight terms generated by the other classes. This information is useful to show the lack of consensus in defining the most important characteristics of personality.

Values.   There are a wealth of issues surrounding personality and psychological assessment that can be experienced and discussed in this exercise, e.g., issues of reliability and validity, difficulty in defining constructs, issues in item construction and test construction, and so forth. We have used the exercise in our course for the past two years and it has

rated as a favorite activity for a number of students. We believe that the assets of the activity are as follows: (a) it teaches students about the complexity of psychological constructs, (b) it taps an area, personality, that is familiar to students and of great interest to them, (c) it gives them first-hand experience with the issue of face validity, (d) it gives them an opportunity for participation in some small group (2-4 students) activities, (e) it provides them with an opportunity to actually collect some data, (f) it gives them some experience in thinking about the meaning of questionnaire results, (g) it shows them some of the problems inherent in psychological assessment, (h) it gives students a closer look at some of the problems of the trait approach to personality, and (i) it provides an excellent vehicle for class discussion with minimal involvement from the instructor. The feedback we have received in written evaluations from students indicates that they view those two weeks as a significant learning experience.

Of course the activity that has been described here can be modified in a number of ways, even to fit larger classes. Instructors should make whatever modifications they desire to best fit their teaching situation.

---

# Testing the Validity of Astrology in Class

William R. Balch
*The Pennsylvania State University at Altoona*

According to recent evidence on student beliefs, most undergraduates entering an introductory course in psychology are anything but "blank slates." For example, Vaughan (1977) has identified a variety of common misconceptions held among members of introductory classes. These beliefs include agreement with popular myths, or outmoded cliches such as: "A high forehead is a sign of intelligence." Such prior "knowledge" may have an adverse effect on grades (Gutman, 1979).

Belief in the occult is also popular among introductory students. For instance, Shepard (1977) has conducted a survey of 400 freshmen at Southern Methodist University. Of this sample, 40% reported believing in witchcraft; and 36% in astrology. Here at the Altoona Campus of the Pennsylvania State University, Jensen (Note 1) found 53% endorsement of astrology; and 33% of witchcraft. In more general terms, Roll (1973) has written about the recent increase in the popularity of non-rational beliefs; especially among young people. He suggests that they are reacting against the depersonalization they perceive in Western technology.

Whatever the reasons, it is difficult to deny that a considerable number of students are predisposed toward non-scientific modes of thought. Furthermore, their prior beliefs may be quite deep-rooted. For example, both Vaughan

(1977) and Gutman (1979) found that course instruction did little to dispel undergraduates' misconceptions about psychology. Similarly, it may be optimistic to assume that students will stop believing in astrology and witchcraft just because "teacher says so."

With these points in mind, I have developed a non-partisan classroom test of a most persistent student belief: astrology. Under the assumption that they are taking an ordinary "personality test," students rate how much twelve different personality "types" apply to themselves. Each type consists of three descriptive adjectives. After taking the test, students are told its real purpose. The adjectives defining each type are those most commonly used by astrologers to describe the different zodiac "personalities." The question is: how many students rate the description of their own sign as applicable to themselves? The test is scored so that the astrologer's point of view is supported if significantly more than half the class members agree with their zodiac types.

The twelve personality types used in the test are given in Table 1. In the left-hand column are the 12 signs and their birth dates. In the adjacent column, the three most frequently occurring adjectives describing that sign type are italicized. These norms are based on a count from 11 different books on astrology (Chambertin, 1970; Cooper & Weaver, 1975; Gettings, 1972; Goodman, 1968; King, 1976; Lee; 1968; Leek, 1970; Lynch, 1969; MacNiece, 1964; Octopus Books (eds.), 1973; and Sakoran & Acker, 1973). All of these books had short sections describing the character traits presumed to be associated with the various zodiac signs. The italicized adjectives in the table are those which were used for the test reported here. Synonyms of these adjectives, which counted as occurrences of the ones italicized, are shown in parentheses. The normative frequency of each adjective (maximum of 11) is given in the right-hand column.

For several years now, I have been using the astrology test in my introductory classes. The details have varied as I developed my materials and procedures. In the fall of 1979, I performed a standardized version of the demonstration on two sections of introductory psychology taught by a colleague. The personality types shown in Table 1 were employed. For purposes of control, mimeographed booklets were prepared containing instructions and rating scales for the personality types. The method and results of this test are described below.

Method. The subjects were freshmen or sophomore undergraduates enrolled in two different sections of introductory psychology, neither of which I taught. There were 76 students (39 males and 37 females) in one section; and 88 (56 females and 36 males) in the other. On the first day of class, I introduced myself to each group as another psychology instructor on the campus, and asked for their participation in a research project. I explained that I had just developed a new personality test, and would like them to take it in class. A small amount of extra credit was offered for anyone who wished to volunteer. All students in each section indicated willingness to participate.

Booklets were then passed out. The first page of these booklets was labeled "The Altoona Campus Personality Test." It was explained that some biographical information would be necessary to help evaluate the results of the test. The information requested was name; sex; date of birth; number of states lived in; academic subjects not enjoyed; hobbies; number of brothers; and number of sisters. Verbally, students were requested not to fill in their names on the forms, since they were serving as "preliminary, trial subjects."

After completing the biographical information, students turned to the second page of the booklet, labelled "Instructions." On this page, they were instructed that they would be rating 12 personality types for applicability to their own personalities. Every type would consist of three adjectives, which would be printed below a horizontal line that served as a personality scale. The left end of the scales was marked "INAPPLICABLE;" and the right end, "APPLICABLE." Subjects were to rate each type by marking a vertical mark anywhere on the scale, from completely inapplicable to completely applicable. They were asked to respond reasonably quickly and naturally; and to try to use the full range of the scales in making their 12 ratings. Finally, the instructions stated that although not every adjective in a type would necessarily apply equally, students should respond to each set of three as one description. That is, they were to rate how well the entire type fit their personalities.

At this point, students were requested to turn to the last page of their booklets, on which the 12 personality types appeared in a random order. They were asked if they had any questions before beginning (which nobody did). Instructions to begin were then given.

Table 1. Three-Adjective Personality Types Used in the Zodiac-Based "Personality Test"

| Sign | Adjectives[a] | Normative Frequency |
|---|---|---|
| Aries | 1. *pioneering* (adventurous) | 10 |
| March 21- | 2. *enthusiastic* | 7 |
| April 19 | 3. *courageous* (fearless, daring, dauntless) | 7 |
| Taurus | 1. *stable* (steadfast, steady) | 6 |
| April 20- | 2. *stubborn* (head-strong) | 6 |
| May 20 | 3. *well-organized* (well-ordered, systematic) | 4 |
| Gemini | 1. *intellectual* | 7 |
| May 21- | 2. *adaptable* (mutable, versatile) | 6 |
| June 21 | 3. *clever* (ingenious) | 4 |
| Cancer | 1. *sensitive* | 9 |
| June 22- | 2. *nurturing*[b] | 9 |
| July 22 | 3. *sympathetic* (compassionate) | 7 |
| Leo | 1. *extroverted* (out-going) | 5 |
| July 23- | 2. *generous* | 5 |
| August 22 | 3. *authoritative* (masterful, leading) | 5 |
| Virgo | 1. *critical* (analytical) | 10 |
| August 23- | 2. *exacting* (painstaking, perfecting, precise) | 8 |
| Sept. 22 | 3. *intelligent* (ingenious) | 7 |
| Libra | 1. *harmonizing* (mediating, co-operative) | 6 |
| Sept. 23- | 2. *just* (lawful, impartial) | 5 |
| Oct. 22 | 3. *sociable* (popular, likeable, friendly) | 5 |
| Scorpio | 1. *secretive* | 7 |
| Oct. 23- | 2. *strong* (forceful, powerful) | 5 |
| Nov. 21 | 3. *passionate* (romantic, erotic) | 5 |
| Sagittarius | 1. *honest* (frank, truthful, candid) | 8 |
| Nov. 22- | 2. *impulsive* (restless) | 6 |
| Dec. 21 | 3. *optimistic* | 5 |
| Capricorn | 1. *ambitious* | 8 |
| Dec. 22- | 2. *hard-working* (persevering) | 6 |
| Jan. 19 | 3. *cautious* (conservative) | 5 |
| Aquarius | 1. *original* (non-traditional, creative, unconventional) | 7 |
| Jan. 20- | 2. *open-minded* (broad-minded) | 5 |
| Feb. 18 | 3. *independent* | 4 |
| Pisces | 1. *kind* (loving, warm) | 5 |
| Feb. 19- | 2. *sensitive* | 5 |
| March 20 | 3. *creative* (artistic) | 5 |

Note: These norms are based on 11 Astrology books. [a]Words appearing in parentheses are alternate synonyms found in the astrology books. [b]This word is substitute for "maternal."

In Figure 1, the format of the rating sheet is illustrated. Only four of the 12 scales are shown (see Table 1 for the complete set of 12 types). Each of the scales was labelled only by a number. The figure illustrates the vertical marks made by a hypothetical subject. Lines A and B did not appear on the rating sheet; and are shown only to illustrate the scoring procedure.

After completing the test, students were given scoring instructions. Each subject was to draw a median line through the scales, which divided his or her responses into six on either side. For example, line A in Figure 1 divides the responses into half, with an equal number (2) on either side. Note that the median line is not necessarily the midpoint of the scales (which is marked by line B).

Finally, students were fully debriefed. The astrological purpose of the test was revealed. Then the zodiac signs for

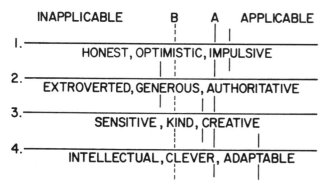

| INAPPLICABLE | B | A | APPLICABLE |

1. ────────────────────────────────────
HONEST, OPTIMISTIC, IMPULSIVE

2. ────────────────────────────────────
EXTROVERTED, GENEROUS, AUTHORITATIVE

3. ────────────────────────────────────
SENSITIVE , KIND, CREATIVE

4. ────────────────────────────────────
INTELLECTUAL, CLEVER, ADAPTABLE

Figure 1. An illustration of the rating scales used in the astrology demonstration. The short vertical marks are responses made by a hypothetical subject. Lines A and B (explained in text) are for scoring purposes only.

each type were read to students, along with the corresponding dates. I instructed them each to make an asterisk by the scale representing her or his own zodiac sign. Then they determined whether their response to this personality type was "applicable" (on the right side of the median line) or "inapplicable" (to the left of the median). A showing of hands revealed that approximately equal numbers of students fell into each category.

The booklets were collected to ensure correct scoring, and to allow for statistical analysis. The results are discussed below.

Results. For each class, the split was close to even between applicable and inapplicable responses to the students' own zodiac signs. Of the 164 students in both sections, 88 signs were "applicable" (39 and 49 in the first and second sections, respectively). Almost as many were "inapplicable," totalling 76 for both sections (35 and 41 for sections one and two, respectively).[2] Because the rating sheets were scored by a median line (see line A in Figure 1), the split expected by chance should be even. However, the proportion of applicable signs obtained in this demonstration was not significantly more than half, $\chi^2(1) = .88, p > .20$. Thus the students showed no tendency to recognize their own zodiac descriptions as being particularly relevant to their personalities.

Although no significant "zodiac effect" was found, one striking phenomenon did occur. Regardless of the students' own zodiac, their responses to all the signs were skewed toward the positive end of the scales. With respect to the *midpoint* of the scales (line B in Figure 1), an average of 8.29 out of 12 were made toward the applicable end of the scale. However, if subjects were unbiased in their responding, only half the responses (i.e., 6) should occur on the positive side end. This tendency to agree with all the personality descriptions was highly significant, $t(163) = 14.126, p < .0001$. Thus a strong response set of acquiescence was found. The general acceptability of these personality types surely must be one important cause of the popular belief in astrologers' claims.[3]

Discussion. This demonstration can be combined with course instruction in a variety of ways, depending on the objectives of the teacher. In my own classes, I have inte-

grated it into an introductory lecture-discussion on the value of scientific method in psychology. The opening lecture material expresses the usual skepticism toward "common sense" and "popular belief;" and the standard arguments for scientific research in psychology. I then present the "personality test," which is offered as an example of "my own research." The subsequent debriefing and showing of hands is orchestrated so as to create as much suspense as possible. By the way, the numbers of "applicable" and "inapplicable" zodiac sign has always turned out to be nearly even.[4]

With a few strategic remarks by the instructor, a spirited discussion (to say the least) can almost always be elicited. In particular, there will be advocates of astrology, who will not passively accept any embarrassment of their own beliefs. They will offer a variety of surprisingly good methodological arguments against the demonstration. For instance, they will point out that people may not always be the most accurate judges of their own personalities. Thus a zodiac description may be true of somebody, yet not be recognized as such by that person. As a matter of fact, Silverman and Whitmer (1974) have used ratings by a friend of the individual as an index of personal characteristics. They found no significant relation between their subjects' zodiac signs and this more objective measure of personality. Actually, the validity of astrology has been tested in a number of different studies. Any student wishing to pursue the topic as an individual project may be interested in some of the following books and articles: (Delaney & Woodyard, 1974; Illingworth & Syme, 1977; Hume & Goldstein, 1977; Jerome, 1977; Pellegrini, 1973; Shaffer, Nurco & Bonito, 1978; Snyder, 1974; Tyson, 1977).

In general, testing popular beliefs in class may be an effective method of addressing predispositions on the part of many students toward non-scientific thought. The astrology demonstration reported here has some attractive features: (a) The students themselves help participate in resolving the issue of a belief's validity. (b) The outcome of the test is not known in advance, generating an element of suspense. (c) This type of demonstration can give the class a first-hand look at objective research methods. (d) The final decision to accept or reject the belief is up to the students. After all, don't we tell them in our own classes that one study alone can never be considered conclusive?

## References

Chambertin, D. *Astro analysis.* New York: Lancer, 1970.

Cooper, M., & Weaver, A. *An astrological index to the world's famous people.* Garden City: Doubleday, 1975.

Delaney, J. G., & Woodyard, H. D. Effects of reading an astrological description on responding to a personality. *Psychological Reports,* 1974, *34,* 1214.

Gettings, F. *The book of the zodiac.* London: Triune, 1972

Goodman, L. *Sun signs.* New York: Taplinger, 1968.

Gutman, A. Misconceptions of psychology and performance in the introductory course. *Teaching of Psychology,* 1979, *6,* 159-161.

Hume, N., & Goldstein, G. Is there an association between astrological data and personality? *Journal of Clinical Psychology,* 1977, *33,* 711-713.

Illingworth, D. J., & Syme, G. J. Birthdate and feminity. *Journal of Social Psychology,* 1977, *103,* 153-154.

Jerome, L. E. *Astrology disproved.* Buffalo: Promethus, 1977.

King, F. *The cosmic influence.* New York: Doubleday, 1976.

Lee, D. *Dictionary of astrology.* New York: Coronet, 1968.

Leek, S. *How to become your own astrologer.* New York: Cowles, 1970.

Lynch, J. *Table book of astrology.* New York: Viking, 1969.

MacNiece, L. *Astrology.* New York: Doubleday, 1964.

Octopus Books (Eds.). *Understanding astrology.* London: Octopus, 1973.

Pellegrini, R. J. The astrological theory of personality: An unbiased test by a biased observer. *Journal of Psychology,* 1973, *85,* 21-28.

Roll, W. G. Science looks at the occult. *Psychic,* 1973, *4,* 50-55.

Sakoran, F., & Acker, L. *The astrologer's handbook.* New York: Harper & Row, 1973.

Shepard, D. L. *Psychology: The science of human behavior (Instructor's guide).* Chicago: Science Research Associates, 1977.

Silverman, B. J., & Whitmer, M. Astrological indications of personality. *Journal of Psychology,* 1974, *87,* 89-95.

Shaffer, J. W., Nurco, D. N., & Bonito, A. J. Is there a relationship between astrology and addiction? *Drug Forum,* 1977-78, *6,* 137-141.

Snyder, C. R. Why horoscopes are true: The effects of specificity on the acceptance of astrological interpretations. *Journal of Clinical Psychology,* 1974, *30,* 577-580.

Snyder, C. R., & Larson, G. R. A further look at student acceptance of general personality interpretations. *Journal of Consulting and Clinical Psychology,* 1972, *38,* 384-388.

Tyson, G. A. Astrology or season of birth: A "split-sphere" test. *Journal of Psychology,* 1977, *95,* 285-287.

Ulrich, R. E., Stachnik, T. J., & Stainton, N. R. Student acceptance of generalized personality interpretations. *Psychological Report,* 1963, *13,* 831-834.

Vaughan, E. Misconceptions about psychology among introductory psychology students. *Teaching of Psychology,* 1977, *4,* 138-141.

## Notes

1. Jensen, P. *Beliefs of today's college student: Where has science gone?* Unpublished manuscript, The Pennsylvania State University at Altoona, 1979.

2. There were four rating sheets excluded from the analysis, because responses were made too close together to draw a median line.

3. In fact, subjects tend to agree with any generalized personality descriptions (Snyder & Larson, 1972; Ulrich, Stachnik & Stainton 1963).

4. With smaller groups, under 30 students or so, splits may appear less even. However, I have never found a significantly above-chance proportion of applicable signs in any of my classes—even small sections. Yet interestingly, there are usually slightly more applicable signs than inapplicable ones. Note that the test does not rule out the possibility that students may already be influenced by prior knowledge of astrological claims. For instance, Pisces may have heard they were "sensitive" enough times to be influenced in their perception of themselves.

5. The normative materials, demonstration techniques, and research reported in this article were developed with the aid of funding from The Pennsylvania State University. The author gratefully acknowledges assistance and helpful advice from Kathy Geiger, Jean Emery, Carole Bookhamer, Patricia Datris, and Drs. Valerie Stratton and Paul Jensen.

# 17. ABNORMAL PSYCHOLOGY

## An Abnormal Psychology Community-Based Interview Assignment

Geoffry D. White
*California State University, Fullerton*

Activities and projects of various kinds have been suggested as important adjuncts to classroom teaching of Abnormal Psychology (e.g., Hansen, Hansen, D'Angelo & Smart, 1972; Price & Price, 1974). Instructors have struggled with new ways to make the subject matter interesting, involving, and more meaningful for their students. One hopes that students will make their own discoveries from an involving experience and that these will be remembered longer than material that is simply read.

The project described and evaluated in this report was offered as one of several options in the course. It involves students interviewing and observing the activities of individuals in the off-campus community who are concerned or involved with some topic in abnormal psychology (e.g., child abuse, transsexualism, drug abuse). The evaluation consists of anonymous student and interviewee ratings and comments concerning the project.

**Method.** At the beginning of the semester, students are informed that there are several term project options open to them. The interview project is presented as a way for students to combine two different kinds of sources of information on a topic of their choosing. First, they read from current books and journals in their area of interest. Secondly, students contact and interview an individual or group for a closer and more intimate look at the topic. The interviewees can either be mental health professionals or people who have or had any of the conditions described in the text (Davison & Neale, 1974). It is the students' responsibility to discover and meet with prospective interviewees. They are asked not to select someone they currently know, such as employers, coworkers, or family friends. An important part of the assignment is learning to be resourceful and assertive in interactions within the community. The process of locating interviewees, a brief literature review, and the interview report is submitted at the end of the course in a ten to twenty page paper.

Several steps are involved before the interview is conducted and observations made. First of all, students submit a one page proposal early in the semester which identifies their topic, their reasons for selecting it, how they plan to meet interviewees, and five literature references which must have been published after 1970. The latter requirement helps guarantee that current literature and theories are being explored and that students become familiar with publications in major psychology journals. Students are encouraged to consult with the instructor and text for suggested sources of information.

This first step serves initial screening purposes. For example, students who select sensitive topics are asked to discuss them personally with the instructor. Projects which are too large, and are therefore unlikely to be covered adequately in an interview based paper, are given suggestions for narrowing their focus. Students are also given ideas and leads for finding someone interesting to interview.

The second step is that after the topic is approved students submit a five page paper with abstracts and discussion of at least ten journal articles and/or books related to the topic. Students can elect to make alterations in their proposal at this time. Also, at this time a one page outline of questions and issues to be discussed with the interviewee is attached to the review. This is returned with comments and suggestions from the instructor (e.g., students typically ask too many "closed-ended" questions requiring only a yes or no response). At this point students arrange an appointment with potential interviewees.

Finally, students are asked to submit the name, address, and phone number of the individuals they interview. They are also asked for at least a one page verbatim transcript of their interaction with the interviewee. Students are encouraged to audiotape their interview, if possible, and to erase the tape after submitting the final paper.

It is explained that the instructor may question the interviewees for further information, to arrange to have them as guest speakers, or to clarify some aspect of the interview. In some ways, this feature may have served to encourage accurate and honest reporting by students since it operates as a spot check procedure.

**Subjects.** Twenty-three out of 35 students taking Abnormal Psychology in the Fall 1976 semester selected and completed the interview project option. The remaining students in the course contracted for a variety of other term project options. Of the 23 students, 11 were Psychology majors. The remaining 12 were divided among other Humanities majors with a few students from Business and the Physical Sciences. This mix is fairly representative of the balance of psychology to non-psychology majors who take this course.

Twenty of the 23 (87%) interviewees responded by completing and returning the evaluation form mailed to them at the end of the semester. Only one of the respondents failed to include his or her name even though the form indicated that this was optional.

There were 11 male and eight female respondents. With the exception of two transsexuals, all respondents were providers of mental health services. The highest academic degrees obtained included: two MDs, three PhDs, seven Masters-level professionals, two BA degreed individuals, and five with two-year college degrees. The average age of the respondents was almost 41 years, with a range from 27 to 60 years.

**Interview Topics.** Topics concerned with children were the most numerous in this study, a result that is highly consistent over the four semesters that this project option has been used. Some of these topics included: hyperactivity, infantile autism, child abuse, the negative effects of divorce and of adoptions, and play therapy. Concern with adult topics usually ranks second among undergraduate students, which held up this semester as well. Topics here were: drug abuse, transsexualism, pedophilia, and the abuse of the aged in institutional settings.

It should be noted that over the last few years there has yet to be an instance where a student proposed to interview someone who was involved in a previous semester's projects. This may not be surprising considering that the Southern California area surrounding the instructor's university contains millions of people and hundreds of mental health facilities.

**Results.** The items and mean ratings for the students' evaluation of the assignment are presented in Table 1 along

imposition on their time. They perceived the student interviewers as having prepared for the interview and very interested in the topic. On the other hand the interviewees reported that they themselves did not learn too much from the experience, which might have been expected.

Some representative comments made by several interviewees are the following:

"... I would be glad to be the subject of an interview at any time. I think it's one of the best possible ways for students to learn 'straight from the horse's mouth'." "The student who interviewed me was very interested, polite, and seemed better prepared than some professionals have been who've interviewed me in the past." "A pleasant experience and a good assignment. Students find out that professionals don't know all the answers nor do they "win" all cases!"

**Discussion.** The small sample of data suggests that the interview project described in this paper was generally a successful experience as evaluated by students and their interview subjects. The discussion to follow focuses on important factors to be considered in assigning this or

Table 1
Evaluations of the Interview Project

| Rating | | |
|---|---|---|
| Mean | Range | Item |
| | | **By Students** |
| 5.8 | 4 - 7 | 1. Compared to other term projects, how much time was devoted to this one? |
| 6.3 | 5 - 7 | 2. Compared to other term projects, how much was learned from this one? |
| 5.6 | 3 - 7 | 3. Compared to other term projects, how much did you enjoy this one? |
| 5.6 | 4 - 6 | 4. To what extent do you think that other courses could benefit from this type of project? |
| 4.3 | 1 - 7 | 5. How difficult did you find the role of interviewer? |
| 5.6 | 3 - 7 | 6. How enjoyable did you find the role of interviewer? |
| 3.6 | 1 - 7 | 7. How much difficulty did you have locating an interviewee? |
| 5.3 | 4 - 7 | 8. How helpful was the interviewee in providing you with desired information? |
| 6.2 | 5 - 7 | 9. Did the interviewee seem interested in talking to you? |
| | | **By Interviewee** |
| 5.3 | 4 - 7 | 1. How prepared was the interviewer? |
| 5.8 | 3 - 7 | 2. How much did you enjoy being interviewed? |
| 5.7 | 4 - 7 | 3. What kind of an impression did the interviewer make on you? |
| 6.3 | 5 - 7 | 4. Did the interviewer seem interested in the topic? |
| 3.2 | 1 - 7 | 5. How much did you learn from the interview? |
| 5.7 | 4 - 7 | 6. Would you be willing to participate in another interview like this in the future? |
| 3.1 | 1 - 7 | 7. To what extent was the interview an imposition on your time? |

| Rating scale: | 1 | 2 | 3 | 4 | 5 | 6 | 7 |
|---|---|---|---|---|---|---|---|
| | very poor/ very little | | | adequate/ average | | | very good/ very much |

with the rating scale. A seven point rating scale was employed as shown in the Table. Only points 1, 4, and 7 had labels and respondents were asked to evaluate the question or item by circling the appropriate numerical rating. As can be seen from these results, students felt that they had learned quite a bit compared to term projects in other courses. They enjoyed it, thought other courses could benefit from a similar assignment, but that it required more work than other projects. They thought the interviewees were interested in talking to them.

The items and mean ratings for the evaluations obtained from the interviewees are presented in the lower part of Table 1. The results indicate that the interviewees generally enjoyed being interviewed, would be happy to repeat the experience, and did not particularly find the interview an

similar projects and several side benefits which occurred.

The preparation required by students for the current project was greater than in previous semesters. For example, students were required to submit a five page literature review and an interview outline, both of which were edited and critiqued by the instructor. These assignments were aimed at producing students who were better organized and prepared to conduct the interview. It is suspected that lower ratings would have been obtained had the current evaluation procedures been carried out on previous semesters' projects. Indeed, in those cases where the interviewee commented that the student was not very well organized, the quality of the student's final papers was of lower overall quality than students receiving higher ratings on "preparation."

Instructors who plan to use these procedures should be

prepared to spend more time than they may currently devote to reading and grading traditional projects and papers. In addition to reading the final papers, the instructor must screen the initial one-page proposals and then the five-page reviews and interview outline. Finally, personal interviews must be made with those students selecting sensitive or difficult topic areas.

Greater time is also required for projects which raise certain ethical and logistical difficulties. That is, while innovative projects have greater possibilities they also have greater risks. Such projects require additional supervision by the instructor compared to the traditional library research review paper. Issues of confidentiality, invasion of privacy, being exposed to individuals with intense feelings about a particular project, and other potential hazards must be considered and discussed with students. In short, innovations in teaching, as in any area of psychology (e.g., clinical practice and testing), must be taken seriously for maximum benefit and minimum negative effects. The project described here was approved by the department's human subjects review committee. It is recommended that this procedure be used when nontraditional projects involve unsupervised students who have interviews with individuals who are not specifically provided by or known to the instructor.

It has been suggested that students might benefit from interviewing individuals whose socioeconomic status is considerably lower than that in the present sample. This experience would provide students with exposure to individuals who are not traditionally thought of as providing

mental health services. For example, psychiatric technicians in hospital settings, members of minority groups hired as paraprofessionals in public mental health clinics, and low socioeconomic status volunteer workers in various community psychology programs would all be available for interviews.

The additional time and energy required of the instructor was more than made up by several positive side effects of the project. It is gratifying to introduce students to a new form of term project which they enjoy and where learning occurs. In addition, several students have found employment as a result of the interview and observation of the interviewee's agency and activities.

Another tangible result is that the instructor has become much more familiar with the local community and its mental health resources. This information has been used to obtain interesting guest speakers for Abnormal Psychology and other courses. Knowledge about the variety of mental health services has also been helpful in directing graduate students in an applied psychology training program to potential fieldwork settings.

## References

Hansen, P., Hansen, S., D'Angelo, B., & Smart, K. *Instructor's Resource Book for Coleman, Abnormal Psychology and Modern Life*. Glenview, IL: Scott, Foresman, 1972.

Price, G. H., & Price, K. P. *Instructor's Manual and Resource Book for Davison & Neale, Abnormal Psychology: An Experimental Clinical Approach*. New York: Wiley, 1974.

---

# Feeling Abnormal: Simulation of Deviancy in Abnormal and Exceptionality Courses

Charles D. Fernald
*University of North Carolina at Charlotte*

Most courses and text books on abnormal psychology and psychology of exceptional children discuss research on the social and personal consequences of classifying and labeling individuals as abnormal, disturbed or exceptional. However, the mere reporting of research findings may have little personal impact upon students. This is unfortunate because many of these students will later become teachers and mental health paraprofessionals who will be involved in screening, referring and evaluating individuals, perhaps without careful consideration of the consequences of classifying people as deviant. I have incorporated an experiential activity into my abnormal and exceptional child courses to give students a personal glimpse of what it's like to be considered abnormal or exceptional. The rational for including this activity is that if students personally experience being judged abnormal, they will more likely (a) remember relevant research literature better; (b) become sensitized to the feelings of individuals who are classified as deviant; (c) use care and caution in classifying as abnormal, individuals they will later work with. Students who have participated in this procedure generally report that it did make them feel

deviant and that it was a very worthwhile activity. The procedure is basically a replication of the study of the effects of experimentally induced deviancy by Freedman and Doob (1968) adapted for classroom use.

Because this procedure can induce mental stress and because deception is involved, an instructor should employ the technique only after careful consideration of the ethical issues involved. Although most students have felt that I was unduly concerned about possible negative side effects, students could become angered at being deceived or become distressed at being told they are poorly adjusted. Although the procedure is an instructional, not research technique, it is useful to review the APA Ethical Principles on Research (APA, 1973) especially the sections on mental stress, deception and obtaining informed consent. Consultation with colleagues, the department chairperson or an ethics committee would also be wise. When a decision is made to use this technique, care must be taken, as described below, to insure that participation is voluntary, to warn students before they begin that learning the results of the personality test may be stressful, to minimize stress by quickly revealing the deception, and to thoroughly debrief students so they understand the nature and rationale for the deception.

**Method.** 1. Administer a "personality test" to students. During a class period early in the semester students are given test booklets called "Haley Brief Personal Adjustment Inventory," to complete on computer scored answer sheets. (This Inventory was constructed by selecting 50 items from several published personality tests.) Students are told that participation is entirely voluntary and that the purpose of the test is to expose them to personality testing similar to what will be discussed later in the course. They are told that test scores will be returned and they may enter their name or a private identification number to guarantee confidentiality of results. They are told that receiving results can be mentally stressful and for that reason they should feel free not to participate. It is emphasized that there are no penalties for not participating.

2. Low adjustment scores are recorded on each individual student feedback sheet. Each student's name or i.d. number is copied onto an individual test results form. A very low adjustment score is assigned to each sheet without regard to actual responses on the Inventory. If a control group is used, low and average scores can be randomly assigned to the two groups.

3. Prepare bogus summary of class results showing most students obtained good adjustment scores. A frequency distribution supposedly showing class test results is prepared and duplicated. The horizontal axis of the graph is labeled "Poor Prognosis" at the low end and "Excellent Prognosis" under the high scores. Two scores are located at the extreme low end, clearly away from the other scores which are rather normally distributed and clustered around the central, "good adjustment" portion of the graph.

4. Distribute bogus graph to class members and explain class results. Just before lecture material relevant to the effects of classification and labeling is discussed, I return the "results" of the test. I start by discussing the personality inventory to make the results appear credible. For example, I emphasize that the Haley Inventory is a well constructed psychometric device, highly reliable and empirically validated. I also note that the test measures primarily long term personal adjustment (i.e., it has good predictive validity) so that even if the present test score indicates good adjustment, the student may currently be experiencing temporary stress, and conversely, the student may perceive himself well adjusted now, but receive a poor score, since the test shows eventual, not present status. The graph supposedly showing class results is then distributed and explained in detail, emphasizing that a few students received very poor scores but most were normal.

5. Return individual "adjustment scores" to students. Individual forms reporting their "scores" are returned to students after "computer analysis." They are told not to reveal scores to other students in order to "maintain confidentiality." Students are told how to locate their scores on the class distribution. There are usually questions about the interpretation of very low scores and the explanation of poor prognosis is repeated along with statement about the empirical validity of the test.

6. Solicit reaction to adjustment scores and discuss. I have usually distributed a questionnaire concerning student responses to receiving poor scores, to determine whether the procedure induced a feeling of deviancy and then the nature of responses to this feeling. Student reactions are also discussed in class. If control, "good score" subjects are also included, the reactions of the two groups can be compared, in a class discussion, as well as quantitatively from questionnaire results.

7. Debrief the students. After discussion and data collection, the deception is disclosed and much effort is spent in thoroughly debriefing the students. The procedure and rationale is explained in detail and a written debriefing explanation is also distributed. Students are questioned to insure they understand the deception. There will also be class discussion relating their personal reactions to induced deviancy with findings in the literature. During the subsequent class period, the debriefing information is repeated and students are again questioned to clarify any misconceptions.

**Results.** Data were collected from 83 students during three recent semesters of my course, Psychology of Exceptional Children, for advanced psychology undergraduates and master's level graduate students in education. Students in each class were randomly assigned either a poor adjustment score (N = 50) or a good adjustment score (N = 33). Subjects responded to the seven items of a 5-point, Likert-type questionnaire concerning their reactions upon learning their adjustment scores.

Analysis of variance comparing total questionnaire scores revealed that the two groups responded with significant differences in the predicted direction, $F(1, 44) = 7.61, p < .008$. Significant differences appeared in a number of individual questions as well. The poor adjustment score subjects indicated they had more doubts about their normality, $F(1, 49) = 9.176, p < .004$, felt the test was less valid, $F(1, 81) = 8.011, p < .006$, and felt more angry and hostile about the test results, $F(1, 49) = 6.45, p < .01$, than did control subjects. These results are generally consistent with the research literature. There were no significant differences on other questions concerning desire to change aspects of oneself, or willingness to disclose results to class members.

Informal feedback from students has indicated that most were glad they had participated, most felt it had a powerful effect upon them and felt it sensitized them to the problems of people who are classified as deviant.

### References

American Psychological Association. *Ethical principles in the conduct of research with human participants*. Washington, DC: Author, 1973.

Freedman, J. L., & Doob, A. N. *Deviancy: The psychology of being different*. New York: Academic Press, 1968.

# The Myth of Mental Illness Game: Sick Is Just a Four Letter Word

**James M. Gardner**
*University of Queensland*

Though the medical model remains a potent force, in recent years alternative conceptions of human behavior have emerged. In regard to the issue of institutionalization, the major alternative conceptions (e.g., Szasz, Goffman, Scheff, Braginsky, Blatt) postulate that (a) there is no such thing as mental illness, and (b) the label "mentally ill" and the use of involuntary institutionalization are best viewed as socioeconomic/political instruments designed to repress various groups. Although this model gains increasing attention within the field, the general public remains shackled to the belief that "mental illness" is an illness like any other.

In the course of research on the attitudes of high school students, I developed an exercise which has proven very useful in illustrating the "myth of mental illness" to the students. The exercise takes place during the third of six 40 minute sessions (an expanded version of 10 sessions at the college level is now being developed). In the first session the students are asked to name every possible synonym for mental illness. Students who come up with unusual names are asked to provide the etiology of the term.

In the second session the class is divided into small groups (4-5 each) and half are given the assignment of defining mental illness (without using any of the synonyms used in the first session), and the other half try to define mentally healthy (without recourse to mental illness or any synonym). Group leaders are elected and then report back their definitions, and the rest of the session is spent pointing up the difficulties (impossibilities) in satisfactorily defining either term.

In the third session, the Mental Illness Game (MIG) is introduced, followed in subsequent sessions by a 30-minute videotape dramatization of Szasz's (1970) *The Manufacture of Madness,* then a review of local conditions in psychiatric institutions, and the final session is a 40-minute meeting with ex-inmates of institutions. Evaluation takes place pre- and post-course.

To begin the MIG, six volunteers are selected and along with the author, they leave the room. Once outside they randomly choose role identifications from a group of six 3 x 5 in. index cards. The roles are:

1. An escaped convict, previously convicted of murder.
2. A successful business executive whose spouse has just announced the existence of a love affair, whose child is in the hospital, and whose car just broke down this morning.
3. An unemployed person married with two children, who desperately needs a job, and is on the way to an interview.
4. A person on the way to a sale.
5. A lonely person, who has few friends, is depressed, became bored watching TV, and is going somewhere just to have "something to do."
6. The sixth card reads as follows:

"You are waiting at the bus stop for the Valley bus. Your role is to try to engage each of the waiting passengers in conversation so that the class can observe how they act. Some of the helpful questions you might use are: Is this the bus to the Valley? Do you have the proper time? Does the bus usually run late? Do you have change for a dollar? etc."

While each student volunteer studies the role chosen, the class is instructed to watch and observe the behavior of each person. After sufficient time to study the roles, the catalyst student (sixth card) comes back to the classroom, followed one-by-one by each of the others (the identity of each student is unknown to everyone). Each student is given about one minute of interaction with the catalyst, with complete freedom to interpret the role in their own way. The entire skit takes approximately 10 minutes.

Once the skit is completed, each of the six cards is collected, the actors return to their seats, and the class is then informed of the purpose of the skit. Then the names of each student-actor are placed on the board in the left hand column of a seven by seven table and the class is invited to vote on which role they think each student played (the catalyst is listed last). The roles are listed sequentially (not simultaneously) at the top of each column and the class is polled to determine how many believe each participant could have played that role, then the next role is considered, and so on. The roles are presented in the order described earlier, except that the non-existent role "a mentally ill person" is inserted as the fourth role voted upon.

Once the voting is completed, the total picture is examined. The first step is to inspect the data across participants to see which students appeared to play several roles and which were identified with only one role. Next, we look at the roles to see which ones were clearly identified or which appeared to be played by many actors. Then, we ask the actors to inform us which role they played, and we discuss the accuracy of the decisions. When the last actor (the catalyst) describes his/her role, I note that I have "tricked" the class—i.e., the catalyst played him/her self, and therefore, does not appear in the six listed roles. We then focus on the fourth column headed "mentally ill" and count up the total number of responses here, and compare this with the other column totals (usually it is one of the highest totals). We note how easy it is for people to be labelled "mentally ill" even when there is no mental illness.

The high school course has been evaluated twice, each time with groups of similar students, and in each case it has been compared with a traditional medical model course which emphasized diagnostic nosology, assessment of psychiatric disorders, and methods of treatment and cure. Two measures were used to assess the impact of the different approaches: a composite 7-point opinion survey including items from established inventories (Altrocchi & Eisdorfer, 1961; Gilbert & Levinson, 1957; Rabkin, 1972; Cohen & Struening, 1962), and a request for volunteers to spend one-half day per week working with inmates of similar age and sex.

Though both courses resulted in reduced authoritarianism, the medical model course increased students' feelings that causal determinants of problems in living were rooted in childhood, whereas the MIG-centered course resulted in increased emphasis on psychosocial influences and in social tolerance. Moreover, the interaction with ex-inmates had no impact at all upon students completing the medical course, but students in the MIG-centered course continued to develop changes in attitudes (e.g., decreased authoritarianism, increased psychosocial orientation). The greatest difference between the two courses occurred in the number of volunteers: only 64% of the students from the medical courses were willing to spend one-half day per week with inmates, whereas 94% of the MIG students volunteered.

Theoretical advances in recent years have offered a viable alternative to the traditional medical model explanation of problems of living. Despite this fact, practical applications have lagged behind, particularly in the area of teaching. The MIG-centered course described here offers one alternative teaching approach which appears not only to convey the theoretical implications, but is superior in some respects to the traditional medical orientation.

## References

Altrocchi, J., & Eisdorfer, C. Changes in attitudes towards mental illness. *Mental Hygiene,* 1961, *45,* 563-570.

Cohen J., & Struening, E. L. Opinions about mental illness in the personnel of two large mental hospitals. *Journal of Abnormal and Social Psychology,* 1962, *64,* 349-360.

Gilbert, D. C., & Levinson, D. J. "Custodialism" and "humanism" in staff ideology. In M. Greenblatt, D. J. Levinson, & R. H. Williams (Eds.). *The patient and the mental hospital.* Glencoe, Ill.: Free Press, 1957.

Rabkin, J. S. Opinions about mental illness: A review of the literature. *Psychological Bulletin,* 1972, **77,** 153-171.

Szasz, T. *The manufacture of madness.* New York: Harper & Row, 1970.

## Note

1. The evaluation components in this report were completed as part of an honours thesis by Mrs. C. Schultz.

# The Use of Role-Playing in a Classroom Demonstration of Client-Centered Therapy

William R. Balch
*Pennslvania State University*

Of the dozen or more main topics covered in the typical course in introductory psychology, psychotherapy presents a unique problem for the instructor. On one hand, it is an area in which most students who enter the course seem particularly interested. On the other, the topic is essentially a clinical one. Therefore, it is difficult to convey the various therapeutic techniques and processes through textbooks or conventional classroom instruction. Many books do include sample dialogues between therapist and client (e.g., Wortman & Loftus, 1981; Morris, 1982; Smith, Sarason & Sarason, 1982). Moreover, there are a number of films which depict different types of therapy. However, I have found that putting on a live demonstration involving the students themselves is the most effective teaching tool in terms of the enthusiasm and class participation it generates.

In this demonstration four student volunteers play roles in front of the class, much in the manner of improvisatory theatre. Client-centered therapy was chosen as the method to be illustrated, because its non-directive approach is well-suited for role-playing. One student plays the role of Pat, who is faced with several conflicts. Three other students play Pat's father, mother, and best friend. Each person discusses Pat's problems with Pat in a series of improvised two-way dialogues. In particular, each offers some directive advice to Pat, who remains confused and indecisive. Finally, a non-directive therapist talks to Pat using client-centered techniques (Rogers, 1965) to help clarify Pat's own feelings. This therapist can be played by the instructor. However, a counseling or clinical psychologist on the instructor's campus is a particularly ideal person to play the role.

A day or two before the demonstration, I recruit volunteers; and pass out a hand-out explaining the situation and roles to be enacted by the participants. I shall present the essential content of the scenario here in brief form.

*Pat* may be male or female. (From here on in "he" will be used in the general sense, meaning he or she). He is enrolled in a tough pre-medical program, but his grades are beginning to drop sharply. No longer sure he wants to be a doctor, Pat is considering acting on his long-standing interest in art and applying to a nearby school of art and design. The deadline for applications is drawing near. To add to his troubles, Pat has been having a problem with his girlfriend (or her boyfriend), *Lee.* Because Lee feels that Pat is selfishly preoccupied with his own concerns, she is threatening to break off with him unless he spends more time with her. Note that Lee serves as an off-stage presence, and does not appear as a role-player.

*Pat's father* is a struggling insurance salesman, who

thinks that he could have been a doctor himself if he had applied himself a little more in school. He feels that Pat could make it through the pre-med program if he simply pulled himself together and worked a bit harder. Opposed to Pat's idea of going to art school, Pat's father is convinced that his son could be a fine doctor.

*Pat's mother* is a housewife who would also like to see him become a doctor. However, she may be a little more sympathetic than her husband to Pat's interest in art. She herself was told by her high school English teacher that she had a flair for writing. But rather than develop it, she married Pat's father at age 18. Her main concern about Pat is that she fears Lee will pressure him into an early marriage; the same mistake she feels she made.

*Pat's best friend* Jack (or Jackie) dropped out of high school, and is now working as a gas station attendant (or stock clerk, waiter, etc.). He is fed up with the middle-class values of education, hard work and success. According to Jack, either medical or art school would be equally a waste of time for Pat. Pat should simply take any old job, make enough to live on and get out of the rat race.

*Pat's therapist* uses client-centered techniques (unconditional positive regard, non-directiveness, clarification of feeling, restatement of content, etc.) to help Pat see what his *own* thoughts are. He avoids telling Pat what to do, even though Pat hopes the therapist has some answers for him.

During the demonstration, *the instructor* serves as more or less a stage manager. This function includes: introducing Pat; then ushering in and out, in turn, the father, mother, best friend and therapist; and providing any commentary deemed appropriate. Afterwards, the instructor should moderate an interactive discussion between the participants in the demonstration and the rest of the class.

To date, I have not quantitatively evaluated this demonstration. However, I believe that instructors who try it will find it has some benefits not always shared by the traditional methods of text, film or lecture. First, the role-playing scenario described above has been designed to be under-

standable and fairly familiar to college freshmen. Secondly, the student participants usually play their roles spontaneously, plausibly and creatively. In some classes, they even appear to become quite emotionally involved: particularly in the case of Pat's role. This feature of the demonstration raises the ethical problem of potential psychological risk. Though I've seen no evidence that any harmful aftereffects occur, the risk may be dealt with by a common sense screening of volunteers; and, by encouraging the participants to discuss afterwards their feelings during the demonstration. On the distinctly positive side, the involvement of the participants in their roles definitely seems to influence the rest of the class. Thus, the audience and role-players alike experience first-hand some of the emotional dynamics of a plausible therapy situation.

One particularly interesting set of phenomena I have noticed relates to behavioral changes in the student playing Pat. When talking to the client-centered therapist, Pat often speaks more softly and at a lower pitch than when talking to the more "directive" players. Usually Pat also engages in more eye contact with the therapist. Generally he or she gives the impression of being much more relaxed. This potentially measurable effect could serve as a discussion ice-breaker, or perhaps as the basis of some student projects.

## References

Morris, C. G. *Psychology: An introduction* (4th ed). Englewood Cliffs, NJ: Prentice-Hall, 1982.

Rogers, C. R. *Client-centered therapy.* Boston: Houghton Mifflin, 1965.

Smith, R. E., Sarason, I. G., & Sarason, B. R. *Psychology: The frontiers of behavior.* New York: Harper and Row, 1982.

Wortman, C. B., & Loftus, E. F. *Psychology,* New York: Knopf, 1981.

## Note

1. The author wishes to thank Dr. Charles Kormanski, who has played the role of therapist in many demonstrations put on in my classes.

# Teaching Abnormal Psychology Concepts Using Popular Song Lyrics

Charles R. Potkay
*Western Illinois University*

Psychology instructors have adopted a variety of popular media as supplemental teaching techniques. Among those previously reported in this journal have been "psychological thriller" books, magazines, popular films, television commercials, newspaper features and radio programming. Instructors of abnormal psychology also have reported using popular films and literature excerpts.

Music represents an additional popular culture media with classroom advantages. It has a theoretical basis in educational literature on open classrooms, aimed at enhancing student motivation and personal involvement in the learning process (Silberman, Allender, & Yanoff, 1972). Song lyrics may be used to (a) highlight the importance of a concept; (b) provide a concrete illustration of the concept; (c) demonstrate the relevance of an idea in a contemporary context; (d) increase general awareness of psychological aspects of everyday media; (e) stimulate classroom discussion; (f) encourage personal involvement by students, who also may find new songs on their own; (g) add an alternative to film, television and print media for use in the classroom; and, (h) offer a novel, entertaining stimulus with which to break fatigue or monotony during lengthy class sessions.

Computer searches of three literature bases, PsycINFO, ERIC and RILM failed to identify any uses of popular, folk, rock, musical comedy or opera music genre as psychology course supplements at the college level. However applications of music were reported in other fields (Cooper, 1973; Schiff & Frances, 1974; Freudiger & Almquist, 1978).

The author's interest in linking popular music and abnormal psychology was sparked by *The Bestiary of Flanders and Swann*. This album contained a song about "an introverted, elephocentric, hypochondriac" elephant who decided to feign amnesia and remain in a nursing home to avoid the labors of dutiful life. Textbook concepts came readily to mind: psychiatric classification, secondary gain, self-labelling, malingering and iatragenic treatment effects. A Joni Mitchell song, *Twisted*, illustrated all six of Scott's research definitions of mental illness. In *Glory, Glory Psychotherapy*, Melanie's "eyes have seen the glory of the theories of Freud." An Alan Parsons Project album, *I Robot*, offered lyrics relevant to schizophrenia, including cognitive slippage, referential ideas and paranoid thinking. An entire album, *The Wiz*, provided story-line continuity to help students understand Gestalt therapy concepts of dream interpretation, projection, and maturation in a storm-and-stress adolescent (Potkay, 1979).

In my abnormal psychology class, following presentation of lecture material, students listened to a song on a portable stereo cassette tape player. Students then were asked to identify ways in which the lyrics illustrated lecture or textbook ideas. A handout directed students to write down the song title, main psychology concept illustrated, brief supporting rationale from the lyrics and any personal reactions or comments. The handout also contained two 7-point rating scales anchored by the labels "Definitely No" (0) and "Definitely Yes" (6), for evaluation purposes: "This song has aided my understanding or learning of the psychology concept" and "This song should be used in future classes." It has been helpful to display lyrics visually, by handout or overhead projector, to aid comprehension and recall of lyrics.

During the 1980 spring semester, 13 lyrics were played and evaluated in each of two upper division abnormal psychology sections. A daytime section met twice weekly and an evening section met once weekly. End-of-course student ratings of the songs for "Aided my understanding or learning" and "Should be used in future classes" averaged 4.63 (SD = 1.37) and 4.97 (SD = 1.06), respectively. The "Suggested frequency of songs per week" averaged 1.52 (SD = .85). Overall reactions to the use of popular songs as a teaching technique averaged 4.46 (SD = 1.26), statistically equivalent to overall reactions to use of films as a teaching technique in all past psychology courses (M = 4.97, SD = 1.17). No significant differences in ratings were observed between sections. Results were conservative, in that all omitted ratings were systematically assigned the lowest scale value (0).

In sum, student ratings supported continued use of popular music lyrics as a supplemental teaching technique. Future use of popular songs in my own courses will involve the playing of 8-10 preselected songs per semester, adding a more contemporary balance to the selections, and encouraging students to bring personal selections of their own into the classroom.

## References

Cooper, B. L. Social change, popular music, and the teacher. *Social Education*, 1973, 37, 776-781.

Freudiger, P., & Almquist, E. M. Male and female roles in the lyrics of three genres of contemporary music. *Sex Roles*, 1978, 4, 51-65.

Schiff, M., & Frances, A. Popular Music: A training catalyst. *Journal of Music Therapy*, 1974, 11, 33-40.

Silberman, M. L., Allender, J. S., & Yanoff, J. M. (Eds.). *The psychology of open teaching and learning: An inquiry approach.* Boston: Little, Brown, 1972.

## Note

1. Potkay, C. R. "The Wiz": A Gestalt therapy "interpretation." Paper presented at the 87th Annual Convention of the American Psychological Association, New York, 1979.

# 18. SOCIAL PSYCHOLOGY

## The Risky Shift Is a Sure Bet

George R. Goethals
and Amy P. Demorest
*Williams College*

For nearly twenty years students of social psychology have been interested in the phenomenon known as the risky shift. These students include both social psychologists themselves, who are still exploring and debating the causes of the shift (cf. Sanders & Baron, 1977; Burnstein & Vinokur, 1977), and undergraduates in social psychology courses who are learning about fundamental interpersonal processes. The risky shift, it will be recalled, is the phenomenon whereby individuals in a group make decisions which are riskier than the ones they make individually. It was discovered by James Stoner (1961) who showed specifically that when subjects in a group are asked to make a unanimous decision on an issue involving risk, their decision is riskier than the average of the decisions they had made individually at an earlier time. This paper reports the results of a series of attempts over eight years to demonstrate the risky shift in social psychology classes as a way to elicit student involvement and interest in the course. These attempts have been highly successful.

Procedure.    Risky shift demonstrations were attempted in eight classes varying in size from 28 to 68. In all but one case, these classes were composed of male and female undergraduates at Williams College. In the other case the students were enrolled in an adult education class and they represented men and women in the Williamstown area of various ages, occupations, and educational levels.

The ten items from Kogan and Wallach's (1964) Choice Dilemma Questionnaire II (CDQ) which had been found to reliably produce shifts to risk (Items 1-4 and 6-11) were used in the demonstrations. Each item describes a situation in which two alternative courses of action are available to an individual who must choose between them. One of the alternatives has a more desirable outcome than the other but it is also less likely to be successful. For example, in one choice dilemma the captain of a football team must choose between a play that would almost certainly work and produce a tie for his team and another play that is less likely to be successful but would produce a victory. For each dilemma subjects must choose the minimum odds of success they would demand before recommending that the risky course of action be taken. They must choose between probabilities of 1, 3, 5, 7, and 9 out of ten or indicate that they would not select

the risky course of action under any circumstances (scored as 11). The lower the minimum odds of success a person is willing to accept before attempting the risky course of action, the more risk that person is taking.

The demonstration is conducted as follows: At the end of the first meeting of the class students are asked to complete the ten CDQ items and are then dismissed. When they arrive for the next meeting they are divided into small groups and each group is given one CDQ item to discuss, and is asked to make a recommendation for that item. Typically, students are assigned to groups alphabetically to facilitate keeping track of which students are in what groups and to ensure some mix of students. In most cases there have been ten groups, each one discussing one of the ten problems, and group size has ranged from three to seven members. Our experience has been that group size makes little difference in producing the shift.

Following the usual instructions, the groups are asked to discuss the dilemma until they have reached a unanimous decision as to what odds to recommend to the person in the vignette. While the students are discussing the CDQ problems, the instructor calculates the average of the individuals' scores in each group for the item the group is working on. If any group finishes early they can be given another problem to discuss. Most groups can complete the task easily in fifteen minutes, and any group which cannot make a unanimous decision in that time is asked to decide by majority vote. After all groups have turned in their decision, the following date for each of the ten items are put on the blackboard: First, the overall class average for the item; second, the mean score of the individuals in the group discussing that item; and, finally, the group decision. Sometimes more than one group will have discussed a given problem and the data for both groups are recorded. Once these data are recorded the students in the class are asked to discuss them.

Results.    The data for the first year's demonstration (1970) were not recorded. It was successful, however, so that plans were made to keep data thereafter. There were no significant differences between the results for undergraduates and adults, so the data for both groups were considered together. Table 1 presents the mean of the individual group members' individual scores and their group decision for each problem in the demonstrations conducted from 1971 to 1977. Shifts to risk or caution are indicated according to the following criterion: A group was considered to have shifted to risk or caution if its decision was riskier or more cautious than the closest available compromise position. Thus, for example, a

# Table 1
## Results of Risky Shift Demonstrations, 1971-1977

| Year | Problem Number | | | | | | | | | |
|------|------|------|------|------|------|------|------|------|------|------|
|      | 1 | 2 | 3 | 4 | 6 | 7 | 8 | 9 | 10 | 11 |
| 1971 | 5.00-5 | 5.00-7** | 6.00-7** | 5.00-3* | 5.00-1* | 5.00-3* | 6.20-5* | 5.00-5 | -- | 5.50-3* |
| 1972 | 5.40-5 | 6.20-5* | -- | 3.80-1* | 5.40-5 | 4.20-3* | 5.00-3* | 5.80-5 | 5.00-5 | 5.00-3* |
| 1973¹ | 4.33-3* | 5.00-7** | 9.00-7* | -- | 3.00-1* | 7.28-5* | -- | -- | 7.28-7 | 5.00-3* |
| 1974 | 5.00-5 | 5.00-5 | 6.00-3* | 4.00-5** | 5.40-5 | 3.00-2* | 7.00-7 | 8.00-5* | 6.00-5* | 3.50-1* |
| 1975 | 4.50-4 | 7.00-7 | 8.60-3* | 4.00-3* | 7.50-7 | 2.50-3 | 6.20-5* | 6.20-5* | 4.00-3* | 3.50-3 |
| 1976 | 7.00-7 | 8.50-9 | 5.00-5 | 5.33-3*<br>2.60-1* | 4.67-3* | 4.33-2*<br>4.33-3* | 7.00-5* | 5.33-7** | 5.00-3* | 4.70-3* |
| 1977 | 4.00-3* | 9.00-7*<br>9.00-7* | 6.33-7 | 3.33-3 | 5.00-1*<br>8.33-7* | 6.33-3*<br>4.00-1* | 5.67-5<br>7.00-7 | 7.33-5* | 5.00-5 | 4.20-3* |

¹Adult Education class.
*Risky shift
**Cautious shift
First values given are the means of the individuals; second values are group decisions.

group whose average individual score was 5.8 was not considered to have shifted to risk if the group decision was 5 since 5 is the compromise choice closest to 5.8. However, if a group's average score was half-way between two choices it was considered to have shifted to caution if it chose the higher available choice and to have shifted to risk if it chose the lower available score. Thus a group whose average individual score was 6 was considered to have shown a risky shift if it chose 5 or below and a cautious shift if it chose 7 or above.

Using this criterion for shifts, among the total of 70 group decisions there were 41 shifts to risk (59%), 24 compromise or no-shift decisions (34%), and five shifts to caution (7%). It can be seen that the items which most reliably produced the shift in these demonstrations were number 7 (the chess player deciding whether to make a daring move), number 11 (the research physicist deciding between a challenging project and a more certain but less important one), and number 4 (the football captain deciding whether to attempt a risky play). The items least reliably producing a risky shift are numbers 1 and 2 (the engineer who could become an executive in a new firm and the accountant deciding on a heart operation).

Discussion.   The data above show that the shift to risk is a robust social psychological phenomenon that can be reliably demonstrated in a classroom setting. The students themselves are quick to recognize that it has occurred. When they are asked to comment on their own data on the board, several invariably point out that the odds recommended by the groups are lower on the whole, that is, riskier than the odds recommended individually prior to the discussion. Because the risky shift is inherently interesting and because the students are highly involved with data that they have generated themselves, it is easy to move directly into an animated discussion of choice shifts.

There are many facets of the history of the risky shift, its occurrence in real life decision-making groups, and its causes that students seem to enjoy discussing. Several specific topics can be mentioned: First, students are interested to learn that the risky shift was discovered more or less accidentally. It had been predicted that group discussions of the CDQ items would produce compromise deci-

sions based on the average of individual scores or a slight shift toward cautiousness. Also, students are highly interested in knowing that the risky shift occurs with students who are risking painful physical side effects (Bem, Wallach, & Kogan, 1965) and with state trial judges at gambling establishments in Nevada (Blascovitch & Ginsburg, 1973). Accounts of decision making in government which seemed to have shown a risky shift elicit the most interest. One example is Arthur Schlesinger's (1965) account of the recommendations of President Kennedy's advisers regarding the Bay of Pigs invasion of Cuba in 1961.

Possible explanations for the shift can also be discussed. Experience has indicated that students are fairly adept at generating explanations and will quickly suggest the ideas that have been examined in risky shift research. These include the diffusion of responsibility in groups (Wallach, Kogan, & Bem, 1964), the notion that group discussions will contain more risky arguments (Burnstein & Vinokur, 1975; Burnstein, Vinokur, & Trope, 1973), and the idea that risk is a cultural value (Brown, 1965; Baron & Roper, 1976). After demonstrating the phenomenon themselves and listing several competing explanations, students are usually eager to hear about the relevant research.

Other aspects of the data can also be discussed. One such topic of discussion may be why certain groups failed to shift to risk or why others showed a particularly large shift. Sex differences can also be discussed. Our experience shows only that women are initially more risky on some items and men on others. Usually the difference can be understood in terms of subjects being more cautious when they perceive the interests of their own sex to be involved. It can also be valuable to discuss how the data collected in class relate to particular explanations of the shift. For example, Jellison and Riskind (1970, 1971) have proposed a social comparison of abilities explanation, which suggests that subjects would be more likely to shift on CDQ items where the ability of the protagonist can determine whether or not the risky course of action succeeds. This can be examined by deciding which items depend more on the individual's ability and which on external circumstances, and then considering the shifts for each type of item.

The risky shift is a simple and reliable classroom demonstration. It is also a valuable resource for class discussion. It can capture student interest at the beginning of the course and get it off to a good start. Whenever one conducts a classroom demonstration, particularly of a social psychological phenomenon, one goes out on a limb. The risky shift demonstration comes as close as any to being a sure bet.

## References

Baron, R. S., & Roper, G.  A reaffirmation of a social comparison view of choice shifts, averaging, and extremity effects in autokinetic situations. *Journal of Personality and Social Psychology*, 1976, *33*, 521-530.

Bem, D. J., Wallach, M. A., & Kogan, N.  Group decision-making under risk of aversive consequences. *Journal of Personality and Social Psychology*, 1965, *1*, 453-460.

Blascovitch, J., & Ginsburg, G.  Blackjack and the risky shift. *Sociometry*, 1973, *36*, 42-55.

Brown, R.  *Social psychology*. New York: Free Press of Glencoe, 1965.

Burnstein, E., & Vinokur, A.  What a person thinks upon learning he has chosen differently from others: Nice evidence for the persuasive-arguments explanation of choice shifts. *Journal of Experimental Social Psychology*, 1975, *11*, 412-426.

Burnstein, E., & Vinokur, A.  Persuasive argumentation and social comparison as determinants of attitude polarization. *Journal of Experimental Social Psychology*, 1977, *13*, 315-332.

Burnstein, E., Vinokur, A., & Trope, Y.  Interpersonal comparison versus persuasive argumentation: A more direct test of alternative explanations for group induced shifts in individual choice. *Journal of Experimental Social Psychology*, 1973, *9*, 236-245.

Jellison, J. M., & Riskind, J.  A social comparison of abilities interpretation of risk taking behavior. *Journal of Personality and Social Psychology*, 1970, *15*, 375-390.

Jellison, J. M., & Riskind, J.  Attribution of risk to others as a function of their ability. *Journal of Personality and Social Psychology*, 1971, *20*, 413-415.

Kogan, N., & Wallach, M. A.  *Risk taking: A study in cognition and personality*. New York: Holt, Rinehart and Winston, 1964.

Sanders, G. S., & Baron, R. S.  Is social comparison irrelevant for producing choice shifts? *Journal of Experimental Social Psychology*, 1977, *13*, 303-314.

Schlesinger, A.  *A thousand days: John F. Kennedy in the White House*. Boston: Houghton Mifflin, 1965.

Stoner, J. A. F.  A comparison of individual and group decisions including risk. Unpublished master's thesis, School of Industrial Management, MIT, 1961.

Wallach, M. A., Kogan, N., & Bem, D. J.  Group influence on individual risk taking. *Journal of Abnormal and Social Psychology*, 1962, *65*, 75-86.

# Teaching About Crowding: Students as an Independent Variable

George Banziger
*Marietta College*

Research on crowding has come a long way since Calhoun's (1962) postulations on the "behavioral sink." The introductory psychology student, however, comes to this issue with some popular misconceptions about the causative effect of crowding and high density on negative behaviors in all species and is reinforced in this view by exposure to the Calhoun studies on rats. Yet studies done on other infrahuman species and other investigations done with humans (see Freedman, 1979) have demonstrated that the effects of crowding are more complicated than Calhoun's studies suggest. The purpose of the classroom exercise described here was to demonstrate the importance of situational and attributional cues in determining people's response to crowding. In summarizing studies of crowding done with many species, Freedman (1979) concluded that the effects of high density depend on the situation and are not necessarily harmful. In reference to crowding in humans, Patterson (1978) has noted that the evaluation of the meaning of crowding (cognitive labeling) is critical in people's adjustment to such events and that such evaluations may show positive or negative affect. Other studies have indicated that the sex of the subject and degree of familiarity among subjects are important variables in determining the evaluation of a crowded environment (see Zlutnik & Altman, 1972). It was assumed that students would appreciate a more sophisticated view of the psychology of crowding if they themselves were to experience high density under varying circumstances—that is, if the students were collectively involved as the independent variables.

**Methods and Procedure.**  A brief five-question survey was given to a class of 43 male (n = 20) and female (n = 23) students of introductory psychology at Marietta College in the Spring Semester 1980. The students were asked to indicate first their sex and then on 10-point scales, show how comfortable, friendly, happy, and satisfied they felt about the physical arrangement of the classroom. The classroom has 55 movable chairs, a width of 21 feet and a length of 35 feet; the approximate distance between chairs is two feet. There were three conditions of physical arrangement: (1) the regular seating pattern with the usual spacing of seats which students voluntarily assumed—measured on the first day of class; (2) the same seating pattern as (1), but pressed into half the space, also measured on the first day of class; (3) the same as (2), but measured at the end of the semester. Presumably familiarity between students was greater at the end of the semester and affective reactions to crowding differed from those experienced earlier.

**Results and Discussion.**  A 3 x 2 (Physical Arrangement by Sex) analysis of variance was computed four times using each question on affect as a dependent variable. Significant main effects of Physical Arrangement were obtained for Comfortable ($p < .01$), Satisfying ($p < .01$), and Happy ($p < .05$), but there were no main effects or interaction effects of Sex. Scheffé a posteriori comparisons indicated that the regular seating arrangement was judged to be significantly more comfortable ($p < .01$) and more satisfying ($p < .01$) than either of the crowded conditions and happier ($p<.01$) than the early crowded arrangement. Measures of crowding at the two different times in the semester were not significantly different on any of the a posteriori tests.

Although the instructor's intention in the class exercise was to demonstrate the complexity and possible interactive effects of crowding variables, the results appeared to be fairly straightforward. Crowding, regardless of time of measurement and sex, seemed to produce more negative affect than normal seating arrangements in a classroom. The results were brought up in the class where the experiment was performed during a discussion on the psychology of crowding. Students and the instructor generated the following interpretations of the results: (a) there may have been some kind of reactance effect and, as a result, negative affect in the high density conditions; that is, students might have experienced some restriction on their freedom by being told to squeeze into half the space of a normal classroom; (b) because the students were part of the independent variable, demand characteristics might have led them to respond in the way they did; some students indicated in the discussion that there was the expectation that psychologists will find negative effects of crowding; (c) other manipulations and measures, such as perceived familiarity, taking a measurement of regular density at the end of the semester, measuring autonomic responses, performance measures, anticipated duration of the arrangement, or changes in the expectation about interaction, might have reflected some of the nuances of human crowding suggested in previous literature that were not shown in the present experiment.

This classroom experiment on crowding did not demonstrate the complexity of effects it was intended to show, but it did allow students to participate in an experiment both as subjects and as part of the independent variable. Subsequent class discussion indicated that this event brought additional insight into the subject matter of crowding, an understanding of experimental design, and an experience with which to provide helpful interpretations of experimental findings.

## References

Calhoun, J. B. Population density and social pathology. *Scientific American,* 1962, *206,* 139-148.

Freedman, J. L. Reconciling apparent differences between the responses of humans and other animals to crowding. *Psychological Review,* 1979, *86,* 80-85.

Patterson, M. L. Arousal change and cognitive labeling: Pursuing the mediators of intimacy exchange. *Environmental Psychology and Nonverbal Behavior,* Fall, 1978, *3,* 17-22.

Zlutnik, S., & Altman, I. Crowding and human behavior. In J. Wohlwill & D. Carson (Eds.), *Environment and the social sciences: Perspectives and applications.* Washington, DC: American Psychological Association, 1972.

# 19.  STATISTICS AND METHODOLOGY

## Rewards, Costs, and Helping:
## A Demonstration of the Complementary Nature of
## Experimental and Correlational Research

Kenneth W. Kerber
*College of the Holy Cross*

Cronbach (1957) maintained that there are two principal research strategies in psychology: the experimental and the correlational. Textbooks in psychology often provide discussions of these two methods. Although many psychologists prefer the greater control of experiments, some researchers believe that it is desirable to use both methods when feasible because the disadvantages of one are frequently offset by the advantages of the other. For example, in their textbook on social psychology, Baron and Byrne (1977, pp. 18-24) give an interesting example of how the same psychological relationship, specifically, the relationship between the exposure of young children to violent television shows and their level of aggression toward peers, has been examined by using both the correlational (Eron, 1963) and the experimental (Liebert & Baron, 1972) methods.

In this article, I will describe a two-part research project which I have used in a social psychology laboratory course. The major purpose of the project is to demonstrate how the correlational and experimental methods can be used to explore the same psychological relationships. The project can be employed in general laboratory courses or in lecture courses where an understanding of the correlational and experimental methods is important.

The project focuses on a set of relationships from Piliavin and Piliavin's (1972) reward-cost model of helping behavior in emergency situations. In a very simplified form, their model suggests that the probability that an observer will provide help to a victim depends upon the relative strength of the costs and rewards for providing help. For example, if the costs for providing help are low and the rewards are high, direct help would be expected in the situation. On the other hand, if the costs are high and the rewards are low, the observer may attempt to escape from the situation rather than provide help.

According to Piliavin and Piliavin (1972), the costs for providing help are a function of the costs for helping and the costs for *not* helping. Costs for helping may include personal danger, expenditure of effort, lost time, embarassment, disgusting or sickening experiences, and feelings of inadequacy or failure if the help is not effective. Costs for

not helping may include self-blame, public censure, loss of rewards for helping, and continued empathic arousal. Similarly, the rewards for providing help are a function of the rewards for helping and the rewards for *not* helping. Rewards for helping may include feelings of competence, self-congratulations, thanks from the victim, praise and admiration from bystanders, money, and fame. Rewards for not helping refer to rewards associated with the activities that would be interrupted were the individual to help and any rewards associated with personal freedom and lack of involvement.

A very important feature of this model is that rewards and costs are in the eye of the beholder (Walster & Piliavin, 1972). Thus, any assessment of rewards and costs must be from the point of view of the person who provides the help.

Although this model explicitly refers to responses in emergency situations, which are, by definition, an important context in which to study helping, one might argue that non-emergency situations are a more common and no less valid context in which to study altruistic behavior. A request for help in a non-emergency situation requires some response on the part of the person who is asked. A person who is asked for help may respond with different degrees of help from no help at all to very much help. The present research project examines the possibility that the amount of help provided in a non-emergency situation may depend upon the strength of the costs and rewards for providing help. Specifically, the research question to be explored in the current project is: What are the relationships between rewards and helping and between costs and helping in a non-emergency situation where help is requested?

On the basis of the model of helping presented by Piliavin and Piliavin (1972), hypotheses were derived for a correlational study and for an experimental study. For the correlational study, it was hypothesized that there would be a positive correlation between rewards and helping and a negative correlation between costs and helping in a non-emergency situation. For the experimental study, it was hypothesized that high rewards would lead to more helping than low rewards and that high costs would lead to less helping than low costs in a similar non-emergency situation.

### Method

**Correlational Study.**  Subjects in this study were recruited by the thirteen students in my social psychology laboratory course. Each student obtained data from four subjects who were friends or acquaintances of the students. In order to have the same number of male and female subjects, each student recruited two males and two females. All 52 subjects completed a two page questionnaire that was prepared especially for this study. On the first page of the questionnaire, subjects were told to read the following situation:

> One evening, just as you settle down to study for an important test, an acquaintance from down the hall in your dormitory enters your room. He/she asks for assistance with some homework which is due the next morning. It turns out that you have already taken the same course in which your acquaintance needs assistance.

Subjects then rated how much help they would give to the person who asked for assistance (1 = No help at all; 7 = Very much help).

On the second page of the questionnaire, subjects gave their estimates of the rewards (1 = No rewards at all; 7 = Very high rewards) and the costs (1 = No costs at all; 7 = Very high costs) of helping the person in the situation. Above the appropriate rating scale, subjects were given the following brief definitions of rewards and costs:

> When helping a person, we sometimes experience *rewards* as a result of our behavior. For example, we may feel better about ourselves, we may receive thanks from the person we help, we may receive praise for our behavior, we may receive assistance at a later time from the person we helped.
>
> When helping a person, we sometimes experience *costs* as a result of our behavior. For example, we may lose valuable time, we may receive no thanks for our help, we may have to expend a lot of effort, we may never receive assistance at a later time from the person we helped.

The data from this study were compiled in class, and each student performed an analysis of the results.

Experimental Study.  This study consisted of a 2 X 2 factorial design with costs and rewards as the independent variables. The study was divided into two parts: (a) a check on the manipulation of rewards and costs; and (b) the effect of the manipulation of rewards and costs on helping.

For both parts of this study, subjects were told to read the following situation:

> It is 8 o'clock on a Monday evening, and you have just begun to study for a very important examination. The examination is scheduled for tomorrow morning at 10 o'clock. You need an excellent performance in order to make up for a poor showing on the previous test in this class.
>
> Just as you settle down to work, an acquaintance from down the hall enters your room and asks for some assistance with his/her mathematics homework which is due the next morning. You took the same mathematics course last semester.
>
> Before responding to his/her request, you ask if your acquaintance will do a favor for you in return for your help. Your acquaintance says that he/she is willing to do a favor of your choice in return for your assistance with the homework.

The cost manipulation was accomplished by changing the day of the examination from tomorrow morning (High Cost) to Thursday morning (Low Cost). The reward manipulation was accomplished by stating that the acquaintance was willing to do a favor (High Reward) versus was *not* willing to do a favor (Low Reward) in return for assistance with the homework.

To check the manipulations of the independent variables, 52 subjects gave their estimates of the rewards and the costs of helping the person in the situation. The rating scales and the definitions of rewards and costs were the same as those in the correlational study. Subjects were recruited by the students in the course. Each student recruited four subjects, one in each of the four conditions of the study. In order to have the same number of male and female subjects in each condition, each student recruited only persons of his or her own sex.

To assess the effect of the manipulation of rewards and costs on helping, 52 subjects rated how much help they would give to the person who asked for assistance by using the same rating scale as that in the correlational study. A new group of subjects was recruited for this part of the study. Once again, each student in the class obtained data from four subjects, one in each of the four conditions of the study, and each student recruited all male or all female subjects to control for sex.

The data from both parts of this study were compiled in class, and each student performed the analyses of the results.

## Results

Correlational Study.  The correlation between rewards and helping in this study was statistically significant in the predicted direction, $r = .57$ ($df = 50$, $p < .01$). However, the correlation between costs and helping, although in the predicted direction, did not reach conventional levels of significance, $r = -.24$ ($df = 50$, $p < .10$).

Experimental Study.  For the manipulation check, separate 2 X 2 analyses of variance were performed for the dependent variables of rewards and costs. In the analysis of rewards, the High Reward condition (4.77) was rated as significantly more rewarding than the Low Reward condition (3.62), $F(1, 48) = 8.78$, $p < .01$, and neither the main effect for costs, $F(1, 48) = 3.16$, nor the interaction of rewards and costs, $F(1, 48) = .98$, were significant. In the analysis of costs, the High Cost condition (5.39) was rated as significantly more costly than the Low Cost condition (3.12), $F(1, 48) = 31.74$, $p < .01$, and neither the main effect for rewards, $F(1, 48) = .01$, nor the interaction of rewards and costs, $F(1, 48) = .74$, were significant. Therefore, the manipulation of rewards and costs was highly successful.

Finally, a 2 X 2 analysis of variance was performed for the dependent variable of helping. Subjects indicated that they would give significantly more help in the High Reward (5.31) as opposed to the Low Reward (3.00) condition, $F(1, 48) = 31.08$, $p < .01$. In addition, there was a trend toward greater helping in the Low Cost (4.54) as opposed to the High Cost (3.77) condition, $F(1, 48) = 3.45$, $p < .10$. The interaction between rewards and costs was not significant, $F(1, 48) = 2.21$.

## Discussion

The purpose of this research project was to demonstrate how a correlational study and an experimental study can explore the same psychological relationships. The two studies described here present a correlational and an experimental investigation of the relationships between rewards and helping and between costs and helping in a non-emergency situation. The results of the project show how the findings from these two types of studies may complement one another. The results of the correlational study support the hypothesis that there is a positive relationship between rewards and helping. One advantage of this study was that the subjects themselves estimated the rewards and costs of the situation, as they perceived them, as well as the extent of their helping. Of course, statements about causality in this study are problematic. The experimental study supports the hypothesis that increases in reward *cause* increases in helping, although in this study the rewards and costs were contrived by the experimenter. Taken together, these studies indicate that in at least one non-emergency situation, helping is strongly related to the rewards in the situation but is not clearly related to the costs in the same situation. With respect to the model proposed by Piliavin and Piliavin (1972), perhaps the relative importance of rewards and costs varies in non-emergency as opposed to emergency situations.

The only materials necessary to use this research project in the classroom are the questionnaires described in the method section. The amount of time that students devote to the project could be reduced if the instructor instead of the students analyzed the data. In addition, with larger classes, the students themselves could be the subjects, thus eliminating the need for data collection outside of class.

This project could initiate the discussion of many important aspects of psychological research: (a) differences between correlational and experimental research; (b) ad-

vantages and disadvantages of each of these methods; (c) the generation of hypotheses on the basis of previous research; (d) operational definitions; (e) manipulation checks; (f) the adequacy of subject samples; (g) generalization of research findings; and (h) statistical analysis and inferences from data. In short, this project could be a valuable tool when teaching courses that require an understanding of research methods in psychology.

### References

Baron, R. A., & Byrne, D. *Social psychology: Understanding human interaction* (Second edition). Boston: Allyn & Bacon, 1977.

Cronbach, L. J. The two disciplines of scientific psychology. *American Psychologist,* 1957, *12*, 671-684.

Eron, L. D. Relationship of TV viewing habits and aggressive behavior in children. *Journal of Abnormal and Social Psychology,* 1963, *67*, 193-196.

Liebert, R. M., & Baron, R. A. Some immediate effects of televised violence on children's behavior. *Developmental Psychology,* 1972, *6*, 469-475.

Piliavin, J. A., & Piliavin, I. M. Effect of blood on reactions to a victim. *Journal of Personality and Social Psychology,* 1972, *23*, 353-361.

Walster, E., & Piliavin, J. A. Equity and the innocent bystander. *Journal of Social Issues.* 1972, *28*, 165-189.

### Note

1. The author wishes to thank Dr. Royce Singleton, Jr., for his helpful comments.

# Operational Definitions Made Simple, Lasting, and Useful

Larry R. Vandervert
*Spokane Falls Community College*

One of the most difficult things to get across to beginning psychology students is a reasonable understanding of the usefulness and limitations of operational definitions. To be sure, there are always students who quickly grasp these ideas and see their significance, but those students always seem to be in the minority. Should we go to a lot of trouble for operational definitions? I believe we should. One of the deeper appreciations for modern psychology, in my estimation, comes from the way psychologists have dealt with "mind" while attempting to maintain a scientific framework of activity. This is a perspective on psychology that students cannot afford to miss, and psychology probably cannot afford to have them miss it.

My goal, when dealing with difficult concepts, is to *find something that is in the background of all of my students* that will recognize the new as something already well understood. One way to help break down ideas involved in

operational definitions has been to relate the entire process by story-like analogy to something all of the students are familiar with. I have used the household kitchen and kitchen recipes as analogies to the scientific laboratory and the operational definition. The analogy becomes so thoroughgoing, and the students' understanding so great, that many students become able to write fairly good definitions for certain psychological concepts. Some students, perhaps the more creative ones, are even able to originate fictitious psychological concepts and write operational definitions for them. I will give an example of these student efforts later.

**Kitchen Analogy.** The purpose of the kitchen-analogy is to show students that they are already familiar with the important ideas related to operational definitions of psychological concepts. The main ideas covered are: Constructs, Empirical Referents, Quantification, Conditions of Control, and Scientific Agreement.

Most people don't think about it, but we all grow up (in this country anyway) in homes that contain highly sophisticated *scientific* laboratories—the household kitchen. Stretching the point, you say? Let's take inventory: (a) Hot and cold running water—into a temperature and corrosive resistant basin; (b) An adjustable cooling chamber; (c) An adjustable heating chamber; (d) A motorized, variable-speed mixing device; (e) A high-speed blending device; (f) A long list of reasonably accurate measuring devices and containers; (g) Containers for use in the heating and cooling chambers; (h) A great collection of substances which may be combined in accordance with empirically established (often internationally) methods and rules; (i) Handling and cutting tools.

Now, we begin to have a little more appreciation for the old kitchen. Have we left anything out? (Students will supply the entire list if you simply ask them how a kitchen is like a scientific laboratory.) Oh yes, one of the most important things, a shelf of specialized texts, handbooks, and manuals of methods. There might even be a procedures book written by a team of French experts, perhaps one by a Japanese expert. Yes, we seem to have a complete scientific laboratory. (Ask students if they think the term "scientific" is really appropriate here.)

Most of the things we prepare in the kitchen require a combination of activities or *building operations* in the combining of ingredients. Therefore, we might easily refer to the things we prepare as things we construct—or simply refer to them as *constructs*. For example, we might refer to a cake prepared in our scientific kitchen as a physical construction, much like a building is a physical construction. More simply, we may refer to a cake (or a building) as a *physical construct*. We usually follow a precise recipe in constructing a cake. The recipe lists specific activities or *operations* we must perform to obtain the desired physical cake. The recipe can be referred as a definition of the cake in terms of operations. More simply, the recipe is an *operational definition* of the cake. Now, we have two ways of saying the same thing: "recipe for a cake," OR "operational definition for a physical construct."

As we all know, the operational definition (recipe) for a cake consists of written instructions including specification of the substances to be mixed in relation to one another (empirical referents), the apparatus to be used (conditions of control), the various amounts of substances and apparatus used (quantification), and the operations one must perform to mix things in the proper relationship. If the operational definition is followed carefully, the result will be the specific, desired cake. Perhaps the operations have defined a chocolate cake with vanilla frosting—first defined by that team of French experts in 1938.

The perfect cake obtained by sticking closely to the *operational definition* for the *physical construct*, "cake," should be identical to the one the French creators had in mind in 1938. We might conclude that the motive behind writing operational definitions for cakes is to insure that anyone, anywhere who wished to follow the operations could produce and observe the same cake. This result is a type of scientific agreement. Personally, I would say it *is* scientific agreement. One may not like this particular cake, or think anyone ought to eat it, but he certainly could produce what the French experts had in mind.

These ideas about converting the making of a cake into a set of operations to be carried out in scientific laboratore are: (a) *Physical Construct*—"Cake"; (b) *Operational Definition*—Recipe; (c) *Empirical Referents*—Ingredients, aspects of apparatus; (d) *Quantifications of Control Conditions*—Cups, teaspoons, ounces, etc. Specification of apparatus conditions, e.g., 350° for 45 minutes; (e) *Scientific Agreement*—Identical cakes produced in France and United States 39 years apart. (This all assumes very close control over specifications of ingredients and apparatus. Surely, if all possible factors were controlled, there would be no reason for the cakes not to be identical.)

At this point in the analogy two very important points should be made. Both of them refer to the limitations of operational definitions, and the limitations apply to both the constructing of cakes and to the construction of psychological concepts. We normally would not think about these points in relation to recipes and cakes, but they are of crucial importance when discussing operational definitions and psychological constructs. *First*, it is worth noting that cakes never occur naturally, they must be constructed. The same may be said of psychological constructs. At least three ideas (in analogy form) are important here: (a) Cakes can only be constructed by the following the appropriate operational definition (recipe), (b) In reality, then, the recipe can not be separated from the cake—the operational definition cannot be separated from the construct, and (c) It would be a mistake to assume that the recipe carried some "real" meaning beyond the cake it produced. *Second,* the writing of recipes for the constructing of cakes may tend to fix the way cakes are generally constructed, as well as the way we think about them, *but it certainly does not fix the way they can be made in the future.* Actually, if one realizes that the set of operations is always open to alteration, it can be seen that the operational definition can serve as a basis for the continual refinement of the construct in question. We can always attempt to produce a better cake by adding a little extra of this or that. Also, it sometimes happens that we follow the recipe perfectly, except for one mistake or accident, and we stumble onto a new treat. A new construct has come into being, and if we are smart, we'll immediately write a set of operations that will reproduce it.

**Psychological Concepts (Ideational Constructs).** In the same way we talk about a cake as a *physical construct,* we can talk about certain psychological concepts such as "fear" or "intelligence" as *ideational constructions.* With the appropriate operational definition a particular version of the psychological concept can be produced for observation.

Through the kitchen-analogy we have been brought very close to what P. W. Bridgeman was expressing in his *The Logic of Modern Physics* (1927), "We mean by any concept nothing more than a set of operations: *the concept is synonymous with the corresponding set of physical operations.*" Students do not find it too difficult to interpret Bridgeman's statement in terms of cakes and recipes.

A summary which point-by point matches the ideas presented in the physical construction of a cake with the ideational construction of a version of the psychological concept of "fear" is as follows: (a) *Ideational Construct*—"fear"; (b) *Operational Definition*—written statement of operations to perform to observe; (c) *Empirical Referents*—stimuli, responses, and organismic variables; apparatus. (One may wish to equate S, R, and O with machine versions of them.); (d) *Quantifications of Control Conditions*—

amplitude, frequency, duration, latency, type; specification of apparatus conditions; (e) *Scientific Agreement*—Identical observations of "fear," and possible identical notions of fear in observers. At this point, for the explication of the relation between operational definition and psychological construct, I begin to move from lecture-discussion to a classroom exercise.

In a scientific psychology, ideational constructions such as "fear" are constructed from such empirical "ingredients" as stimulus, response, and organism variables. These variables are expressed in a particular relationship to one another (mixed and baked) to stand for, for example, "fear." Notice that the S, O, and R variables serve as the building blocks in the derivation of the construct of *fear*. The point that these variables can be taken as the counterparts of the ingredients of the cake is critical in helping students understand what is necessary in the writing of new operational definitions for new psychological conceptions.

Classroom Exercise. I have found that student enjoy this classroom exercise on operational definitions tremendously. Not only do they enjoy it, but the exercise illustrates in a simple way the necessity of reaching agreement as to what set of operations will be used to define the psychological concept in question.

Having been exposed to the kitchen-analogy, students are asked to write an operational definition for the construct "fear," (since they have not yet been given a complete definition of it). If they are cautioned to think through the analogy and to carefully restrict themselves to statements about stimuli, responses, and organismic variables, they will find that they can do quite well. They might even find they have improved upon the definition for "fear" provided by William S. Verplanck in his "A Glossary of Some Terms Used in the Objective Science of Behavior" (1957):

> FEAR: 1. *(empirical, behavior theory)* the behavior produced either by sudden and intense stimulation or by specific classes of stimuli that must be identified empirically for each species studied. Responses include alterations of sphincter control, flight behavior, respiratory changes, and the suppression of behavior occurring at the onset of stimulation. (p.15).

The fear definition has been used because it illustrates the S-O-R construct so well. Also students can identify in a humorous way with *alterations of sphincter control,* and *suppression of behavior occurring at the onset of stimulation* (just say, BOO!). Students become particularly fascinated when given a chance to try their hand at writing operational definitions for such concepts as love or religion, etc. They also now have a clear mental-set to ask critical questions about what sub-sets of S's are mixed with what sub-sets of R's and O's to produce what psychologists are talking about.

The most exciting things the kitchen-analogy has produced for me have been occasions when students have gone beyond the classroom activity of writing operational definitions for already defined pieces of "mind," and have attempted to produce new operational expressions of "mind" that have never before been written (as far as they know). For example, one student decided (after a discussion of how intelligence might be operationalized) that *belief* was an ability, and, further, was normally distributed. He suggested that some people had a greater *ability* to believe than others, and the variations in the ability to believe accounted for a number of everyday observations on human behavior. He felt he could eventually define belief as an ability and develop a test for it. I don't know whether or not he ever did. But I have the satisfaction of knowing that his belief about *belief* was originally cultured into existence by a discussion of intelligence within the context of the kitchen-analogy. I also know that the student came to grips with one of the deeper appreciations of modern scientific psychology.

### References

Bridgeman, P. W. *The logic of modern physics.* New York: Macmillan, 1927.
Verplanck, W. S. A glossary of some terms used in the objective science of behavior. *Supplement to the Psychological Review,* 1957, *64*(6, Part 2, November).

### Note

Reprinted from *Understanding Student Behavior: A newsletter for Teachers Using UNDERSTANDING HUMAN BEHAVIOR,* by James V. McConnell, Vol. 2; No. 1, Spring 1978, published by Holt, Rinehart and Winston. By permission of the publisher.

---

# Science, Psychology and Self: A Demonstration Experiment for Introductory Psychology

Judith Candib Larkin,
and Harvey A. Pines
*Canisius College*
James W. Julian
*State University of New York*

It's a wonder more students are not turned off after their first week in psychology. At the beginning of every science course from grammar school on, our students have read and heard lectures about The Scientific Method. At last in psychology where they are finally expecting to learn about themselves, the first thing they hear is one more definition of a hypothesis, a theory, and the four (or is it five?) steps in the Scientific Method.

Teachers can do something to liven up the methodology section of their course. Although *we* know that the tenets of science are the foundation of psychology, the student who seeks self-insight and better understanding of others needs more than a lecture to tune in to the relationship between science, psychology, and self. The answer we propose is to capitalize on students' interest in themselves by involving them at the beginning in an experimental study of their own behavior.

The demonstration described in this paper is a student-oriented introduction to psychology as science. The behavior we investigated, and later discussed with our students, is social comparison—in particular, what goes on in the classroom when the teacher returns the graded exam. Getting back one's own exam and finding out how others did may be the most universal of all classroom activities. How much comparing of grades actually does take place? Why does it occur? Where? When? By whom? Even in the largest of lecture sessions, students will involve themselves in discussing this widely shared experience.

**From Observation to Theory.** The starting point of many a research project is a simple observation—in this case, that students compare grades. However, when we ask *why* the behavior occurs, we are looking for explanations, and this is where a ready-made theory is helpful. For our purposes, Festinger's (1954) theory of social comparison[1] is not only appropriate, it is clear, easily understood, and handily facilitates the demonstration of scientific thinking. According to this theory, people have a need to evaluate their abilities (and beliefs); to find out how good they are. Although some abilities are tested against a recognizable physical standard, many can only be evaluated by comparing with other people. When there are no absolute standards or when we don't have enough information, we look to others to find out how we're doing. Festinger goes on to theorize that we will compare with others who are similar to us in ability, and that the more similar they are to us, the more accurate and stable our self-evaluations will be.

**From Theory to Hypotheses.** With no more theory than is given above, we can demonstrate the scientific thinking of a research psychologist. Using the theory as a starting point, we discussed in class how to make hypotheses and predictions about behavior and test them out in an experiment. We decided to investigate how, when and where social comparison occurs. Our first hypothesis was that the *less* information students have about their test performance, the *greater* will be their need to compare, and consequently they should find out more grades of other students. On the other hand, if provided with rather complete information about their performance, students will be better able to evaluate it, will have less need to find out how others performed and, we predict, would do less comparing of grades.

The first hypothesis helps us understand how high or low information about performance affects social comparison. Our second hypothesis was concerned with the opportunity for social comparison. There should be more opportunity for comparing when exams are returned at the beginning rather than the end of the class. We hypothesized, then, that when the corrected exam was returned early in the period, there would be a greater amount of comparison behavior and, consequently, students would know more of their classmates' grades.[2]

**Gathering Data.** We solicited the cooperation of the teachers of eight sections[3] of introductory psychology (other than our own) who agreed to return their next exam at a time determined by us and provide students (a total of 442) with a greater or lesser than usual amount of information about their performance. The amount of *opportunity for social comparison* in the classroom was varied by returning the exams either at the beginning of the class period (high opportunity) or just before the end (low opportunity). The *amount of performance information* was varied by giving subjects in the low information condition only their raw score, but subjects in the high information sections received their raw score, a letter grade, and the class distribution of scores which was written on the blackboard.

We collected the data at the first class meeting following return of the exams. The students in the experimental sections filled out a one-page form to provide detailed information about social comparison: they were asked to list everyone whose grade they knew, the location of the person, relationship to the person, as well as how, when, and where they learned the grades.[4]

**Presenting the Results.** To increase student involvement in the presentation of data, we asked our students to predict the results and then presented those that we actually obtained. Summarizing the results provides a high interest opportunity for demonstrating the purpose and calculation of descriptive statistics. Teachers who do this study may want to compare their students' results with ours.

**Results.** First of all, how much comparison really goes on in the classroom? We found that on the average in our classes (size 40-50 students), a student knows the grades of 3.24 other students. If a professor returns an exam at the beginning of class, students on the average know markedly more scores (3.99) than if exams are returned at the end of class (2.50). It appears that there is more opportunity to compare when the exam is given back early in the period.

Comparison does appear to be affected by the amount of information one knows about one's score. For example, if students know their score, letter grade and the distribution of scores, there is apparently less motivation to find out other people's grades. (Mean number of comparisons = 2.66.) If only the score is known, and not the other information, there is apparently more motivation to find out other's grades. (Mean number of comparisons = 4.17.)

Whom do students compare with? Is sheer distance an important factor? Apparently so because 60% of the comparisons were made with people sitting in adjoining seats (front, back and side); only 30% of comparisons were made with students who did not sit nearby. The remaining 10% of comparisons were with students in other class sections.

Is one more likely to know the grades of friends than of people who are slight acquaintances? Forty-two percent of the people whose grades students knew were friends, but 33% were people known only by sight or name (seldom interacted with). The remaining comparisons were made with people who were acquaintances.

When does comparison take place? An average of 67% of the comparisons were made during the class period in which the exam was returned. The remaining 33% were divided fairly evenly among the following categories: 1 hour after class; from then until midnight; the next day; and later.

How does the comparison actually take place? Students typically learned another's grade in three different ways: by directly asking the person (35%); seeing the person's grade (28%); and the person volunteering the grade without being asked (25%). Only 8% of the scores were found out second hand, i.e., by someone else passing on the information.

Discussion and Conclusion. The final step in an experiment is to "discuss" its findings: to relate them back to theory and to show how the results raise questions for further research. In our case it appeared, at first, that we had obtained clear support for Festinger's theory. But, through discussion, we discovered that pre-existing experimental group differences raised some question about the opportunity and information manipulations and made evident the need for a better controlled replication. This observation, as well as questions like "Would the results be the same in a smaller class?" provided a good opportunity for showing the importance of skeptical and critical evaluation in the scientific process.

### References

Festinger, L. A theory of social comparison processes. *Human Relations*, 1954, 7, 117-140.
Latané, B. (Ed.). Studies in social comparison. *Journal of Experimental Social Psychology*, 1966, Suppl. 1.
Suls, J. M. & Miller, R. L. (Eds.). *Social comparison processes: Theoretical and empirical perspectives*. Washington: Hemisphere, 1977.
Wheeler, L., Shaver, K. G., Jones, R. A., Goethals, G. R., Cooper, J., Robinson, J. E., Gruder, C. L., & Butzine, K. W. Factors determining choice of a comparison other. *Journal of Experimental Social Psychology*, 1969, 5, 219-232.

### Notes

1. Recent empirical studies based on the theory are included in the references, although not all are cited.
2. For the more advanced students, teachers may discuss experimental design in greater detail. This demonstration is a 2 x 2 factorial design, with two levels of opportunity for comparison, and two levels of information. Using this design, one can demonstrate main effects and the difficult concept of interaction.
3. We want to thank Drs. Dewey Bayer, Clifford Mahler, Frank Merigold, Donald Tollefson, and Richard Weisman for their cooperation and allowing the use of their class time for this project.

# The Student as Data Generator

Paul Hettich
*Barat College*

Among the leading concerns of Statistics teachers is the creation or location of examples, problems and exercises which generate student interest above the level of "learn-it-or-else." Wanted is not just any problem or example which is valid, but rather ones which spark a student's enthusiasm for learning. Many statistics texts do contain problems extracted from actual behavioral science research; however, "real" research examples are frequently remote from the student's immediate frame of reference. For instance, the calculation of standard scores derived from an eighth grade science test represents an actual problem, but what *immediate* meaning does the problem contain for the statistics student, unless the student expects to teach? The writer certainly is not assuming that such "immediacy" is a necessary criterion for selecting problems, but it *is* an aid to learning. The following details a technique which integrates the student with the subject matter: the utilization of student produced data and student centered examples.

On the first day of class students are given 3 x 5 cards on which they print their names (on the top line) and class (sophomore, junior, etc.), academic major, number of psychology courses completed, and height on subsequent lines. In addition, students are administered Pressey's survey of study habits (Morgan & Deese, 1969) and the Test Anxiety Scale (TAS) described in Sarason and Ganzer (1962). The completed 3 x 5 cards are assembled to form 8½ x 11 sheets (student names are covered) and then Xeroxed. Students' scores on the two questionnaires are paired on a master summary sheet. Finally, a copy of the card and questionnaire data along with the original questionnaires are returned to the students. Besides supplying the students with data and the teacher with information about his class, the cards function as a ready reference for student advisement.

Statistics Generation. How does the student generated data become incorporated into statistics?
1. The variables which formed the data (e.g., class, major, questionnaire scores) are introduced as examples in discussions of the four *levels of measurement* (nominal, ordinal, interval, ratio).
2. Class, academic major and questionnaire data are used in exercises requiring the preparation of *frequency distributions*.
3. To recognize that the type of graph employed in a particular situation depends on the corresponding level of measurement and that various *shapes of distributions* (e.g., mesokurtic, skewed, normal) occur, students are instructed to construct graphs for the variables of class, academic major and test anxiety.
4. Concepts and problems pertaining to *percentile ranks* and *standard scores* utilize the study habits and TAS scores.
5. The measures of *central tendency* and *dispersion* and the relation of each to the levels of measurement can be illustrated using card and questionnaire data.
6. Comparisons of student performance on the study habits and test anxiety measures provide an excellent opportunity for presenting concepts, techniques and questions related to *correlation* (e.g. Which coefficient of correlation is best suited for these data? How do Pearson and Spearman coefficients differ on the same data?). Discussions of the relationship between study

habits and test anxiety illustrate the concepts of correlation in a manner that can be personally meaningful and potentially useful to students. For the past two classes low negative correlations between these measures were obtained, providing an opportunity to critically examine the underlying behaviors and the instruments used to measure them.

7. When classes are too large to realistically permit the use of all student scores in calculations of correlation coefficients, 10, 15 or 20 pairs can be selected from the population, a procedure that can open an examination of *sampling techniques*.

8. After the concepts of *sampling distribution* and the *central limit theorem* are explained, students are instructed to cut the height data from their Xeroxed sheets, mix it in a container, and draw samples of N=2, N=5 and N=10. Means and grand means are calculated and subsequently related to these concepts.

By now you may have identified additional concepts or problems suitable for the employment of student produced data; the examples summarized here are not exhaustive.

**Values.** What are the effects of using student generated data? Because statistics is taught annually at this school to only one section it has not yet been possible to collect "outcome" data on learning effectiveness of comparison groups. However, tutor assistants and students frequently remark that reading statistics and completing homework assignments are more interesting when student centered problems are used than when text examples or exercises are given.

Additional advantages accrue using this teaching technique. Because student generated data is not contrived it possesses characteristics of actual data: occasional ambiguity and complexity. For instance, when constructing a frequency distribution, in what category of "major" would an "Art-Psychology" student be assigned? Or, what is done with illegible or confusing data (student cards are Xeroxed)? Also, means and standard deviations seldom occur in easily calculated whole numbers when using actual data: decimals do exist. Furthermore, students can ponder why so-called normally distributed variables (e.g., height) may occasionally produce a skewed distribution for a given group. Or, as happened last semester when three students obtained a closer approximation to the population mean using sample sizes of two than with sample sizes of five and ten, a particular concept may not hold true for a particular instance.

Besides developing interest and critical thinking, students can begin to realize that the use of statistics and scientific methodology is not restricted to textbooks and laboratories. On one occasion when the writer was describing pretest-posttest designs, student attention increased markedly when it was mentioned that many seniors were participating in a school-wide pretest-posttest questionnaire attitude study. Many students are surprised to learn that questions regarding their likes or gripes about student life can be translated into testable hypotheses capable of producing data which can be analyzed by tests of significance.

When the teacher presents statistical concepts in a meaningful manner, students are likely to become interested in this traditionally abstract area of psychology. If principles relating motivation to learning hold true in the statistics classroom, it is reasonable to expect that the use of student generated data and student centered problems can result in an increment of learning.

### References

Morgan, C. T. & Deese, J. *How to study* (2nd ed.). New York: McGraw-Hill, 1969.
Sarason, I. G. & Ganzer, W. J. Anxiety reinforcement, and experimental instructions in a free verbalization situation, *Journal of Abnormal and Social Psychology*, 1962, 65, 300-307.

# Tables to Help Students Grasp Size Differences in Simple Correlations

John Daniel Duke
*Appalachian State University*

When the writer was enrolled in a beginning psychology class back near mid-century, his instructor tried to explain what simple correlations measure. After describing direct and inverse relationships, he made the usual cautions. Correlations are not percentages. The sign indicates the kind of association between X and Y, and a minus sign certainly does not indicate a low or an absent or deficient relationship. Correlations neither imply nor preclude causal relationships. On scatter diagrams, straight lines of dots indicate perfect relationships, circular clusters indicate zero relationships, while elliptical clusters indicate some degree of linear association. Even verbal labels were applied: 0.00 to 0.25 indicated from no to a very low relationship; 0.25 to 0.50 indicated from a low to a moderate relationship; 0.50 to 0.75 indicated from a moderate to a high relationship; and 0.75 to 1.00 indicated from a high to a perfect relationship.

Although the instructor did not mention that the amount of the covariation between X and Y was approximately the square of the correlation coefficient, he did all he reasonably could to give beginning students an intuitive appreciation of what correlations measure. Despite his efforts, however, subsequent tests showed that he attained limited success. The statistics items had the highest rate of failure then, and they still do today.

Later that quarter a generation ago, the instructor mentioned IQ scores and their correlates. Among other generalizations, he mentioned that there was a small but significant correlation (about +.20) between IQ scores and ratings of physical attractiveness. The attractive male and female students forgot the early qualifications. Here was a discipline suggesting not only that they were attractive and bright, but psychologists said that the relationship was "significant" (garbled in their minds to mean "important" or "impressive"). The less attractive students also failed to comprehend. Aware that some of their attractive peers were definitely not very bright, many of these not so attractive students decided that class content had little or any reference to events in the real world. Of course, some of the students had a reasonable understanding of the many exceptions to a generalization implied by a low correlation, but not many. Then and now, instructors have difficulty teaching students to appreciate size differences in correlation. Today and then, students overestimate how often relationship generalizations will apply, and underestimate how many exceptions there will be.

Based upon a brief discussion of tetrachoric correlations found in Edwards (1960) and a table itself originally published by Davidoff and Goheen (1953) and reproduced in Edwards, the writer derived a table which might help students become both aware of size differences in correlations and of frequency of exceptions implied by various correlation coefficients. Given 2 x 2 cell entries on dichotomized variables X and Y, the Davidoff and Goheen table uses the larger ratio of diagonal cell products, one to the other, for rapid estimation of the tetrachoric correlation. Working backward from the Davidoff and Goheen table, Table 1 derived the expected percentages of "fits" and "exceptions" to relationships defined by correlations varying from 0.00 to 1.00.

Now consider the correlation of +0.20 between IQs and attractiveness. Table 1 reveals that for all those above the median in IQ, *only 56% are at the same time above the median in rated attractiveness.* The remaining 44% are below the median in rated attractiveness. Conversely, for those below median in IQ, 44% are above the median in rated attractiveness, and 56% are below the median. Thus for correlations as low as +0.20, Table 1 shows that there will be about 44 "exceptions" (less attractive bright people) per 100 people for all those above the median level of intelligence, and another 44 "exceptions" (attractive dull people) per 100 people among all those below the median level of intelligence. The expected percentage of exceptions to a generalization relating X to Y is a concrete analysis of correlational data that most college students can digest.

Here is another example. Suppose a correlation of +.69 is found between height and weight. Table 1 entries show us that for all those people above the median on one variable, 74%, approximately, are expected to be above the median on the other variable. Or 26% of all people would be exceptional cases (below median on one variable while above median on the other).

If the correlation is negative, column percentage entries are reversed for all tables recorded in this paper. Suppose in the open field test using rat subjects, an experimenter found a correlation of -0.88 between activity level (number of grids crossed per unit time) and number of boluses defecated per unit time. Table 1 now shows that for all rats

with an above median level of activity, 84% are expected to defecate a below median number of boluses. Since the correlation describes an inverse relationship as the general trend in the association between X and Y, those rats above or below median on both variables at the same time are the

Table 1
Minimum Probable Percentages of
Above and Below Median Cases
on a Second Variable of All Cases
Above the Median on the First Variable
(Assuming True Correlations From 0.00 to 1.00)

| True Correlation | % Expected on 2nd Variable* | | True Correlation | % Expected on 2nd Variable* | |
|---|---|---|---|---|---|
| | Above Med | Below Med | | Above Med | Below Med |
| 0.00 | 50.0 | 50.0 | 0.51 | 66.9 | 33.1 |
| 0.01 | 50.2 | 49.8 | 0.52 | 67.3 | 32.7 |
| 0.02 | 50.5 | 49.5 | 0.53 | 67.6 | 32.4 |
| 0.03 | 50.8 | 49.2 | 0.54 | 68.0 | 32.0 |
| 0.04 | 51.1 | 48.9 | 0.55 | 68.4 | 31.6 |
| 0.05 | 51.4 | 48.6 | 0.56 | 68.8 | 31.2 |
| 0.06 | 51.7 | 48.3 | 0.57 | 69.1 | 30.9 |
| 0.07 | 52.1 | 47.9 | 0.58 | 69.5 | 30.5 |
| 0.08 | 52.4 | 47.6 | 0.59 | 69.9 | 30.1 |
| 0.09 | 52.7 | 47.3 | 0.60 | 70.3 | 29.7 |
| 0.10 | 53.1 | 46.9 | 0.61 | 70.7 | 29.3 |
| 0.11 | 53.4 | 46.6 | 0.62 | 71.1 | 28.9 |
| 0.12 | 53.7 | 46.3 | 0.63 | 71.5 | 28.5 |
| 0.13 | 54.0 | 46.0 | 0.64 | 71.9 | 28.1 |
| 0.14 | 54.3 | 45.7 | 0.65 | 72.4 | 27.6 |
| 0.15 | 54.6 | 45.4 | 0.66 | 72.8 | 27.2 |
| 0.16 | 55.0 | 45.0 | 0.67 | 73.2 | 26.8 |
| 0.17 | 55.3 | 44.7 | 0.68 | 73.6 | 26.4 |
| 0.18 | 55.6 | 44.4 | 0.69 | 74.1 | 25.9 |
| 0.19 | 55.9 | 44.1 | 0.70 | 74.5 | 25.5 |
| 0.20 | 56.2 | 43.8 | 0.71 | 75.0 | 25.0 |
| 0.21 | 56.6 | 43.4 | 0.72 | 75.4 | 24.6 |
| 0.22 | 56.9 | 43.1 | 0.73 | 75.9 | 24.1 |
| 0.23 | 57.2 | 42.8 | 0.74 | 76.3 | 23.7 |
| 0.24 | 57.6 | 42.4 | 0.75 | 76.8 | 23.2 |
| 0.25 | 57.9 | 42.1 | 0.76 | 77.3 | 22.7 |
| 0.26 | 58.2 | 41.8 | 0.77 | 77.8 | 22.2 |
| 0.27 | 58.5 | 41.5 | 0.78 | 78.3 | 21.7 |
| 0.28 | 58.9 | 41.1 | 0.79 | 78.8 | 21.2 |
| 0.29 | 59.2 | 40.8 | 0.80 | 79.3 | 20.7 |
| 0.30 | 59.5 | 40.5 | 0.81 | 79.8 | 20.2 |
| 0.31 | 59.9 | 40.1 | 0.82 | 80.4 | 19.6 |
| 0.32 | 60.2 | 39.8 | 0.83 | 80.9 | 19.1 |
| 0.33 | 60.5 | 39.5 | 0.84 | 81.5 | 18.5 |
| 0.34 | 60.9 | 39.1 | 0.85 | 82.1 | 17.9 |
| 0.35 | 61.2 | 38.8 | 0.86 | 82.7 | 17.3 |
| 0.36 | 61.6 | 38.4 | 0.87 | 83.3 | 16.7 |
| 0.37 | 61.9 | 38.1 | 0.88 | 84.0 | 16.0 |
| 0.38 | 62.3 | 37.7 | 0.89 | 84.6 | 15.4 |
| 0.39 | 62.6 | 37.4 | 0.90 | 85.3 | 14.7 |
| 0.40 | 63.0 | 37.0 | 0.91 | 86.1 | 13.9 |
| 0.41 | 63.3 | 36.7 | 0.92 | 86.8 | 13.2 |
| 0.42 | 63.7 | 36.3 | 0.93 | 87.6 | 12.4 |
| 0.43 | 64.0 | 36.0 | 0.94 | 88.5 | 11.5 |
| 0.44 | 64.4 | 35.6 | 0.95 | 89.4 | 10.6 |
| 0.45 | 64.7 | 35.3 | 0.96 | 90.5 | 9.5 |
| 0.46 | 65.1 | 34.9 | 0.97 | 91.6 | 8.4 |
| 0.47 | 65.4 | 34.6 | 0.98 | 92.9 | 7.1 |
| 0.48 | 65.8 | 34.2 | 0.990 | 94.5 | 5.5 |
| 0.49 | 66.2 | 33.8 | 0.995 | 96.9 | 3.1 |
| 0.50 | 66.5 | 33.5 | 1.000 | 100.0 | 0.0 |

*For negative correlations, column entries are reversed.

exceptions. With a correlation of -0.88, only 16% of the rats behave exceptionally.

Table 1 is overly long but is included for those who might want to reproduce it for a set of statistical tables. For pedagogical purposes, and perhaps for reproduction in introductory text discussions, Table 2 will suit the purposes of most users. Table 2 uses only correlation coefficients round to tenths or twentieths (left side), and correlations to hundredths which produces multiples of 5 in the percentage splits of fitting and nonfitting cases (right side). Table 2 shows that with a correlation of 0.10, 0.40, and 0.95, for

### Table 2
### Given All Cases Above the Median on Variable 1, Concurrent Percentages of Above and Below Median Cases on Variable 2 for Selected Values

| Correlation Intervals | | | Percent Intervals | | |
|---|---|---|---|---|---|
| True | % Expected on 2nd Variable* | | True | % Expected on 2nd Variable* | |
| Correlation | Above Med | Below Med | Correlation | Above Med | Below Med |
| 0.10 | 52.7 | 47.3 | 0.00 | 50 | 50 |
| 0.20 | 56.2 | 43.8 | 0.16 | 55 | 45 |
| 0.30 | 59.5 | 40.5 | 0.31 | 60 | 40 |
| 0.40 | 63.0 | 37.0 | 0.46 | 65 | 35 |
| 0.50 | 66.5 | 33.5 | 0.59 | 70 | 30 |
| 0.60 | 70.3 | 29.7 | 0.71 | 75 | 25 |
| 0.70 | 74.5 | 25.5 | 0.81 | 80 | 20 |
| 0.80 | 79.3 | 20.7 | 0.90 | 85 | 15 |
| 0.85 | 82.1 | 17.9 | 0.96 | 90 | 10 |
| 0.90 | 85.3 | 14.7 | 0.99 | 95 | 5 |
| 0.95 | 89.4 | 10.6 | 1.00 | 100 | 0 |

*For negative correlations, column entries are reversed.

example, that there are, respectively, 47%, 37%, and 11% of the cases expected to be exceptions, and that it takes a correlation of +0.16 to hold down the percentage of exceptions to 45%, a correlation of +0.31 to reduce the exceptions to 40%, etc.

Most correlations are estimates based on limited observations, not parameter values. Table estimates assume parameter correlations. The tables are still useful with nonparameter estimates, however, provided only that the user remember that the "true" correlation may vary somewhat from the estimated value. Advanced students can obtain confidence limits for their statistics. Suppose on a limited sample size, a negative correlation is found between husbands' incomes and wives' waist lines, measured in inches. Suppose the 99 percent confidence interval places the true correlation somewhere between -0.28 and -0.46. From Table 1, one could estimate that for all husbands earning above median incomes, between 35 and 41 percent would expect to have wives with above median waist lines.

**Assumptions and Cautions in Use of the Tables.** Technical assumptions for use of all tables in this paper are that the dichotomized variables be essentially continuous and normally distributed. Percentages apply only if both variables have been divided at their medians and if the

correlation is "true," that is, without any error of measurement.

But even if the assumptions are only approximately met, and even if nonparameter estimates are used, the tabled data should still provide "ballpark estimates" which should give students some idea of the percentages of fitting and nonfitting cases suggested by different sized correlations. These rough estimates should improve on the uninformed and usually exaggerated estimates of fitting cases now guessed at by students.

The caution should be made, however, that there are quite technical analyses of what correlations measure, and that the tables presented offer only beginning insight into understanding of relationships between paired variables. When appropriate, students should be exposed to technical discussions about regression, and they should learn how $r$ and $r^2$ relate to the slope of, and variability around, the regression line. Usually, however, complex analyses of the meaning of correlation measures will be reserved for a second or third course in statistics.

**How the Tables were Derived.** As already noted, the tables were derived by working backward from the Davidoff and Goheen table to estimate tetrachoric correlations. A 2 x 2 cell matrix is created by dividing two variables at the median. Cell $a$ stands for being below the median on both variables. Cell $b$ stands for being above the median on the second variable but below the median on the first. Cell $c$ stands for being above the median on the first variable, but below on the second. Cell $d$ stands for being above the median on both variables. Davidoff and Goheen instruct readers to take the ratio of bc/ad, or its reciprocal (whichever is larger), and to look up in their table to find what correlations are associated with what ratios.

By varying $a$ from 0 to 1000, while making $c$ the result of subtracting $a$ from 1000, and by reversing $b$ and $d$ systematically with changes in $a$ and $c$, Table 1 can be created. Beside the correlation of +0.38 in Table 1, for example, the percentages cited are 62.3% ("fits") and 37.7%("exceptions"). In a 2 x 2 matrix with a total frequency of 1000, $a$ and $d$ would both be 623 and $b$ and $c$ would both be 377. The ratio of ad/bc is larger than the ratio of bc/ad, and from the Davidoff and Goheen table, the resulting ratio is best associated with a correlation of 0.38. It took 1000 calculations to produce the 102 sets of entries in Table 1. Table 2, of course, was directly abstracted from Table 1 entries.

**Summary.** Two tables are presented to help students and others better understand size differences in correlations. The tables were independently developed by the author who does not know if they have been created or presented by others. The pedagogical value of the tables was illustrated and stressed. Technical assumptions and cautions in use of the tables were noted, and a brief explanation was given of how the tables were derived.

### References

Davidoff, M. D., & Goheen, M. W. A table for the rapid determination of the tetrachoric correlation coefficient. *Psychometrics*, 1953, *18*, 115-121.

Edwards, A. L. *Statistical methods for the behavioral sciences.* New York: Rinehart, 1960.

# Subject Index

# Appendix

All articles in this book appeared originally in the journal, *Teaching of Psychology*. This appendix provides the year and volume of original publication, plus page numbers, to facilitate proper citation of these articles.

COURSE ORGANIZATION
Senn, 1977, *4*, 124–127.
Lenthall & Andrews, 1983, *10*, 137–139.
Stanners & Brown, 1982, *9*, 74–77.
Bare, 1982, *9*, 42–45.
Dimond & Senter, 1976, *3*, 181–182.

A VARIETY OF APPROACHES TO THE INTRODUCTORY
  COURSE
Chase, Sulzer-Azaroff, & Well, 1983, *10*, 7–11.
Silverstein, 1982, *9*, 150–155.
Walker & Inbody, 1974, *1*, 29–31.
McKeachie, Yi-Guang, Moffett, & Daugherty, 1978, *5*, 193–194.
Arkes, 1980, *7*, 22–24.
Splane & Kushner, 1978, *5*, 186–188.
Gorman, Law, & Lindegren, 1981, *8*, 164–166.
Brown & Engram, 1979, *6*, 234–235.
Brender, 1982, *9*, 222–224.

TEAM TEACHING APPROACHES
Levine, 1977, *4*, 132–134.
Kirschenbaum & Riechmann, 1975, *2*, 72–76.
Ware, Gardner, & Murphy, 1978, *5*, 127–130.

PSI, MASTERY, AND OTHER INDIVIDUALIZED APPROACHES
Hobbs, 1981, *8*, 209–211.
Nation & Roop, 1975, *2*, 108–111.
Terman, 1978, *5*, 72–75.
Fernald, Chiseri, Lawson, Scroggs, & Riddell, 1975, *2*, 147–151.
Goldwater & Acker, 1975, *2*, 152–155.
Nation, Massad, & Wilkerson, 1977, *4*, 116–119.

SELECTING A TEXTBOOK
Morris, 1977, *4*, 21–24.
Jacobs, 1983, *10*, 183–184.

CONCEPTIONS OF STUDENTS IN INTRODUCTORY
  PSYCHOLOGY
Vaughan, 1977, *4*, 138–141.
Lamal, 1979, *6*, 155–158.
Gutman, 1979, *6*, 159–161.
Brown, 1983, *10*, 207–210.
Brown, 1980, *7*, 215–218.

MOTIVATING STUDENTS IN INTRODUCTORY PSYCHOLOGY
Lamberth & Knight, 1974, *1*, 16–20.
Batson & Johnson, 1976, *3*, 155–159.
Solomon, 1979, *6*, 77–80.
Bebeau, Eubanks, & Sullivan, 1977, *4*, 141–143.

USE OF STUDENT TEACHING ASSISTANTS
Wortman & Hillis, 1976, *3*, 69–72.
Gnagey, 1979, *6*, 80–82.
Kohn & Brill, 1981, *8*, 133–138.
White & Kolber, 1978, *5*, 6–9.

TESTING IN THE INTRODUCTORY COURSE
Diekhoff, 1984, *11*, 99–101.
Lore, 1978, *5*, 152–154.

Fulkerson & Martin, 1981, *8*, 90–93.
Tauber, 1984, *11*, 48–49.
Carroll & Senter, 1979, *6*, 233–234.

GENERAL
Hettich, 1976, *3*, 60–63.
Kellogg, 1980, *7*, 41–44.
Schwartz, 1980, *7*, 192–193.
Gardner, 1977 *4*, 89–91.
Wortman & Hillis, 1975, *2*, 134–135.
Sorensen, 1976, *3*, 140–141.
Bare, 1982, *9*, 236–237.
Winzenz & Winzenz, 1978, *5*, 159–160.
Berg, 1979, *6*, 242–243.
Baldwin, 1978, *5*, 41–42.
Flanagan, 1978, *5*, 209–210.

PHYSIOLOGICAL PSYCHOLOGY
Rozin & Jonides, 1977, *4*, 91–94.
Daniels, 1979, *6*, 175–177.

PERCEPTION AND SENSORY PROCESSES
Solomon, 1980, *7*, 3–8.
Mason, 1981, *8*, 117–119.
Benjamin, 1976, *3*, 37–39.
Beins, 1983, *10*, 113–114.
Cowan, 1974, *1*, 80–82.
Mershon, 1980, *7*, 183–184.
Lumsden, 1976, *3*, 143–144.

LEARNING
Edwards, 1976, *3*, 35–37.
Kemble & Phillips, 1980, *7*, 246–247.
Kling, 1981, *8*, 166–169.
Gibb, 1983, *10*, 112–113.
Katz, 1978, *5*, 91–93.
Plant, 1980, *7*, 109.

MEMORY AND COGNITION
Chaffin & Herrmann, 1983, *10*, 105–107.
Katz, 1979, *6*, 173–175.
Shaffer, 1982, *9*, 116–117.

DEVELOPMENTAL PSYCHOLOGY
Dillon & Goodman, 1980, *7*, 96–99.
LeUnes, 1977, *4*, 86.
Dollinger & Brown, 1979, *6*, 180–181.

PERSONALITY
Benjamin, 1983, *10*, 94–95.
Balch, 1980, *7*, 247–250.

ABNORMAL PSYCHOLOGY
White, 1977, *4*, 200–202.
Fernald, 1980, *7*, 46–47.
Gardner, 1976, *3*, 141–142.
Balch, 1983, *10*, 173–174.
Potkay, 1982, *9*, 233–234.

## SOCIAL PSYCHOLOGY
Goethals & Demorest, 1979, *6*, 177–179.
Banziger, 1982, *9*, 241–242.

## STATISTICS AND METHODOLOGY
Kerber, 1980, *7*, 50–52.
Vandervert, 1980, *7*, 57–59.
Larkin, Pines, & Julian, 1979, *6*, 237–238.
Hettich, 1974, *1*, 35–36.
Duke, 1978, *5*, 219–221.